W9-BAW-594

CHILD ABUSE

A Multidisciplinary Survey

Series Editor

BYRGEN FINKELMAN, J.D.

A GARLAND SERIES

SERIES CONTENTS

VOLUME
9

PERPETRATORS, VICTIMS AND THE COURTS

Edited with introductions by

BYRGEN FINKELMAN, J.D.

GARLAND PUBLISHING, INC.
New York & London
1995

Library of Congress Cataloging-in-Publication Data

Child abuse : a multidisciplinary survey / series editor, Byrgen
Finkelman.
    p.   cm.
    Includes bibliographical references and indexes.
    Contents: v. 1. Physical and emotional abuse and neglect
— v. 2. Sexual abuse — v. 3. Causes, prevention, and remedies
— v. 4. Short- and long-term effects — v. 5. Treatment of child
and adult survivors — v. 6. Treatment of offenders and
families — v. 7. Protecting abused children — v. 8. Victim as
witness — v. 9. Perpetrators, victims and the courts — v. 10.
Child abuse legislation.
    ISBN 0-8153-1813-8 (v. 1 : acid-free paper). — ISBN
0-8153-1814-6 (v. 2 : acid-free paper). — ISBN 0-8153-1815-4
(v. 3 : acid-free paper). — ISBN 0-8153-1816-2 (v. 4 : acid-
free paper). — ISBN 0-8153-1817-0 (v. 5 : acid-free paper).
— ISBN 0-8153-1818-9 (v. 6 : acid-free paper). — ISBN 0-8153-
1819-7 (v. 7 : acid-free paper). — ISBN 0-8153-1820-0 (v. 8 :
acid-free paper). — ISBN 0-8153-1821-9 (v. 9 : acid-free paper). — ISBN 0-8153-1822-7 (v. 10 : acid-free paper)
    1. Child abuse—United States.   I. Finkelman, Byrgen.
HV6626.52.C54   1995
362.7'62'0973—dc20   95-753
                                                  CIP

Printed on acid-free, 250-year-life paper
Manufactured in the United States of America

CONTENTS

ANATOMICAL DOLLS

AGENCY LIABILITY

ALLEGATIONS IN CUSTODY CASES

PREVENTION AND THE COURTS

SERIES INTRODUCTION

In 1960 Elizabeth Elmer said of child abuse "little is known about any facet of the problem and that methods for dealing with it are random and inadequate." She spoke of a "professional blind-spot" for abuse and of "the repugnance felt by most of our society for the entire subject of abused children."[1] Two years later, Dr. C. Henry Kempe and his colleagues brought national attention to the problem of child abuse with their article, "The Battered-Child Syndrome."[2] Prior to the publication of that landmark article, the literature on child abuse was almost non-existent. In the three decades since its publication, the research and literature on child abuse have become vast and daunting.

Social workers, psychologists, psychiatrists, counselors, and doctors have studied child abuse in great detail. As a result, we know that child abuse includes physical, emotional, and sexual abuse as well as neglect. Researchers have studied the causes of abuse from both the individual and societal perspectives. There are effective interventions for tertiary remediation of the problem, and there are many prevention models that hold out hope that child abuse can be stopped before it starts. Studies of the short- and long-term effects of child abuse show a range of maladies that include infant failure-to-thrive, learning disabilities, eating disorders, borderline personality disorders, violent behavior, delinquency, and even parricide. We now recognize the need for treatment of child victims, adult survivors, and adult perpetrators of all forms of abuse. Lawyers, legislators, and judges have grappled with the profusion of legal problems raised by protective services and proceedings, foster care, and the termination of parental rights to free abused children for placement in permanent homes. Legislatures have passed and amended statutes requiring various health, education and child care professionals to report suspected abuse, and they have dealt with the difficult problem of defining abuse and determining when the state should intervene to protect children from abusive parents. They have also struggled with the legal and psychological issues that arise when the child victim becomes a witness against his or her abuser. Even the Supreme Court has been called upon to sort out the constitutional rights of victims and criminal defendants and to determine the extent of government liability for failure to adequately protect children from abuse.

The articles in this series document our passage through five of the six stages that C. Henry Kempe identified in his 1978 commentary "Recent Developments in the Field of Child Abuse" as developmental stages in addressing the problem of child abuse:

> Stage One is denial that either physical or sexual abuse exists to a significant extent . . . Stage Two is paying attention to the more lurid abuse . . . Stage Three comes when physical abuse is better handled and attention is now beginning to be paid to the infant who fails to thrive . . . Stage Four comes in recognition of emotional abuse and neglect . . . and Stage Five is the paying attention to the serious plight of the sexually abused child, including the youngster involved in incest . . .

In spite of the voluminous research and writing on child abuse, the sixth and final of Kempe's stages, "that of guaranteeing each child that he or she is truly wanted, is provided with loving care, decent shelter and food, and first class preventive and curative health care," remains elusive.[3] There are many explanations for our inability to conquer the problem of child abuse. In reality, the explanation for our continued inability to defeat this contemptible social problem is as complex as the problem itself.

We continue to sanction the use of violence in the name of discipline. We put our societal stamp of approval on "punishment inflicted by way of correction and training" and call it discipline. But discipline also means "instruction and exercise designed to train to proper conduct or action."[4] It is not difficult to see the inherent conflict in these two definitions when applied to child-rearing. How can we "train to proper conduct or action" when we use physical punishment as a means of training, punishment that we would not inflict upon an adult under the same circumstances?

The courts and legislatures have been unable to find the correct balance between a family's right to privacy and self governance and the need of children for protection. We are unable or unwilling to commit sufficient revenue to programs that combat abuse.

There is also the tendency among many professionals working with abused children and abusive parents to view the problem and solution through specialized cognitive lenses. Doctors, social workers, lawyers, psychologists, psychiatrists, counselors, and educators are all striving to defeat child abuse. However, for the most part, these professionals focus on the problem of child abuse from the perspective of their own field of expertise. The literature on child abuse is spread throughout journals from these fields and in more specialized journals within these fields. It would be impossible for any single person to remain abreast of the developments in all other disciplines working toward a solution to child abuse. But it is also patently clear that the solution to the problem of child abuse is not going to come from any one individual or discipline. It is going to take professionals and lay people from all disciplines, working with knowledge from all disciplines.

An interdisciplinary examination is important in the fight against child abuse. The more professionals know about all aspects of the problem of child sexual abuse, the better equipped they will be to do work within their area of expertise. It is important, for example, for lawyers, working in the midst of the current backlash against child sexual abuse claims, to understand that there is a long history of discovery and repression of childhood sexual abuse. With a full understanding of why this backlash is occurring, lawyers and social service professionals can continue to effectively work against child sexual abuse.

Child abuse is a complex social problem. The issues confronted in these volumes are interconnected and overlapping. It is my hope that bringing together the articles in this series will aid in the fight against child abuse by facilitating a multidisciplinary search for a solution.[5]

NOTES

1. Elizabeth Elmer, M.S.S., "Abused Young Children Seen in Hospitals," *Social Work* 5(4), pp. 98–102 (October 1960).

2. C. Henry Kempe, M.D., F.N. Silverman, M.D., Brandt F. Steele, M.D. and others, "The Battered-Child Syndrome," *JAMA* 181, pp. 17–24 (1962).

3. C. Henry Kempe, M.D., "Recent Developments in the Field of Child Abuse," *Child Abuse & Neglect* 3(1), pp. ix–xv (1979).

4. *The Random House Dictionary of the English Language*, unabridged edition.

5. The articles in this collection may give the impression that child abuse and neglect and child sexual abuse are uniquely American

phenomena. They are not. There is a wealth of similar articles from almost every country imaginable. American sources have been used mainly because of the space limitations and because understanding the American child welfare system is vital to developing a cure for the problem.

VOLUME INTRODUCTION

This volume contains articles addressing many legal issues and barriers faced by child abuse victims and survivors: (1) statutes of limitations in criminal prosecution and civil damage claims; (2) the use of expert testimony in physical and sexual abuse prosecutions; (3) the use of anatomically correct dolls in investigation and prosecution of sexual abuse cases; (4) liability of state agencies for failure to protect children in the protective services system; (5) the problem of sexual abuse allegations in child custody cases; and finally, (6) the effort by some courts to prevent child abuse by requiring birth control or sterilization as a condition of probation for perpetrators of child abuse.

Statutes of Limitations

The secret of child sexual abuse is carried by many childhood victims into adulthood. For a variety of reasons, victimized children often don't tell about the abuse. Many adult survivors have repressed the memory of their abuse; others—grateful to have survived their abusive upbringing—fail to appreciate the continuing destructive impact of their childhood abuse.[1]

Eventually, many of these adults will seek treatment. Often, once the victim is recovered enough from the abuse, she or he may want to bring criminal charges against the abuser or seek monetary compensation for pain and suffering and for costly therapy. Many of these survivors find that they cannot pursue a legal remedy against their abusers because statutes of limitations[2] often bar both criminal prosecution of perpetrators and civil actions for monetary damages. Some state legislatures have attempted to alleviate the barrier to prosecution by modifying the statutes of limitations in the case of child sexual abuse either by extending the statutory period until the child reaches the age of majority or until the time abuse is "discovered" or remembered by the victim. In other states, the statutes of limitations for sexual abuse does not begin to run until the victim discovers the damage caused by the abuse. Still other state legislatures have extended the applicable limitation period, in some cases to as long as twenty-two years after majority, to allow for criminal prosecution of more cases. None of these solutions is without its problems, but all recognize the unfairness of shielding an adult perpetrator of child sexual abuse from prosecution simply because of the passage of time.

Brian L. Porto (1991) discusses the constitutional problems with New Hampshire's new statute of limitations for child sexual assault, which extends the limitation period (which begins to run on the victim's eighteen birthday) from six to twenty-two years. Porto further discusses alternatives to retroactively changing the limitations period.[3]

Tina Snelling and Wayne Fisher (1992) discuss the "inescapable tension" between "policies favoring unenforceability of stale [civil] claims, as reflected in statutes of limitations, compared with those allowing a remedy to survivors of childhood sexual abuse (CSA), as reflected in the principles of delayed discovery and other equitable tolling provisions."[4]

Syndrome Evidence

Even when child abuse is reported in a timely fashion and prosecution is pursued, child abuse is often difficult to prove. A physically abused child may be too young or too frightened to give evidence against an abusive parent. Still, their medical records may contain a wealth of evidence of ongoing and often brutal maltreatment. Children who are sexually abused may have few or no physical symptoms. Still their conduct speaks volumes about the abuse they have endured.

In cases of physical abuse, doctors rely on evidence of "battered-child syndrome" to help in the diagnosis of abuse. In cases of sexual abuse, children often display evidence of Child Sexual Abuse Accommodation Syndrome (CSAAS). CSAAS is a predictable series of behaviors which help professionals determine that sexual abuse has occurred.

The question of whether this "syndrome" evidence is admissible in a court of law—and what it may be used to prove—has been addressed by many courts and scholars.

Many courts have allowed the use of "battered-child syndrome" evidence to be admitted as proof that a child has been battered. This is important because, without such evidence, it is often extremely difficult to prove ongoing child abuse. This is especially true when the victims are young children who are either incapable or unwilling to give testimony. Once evidence that a child is a victim of "battered-child syndrome" is admitted, many courts will allow the presumption that the parents are the perpetrators absent evidence to the contrary.

Roland C. Summit (1983) discovered in "clinical study of large numbers of children and their parents in proven cases of sexual abuse" the emergence of "a typical behavior pattern or syndrome of mutually dependent variables which allows for immediate survival of the child within the family but which tends to isolate the child from eventual acceptance, credibility or empathy within the larger society." He dubbed this behavior Child Sexual Abuse Accommodation Syndrome. These behaviors need explanation because:

> the accommodation process intrinsic to the world of child sexual abuse inspires prejudice and rejection in any adult who chooses to remain aloof from the helplessness and pain of the child's dilemma or who expects that a child should behave in accordance with adult concepts of self-determinism and autonomous, rational choices.

Summit felt that "clinical awareness of the CSAAS is essential to provide counterprejudicial explanation to the otherwise self-camouflaging and self-stigmatizing behavior of the victim."[5]

He explained the child sexual abuse accommodation syndrome as including five categories:

1. Secrecy
2. Helplessness
3. Entrapment and accommodation
4. Delayed, conflicted and unconvincing disclosure
5. Retraction.[6]

Secrecy plays a role in enabling sexual abuse to begin and in allowing it to continue. The child is told by the perpetrator that what they are doing is a secret. They are also often told of the sometimes severe consequences of their disclosure. The perpetrator, who knows the child, will know whether to play on the child's fear of rejection or punishment or violence in determining why the secret must be kept. The child is also led to believe that not telling will be better, especially since the child knows that what is happening is bad; that she is bad. Children are helpless against the inappropriate sexual behavior of the perpetrator who is often a trusted and loved parent or other close relative.

Once the child realizes that he or she has no way out of the relationship he or she is forced to come to an accommodation of the situation. This usually involves determining that the conduct must be their fault. This happens because the world would be too frightening if the child believed the parent is to blame. Also, "in the classic role reversal of child abuse, the child is given the power to destroy the family and the responsibility to keep it together. The child, *not the parent*, must mobilize the altruism and self-control to insure the survival of the others. The child, in short, must secretly assume many of the role-functions ordinarily assigned to the mother."[7]

"Most ongoing sexual abuse is *never* disclosed, at least not outside the immediate family. . . ."[8] If a child does tell, he or she is often met with disbelief:

> Whether the child is delinquent, hypersexual, countersexual, suicidal, hysterical, psychotic, or perfectly well-adjusted, and whether the child is angry, evasive or serene, the immediate effect and the adjustment pattern of the child will be interpreted by adults to invalidate the child's complaint.

And disclosure is quite often followed by retraction. According to Summit, *"whatever a child says about sexual abuse, she is likely to reverse it."* Once the abuse is out in the open, the child discovers that, in many ways, things were better when it was a secret. Families are often fragmented (or joined in force against the child), and the child is often removed from the home (which seems both blaming and punishing to the child). Thus retraction is a natural reaction to a bad situation.[9]

Often this retraction does not occur until criminal proceedings are imminent or even underway. Courts must determine whether to admit expert testimony on Child Sexual Abuse Accommodation Syndrome to explain the counter-intuitive behaviors of victims of sexual abuse.

Patrick Larson (1989) discussed the admissibility of expert testimony of CSAAS as proof that a child has been sexually abused and the split of authority in this regard. He further discussed the possible use of Child Sexual Abuse Accommodation Syndrome evidence to explain the child/victim/witness' unusual behavior where it is inadmissible as proof of abuse.[10]

Use of Anatomically Correct Dolls

Not only is the use of anatomically correct dolls as evidence of abuse controversial, there is considerable disagreement among professionals working with sexually abused children about their usefulness and effectiveness.

Helen L. Britton and Mary Allyce O'Keefe (1991) compared two groups of children referred for medical evaluation of sexual abuse.

One group of 67 children was given nonanatomical dolls to play with and a second group of 69 children was given anatomically correct dolls to play with. Britton and O'Keefe found that "children being evaluated for suspected sexual abuse will demonstrate a similar frequency of sexually explicit behavior to describe what happened to them when being interviewed with either anatomical dolls (those with specific genital organs) or nonanatomically specific ones (i.e., Cabbage Patch, Ken, and Barbie)." They found that anatomical dolls *did not* "provoke sexualized behavior" and that "children who have been sexually victimized will act out situations that have occurred to them with dolls that are familiar, often naming and pointing to body parts that may not be physically apparent on whatever doll they use."[11] They concluded that dolls in general "are useful in the child sexual abuse interview study, not because they may have anatomically detailed genital organs, but because they are props that allow children to express themselves more accurately and completely."[12]

Cathy Maan (1991) reviewed empirical studies comparing the responses of sexually abused and non-abused children to anatomically detailed dolls. She found that researchers and clinicians tend to fall into one of two camps. They either tend to think that all clinicians who interact with sexually abused children will find the use of anatomically correct dolls useful or that the dolls tend to serve the function of a suggestive question with young children. Maan suggested that "given the empirical evidence to date, the third perspective, that of cautious optimism, seems fitting." She advised professionals who use anatomically detailed dolls, or the results of anatomical doll interviews, to "be aware of the strengths and limitations of these techniques to insure that their input into sexual abuse investigations is appropriate and beneficial."[13]

Agency Liability

From the initial discovery of battered child syndrome and the enactment of reporting statutes as a panacea, "legislative focus has changed from requiring mere reporting of suspected abuse to initiating investigation and intervention proceedings." State, county, and municipal child protective service agencies are charged with legal responsibilities for investigating reports of abuse and neglect, often substantiating such reports, and finally assisting the child and family."[14]

One of the most disturbing problems is the failure of many agencies to adequately protect children under their auspices. Shelley Urban (1985) discussed the problem of children who are subjected to further abuse after their plight is reported to child protective agencies. Urban notes that "until recently, recurrent malfeasance by child welfare agencies was attributed to inadequate funding and poor regulation. This conclusion in turn sparked legislative reform. But increased regulation did not ensure that these problems would be solved. As a result, civil and even criminal liability of child protective service agencies has emerged as a powerful deterrent to negligent performance of their duties."[15]

The Supreme Court, however, put a dent in the use of agency liability as a deterrent to agency malfeasance when it failed to hold the child protective agency liable in the now infamous case of Joshua DeShaney, who was beaten by his father into a permanent vegetative state after the child protective agency was aware of his plight and the father's brutal treatment of Joshua.[16]

Allegations in Custody Cases

Allegations of child sexual abuse often occur during divorce or custody disputes or sometimes precipitate a request for a change in an established custody or visitation order. There are many possible explanations why allegations arise at this time. Kathleen C. Faller discussed:

> four identified dynamics resulting in allegations of sexual abuse during or after dissolution of the marriage . . . : 1) the mother finds out about the sexual abuse and decides to divorce her husband; 2) long-standing sexual abuse is only revealed during the marital breakup; 3) sexual abuse has been precipitated by the marital dissolution; or 4) the allegation is false.[17]

She points to possible explanations for false allegations:

> Under the stress of divorce and its aftermath, parental perceptions may become distorted . . . and the behavior of former partners perceived as pathological. . . . Second, the parent or others may observe behavior by the child that could indicate sexual abuse, but could just as well have other explanations. . . . Third, parents may correctly perceive that their children have been sexually abused, but incorrectly attribute it to their ex-partners. . . . Finally, the parent may consciously lie in making the allegation, although this seems to be quite rare. . . .[18]

In these situations Faller reminds us that, "as with other sexual abuse cases, the child interview is the most important factor in determining the truth of the allegation." She cautions, however, that when the accusation is made by an estranged or former spouse, "evaluating that parent appears to be the second most important aspect of assessment."[19]

Kerin S. Bischoff (1990) argued that "the child's dual interests in avoiding continued molestation and in maintaining healthy relationships with non-abusing parents merit legal recognition." She believes the child's interests in custody disputes involving allegations of sexual abuse are sufficiently different from the parents that the child needs independent legal representation.[20]

Prevention Efforts and the Courts

Emily Campbell (1992/93) discusses the requirement of birth control as a condition of probation for those convicted of child abuse. She discusses the trend of courts to require women convicted of child abuse to use birth control in an effort to rectify the pervasive problem of child abuse. She argues, however, that "such a condition is not proper. First, the empirical evidence does not support the assumptions underlying the condition, that is, that a woman who has abused a child will abuse again and that she will abuse that *particular* child who is yet unborn. Second, and more important, the constitutional right of privacy confers upon these women a right to bear children."[21]

The issues addressed by the articles in this volume are difficult ones, and ones which professionals, scholars, and courts must continue to grapple with.

NOTES

1. Volume 4 of this series contains articles on the short- and long-term effects of abuse.

2. Statutes of limitations set forth the limitation period for bringing a cause of action (civil or criminal). After the time prescribed, no legal action can be maintained.

3. Brian L. Porto, "New Hampshire's New Statute of Limitations for Child Sexual Assault: Is It Constitutional and Is It Good Public Policy?" *New England Law Review* 26, pp. 141–172 (1991).

4. Tina Snelling, and Wayne Fisher, "Adult Survivors of Child Sexual Abuse—Civil Remedies," *South Texas Law Review* 33, pp. 377–415, 414 (1992).

5. Roland C. Summit, M.D., "The Child Sexual Abuse Accommoda-

tion Syndrome," *Child Abuse & Neglect* 7, pp. 177–93, 179 (1983).

6. Id. at 181.

7. Id. at 185.

8. Id. at 186.

9. Id. at 187.

10. Patrick Larson, "The Admissibility of Expert Testimony on Child Sexual Abuse Accommodation Syndrome as Indicia of Abuse: Aiding the Prosecution in Meeting Its Burden of Proof," *Ohio Northern University Law Review* 16, pp. 81–91 (1989).

11. Helen L. Britton, and Mary Allyce O'Keefe, "Use of Nonanatomical Dolls in the Sexual Abuse Interview," *Child Abuse & Neglect* 15(4), pp. 567–73, 571 (1991).

12. Id. at 572.

13. Cathy Maan, "Assessment of Sexually Abused Children With Anatomically Detailed Dolls: A Critical Review," *Behavioral Sciences and the Law* 9(1), pp. 43–51, 50 (Win 1991).

14. Shelley Urban, "Trapped Within the System: Abused Children and Protective Service Agencies," *Dickinson Law Review* 89, pp. 773–96, 773–74 (1985).

15. Id. at 774.

16. *DeShaney v. Winnebago Dept of Social Services*, 489 U.S. 189 (1989).

17. Kathleen C. Faller, "Possible Explanations for Child Sexual Abuse Allegations In Divorce," *American Journal of Orthopsychiatry* 61(1), pp. 86–91, 87 (Jan 1991).

18. Id. at 89.

19. Id. at 90.

20. Kerin S. Bischoff, "The Voice of a Child: Independent Legal Representation of Children in Private Custody Disputes When Sexual Abuse Is Alleged," *University of Pennsylvania Law Review* 138, pp. 1383–1409, 1408 (1990).

21. Campbell, "Birth Control as a Condition of Probation," *Gonzaga Law Review* 28, pp. 67–102, 101 (1992/93).

FURTHER READING

Burroughs, Thomas G. "Retroactive Application of Legislatively Enlarged Statutes of Limitation for Child Abuse: Time's No Bar to Revival." *Indiana Law Review* 22, pp. 989–1019 (1989).

Davenport, Kristen L. "Due Process-Claims of Abuse Children Against State Protective Agencies—The State's Responsibility After *DeShaney v. Winnebago County Department of Social Services*, 489 U.S. 189 (1989)." *Florida State University Law Review* 19, pp. 243–253 (1991).

Green, Arthur H., M.D. "True and False Allegations of Sexual Abuse in Child Custody Disputes." *Journal of the American Academy of Child Psychiatry* 25(4), pp. 449–456 (1986).

Jones, et al., "Reliable and Fictitious Accounts of Sexual Abuse of Children." *Journal of Interpersonal Violence* 2, pp. 27–45 (1987).

McCord, David. "Expert Psychological Testimony About Child Complainants in Sexual Abuse Prosecutions: A Foray into the Admissibility of Novel Psychological Evidence." *Journal of Criminal Law & Criminology* 77, pp. 1–68 (1986).

Myers, J.E.B., et al. "Proof of Physical Child Abuse." *Missouri Law Review* 53, pp. 189–225 (1988).

Perpetrators, Victims and the Courts

0091-4169/89/8003-842
The Journal of Criminal Law & Criminology
Copyright © 1989 by Northwestern University, School of Law

Vol. 80, No. 3
Printed in U.S.A.

STATUTE OF LIMITATIONS FOR CHILD SEXUAL ABUSE OFFENSES: A TIME FOR REFORM UTILIZING THE DISCOVERY RULE

I. Introduction

A child at the age of nine had been sexually abused two to three times a week by her stepfather. Because of her stepfather's threats of further abuse and her mother's disregard for the criminal, sexual activities, the child was prevented from disclosing the wrongful acts to others. Her natural father became aware of the criminal, sexual acts against his daughter only after the child attempted suicide. By that time, it was too late. The stepfather escaped prosecution because the statute of limitations had expired, barring the state from commencing the criminal proceedings.[1]

The above scenerio is a repeated occurence in today's society. Child sexual abuse[2] itself is a societal injustice which has long plagued our nation. Recently, this crisis has gained the attention of legislatures throughout the country. Since the early 1980s, a number of states have undertaken statutory reform efforts to improve the handling of child sexual abuse cases in the legal system.[3] This recent proliferation of legislation is predominantly directed at the procedures utilized in criminal prosecution of child abuse offenders. Some of these reforms include the adoption of hearsay exceptions for the child's out-of-court statements of abuse, the removal of competency tests for child witnesses, the giving of testimony through videotape or closed circuit television, and the use of

---

[1] These facts are taken from State v. Danielski, 348 N.W.2d 352, 354 (Minn. Ct. App. 1984). In *Danielski*, the district court dismissed the complaint on the ground that it was barred by the statute of limitations. *Id.* at 352. However, the appellate court, recognizing the injustice created an implied exception to toll the statutory period. *Id.* at 357.

[2] For purposes of this comment, the term "child sexual abuse" refers to any sexual contact ranging from fondling to intercourse with a minor.

[3] Bulkley, *Evidentiary and Procedural Trends in State Legislation and Other Emerging Legal Issues in Child Sexual Abuse Cases*, 89 Dick. L. Rev. 645 (1985) (suggests that the recent reform movement in child abuse matters is the result of a greater awareness of child sexual abuse and an increase in the number of reported incidents of abuse).

closed courtrooms during the child's testimony.[4]

Other legislative innovations concerning child sexual abuse include a statutory requirement of reporting abuse. For example, in North Carolina[5] any person or institution who has cause to suspect that any juvenile is abused or neglected is required to report such cases. Statutes requiring that abuse be reported specify that upon receipt of such reports the social service division must immediately inform the appropriate law enforcement agency.[6] Many states impose criminal sanctions or fines upon those professionals who fail to report possible cases of child abuse.[7] Further, the states of Ohio[8] and Utah[9] have mandated that sex offenders register their whereabouts with local and state officials.[10]

Despite these measures, prosecuting cases of child victimization remains difficult. This difficulty arises from the fact that many of these cases go unreported for years. Because children are often very young, confused, and feel responsible for the acts, they are afraid to report the assaults or may not even realize that what happened to them is a crime. This is especially true in incest cases, but it also occurs in cases involving molestation by nonfamily members. As a result, many cases of child sexual abuse cannot be prosecuted simply because the child did not report the abuse until years later, after the statute of limitations had expired.[11]

Faced with this awareness of the difficulties associated with the statute of limitations in prosecuting child sexual abuse offenses, many state legislatures have amended applicable legislation by the implementation of new exceptions to toll the running of the limitations period and by extending the period during which prosecution may be commenced. This Comment analyzes the procedures and exceptions to the statutes of limitations adopted in each state. It then endorses a procedure that grants discretion to the courts to toll the limitation period until discovery of the offense is made. This procedure takes into consideration the purposes of a statute of limitations as well as the circumstances common in child sexual abuse

---

[4] *See* Comment, *The Young Victim as Witness for the Prosecution: Another Form of Abuse?*, 89 DICK. L. REV. 721 (1985).

[5] N.C. GEN. STAT. § 7A-543 (1986).

[6] *See, e.g.,* D.C. CODE ANN. § 6-2102(a) (1989).

[7] *See* NATIONAL CENTER FOR MISSING AND EXPLOITED CHILDREN, SELECTED STATE LEGISLATION: A GUIDE FOR EFFECTIVE STATE LAWS TO PROTECT CHILDREN (Jan. 1985) [hereinafter GUIDE].

[8] OHIO REV. CODE ANN. § 2950.02 (Baldwin 1986).

[9] UTAH CODE ANN. § 62A-4-512 (1989).

[10] *See* GUIDE, *supra* note 7, at 18.

[11] *Id.* at 17.

offenses. Through the reformed exception, justice can be served against child sexual abusers who in the past were able to utilize statutes of limitations to their benefit.

II. SURVEY OF THE STATE STATUTES OF LIMITATIONS FOR CHILD SEXUAL ABUSE OFFENSES

State legislatures, recognizing the social harm eminating from child abuse, have enacted legislation providing criminal sanctions against child abuse offenders.[12] However, to a certain degree, the effectiveness of any criminal legislation is determined by the enforceability of the laws against child abuse. In most states enforceability is limited by another provision, generally entitled "limitation of prosecution." A limitation of prosecution provision, or a statute of limitations, limits the enforcement of criminal legislation by limiting the period of time in which a prosecutor can bring the case to court. Thus, upon the expiration of the statutory limitation period, the state is prevented from prosecuting an alleged offender.

The limitation period for sexual offenses committed against children is predominantly prescribed by statute. Statutes of limitations are typically divided into subprovisions based upon the grade of the offense. Each gradation is provided with a specific time pe-

---

12 *See* ALA. CODE § 13A-6-66 (1975); ALASKA STAT. § 11.41.434 (1962 & Supp. 1988); ARIZ. REV. STAT. ANN. § 13-1405(8) (1978 & Supp. 1988); ARK. STAT. ANN. § 5-14-108 (1987); CAL. PENAL CODE § 261.5 (West 1980); COLO. REV. STAT. § 18-3-405 (1986); CONN. GEN. STAT. ANN. § 53a-70 (West 1958); DEL. CODE ANN. tit. 11 § 768 (1978); D.C. CODE ANN. § 22-3501 (1981); FLA. STAT. § 794.011 (1976 & Supp. 1989); GA. CODE ANN. § 26-2019 (1981); HAW. REV. STAT. § 707-736 (1985); IDAHO CODE § 18-1506 (1987 & Supp. 1989); ILL. REV. STAT. ch. 38, para. 12-15 (1979 & Supp. 1989); IND. CODE ANN. § 35-42-4-4 (West 1986); IOWA CODE § 709.3 (1979); KAN. STAT. ANN. § 21-3503 (1988); KY. REV. STAT. ANN. § 510.110 (Michie/Bobbs-Merrill 1987); LA. REV. STAT. ANN. § 14:80 (West 1986); ME. REV. STAT. ANN. tit. 17A, §·254 (1964 & Supp. 1989); MD. CRIM. LAW CODE ANN. § 27-464A (1987); MASS. GEN. LAWS ANN. ch. 265, § 24B (Law. Co-op. 1980); MICH. COMP. LAWS ANN. § 750.520(b) (West 1968 & Supp. 1989); MINN. STAT. ANN. § 609.342 (West 1987); MISS. CODE ANN. § 97-5-21 (1972 & Supp. 1989); MO. ANN. STAT. § 566.100 (Vernon 1979); MONT. CODE ANN. § 45-5-625 (1989); NEB. REV. STAT. § 28-320,01 (1985); NEV. REV. STAT. § 200.366(2)(c) (1986); N.H. REV. STAT. ANN. § 632A:2 (1986 & Supp. 1988); N.J. STAT. ANN. § 2C:24-4 (West 1982 & Supp. 1989); N.M. STAT. ANN. § 30-9-13 (1983); N.Y. PENAL LAW § 130 (McKinney 1987); N.C. GEN. STAT. § 14-27.7 (1986); N.D. CENT. CODE § 12.1-20-03 (1985 & Supp. 1989); OHIO REV. CODE ANN. § 2907.04 (Baldwin 1986); OKLA. STAT. ANN. tit. 21, § 1123 (West 1983 & Supp. 1989); OR. REV. STAT. § 163.415 (1971 & Supp. 1987); PA. STAT. ANN. tit. 18, § 3122 (Purdon 1981); R.I. GEN. LAWS § 11-37-8 (1961 & Supp. 1988); S.C. CODE ANN. § 16-3-655 (Law. Co-op. 1976); S.D. CODIFIED LAWS ANN. § 22-22-7 (1988); TENN. CODE ANN. § 39-2-600 (1982 & Supp. 1987); TEX. PENAL CODE ANN. § 21.11 (Vernon 1989); UTAH CODE ANN. § 76-5-404.1 (1978 & Supp. 1989); VT. STAT. ANN. tit. 13, § 2602 (1974); VA. CODE ANN. § 18.2-370 (1988); WASH. REV. CODE ANN. § 9A.44.083 (1983 & Supp. 1989); W. VA. CODE § 61-8D-5 (1989); WIS. STAT. ANN. § 948.02 (West 1982 & Supp. 1989); WYO. STAT. § 6-2-300 (1977 & Supp. 1988).

riod during which commencement of prosecution against an offense of that grade may take place. For example, Hawaii's statute of limitations provides:

Time Limitations.

(1) A prosecution for murder may be commenced at any time.

(2) Except as otherwise provided in this section, prosecution for other offenses are subject to the following periods of limitation:

(a) A prosecution for a class A felony must be commenced within six years after it is committed;

(b) A prosecution for any other felony must be commenced within three years after it is committed;

(c) A prosecution for a misdemeanor or a parking violation must be commenced within two years after it is committed;

(d) A prosecution for a petty misdemeanor or a violation other than a parking violation must be commenced within one year after it is committed.[13]

The applicable limitation period for a child sexual abuse offense[14] in Hawaii would be three years. However, not every state's statute of limitations provision is this simple.

State legislatures have created a wide range of statutory limitation periods. Nationally, there is no consensus of an ideal limitation period or applicable exceptions. State statutes of limitations vary in the number of years, the time at which the limitation period commences, and exceptions which toll the limitation period. This Comment will first examine states with the simplest legislation and then proceed to the states with more complex statutes of limitations. States with similar legislation are categorized under general headings and analyzed accordingly.

A.   NO STATUTORY PERIOD

Not all states have a specified statute of limitations period applicable to child sexual abuse offenses. In Alambama,[15] Kentucky,[16] and Rhode Island[17] there is no statute of limitations for felonies.

---

[13] HAW. REV. STAT. § 701-108 (1985).

[14] In Hawaii a child sexual abuse offense is a class C felony. *See* HAW. REV. STAT. § 707-736(2) (1985). Likewise, the majority of the states classify sexual abuse of children as a felony. *See supra* note 12 and accompanying text.

[15] ALA. CODE § 15-3-5 (1975) states in pertinent part: "Offenses having no limitations. (a) Prosecution may commence at any time for . . . (4) Any sex offense involving a victim under sixteen years of age, regardless of whether it involves force or serious injury or death."

[16] KY. REV. STAT. ANN. § 500.050(1) (Michie/Bobbs-Merrill 1985) states in pertinent part: "Except as otherwise expressly provided, the prosecution of a felony is not subject to a period of limitation and may be commenced at any time."

[17] R.I. GEN. LAWS § 12-12-17(1) (1956 & Supp. 1988) states in pertinent part: "Stat-

Accordingly, prosecution may be commenced at any time for felonious child sexual abuse offenses in these three states.

Likewise in North Carolina, South Carolina, Virginia, West Virginia, and Wyoming, the state legislatures have remained silent with regard to any applicable statutory period of limitations.[18] Therefore, it is implied that prosecution may commence at any time.[19] The underlying rationale for not providing a bar to prosecution of certain felonies is that the interest of the state in prosecuting those crimes outweighs the benefits derived from the implementation of a limitation period.[20]

B. GENERAL STATUTORY PERIOD FOR FELONIES

Several states have enacted a specified statutory limitation period for felonies in general. In these states, the limitation period for sexual offenses committed against children is defined within the general statutes of limitations for felonies.[21] Generally, the period for felony statutes of limitations range between two and fifteen years.[22] These variations arise because states assign different weights to factors influencing a longer or shorter period of limitation: each state balances those interests supporting a longer period of limitations against those interests justifying a shorter period of

---

ute of Limitations. (a) There shall be no statute of limitations for the following offenses . . . first degree child molestation sexual assualt . . . ."

[18] In North Carolina, N.C. GEN. STAT. § 15-1 (1983), Virginia, VA. CODE ANN. § 19.2-8 (1989) and West Virginia, W. VA. CODE § 61-11-9 (1989), the statutory limitation provisions apply to prosecutions of misdemeanors only and not felonies. The penal code sections of the South Carolina and Wyoming statutes, however, do not have statutes of limitations.

[19] Note, *The Statute of Limitations in Criminal Law: A Penetrable Barrier to Prosecution*, 102 U. PA. L. REV. 630 (1954) (where a statute limiting the time period for prosecution is absent, a criminal act may be prosecuted at any time after its commission).

[20] Reed v. Commonwealth, 738 S.W.2d 818, 819-20 (Ky. 1987). The indictment charged that upon five occasions, defendant engaged in sexual intercourse with his neice, a female under fourteen years of age, by forcible compulsion. Defendant contended that he was prejudiced by a delay of eight years in the bringing of charges against him. The court, however, held that under Kentucky statutes there is no time bar for commencement of prosecution when the offense is classified as a felony.

[21] *See supra* notes 13-14 and accompanying text.

[22] *See, e.g.*, ME. REV. STAT. ANN. tit. 17-A, § 8(2)(B) (1983), NEB. REV. STAT. § 29-110 (1985), OR. REV. STAT. § 131.125 (1987) (three years); HAW. REV. STAT. § 701-108(2) (1986) (a class A felony is six years, any other felony is three years); N.Y. CRIM. PROC. LAW § 30.10(2)(b) (McKinney 1981) (five years); LA. CODE CRIM. PROC. ANN. § 572(1) (West 1981 & Supp. 1989), OHIO REV. CODE ANN. § 2901.13 (Anderson 1983), WIS. STAT. ANN. § 939.74(1) (West 1982) (six years); MISS. CODE ANN. § 99-1-5 (1989), S.D. CODIFIED LAWS ANN. § 23A-42-2 (1988) (seven years); N.M. STAT. ANN. § 30-1-8 (1978 & Supp. 1984) (a first degree felony is 15 years, a second degree felony is six years and a third degree felony is five years).

limitations. For instance, both Hawaii[23] and New Mexico[24] provide a longer limitation period for a more serious offense and a shorter limitation period for a lesser offense. Under New Mexico's statute of limitations,[25] sexual penetration involving a child under thirteen years of age is a felony of the first degree,[26] which has a limitation period of fifteen years. Where the victim is between the age of thirteen and sixteen, the same conduct is a second degree felony,[27] and the period of limitation is reduced to six years. Finally, if only sexual contact occurs with a minor, it is a third degree felony[28] and thus subject to a three year limitation period.

In addition to the general specified periods of limitation for felonies, many state legislatures have provided specific time periods for offenses committed against minors. The Georgia[29] and Idaho[30] legislatures have provided for a longer period of limitation when an offense has been committed against a minor. North Dakota[31] and Pennslyvania[32] have also recognized the special need for a longer

---

[23] HAW. REV. STAT. § 701-108(2) (1985). "For the most serious class of felonies, other than murder, a six year period is set, while for the other classes of felonies, three years is deemed sufficient." Commentary on HAW. REV. STAT. § 701-108(2) (1985).

[24] N.M. STAT. ANN. § 30-1-8 (1978 & Supp. 1984) states in pertinent part:

No person shall hereafter be prosecuted, tried or punished in any court of this state unless the indictment shall be found or information or complaint filed therefore within the time hereinafter provided:

    A. for a capital felony, within fifteen years from the time the crime was committed;

    B. for a first degree felony, within fifteen years from the time the crime was committed;

    C. for a second degree felony, within six years from the time the crime was committed;

    D. for a third or fourth degree felony, within five years from the time the crime was committed . . . .

[25] Id.

[26] Id. at § 30-9-11(A)(1).

[27] Id. at § 30-9-11(B)(1).

[28] Id. at § 30-9-13(A).

[29] GA. CODE ANN. § 26-503 (Harrison 1988) states in pertinent part:

Limitation of criminal prosecution, generally . . . (c) Prosecution for felonies . . . must be commenced within four years after the commission of the crime, provided that prosecution for felonies committed against victims who are at the time of the commission of the offense under the age of fourteen years must be commenced within seven years after the commission of the crime.

[30] IDAHO CODE § 19-402 (1985) states in pertinent part: "Commencement of prosecutions for crimes against children and other felonies. A prosecution for . . . any felony committed upon or against a minor child must be commenced within five years after the commission of the offense . . . ."

[31] N.D. CENT. CODE § 29-04-03.2 (1974 & Supp. 1989) states in pertinent part: "Statute of limitations as to child victim. If the victim . . . is under the age of fifteen, the applicable period of limitation, if any, does not begin to run until the victim has reached the age of fifteen."

[32] PA. STAT. ANN. tit. 42, § 5554(3) (Purdon 1981 & Supp. 1988) states in pertinent part:

limitation period for crimes committed against children and thus have enacted an exception applicable under such circumstances which tolls the running of the applicable limitations period for a specified number of years when the offense is committed against a minor.

C. SPECIFIED STATUTES OF LIMITATION FOR CHILD SEXUAL ABUSE

Even a greater number of states have enacted specific legislation for limitation of prosecution for sexual offenses involving minor victims.[33] An examination of these statutes indicates how the legislature of individual states evaluate the various factors that determine the limitation period for child sexual abuse offenses.

Several states, in enacting a limitation period for sexual abuse offenses committed against minors, have simply specified a certain number of years in which prosecution against the alleged offender may be commenced. The specified number of years represents how each state legislature defines the ideal time period. This period takes into consideration factors of stale evidence, motivation for prosecution, and repose, and measures these factors against the state's desire for retribution, concealment of the wrongful acts, and the seriousness of the crime.[34] The range in the length of the statutory limitation periods illustrates the different mode of evaluation of the individual factors utilized by the different state legislatures.

Iowa[35] and Tennessee[36] have the shortest limitation period,

---

Tolling of statute. Except as provided by section 5553(e) . . . the period of limitation does not run during any time when . . . (3) a child is under eighteen years of age, where the crime involves injuries to the person of the child caused by the wrongful act, or neglect, or unlawful violence, or negligence of the child's parents or by a person responsible for the child's welfare, or any individual residing in the same home as the child, or a paramour of the child's parent.

[33] *See, e.g.,* ALASKA STAT. § 12.10.020 (1962 & Supp. 1989) which states in part:

Specific Time Limitation . . . (c) Even if the general time limitation has expired, a prosecution under A.S. § 11.41.410 - 11.41.460 [sexual offenses] . . . for an offense committed against a person under the age of sixteen may be commenced within one year after the crime is reported to a peace officer or the person reaches the age of sixteen, whichever occurs first. This subsection does not extend the period of limitation by more than five years.

[34] Uelmen, *Making Sense Out of the California Criminal Statute of Limitations,* 15 PAC. L.J. 35 (1983) (examines the factors for and against a longer or shorter period of limitations for various crimes and then compares these factors to current California law).

[35] IOWA CODE ANN. § 802.2 (West 1976 & Supp. 1989) states in pertinent part: "Sexual abuse of child. An information or indictment for sexual abuse in the first, second or third degree committed on or with a child under the age of ten years shall be found within four years after its commission."

[36] TENN. CODE ANN. § 40-2-101(c) (1977 & Supp. 1989) states in pertinent part: "Prosecution for any offense committed against a child that constitutes a criminal offense under the provisions of . . . [sexual offense listed] . . . shall be commenced no later

four years, while Massachusetts[37], Missouri,[38] and Texas[39] have the longest limitation period, ten years. The remaining eight states[40] have enacted limitation periods which fall within these two extremes. Three of these states have determined that the optimal limitation period for child sexual abuse offenses is five years.[41]

Colorado also has a specific statute of limitations provision for the offense of sexual assault on a child. In Colorado the general limitation period of three years is extended to ten years when the offense is one of child sexual abuse.[42]

D.   TOLLING THE STATUTE OF LIMITATIONS

An alternative approach to extending the limitation period is to provide exceptions to the prevailing general provisions when the of-

---

than the date the child attains the age of majority or within four (4) years next after the commission of the offense, whichever occurs later . . . ."

[37] MASS. ANN. LAWS ch. 277, § 63 (Law Co-op 1980 & Supp. 1988) states, "An indictment for a crime set forth in sections . . . [sex offenses] . . . may be found and filed within ten years of the date of commission of said crime."

[38] MO. ANN. STAT. § 556.037 (Vernon 1979 & Supp. 1989) states that "prosecutions for unlawful sexual offenses involving a person seventeen years of age or under must be commenced within ten years after commission of the offense if the offense charged is a felony and within five years after commission of the offense if the offense is a misdemeanor."

[39] TEX. CRIM. PROC. CODE ANN. § 12.01(2)(d) (Vernon 1965 & Supp. 1989) (provides that prosecution for child sexual abuse offense must be commenced within 10 years from the date of the commission of the offense).

[40] See KAN. STAT. ANN. § 21-3106(2) (1969 & Supp. 1987), MONT. CODE ANN. § 45-1-205(1)(b) (1989) (provides a five year limitation period during which commencement of prosecution is permitted where the victim was under 18 years of age at the time the offense was committed.); PA. STAT. ANN. tit. 42, § 5552(b) (Purdon 1981 & Supp. 1989) (provides a five year limitations period); MICH. COMP. LAWS ANN. § 767.24(2) (West 1982 & Supp. 1989) (provides that prosecution may commence up until six years after the commission of the offense or until the victim reaches 21 years of age, whichever is later); VT. STAT. ANN. tit. 113, § 4501(c) (1974 & Supp. 1989) (provides a six years period of limitation if victim is under 16 years of age at the time of offense); MINN. STAT. ANN. § 628.26(c) (West 1983 & Supp. 1989) (provides a limitation period of seven years); N.D. CENT. CODE § 29-04-03.1 (1974 & Supp. 1989) (provides that prosecution may be commenced within seven years where victim is under 18 years of age); WASH. REV. CODE ANN. § 9A.04.080(1)(c) (1988 & Supp. 1989) (provides a seven year period of limitation).

[41] See KAN. STAT. ANN. § 21-3106(2) (1988); MONT. CODE ANN. § 45-1-205(1)(b) (1989); PA. STAT. ANN. tit. 42, § 5552(b) (Purdon 1981 & Supp. 1989).

[42] COLO. REV. STAT. § 16-5-401(7) (1984 & Supp. 1988) states:

When the victim at the time of the commission of the offense is a child under fifteen years of age, the period of time during which a person may be prosecuted shall be extended for an additional seven years as to a felony charged under section 18-3-404 . . . .

. . . .

. . . The intent of the general assembly in enacting enacting § 16-5-401 (6) and (7) in 1982 was to create a ten year statute of limitations as to offenses specified in said subsections committed on or after July 1, 1979.

fense is one of child sexual abuse. These exceptions toll the applicable time period defined in the general provisions until the victim attains majority (or soon thereafter)[43] or until discovery of the wrongful act is made by a guardian or law enforcement agency.[44] A few states have utilized both types of tolling provisions, with the applicable period being the shortest of the two periods.[45] However, states which permit tolling the statutory period preserve a maximum time period during which prosecution must commence.[46]

1. Attaining Majority

For crimes involving minors and, in particular, child sexual abuse offenses, several state legislatures have extended the statutory period of limitations until the victim attains majority.[47] Generally, the limitation period provided by this exception will not be shorter than the general limitation period; otherwise, the latter provision applies.[48]

A few states[49] have taken this exception one step further and

---

[43] *See infra* notes 47-49 and accompanying text.

[44] *See infra* notes 67-69 and accompanying text.

[45] *See* ALASKA STAT. § 12.10.020(c) (1962 & Supp. 1989) (permits commencement of prosecution for a sexual offense committed against a minor, even though the general time limitation has expired, until one year after the victim reaches the age of 16 or the violation is reported to a peace officer, whichever occurs first); MASS. ANN. LAWS ch. 277, § 63 (Law. Co-op. 1980 & Supp. 1989) (provides that if the victim is under 16 years of age at the time of the commission of the offense, the limitation period is tolled until the victim reaches 16 years of age or until it is reported to a law enforcement agency, whichever occurs first); NEV. REV. STAT. ANN. § 171.095(2) (1986 & Supp. 1987) (prosecution may be commenced any time until the victim is 18 years old or until reported to the appropriate authority, whichever is earlier).

[46] *See, e.g.,* ALASKA STAT. § 12.10.020(c) (1962 & Supp. 1989) states, "This subsection does not extend the period of limitation by more than five years."

[47] *See* MICH. COMP. LAWS ANN. § 767.24(2) (West 1982 & Supp. 1989) (permits commencement of prosecution within six years from the date of the commission of the crime or by the victim's twenty-first birthday, whichever is later); NEV. REV. STAT. ANN. § 171.095(2) (1986 & Supp. 1987) (permits prosecution of the offense until the victim is 18 years old if not previously reported); N.J. STAT. ANN. § 2C:1-6(b)(4) (West 1982 & Supp. 1989) (permits commencement of prosecution until two years after the victim attains eighteen years of age or within five years from the date of the commission of the crime, whichever occurs later); TENN. CODE ANN. § 40-2-101(c) (1982 & Supp. 1989) (permits commencement of prosecution at any time until the victim attains majority or within four years).

[48] *See, e.g.,* ILL. ANN. STAT. ch. 38, para. 3-6(d) (Smith-Hurd 1989) which states:

When the victim is under eighteen years of age, a prosecution for criminal sexual assualt . . . may be commenced within one year of the victim attaining the age of eighteen years. However, in no such case shall the time period for prosecution expire sooner than three years after the commission of the offense.

[49] ARK. STAT. ANN. § 5-1-109(h) (1987) states in pertinent part:

If the period prescribed in subsection (b) [three years] has expired, a prosecution may nevertheless be commenced for violations of the following offenses if, when the alleged violation occurred, the offense was committed against a minor, the violation

have tolled application of the statutory period until the victim attains majority. Thus, the applicable statutory period does not begin to run until the victim becomes of age.

2. Discovery

a. In General

Statutes of limitations may also be tolled until discovery of the alleged offense is made by the victim or a law enforcement agency. This exception is based upon the common law "discovery rule" principle.[50]

Ordinarily, a statute of limitations begins to run "upon the occurence of the last fact essential to the cause of action."[51] However, in jurisdictions in which the discovery rule is applicable, courts have held that the limitation period does not begin to run until the plaintiff discovered or in the exercise of diligence should have discovered all of the facts essential to the cause of action.[52]

The underlying rationale of the discovery rule focuses on the inequity in foreclosing a cause of action where the victim may not know of the injury or harm.[53] The interests of the defendant, on the other hand, are protected by employing a balancing test to determine the applicability of the discovery rule. This balancing test weighs the harm to the defendant of being forced to prosecute stale claims against the harm to a plaintiff of being deprived of a rem-

---

has not previously been reported to a law enforcement agency or prosecuting attorney, and the period prescribed in subsection (b) has not expired since the victim has reached the age of eighteen (18): . . . (8) Sexual abuse in the fist degree as prohibited in § 5-14-108.

FLA. STAT. ANN. § 775.15(7) (West 1976 & Supp. 1989) states, "If the victim of a violation of . . . [sex offenses listed] . . . is under the age of sixteen, the applicable period of limitations, if any, does not begin to run until the victim has reached the age of sixteen . . . ."; MASS. GEN. LAWS ANN. ch. 277, § 63 (1980 & Supp. 1988) states:

Nothwithstanding the foregoing provisions, if a victim of a crime set forth in . . . [includes sex offenses] . . . is under the age of sixteen at the time such crime is committed, the period of limitations for prosecution shall not commence until the victim has reached the age of sixteen or the violation is reported to a law enforcement agency, whichever occurs earlier.

[50] See Comment, *Adult Incest Survivors and the Statute of Limitations: The Delayed Discovery Rule and Long-Term Damages*, 25 SANTA CLARA L. REV. 191 (1985) (The discovery rule permits tolling of the statue of limitations until all the elements of the crime have been discovered. The comment argues that the application of the delayed discovery exception is appropriate for damages suffered by adult incest survivors.).

[51] E.W. v. D.C.H., 754 P.2d 817, 819 (Mont. 1988) (The court refused to apply the discovery rule to extend the statutory limitation period in a civil action to recover damages for emotional distress resulting from sexual abuse committed against the plaintiff as a child.).

[52] Note, *Evidence: Discovery Rule Application in Child Abuse Actions*, 23 GONZ. L. REV. 223, 226 (1987/88).

[53] *Id.* at 224-225.

edy.[54] Therefore, the discovery rule "should be adopted only when the risk of stale claims is outweighed by the unfairness of precluding justified causes of action."[55]

Attempts to apply the discovery rule to toll the statute of limitations for sexual offenses committed against children have been made by plaintiffs in civil actions seeking to recover damages for emotional distress.[56] In the landmark case of *Tyson v. Tyson*,[57] the issue presented to the court was whether the discovery rule should be applied to toll the statute of limitations until the plaintiff discovers the cause of action, where the victim had blocked the illicit incidents from her conscious memory for a period extending beyond the duration of the limitation period.[58]

The court, in addressing its concern about the evidentiary problems surrounding stale claims, examined other fact scenerios in which the discovery rule had been applied, such as medical malpractice, products liability, and asbestos cases, and found that in each instance there was "objective, verifiable evidence" of the wrongful conduct.[59] The court determined that existence of this evidence diminished the risk of stale evidence by increasing the possibility that the fact finder would be able to determine the truth despite the passage of time.[60] However, due to the absence of such objective evidence of the allegations, the *Tyson* court refused to apply the discovery rule.[61] Since *Tyson*, the existence of objective, verifiable evidence as a prerequisite to application of the discovery rule has

---

[54] *See* Glimcher, *Statute of Limitations and the Discovery Rule in Latent Injury Claims: An Exception or the Law*, 43 U. Pitt. L. Rev. 501 (1982).

[55] Tyson v. Tyson, 107 Wash.2d 72, 76, 727 P.2d 226, 228 (1986) (citing United States Oil & Refinery Co. v. Dep't. of Ecology, 96 Wash.2d 85, 93, 633 P.2d 1329, 1334 (1981)).

[56] *See, e.g., Tyson*, 107 Wash.2d at 72, 727 P.2d at 226; John R. v. Oakland Unified School Dist., 206 Cal. App. 3d 1473, 240 Cal. Rptr. 319 (1987); E.W. v. D.C.H., 754 P.2d 817 (Mont. 1988); DeRose v. Carswell, 196 Cal. App. 3d 1011, 242 Cal. Rptr. 368 (1987).

[57] 107 Wash.2d at 72, 727 P.2d at 206.

[58] *Id.* at 73-74, 727 P.2d at 227. The plaintiff-victim was subject to multiple acts of sexual assault during her childhood from 1960 through 1969 but failed to file a complaint until 1983. The cause for the delay was the suppression of the alleged acts by the victim, which resurfaced only through psychological therapy undertaken several years later in 1983. *Id.* at 74, 727 P.2d at 227.

[59] *Id.* at 76, 727 P.2d at 228.

[60] "Because of the availability and trustworthiness of objective, verifiable evidence in the above cases, the claims were neither speculative nor incapable of proof. Since the evidentiary problems which the statute of limitations is designed to prevent did not exist or were reduced, it was reasonable to extend the period for bringing the actions." *Id.* at 77, 727 P.2d at 228.

[61] *Id.* at 77, 80, 727 P.2d at 229, 230.

been followed by several courts in other jurisdictions.[62]

Nevertheless, the five-four decision in *Tyson* is not without controversy. Many critics, supporting the views expressed in the dissent,[63] suggest that the need for objective, verifiable evidence ignores the balancing of interests test. At the very least, the balancing of interests test essentially becomes biased towards the accused when objective, verifiable evidence is required.[64] Furthermore, many of the courts following the *Tyson* decision have noted that the application of the discovery rule to a particular offense is the province of the legislatures and not the courts.[65] Other courts have suggested that legislatures should give special attention to the applicability of the discovery rule for cases involving the sexual abuse of children.[66]

In response to the courts, the state legislatures of Alaska, Oklahoma, and Utah[67] have recognized the applicability of the discovery rule to child sexual abuse offenses. For example, in Utah the statutory limitation provision provides that if the four-year period has expired, "a prosecution may nevertheless be commenced for . . . (c) sexual abuse of a child within one year after the report of offense to law enforcement officials, so long as no more than eight years has elapsed since the alleged commission of the offense."[68]

---

[62] *See* John R. v. Oakland Unified School Dist., 206 Cal. App. 3d 1473, 240 Cal. Rptr. 319 (1987); DeRose v. Carswell, 196 Cal. App. 3d 1011, 242 Cal. Rptr. 368 (1987); E.W. v. D.C.H., 754 P.2d 817 (Mont. 1988).

[63] *See, e.g.*, Note, *supra* note 52, at 229-34.

[64] "Fundalmental fairness, not availability of objective evidence, has always been the linchpin of the discovery rule." *Tyson*, 107 Wash. 2d at 82, 727 P.2d at 231 (Pearson, J., dissenting). The dissent suggested that the issue was simply to decide "whether notions of fundamental fairness entitle the plaintiff to try to convince a court or jury that she discovered or should have discovered her cause of action after it would otherwise have been foreclosed by the statute of limitations." *Id.* at 231 (Pearson, J., dissenting). According to the dissent, the evidentiary problems encountered by the plaintiff in trying to convince the trier of fact of the reasonableness of her late discovery should not be the court's concern. *Id.* at 231 (Pearson, J., dissenting).

[65] *See, e.g., id.* at 80, 727 P.2d at 230 (5-4 decision) (Goodloe, J., concurring) (concluded that it was a policy decision that should be determined by the legislature).

[66] *See, e.g.*, E.W. v. D.C.H. 754 P.2d at 821. "While this Court is aware of the horrifying damage inflicted by child molesters, it is not for us to rewrite the statute of limitations to accomodate such claims through judicial fiat. Such a task is properly vested in the legislature."

[67] *See infra* note 68 and accompanying text.

[68] UTAH CODE ANN. § 76-1-303 (1978 & Supp. 1989). See also ALASKA STAT. § 12.10.020 (1962 & Supp. 1988), which states in pertinent part:

Specific Time Limitations . . . (c) Even if the general time limitation has expired, a prosecution under Alaska statutes § 11.41.410 - 11.41.460 [sexual offenses] for an offense committed against a person under the age of sixteen may be commenced within one year after the crime is reported to a peace officer or the person reaches the age of sixteen, whichever occurs first. This subsection does not extend the period of limitation by more than five years.

Similarly, Georgia statutorily provides for the application of the discovery rule for general offenses.[69] However, courts in Georgia have denied tolling the statutory period for child sexual abuse offenses by imputing the victim's knowledge of the acts to knowledge of the state. In *Sears v. State*,[70] for example, the victim testified that she knew of the sexual acts wrongfully committed against her when she was eleven years old, but she was not specifically aware that such conduct was criminal. She only became aware of the criminality of the conduct four years later as the result of radio and television news broadcasts.[71] The court held:

> Where, as here the undisputed record evidence shows that the victim had knowledge of the offenses (if not their criminality) allegedly committed upon her by the appellant 'in the year 1980,' such knowledge is imputed to the State, and precludes the State from obtaining an indictment against appellant for those alleged crimes more than four years after both the offenses and the offender were known.[72]

Georgia, however, as a discovery rule state, stands alone on this view.

Several state legislatures have qualified the application of the discovery rule by requiring that there be either a breach of a fiduciary relationship or concealment of the crime by the accused.[73]

b. Breach of Fiduciary Obligation

A common circumstance under which several states permit toll-

---

OKLA. STAT. ANN. tit. 22, § 152 (1978 & Supp. 1989) states, "Limitations in General . . . the crime of lewd or indecent proposals or acts against children, pursuant to § 1123 of Title 21 of the Oklahoma statutes, [lists other child sexual abuse offenses and other offenses] shall be commenced within five years after the discovery of the crime."

69 GA. CODE ANN. § 26-503 (Harrison 1988) states, "The period within which a prosecution must be commenced under Code Section 17-3-1 . . . does not include any period in which: . . . (2) The person committing the crime is unknown or the crime is unknown. . . ."

CONN. GEN. STAT. ANN. § 53a-69 (1976) provided that where the alleged victim was under 16 years old, the offense must be brought within one year after a parent, guardian, or other competent person especially interested in the alleged victim learns of the offense. However, this section was repealed in 1987. The current applicable provision, CONN. GEN. STAT. ANN. § 54-193(b) (West 1985 & Supp. 1989) provides a one year statutory period of limitations.

70 182 Ga. App. 480, 356 S.E.2d 72 (1987).

71 *Id.* at 481, 356 S.E.2d at 74.

72 *Id. see also* People v. Strait, 152 Ill. App. 3d 599, 367 N.E.2d 768 (1977). Charges of indecent liberties with a child were dismissed because prosecution of the offense was barred by the staute of limitations. Here again, the court held that the crime was easily discoverable because the victim had knowledge. The court further stated that because the victim did not immediately report the incident to the authorities, the statutory discovery rule exception would not operate to extend the period of limitations. *Id.* at 602, 367 N.E.2d at 771.

73 *See infra* notes 74-101 and accompanying text.

ing the statute of limitations until discovery of the offense is made is when a breach of a fiduciary obligation or relationship occurs. For instance, Delaware's limitation provision provides:

> If the period . . . has expired, a prosecution for any offense in which the accused's acts include or constitute . . . breach of fiduciary duty . . . may be commenced within two years after discovery of the offense has been made or should have been made in the exercise of ordinary diligence by an aggrieved party or by an authorized agent, fiduciary guardian, personal representative or parent . . . who is not a party to the offense. In no case shall this provision extend the period of limitation otherwise applicable by more than an additional three years beyond the period specified in subsection (b) of this section.[74]

Such an exception may arguably be applied to sexual offenses committed against children. The existence of a fiduciary relationship between the accused and the child imposes an affirmative obligation upon the dominating party to make full disclosure. The failure to disclose is treated as fraudulent concealment of the cause of action by the defendant, even though no active misrepresentation is ever made.[75]

In Illinois, the legislature has specifically applied this discovery exception to sexual offenses:

> A prosecution for any offense involving sexual conduct or sexual penetration, as defined in § 12-12 of this Code, where defendant was within a professional or fiduciary relationship with the victim at the time of the commission of the offense may be commenced within one year after discovery of the offense by the victim.[76]

However, in many of the other states, breach of the fiduciary obligation must be a "material element of the offense" before the limitation period may be tolled.[77] In *State v. Mills*,[78] the court de-

---

[74] DEL. CODE ANN. tit. 11, § 205(c) (1987). HAW. REV. STAT. § 701-108(3)(a) (1985 & Supp. 1988) states:
If the period . . . has expired, a prosecution may nevertheless be commenced for:
(a) Any offense an element of which is either fraud or a breach of a fiduciary obligation within two years after discovery of the offense by a person who has a legal duty to represent an aggrieved party, and who is himself not a party to the offense.
ME. REV. STAT. ANN. tit. 17A, § 8(5)(a) (1978) states, "If the period of limitation has expired, a prosecution may nevertheless be commenced for: (a) Any crime based upon breach of fiduciary obligation, within one year after discovery of the crime by an aggrevied party . . . ."

[75] *See* Comment, *supra* note 50, at 204.

[76] ILL. ANN. STAT. ch. 38, para. 3-6(e) (Smith-Hurd 1989).

[77] HAW. REV. STAT. § 701-108(3)(a) (1985 & Supp. 1988) states:
If the period . . . has expired, a prosecution may nevertheless be commenced for:
(a) Any offense an element of which is either fraud or breach of a fiduciary obligation within two years after discovery of the offense by an aggrieved party or by a person who has a legal duty to represent an aggrieved party and who is himself not a party to the offense . . . but in no case shall this provision extend the period of limitation otherwise applicable by more than six years.

fined material elements as "[t]hose constituent parts of a crime which must be proved by the prosecution to sustain a conviction.' "[79] In *Mills*, the state argued that the deviate sexual intercouse of defendant upon his daughter, a person under the age of sixteen years, constituted a breach of the fiduciary obligation that a father owes to his daughter.[80] The court, however, held that the breach of a fiduciary obligation is not a material element of the offense; thus, the exception to toll the statutory period is not applicable.[81] According to the statutory language, the offense of sodomy only requires that the victim be a close family relation of the defendant.[82] There is no explicit requirement to prove breach of a fiduciary obligation in order to obtain a conviction.[83] Further, the *Mills* court stated that if the legislature desired to extend the limitation period for crimes involving sexual abuse of minors, it would have done so in a clear and straightforward manner.[84]

c. Concealment

Concealment of a crime is a another recognized cause for tolling the statute of limitations until discovery is made. In *State v. Danielski*,[85] a Minnesota court utilized the doctrine of concealment as a means to toll the running of the statutory period in order to overcome certain injustices in child sexual abuse cases. Prosecution for child sexual abuse under Minnesota statute requires that the defendant both be in a position of authority over the victim and use that authority to coerce the victim to submit to the acts.[86] The Min-

---

OR. REV. STAT. § 131.125(3)(a) (1987) states:

If the offense has as a material element either fraud or the breach of a fiduciary obligation, prosecution may be commenced within one year after discovery of the offense by the aggrieved party . . . but in no case shall the period of limitation otherwise applicable be extended by more than three years.

PA. STAT. ANN. tit. 42, § 5552(c)(1) (Purdon 1981) states, "If the period prescribed . . . has expired, a prosecution may neverthless be commenced for: (1) Any offense a material element of which is either fraud or breach of fiduciary obligation within one year after discovery of the offense . . . ."

[78] 77 Or. App. 125, 711 P.2d 207 (1985).
[79] *Id.* at 129, 711 P.2d at 209 (quoting BLACK'S LAW DICTIONARY 467 (5th ed. 1979)).
[80] *Id.* at 128-29, 711 P.2d at 208.
[81] *Id.* at 129, 711 P.2d at 209.
[82] *Id.* at 128, 711 P.2d at 208.
[83] *Id.*; *accord*, Commonwealth v. Goldhammer, 507 Pa. 236, 241-42, 489 A.2d 1307, 1311-12 (1985) (The court held that for purposes of tolling the statute of limitations, the definition of the offense must include fraud or breach of fiduciary obligation as one of its elements. Theft by unlawful taking does not contain as a material element either fraud or breach of fiduciary obligation.).
[84] *Mills*, 77 Or. App. at 130, 711 P.2d. at 209.
[85] 348 N.W.2d 352 (Minn. Ct. App. 1984).
[86] MINN. STAT. § 609.342(b) (1980).

nesota court held that commission of the offense is continuing as long as the accused abuses his or her position of authority and thus the statutory period of limitation does not commence until the coercion ceases.[87]

The court's application of the concealment exception is justified under the doctrine of continuing offenses. The Supreme Court has held that the "[s]tatute of limitations normally begins to run when the crime is complete.' "[88] A crime is said to be complete upon the satisfaction of all of the elements of the offense.[89] However, under the doctrine of continuing offenses, even though all the elements of the crime have occured, if one of the elements persists, the crime is not complete but is a continuing offense.[90]

In child sexual abuse cases, although each act of penetration may constitute a separate offense, as long as the same authority "that is used to accomplish criminal sexual acts against a child is used to prevent the reporting of that act," the offense is continuous and "the statute of limitations does not begin to run until the child is no longer subjected to that authority."[91]

Furthermore, the concealment of a crime which suspends the operation of the statute of limitations must be the result of positive acts done by the accused, calculated to prevent the discovery of the commission of the offense.[92] Mere silence, inaction, or nondisclo-

---

[87] *Danielski*, 348 N.W.2d at 357.

[88] Toussie v. United States, 397 U.S. 112, 115 (1970) (quoting Pendergast v. United States, 317 U.S. 412, 418 (1943)) (Court acknowledged that whether a particular criminal offense is a continuing offense is a question of statutory interpretation).

[89] *See, e.g.*, ALASKA STAT. § 12.10.030 (1984) (statutory period starts running when every element of the offense occurs or the prohibited conduct is terminated).

[90] Note, *supra* note 19, at 642.

[91] *Danielski*, 348 N.W.2d at 356. The court found that the offense was a continuing one because the defendant who was in a position of authority over the victim used that authority, by means of threats, to coerce the victim to submit to the sexual acts. The defendant's conduct and use of authority was found sufficient to toll the statutes of limitations until the child was no longer subjected to such authority. *Id.* at 357; *see also* State v. Johnson, 422 N.W.2d 14, 17-18 (Minn. Ct. App. 1988) (The court, in following *Danielski*, affirmed the trial court's determination that the defendant actively coerced his victim by threatening to throw her into jail along with threats of other physical abuse. The court also noted that the lapse of time after the statute had run was irrelevant. *But see* State v. Bentley, 239 Kan. 334, 339, 721 P.2d 227, 230 (1986). (an uncle's threat to repeat the act if his nine year old niece revealed the sexual incidents did not constitute concealment and thus did not toll the statute of limitations).

[92] State v. Mills, 238 Kan. 189, 190, 707 P.2d 1079, 1081 (1985). (threats issued by a third party not to reveal incidents of fondling did not constitute concealment to toll the running of the statute of limitations); State v. Shamp, 422 N.W.2d 736, 740 (Minn. App. 1988) (the court held that where the accused, here the victim's sister, did not control the victim's day to day movements and did not reside with the victim, the statute of limitations is not tolled).

sure alone does not constitute concealmeant.[93]

Many courts have rejected the concealment exception, claiming that "it is not the province of the court to fashion exceptions to the statute of limitations as that task is left to the legislature."[94] However, a few state legislatures, recognizing that many child sexual abuse acts are in fact concealed by the abuser, have enacted legislation to counter this result. The Louisiana concealment exception to the four-year statutory limitation period for child sexual abuse offenses reads as follows:

> The time limitations established by Article 572 shall not commence to run as to the following offenses until the relationship or status involved has ceased to exist where: . . .
>
> (4) The offense charged is one of the following . . . indecent behavior with juveniles (R.S. 14:81) . . . and the victim is under the domination or control of the offender while under seventeen years of age.[95]

Emphasis is placed upon the existence of control.[96] Thus the limitation period is tolled only until the coercion or domination ceases.

In Nevada,[97] Indiana,[98] and Kansas,[99] general provisions for concealment exceptions have been enacted. Although these provisions are not explicitly applicable to cases regarding child sexual abuse, the courts in Nevada[100] and Indiana[101] have applied the gen-

---

[93] *Id.*

[94] *Id.* at 191, 707 P.2d at 1081; *Bentley*, 239 Kan. at 339, 721 P.2d at 230.

[95] La. Code Crim. Proc. Ann. art. 573 (West 1981 & Supp. 1989).

[96] State v. Barre, 532 So. 2d 842, 843 (La. Ct. App. 1988). Application of the Louisiana statutory exception "requires a showing of a relationship or status and proof of 'domination or control' by the offender over his victim while the victim is under the age of seventeen." Here the court held that the record failed to support a finding that the victim was under the domination of her father, the defendant. The victim stated that she was never forced to visit her father and would often call him and arrange to see him even after the alleged offense. She also testified that she did not fear physical harm from her father if she revealed his behavior.

[97] Nev. Rev. Stat. Ann. § 171.095(1) (Michie 1986 & Supp. 1988) ("If a felony . . . is committed in a secret manner . . . an information [must be] filed [within three or four years] after the discovery of the offense.").

[98] Ind. Code Ann. § 35-41-4-21(d) (West 1986) states:
The period within which a prosecution must be commenced does not include any period in which: . . . (2) the accused person conceals evidence of the offense, and evidence sufficient to charge him with that offense is unknown to the prosecuting authority and could not have been discovered by that authority by exercise of due diligence.

[99] Kan. Crim. Proc. Code Ann. § 21-3106(4)(c) (Vernon 1988) ("The period within which a prosecution must be commenced shall not include any period in which . . . (c) the fact of the crime is concealed; . . . .").

[100] *See, e.g.*, Walstrom v. State, 752 P.2d 225, 228 (Nev. 1988):
We conclude that a crime is done in a secret manner, under NRS 171.095, when it is committed in a deliberately surreptitious manner that is intended to and does keep all but those committing the crime unaware that an offense has been committed . . . given the inherently vulnerable nature of a child, we conclude that the crime of

eral statutory exception to child sexual abuse offenses. However, the courts in Kansas have consistently held that their statutory concealment exception does not apply to child sexual offenses. In *State v. Bentley*,[102] the Kansas Supreme Court held that "[c]rimes against persons, by their very nature, cannot be concealed."[103] The court concluded that threats by an uncle to repeat the offensive acts if the nine year old victim revealed the incidents to anyone did not amount to concealment of a crime.[104] However, the court noted that the uncle's ability to control the child victim in this case was too remote.[105]

E.- AMENDMENT TO STATUTE OF LIMITATIONS

In recent years many state legislatures have amended their legislation for offenses committed against minors by extending the applicable limitation period.[106] The constitutionality of these amendments have been upheld.[107]

In absence of language to the contrary, these extended periods

---

lewdness with a minor can be committed in a secret manner, even though a victim is involved.

[101] *See, e.g.,* Crider v. State, 351 N.E.2d 1151, 1154 (Ind. 1988). Defendant who was convicted of child molesting threatened his daughter with bodily harm if she revealed the acts. The court held that the defendant concealed the fact of his crime by her positive acts of intimidation of his victim. The statute of limitations did not run until the victim made her disclosure to authorities.

[102] 239 Kan. 334, 721 P.2d 227 (1986).

[103] *Id.* at 339, 721 P.2d at 230.

[104] *Id.; accord* State v. Miller, 11 Kan. App.2d 410, 413-14, 722 P.2d 1131, 1134 (1986) (threats by defendant to step-daughters that he would hurt them if they told anyone about the alleged aggravated incest did not constitute concealment).

[105] State v. Bentley, 239 Kan. 334, 339, 721 P.2d 227, 230 (1986).

[106] *See, e.g.,* ALA. CODE § 15-3-5(a)(4) (1975) (extended the general provision of three years to a no limitation period in 1985); ALASKA STAT. § 12.10.020 (1984) (in 1983 extended a five year period to a one year period after the child reaches 16 or after the crime is reported to a peace officer, whichever occurs first); ARK. STAT. ANN § 5-1-109(h) (1987) (in 1987 added an exception to the three year limitation period in which prosecution may be commenced within three years of the victim attaining the age of 18, where the offense was committed against a minor and the violation had not been previously reported to a law enforcement agency); FLA. STAT. ANN. § 775.15 (1976 & Supp. 1989) (in 1984 added that if the victim is under the age of 16, the period of limitations does not begin to run until the victim has reached the age of sixteen or the violation is reported to a law, enforcement agency, whichever occurs first); WASH. REV. CODE ANN. § 9A.040.080(1)(c) (in 1985 extended the period in which prosecution may be commenced for crimes of indecent liberties from five to seven years).

[107] The Seventh Circuit, in upholding the constitutionality of these amendments, explicitly held that the extension of a statute of limitations was merely a procedural alteration which did "not increase the punishment nor change the ingredients of the offense or the ultimate facts necessary to establish guilt.' " United States *ex rel.* Massarella v. Elrod, 682 F.2d 688, 689 (7th Cir. 1982) (quoting Weaver v. Graham, 450 U.S. 24, 29 n. 12 (1981)).

apply not only to crimes committed subsequent to the date the statute was amended, but encompass those offenses not barred by the previous legislative period.[108] However, where the statute explicitly states that the provision of this section (or act) does not apply to any offense committed before the effective date of the section, the limitation period only operates prospectively.[109]

III. LEGISLATIVE RECOMMENDATION

A period of limitation should be determined by the legislative goals and purposes underlying statutes of limitations. The main purpose of any statute of limitations is "to protect the accused from the burden of defending himself against charges of long completed misconduct."[110] Likewise, criminal prosecution should be based on evidence that is reasonably fresh and trustworthy.[111] To allow otherwise would infringe upon the accused's rights to a fair trial due

---

[108] *See* State v. Creekpaum, 753 P.2d 1139 (Alaska 1988) (Defendant who allegedly sexually assaulted a nine year old girl filed a motion to dismiss the case on the grounds that the applicable statute of limitations had run. The court held that the extension of the statute of limitations before the original limitation period had run on defendant's alleged offense was not an unconstitutional ex post facto law.); People v. Callan, 174 Cal. App. 3d 1011, 220 Cal. Rptr. 339 (1985) (statutory amendments lengthening the statute of limitations for bringing prosecution to six years for lewd and lascivious conduct with a child under the age of 14 years was not time barred where statutory amendents were enacted before the old statutory period expired); People v. Whitesell, 729 P.2d 985 (Colo. 1986) (Defendant was charged with sexual criminal assault on a child. The Colorado Supreme Court held that the amendment increasing the applicable statute of limitations for an additional three years applied to all offenses not time barred as of the amendment's effective date.).

The court in Commonwealth v. Thek, 376 Pa. Super. 390, 401, 546 A.2d 83, 89 (1988) stated:

Where the legislature amends a statute of limitations to provide a longer limitations period or enacts [an amendment] which tolls the running of the statute of limitations before prior limitations period has expired, in the absence of language in the statute to the contrary, the amendments will be construed to apply so as to extend the period within which prosecution is to be commenced.

However, an amendment would be in violation of the state constitution's ex post facto clause if it extends the statute of limitations to resurrect a case for which the statury period has already run. *Id.* at 401, 546 A.2d at 89.

The court in State v Traczyk, 421 N.W.2d 229 (Minn. 1988), however, held that the amended statute of limitations is not to be applied retroactively to any offense committed prior to the effective amendment date.

[109] *See* Martin v. Superior Court, 135 Ariz. 99, 100, 659 P.2d 652, 653 (1983). The language specifying the applicability of the act was not explicit in the statute of limitations provision but in another section of the act. Nevertheless, the court held that all provisions of the new criminal code applied prospectively and not retroactively. Thus, the court dismissed the indictment on the grounds that the old applicable statutory period had expired.

[110] Note, *supra* note 19, at 632.

[111] *Id.*

to evidentiary problems of obtaining witnesses,[112] forgotten events,[113] and lost records.[114] This general goal of a statute of limitations is further supplemented by a defendant's constitutional right to a speedy trial.[115]

Generally, to determine the length of a statute of limitations, state legislatures weigh factors supporting a shorter period of limitation against factors justifying a longer limitation period. Factors which justify a short period of limitation are staleness of evidence, motivation, and repose. A short period of limitation overcomes many of the problems associated with stale evidence.[116] A brief limitation period also motivates the state to be efficient in prosecuting criminal offenses.[117] Furthermore, a shorter period of limitation fosters rehabilitation by assuring a criminal that any rehabilitative progress will not be shattered by the enforcement of some long-dormant claim.[118]

Factors which support a long period of limitation are concealment, investigation, and the seriousness of the offense.[119] The very nature of certain crimes, particularly child sexual abuse, makes detection of the offense especially difficult. A long period of limitation

---

[112] *Id.* (As time lapses, witnesses may be difficult to locate because they might have moved or passed away.).

[113] *Id.* (As memories fade, testimonies become less reliable.). *But see* Uelmen, *supra* note 34, at 46 ("Some research suggests that passage of time assumes less significance as more time passes, since loss of memory is most accute in the period immediately following the events while long term memory is more of a gradual process.").

[114] *See* Tyson v. Tyson, 107 Wash.2d 72,75-76, 727 P.2d 226, 228 (1986) (Physical evidence is more likely to be lost when a claim is stale either because it has been misplaced or because its significance was not comprehended at the time of the alleged wrong.).

[115] Note, *supra* note 19, at 633 (Statutes of limitations provide no assurance as to the time of the trial. A limitation period only assures that an indictment will be issued within a specified time.).

[116] *See* Uelman, *supra* note 34, at 46-47.

[117] *See* Uelmen, *supra* note 34, at 48-49 (This is to insure against bureacratic delays. However, the author also suggests that the statute of limitations may be a negligible factor in motivating, as priority in investing and prosecuting is determined by other means such as the seriousness of the offense.).

[118] Note, *supra* note 19, at 634. (Society will have more to lose than to gain in prosecuting a criminal unlikely to commit another crime. Desirable to bar prosecution where there is a strong possibility that self rehabilitation has taken place.) *Id.* at 638. Uelman, *supra* note 34, at 51 (quoting Model Penal Code § 1.07 at 16) states:

   If the person refrains from further criminal activity, the likelihood increases with the passage of time that he has reformed, diminishing pro tanto the necessity for imposition of the criminal sanction. If he has repeated his criminal behavior, he can be prosecuted for recent offenses committed within the period of limitations. As time goes by, the retributive impulse which may have existed in the community is likely to yield place to a sense of compassion for the person prosecuted for an offense long forgotten.'

[119] Uelmen, *supra* note 34, at 52.

insures that a perpetrator does not escape punishment simply by successfully concealing his acts. Besides, concealed crimes generally require a longer period of investigation and thus justify a longer limitation period.[120] Generally, the seriousness of the offense correlates with the duration of a limitation period regardless of whether the purpose of criminal law is deterrence, incapacitation, or rehabilitation.[121]

The extent to which current states' statute of limitations for child sexual abuse offenses reflect and satisfy these purposes and factors merits discussion.

Statutes of limitations which permit commencement of prosecution up until a specified number of years after the commission of the offense are inflexible and ineffective. Such an approach is advantageous only to the extent that it is expedient and cost efficient in determining whether a certain case may or may not be prosecuted.[122] However, to screen worthy causes of action at the pleading stage rather than through the trier of fact would be an "elevation of procedural efficiency over substantive justice."[123]

States adopting this approach have failed to consider the special circumstances that arise in child sexual abuse cases. In many instances, for example, report of the abuse is delayed because of coercion employed by the accused.[124] This coercion generally results in the child becoming confused and guilt-ridden.[125] An incest victim may also fear losing the affection of those from whom he or she is accustomed of regularly seeking comfort.[126] Furthermore, the mystique surrounding sex often causes the child to fear that he or she will not be believed or is somehow personally responsible for the sexual incident(s).[127] Finally, because of his or her youth and ignorance, a child may not fully comprehend the criminal nature of

---

[120] *Id.* There is an obvious correlation between crimes that require a lengthy investigation and those associated with concealment. *Id.* at 55. In a survey to identify the crimes most likely to be concealed, child molesting was ranked seventh out of 26 crimes. *Id.* at 53. However, the author suggests that the concealment factor can be accomodated by suspending the limitation period until discovery. *Id.* at 54.

[121] *Id.* at 56. (Generally the more serious the offense, the longer the period of limitation.).

[122] Comment, *Accural of Statutes of Limitations: California's Discovery Exceptions Swallow the Rule*, 108 CALIF. L. REV. 106, 118 (1988).

[123] *Id.; see also* Note, *supra* note 52, at 228.

[124] *See* HIGHLIGHTS OF OFFICIAL CHILD NEGLECT AND ABUSE REPORTING (1985) [hereinafter HIGHLIGHTS].

[125] *See* Comment, *Civil Claims of Adults Molested as Children: Maturation of Harm and the Statute of Limitations Hurdle*, 15 FORDHAM L. REV. 709 (1987).

[126] *Id.*

[127] *Id.*

the defendant's behavior.[128]

States which have recognized the need for special consideration for offenses committed against children have enacted statutes of limitations which extend or toll the limitation period until the victim attains the age of majority or soon thereafter.[129] This approach attempts to remedy the inequity associated with the inability of minors to commence prosecution on their own behalf or to inform the state of the criminally committed acts due to coercion, dependence, or ignorance.[130]

However, even this approach is inflexible and fails to serve satisfactorily the purposes underlying the statute of limitations. Under such a statute of limitations, there is a possibility that a prosecutor might obtain sufficient evidence against the accused soon after the crime is committed but waits until a time just before the victim attains majority to commence prosecution. Such strategizing may prevent a defendant from effectively and equitably establishing a defense, and will undermine many of the purposes of the statute of limitations.[131]

Many of the problems associated with the above two methods could be overcome by providing exceptions to toll the running of the statutory provision.[132] By means of exceptions, particular circumstances that may arise can be accommodated without sacrificing the purposes and factors of the statute of limitations.

The discovery approach—tolling the statute of limitations until discovery of the offense has been made—is superior to the fixed time approach of the prior two methods. Discovery of the offense is said to occur when a third person, who is not a party to the offense, becomes aware of the offense.[133] The fact that the victim may real-

---

[128] See Comment, *The Young Victim as Witness for the Prosecution: Another Form of Abuse?* 89 DICK. L. REV. 721, 731 (1985). According to a study conducted by the Amercian Humane Society and the National Center on Child Abuse and Neglect approximately 28.5% of child sexual victims are under the age of five and therefore do not realise the wrongfulness of the sexual act. HIGHLIGHTS, *supra* note 124, at 19.

[129] See *supra* notes 47-49 and accompanying text.

[130] The preamble to the 1987 amendment of ARK. STAT. ANN. § 5-1-109 (1978) states, "[W]hereas, in many instances, child victims are threatened or intimidated to prevent the prompt reporting of abuse or sexual offenses; and whereas, it is in the best interest of the State to extend the statute of limitations for certain offenses involving child victims; now therefore . . . ."

[131] Note, *supra* note 19, at 639.

[132] Uelman, *supra* note 34, at 63.

[133] See John R. v. Oakland Unified School Dist., 206 Cal. App. 3d 1473, 240 Cal. Rptr. 319 (1987). The court determined that the statutory period commenced from the date of the parents' discovery even though the child was aware of the criminal act because under those circumstances the timeliness of the action for sexual assault depended upon the knowledge of someone other than the plaintiff-victim.

ize that the conduct is of a criminal nature prior to discovery by a third party should not be determinative for statute of limitations purposes because the victim may not report such conduct due to coercion, self-blame, or fear of destroying the family.

Suspension of the statute of limitations until discovery of the offense where the crime is concealed should be preferred over a longer limitation period.[134] Under this approach, the accused is arguably no more prejudiced in his or her attempt to gather evidence than would be the victim.[135] Futhermore, the desire for motivation is satisfied by limiting the prosecution period following discovery. The state would be able to prosecute only to the point of discovery plus a reasonable time thereafter to properly investigate.[136]

However, under the present statutory discovery rule approach, the interests of the accused are not fairly considered. The state's interest in prosecution unjustly takes automatic precedent over the interests of the defendant.

Historically, courts have employed a balancing of interests test to determine the applicability of the discovery rule to toll a statute of limitations.[137] A balancing test enables a court to avoid sacrificing one factor of a limitation period to accommodate another factor. To accommodate both the circumstances that may arise in child sexual abuse cases as well as the purposes of a statute of limitations, focus must be on the reasons for delay.[138] Therefore, the following provision should be utilized:

> *No person shall be prosecuted, tried or punished for the offense of child sexual abuse unless an indictment is issued or information is filed within x years after the commission of the offense.*
>
> *If the above period has expired, a court has discretion to toll the limitation period until one year after discovery of the offense has been made by a law enforcement agency or any other person who is not a party to the offense.*

Factors to be taken into consideration and balanced by the court to determine whether to apply the discovery rule exception should include:

> *1) the time elapsed since the offense was committed;*
>
> *2) whether the victim and the state acted reasonably or in good faith in making the discovery;*

---

134 Uelman, *supra* note 34, at 51.

135 The state is unaware of the offense until informed by the victim or a third party. Furthermore, unlike a manufacturer who does not know that an injury has occured, a sexual abuse offender is completely aware of the abuse. *See* DeRose, *Adult Incest Survivors and the Statute of Limitations: The Delayed Discovery Rule and Long-Term Damages*, 25 Santa Clara L. Rev. 191, 222 (1985).

136 *See supra* notes 74-77 and accompanying text.

137 *See supra* note 54-55 and accompanying text.

138 Note, *Supra* note 52, at 233.

3) whether the victim, under the circumstances, was diligent in informing a third party and that any delay in so doing was done in good faith;

4) whether timely notice was given to the defendants when the offense was discovered;

5) whether there was a rational basis for the delay in discovery;

6) the extent the defendant will suffer prejudice, if at all, in his right to gather evidence if discovery accrual is allowed;

7) whether there was a fiduciary relationship involved;

8) whether coercion was employed; and

9) the grievousness of the act.[139]

IV. CONCLUSION

In the midst of statutory reform efforts to improve the handling of child sexual abuse cases in the legal system, legislative attention must be given to the statute of limitations. Courts troubled by the injustice that have arisen due to the inflexible nature of present statutes of limitations have looked to the legislatures for relief.[140] By adopting the proposed legislation, relief can accommodate both the purposes of a statute of limitations as well as the circumstances common in child sexual abuse cases.

DURGA M. BHARAM

---

[139] *See* Comment, *supra* note 50, at 220-21; Note, *supra* note 19, at 638-39.
[140] *See Supra* notes 66, 84 and 94 and accompanying text.

25

New Hampshire's New Statute of Limitations for Child Sexual Assault: Is It Constitutional and Is It Good Public Policy?

Brian L. Porto*

I. INTRODUCTION

On April 27, 1990, the New Hampshire General Court enacted Chapter 213, formerly House Bill 1245, an act relating to the statute of limitations on prosecutions for sexual assault offenses against children.

Chapter 213:2 creates New Hampshire Revised Statutes Annotated 625:8, III (d), which provides that "[f]or any offense under RSA 632-A, [namely, sexual assault and related offenses] where the victim was under 18 years of age when the alleged offense occurred, [prosecutions shall commence] within 22 years of the victim's eighteenth birthday."[1] Prior to the enactment of Chapter 213, prosecutions for aggravated felonious sexual assault and felonious sexual assault had to be brought no later than six years after the victim's eighteeth birthday. In cases of misdemeanor sexual assault, prosecutions had to be commenced within one year from the victim's eighteenth birthday.[2] The impetus for changing the statute resulted from the General Court's findings that "juvenile victims of sexual assault often suffer profound psychological harm resulting in repression of memory of the assault"[3] and that "[a]s a result, charges for sexual assault against youthful victims are frequently not brought because the criminal conduct is not brought to light within the current statute of limitations."[4]

Aside from extending the limitations period for sexual assaults, chapter 213 is designed to apply retroactively. Chapter 213:4 provides that the new, extended limitations period contained in Chapter 213:2 "shall apply to victims injured under RSA 632-A before, on, or after

---

* Assistant Professor of Political Science, Norwich University, Northfield, Vermont. J.D. 1987, Indiana University; Ph.D. 1979, Miami University (Ohio); B.A. 1974 University of Rhode Island.
1. N.H. REV. STAT. ANN. § 625:8, III (d) (1990).
2. *See* N.H. REV. STAT. ANN. § 625:8 (1987), *amended by* 1990 N.H. Laws 213.
3. 1990 N.H. Laws 213:1.
4. *Id.*

April 27, 1990."[5]

It is likely that the extended limitations period will be challenged as violative of both the Due Process and Ex Post Facto Clauses of the United States and New Hampshire Constitutions, respectively.[6] After outlining the legislative history of Chapter 213, this comment will examine the legal issues likely to be raised and assess their prospects for success. Furthermore, this comment will propose alternate legislative prescriptions concerning limitations on prosecutions that strike an even balance between the respective rights of the alleged victim and the accused in child sexual assault cases.

II. The Legislative History of Chapter 213

Chapter 213 was introduced in the New Hampshire House of Representatives as House Bill 1245 [hereinafter H.B. 1245] on January 3, 1990, whereupon it was referred to the House Judiciary Committee [hereinafter the House Committee].[7] On January 23, 1990, the House Committee held a public hearing on H.B. 1245, during which numerous police officers, social workers and mental health professionals spoke in favor of the Bill. The House Committee also heard testimony from no less than a dozen adults who had been victims of sexual assault as children, and who also supported the Bill.[8]

Throughout the hearing, the proponents of the Bill repeatedly espoused a common objective: it was necessary to substantially increase the time period during which prosecutions for child sexual assault could be commenced in New Hampshire. Likewise, they reasoned that child victims commonly repress memories of such assaults and only become conscious of those memories as adults after the statute of limitations has expired.[9]

The testimony of Dr. Sheila Stanley, Director of the Contoocook Valley Counseling Center in Henniker, New Hampshire, was particularly illustrative of the supporters' view. Dr. Stanley stated:

> The current law provides victims with an inappropriate meaningless period in which to act. It usually takes years for incest victims to begin to face and deal with what has happened to them. In my twenty years of experience as a clinician, most of the three dozen or so incest survi-

---

5. 1990 N.H. Laws 213:4.

6. The Ex Post Facto Clauses of the Federal Constitution appear at U.S. Const. art. I, § 9, cl. 3 and § 10, cl. 1. The New Hampshire Constitution's Ex Post Facto Clause appears at N.H. Const. pt. I, art. 23. The Due Process Clauses of the Federal Constitution are contained in U.S. Const. amends. V and XIV, respectively. The Due Process Clause of the New Hampshire Constitution is contained in N.H. Const. pt. 1, art. 15.

7. N.H. H.B. 1245, 1990 Sess., 1990 Journal of the House of Representatives, at 55.

8. See Senate Research File No. 1138, Senate Research Office, Concord, N.H.

9. Id.

vors I've worked with have not begun to face the trauma until their thirties and forties, and in several cases, their fifties.[10]

To explain why victims of child sexual abuse require years "to face and deal with what has happened to them," Dr. Stanley asserted:

> One creative way a small child deals with (the despair resulting from the violation of parent-child trust by the abuser) is to convince herself [it] isn't really happening or that it didn't happen. Another reason why memories are repressed is that the child is often threatened by the perpetrator . . . . It is often only many years later, well past age 24 (when the current statute of limitations runs out), that memories return - often only with the help of counseling. By the time incest victims are psychologically able to take action, it is almost always too late. The perpetrator continues to avoid responsibility for his or her crime while the victim [] suffers the consequences of it.[11]

In the New Hampshire Legislature, when a proposed bill is sent to a committee for a public hearing, a representative of the State Attorney General will frequently appear. The representative discusses the legal ramifications of the proposed legislation and presents the Attorney General's views. No representative of the Attorney General appeared at either the House or the Senate Judiciary Committee's hearings concerning H.B. 1245, nor did any such representative submit written testimony to either committee about H.B. 1245.[12] Indeed, no one spoke against H.B. 1245 at the House Committee hearing.

On February 14, 1990, by a vote of 15-1, the House Committee recommended that the House of Representatives pass H.B. 1245 as amended.[13] The amendments that the House Committee adopted included: 1) a statement of findings and purpose;[14] 2) an extension of the applicable limitations period to twenty-two years from the victim's eighteenth birthday, replacing the unlimited time period allowed in the original version of the bill,[15] and; 3) the inclusion of a severability clause that provides that if any provision of H.B. 1245 or its application to any particular person were held invalid, the remaining provision that "can be given effect without the invalid provisions or applications"

---

10. Letter from Sheila Stanley, Ed.D., Director, Contoocook Valley Counseling Center, to Eleanor Podles, Senator, *Senate Judiciary Committee* 1 (Mar. 14, 1990) (Senate Research File No. 1138, Senate Research Office, Concord, N.H.). The proponents therefore asked, in the original version of the bill, for an unlimited time period within which prosecutions could commence.

11. *Id.* at 2.

12. *See* Christine M. Gardner, *Statute of Limitations Ruling on Abuse Law Decried*, BOSTON GLOBE, February 24, 1991, at N.H. 1 and Norma Love, *State Questions Child Rape Law*, Concord Monitor, February 19, 1991, at A-1.

13. N.H. H.B. 1245, 1990 Sess., 1990 Journal of the House of Representatives, at 702.

14. *Id.* at 714.

15. *Id.* at 715.

would still be valid.[16]

On February 15, 1990, the New Hampshire House of Representatives passed H.B. 1245 as amended, while the Bill was simultaneously[17] being introduced in the Senate.[18]

On March 14, 1990, the Senate Judiciary Committee [hereinafter the Senate Committee] held a public hearing concerning H.B. 1245, during which it heard testimony from most of the same supporters who spoke before the House Committee.[19]

The author of this comment, then serving as the attorney for the Senate Committee, cautioned the six Committee members, none of whom was an attorney, that the language of H.B. 1245 raised " 'potentially serious constitutional questions' "[20] that could cause the Bill to be challenged in court and declared unconstitutional by the New Hampshire Supreme Court.[21] The problematic language in the Bill concerned: 1) the applicability of the extended limitations period to victims injured "before" the act's effective date, which rendered the act potentially violative of the Ex Post Facto Clauses of the United States and New Hampshire Constitutions,[22] respectively, and 2) the extension of the limitations period for child sexual abuse prosecutions to twenty-two years from the alleged victim's eighteenth birthday, which might so hinder a defendant's ability to mount a defense as to violate the Due Process Clauses of the United States[23] and New Hampshire[24] Constitutions, respectively.[25]

In an executive session following the hearing, the Senate Committee recommended by a vote of 6-0, that the Senate pass H.B. 1245.[26] While members of the Senate Committee did consider the potential constitutional problems associated with the Bill, they nonetheless concluded that those problems were insufficient to justify a recommendation against passing it.[27] One member noted that the constitutional issues were best resolved in the context of a challenge to the act in the State Supreme Court. Hence, the Senate Committee could facilitate

---

16. *Id.*

17. *Id.*

18. *Id.; see also* 1990 Journal of the Senate, at 549.

19. *Statute of Limitations on Prosecutions for Sexual Assault Offenses Against Children, 1990: Hearings on H.B. 1245 Before the House Judiciary Committee* (1990).

20. Nancy West, *Senate Panel Backs Extending Prosecution Time in Child Abuse,* MANCHESTER UNION LEADER, Mar. 15, 1990, at 20 (quoting Committee Attorney Brian Porto).

21. *Id.*

22. *See supra* note 6.

23. *Id.*

24. N.H. CONST. pt. 1, art. 15 (Law of the Land Clause).

25. *See also* West, *supra* note 20.

26. *See* Senate Research File No. 1138, *supra* note 8.

27. 1990 Journal of the Senate, at 662-64.

that resolution by recommending passage of H.B. 1245.[28] The Senate Committee Chair expressed reservations about the Bill because of its potential constitutional deficiencies and observed that the appropriate course of action might be to seek an advisory opinion from the State Supreme Court. The chair nevertheless voted to recommend passage of the Bill.[29]

On March 20th, the Chair of the Senate Committee discussed her reservations with the Senate Committee's attorney. The chair subsequently learned that the Supreme Court would be unable to issue an advisory opinion about the constitutionality of H.B. 1245 until after the legislative session had ended. The chair then offered a floor amendment to the bill.[30] That amendment eliminated the bill's retroactive application by striking the word "before" from section 4, thereby limiting its application to "victims injured under RSA 632-A on or after the effective date of this act."[31] The Senate adopted the floor amendment of March 20th,[32] and later that same day, the Senate passed H.B. 1245.[33]

On March 29th, the Chair of the House Committee moved that the House "nonconcur" with the Senate version of H.B. 1245 and request the establishment of a Conference Committee in order that a compromise could be reached between the two chambers.[34] The House adopted the motion and the Speaker appointed conferees from among the House membership.[35] On April 10th, the Senate acceded to the House's request.[36]

The Conference Committee, comprised of three Senators and four Representatives,[37] reached agreement on April 19th by adopting the House-passed version of H.B. 1245, which applied the new limitations period to cases involving "victims injured under RSA 632-A before, on, or after the effective date of this act."[38]

---

28. *Id.*; *see also* West, *supra* note 20.

29. *See* Senate Research File No. 1138, *supra* note 8. The New Hampshire Constitution provides that "[e]ach branch of the legislature as well as the governor and council shall have authority to require the opinions of the justices of the supreme court upon important questions of law and upon solemn occasions." N.H. CONST. pt. 2, art. 74.

30. 1990 Journal of the Senate, at 662-64.

31. *Id.* at 664.

32. *Id.*

33. *Id.* at 679.

34. N.H. H.B. 1245, 1990 Sess., 1990 Journal of the House of Representatives, at 860.

35. *Id.*

36. 1990 Journal of the Senate, at 990.

37. *Id.* at 1148. The three Senators included: Sen. Podles (Dist. 16), Sen. Nelson (Dist. 13), and Sen. Roberge (Dist. 9). The four Representatives included: Rep. Lown (Hills. 9), Rep. Jasper (Hills. 19), Rep. Hollingsworth (Rock. 17), and Rep. Moore (Hills. 5). *Id.*

38. *Id.*

Because only the conferees were present at the conference, it is not possible to determine with any certainty why the Senate conferees agreed to adopt the retroactive language of the House Bill. Nevertheless, given the discussion that occurred at the Senate Committee hearing on March 14th, one can confidently hypothesize that the Senators concluded that by accepting the House language, not only could they respond effectively to a serious social problem, but they also could be assured that the State Supreme Court would resolve any constitutional questions raised by the retroactive application of the new law.[39]

On April 19th, both the House and the Senate adopted the Conference Report,[40] and on April 27th, Chapter 213, formerly H.B. 1245, became law.[41]

III. Likely Constitutional Challenges to Chapter 213

A. *The Ex Post Facto Challenge*

1. The Governing Standards

The United States Constitution contains two separate clauses that prohibit the passage of ex post facto laws. Article I, section 9, clause 3 prohibits the United States Congress from passing such laws and Article I, section 10, clause 1 prohibits the states from doing so. Similarly, Part 1, Article 23 of the New Hampshire Constitution prohibits the enactment by the General Court of "retrospective laws," for "the punishment of offenses."[42]

Both the United States and New Hampshire Supreme Courts have struck down ex post facto laws. The New Hampshire Court, in paraphrasing the Supreme Court, stated:

> [E]very law, which makes an action done before the passing of the law, and which was innocent when done, criminal, and punishes such action; or which aggravates a crime, and makes it greater, than it was when committed; or which changes the punishment, and inflicts greater punishment, than the law annexed to the crime when committed; or which alters the legal rules of evidence, and receives less or different testimony, than the law required at the time of the commission of the [offense], in order to convict the offender, is an *ex post facto* law.[43]

The definition of an ex post facto law is well-established in American law, as New Hampshire case law demonstrates. Under both the United States Constitution and the New Hampshire Constitution, "two critical elements must be present for a criminal or penal law to be ex post facto: it must be retrospective, that is, it must apply to events oc-

---

39. *See* Senate Research File No. 1138, *supra* note 8; *see also* West, *supra* note 20.
40. 1990 Journal of the Senate, at 1147-48, 1243.
41. *See* 1990 N.H. Laws 213.
42. N.H. Const. pt. 1, art. 23.
43. Woart v. Winnick, 3 N.H. 473, 475 (1826) (citing Calder v. Bull, 3 U.S. 386, 390 (1798)).

curring before its enactment, and it must disadvantage the offender affected by it."[44]

Notwithstanding the firmly entrenched prohibition against ex post facto laws, the United States Supreme Court has held that " '[t]he inhibition upon the passage of ex post facto laws does not [necessarily] give a criminal a right to be tried, in all respects, by the law in force when the crime charged was committed.' "[45] The Court has also opined that " 'the constitutional provision was intended to secure substantial personal rights against arbitrary and oppressive legislation, [and this provision was not intended] to limit the legislative control of remedies and modes of procedure which do not affect matters of substance.' "[46] Therefore, even though it may work to the disadvantage of a defendant, a procedural change is not ex post facto.[47]

In the Supreme Court's view, a change in the law is merely "procedural" if it does "not increase the punishment, nor change the ingredients of the offence or the ultimate facts necessary to establish guilt."[48] This draconian view was subsequently tempered when the court held that "a change in the law that alters a substantial right can be ex post facto 'even if the statute takes a seemingly procedural form.' "[49]

2. Applying the Standards: United States Supreme Court
   Decisions

In applying the aforementioned standards, the United States Supreme Court has held that a Florida statute, which altered the availability of reductions in prison time in return for good conduct, was an ex post facto law when applied to a petitioner who committed a crime before the enactment of the statute.[50] When it analyzed the facts of the case, the Court noted that application of the new law to the petitioner would result in an extension of his confinement by more than two years on a fifteen year sentence. Such a result, said the Court, substantially altered the consequences attached to a crime already committed and disadvantaged the petitioner by reducing his opportunity to shorten his period of confinement through good conduct.[51]

Similarly, the Supreme Court struck down another Florida statute establishing sentencing guidelines which applied to a petitioner whose

---

44. Weaver v. Graham, 450 U.S. 24, 29 (1981) (citing *Calder* at 390).
45. Dobbert v. Florida, 432 U.S. 282, 293 (1977) (quoting Gibson v. Mississippi, 162 U.S. 565, 590 (1896)).
46. *Id.* (quoting Beazell v. Ohio, 269 U.S. 167, 171 (1925) and citing Malloy v. South Carolina, 237 U.S. 180, 183 (1915)).
47. *Id.*
48. Miller v. Florida, 482 U.S. 423, 433 (1987) (quoting Hopt v. Utah, 110 U.S. 574, 590 (1884)).
49. *Id.* (citing Weaver v. Graham, 450 U.S. 24, 29 n.12 (1981)).
50. Weaver v. Graham, 450 U.S. 24 (1981).
51. *Id.* at 35-36.

conviction had preceded their enactment, as an ex post facto law.[52] Here, the Court based its conclusion upon the fact that when applied, the new law increased the presumptive sentence for the petitioner's offense from a three-and-a-half to four-and-a-half year period to a five-and-a-half to seven year period, an increase for the petitioner of two-and-a-half years over the sentence that applied when he committed the crime.[53]

In a third Florida case, however, the Supreme Court held that a statute that altered the roles played by judge and jury in the imposition of the death penalty, was not an ex post facto law when applied to the petitioner, whose offense had been committed prior to the law's enactment.[54] Specifically, the new statute provided for a post conviction sentencing hearing in capital cases, to be followed by the jury's rendering of a non-binding advisory sentencing decision to the trial judge.[55] This represented a change from the prior law under which a recommendation of mercy by the jury was not reviewable by the trial judge.[56] Pursuant to this change, the judge in *Dobbert* "overruled the jury's recommendation"[57] of a sentence of life imprisonment, and imposed a death sentence.[58]

The Court rejected the petitioner's argument that the statutory change constituted an ex post facto violation because it deprived him of the substantial right to have the jury determine, without review by the trial judge, whether the death penalty should be imposed.[59] The Court concluded that while the new statute altered the methodology of "determining whether the death penalty [should] be imposed,"[60] it did not change, to the petitioner's detriment, "the quantum of punishment attached to"[61] his offense. Therefore, the change effected by the new law was procedural rather than substantive.[62]

3. Applying the Standards in the First Circuit

Within the past fifteen years, the United States District Court for the District of New Hampshire and the United States Court of Appeals for the First Circuit have each decided cases originating in New Hampshire where a criminal defendant argued that he had been punished by an ex post facto law.

---

52. Miller v. Florida, 482 U.S. 423 (1987).
53. *Id.* at 424.
54. Dobbert v. Florida, 432 U.S. 282 (1977).
55. *Id.* at 287.
56. *Id.* at 288 n.3.
57. *Id.* at 287.
58. *Id.*
59. *Id.* at 296-97.
60. *Id.* at 293-94.
61. *Id.*
62. *Id.* at 293.

In *Piper v. Perrin*,[63] the district court invalidated the application of a new rule establishing a more stringent method of calculating good conduct credits to a prisoner whose offense had been committed prior to the new rule's enactment.[64] The new system changed the petitioner's eligibility date for parole from November 28, 1982 to March 23, 1983.[65] After applying the "retrospective and disadvantageous" standard used by the United States Supreme Court two years earlier in *Weaver v. Graham*,[66] the district court concluded that the modified mechanism for calculating good conduct credits violated the ex post facto prohibition, because "it [was] both retrospective and more onerous than the law in effect on the date of the offense."[67] In the Court's view, "[t]he new method [was] retrospective since it reache[d] back to crimes committed before its adoption."[68] Further, "it [was] more onerous [than its predecessor] because it " 'change[d] the punishment, and inflict[ed] a greater punishment, than the law [affixed] to the crime, when committed.' "[69]

In *Breest v. Helgemoe*,[70] the Court of Appeals for the First Circuit rejected a petitioner's argument that a new statute that permitted a person serving a life sentence to be eligible for parole after having served eighteen years (unless that person had been convicted of a first degree, psychosexual murder) was an ex post facto law when applied to him.[71] The Court based its conclusion upon the fact that the new law, as applied to the petitioner, was "neither more onerous than the prior law nor disadvantageous in any respect."[72]

The Court noted that when the petitioner committed the offense, (a first-degree murder that was psychosexual in nature), the penalty for first degree murder was life imprisonment without parole.[73] The law that the petitioner challenged stated that one who was serving a life sentence, and who had committed first degree murder, would henceforth be eligible for parole after having served eighteen years *and* that one who was serving a life sentence for a psychosexual murder would henceforth be eligible for parole after serving forty years.[74]

Therefore, although the punishment affixed to the petitioner's of-

---

63. 560 F. Supp. 253 (D.N.H. 1983).
64. *Id.* at 258.
65. *Id.* at 255.
66. 450 U.S. 24, 29 (1981).
67. Piper v. Perrin, 560 F. Supp. 253, 255 (citing Weaver v. Graham, 450 U.S. 24, 30-31 (1981)).
68. *Id.* at 255.
69. *Id.* (citing Calder v. Bull, 3 U.S. (3 Dall.) 386, 390 (1798)).
70. 579 F.2d 95 (1st Cir. 1978), *cert. denied*, 439 U.S. 933 (1978).
71. *Id.* at 103.
72. *Id.*
73. *Id.* at 102. At that time, there was no distinction made between the crime of first degree murder, and a murder that was psychosexual in nature.
74. *Id.*

fense had been altered retrospectively, the result of the alteration advantaged the defendant, instead of working to his detriment, because the change enabled him to realize a parole eligibility that prior law had denied him. Accordingly, "[n]o violation of the bar against ex post facto laws occurred."[75]

4. Applying the Standards in New Hampshire

The New Hampshire Supreme Court also addressed an ex post facto claim in *Breest v. Helgemoe*.[76] In *Breest*, the court held that no ex post facto violation had occurred where a bill that might have eased parole eligibility requirements for the petitioner was rejected by the legislature, and was replaced by a bill, later enacted, that did not ease parole eligibility requirements for the petitioner.[77] The court noted that, as a result of the enactment of the substitute measure, the petitioner was "no worse off than before."[78] It concluded that "he was entitled to nothing, he lost nothing, and he is in no position to complain."[79]

Several years later, the New Hampshire Supreme Court rejected another ex post facto claim in *State v. Theodosopoulos*.[80] There, the petitioner argued that sentence suspension provisions enacted after he committed an offense were invalid when applied to him.[81] The court held that applying the new provisions to the petitioner did not violate the ex post facto prohibition.[82]

The court noted that although a 1979 amendment to the sentencing provision prevented the petitioner from seeking a suspended sentence and a 1981 amendment required him to serve two years before seeking suspension (he had only served one year), neither change deprived him of a "meaningful opportunity to seek a suspension of his sentence."[83] Thus, the new provisions, according to the court's analysis, did not substantially disadvantage the petitioner "so as to be deemed an increase in the quantum of punishment attaching to his crime."[84]

The foregoing cases establish that when criminal statutes are enacted subsequent to the commission of offenses and are applied retrospectively, they are likely to be invalidated as ex post facto laws if, when applied, they disadvantage offenders by increasing the quantum of punishment to which offenders will be subjected.

---

75. *Id.* at 103.
76. 369 A.2d 612 (N.H. 1977).
77. *Id.* at 613.
78. *Id.*
79. *Id.*
80. 461 A.2d 100 (N.H. 1983).
81. *Id.*
82. *Id.* at 103.
83. *Id.*
84. *Id.* at 102.

The next question to be addressed, therefore, is whether Chapter 213:4,[85] in its effort to apply an extended statute of limitations to child sexual assaults that occurred prior to its enactment, disadvantages pre-enactment offenders by increasing the quantum of punishment to which they will be subjected. The following analysis of cases from other jurisdictions that have addressed this issue will facilitate an answer for New Hampshire.

5. Applying the Standards to Limitations Extensions in Cases of Sexual Assaults

State courts have had numerous occasions in recent years to apply the aforementioned standards governing ex post facto claims to extensions of limitations periods for the prosecution of sexual assaults, including those committed against children. It has consistently been held that the enactment of a provision extending a limitations period for an offense that occurred prior to the enactment of the extension and that was actionable under the previous limitations period, *does not* violate the ex post facto prohibition.[86] That is, it is constitutionally permissible to extend a limitations period *before* a particular prosecution has been barred by an existing limitations period.

The reverse side of this constitutional coin, however, is that state courts have also consistently held that it is *not* constitutionally permissible to apply an extended limitations period to an offense for which the previous statute of limitations has expired.[87] To do so is to violate the controlling standard of ex post facto jurisprudence announced by the Supreme Court in *Weaver v. Graham.*[88] In *Weaver* the Court stated that:

> Critical to relief under the *Ex Post Facto* Clause is not an individual's right to less punishment, but the lack of fair notice and governmental restraint when the legislature increases punishment beyond what was prescribed when the crime was consummated. Thus, even if a statute merely alters penal provisions accorded by the grace of the legislature, it violates the Clause if it is both retrospective and more onerous than the law in effect on the date of the offense.[89]

For example, in *Commonwealth v. Rocheleau,*[90] the Massachusetts

---

85. 1990 N.H. LAWS 213:4.

86. *See* State v. Creekpaum, 753 P.2d 1139 (Alaska 1988); People v. Callan, 220 Cal. Rptr. 339 (1985); People v. Whitesell, 729 P.2d 985 (Colo. 1986); Commonwealth v. Rocheleau, 533 N.E.2d 1333 (Mass. 1989); Commonwealth v. Bargeron, 524 N.E.2d 829 (Mass. 1988); Commonwealth v. Johnson, 553 A.2d 897, (Pa. 1989).

87. For an argument that it is constitutionally permissible for state legislatures to "apply the extended limitation period to revive time-barred claims," *see* Thomas G. Burroughs, Note, *Retroactive Application of Legislatively Enlarged Statutes of Limitations for Child Abuse: Time's No Bar to Revival,* 22 IND. L. REV. 989, 1011 (1989).

88. 450 U.S. 24 (1981).

89. *Id.* at 30-31.

90. 533 N.E.2d 1333 (Mass. 1989).

Supreme Judicial Court invalidated an indictment against an individual for having unnatural sexual intercourse with a child under the age of sixteen, because the applicable six-year limitations period had expired more than seven months before the passage of an amendment extending it to ten years.[91] Conversely, in *Commonwealth v. Bargeron*,[92] the same court upheld an indictment against an individual for assault with intent to rape, where the amendment extending the relevant statute of limitations from six to ten years went into effect within six years of the offenses. Thus, the individual was still subject to prosecution under the previous limitations period.[93]

Similarly, the Pennsylvania Supreme Court, in *Commonwealth v. Johnson*,[94] held that the five-year statute of limitations on prosecutions for rape, which the Legislature had enacted to replace the earlier two-year statute, applied to offenses not already time-barred by the prior statute on the date that the new law became effective.[95] The court noted that "[t]here is nothing 'retroactive' about the application of an extension of a statute of limitations, so long as the original statutory period has not yet expired."[96]

The Supreme Courts of Alaska and Colorado, as well as the California Court of Appeals, have also recently held that extensions of limitations periods for the prosecution of sexual assaults committed against minors were not ex post facto laws under either the United States Constitution or their respective state constitutions when applied to offenses that were still eligible for prosecution under the old limitations statute on the date the new statute took effect.[97]

6. Applying the Standards to Chapter 213:4

The extended statute of limitations under Chapter 213 will apply to all sexual assault offenses against children.[98] The foregoing discussion, therefore, strongly suggests that if a prosecutor in the State of New Hampshire seeks to prosecute one for aggravated felonious sexual assault or felonious sexual assault using Chapter 213, the indictment of one whose alleged offense was supposedly committed more than six years prior to the 1990 enactment of Chapter 213 is likely to be dis-

---

91. *Id.* at 1334.

92. 524 N.E.2d 829 (Mass. 1988).

93. *Id.* at 830.

94. 553 A.2d 897 (Pa. 1989).

95. *Id.* at 898.

96. *Id.* at 900 (quoting United States v. Kurzenknabe, 136 F. Supp. 17, 23 (D.N.J. 1955)).

97. State v. Creekpaum, 753 P.2d 1139 (Alaska 1988); People v. Whitesell, 729 P.2d 985 (Colo. 1986); People v. Callan, 220 Cal. Rptr. 339 (1985).

98. The statute of limitations for child sexual assault prior to the passage of Chapter 213 was six years from the alleged victim's eighteenth birthday. *See* N.H. REV. STAT. ANN. § 625:8 (1987), *amended by* 1990 N.H. LAWS 213.

missed as violative of the Ex Post Facto Clauses of both the United States and New Hampshire Constitutions. The identical result is also likely in the event of a prosecution for misdemeanor sexual assault of one whose alleged offense occurred more than one year prior to the enactment of Chapter 213.[99] Although the language of Chapter 213:4 extends its applicability to victims injured "before, on, or after [its] effective date,"[100] the prevailing constitutional standards announced by the United States Supreme Court and consistently implemented by state courts in recent years instruct that the word "before," as used in Chapter 213:4, means within the previously applicable six-year limitations period.

Based on the previous case law, prosecutors in New Hampshire will be barred from prosecuting anyone for aggravated felonious sexual assault or felonious sexual assault who allegedly committed a final offense against a complainant who reached the age of 18 prior to April 27, 1984, and will be barred from prosecuting for misdemeanor sexual assault anyone whose alleged final offense against a complainant who reached the age of 18 before April 27, 1989. Attorney General John P. Arnold acknowledged this in a January 7, 1991 "[m]emorandum To All Law Enforcement Agencies,"[101] wherein he noted his conclusion that the prosecution of cases for which the prior limitations period had expired "would violate the constitutional prohibition against *ex post facto* legislation under the United States and New Hampshire Constitutions."[102] Accordingly, Attorney General Arnold advised the county attorneys of New Hampshire that "[n]o prosecution should be instituted for a felony offense, under RSA 632-A, committed against a minor victim, in which the victim turned 18 on or before April 27, 1984."[103] He added that "[n]o prosecution should be instituted for a misdemeanor offense under RSA 632-A, committed against a minor victim, in which the victim turned 18 on or before April 27, 1989."[104]

---

99. The statute of limitations for misdemeanor child sexual assault prior to Chapter 213 was one year from the alleged victim's eighteenth birthday. *See* N.H. REV. STAT. ANN. § 625:8 (1987), *amended by* 1990 N.H. LAWS 213.

100. N.H. REV. STAT. ANN. § 213:4 (1990).

101. Memorandum from New Hampshire Attorney General John P. Arnold to All Law Enforcement Agencies, January 7, 1991 [hereinafter Arnold Memo].

102. *Id. See* Senate Research File No. 1138, *supra* note 8.

103. Arnold Memo, *supra* note 101.

104. *Id.* For discussions of the criticisms that mental health professionals in New Hampshire have levelled at Attorney General Arnold as a result of the January 7, 1991 Memorandum, see *supra* note 8; *see also* Kate F. Hays, *Doubling the Trauma*, Concord Monitor, March 9, 1991, at 10 and Norma Love, *Advocates Charge AG Ignores Longer Statute of Limitations in Child Rape*, Manchester Union Leader, February 20, 1991, at 7. The Attorney General's critics are chagrined not only because of his memorandum, but because he did not send a representative to testify at hearings about H.B. 1245 and did not comment publicly about Chapter 213 until nine months after it had become law. *Id.*

B. *The Due Process Challenge*

1. Introduction

Chapter 213:2, which extends the limitations period to twenty-two years from the alleged victim's eighteenth birthday in prosecutions for sexual assault against a minor, is also likely to be challenged on constitutional grounds in the years ahead. Specifically, the provision is susceptible to a challenge that it violates the Due Process Clause of the Fourteenth Amendment to the United States Constitution and the "Law of the Land" Clause (or Due Process Clause, Part 1, Article 15) of the New Hampshire Constitution, based on a pre-indictment delay that results in substantial prejudice to a petitioner's right to a fair trial.[105] The basis for this argument is the lengthy limitations period provided for in Chapter 213:2. Such a long delay between the alleged commission of the crime and the indictment arguably deprives the accused of the protection against stale charges that statutes of limitation customarily afford. Consequently, the right to a fair trial guaranteed by the Sixth Amendment to the United States Constitution and made applicable to the states by the aforementioned Due Process Clause, is compromised.

2. The Governing Standard

The United States Supreme Court has observed that statutes of limitation are "the primary guarantee against bringing overly stale criminal charges."[106] Nonetheless, the Second Circuit has recognized that: "[e]vents predating the filing of an indictment and occurring within the limitation time-frame . . . may result in actual prejudice. In such case an accused's rights are not fully fixed by the statute of limitations and the Due Process Clause[s] of the Fifth [and Fourteenth] Amendment[s] [are] considered."[107]

For the petitioner claiming prejudicial pre-indictment delay, "[p]roof of [actual] prejudice is a necessary element in stating a valid due process claim, though it is not sufficient by itself since the inquiry focuses not only on prejudice to the accused but also on the reasons for the claimed oppressive delay."[108] Therefore, dismissal of an indictment on due process grounds is warranted if it is shown "that the pre-indictment delay . . . caused substantial prejudice to [the defendant's] rights to a fair trial and that the delay was an intentional device to gain tactical advantage over the accused."[109]

The petitioner is required to demonstrate such actual prejudice and

---

105. U.S. CONST. amend. XIV, § 1, cl. 3; N.H. CONST. part 1, art. 15.
106. United States v. Ewell, 383 U.S. 116, 122 (1966).
107. United States v. Birney, 686 F.2d 102, 105 (2d Cir. 1982).
108. *Id.*
109. United States v. Marion, 404 U.S. 307, 324 (1971).

unreasonable delay in order to raise a successful due process claim[110] "because it can be presumed that timely prosecution has commenced if charges are brought within the applicable statute of limitations . . . ."[111]

It is also presumed that:

> the assertion that memories have dimmed with the passage of time cannot establish actual substantial prejudice . . . . This is especially true where the failure to recall is by *prosecution* witnesses, whose faltering testimony works to the advantage of the defense. . . . Where, however, the defense can show that actual impairment of witnesses' recollections resulted from the pre-indictment delay . . . and that the memory flaws were so egregious that the defendant is essentially "convicted on failing memories," he may be able to establish substantial prejudice.[112]

3. Applying the Governing Standard in the Federal Courts

Application of the governing standard, the so-called *"Marion test,"* to specific cases, has resulted in consistent rejection of petitioners' due process claims.[113]

In *United States v. Marion*,[114] the Supreme Court rejected the due process claims of two defendants charged with and indicted on nineteen counts of engaging in fraudulent business practices three years prior.[115] The Court observed that the defendants alleged no actual prejudice or intentional, tactical delay, but rather, only the possibility of dimmed memories and inaccessible witnesses.[116] The majority reasoned that since the delay between the end of the fraudulent conduct and the date of the indictment did not exceed the statute of limitations, the aforementioned possibilities did not demonstrate the defendants' inability to receive a fair trial.[117]

Subsequently, in *United States v. Lovasco*,[118] the High Court denied the due process claim of a defendant who was indicted more than eighteen months after he had taken possession of eight firearms stolen from the mails and had dealt in firearms without a license.[119] The Justices held that investigative delay resulting from the prosecutor's refusal to

---

110. State v. Philibotte, 459 A.2d 275, 277 (N.H. 1983).

111. United States v. Lieberman, 608 F.2d 889, 902 (1st Cir. 1979), *cert. denied*, 444 U.S. 1019 (1980).

112. United States v. Marler, 756 F.2d 206, 214 (1985) (citations omitted) (quoting Dufield v. Perrin, 470 F. Supp. 687, 692 (D.N.H. 1979)).

113. *See, e.g.*, United States v. Lovasco, 431 U.S. 783 (1977), *reh'g denied*, 434 U.S. 881 (1977); United States v. Marion, 404 U.S. 307 (1971); United States v. Birney, 686 F.2d 102 (2d Cir. 1982); United States v. Lieberman, 608 F.2d 889 (1st Cir. 1979), *cert. denied*, 444 U.S. 1019 (1980).

114. 404 U.S. 307 (1971).

115. *Id.* at 308-09.

116. *Id.* at 325-26.

117. *Id.*

118. 431 U.S. 783 (1977), *reh'g denied*, 434 U.S. 881 (1977).

119. *Id.* at 784.

seek indictments until he is satisfied that he will be able to promptly establish guilt beyond a reasonable doubt does not violate the Due Process Clause.[120]

In *United States v. Lieberman*,[121] the Court of Appeals for the First Circuit applied the *Marion* standard and rejected the defendant's due process claim despite a four-year hiatus between the start of a Securities and Exchange Commission investigation (of a corporation of which the defendant was Financial Vice-President) and the indictment of the defendant.[122] In the court's view, the defendant failed to prove actual prejudice had resulted from the hiatus because he did not show his defense had been "impaired" by the delay between investigation and indictment.[123]

In *United States v. Birney*,[124] the Second Circuit Court of Appeals rejected the petitioner's claim that several counts of making false entries ought to be dismissed from her indictment because pertinent records had been lost or destroyed between the time of the offenses and the issuance of the indictment.[125] The court reasoned that the absence of the records did not impair her defense enough to establish actual prejudice because, even absent the records, the Government had produced sufficient evidence to prove her guilt beyond a reasonable doubt.[126]

4. Applying the Governing Standard in the New Hampshire Courts

When addressing due process claims arising out of pre-indictment delay, the New Hampshire Supreme Court has applied the *Marion* test and achieved results similar to the federal courts conclusions, namely, consistent rejection of due process claims.[127]

In *State v. Philibotte*, for example, the court rejected the defendant's due process argument that he was deprived of a fair trial due to a nine-month delay between the date of his alleged offense and his indictment.[128] Citing *Marion*, the court observed that "the defendant's sole claim of prejudice was his purported inability to remember his whereabouts at the time of the alleged offenses"[129] and that "the possibility of prejudice due to the dimming of memories is inherent in any delay and,

---

120. *Id.* at 796.
121. 608 F.2d 889 (1st Cir. 1979), *cert. denied*, 444 U.S. 1019 (1980).
122. *Id.* at 899.
123. *Id.* at 902.
124. 686 F.2d 102 (2d Cir. 1982).
125. *Id.* at 105-06.
126. *Id.* at 106-07.
127. *See, e.g.*, State v. Varagianis, 512 A.2d 1117 (N.H. 1986); State v. Philibotte, 459 A.2d 275 (N.H. 1983).
128. *Philibotte*, 459 A.2d at 277.
129. *Id.*

alone, is insufficient to constitute a denial of due process."[130]

Similarly, in *State v. Varagianis*,[131] the court turned down a defendant's claim that a two-year delay between offense and indictment had deprived her of due process. Here the defendant argued that the delay dimmed the memory of a police informant, thus causing her to be deprived of two potential defense witnesses by virtue of the informant's inability to remember their names.[132] In rejecting this argument, however, the court observed that there was no evidence in the record that the informant had ever even known the names of the two potential witnesses. Consequently, said the court, the defendant's claim that she had been deprived of their testimony as a result of pre-indictment delay was highly speculative.[133] Moreover, the two-year investigative delay in this case was necessary to maintain the secrecy of the informant's identity pending completion of the investigation. Accordingly, the court held that the delay was reasonably necessary under the *Marion* standard and dismissed the defendant's claim.[134]

5. Applying the Governing Standard for Due Process Challenges to Chapter 213

The foregoing discussion clearly establishes that the criminal defendant who challenges Chapter 213:2 as violative of the Due Process Clauses of the United States and New Hampshire Constitutions faces formidable obstacles. Granted, the limitations period of twenty-two years from the alleged victim's eighteenth birthday provided therein will frequently result in long delays between alleged offenses and indictment. However, given the *Marion* standard, as heretofore applied in New Hampshire, the defendant must prove not only that the delay caused actual prejudice, but also that it was unrelated to any investigative necessity, and was employed merely to gain a tactical advantage over the defendant.

Nonetheless, the obstacle that the *Marion* standard places before the defendant is not insurmountable. The limitations period contained in Chapter 213:2 would permit forty-year-old complainants to bring charges of child sexual assault against defendants for assaulting them when they were four or five years old. Under these circumstances, one can certainly argue that such a case would be distinguishable from the cases examined in the foregoing discussion. Indeed, the protections against stale charges customarily provided by a limitations period would be significantly diminished in the hypothesized case. In light of those reduced protections, one could argue further that increased judi-

---

130. *Id.*
131. 512 A.2d 1117 (N.H. 1986).
132. *Id.* at 1118-19.
133. *Id.* at 1119.
134. *Id.*

cial scrutiny ought to be accorded to the defendant's claim of actual prejudice and to the state's explanation of the reasons for the pre-indictment delay.

With the benefit of such heightened scrutiny, a New Hampshire petitioner in circumstances such as those posited above might be able to demonstrate that actual impairment of witnesses' recollections resulted from the pre-indictment delay engendered by Chapter 213:2. Accordingly, a petitioner could argue that the memory flaws due to the delay were so egregious that the petitioner was convicted on the basis of failed memories, thereby establishing substantial prejudice.[135] A federal court in New Hampshire recognized the potential for this argument's success as far back as 1979 in *Dufield v. Perrin*.[136]

The aforementioned argument, of course, could succeed even if the court does not conclude that Chapter 213:2 per se violates the respective Due Process Clauses by imposing a limitations period that is inherently prejudicial to defendants.

Moreover, a New Hampshire petitioner who challenges Chapter 213:2 on due process grounds might be able to satisfy the second prong of the *Marion* test, which requires a showing that the state has delayed an indictment in order to gain a tactical advantage over the defendant. Again, a credible argument could be made for heightened judicial scrutiny on the ground that Chapter 213:2 diminishes the protections customarily provided to a defendant by a statute of limitations. By employing such scrutiny, the court, even if it does not find that Chapter 213:2 violates the Due Process Clause by imposing a limitations period that gives prosecutors an inherent tactical advantage, could nevertheless conclude that the prosecutor used that statute to gain such an advantage.

IV. LEGISLATIVE ALTERNATIVES TO CHAPTER 213

The discussion just concluded inspires the observation that even if Chapter 213 is found to be constitutional, it is hardly the best statutory scheme available for balancing the respective rights of victims of child sexual assaults and their accused assailants. The "balance" it attempts to strike weighs so heavily in favor of the victims that the statute is likely to be the object of due process challenges for years to come. To make matters worse, its lengthy limitations period could invite some prosecutors to orchestrate tactically motivated pre-indictment delays under the guise of investigative necessity. Finally, alternative legislative schemes exist that more effectively balance the respective rights of victims against the rights of the accused. Hence, the necessity for Chapter 213 is certainly open to debate.

---

135. *See supra* notes 108-12 and accompanying text.
136. 470 F. Supp. 687, 692 (D.N.H. 1979).

Several of the alternative legislative schemes to be discussed below are preferable to Chapter 213 because they recognize that the problem caused by time-barred prosecutions in cases of sexual assault against children does not arise from the length of the limitations period involved.[137] Instead, the problem arises from the inability of child victims to report the assaults due to either emotional trauma or fear of retaliation.[138] When a legislature responds to this problem solely by increasing or by eliminating limitations periods, it extends the reporting period in *all* child sexual assault cases, including those in which the offender has not prevented the victim from reporting the assault.[139] In the latter circumstance, the extended limitations period is of questionable necessity and thus it may diminish the accused's due process protection without a good reason.[140] The following discussion enumerates a full menu of legislative alternatives to Chapter 213, including measures that strike a more equitable balance between the respective rights of the alleged victim and those of the accused.

A.   *A Survey of the States*

The fifty states address the statute of limitations issue relative to child sexual assault in a wide variety of ways. Two states, Wyoming and South Carolina, impose no statutes of limitation for criminal offenses, including child sexual abuse. Seven other states, namely Alabama, Kentucky, Maryland, North Carolina, Rhode Island, Virginia and West Virginia, impose no statutes of limitation for certain felonies, including felony sex offenses committed against children.[141]

Eleven states have enacted specific limitations periods for all felonies, including felony sex offenses against children. Here the limitations periods range from two years to fifteen years from the commission of the alleged crime.[142] These statutes typically assign longer or shorter limitations periods to offenses based upon the rela-

---

137. Jessica E. Mindlin, Note, *Child Sexual Abuse and Criminal Statutes of Limitation: A Model for Reform*, 65 WASH. L. REV. 189, 201 (1990).

138. *Id.*

139. *Id.*

140. *Id.* at 201-02.

141. *See* ALA. CODE § 15-3-5(a)(4) (1990); KY. REV. STAT. ANN. § 500.050 (Michie/Bobbs-Merril 1990); MD. CTS. & JUD. PROC. CODE ANN. § 5-106 (1990); N.C. GEN. STAT. § 15-1 (Michie 1990); R.I. GEN. LAWS § 12-12-17 (Michie Supp. 1990); VA. CODE ANN. § 19.2-8 (Michie 1990); W. VA. CODE § 61-11-9 (Michie 1990).

142. *See* HAW. REV. STAT. § 701-108(2) (1985); LA. CODE CRIM. PROC. ANN. art. 572 (West 1991); ME. REV. STAT. ANN. tit. 17-A, § 8(2)(B) (West 1983 & Supp. 1990); MISS. CODE ANN. § 99-1-5 (1990); NEB. REV. STAT. § 29-110 (Supp. 1990); N.M. STAT. ANN. § 30-1-8 (Michie 1984); N.Y. CRIM. PROC. LAW § 30.10(2)(b) (McKinney 1981 & Supp. 1991); OHIO REV. CODE ANN. § 2901.13 (Anderson 1987); OR. REV. STAT. § 131.125 (1989 & Supp. 1990); S.D. CODIFIED LAWS ANN. § 23A-42-2 (Allen-Smith 1988); WIS. STAT. ANN. § 939.74(1) (West 1990).

tive severity of those offenses. For example, under New Mexico law, sexual penetration of a child under the age of thirteen is a first degree felony that carries a limitations period of fifteen years; the same conduct with a child between the ages of thirteen and sixteen is a second degree felony with a six-year limitations period. Furthermore, under the New Mexico statute, sexual contact with a minor, absent penetration, is a third degree felony with a three-year limitations period.[143]

Several states have enacted specific limitations periods for offenses committed against minors. For example, Georgia and Idaho have established longer limitations periods for offenses committed against minors.[144] In North Dakota, when an offense has been committed against a child under the age of fifteen, the statute of limitations is tolled and does not begin to run until the child reaches the age of fifteen.[145] Pennsylvania tolls its statute until a victim under the age of eighteen reaches eighteen.[146]

Eleven states have enacted limitations periods specifically for sexual offenses against minors. Generally, these statutes range from four years in Tennessee to ten years in Missouri and Texas.[147]

Two states have extended the limitations period pertaining to child

---

143. *See* N.M. STAT. ANN. §§ 30-9-11(A)(1), 30-9-11(B)(1), and 30-9-13(A) (Michie Supp. 1991).

144. GA. CODE ANN. § 17-3-1(c) (Michie 1990) states:

Prosecution for felonies . . . must be commenced within four years after the commission of the crime, provided that prosecution for felonies committed against victims who are at the time of the commission of the offense under the age of 14 years must be commenced within seven years after the commission of the crime.

IDAHO CODE § 19-402(1) (Michie Supp. 1991) states in pertinent part: "Commencement of prosecutions for crimes against children and other felonies. —(1) . . . a prosecution for any felony . . . committed upon or against a minor child must be commenced within five (5) years after the commission of the offense. . . ." Section 19-402(2) of the IDAHO CODE states that prosecutions for sexual abuse of a child under the age of 16 or for lewd conduct with a child under the age of 16 "must be commenced within five (5) years after the date the child reaches eighteen (18) years of age."

145. *See* N.D. CENT. CODE § 29-04-03.2 (Michie 1974 & Supp. 1989). *See also* MASS. ANN. LAWS ch. 277, § 63 (Law. Co-op. 1980 & Supp. 1991) (statute tolls until the victim turns 16).

146. *See* PA. CONS. STAT. ANN. tit. 42, § 5554(3) (Purdon 1981 & Supp. 1991).

147. *See* KAN. STAT. ANN. § 21-3106(2) (1988 & Supp. 1990) (five years); MINN. STAT. ANN. § 628.26(c) (West 1983 & Supp 1991) (seven years); MO. ANN. STAT. § 556.037 (Vernon Supp. 1991) (ten years); PA. CONS. STAT. ANN. tit. 42 § 5552(b) (Purdon 1981 & Supp. 1991) (five years); TENN. CODE ANN. § 40-2-101(d) (1990); TEX. CRIM. PROC. CODE ANN. § 12.01(2)(d) (West Supp. 1991); VT. STAT. ANN. tit. 13, § 4501(c) (Supp. 1991) (six years or when the victim reaches age twenty-four, whichever occurs first); WASH. REV. CODE ANN. § 9A.04.080(1)(c) (West Supp. 1991) (seven years after commission or three years after the victim's eighteenth birthday, whichever is later).

sexual abuse until the alleged victim reaches the age of majority.[148]

Other states, including New Hampshire, when in 1987 it enacted R.S.A. 632-A:7, (the predecessor of Chapter 213), have tolled the application of their statutory limitations periods until the alleged victim reaches the age of majority.[149] Under these statutes, the limitations period does not begin to run until the alleged victim reaches majority, which is typically *eighteen*.

Two states toll the application of the statute of limitations until the alleged offense is reported to law enforcement authorities[150] and three others toll the statute until the victim reaches majority, the crime is reported, or until the earlier of those events occurs.[151]

In total, sixteen states toll the statute of limitations until an offense is discovered, the alleged victim reaches a minimum age, or the alleged abuse is reported to a law enforcement agency.[152]

---

148. *See* NEV. REV. STAT. ANN. § 171-095(2) (Michie Supp. 1989); TENN. CODE ANN. § 40-2-101(d) (1990).

149. *See* ARK. CODE ANN. § 5-1-109(h) (Michie Supp. 1991); FLA. STAT. ANN. § 775.15(7) (West Supp. 1991); MASS. GEN. LAWS ANN. ch. 277, § 63 (West Supp. 1991); MONT. CODE ANN. § 45-1-205(1)(b) (1991); N.J. STAT. ANN. § 2C:1-6(b)(4) (West Supp. 1991).

150. *See* ARIZ. REV. STAT. ANN. § 13-107 (West 1989); OKLA. STAT. ANN. tit. 22, § 152 (West Supp. 1991).

151. *See* ALASKA STAT. § 12.10.020(c) (Michie 1990); MASS. ANN. LAWS ch. 277, § 63 (Law. Co-op Supp. 1991); NEV. REV. STAT. ANN. § 171.095(2) (Michie 1989).

152. ALASKA STAT. § 12.10.020 (Michie 1990) requires that an offense committed against a victim under the age of 16 be commenced within one year after the crime is reported to a peace officer or one year after the victim reaches 16, whichever occurs first but, in so doing, does not extend the period of limitation by more than five years. ARIZ. REV. STAT. ANN. § 13-107 (West 1989) states that criminal statutes of limitation do not begin to run until after discovery by the state, or from the time discovery should have occurred with the exercise of reasonable diligence. ARK. CODE ANN. § 5-1-109(h) (Michie Supp. 1991) tolls the statute until the victim reaches 18. FLA. STAT. ANN. § 775.15(b)(7) (West Supp. 1991) tolls the statute until the victim reaches 16. ILL. ANN. STAT. ch. 38, 3-6(c) (Smith-Hurd 1989) tolls the statute until the victim reaches 18. MASS. ANN. LAWS ch. 277, § 63 (Law. Co-op. Supp. 1991) tolls the statute until the victim reaches 16. NEV. REV. STAT. § 171.095 (Michie Supp. 1989) tolls the statute of limitations until the victim reaches 21. N.H. REV. STAT. ANN. § 625:8, III(d) (Supp. 1990) tolls the statute until the victim reaches 18. N.J. STAT. ANN. § 2C:1-6-b(4) (West Supp. 1991) tolls the statute until the victim reaches 18. N.M. STAT. ANN. § 30-1-9.1 (Michie Supp. 1991) tolls the statute until the victim reaches 18. N.D. CENT. CODE § 29-04-03.2 (Michie Supp. 1989) tolls the statute until the victim reaches age 15. OKLA. STAT. ANN. tit. 22, § 152(A) (West Supp. 1991) provides that criminal prosecutions for sexual acts against children must begin within five years after the discovery of the crime. PA. CONS. STAT. ANN. tit. 42, § 5554(3) (Purdon Supp. 1991) tolls the statutes of limitations until the victim reaches 18. UTAH CODE ANN. § 76-1-303 (Michie 1990) provides that a prosecution for sexual abuse of a child may be commenced within one year after the offense is reported to law enforcement officials, so long as no more than eight years have elapsed since the offense. WASH. REV. CODE ANN. § 9A.04.080 (West Supp. 1991) provides that prosecution must commence within three years after the victim's 18th birthday or seven years after the commission of

Three states have criminalized the use of one's authority to coerce a child victim into an abusive relationship.[153]

One state, Louisiana, has enacted a "concealment exception" to its four-year limitations period for child sexual abuse, whereby the statute of limitations is tolled where the victim is under 17, until the coercion or domination of the victim by the abuser ceases, thereby facilitating disclosure of the offense.[154] Nevada, Indiana and Kansas have enacted general concealment exceptions to their respective statutes of limitations that are applicable not only to cases of child sexual abuse, but to all offenses to which the respective limitations periods pertain.[155] The courts in Nevada and Indiana have applied these general concealment exceptions to child sexual abuse.[156] In Kansas, however, the State Supreme Court has held that "[c]rimes against persons, by their very nature, cannot be concealed."[157]

Finally, in recent years, five states have extended their limitations periods pertaining to offenses against minors.[158]

---

the offense, whichever is later. LA. CODE CRIM. PROC. ANN. art. 573(4) (West Supp. 1991) tolls the statute until the victim reaches 17.

153. WASH. REV. CODE ANN. §§ 9A.44.093, 096 (West Supp. 1991) created the offense of Sexual Misconduct With a Minor. In the first degree, it involves a perpetrator at least sixty months older than the victim, who is in a supervisory relationship to the victim and who commits an offense by abusing that supervisory capacity. MINN. STAT. ANN. § 609.342(b) (West 1980 & Supp. 1991) creates the offense of Criminal Sexual Misconduct, which consists of using a position of authority to coerce a victim into an abusive relationship. COLO. REV. STAT. § 18-3-405.3 (1984 & Supp. 1990) increases from four years to eight years the maximum jail term for sexual abuse of a child by a person in a position of trust concerning the child.

154. See LA. CODE CRIM. PROC. ANN. art. 573 (West Supp. 1991).

155. See NEV. REV. STAT. ANN. § 171.095(1) (Michie 1989); IND. CODE ANN. § 35-41-4-2 (d) (West 1990); KAN. CRIM. PROC. CODE ANN. § 21-3106(4)(c) (Vernon 1988 & Supp. 1989).

156. See, e.g., Walstrom v. State, 752 P.2d 225 (Nev. 1988) and Crider v. State, 531 N.E.2d 1151 (Ind. 1988).

157. State v. Bentley, 721 P.2d 227, 230 (Kan. 1986).

158. ALA. CODE § 15-3-5(a)(4) (Michie 1985) extended a three-year limitations period to an unlimited period in 1985. In 1984, Alaska extended a five-year period to one year after the child reaches age 16 or after the crime is reported, whichever occurs first. ALASKA STAT. § 12.10.020 (Michie 1990). In 1987, Arkansas extended a three-year period to three years from the victim's 18th birthday. ARK. CODE ANN. § 5-1-109(h) (Michie 1987). In 1984, Florida provided that if a victim is under age 16, the applicable limitations period does not begin to run until the victim reaches 16 or the offense is reported, whichever occurs first. FLA. STAT. ANN. § 755.15 (West 1991). In 1989, Washington extended the limitations period for crimes of indecent liberties from five years to seven years after the offense, or three years after the victim reaches age 18, whichever is later. WASH. REV. CODE ANN. § 9A.04.080(1)(c) (West 1989).

B. *Alternative 1: The Continuing Crime Doctrine*

One alternative to Chapter 213 is to enact a statute that designates child sexual assault as an offense that may be treated as a continuing crime. Generally, the statute of limitations begins to run from the commission of an offense or when the crime is complete, not from the date the crime is discovered.[159] However, for continuing crimes the statute does not begin to run with the occurrence of the initial act (which may in itself embody all the elements of the crime); instead, it runs from the occurrence of the most recent act.[160]

Where an offense is a continuing one, and so continues to a date within the statute of limitations, it is immaterial that the crime began on a date not within the statute.[161] A crime is not "continuing," however, unless it is either designated as such by statute, or its nature is such that the legislature clearly must have intended that it be treated as continuing.[162]

The Minnesota Court of Appeals has applied the continuing crime doctrine to extend the limitations period in the case of a child sexual assault. In *State v. Danielski*,[163] the victim's mother and stepfather violated a specific statutory prohibition against the use of one's authority over a child to sexually abuse that child.[164] In so doing, the court acted independently of the state legislature in creating a common law exception that tolls the statute of limitations.[165]

The *Danielski* court[166] reasoned that where an element of a sexual offense against a child is the perpetrator's exercise of authority over the victim, the use of such authority to sexually assault the victim and to prevent the victim from reporting the assault is a continuing crime. Therefore, the statute, said the court, does not begin to run until the victim is no longer subject to the assailant's authority. To hold otherwise would be to "completely thwart" the legislature's attempt to punish those who use their authority to sexually abuse children.[167]

The codification of the continuing crime doctrine is, however, a limited solution to the statute of limitations problem in cases of child sexual assault. This is because the United States Supreme Court has held that a criminal offense should not be considered a continuing crime unless either the explicit language of the governing statute compels such a conclusion, or the framers of the law intended that the offense

---

159. 21 Am. Jur. 2D *Criminal Law* § 226 (1981).
160. *Id.*
161. *Id.*
162. 22 C.J.S. *Criminal Law* § 200 (1989).
163. 348 N.W.2d 352 (Minn. Ct. App. 1984).
164. Mindlin, *supra* note 137, at 198-99.
165. *Id.* at 191-92.
166. 348 N.W.2d 352.
167. *Id.* at 356.

be treated as a continuing crime.[168]

In Minnesota, the state's criminal sexual misconduct statute requires that the defendant occupy a position of authority over the victim and use that authority to coerce the victim to submit to sexual abuse.[169] Accordingly, the conduct of the defendant in *Danielski* was ideally suited to fit within a continuing crime exception to a statute of limitations.[170] In the absence of a child sexual abuse statute that so clearly satisfies the *Toussie* requirement, a state court would not be able to apply the *Danielski* reasoning to create a continuing crime exception to its statute of limitations.[171] This problem could be solved by amending sexual abuse statutes to include "abuse of authority" as an element of the offense. However, in so doing, legislators would increase the state's burden of proof in child sexual assault cases, thereby making the state's task more difficult. Indeed, given that the purpose of a continuing crime exception is to facilitate, not hinder, prosecution,[172] such a measure would fly in the face of legislative intent.

C. *Alternative 2: Tolling the Statute for Secretive or Concealed Offenses*

Another alternative to Chapter 213 would be to toll the statute of limitations in child sexual assault cases if the offense is committed in a secretive manner or if the perpetrator concealed the fact that the crime occurred. Nevada, Indiana and Kansas have enacted statutory provisions to achieve this end.[173]

Such provisions recognize that the very nature of child sexual assault makes its detection especially difficult. Hence, a tolling of the statute during a demonstrated period of concealment is warranted in order to prevent offenders from escaping punishment by successfully concealing their conduct.[174] According to one commentator, "[w]hile there is motivation for the concealment of *all* crime, ordinarily it is desirable to start the period of limitation at the time of commission. When specific types of crimes present an opportunity for prolonged concealment, however, different treatment is warranted."[175]

---

168. Toussie v. United States, 397 U.S. 112, 115 (1970).

169. MINN. STAT. ANN. § 609.342(1)(b) (West Supp. 1991).

170. *See* Mindlin, *supra* note 137; at 204.

171. *Id.*

172. *Id.*

173. *See* NEV. REV. STAT. ANN. § 171.095(1) (Michie 1989); IND. CODE ANN. § 35-41-4-21(d)(2) (Burns 1990); KAN. CRIM. PROC. CODE ANN. § 21-3106(4)(c) (Vernon 1988 & Supp. 1989).

174. For a discussion of the forces that hinder the reporting of child sexual abuse and of legislative responses to the reporting problem, see Mindlin, *supra* note 137, at 197-98 and Durga M. Bharam, Comment, *Statute of Limitations for Child Sexual Abuse Offenses: A Time for Reform Utilizing the Discovery Rule*, 80 J. CRIM. L. & CRIMINOLOGY 842, 843 (1989).

175. Gerald F. Uelmen, *Making Sense Out of the California Criminal Statute of Limitations*, 15 PAC. L.J. 35, 63 (October 1983).

New Hampshire presently tolls its statute of limitations when a defendant is absent from the state, has no reasonably ascertained place of abode or employment in the state or when another prosecution is pending in the state against that defendant as a result of the same conduct.[176] The General Court could also toll the statute when the crime at issue was committed in a secretive manner or with intent to conceal. Under such circumstances, the statute would be tolled until the crime is discovered, although the legislators would be free to add a maximum time period from the date of the last offense within which prosecution must commence.

Concealment statutes, though, rather like continuing crime statutes, are an imperfect solution to the statute of limitations problem in cases of child sexual assault. This is because courts typically hold that the concealment of a crime that suspends the operation of a statute of limitations must be the product of acts by the accused that were calculated to prevent discovery of the alleged abuse.[177] Therefore, mere silence, inaction or nondisclosure does not constitute concealment.[178] In addition, the Kansas Supreme Court has held that Kansas's general concealment statute does not toll the limitations period in cases of child sexual assault because "[c]rimes against persons, by their very nature, cannot be concealed."[179] Most importantly, concealment statutes would not

---

176. N.H. REV. STAT. ANN. § 625:8, VI(a) and (b) (1990).

177. *See, e.g.*, State v. Shamp, 422 N.W.2d 736 (Minn. Ct. App. 1988), where the court held that the statute of limitations is not tolled where the accused, the victim's brother, neither resided with the victim nor controlled the victim's daily movements, and State v. Mills, 707 P.2d 1079 (Kan. 1985), wherein the court held that a third party's threats to the victim, designed to prevent the victim from revealing incidents of fondling, were not "concealment," hence, did not cause the statute to be tolled.

178. *Id.*

179. In State v. Bentley, 721 P.2d 227, 230 (Kan. 1986), the Kansas Supreme Court held that an uncle's threat to his nine-year-old niece to sexually abuse her again if she revealed the earlier abuse did not constitute concealment, and hence, did not toll the statute of limitations. The court stated:

Crimes against persons, by their very nature, cannot be concealed. Other people may not know a crime has occurred, but the victim necessarily knows that a crime has been committed. On the facts in this case, we cannot equate a threat made to a child victim with concealment of a crime. Even assuming this court recognized control over a child victim as bearing upon the fact of concealment, as the Minnesota Court of Appeals did in *State v. Danielski*, 348 N.W.2d 352, the uncle's ability to control the child victim (the uncle did not live with the victim) in this case was too remote for recognition.

Id. at 230.

Similarly, in Sears v. State, 356 S.E.2d 72 (Ga. 1987), the Georgia Supreme Court held that the eleven-year-old victim's knowledge that the offenses committed against her were wrong (although she did not know that they were crimes) was imputed to the State, thereby precluding the State from obtaining an indictment after the statute of limitations had expired. The court concluded that the statute

serve to toll statutes of limitations in cases of child sexual abuse where the abuser did not take affirmative steps to coerce the victim into silence. They would toll the limitation period, however, where the victim was too young and/or frightened to report the crime within the requisite statutory period.[180]

D. *Alternative 3: Tolling the Statute as It Applies to Child Sexual Assault*

A third and final alternative is to enact exceptions solely for child sexual assault to the limitations periods generally applicable to crimes under New Hampshire law. The principal means of accomplishing this are: 1) tolling the statute until the complainant reaches the age of majority, 2) tolling the statute until the wrongful act is discovered by the victim, a guardian or a law enforcement agency, or 3) using both types of tolling provisions, with the shorter period of the two controlling.[181]

New Hampshire's prior statute of limitations for child sexual assault employed the first means, tolling the statute, but extending the limitations period only six years beyond the complainant's eighteenth birthday.[182] In so doing, the prior statute attempted to strike a balance between the rights of the complainant and those of the accused. It mirrored the tolling provisions contained in statutes of limitations for child sexual assault enacted in other states in recent years.[183]

This approach is commendable for recognizing that child victims of sexual abuse are commonly unable to report that they have been victimized because they have been coerced into silence by their abusers, upon whom they are often dependent for financial, and/or emotional, sustenance.[184] Nevertheless, this approach is inflexible, resulting in unjustly delayed prosecutions where the state has sufficient evidence of guilt soon after the commission of the offense, but waits to commence prosecution until shortly before the complainant reaches the age of majority.[185] Conversely, this approach would also prohibit a prosecution commenced after the complainant's twenty-fourth birthday where, under the discovery rule approach, a judge could reasonably conclude that the prosecution could go forward without prejudice to the defendant's efforts to gather evidence.

Thus, tolling the statute of limitations until a fixed date after the

---

was not tolled (Georgia law tolled the statute during the period in which the perpetrator or the existence of the crime itself was not known) by the victim's infancy, ignorance of the criminality of the defendant's alleged acts, or fear of the defendant.

180. *See* Mindlin, *supra* note 137, at 205.

181. *See* Bharam, *supra* note 174, at 849-50.

182. N.H. Rev. Stat. Ann. § 632-A:7 (1987).

183. *See supra* notes 152 and 154.

184. For a thoughtful, concise discussion of the "dynamics of sexually abusive relationships," see Mindlin, *supra* note 137, at 193-94.

185. *See* Bharam, *supra* note 174, at 863.

alleged victim reaches the age of majority is not the best solution available to the statute of limitations problem in cases of child sexual abuse.

The second tolling mechanism identified above, tolling the statute of limitations until discovery of the crime, results from codification in criminal law of the common law discovery rule long used in the civil context.[186] That rule recognizes that there is inequity in foreclosing a cause of action where the victim might not know of the injury or harm until long after the events that precipitate it are over.[187] Where the discovery mechanism is provided for by statute, in the criminal setting, a limitations period does not begin to run until the alleged offense is discovered or it is reported to a law enforcement officer.[188]

In the civil context, the defendant's interests can be protected by the use of a balancing test to determine the discovery rule's applicability in each case. This test weighs the harm to the defendant occasioned by the litigation of stale claims, against the harm to the plaintiff of being denied a remedy against his or her abuser.[189] The discovery rule will apply when the unfairness of denying the plaintiff an opportunity to pursue that remedy outweighs the risks to the defendant associated with the litigation of old claims.[190]

California courts employ a balancing test that considers the following factors before deciding whether to invoke the discovery rule in civil actions:

---

186. For discussions of state courts' responses to the efforts of child sexual abuse victims to employ the discovery rule in civil actions, see Elaine M. Hartnett, Note, *Use of the Massachusetts Discovery Rule by Adult Survivors of Father-Daughter Incest*, 24 NEW ENG. L. REV. 1243 (1990); Charles J. Duffy III, Note, *Use of the Discovery Rule in Cases of Alleged Child Sexual Abuse: Does the Statute of Limitations Ever Run?* 28 DUQ. L. REV. 777 (1990); Alan Rosenfeld, *The Statute of Limitations Barrier in Childhood Sexual Abuse Cases: The Equitable Estoppel Remedy*, 12 HARV. WOMEN'S L.J. 206 (1989); and Martha Jean Zackin, Note, *The Discovery Rule and Father-Daughter Incest: A Legislative Response*, 29 B.C. L. REV. 941 (1988).

187. *See* Mark D. Kamitomo, Note, *Discovery Rule Application in Child Abuse Actions*, 23 GONZ. L. REV. 223, 226 (1987-88). In the criminal context,

[a]s a general rule, exceptions will not be implied to statutes of limitations for criminal offenses, and hence, . . . unless the statute of limitations contains an exception or condition that will toll its operation, the running of the statute is not interrupted, save only by indictment or other sufficient procedure commencing the prosecution of the offense.

22 C.J.S. *Criminal Law* § 202 (1989). "Under various statutes, however, definite exceptions or conditions are provided which will toll their operation." *Id.* This is precisely the case where a statute of limitations is tolled, in cases of child sexual assault, until discovery of the assault.

188. 22 C.J.S. *Criminal Law* § 202 (1989).

189. *See* Denise M. DeRose, Comment, *Adult Incest Survivors and the Statute of Limitations: The Delayed Discovery Rule and Long-Term Damages*, 25 SANTA CLARA L. REV. 191, 221 (1985).

190. *See generally* Susan D. Glimcher, Comment, *Statutes of Limitations and the Discovery Rule in Latent Injury Claims: An Exception or the Law?*, 43 U. PITT. L. REV. 501 (1981-82).

1.   whether, upon discovery of the injury, the defendant received timely notice of the victim's complaint;

2.   whether the defendant will suffer prejudice in attempting to gather evidence if the discovery rule is invoked;

3.   whether the complainant acted reasonably or in good faith in making the discovery;

4.   whether a fiduciary relationship existed between the parties;

5.   whether the complainant used reasonable diligence in seeking professional advice upon discovery of the injury; and

6.   whether there was a rational basis for delay in discovery.[191]

New Jersey courts consider similar factors in civil cases wherein the plaintiff seeks to use the discovery rule to toll a statute of limitations. These factors "may include but need not be limited to: the nature of the alleged injury, the availability of witnesses and written evidence, the length of time that has elapsed since the alleged wrongdoing, whether the delay has been to any extent deliberate or intentional [and] whether the delay may be said to have peculiarly or unusually prejudiced the defendant.[192]

These factors could be adapted to criminal prosecutions for child sexual abuse, thereby implementing a tolling exception to the statute of limitations that judges could invoke when the balance of interests in a particular prosecution so demanded. In such circumstances, prosecution would be required to commence within a reasonable time after the date of discovery, such as one year, in order to eliminate prosecutorial motivation to delay.[193]

The third tolling alternative, tolling the statute of limitations until either the victim reaches majority or the offense is discovered, whichever period is shorter, is as problematical as merely tolling the statute until the complainant reaches majority would be. This is because it would not, in all likelihood, produce a limitations period long enough to aid the victim for whom discovery occurs long after reaching majority. Yet, such a device may produce a limitations period short enough

---

191. Mindlin, *supra* note 137, at 220-21 (citing Electronic Equip. v. Sailer & Co., 176 Cal. Rptr. 239 (1981); Velasquez v. Fibreboard Paper Products Corp., 159 Cal. Rptr. 113 (1979); Bedolla v. Logan & Frazier, 125 Cal. Rptr. 59 (1975); United States Liab. Ins. Co. v. Haidinger-Hayes, Inc., 463 P.2d 770 (Cal. 1970); Bennet v. Hibernia Bank, 305 P.2d 20 (Cal. 1956); Hobart v. Hobart Estates, 159 P.2d 958 (Cal. 1945)).

192. *See* Lopez v. Swyer, 300 A.2d 563 (N.J. 1973).

193. *See, e.g.*, UTAH CODE ANN. § 76-1-303 (Michie 1990) and ALASKA STAT. § 12.10.020 (Michie 1990), both of which permit the commencement of a prosecution within one year after the discovery of the offense. However, the Utah statute does not permit a prosecution to commence more than eight years after the alleged offense and the Alaska statute prohibits the commencement of a prosecution more than one year after the alleged victim reaches the age of 16.

to permit prosecution in a case where the threat of a denial of due process to the defendant is substantial.

The best of all the alternatives considered heretofore is the tolling exception based upon the codified discovery rule. This is because it balances the respective rights of the complainant and the accused more effectively than fixed-date extensions of the statute of limitations and it does not suffer from the limitations peculiar to the continuing crime doctrine and the concealment exception, respectively.[194]

V. LEGISLATIVE RECOMMENDATION

All of the alternative legislative prescriptions to Chapter 213 are preferable because at minimum they reduce the likelihood of, if not avoiding entirely, the potential due process violations engendered by a lengthy, fixed statute of limitations. However, the most desirable alternative to Chapter 213 is the enactment of a tolling exception that accords to judges in prosecutions for child sexual assault discretion to determine whether to toll the statute and invoke the discovery rule.

The wisdom of the discovery rule lies in the fact that it does not establish a limitations period with a fixed date of conclusion that might arrive sooner than equity would favor in some cases and later than due process would require in others. Instead, the discovery rule provides for a careful weighing of the respective interests of the complainant and the accused before the decision of whether or not to toll the customary limitations period is made.

Both prosecution and defense will have an opportunity to demonstrate that the balance of interests in a particular case compels a specific result regarding the tolling of the statute. In some cases, no doubt, that balance will weigh in favor of tolling the statute even when the prosecution is commenced twenty-five years after the alleged offense. In others, the balance might weigh against tolling the statute, even when the prosecution is commenced eight-to-ten years after the commission of the alleged offense. Either way, the decision to toll or not to toll the statute of limitations will result from the careful consideration of the circumstances of the case rather than from adherence to a legislative requirement. Similarly, in either case, the accused will sacrifice a measure of the certainty of repose customarily afforded by statutes of limitation and the alleged victim will sacrifice a measure of the certainty of prosecution afforded by a lengthy limitations period.[195]

Accordingly, the New Hampshire General Court should consider amending R.S.A. 625:8, III to state that

[i]f the (limitations) period prescribed in paragraph I (6 years from the

---

194. *See supra* notes 159-80 and accompanying text.

195. For a thorough treatment of the competing interests implicated in statutes of limitations, see generally Uelmen, *supra* note 175.

date of the offense for class A and class B felonies, 1 year from the date of the offense for misdemeanors and 3 months from the date of the offense for violations) has expired, a prosecution may nevertheless be commenced: (d) For any offense under R.S.A. 632-A, where the victim was under 18 years of age when the alleged offense occurred, until 1 year after the discovery of the offense by a law enforcement agency or by any other adult person who is not a party to the offense, so long as the court, using the discretion that is accorded to it by this provision, orders that the period prescribed in paragraph I be tolled until 1 year from discovery.[196]

The amended statute should also state that:

In deciding whether to order that the period prescribed in paragraph I be tolled until 1 year after discovery, the court shall consider and weigh the following factors:

1.   whether the alleged victim and the state acted reasonably in making the discovery;

2.   whether the alleged victim, under the circumstances, was diligent in informing a third party of the alleged offense (including whether the delay has been to any extent deliberate or intentional);

3.   whether the state gave the defendant[s] timely notice after discovering the alleged offense;

4.   whether the defendant[s] will suffer prejudice in attempting to gather evidence if the discovery rule is invoked (taking into account the length of time that has elapsed since the alleged offense);

5.   whether there was a rational basis for delay in discovery of the alleged offense; and

6.   whether a fiduciary relationship existed between the accused and the alleged victim.[197]

The recommended legislation would reduce the likelihood of violations of defendants' due process rights because it would give judges discretion to bar criminal actions wherein pre-indictment delay will cause the defendant to suffer prejudice. This would occur regardless of the number of years that have passed since the alleged offense. This is preferable to a limitations period of twenty-two years from the alleged victim's eighteenth birthday because it makes prejudice to the defendant, rather than the number of years since the alleged offense, the determinant of whether the action should be barred.[198] Such a law more clearly reflects the limitations period's purpose of barring stale claims based on unreliable evidence than does the fixed date limitations period contained in Chapter 213.[199]

The recommended legislation would also discourage unnecessary delay in reporting alleged offenses and commencing prosecutions because such delay would plainly hinder the prosecution's effort to con-

---

196. *See* N.H. REV. STAT. ANN. § 625:8, III(d) (1990).

197. *See supra* notes 176-77.

198. *See supra* text accompanying note 185.

199. *See supra* notes 138-40 and accompanying text.

vince the court that the case should proceed despite potential prejudice to the defendant. Alleged victims would know that prosecution is not a certainty merely because the case is commenced within a requisite number of years after the alleged offense. Ironically, this feature may well prove a great boon to alleged victims because, by encouraging prompt reporting and expeditious commencement of prosecutions, it is likely to make the defendant's task of demonstrating prejudice more difficult.

Moreover, the recommended legislation would benefit alleged victims by permitting them to prosecute their alleged abusers within a reasonable time after discovering the offense, rather than restricting prosecutions to some arbitrarily determined time frame after the alleged offense. Under the proposed law, for example, a forty-one year-old victim who had last been abused at age ten could prosecute the abuser provided the victim's legitimate expectation of prosecution outweighed the potential prejudice to the defendant occasioned by long-dormant evidence. Under Chapter 213 though, this victim would be denied the right to prosecute, even if the balance of relevant factors weighed in favor of prosecution, merely because discovery of the offense occurred one year too late.[200]

Thus, the proposed legislation, unlike the existing limitations period in New Hampshire, would: 1) encourage alleged victims to report offenses promptly and prosecutors to commence prosecutions in a timely fashion; 2) protect the due process rights of defendants by barring prosecutions wherein the defendant's ability to build a case will be seriously jeopardized; and 3) still achieve the overriding goal of Chapter 213, namely, removing the formidable barrier to criminal prosecutions for child sexual abuse long erected by statutes of limitations.[201] In so doing, it would achieve the ends sought by Chapter 213 without imposing the burdens that Chapter 213 imposes on alleged victims and defendants alike.

It would, moreover, achieve those ends by adapting, for the criminal context, the discovery rule-based tolling exception that already applies in personal injury actions brought under New Hampshire law. N.H.R.S.A. 508:4, I, provides that personal injury actions, unless otherwise provided by law, must be brought within three years of the act or omission complained of,

> except that when the injury and its causal relationship to the act or omission were not discovered and could not reasonably have been discovered at the time of the act or omission, the action shall be commenced within 3 years of the time the plaintiff discovers, or in the exercise of reasonable diligence should have discovered, the injury and

---

200. *See supra* text accompanying note 185.
201. *See* 1990 N.H. Laws 213:1.

its causal relationship to the act or omission complained of.[202]

The proposed legislation would apply the above provision, in a modified form, to the criminal context, in place of Chapter 213.

VI. CONCLUSION

Chapter 213, relating to the statute of limitations on prosecutions for sexual assault offenses against children, is likely to be challenged in the New Hampshire courts during the coming years on due process grounds and is vulnerable to challenge on ex post facto grounds. It is likely that most of the due process challenges will fail, but those failures may be better explained by the pressure of formidable doctrinal barriers to success than by the clarity or equity of Chapter 213. Accordingly, the New Hampshire General Court should consider replacing Chapter 213 with one of the alternative legislative prescriptions outlined above, preferably the discovery rule-based tolling exception to the statute of limitations. Of the available alternatives, the discovery tolling exception is best able to achieve the aims of Chapter 213 without producing the adverse consequences that flow from it for victims and defendants alike.

---

202. N.H. REV. STAT. ANN. § 508:4, I (1986).

Adult Survivors of Childhood Sexual Abuse: Should Texas Courts Apply the Discovery Rule?

Tina Snelling*
Wayne Fisher**

---

   *   Tina Snelling is a graduate of South Texas College of Law and the University of Houston Law Center. After graduation from the University of Houston Law Center in 1987, she served as a briefing attorney for the Fourteenth Court of Appeals. She authored this article while working as an attorney with Fisher, Gallagher & Lewis. Ms. Snelling is now an associate in the appellate department of the firm Hirsch, Glover, Robinson & Sheiness, P.C. of Houston, Texas.
   **   Wayne Fisher, certified in personal injury trial law, is founder of the law firm of Fisher, Gallagher & Lewis, L.L.P. of Houston, Texas. He is the former president of the State Bar of Texas, Texas Trial Lawyers Association, and Houston Trial Lawyers Association, and is the current president-elect of the International Academy of Trial Lawyers. Mr. Fisher has presented papers and lectured for various legal organizations throughout the United States.

59

INTRODUCTION

This year, as in years past, thousands of young girls and boys will be sexually abused in the United States. Every aspect of their emotional, mental, spiritual and physical well-being will be greatly affected by such abuse. When these children reach adulthood they will suffer a myriad of dysfunctions, ranging from troubled relationships, poor self-esteem, substance abuse and self-destructive behavior. Some will become so overwhelmed by their suffering that they will destroy themselves. Others will unknowingly suffer the effect of the childhood sexual abuse [hereinafter "CSA"] for many years, if not for the balance of their lives. If and when these adult survivors are able to understand the devastating connection between their suffering and the CSA, there will be generally no mechanism to hold their abusers accountable: they will be barred from seeking redress in many jurisdictions by the statute of limitations.

This article discusses the inherent problems encountered in applying the traditional limitation period for personal injury actions to tort claims brought by CSA survivors. Part I of this article gives an overview of the background and nature of CSA, focusing on the factors that prevent a survivor from seeking redress within the traditional time constraints of an ordinary civil tort action. Part II discusses the current treatment of CSA suits in those legal forums which have encountered these causes of action. Part III analyzes mechanisms, including use of the discovery rule, to surmount the bar of limitations. Finally, Part IV sets forth possible causes of action for the redress of CSA and suggests several strategies to consider in pursuing a CSA suit in the Texas judicial system.

II. THE BACKGROUND AND NATURE OF CHILDHOOD
SEXUAL ABUSE

A. The Background of CSA

CSA is not a product of modern society. In fact, current recognition of CSA follows a historic tradition of avoidant prejudice where the same factors that have trapped a child victim into helpless silence have become institutionalized in society at large. Before our society's latest discovery of CSA, there were at least three previous attempts to study and respond to it before 1978, all of which were suppressed.[1] The first attempt was in 1860, when Amboise Tardieu discovered and published the equivalent of the battered child syndrome and publicized the high incidence and tragic effects of CSA.[2] Tardieu was discredited immediately by his academic predecessors who chose to restore the concept of victim-blame by focusing on the ulterior motives of children to make false accusations against their innocent parents.[3] In 1896, Sigmund Freud deduced that early childhood seduction was the central basis for neurosis.[4] His claim brought scorn and rejection from his peers. Freud subsequently repudiated his observations and developed the theory that such descriptions by victims were fantasies.[5] By retracting his earlier theories, Freud reinforced a climate of prejudice toward the discovery of the reality and devastating effects of CSA.[6] In 1932, Sandor Ferenczi attempted to present his findings on CSA, in return he received isolation from his peers.[7]

Ironically, in 1962, the nation "rediscovered" child abuse.[8] Fifteen years later, CSA was acknowledged as a concomitant form of such

---

1. John Meyers, *Protecting Children From Sexual Abuse, What Does The Future Hold?*, 15 J. CONTEMP. L. 31 (1989).

2. Roland C. Summit, *The Centrality of Victimization, Psychiatric Clinics of N. America*, 413-14, Vol. 12, No. 2 (June 1989) [hereinafter "Summit"].

3. *Id.*

4. *Id.*; *see also* SIGMUND FREUD, THE AETIOLOGY OF HYSTERIA (1896) *in* THE STANDARD EDITION OF THE COMPLETE PSYCHOLOGICAL WORKS OF SIGMUND FREUD (1962) [hereinafter "Freud"].

5. M. HUNTER, ABUSED BOYS, THE NEGLECTED VICTIMS OF SEXUAL ABUSE 27-28 (1990) [hereinafter "HUNTER"].

6. FLORENCE RUSH, THE BEST KEPT SECRET: SEXUAL ABUSE OF CHILDREN 80-104 (1980) [hereinafter "Rush"]. Freud's impact on the law was immediate, as evinced by John Wigmore's treatise on evidence, which warned that, in sex offense cases, women and young girls were not to be believed absent careful psychiatric scrutiny. *See* Duckett v. State, 797 S.W.2d 906 (Tex. Crim. App. 1990). One vestige of Wigmore's influence can be seen in evidentiary rules which require corroboration of a sex victim's testimony, as compared to admissibility of other crime victim's testimony. *Id.* at 916 n.15.

7. Summit, *supra* note 2, at 414.

8. *Id.*

abuse.[9] Yet, despite growing national recognition, CSA has been slow to gain acceptance. Even today, its victims are likened to persecutors in modern-day Salem witch trials.[10] Until recently, if a CSA victim disclosed the fact of the CSA, relatives, friends, therapists[11] and professionals charged with the duty to protect these victims either did not believe it[12] or were ill-equipped to challenge the patriarchal prerogative.[13] Even our legal system has provided evidentiary obstacles to CSA claims, which still persist under current jurisprudence.[14]

In light of the historical cycle of discovery and rejection, it is little wonder CSA reports appear only recently to have exploded in numbers.[15] Despite what the "trends" indicate, the incidence rate of CSA has not risen. What has happened is a revolution in consciousness, where, because of changed mores, professionals are now more sensitive to identifying instances of CSA. Further, the victims and their families are more willing than before to seek help.[16] All that remains to be accorded to such victims is the consistent judicial recognition of their claims.

---

9. *Id.*; Melissa G. Salten, *Statutes of Limitations in Civil Incest Suits: Preserving The Victim's Remedy*, 7 HARV. WOMEN'S L. J. 189, 192-93 (1984) [hereinafter "Salten"]. Recognition of CSA is primarily attributed to the efforts of feminist scholars, health professionals and survivors who have written about their CSA. *Id.* at 192.

10. Joseph B. Cheshire, *Child Sex Cases: The Salem Witch Trials Of The 20th Century?*, 1991 A.T.L.A. Winter Convention at 237 [hereinafter "Cheshire"].

11. Until recently, psychotherapists and other mental health professionals accepted and fostered the double myth that sexual abuse of children was uncommon and, if it occurred, was unlikely to cause long-term harm. Salten, *supra* note 9, at 192. Also, society and persons otherwise able to assist the child did not believe in the possibility that such an act could occur. *Id.* at 198; *see also* Elaine E. Barney, *A Clinical Practice Model For Treatment Of College-Aged Incest Survivors*, 38 J. AM. COLLEGE HEALTH 279-82 (1990) [hereinafter "Barney"].

12. Researchers have termed this lack of response at the "second injury" to the victim. HUNTER, *supra* note 5, at 50.

13. *Id.* at 54-55; Salten, supra note 9, at 194-196.

14. Fitzgerald v. United States, 443 A.2d 1295, 1307-1309 (D.C. 1982) (Newman, C.J., dissenting) (justification for majority's distinguishing between "mature" females and other complainants is its belief that there is a greater danger of false accusations in sex offense cases involving child victims); Tyson v. Tyson, 727 P.2d 226, 229 (Wash. 1989) (expert testimony concerning psychoanalysis of CSA victim cannot be assumed to produce an accurate account of events in the individual's past); *see also* Durga M. Bharam, *Statute of Limitations For Child Sexual Abuse Offenses: A Time For Reform Utilizing The Discovery Rule*, 80 J. CRIM. L. & CRIMINOLOGY 842-43 (1989) (hereinafter "Bharam"). Even though, for almost thirty years, our legal community has been preoccupied with the immediate impact of CSA, it is only of late that attention has been given to the future harm which occurs in CSA. Elaine M. Hartnett, *Use Of The Massachusetts Discovery Rule By Adult Survivors Of Father-Daughter Incest*, NEW ENGLAND L. REV. 1243, 1249 (1990) [hereinafter "Hartnett"].

15. DAVID FINKELHOR, SEXUALLY VICTIMIZED CHILDREN 131 (1979) [hereinafter "Finkelhor"].

16. *Id.* at 131-132, 144.

B.   The Nature of CSA

The most prevalent type of CSA is that of incest.[17] Although the Texas Penal Code defines incest as a criminal proscription of intercourse within certain degrees of consanguinity,[18] in the CSA context, incest is defined as sexual contact between a child and other family member in a position of power or control over the child, where the child is being used for the sexual stimulation of the perpetrator or another person.[19] In one study of 583 cases of CSA, the offender was a family member in forty-seven percent of the cases; an acquaintance of the child in forty-two percent; and a stranger in only eight percent.[20] Incest involving fathers[21] and daughters or that involve girls and a father figure is the most frequently reported type of incestuous CSA.[22] Mother-son incestuous CSA is considered to be very rare and instances of same-sex incestuous CSA that involves fathers and sons or mothers and daughters are rarely re-

---

17.   Salten, *supra* note 9, at 193 n.18.

18.   In Texas, incest is defined as sexual intercourse or deviate sexual intercourse by an individual with a person he knows to be, without regard to legitimacy:

(1)   his ancestor or descendant by blood or adoption;

(2)   his stepchild or stepparent, while the marriage creating that relationship exists;

(3)   his parent's brother or sister of the whole or half blood;

(4)   his brother or sister of the whole or half blood or by adoption; or

(5)   the children of his brother or sister of the whole or half blood or by adoption.

TEX. PENAL CODE ANN. § 25.02(a) (Vernon 1989).

19.   Hartnett, *supra* note 14, at 1245-46; Margaret J. Allen, *Tort Remedies For Incestuous Abuse*, 13 GOLDEN GATE U. L. REV. 609, 610-11 (1983) [hereinafter "Allen"]. There are three recent definitions of incestuous CSA:

(1)   any physical contact between a child and an adult in a position of paternal authority that has to be kept a secret;

(2)   sexual contact between family members; and

(3)   any manual, oral or genital sexual contact or other explicit behavior that an adult family member imposes on a child which results in emotional, physical or sexual trauma.

Id. at n.7.

20.   Note, *Testimony of Child Victims in Sex Abuse Prosecutions: Two Legislative Innovations*, 98 HARV. L. REV. 806, 807 n.14 (1985) [hereinafter "Note, *Testimony of Child Victims*"]; *cf.* FINKELHOR, *supra* note 15, at 3 (noting "the vast majority of reported sexual abusers of children are friends or family: 30 percent relatives and 45 percent acquaintances").

21.   A father is defined as "any man functioning in the paternal, parental role in the family" and includes biological fathers, step-fathers, adoptive fathers, or male partners of the mother whose relationship with the mother is not legally formalized. Brunngraber, *Father-Daughter Incest: Immediate and Long-Term Effects of Sexual Abuse*, 8 ADVANCES IN NURSING SCIENCE 15, 20-21 (1986).

22.   Hartnett, *supra* note 14, at 1246; *see also* Phyllis Coleman, *Incest: A Proper Definition Reveals The Need For A Different Response*, 49 MO. L. REV. 251, 251 n.1 (1984) [hereinafter "Coleman"] (stating that approximately 75% of incest cases are between father and daughter); Roland Summit, *The Child Sexual Abuse Accommodation Syndrome*, 7 CHILD ABUSE & NEGLECT 177-180 (1983) (stating most incest victims are females).

ported.[23] While the exact incidence-rate of CSA is unknown, estimates range that as many as one in three girls and one in six boys are the victims of CSA.[24]

In the average case, CSA begins when the child is eight or nine years old.[25] However, sexual relations and intercourse may begin even earlier.[26] In order to ensure the child's availability and to provide a cover for the lascivious conduct, the child's abuser demands secrecy.[27] This often is accomplished by threats of harm to the child or to the child's family's well-being.[28] Because the child is forced to cope in silence, the child is likely to internalize self-blame, anger, fear, confusion and sadness resulting from the sexual contact(s).[29] This internalization is referred to as "accommodation."[30] In accommodating an intolerable situation, the victim often "blocks out" or represses the experience for years, often

---

23. Hartnett, *supra* note 14, at 1246 n.25. One author cites a Minnesota survey which reveals that one of every twenty-five male high school students and one of every fourteen male college students reports that he is a victim of sexual abuse. Also, if the rate were to remain constant, at least 46,000 to 92,000 boys under the age of thirteen are sexually abused in the United States on an annual basis. HUNTER, *supra* note 5, at 26. Another commentator suggests that these forms of CSA are more frequent than reported but, even allowing for under-reporting, the conclusion is that these forms of CSA are relatively rare compared to other forms of CSA. Hartnett, *supra* note 14, at 1246 n.25 (citing DAVID FINKELHOR, CHILD SEXUAL ABUSE: NEW THEORY AND RESEARCH 23, 223-227 (1981)).

24. Bonnie Gangelhoff and Lersh Hopper, *Incest—The Last Secret*, HOUSTON POST, Nov. 10, 1991, at E-1, 3-4; Judith Herman, Diana Russell, et al., *Long-Term Effects of Incestuous Abuse in Childhood*, 143 AM. J. PSYCHIATRY 1293 (1986) (citing one in ten chance for boys under age eighteen). In Texas, the State's Department of Human Services reports a total of 8,162 confirmed cases of CSA for fiscal year 1989. Of the 8,162 cases, 84.1% were girls and 15.9% were boys. For fiscal year 1990, 8,916 cases were confirmed, nearly a ten percent increase in confirmed cases of CSA. Of the 8,916 cases, 82.4% were girls and 17.6% were boys. TEXAS DEPARTMENT HUMAN SERVICES PROTECTIVE SERVICES FOR FAMILIES AND CHILDREN STATUS REPORT FISCAL YEAR 1989 AND 1990.

25. HUNTER, *supra* note 5, at 46; Denise M. DeRose, *Adult Incest Survivors and the Statute of Limitations: The Delayed Discovery Rule and Long-Term Damages*, 25 SANTA CLARA L. REV. 191, 192 n.3 (1985) [hereinafter "DeRose"] (citing JUDITH HERMAN, FATHER-DAUGHTER INCEST 83 (1981) [hereinafter "HERMAN"].

26. Salten, *supra* note 9, at 194-95; DeRose, *supra* note 25, at 192 n.3. It is reported that hospitals have treated three-month-old babies for venereal disease of the throat. ELLEN BASS, *Introduction: In The Truth Itself, There is Healing*, in I NEVER TOLD ANYONE (1983); *see also* In Interest of LS, 748 S.W.2d 571, 573 (Tex. App.— Amarillo 1988, no writ) (eighteen-month-old baby treated for gonorrhea).

27. Salten, *supra* note 9, at 194-95; DeRose, *supra* note 25, at 192 (providing descriptions of incest recollecting); *see also* Duckett v. State, 797 S.W.2d 906, 908 n.6 (Tex. Crim. App. 1990) (describing the expert's testimony as to the six phases of the Child Abuse Syndrome, which include the conditioning-secrecy phase(s)).

28. Allen, *supra* note 19, at 615.

29. Salten, *supra* note 9, at 198; Allen, *supra* note 19, at 616 (describing internalization of anxiety and shame).

30. Salten, *supra* note 9, at 198; Hartnett, *supra* note 14, at 1244 (describing repression of incest memories); Allen, *supra* note 19, at 616 (describing childhood internalization of shame).

many years past adolescence and well into adulthood.[31] These survivors comprise a broad range of ages, ranging from the age of majority to above the age of forty years.[32]

As the victim becomes an adult, she will often begin to exhibit signs of sexual trauma.[33] The most common traumatic symptoms are sexual dysfunctions, low self-esteem, poor capacity for self-protection, feelings of isolation, and an inability to form or maintain supportive relationships.[34] At this time, the victim may realize she is injured.[35] However, until such time as the victim is able to place blame for the CSA upon the offender, it will be impossible for such victim to realize that such behavior caused psychological disorders.[36] It is only through therapy that the victim is able to recognize the causal link between the abuser's conduct and personal damages from the sexual trauma.[37] Oftentimes, the victim may not consciously remember the incidents until undergoing therapy for dysfunctions or until a triggering life event occurs that will unlock the repressed memory of the CSA.[38] Once the CSA victim begins to confront these experiences and link personal damages with the abuser's conduct, the victim has taken the first step towards becoming a *survivor*.[39]

The need for maturity of the survivor before he or she can confront the CSA experience results in a general lack of ability to file suit within the statutory period for civil tort actions.[40] Because the maximum age at

---

31. Summit, *supra* note 2, at 413; DeRose, *supra* note 25, at 212.

32. DeRose, *supra* note 25, at 192 n.5-6; *see also* Frederick H. Lindberg and Lois J. Distad, *Post-Traumatic Stress Disorders In Women Who Experienced Childhood Incest*, 9 CHILD ABUSE & NEGLECT 329-34 (1985) (providing chart showing incest population).

33. Allen, *supra* note 19, at 616. The sexual trauma is also known as Post Traumatic Stress Syndrome ("PTSD"). Patrick Edwards & Mary Ann Donaldson, *Assessment Of Symptoms In Adult Survivors Of Incest: A Factor Analytic Study Of The Responses To Childhood Incest Questionnaire*, 13 CHILD ABUSE & NEGLECT 101, 102 (1989).

34. Salten, *supra* note 9, at 200-201.

35. Allen, *supra* note 19, at 630.

36. *Id.*

37. Hartnett, *supra* note 14, at 1267.

38. DeRose, *supra* note 25, at 212; Salten, *supra* note 9, at 202; Hartnett, *supra* note 14, at 1267 (stating that therapy during adulthood is necessary to discover nature of incest damage); *see also* Meiers-Post v. Schafer, 427 N.W.2d 606 (Mich. Ct. App. 1988) (showing facts where victim had repressed memory of incest).

39. Allen, *supra* note 19, at 610 n.5; Hunter, *supra* note 5, at 93-95; *see also* David Speigel, *Hypnosis in the Treatment of Victims of Sexual Abuse*, 12 PSYCHIATRIC CLINICS OF N. AM. 295-299 (1989) [hereinafter "Spiegel"] (stating victim needs to confront memories of abuse to recover).

40. Allen, *supra* note 19, at 630; *see also* De Rose, *supra* note 25, at 195 (stating that statute of limitations is major stumbling block of incest survivors). Indeed, clinical psychologists who treat incestuous CSA agree that the injury to the incest victim most often does not manifest until the victim's later life. Frequently, the manifestation occurs with the female survivor when she gives birth to her first female child. *Id.* at 212.

which adult survivors of CSA may file suit is age twenty in Texas,[41] they are effectively denied a legal remedy unless they are given the benefit of a tolling mechanism such as the discovery rule.

III. CASE LAW TO DATE

To date, the CSA survivor cases that have been brought are, for purposes of discussion, divisible into two categories:

(1)   those cases where the plaintiff claimed that he or she knew about the sexual assaults at or before majority, but was unaware that physical or psychological problems were caused by the prior sexual abuse (Type 1 cases); and

(2)   cases where the plaintiff claims that, due to the trauma of the experience, he or she had no recollection or knowledge of the sexual abuse until shortly before filing suit (Type 2 cases).[42]

The discussion that follows reflects how courts have sided on the issue according to the type of CSA claim.

A.   *No Recovery for Either Type 1 or Type 2 Cases*

Courts in Washington and Florida have decided that the discovery rule, a protection afforded the plaintiff who does not learn of his or her injury until after the statute of limitations has elapsed, does not apply to either Type 1 or Type 2 cases.[43] In *Tyson v. Tyson*,[44] the Washington

---

41.   TEX. CIV. PRAC. & REM. CODE ANN. § 16.001, § 16.003 (Vernon 1986).

42.   As categorized and discussed by Judge Plunkett in Johnson v. Johnson, 701 F. Supp. 1363 (N.D. Ill. 1988); *see also* Hartnett, *supra* note 14, at 1277 (discussing emergence of different case "types").

43.   Tyson v. Tyson , 727 P.2d at 227; Lindabury v. Lindabury, 552 So. 2d 1117 (Fla. Dist. Ct. App. 1989) (per curiam) (stating that statute begins to run when the injury occurs), *cause dismissed*, 560 So. 2d 233 (Fla. 1990). In *Tyson*, the court was called upon to answer the certified question as to whether the discovery rule could be invoked where the plaintiff alleged that she was the victim of CSA but had blocked the memory of the events during the entire period of the statute of limitations. *Tyson*, 727 P.2d at 227. After the court refused to apply the discovery rule, the Washington legislature swiftly passed legislation to address CSA suits. The legislation, S.S.B. 6305, passed by a unanimous vote of the Senate and the House. Hartnett, *supra* note 14, at 1275-76.

Now, the statute of limitations on CSA or child exploitation states that "[a]ll claims or causes of action based on intentional conduct brought by any person for recovery of damages for injury suffered as a result of childhood sexual abuse shall be commenced within three years of the act alleged to have caused the injury or condition, or three years of the time the victim discovered or reasonably should have discovered that the injury or condition was caused by said act, whichever period expires later: *Provided*, That the time limit for commencement of an action under this section is tolled for a child until the child reaches the age of eighteen years." WASH. REV. CODE ANN. §§ 4.16.340, 4.16.350 (West Supp. 1991). In *Lindabury*, the court reasoned that, notwithstanding repression and taking the 34-year old plaintiff's allegations of the sexual abuses as true, such damaged the plaintiff "at the time they occurred." *Lindabury*, 552 So. 2d at 1117.

It should also be noted that two lower courts in New York have held that there is no

court refused to apply the discovery rule in CSA survivor suits, because there was "no empirical, verifiable evidence . . . of the occurrences and resulting harm which plaintiff alleges."[45] The court believed that faulty recollections, subjective assertions, and the imprecision of psychological evidence prevented civil prosecution of CSA suits.[46] In *Lindabury v. Lindabury*,[47] the Florida appellate court refused to apply the discovery rule to such a suit, holding that "under any conventional application of the statute of limitations . . . the statutory clock began running, no later than 1965," the date of the sexual abuse.[48] The dissent argued that the majority mechanically applied the statute of limitations when the case should have been remanded for an evidentiary determination of the reliability of mental health expert testimony before applying the discovery rule.[49]

B. Type 1 Cases

The California judiciary has specifically held that the discovery rule is inapplicable to Type 1 cases, where the plaintiff was aware of the sexual abuse but was unaware of the causal connection between the sexual abuse and the plaintiff's physical or psychological problems. In *DeRose v. Carswell*,[50] the plaintiff not only was barred from her cause of action against her step-grandfather for assault and battery because she had remembered the sexual assaults rather than repressed them, but she also was not allowed to pursue a separate cause of action for intentional and negligent infliction of emotional distress for her years of trauma resulting from the CSA.[51] In the simplest terms, the court reasoned that her cause of action for emotional distress required an element of perception of

---

equitable tolling rule or discovery rule available for CSA survivors in the New York courts. Burpee v. Burpee, 578 N.Y.S.2d 359 (N.Y. Sup. Ct. 1991); Basile v. Covenant, 575 N.Y.S.2d 233 (N.Y. Sup. Ct. 1991).

44. *Tyson*, 727 P.2d 226 (Wash. 1986), *superseded by statute as noted in* North Coast Air Servs., Ltd. v. Grumman Corp., 759 P.2d 405 (Wash. 1988).

45. *Tyson*, 727 P.2d at 229.

46. *Id.* However, the *Tyson* dissent argued that prior Washington cases regarding the discovery rule centered on "fundamental fairness, not availability of objective evidence." *Id.* at 231. The dissent further reminded the majority that expert testimony by mental health practitioners is an aid for the factfinder and may be accepted or rejected, in whole or in part. *Id.* at 233. Finally, the dissent noted that a CSA survivor is not guaranteed a remedy by the discovery rule, but is given an opportunity to prove that she was abused and that the defendant was her abuser, "but that her suffering was such that she did not and could not reasonably have discovered all the elements of her cause of action at an earlier time." *Id.* at 237.

47. 552 So. 2d 1117 (Fla. Dist. Ct. App. 1989), *dismissed*, 560 So. 2d 233 (Fla. 1990).

48. *Id.*

49. *Id.* at 1120.

50. 242 Cal. Rptr. 368 (Cal. Ct. App. 1987).

51. *Id.*

harm.[52] According to the court, the plaintiff's knowledge of her sexual abuse at the time it occurred was an appreciation of harm (outrageous conduct) that was now time-barred.[53] Moreover, because the plaintiff knew of the sexual abuse (even though she did not know that her trauma was causally connected to it) she was not insane for the purposes of tolling limitations on the basis of disability. In the absence of such a disability the statute of limitations was not tolled.[54] However, in 1990, the California legislature amended the statute of limitations governing suits for CSA, essentially rejecting the *DeRose* holding. Now, any action for CSA in California must be commenced within eight years of attaining majc.ity or within three years of discovery of the psychological injury caused by the CSA, whichever is later.[55]

In *Hammer v. Hammer*,[56] the Wisconsin court applied the discovery rule to allow both Type 1 and Type 2 cases. There, the plaintiff alleged a Type "1-1/2" harm—she had known she was sexually abused but she had been told by her parents at the time that it was not wrong.[57] The *Hammer* court interpreted its discovery rule to include both a factual and causal component so that plaintiffs in both Type 1 and Type 2 cases will have their day in court.[58] Similarly, the Iowa Supreme Court in *Callahan v. State*,[59] interpreted the Iowa accrual rule to allow delayed discovery of the injury *and* its cause in CSA suits.[60] However, in 1990, near the time of the suit, the Iowa legislature amended its statute of limitations to allow delayed discovery in CSA suits.[61] Although the *Callahan* case was not governed by the amended rule, the court considered it as strong evidence of public policy regarding redress available to CSA survivors.[62]

---

52. *Id.*

53. *Id.* at 376-77.

54. *Id.* at 378-79.

55. CAL. CIV. PROC. CODE § 340.1(a) (West 1990). This amendment applies only to actions commenced after January 1, 1991. CAL. CIV. PROC. CODE § 340.1(k).

56. 418 N.W.2d 23, 25 (1987), *rev. denied*, 144 Wis.2d 953, 428 N.W.2d 552 (1988).

57. *Id.* Child victims are frequently mislead by the offender's assertions of propriety. However such victims do not remain deceived for long. The offender's furtive behavior usually indicated that something was wrong in the conduct. HERMAN, *supra* note 25, at 86.

58. *Hammer*, 418 N.W.2d at 27; *see also* United States v. Kubrick, 444 U.S. 111 (1979) (holding statute of limitations began to run when the plaintiff had knowledge of the injury *and* its causative link).

59. 464 N.W.2d 268 (Iowa 1990).

60. *Id.* at 273.

61. IOWA CODE § 614.8A (1990).

62. *Callahan*, 464 N.W.2d at 272.

C. Type 2 Cases

DeRose was the standard the Montana and Illinois judiciary followed. Both the Montana case of *E.W. and D.W. v. D.C.H.*[63] and the Illinois case of *Franke v. Geyer*[64] followed the California court's *DeRose* analysis; the plaintiff was time-barred and it was not necessary to know the total extent of damages that may flow from the original injury because the cause accrued on the date of the injury.[65] The *Franke* court specifically held that the thirty-one year old plaintiff was time-barred where she always knew of her CSA and neither the newly enacted CSA statute nor the rule of equitable estoppel applied against her defendant-parents.[66] On the other hand, the Montana judiciary went one step past *Franke* and expressly reserved the issue of whether *vel non* it would apply the discovery rule in Type 2 cases where the plaintiff may claim repression of the abuse from consciousness.[67]

In *Meiers-Post v. Schafer*,[68] the Michigan Supreme Court reviewed a grant of summary judgment by the lower court against a plaintiff who had repressed her CSA. The *Meiers-Post* court determined that an adult CSA plaintiff could, under the insanity provision, toll the statute of limitations upon a showing that (1) such plaintiff has repressed the memory of the facts upon which the claim is predicated, such that the plaintiff could not have been aware of the rights he or she was otherwise bound to know, and (2) there is corroboration for the plaintiff's testimony that the sexual assault occurred.[69]

Affidavits or testimony of mental health professionals regarding the extent of a plaintiff's disassociation caused by the CSA can establish the

---

63. 754 P.2d 817 (Mont. 1988).

64. 568 N.E.2d 931, 933 (Ill. App. Ct. 1991).

65. *E.W.*, 754 P.2d at 820 (*quoting* Raymond v. Ingram, 737 P.2d 314, 317 (Wash. App. 1987)).

66. *Franke*, 568 N.E.2d at 933.

67. *E.W.*, 754 P.2d at 821. Montana's discovery rule does not require the plaintiff to have complete knowledge before the cause of action accrues, but knowledge of the CSA itself is "sufficient to require inquiry." *Id.* at 820; Hartnett, *supra* note 14, at 1278. Although the *DeRose* court also reserved judgment as to Type 2 cases, in Mary D. v. John D., 264 Cal. Rptr. 633 (Cal. App. 1989), *review dismissed*, 800 P.2d 858 (1990) (a Type 2 case), the court applied the delayed discovery rule.

68. 427 N.W.2d 606 (1988).

69. *Id.* at 610. The *Meiers-Post* majority had no problem accepting psychiatric expert evidence to support an adult CSA claim insofar as the plaintiff's alleged repression is proven through a clinical evaluation. *Id.* at 607. The court reversed the summary judgment for the defendant but did not remand for trial. *Id.* at 610. Instead, the court sent the matter back for further proceedings and dictated that further motions and answers were to be based upon "additional legal and psychiatric authority." *Id.* at 610. From a reading of the case, it appears that the court implicitly prefers psychiatric evidence over psychological evidence.

first prong of the *Meiers-Post* test.[70] Additionally, if the plaintiff previously sent a letter to her abuser, she may establish corroboration by the abuser's signed reply letter which acknowledges the CSA.[71]

In *Johnson v. Johnson*,[72] the district court for the Northern District of Illinois interpreted the Illinois limitations statute to require the application of the discovery rule to Type 2 cases.[73] Because the facts in *Johnson* resembled the *Tyson* case, the court carefully considered the issues of proof that troubled the *Tyson* majority. The Illinois court decried a literal interpretation of the limitations statute and characterized *Tyson* as harshly unfair to the diligent plaintiff who is unable to discover that she has been injured.[74] The court also examined the Illinois discovery rule and found that, while problems of proof were important, such were not determinative on the question of the application of the rule.[75] The court observed that the "strictures [of the statutes of limitations] must sometimes be loosened in order to give the substantive law room to develop."[76] According to the rule announced in *Johnson*, Illinois courts should allow a survivor suit where the victim repressed the CSA from his or her memory.[77] Moreover, the court did not consider any problem of expert testimony which had troubled the *Tyson* majority. According to the court, the equitable considerations surrounding the application of the discovery rule outweigh concerns over proof.[78]

In North Dakota, New Jersey and Nevada, the courts are sympathetic to the plight of CSA survivors. However, neither the North Dakota court nor the Nevada court discussed the distinction between Type 1 or Type 2 cases. Accordingly, parameters will have to be more fully defined in subsequent cases. However, in all three of these decisions, the plaintiffs pleaded repression of their sexual abuse, as in a Type 2 case,

---

70. Nicolette v. Carey, 751 F. Supp. 695, 699 (W.D. Mich. 1990).

71. *Id.* at 699-700.

72. 701 F. Supp. 1363 (N.D. Ill. 1988).

73. *Id.* The *Johnson* plaintiff, in addition to alleging that her father abused her as a child, alleged that her mother had known of the abuse and that she negligently failed to protect her. *Id.* at 1365; *see also* Grace Hubbard, *Mothers' Perceptions of Incest: Sustained Disruption and Turmoil*, Vol. III, No. 1 Archives of Psychiatric Nursing 34 (Feb. 1989).[hereinafter "Hubbard"].

74. *Johnson*, 701 F. Supp. at 1368.

75. *Id.* at 1369.

76. *Id.*

77. *Id.* at 1369; *see also* Franke v. Geyer, 568 N.E.2d 931, 933 (Ill. Ct. App. 1991). Subsequent to *Johnson*, the Illinois legislature created a cause of action for CSA and a statute of repose thereto. The statute contains an outside limitation of twelve years from the age of eighteen. *Id.* (citing Public Act 86-1346, *codified as* § 13-202.2 of the Illinois Code of Civ. P.) The *Franke* court construed the *Johnson* case as the type of case for which the new amendment applied.

78. *Johnson*, 701 F. Supp. at 1369-70.

and sought to toll the statute of limitations.[79]

In *Osland v. Osland*,[80] the North Dakota court rejected the *Tyson* requirement of objective evidence and affirmed the lower court's application of the discovery rule as not "clearly erroneous."[81] The statute of limitations was tolled on the basis that the plaintiff's psychological injuries were so severe as to cause the plaintiff not to discover her cause during the applicable statutory time period.[82] On the other hand, the New Jersey court, in *Jones v. Jones*,[83] stated that a plaintiff may allege either the fact of repression or traumatization to invoke the insanity tolling provision of the state's statute of limitations.[84] Moreover, a plaintiff may urge as an independent tolling mechanism the disability of duress to estop her abuser from asserting the statute of limitations.[85] Similarly, the Nevada court, in *Petersen v. Bruen*,[86] applied the insanity tolling provision where repression was alleged, but espoused its concerns over stale or subjective evidence.[87] The court determined that, in order to come within

---

79.   Osland v. Osland, 442 N.W.2d 907, 908 (N.D. 1989) (noting the plaintiff had "severe emotional trauma" so as to not be "able to fully understand or discover her cause of action"); Jones v. Jones, 576 A.2d 316, 321 (N.J. Super. Ct. App. Div.), *cert. denied*, 585 A.2d 412 (N.J. 1990) (stating mental trauma was so "disabling" as to impair ability to institute the action prior to the expiration of the statute of limitations); Petersen v. Bruen, 792 P.2d 18, 19 (Nev. 1990) (plaintiff "blocked out the eight years of [the defendant's] sexual molestations until vividly recalled during his therapy").

80.   442 N.W.2d at 908.

81.   *Id.* at 909.

82.   *Id.* at 908. The severity of the plaintiff's emotional injuries was not categorized as a mental disability, per se. Instead, such injuries were cause to apply the discovery rule. *Id.* at 908-909.

83.   576 A.2d 316 (N.J. Super.), *cert. denied*, 585 A.2d 412 (1990).

84.   *Id.* at 322.

85.   *Id.* at 322-23 (citing Whatley v. National Bank of Commerce, 555 S.W.2d 500, 505 (Tex. Civ. App.—Dallas 1977, no writ)).

86.   792 P.2d 18 (Nev. 1990).

87.   In *Petersen*, the plaintiff, a 22-year-old male, sued his former "Big Brother" for eight years of molestation he endured from age 7 to age 15. The year before his civil suit, he entered therapy and, shortly thereafter, sought and obtained a criminal conviction against his defendant. Then, in his civil suit, the plaintiff argued that the *Tyson* objective-evidence test was met by virtue of the obtained criminal conviction. The court noted this fact with approval. *Petersen*, 792 P.2d at 21.   Although Nevada's criminal statute of limitations allows for prosecution up to the victim's majority age of twenty-one, in Texas, the criminal statute is within 10 years from the date of the commission of the offense. *Compare* NEV. REV. STAT. §§ 171.095, 432 B.100 (1989) *with* TEX. CODE CRIM. PROC. ANN. art 12.01(2)(d) (Vernon 1965 & Supp. 1990). Thus, even if CSA were committed upon a 17 year-old, in Texas, the case would have to be prosecuted by the time the survivor was 27 years old. Consequently, the argument made by the *Petersen* plaintiff, that the prior criminal conviction served as "objective" evidence of the CSA, is useless to a Texas survivor over the age of twenty-seven. Further, it should be noted the plaintiff Petersen admitted recalling that, as a child, he consented to the assaults, he did not consider them offensive at the time, and he suffered no physical injuries. *Petersen*, 729 P.2d at 9. The court exposed the "irony" of his argument that he repressed the assaults but, at

such a provision, an adult CSA plaintiff must show "by clear and convincing evidence that the plaintiff has in fact been sexually abused during minority by the named defendant."[88] If the plaintiff can do so, there will be "no existing statute of limitations" to surmount.[89] Conversely, if the plaintiff cannot make such a showing, the cause of action "will be subject to the regular two-year period of limitations."[90] In his concurrence, Justice Rose noted that, while the "majority opinion is very persuasive" in eliminating the statute of limitations in CSA cases, he would have preferred the adoption of the discovery rule to keep a check on patently stale claims.[91]

In Pennsylvania, the federal district court, in *Baily v. Lewis*,[92] concluded that all of the plaintiff's claims "stem from what are essentially batteries."[93] Because the plaintiff admitted that he was aware of the CSA when it was occurring and that it was frightening to him, his judicial allegation that, as a child, he did not know such acts were wrongful does not toll the statute of limitations.[94] It is unclear, at this juncture, whether Pennsylvania courts, like Florida and Washington's *Tyson* court, will continuously and strictly apply the legal rule of accrual. However, it appears, for the time being, that the Pennsylvania judiciary insists not only on repression, but also upon the allegation that the survivor did not know the CSA was wrongful when it was inflicted.[95] If the latter hypothesis is correct, Pennsylvania courts have placed an onerous burden upon children to foreknow the consequences of their sexual molestation.[96]

---

the same time, was "not sufficiently traumatized or impressed with the wrongfulness of the acts to make their repression particularly difficult." *Id.* at 23-24.

88.   *Id.* at 25.

89.   *Id.* at 24.

90.   *Id.* at 25.

91.   *Id.*

92.   763 F. Supp. 802 (E.D. Pa. 1991).

93.   *Id.* at 807.

94.   *Id.* at 810.

95.   *Id.* at 808 ("He also testified that at the time the abuse occurred, 'he knew it was horrifying.' He claims rather that he could not bring his claim earlier, because he repressed the memory of the experiences. It was thus plaintiff's own incapacity, albeit, one allegedly caused by the injury, and not the nature of the injury itself that resulted in his inability to pursue his claim").

96.   Hartnett, *supra* note 14, at 1249 n. 52 (*citing* Burgess & Halstrom, *Sexual Trauma of Children and Adolescents*, 10 Nursing Clinics of N. Am. 551, 554 (1975)) (stating "Young people often do not have the ability to consent when confronted with pressure . . . or misrepresentation of moral standards . . . Young children or school-age children have not incorporated sexual standards into their behavior and they acquiesce in the exploitative conduct"); Comment, *The Young Victim As Witness For The Prosecution: Another Form Of Abuse?* 89 Dick. L. Rev. 721, 731 (1985); *cf. Petersen*, 792 P.2d at 23-24.

In summary, adult CSA cases are receiving emerging judicial recognition. Yet, at present, such recognition differentiates between survivors in Type 1 and Type 2 cases. Type 1 cases, on one hand, may achieve successful recognition in those jurisdictions that construe the limitations statute to include both a factual and a causal component. However, if the particular jurisdiction does not construe its accrual rule liberally, the CSA survivor in a Type 1 case must rely upon either a legal disability such as unsound mind or upon equity and public policy in order to toll the statute of limitations.

Type 2 cases, on the other hand, have received the greatest judicial recognition. The element of repression inherent in such cases — that is, ignorance of the injury until a recent "reawakening," makes these cases more easily resolvable under traditional common law principles. Therefore, Type 2 cases generally will be accorded the benefit of the discovery rule. Hence, for now, Type 2 cases will form the foundation of developing CSA law.

IV.   SURMOUNTING THE STATUTE OF LIMITATIONS

Because CSA survivors are well into adulthood before they recognize their injuries, the minority tolling provision in § 16.001(a)(1) of the Texas Civil Practice and Remedies Code has long since expired. It is only later in adulthood, and usually with the help of therapy, that CSA survivors develop enough maturity to perform the introspective analysis to discover that their sexual dysfunctions, substance abuse or repeated failures at interpersonal relationships are not merely products of adolescent adjustment.[97] For this reason, CSA survivors require an alternative mechanism to surmount the general rule of accrual.

Texas courts have yet to address a CSA claim. However, applying the lessons learned in those jurisdictions that have addressed such claims, the following are possible mechanisms in which to "toll" the statute of limitations.

A.   The Discovery Rule

In Texas, the discovery rule is invoked to prevent injustice to a plaintiff who does not learn of his or her injury until the statute of limitations has lapsed.[98] Any civil claim pursued by a CSA survivor is gov-

---

97.   Hartnett, *supra* note 14, at 1267.
98.   Gaddis v. Smith, 417 S.W.2d 577 (Tex. 1967) (foreign object left in body); Hays v. Hall, 488 S.W.2d 412 (Tex. 1972) (negligent vasectomy); Atkins v. Crossland, 417 S.W.2d 150 (Tex. 1967) (accountant malpractice); Grady v. Fraykus, 530 S.W.2d 151 (Tex. Civ. App.— Corpus Christi 1975, writ ref'd n.r.e.) (negligent administration of x-rays); Kelley v. Rinkle,

erned by the limitation provisions set forth in § 16.003(a) of the Texas Civil Practice and Remedies Code.[99]

Section 16.003(a) provides that: "A person must bring suit for trespass for injury to the estate or to the property of another, . . . personal injury, . . . not later than two years after the day the cause of action accrues." When the legislature has not defined the term "accrues," the court determines when the cause of action accrues and, thus, when the statute of limitation commences to run.[100] A cause of action has been construed to accrue when "the wrongful act effects an injury, regardless of when the [plaintiff] learned of such injury."[101] However, when the plaintiff was unable to know of his injury at the time of actual accrual, Texas courts have applied the discovery rule. When applied, the rule tolls the running of the limitations period until the plaintiff discovers, or reasonably should have discovered "the nature of his injury."[102]

There are several ways a CSA survivor may seek application of the Texas discovery rule. First, a CSA claim can arguably be analogized to cases involving toxic torts or latent diseases, such as silicosis and asbestosis under the concept of "maturation of harm."[103] Unlike latent disease

---

532 S.W.2d 947 (Tex. 1976) (libel); Willis v. Maverick, 760 S.W.2d 642 (Tex. 1988) (attorney malpractice); Borel v. Fibreboard Paper Prods. Corp., 493 F.2d 1076 (5th Cir. 1973) (asbestosis); Wise v. Anderson, 359 S.W.2d 876 (Tex. 1962) (fraud).

99.   TEX. CIV. PRAC. & REM. CODE ANN. § 16.003(a) (Vernon 1988). A traditional statute of limitation is intended to compel a plaintiff to bring a claim to court within a reasonable period of time after the cause of action accrues. Robinson v. Weaver, 550 S.W.2d 18, 20 (Tex. 1977); Williams v. Pure Oil Co., 124 Tex. 341, 78 S.W.2d 929, 931 (1935). On the other hand, a statute of repose does not necessarily run from the time a cause of action accrues, but from some other date or event selected by the legislature. Nelson v. Krusen, 678 S.W.2d 918, 926 (Tex. 1984) (Robertson, J., concurring). TEX. CIV. PRAC. & REM. CODE ANN. § 16.003(a) is a traditional statute of limitation.

100.   Moreno v. Sterling Drug, Inc., 787 S.W.2d 348 (Tex. 1990). However, where the legislature has defined clearly the time of accrual, the courts "must seek the intent of the legislature as found in the plain and common meaning of the words and terms used." *Id.* at 352. When "accrual" is clearly expressed, the limitations statute is said to be absolute. *Id.* at 352-53.

101.   Robinson v. Weaver, 550 S.W.2d 18, 19 (Tex. 1977); Williams v. Pure Oil Co., 124 Tex. 341, 78 S.W.2d 929, 931 (1935).

102.   *Moreno,* 787 S.W.2d at 351 (discussing application of the rule in medical malpractice cases); Willis v. Maverick, 760 S.W.2d 642, 646 (Tex. 1988) (applying the discovery rule in legal malpractice case); Gaddis v. Smith, 417 S.W.2d 577, 579-80 (Tex. 1967) (explaining the application of the rule to a fraud cause of action); *see also* Alfaro v. Dow Chemical, 751 S.W.2d 208, 209 (Tex. App.—Houston [1st Dist.] 1988) (explaining when a cause of action for breach of warranty arises), *aff'd,* 786 S.W.2d 674 (Tex. 1990) (explaining when a cause of action for breach of warranty arises), *cert. denied,* 111 S.Ct. 671 (1991); Corder v. A.H. Robins Co., 692 S.W.2d 194, 195-96 (Tex. App.—Eastland 1985, no writ) (applying the rule to a strict liability cause of action for infertility damages caused by the use of a Dalkon Shield).

103.   DeRose, *supra* note 25, at 210 (discussing delayed discovery rule for "inherently undiscoverable injuries"); *see also* Borel v. Fibreboard Paper Prods. Corp., 493 F.2d 1076 (5th

suits where physical evidence remains in the body, such is not the case in CSA suits. In CSA survivor cases, the harm is primarily emotional.[104] But, as discussed in the *Tyson* dissent, this is an evidentiary concern that should not deprive a CSA survivor of his or her day in court.[105]

CSA harm should be given "maturation of harm" status for the following reasons. First, strict adherence to a "physical evidence" standard may deny recovery even in latent disease cases where the deleterious substance no longer remains in the body.[106] Second, no physical evidence standard is currently placed upon survivors who, upon reaching age twenty, sue for injuries from CSA, even though the abuse could have been up to 17 or 18 years prior to the suit.[107] Third, adult CSA claims were not contemplated at the time Texas' civil statute of limitations was enacted.[108] In assessing the accrual of an adult CSA claim, courts are not always bound to take the words of a statute in their literal or ordinary sense when doing so would lead to any absurdity or manifest injustice.[109]

However, before ending this discussion, the concerns of the *Tyson* majority must be addressed. In *Tyson*, the court observed that adult CSA claims do not carry objectively verifiable evidence as in cases in-

---

Cir. 1973) (asbestosis); Urie v. Thompson, 337 U.S. 163 (1949) (silicosis); Allen, *supra* note 19, at 630.

104.   Hartnett, *supra* note 14, at 1248 nn.46-47 (explaining the initial and long-term effects of CSA). *But see* Baily v. Lewis, 763 F. Supp. 802, 810 (E.D. Pa. 1991) ("This is not a case akin to those involving creeping diseases where there were no symptoms of any injury at the time of the plaintiff's exposure. . . . The asserted cause of Baily's subsequent physical and emotional difficulties is the series of batteries committed upon him by the defendant"), *aff'd*, 950 F.2d 721 (3d Cir. 1991).

105.   Tyson v. Tyson, 727 P.2d 226, 232 (Wash. 1986) (Pearson, J. dissenting).

106.   DeRose, *supra* note 25, at 219 n.147.

107.   *Tyson*, 727 P.2d at 232 (Pearson, J., dissenting).

108.   *Accord* Petersen v. Bruen, 792 P.2d 18, 24 n.7 (Nev. 1990) ("We feel assured that the legislature did not contemplate or consider the unique aspects of CSA cases in fixing general periods and categories of limitations"); Salten, *supra* note 9 at 208.

109.   In Hartnett, *supra* note 14, the author discusses a sealed case where the plaintiff alleged sexual assault and battery, intentional or reckless infliction of emotional distress, unlawful incestuous conduct, negligence, breach of fiduciary duty and negligent infliction of emotional distress. The plaintiff was abused by her father from age 10 to age 20, but was unaware of the connection between that abuse and her psychological disorders until entering therapy in her thirties. The court issued a memorandum and order on June 21, 1988, and denied the defendant's motion for summary judgment on five out of six counts. (Summary judgment was granted on sexual assault and battery because she admitted to knowledge of these acts during the period of abuse). In applying the discovery rule to this type of claim Judge Abrams wrote: "Failure to apply the discovery rule . . . would only serve to further punish a plaintiff . . . before the plaintiff reasonably could discover the cause of harm she suffered." *Id.* at 1270. *Accord* Hays v. Hall, 488 S.W.2d 412, 414 (Tex. 1972) (arguing that denying a legal remedy before the injured party can know of any injury is "[a] result so absurd and so unjust ought not to be possible").

volving foreign objects or latent diseases.[110] The court also refused to allow expert psychiatric opinions based upon plaintiff memories to be considered as objective evidence to support a claim that the act occurred or that trauma was suffered.[111]

Hauntingly similar to *Tyson* is the Texas Supreme Court holding in *Robinson v. Weaver*.[112] In *Robinson*, the court refused to apply the discovery rule in cases of alleged misdiagnosis. The court's primary concern rested upon questions regarding credibility and matters of professional diagnosis, judgment or discretion.[113] Moreover, in the court's estimation, prior malpractice suits that applied the discovery rule did so because physical proof existed.[114] Consequently, the *Robinson* majority denied application of the discovery rule to misdiagnosis claims because the "negligent exercise of judgment is subject to proof only by expert hindsight."[115]

Robinson can be distinguished for several reasons. First, adult CSA suits are not suits against a defendant for negligent professional judgment. Thus, the *Robinson* court's fear of erroneous findings of misdiagnoses based on newly existing medical knowledge is misplaced in adult CSA cases. Second, although victim memories and psychological conclusions involve hindsight, our Texas Supreme Court previously announced its acceptance of mental health assessments based upon the plaintiff's psychological profile in *St. Elizabeth Hosp. v. Garrard*.[116] Implicit in *Garrard*, is the court's acceptance of mental health experts' ability to assess CSA.[117] Such acceptance was already established by the Texas Court of Criminal Appeals in *Duckett v. State*,[118] a case involving indecency with a child. The Court of Criminal Appeals held that expert testimony concerning CSA syndrome was admissible under the rule governing admission of expert testimony.[119]

B.   Unsound Mind

If the court disallows the discovery rule, another possible mechanism to surmount the limitations period is the legal disability of "un-

---

110.   *Tyson*, 727 P.2d at 228-29.
111.   *Id*. at 229.
112.   550 S.W.2d 18 (Tex. 1977).
113.   *Id*. at 21.
114.   *Id; see also* Harvey v. Denton, 601 S.W.2d 121, 125 (Tex. Civ. App.—Eastland 1980, writ ref'd n.r.e.).
115.   *Robinson*, 550 S.W.2d at 22.
116.   730 S.W.2d 649, 653 n.4 (Tex. 1987).
117.   *Id*. at 653.
118.   797 S.W.2d 906 (Tex. Crim. App. 1990).
119.   *Id*. at 915-17; *see* also Tex. R. Crim. Evid. 702.

sound mind."[120] However, the disability must exist at or before the time of injury.[121] Otherwise, a disability that arises after a cause of action accrues will not suspend the running of the limitations period.[122] In the same vein, tacking predecessor or personal successive disabilities is not permitted.[123]

Some jurisdictions allow tolling for mental incapacity without regard to whether the disability arose on the same day.[124] Other jurisdictions invoke the equitable maxim that no person should be allowed to profit from the mental incapacity he has inflicted upon his victim.[125] Because CSA survivors suffer from a form of personal intrusion on their mental and emotional makeup that interferes with normal emotional and personality development, they are excellent candidates to employ either maxim.[126]

For example, many CSA survivors exhibit symptoms of post trau-

---

120. TEX. CIV. PRAC. & REM. CODE ANN. § 16.001(a)(2) (Vernon Supp. 1992). Throughout many case discussions, the discovery rule is equated with the tolling rule for recognized legal disabilities. Peterson v. Bruen, 792 P.2d 18, 20 (Nev. 1990); E.W. and D.W. v. O.C.H., 754 P.2d 817, 820 (Mont. 1988). Technically speaking, however, the discovery rule is a legal principle which provides that limitation runs not from the date of injury, but from the date of a plaintiff's reasonable discovery of the nature of his injury. Willis v. Maverick, 760 S.W.2d at 642, 645-46 (Tex. 1988). Conversely, in the case of a disability, the date of injury is the commencing date for the limitations period but such period is tolled, and therefore prevented from accruing until removal of such disability. Whatley v. National Bank of Commerce, 555 S.W.2d 500, 506 (Tex. Civ. App.—Dallas 1977, no writ).

121. Roman v. A.H. Robins Co., 518 F.2d 970 (5th Cir. 1975). In *Roman*, the plaintiff sued for blindness resulting from ingestion of Sulla. The plaintiff developed eye problems in 1968 and was advised that these problems were probably caused by an allergic reaction to Sulla. Thereafter, a "nightmarish" five years of operations caused total blindness. She filed suit in 1973 and urged "unsound mind" from her misfortunes to toll the statute of limitations. The court held that, if she had such a disability, it arose *after* her cause of action had accrued. *Id.* at 972. However, had mental incapacity resulted directly from the injury creating the cause of action *and* arose on the same day, the statute might be tolled. *Id.* at 972 n.4.

122. TEX. CIV. PRAC. & REM. CODE § 16.001(d) (Vernon 1986).

123. TEX. CIV. PRAC. & REM. CODE § 16.001(c) (Vernon 1986).

124. *See supra* notes 68-71, 79-91 and accompanying text. *But see* Baily v. Lewis, 763 F. Supp. 802, 808 (E.D. Pa. 1991) (stating "courts applying Pennsylvania law have consistently stated that the statute of limitations runs against persons under a disability, including one who is mentally incompetent"), *aff'd*, 950 F.2d 721 (3rd Cir. 1991).

125. Corsey v. State, 375 So. 2d 1319, 1321 (La. 1979) (involving brain injury caused by prison staff); Kyle v. Green Acres at Verona, Inc., 207 A.2d 513, 519 (N.J. 1965) (involving nervous disorder after fall on defendant's premises); Klamm Shell v. Berg, 441 P.2d 10, 12 (Colo. 1968) (involving subgaleal hematoma caused by assault and battery).

126. P. Edwards and M. Donaldson, *Assessment of Symptoms In Adult Survivors of Incest: A Factor Analytic Study of The Responses To Childhood Incest Questionnaire*, 13 CHILD ABUSE & NEGLECT 101-110 (1989); Coons, Bowman, et al., *Post-Traumatic Aspects of the Treatment of Victims of Sexual Abuse and Incest*, 12 PSYCHIATRIC CLINICS OF N. AM. 325-35 (1989) [hereinafter "Coons, Bowman et. al."]

matic stress disorder ("PTSD").[127] The symptoms of PTSD "begin immediately or soon after the trauma."[128] The impairment of a CSA survivor may be either mild or severe and affect nearly every aspect of life.[129] "Unsound mind" has been defined to mean that "a person is unable to manage his affairs or to understand his legal rights or liabilities."[130] However, whether a person has suffered from unsoundness of mind ordinarily is a fact question and does not require an adjudication of insanity.[131] Consequently, if it were demonstrated that PTSD began immediately after the sexual trauma, and persisted into adulthood until removal of the disability, CSA survivors should urge the legal disability of unsound mind to toll the limitations period.[132] However, the CSA survivor should give this allegation serious consideration after having already suffered confusion, misdirected blame or other PTSD symptoms.[133]

It should be recalled that the plaintiffs in *DeRose* and *Meiers-Post* experienced differing results under their jurisdictions' insanity tolling provisions. In *DeRose v. DeRose*,[134] the plaintiff remembered her CSA, but did not appreciate the connection between the CSA and her emotional harm until shortly before filing her suit. In California, insanity is defined as "a condition of mental derangement which renders the sufferer incapable of caring for [her] property or transacting business, or under-

---

127. Coons, Bowman, et. al., *supra* note 126, at 325.

128. Diagnostic Statistical Manual [DSM-III-R],[hereinafter "DSM"] American Psychiatric Society, pp. 248, 249 (1989).

129. DSM-III-R, *supra* note 128, at 249; *cf.* Hartnett, *supra* note 14, at 1248 n. 46 ("Initial effects are those which occur within two years of the abusive episode").

130. Helton v. Clements, 832 F.2d 332, 336 (5th Cir. 1987).

131. Smith v. Erhard, 715 S.W.2d 707 (Tex. App.—Austin 1986, writ ref'd n.r.e.).

132. Tex. Civ. Prac. & Rem. Code Ann. § 16.001(a)(3) (Vernon 1988). It should be no moment that the CSA survivor was a minor as well as of "unsound mind" at the time of the injury. At common law, there were three types of disability situations regarding the tolling of statutes of limitation. There were "co-existing" disabilities, successive disabilities and tacking of predecessor disabilities. 51 Am. Jur. 2d, *Limitation of Actions* §§ 197-199 (1970).

Section 16.001 of the Civil Practice and Remedies Code addresses only successive disabilities and tacking. It does not pertain to coexisting disabilities. It is said that where there are two or more coexisting disabilities in the same person, the law allows such person to act when the last disability is removed. Am. Jur. 2d *Limitation of Actions* at § 197. Thus, the expiration of the longer disability fixes the time when the statute commences to run. This rule has not clearly been construed under Texas law. *See* Lotus Oil Co. v. Spires, 240 S.W.2d 357 (Tex. Civ. App.—El Paso 1951, writ ref'd n.r.e.) (holding that plaintiff, who was minor *and* married could not sue during later disability because her suit was governed by adverse possession statutes and not statute for personal actions). *But see* Rittenhouse v. Erhart, 337 N.W.2d 626 (Mich. App. 1983) (holding that suit by father of minor rendered insane by carbon monoxide asphyxiation was not barred because appointment of guardian for insane person did not remove such disability).

133. Salten, *supra* note 9, at 212.

134. 242 Cal. Rptr. 368 (Ct. App. 1987).

standing the nature or effects of [her] acts."[135] The *DeRose* court held that the plaintiff's insanity argument was flawed for the same reason as her delayed discovery argument. That she failed to appreciate the relationship between the CSA and her emotional harm was irrelevant. She was aware at all times of her assaults and knew they were offensive.[136] However, unlike *DeRose*, in *Meiers-Post*, the plaintiff pleaded repression of the CSA. The court therein fashioned the two-part test discussed earlier herein, (i.e. repression and corroboration), to allow the plaintiff's suit under the insanity tolling provisions of the Michigan statutes.[137] Because it is hard to predict how Texas courts will react to the claim of insanity resulting from CSA, repression found in a Type 2 case appears best suited for such a tolling provision.

C. Other Equitable Theories

Several writers advocate usage of the arguments of fiduciary relationship,[138] fraudulent concealment,[139] and undue influence.[140] However, under present usage, the prospect of success on such arguments is hard to predict. For instance, to fit within the fraud exception, the CSA survivor would have to prove that he or she was coaxed into sexual participation by the abuser's misrepresentation of a material fact that was made to such survivor and relied upon with knowing falsity.[141] However, the fraud is only incidentally involved because the plaintiff's claim is for personal injury. Moreover, knowledge of the fraud can be a certain conclusion by the time the survivor reaches majority.[142] However, in *Hildebrand v. Hildebrand*,[143] the federal district court was confronted with the issue of fraudulent concealment.[144] Applying Indiana law, the court held that, where a daughter was sexually abused by her father, who

---

135. *Id.* at 378 (brackets in original).

136. *Id.*

137. Meiers-Post v. Schafer, 427 N.W.2d 606 (Mich. App. 1988). In Michigan, "insanity" is defined as "a condition of mental derangement such as to prevent the sufferer from comprehending rights he or she is otherwise bound to know." Whether a person is insane is a question of fact. *Id.* at 608.

138. Allen, *supra* note 19, at 631; Hartnett, *supra* note 14, at 1264-65; Salten, *supra* note 99, at 208.

139. DeRose, *supra* note 25, at 198; Bharam, *supra* note 14, at 210-11.

140. Santa Clara Law Review, *supra* note 25, at 200.

141. *Id.* at 198; *see also* Bhatam, *supra* note 14, at 855. In a survey to identify the crimes most likely concealed, child molestation was ranked seventh out of twenty six crimes. *Id.* at 862 n. 120. *But see Baily*, 763 F. Supp. at 811 (that plaintiff admits he found the experiences painful at time such occurred belies assertion of reliance).

142. DeRose, *supra* note 25, at 198-99.

143. 736 F. Supp. 1512 (S.D. Ind. 1990).

144. *Id.*

was a doctor, and whose psychological dysfunctions were later diagnosed by her father as a chemical imbalance, her allegation of fraudulent concealment, so as to delay the accrual of her cause, was a matter for the jury.[145] If the fraud exception is to apply, extreme and continuing facts such as those set forth in *Hildebrand*, will have to be utilized.

Undue influence can be inferred from confidential relationships in which a donee exerts power over his or her donor.[146] But, no undue influence can be said to exist after the victim has left the influence of her abuser, which is usually sometime at or after attaining majority.[147] Moreover, if the undue influence persists insofar as keeping the victim from timely filing suit, such victim is obviously aware of the abuse (a Type 1 case) and will probably be, under the majority of current holdings, held to be time-barred.[148] One example of an attempt to utilize undue influence is found in the case of *Doe v. Ainsworth*.[149] In *Doe*, the Louisiana Court of Appeals was confronted with the charge of CSA at the hands of a local minister. The plaintiff, who was a minor and a member of the church at the time of the acts, urged, as an exception to prescription, the minister's psychological domination over him.[150] The operative facts in *Doe* were that the last sexual act took place in 1979, when the plaintiff was almost sixteen. The plaintiff discussed the acts with his parents and psychiatrist in 1982 and filed suit in 1985. From these facts the court found that, in 1982, the plaintiff was at least on constructive notice of the CSA and, for the next three years, was both employed and social. Consequently, there being no extreme level of domination, the plaintiff was time-barred by the one year prescription to his action.[151] However, in Texas, a plaintiff may allege duress, which is an extension of fraudulent concealment.[152] The duress, for purposes of CSA, will be "continuing duress." The test is whether, in reasonable probability, an ordinary person would have lost his free will under the circumstances.[153]

---

145. *Id.* at 1512.

146. DeRose, *supra* note 25, at 201.

147. TEX. CIV. PRAC. & REM. CODE ANN. § 129.001 (Vernon 1986); *cf.* Rothermal v. Duncan, 369 S.W.2d 917, 923 (Tex. 1963).

148. *See supra* notes 50-78 and accompanying text.

149. 540 So. 2d 425 (La. Ct. App. 1989).

150. *Doe,* 540 So. 2d at 427.

151. *Id.* at 427-28; *See also* Bock v. Harmon, 526 So.2d 292 (La. Ct. App. 1988) (holding that father's psychological dominance over the plaintiff did not invoke the equitable rule of *contra non valentem* to suspend prescription).

152. Whatley v. National Bank of Commerce, 555 S.W.2d 500, 505-06 (Tex. Civ. App.—Dallas 1977, no writ).

153. Pierce v. Estate of Haverlah, 428 S.W.2d 422, 428 (Tex. Civ. App.—Tyler 1968, writ ref'd n.r.e.).

Success on the theory of a fiduciary relationship to toll the statute is inconclusive. First, the fiduciary relationship is placed upon the parent-child relationship and mandates a parent to make truthful disclosures to the child.[154] However, not all offenders are parents. Moreover, by the time of majority, the parent-child "fiduciary" relationship technically ends.[155] As noted by the *Franke* court, a plaintiff who asserts the existence of a special relationship with a defendant must also show how such a defendant discouraged the plaintiff from timely filing suit.[156] Nonetheless, in *Evans v. Eckelman*,[157] the California Court of Appeals discussed the special duties of a parent to his child.[158] According to the court, the parental duty is breached by sexually abusing the child and by subsequently enforcing secrecy or otherwise teaching the child that such acts are normal. Although the *Evans* court did not toll the statute of limitations on the premise of mental disability, it held that parental breaches were a major policy justification for invoking the delayed discovery rule in Type 2 cases where the survivor, at the time of childhood, was unaware of the wrongfulness of the sexual acts.[159]

D. Public Policy

Three policy reasons have been utilized to justify the strict application of the statute of limitations. The first is fairness to defendants; the statute is a safeguard against adjudications based upon stale claims.[160] Presently, in Texas, a CSA survivor's remedy is limited to initiation of a tort action on or before such survivor's twentieth birthday. Applying the delayed discovery rule to causes of action by CSA survivors could forcibly facilitate civil actions against abusers at any point in the victim's adult life. However, in CSA situations, the defendant's interest in a guarantee of repose or safety from litigation is poor grounds to deny application of the discovery rule. There are limited instances where repose is necessary, but these do not involve adult CSA claims. For example, doctors are granted repose after two years from the date of breach or tort.[161] Unlimited malpractice liability would drive the cost of malpractice insur-

---

154. DeRose, *supra* note 25, at 205.
155. *Accord* Franke v. Geyer, 568 N.E.2d 931, 934 (Ill. 1991) Under the principle of equitable estoppel and assuming a special relationship existed, "plaintiff still has failed to plead any facts which would indicate that defendant somehow discouraged plaintiff from filing suit." *Id*.
156. *Id*. at 933.
157. 265 Cal. Rptr. 605 (Ct. App. 1990).
158. *Id*. at 609.
159. *Id*. at 610; *see also* Commonwealth v. Snoke, 580 A.2d 295 (Pa. 1990).
160. Robinson v. Weaver, 550 S.W.2d 18, 20 (Tex. 1977); Price v. Estate of Anderson, 522 S.W.2d 690, 692 (Tex. 1975).
161. TEX. REV. CIV. STAT. ANN. art. 4590i § 10.01 (Vernon Supp. 1991).

ance and essential medical services too high. Accordingly, the extension would be contrary to public welfare.[162] However, there is no public benefit in shielding child sexual abusers from the consequences of their actions. Civil suits are remedial deterrents to socially reprehensible behavior. In light of the fact that CSA survivors have suffered emotionally crippling injuries, damages serve as some compensation—at least to pay for therapy. Further, providing access to civil suits allows CSA survivors to take control of their lives rather than remain silent victims.[163]

A second ground supporting strict application of the statute of limitations is the fear of fraudulent claims based upon stale evidence.[164] There is no doubt that memories and recollections are onerous problems in CSA survivor actions. But, the evidentiary reasons for strict date of injury accrual are far different today than in 1623, when the first statute of limitations was enacted.[165] In 1623, parties to lawsuits could not be witnesses. Hence, a plaintiff could wait until the death or departure of a crucial defense witness to bring his suit, knowing that the defendant, himself, could not rebut the charges. The initial statutes were tailored to prevent this problem.[166] Today, evidentiary concerns should not weigh heavily against application of the discovery rule in CSA survivor suits. Modern rules of evidence are sufficient to exclude unreliable or prejudicial evidence at trial.[167]

The third reason supporting strict application of the limitations statute is that it discourages plaintiffs from sleeping on their rights.[168] Applying the delayed discovery rule could erode the CSA survivor's incentive to timely bring suit.[169] In reality, by the time the emotional injury of CSA is finally discovered, the date of injury rule provides no incentive for filing, as it is long since passed. If the date of injury rule is invoked to bar blameless victims from a remedy, their guarantee of justice is violated.[170]

---

162. Morrison v. Chan, 699 S.W.2d 205, 208 (Tex. 1985).

163. Hartnet, *supra* note 14, at 1272 n.250; Allen, *supra* note 19, at 617 n.55, 638.

164. W. PROSSER & W. KEETON, HANDBOOK ON THE LAW OF TORTS, 167 (5th ed. 1984) [hereinafter "Prosser & Keaton"]

165. The Act for Limitation of Actions and for Avoiding of Suits in Law, 21 JAC. I., c. 23 (1623) (cited *in* Note, *Developments in the Law: Statutes of Limitations*, 63 HARV. L. REV. 1177, 1217-18 (1950)).

166. DeRose, *supra* note 25, at 218 (citing Kelly, The Discovery Rule for Personal Injury Statute of Limitations: Reflections on the British Experience, 24 WAYNE L. REV. 1641, 1645-46 (1978)).

167. *Tyson*, 727 P.2d at 233 (Pearson, J., dissenting); *see also* TEX. R. CIV. EVID. 401, 403, 702, 703.

168. DeRose, *supra* note 25, at 220.

169. Petersen v. Bruen, 792 P.2d 18, 25 (Nev. 1990) (Rose, J. concurring).

170. *Id.* at 23. The victim's suffering may be intensified by realization that failure to

IV.   PURSUING A CSA SUIT IN TEXAS

A.   Theories of Liability

1.   Intentional Torts

Three intentional tort theories are available to the CSA survivor: Assault, battery, and intentional infliction of emotional distress.

a.   Assault

An actor is liable for assault if he intends to cause harmful or offensive contact with the person of another . . . or cause an imminent apprehension of such contact. An act is done with the intention of putting the other in apprehension of an imminent harmful or offensive contact if it is done for the purpose of causing such an apprehension or with knowledge that, to a substantial certainty, such apprehension will result.[171] The abuser's intent to commit assault is established if the abuser approached his young victim with the purpose of causing the victim to reasonably believe that harmful or offensive contact with him was imminent, or with knowledge that his victim was substantially certain to have such a reasonable belief.[172]

A child victim may not be aware that a wrong is occurring.[173] However, if the conduct persists or occurs during school-age years or adolescence, the victim generally becomes aware that the act is wrong or shameful.[174] It is suggested that a child who is aware of the wrongfulness of the act, and thus is apprehensive of imminent contact, learns "to distinguish between instances of paternal approach which presage molestation and those which do not" in situations where the act is continually inflicted.[175] Thus, it is reasonable for a victim to apprehend impending sexual contact with her abuser—no sexual contact with a child by an offending adult can be considered desired contact.[176]

---

timely muster the will or courage to seek relief has left the abuser forever immune from accountability. *Id.*; Mary D. v. John D., 264 Cal. Rptr. 633, 639 (Ct. App. 1989) ("[N]o more can she assert her rights if, when, she reaches majority, she is wholly unaware of the facts constituting her cause of action."); Hammer v. Hammer, 418 N.W.2d 23, 27 (Wis. Ct. App. 1987) (In incest abuse cases, "[t]o protect the parent at the expense of the child works an 'intolerable perversion of justice' "); Johnson v. Johnson, 701 F. Supp. 1363, 1370 (N.D. Ill. 1988) (Equitable considerations of discovery rule and fact that incest is a crime allows accrual when injury and cause are discovered.).

171. RESTATEMENT (SECOND) OF TORTS § 21 (1977); *see also* Perkins Bros. Co. v. Anderson, 155 S.W. 556 (Tex. Civ. App.—Dallas 1913, writ ref'd).

172. Allen, *supra* note 19, at 618.

173. Hartnett, *supra* note 14, at 1249 n.52.

174. *Id.*

175. Allen, *supra* note 19, at 622.

176. In Altman v. Eckermann, 132 S.W. 523, 523 (Tex. Civ. App. 1910, no writ) wherein

Recall that, in *DeRose v. Carswell*,[177] the plaintiff brought an action for assault in addition to her battery and infliction of emotional distress claims. According to the *DeRose* court, "the assaults [that the plaintiff alleged] were serious harm as a matter of law."[178] However, because the *DeRose* plaintiff "always knew" of the CSA, she was barred by the statute of limitations.[179] That the plaintiff-survivor did not discover the connection between the abuse and her subsequent emotional harm or mental anguish is, under the logic of *DeRose*, irrelevant. Once such a plaintiff knows of her abuse, she is appreciably harmed enough to sue at that time even if she does not know the extent of her future and subsequent psychological damages.[180]

At present, Texas case law appears to support this same proposition. In *Robertson v. Texas & N.O.R.R.*,[181] the court held that "where an injury, though slight, is sustained in consequence of the wrongful or negligent act of another . . . [i]t is not material that all the damages resulting from the act should have been sustained . . . the running of the statute is not postponed by the fact that the actual or substantial damages do not occur until a later date."[182] This proposition is the legal injury rule.[183] Under Texas law, unless a plaintiff pleads and proves discovery facts, the courts will apply the date of injury in assessing the commencement of limitations.[184] Thus, unless memory of the assault itself were blocked or repressed from the survivor's mind, a survivor who always knew of the assault, but did not know of the subsequently caused emotional harm, is time-barred.[185]

---

the defendant raped his thirteen-year-old ward, the court stated that "the touching of her person with the intent to injure her, she being incapable of giving consent thereto, constituted an assault."

177. 242 Cal. Rptr. 368 (Ct. App. 1987).
178. *Id.* at 371.
179. *Id.* at 373.
180. *Id.* at 373-74.
181. 122 S.W.2d 1098 (Tex. Civ. App.—San Antonio 1938, writ ref'd).
182. *Id.* at 1100; *see also* Albertson v. T.J. Stevenson & Co., Inc., 749 F.2d 223 (5th Cir. 1984) (stating that the plaintiff's cause of action accrues on the date he realized that he had sustained harm from the tortious act, regardless of whether he later discovers that his injuries are more serious than originally thought).
183. Black v. Wills, 758 S.W.2d 809, 816 (Tex. App.—Dallas 1988, no writ).
184. *Id.* at 816.
185. The concept of "continuous injury" also, would not be of benefit to a CSA survivor. This concept originated in trespass to land cases and nuisance. Arquette v. Hancock, 656 S.W.2d 627, 629 (Tex. App.—San Antonio 1983, writ ref'd n.r.e.). It has been expanded to false imprisonment cases to include time detained until the detention ends. Adler v. Beverly Hills Hospital, 594 S.W.2d 153, 155 (Tex. Civ. App. — Dallas 1980, no writ). Although some commentators may analogize CSA survivor trauma to false imprisonment, it is clear that, because at some point after the CSA, the abuser did not control the victim's day to day move-

b.   Battery

"An actor is subject to liability to another for battery if . . . he acts intending to cause a harmful or offensive contact with the person of the other . . . or an imminent apprehension of such a contact."[186] Also, "[i]n order that [an] actor may be liable . . . it is necessary that an act be done for the purpose of bringing about a harmful or offensive contact or an apprehension of such contact . . . or with knowledge that such a result will, to a substantial certainty, be produced by his act."[187]

Liability of the abuser for battery requires a showing that the abuser approached his victim purposefully to cause harmful or offensive contact with the victim, or to cause the victim to believe that such contact was imminent.[188] If the abuser knew that such contact or apprehension was substantially certain to occur as a result of his conduct, tortious intent can be established.[189]

Again, as in assault cases, the statute of limitations begins to run when the defendant's conduct invades the plaintiff's rights. That is, the limitations period commences once the conduct is completed.[190] Hence, under the *DeRose* rationale, if the plaintiff was always aware of the abuse, it matters not that such plaintiff could not anticipate subsequent psychological harm—the "aware" plaintiff will be time-barred.

c.   Intentional Infliction of Emotional Distress

"One who by extreme and outrageous conduct intentionally or recklessly causes severe emotional distress to another is subject to liability for such emotional distress, and if bodily harm to the other results from it, for such bodily harm."[191]

In order to establish that the abuser's conduct renders him liable, the CSA plaintiff must allege that (1) the defendant's conduct was outrageous; (2) the defendant intended to cause or recklessly disregarded the probability of causing severe emotional distress; (3) the plaintiff suffered severe emotional distress; and (4) the defendant's conduct actually and

---

ments. Hence, such an analogy will not be given deference under traditional law concepts. Bharam, *supra* note 14, at 857.

186.   RESTATEMENT (SECOND) OF TORTS § 18 (1977).

187.   *Id.* at comment e.

188.   Allen, *supra* note 19, at 622.

189.   *Id.* at 619.

190.   DeRose, *supra* note 25, at 214.

191.   RESTATEMENT (SECOND) OF TORTS §§ 46, 941 (1977); *see also* Tidelands Auto. Club v. Walters, 699 S.W.2d 939, 941 (Tex. App.—Beaumont 1985, writ ref'd n.r.e.) (severe emotional distress means unpleasant mental reactions such as fright, horror, grief, shame, humiliation).

proximately caused emotional distress.[192] Here, the plaintiff will have to assert that the defendant committed sexual abuse either purposefully or with knowledge that the plaintiff was substantially certain to suffer severe emotional distress.[193] When a trusted relative or father figure abuses a child, his conduct is reckless if he knows or has reason to know of facts from which a reasonable person would realize that such conduct puts his victim at a substantial risk of suffering severe emotional distress.[194] In assessing the severity of the distress, consideration is given to its intensity and duration.[195] If no physical harm is alleged, courts look for more in the way of extreme outrage to ensure the claim is genuine.[196]

CSA survivors typically suffer from guilt, shame, anxiety, low self-esteem and inability to trust or form satisfying relationships with their peers.[197] These and other causal PTSD symptoms persist for years.[198] The multiplicity of symptoms of emotional distress experienced by CSA survivors, in conjunction with the length of time that these symptoms tend to persist, provides compelling evidence of the severe emotional distress suffered. As to the proximate causation element, it follows that the inflicted CSA is *a fortiori* caused emotional distress. This conclusion can be substantiated by psychiatric testimony regarding the nature and cause of the survivor's emotional distress.[199]

2. Negligence

In intentional torts actions such as assault, battery, or intentional infliction of emotional distress, "when the defendant's conduct itself in-

---

192. Allen, *supra* note 19, at 623.

193. *Id.* However, since intentional infliction of emotional distress can be alleged on the basis of reckless conduct alone, the survivor need not prove her abuser intended to cause her severe emotional distress. Proof that he behaved in reckless disregard of that probability is sufficient. *Id.* Also, "reckless" is defined as an act done which would lead a reasonable person to realize that his conduct creates an unreasonable risk of harm to another and that such risk is substantially greater than that which is necessary to make his conduct negligent. RESTATE-MENT (SECOND) OF TORTS § 500 (1977).

194. 699 S.W.2d at 941, 945; *see also* RESTATEMENT (SECOND) OF TORTS, *supra* note 174, at § 46 comment j (the law intervenes only where the distress inflicted is so severe that no reasonable [person] could be expected to endure it). Pursuant to the RESTATEMENT (SECOND) OF TORTS § 46 comment e "[t]he extreme and outrageous character of the conduct may arise from an abuse by the actor of a position, or a relation with the other, which gives him actual or apparent authority over the other, or power to affect his interests."

195. RESTATEMENT (SECOND) OF TORTS § 46 comment j.

196. *Id.* at § 46 comment k.

197. Tsai & Feldman-Summers et. al, *Childhood Molestation: Variables Related To Differential Impacts of Psychosexual Functioning in Adult Women*, 88 J. ABNORMAL PSYCHOLOGY 407, 414 (1979). [hereinafter "Tsai & Feldman-Summers et. al,"]

198. *Id.*

199. Allen, *supra* note 19, at 626; Valdez v. Church's Fried Chicken, 683 F. Supp. 596, 613-15 (W.D. Tex. 1988).

vades the plaintiff's rights, the statute [of limitations] begins to run once the conduct is completed."[200] However, in negligence actions, the general rule is that no cause of action exists unless the plaintiff is injured.[201] Texas courts have painstakingly glossed the negligence rule as follows:

> If the defendant's conduct results in an invasion of the plaintiff's legally protected interest . . . his right of action "accrues" with the invasion, provided some legally cognizable injury however slight, has resulted from the invasion or would necessarily do so. The defendant's conduct is in such case, categorized as "unlawful." Conversely, if no right of redress exists by reason of the defendant's conduct, because no legally protected interest of the plaintiff has been invaded at the time of the conduct complained of, the defendant's conduct is categorized as "lawful" and any cause of action based thereon does not accrue until some invasion of the legally protected interest does occur.[202]

Under such a construction, if the original act of the defendant is "proper" under the law, if any harms come to the plaintiff as a result of it, the discovery rule applies. If, however, the act is, or has always been, considered as improper under the law, immediate harm is inferred, and the statute of limitations accrues at the time of the act.[203]

If this construction is applicable to CSA, then it is a cruel irony. As a child, the survivor possessed a legally protected interest which was invaded improperly by the abuse. However, as a child, the survivor must look to his or her parents or those in control, to protect such interest. In the face of reality, such help is not forthcoming and, thus, the child lives in a conspiracy of debilitating silence.[204] Nonetheless, upon majority, this survivor must overcome debilitation and sue for such wrongs as if he were suing for a breach of contract. Pursuant to the majority of jurisdictions entertaining CSA suits, if the survivor did not, at a minimum, repress consciousness of the abuse, the two-year statute of limitations commences upon majority.[205] Thus, for the time being, a successful

---

200. DeRose, *supra* note 25, at 214 (citing Note, *Developments in the Law: Statute of Limitations*, 63 HARV. L. REV. 1177, 1200-01 (1950)).

201. PROSSER AND KEETON, *supra* note 164, at 165-67.

202. Zidell v. Bird, 692 S.W.2d 550, 555 (Tex. App.—Austin 1985, no writ).

203. Gaddis v. Smith, 417 S.W.2d at 577, 579 (Tex. 1967).

204. David Spiegel, *Hypnosis in the Treatment of Victims of Sexual Abuse*, 12 PSYCHIATRIC CLINICS OF N. AM. 295, 298-99 (1989); Hubbard, *supra* note 73, at 39 (symptoms of avoidance of things associated with traumatic events and numbing of responsiveness to the event); Tsai & Feldman-Summers et. al, *supra* note 197, at 415 (negative feelings associated with molestation).

205. In Mary D. v. John D., a case subsequent to *DeRose*, the plaintiff sued for psychological injuries and alleged repression of the abuse until rediscovering the connection between such abuse and her psychological harm. 264 Cal. Rptr. 633, 635 (Ct. App. 1989). In determining the propriety of the lower court's grant of a summary judgment for the defendant, the court

claim for negligence may require the allegation of repression. And, although repression itself is a nebulous matter, the Texas Supreme Court has previously considered a plaintiff's state of mind in "discovering" his cause of action.[206]

a.   Sexual Molestation

Many authors have described the unique injuries suffered by a CSA victim and the legal awkwardness in analogizing a CSA cause to traditional tort principles.[207] One author has advocated a "tort suit for latent incestuous injuries," to address the special circumstances of CSA.[208] In *Daly v. Derrick*,[209] the California appellate court formally recognized a cause of action for sexual molestation.[210] The cause of action for sexual molestation is not merely another name for assault or battery.[211] Sexual molestation comprises not only sexual touching, the gravamen of a battery, but also "the abuse of [the defendant's] status as an adult in a position of authority and trust."[212] This abuse of trust creates repressive tendencies in CSA survivors, which delays the recognition of the nature of their injuries.[213] This newly created tort was fashioned under prior authority which eventually recognized a cause in negligence for medical malpractice where such was previously classified as a battery.[214] Consequently, sexual molestation is not categorized as an immediate harm, and is best placed as a cause of action under negligence principles.[215] Under such a cause of action, plaintiffs will be allowed the opportunity to demonstrate timely commencement of suit after discovery of the last fact

---

carefully observed that: "Giving the declaration which we do have the benefit of every doubt, it is fairly read as saying not that plaintiff has been delayed in discovering her injury, but that she repressed her contemporaneous awareness of the assaults against her and then later recovered those buried memories." *Id.* at 638.

The above premise states two things. First, it gives the standard of review of a summary judgment: all reasonable doubts are indulged in favor of the nonmovant. Secondly, the court allows a relaxed discovery rule. "Almost all adults molested as children are aware of some emotional or physical trauma at the time" of the abuse. The discovery exception under its standard meaning would be of little use to CSA survivors if the plaintiff's duty of inquiry was not relaxed. DeRose, *supra* note 25, at 206.

206.   Larson v. Cook, 690 S.W.2d 567, 569 (Tex. 1985).
207.   *See supra* notes 9, 14, 19 and accompanying text.
208.   Salten, *supra* note 9, at 220.
209.   281 Cal. Rptr. 709, (Ct. App. 1991).
210.   *Id.* at 716-17.
211.   *Id.* at 716.
212.   *Id.* at 717.
213.   *Id.*
214.   *Id.*
215.   *Cf.* Salten, *supra* note 9, at 190 n.3 (treating the "tort of incest" as an intentional tort which creates unique and long lasting injuries calling for a modified limitation period).

essential to their claim.[216]

b.   Negligent Infliction of Emotional Distress

An actor is liable for negligent infliction of emotional distress if the actor:

> a.   should have realized that his conduct involved an unreasonable risk of causing the distress . . . and
>
> b.   from facts known to him should have realized that the distress, if it were caused, might result in illness or bodily harm.[217]

Texas does not require proof of physical injury to substantiate a claim of emotional distress as long as serious emotional distress to the survivor was a reasonably foreseeable consequence of the abuser's conduct.[218] Children are generally not capable of providing for their own physical and emotional well being. They rely upon their parents, relatives, intimate family friends, and entrusted individuals for the satisfaction of those needs. This creates a tremendously uneven balance of power between the child and the child's caretakers which renders such a child vulnerable to abuse. This vulnerability is exploited when abusers force the child to submit to sexual contact. Such conduct manifestly creates the unreasonable risk that the child will thereby suffer serious emotional distress. It should be noted that, in the case of *Valdez v. Church's Fried Chicken*,[219] the plaintiff brought suit against the defendant for injuries resulting from sexual assault. Although the facts of the molestation supported many tort theories, the plaintiff alleged assault. Her primary injuries were mental injuries called PTSD. The evidence at trial was based primarily upon the plaintiff's and defendant's differing versions as to what occurred. The court found for the plaintiff and also found that it was "reasonably foreseeable that a victim of an attempted rape would suffer mental anguish, even if the particular form of mental anguish — post traumatic stress syndrome—is not understood."[220]

---

216.   *Id.*; *see also* Nicolette v. Carey, 751 F. Supp. 695, 699 (W.D. Mich. 1990) (grace period counted from the termination of the last disability).

217.   RESTATEMENT (SECOND) OF TORTS § 313 (1965).

218.   St. Elizabeth Hospital v. Garrard, 730 S.W.2d 649 (Tex. 1987) (physical injury no longer required to recover for negligent infliction of emotional distress); *cf.* Horace Mann Ins. Co. v. Leeber, 376 S.E.2d 581, 587 (W. Va. 1988) (negligent infliction of emotional distress is not an independent cause of action in West Virginia).

219.   683 F. Supp. 596 (W.D. Tex. 1988).

220.   *Id.* at 615. The defendant in *Valdez*, among other things, argued that the plaintiff's PTSD was pre-existing or latent, as the plaintiff had mental problems at the time of the assault and no evaluation was performed regarding the plaintiff's [bad] childhood experiences. The court observed that the plaintiff's psychological problems and marital difficulties may have made her "more vulnerable" but there was *no evidence* in the record that PTSD existed before the assault or was a latent condition. *Valdez*, 683 F. Supp. at 615.

It cannot be disputed that sexually abused children suffer severe emotional distress as a result of parental, familial, or acquaintance conduct. These symptoms of distress may be verified by expert testimony.[221] Furthermore, no reasonable person should be expected to endure the mental anguish that CSA survivors typically suffer. In conjunction with the reasonable foreseeability of emotional distress as a consequence of sexual contact with one in a position of trust and authority, expert testimony may establish liability for negligent infliction of emotional distress.[222]

c.   Negligent Invasion of Privacy

The right of privacy is difficult to define.[223] It has been coined historically as the "right to be let alone."[224] An unreasonable intrusion upon or interference with another's interest in solitude or seclusion, either as to his person or to his private affairs or concerns, constitutes a negligent invasion of this right.[225] In *C.T.W. v. B.C.G. and D.T.G.*,[226] the Beaumont Court of Appeals held that the sexual abuse of a young child, although an intended act, may be regarded as a negligent invasion of privacy because of its far-reaching consequences.[227]

B.   Strategic Considerations

1.   Insurance Coverage

Insurance policies almost universally use language that excludes coverage for bodily injuries caused intentionally by or at the direction of the insured.[228] In Texas, it is against public policy to insure oneself against the consequences of one's own willful acts, i.e., those committed with the intent to cause injury.[229] In the majority of jurisdictions where the issue of CSA and insurance coverage has been litigated, the court determined that the offender's liability insurer has no duty to defend or

---

221. *See supra* notes 68-70, 79-88 and accompanying text; *see also* Simmons v. United States, 805 F.2d 1363, 1364-65 (9th Cir. 1986) (discussing therapeutic mishandling of psychological phenomena of transference in psychotherapist-client relations, in context of the discovery rule, and likening the same to breach of the parent-child relationship).

222. Allen, *supra* note 19, at 628.

223. PROSSER & KEETON, *supra* note 164, at 849 n.1.

224. *Id.* at 849.

225. *Id.* at 854.

226. 809 S.W.2d 788 (Tex. App.—Beaumont 1991, n.w.h.).

227. *Id.* at 796.

228. BLAKE BAILEY ET. AL., COMPENSATING THE SEXUALLY ABUSED CHILD - HOMEOWNER'S POLICY CAN PROVIDE FUNDS FOR TREATMENT, TRIAL 78 (July 1990) [hereinafter "Bailey"]

229. *See* Travelers Ins. Co. v. Reed Co., 135 S.W.2d 611, 617 (Tex. Civ. App.—Beaumont 1940, writ dism'd judgm't cor.).

indemnify in such circumstances.[230] It is irrelevant that the insured may declare he did not intend the harmful consequences of CSA. Under the majority view, the insured nonetheless intended, as a matter of law, to commit the act of CSA.[231] Recent authors suggest that, under certain circumstances where the abuser was suffering from a mental condition, the CSA survivor should plead, at a minimum, a cause of action for negligent infliction of emotional distress.[232] One jurisdiction has held recently that acts of an insured can trigger policy coverage when the insured suffered from a mental condition which, according to mental health experts, rendered him incapable of intending to inflict bodily harm.[233] Other jurisdictions have held that intoxication or minority age may trigger coverage.[234] Identified disorders such as pedophilia, narcis-

---

230. The following states have adopted the majority rule and have inferred the intent to cause injury as a matter of law in insurance cases involving CSA: Arkansas, California, Colorado, Florida, Georgia, Iowa, Maine, Maryland, Massachusetts, Michigan, Minnesota, Nevada, New Hampshire, Oklahoma, Pennsylvania, Washington, West Virginia and Wisconsin as collected and set forth in Allstate Ins. Co. v. Mugavero, 561 N.Y.S.2d 35, 46 (1990) (Balletta, J. dissenting); *see* Horace Mann Ins. Co. v. Leeber, 376 S.E.2d 581, 585 (W.Va. 1988). *But see* State Auto Mutual Ins. Co. v. McIntyre, 652 F. Supp. 1177, 1220-21 (N.D. Ala. 1987) (declining to follow the majority rule and refusing to give collateral estoppel effect to a prior conviction because expected injury cannot be equated to foreseeable injury); Farmer's Ins. Group and Fire Ins. Exchange v. Dawson, 803 P.2d 211 (Kan. App. 1990) (Unpublished Decision) (finding declaratory judgment action premature when key fact issues remain, including among others, that husband of babysitter had a prior CSA conviction of which babysitter may have been unaware and possibility husband was negligent by participating in babysitting, knowing the presence of children was an irresistible temptation); State Farm Fire & Cas. Co. v. Nycum, 943 F.2d 1100 (9th Cir. 1991) (finding that record supported "touching" as opposed to "molestation," and touching was not, per se, an intentional tort).

231. *Horace Mann*, 376 S.E.2d at 585-586; *see also* Twin City Fire Ins. Co. v. Doe, 163 Ariz. 388, 390, 788 P.2d 121, 123 (Ariz. App. 1989) (holding that in CSA, basic intent to injure will be presumed); J.C. Penny Casualty Ins. Co. v. M.K., 804 P.2d 689, 695 (Cal. 1991) (precluding liability insurance coverage for insured's sexual molestation of the child, no matter whether insured subjectively intended harm); Worcester Ins. Co. v. Fells Acres Day School Inc., 558 N.E.2d 958 (Mass. 1990) (holding that rape and sexual assault are acts of an inherently dangerous kind and reason mandates that harm must have been intended). *Contra* Allstate Ins. Co. v. Mugavero, 561 N.Y.S.2d 35, 36 (1990) (holding that fact finder should determine whether inference of intention to harm arises from nature of act alone).

232. Bailey, *supra* note 228, at 80. In the Allen article, the author discussed the findings of several researchers to the effect that a father who incestuously abused his daughter was motivated more by self-absorption, dominance and power than by offensive sexual pleasure. The conclusion by these researchers was that, in circumstances of incest, the father's or father-figure's mental state did not conform to that required to establish intent in assault or battery. Allen, *supra* note 19, at 619-20.

233. Bailey, *supra* note 228, at 79. (*citing* State Auto Mut'l Ins. Co. v. McIntyre, 652 F. Supp. 1177 (N.D. Ala. 1987)).

234. MacKinnon v. Hanover Ins. Co., 471 A.2d 1166 (N.H. 1984) (admitting evidence of insured's intoxication to determine intent or expectation of bodily injury); Allstate Ins. Co. v. Jack S., 709 F. Supp. 963, 966 (D. Nev. 1989) (holding that it may be too broad a leap in logic to impute intent of harm to a minor who engaged in sexual acts with another minor).

sism, dependent personality, antisocialism, and impulse-control are, by definition, mental disorders in which the offenders are "not fully aware of the effects of their acts and the harm caused."[235]

The case of *C.T.W.*, mentioned above, concerned a similar situation.[236] In *C.T.W.*, the minor plaintiffs sued their step-grandfather for negligent infliction of emotional distress and negligent invasion of privacy resulting from CSA.[237] The Court of Appeals affirmed the jury's finding that the step-grandfather was negligent in failing to seek professional help for his pedophilic disorder and in not avoiding situations where he would be left alone with young children and thus able to act on his desires.[238] Thus, when an abuser suffers or has suffered from a mental condition, it may not be possible to presume the intent to inflict harm so as to preclude insurance coverage.

The nonoffending parent or caretaker is also a potential defendant in a CSA suit.[239] When CSA occurs, the nonoffending parent or caretaker generally is conscious of signs of its existence but nonetheless subconsciously resists acknowledging it.[240] Such behavior reasonably can be defined as negligence.[241] Hence, consideration should be given to including nonoffending, but tacitly consenting, individuals as defendants in a suit seeking compensation from the abuser's homeowner's insurance carrier.

2. Parental Immunity

It is possible that, in the case of incestuous CSA, the abusing parent will raise a parent-child immunity argument to avoid liability. In Texas, the doctrine of parental immunity, first established in 1891, was founded on the public policy premise that family harmony must be preserved.[242] The doctrine of parental immunity has been retained only with regard to "alleged acts of ordinary negligence which involve a reasonable exercise

---

235. Bailey, *supra* note 228, at 78.
236. C.T.W. v. B.C.G. and D.T.G., 809 S.W.2d 788 (Tex. App.—Beaumont 1991, n.w.h.).
237. *Id.* at 790.
238. *Id.* at 797.
239. Johnson v. Johnson, 701 F. Supp. 1363, 1363-1365 (N.D. Ill. 1988) (prosecuting mother and father); Farmers Ins. Group v. Dawson, 803 P.2d 211 (Kans. App. 1990) (per curiam) (unpublished disposition) (litigating assault claims in underlying action against husband and wife babysitters); Allstate Ins. Co. v. Mugavero, 166 A.D.2d 474, 561 N.Y.S.2d 35, 37 (1990) (asserting underlying claims against husband and wife babysitters).
240. Bailey, *supra* note 228, at 80; DeRose, *supra* note 25, at 193 n.8 (asserting that nonoffending mother is afraid of consequences and implications of revealing abuse); G. Hubbard, *supra* note 73, at 38 (finding mothers used denial as most common defense mechanism); *see also* C. ROGERS & T. TERRY, Clinical Intervention With Boy Victims Of Sexual Abuse *in* VICTIMS OF SEXUAL AGGRESSION 98-102 (1984).
241. Bailey, *supra* note 228, at 80.
242. Hewellette v. George, 9 So. 885, 887 (Miss. 1891).

of parental authority or the exercise of ordinary parental discretion with respect to provisions for the care and necessities of the child."[243] In deciding cases on grounds of public policy, courts evidence concern that suits by minor children against one or both parents disrupts the family and interferes with a parent's duty to care for and discipline his or her children.[244] Where family harmony and reasonable parental disciplinary and caretaking discretion are not jeopardized, however, a minor child's suit against her parent has been permitted.[245]

When a child is sexually abused by a family member as a result of a parent's negligence, family harmony is a superficial technicality. "Harmony" in these types of families is nothing more than a hollow coexistence. Such "harmony" is nothing more than compliance predicated on secrecy and corruption of the parent-child relationship. Although Texas courts have yet to address the issue of parental immunity in the context of CSA, it is doubtful that such doctrine would be applied.

3. Case Considerations

There can be no doubt that CSA cases, as currently novel actions at law, may be widely publicized. Because of the threat of publicity and its social implications for the child, counsel should consider the use of pseudonyms or initials in the action or otherwise seek to seal the court records.[246]

Evidentiary concerns will also control the chance of success. The events will have to be primarily reconstructed from memory and, for this reason, counsel must spend considerable time with the client's therapist. This way, counsel can identify and ensure the veracity and foundational strength behind recalled events, times and places before any weaknesses are exposed at trial. It is also important for counsel to ensure that the client's therapist has expertise in CSA cases. The development of the case involves the recall of memories and feelings in the plaintiff that, under the stress of anticipated litigation, may cause such a plaintiff to retreat to "blocking" of recall in order to cope with daily life.[247] Conse-

---

243. Felderhoff v. Felderhoff, 473 S.W.2d 928, 933 (Tex. 1971).

244. Attend, *supra* note 19, at 634.

245. B. Bailey and E. Drott, *The Doctrine of Parental Immunity In Sexual Abuse Cases: The Last Throes of A Texas Dinosaur,* 25 TRIAL LAWYERS' FORUM 27, 28 (1991); *see also* Jilani v. Jilani, 767 S.W.2d 671 (Tex. 1989). In *Jilani,* the Texas Supreme Court recognized, as a matter of public policy, that a parents' conduct can be examined only under limited circumstances. Such circumstances are those of intentional torts or conduct "other than the discharge of parental authority or duties." *Id.* at 672.

246. *See, e.g.,* Unnamed Plaintiff v. Unnamed Defendant, No. Confidential, (Mass. Suffolk County Super. Ct., June 21, 1988); E.W. and D.W. v. D.C.H., 754 P.2d 817 (Mont. 1988).

247. Bailey, *supra* note 228, at 81; Summit, *supra* note 2, at 419.

quently, the therapist must handle the plaintiff carefully to avoid inflicting further damage.[248]

Counsel and client must be prepared to pursue the case to the end. If negligence is alleged, insurance companies will defend vigorously to avoid precedent.[249] Moreover, one experienced practitioner suggests that the trial be made short and to the point. From a plaintiff's counsel perspective, the shorter the case, the less possibility of a jury becoming desensitized to the hideous truths.[250] Further, at least in the case of younger CSA victims, an attorney should be prepared to call in a fashion consultant; as the premature sexual initiation of young victims may cause them to wear inappropriate cosmetics and/or clothing to appear older than their age.[251]

Because of the "newness" of this cause of action, jury awards are uncertain and settlement prospects are difficult to predict.[252] In *Osland v. Osland*,[253] the plaintiff was awarded $12,000 plus costs. However, in an unreported Colorado case, the female plaintiff was awarded $1.2 million by an all-female jury.[254] Insofar as known settlements, in Massachusetts, the plaintiff and defendant in *Unnamed Plaintiff v. Unnamed Defendant*,[255] settled out of court in 1989. Unfortunately, the amount of settlement is currently unknown.

CSA plaintiffs should be prepared to produce corroborative evidence; the majority of courts desire some objective proof to invoke the discovery rule. The more objective the evidence appears to be, the better the chance of taking the case to a trial. Corroborative evidence may be a letter from the abuser, responding to the survivor's earlier written complaint regarding the CSA; a documented medical history indicative of

---

248. Bailey, *supra* note 228, at 81.

249. *Id.*

250. Telephone Interview with Dale Williams, Atorney for Plaintiff in Sessions v. Sessions, No. 85-542-3 (74th Dist. Ct., Waco Texas 1985) (Judge Derwood Johnson presiding). In Sessions, the victim, Shelley Sessions, was sexually abused by her father, Bobby Sessions, from age thirteen to sixteen. Suit was commenced when Shelley Sessions was aged eighteen. The plaintiff's case was premised upon assault and battery with the only damage issues being the award of five million dollars for mental anguish and the grant of five millions dollars in punitive damages. After two hours of deliberation the jury awarded the plaintiff Shelley Sessions, a ten million dollar judgment.

251. *Id.*

252. *Id.*

253. 442 N.W.2d 907, 909 (N.D. 1989).

254. *See, e.g.*, Hartnett, *supra* note 14, at 1270-71 n.239 (citing Bass, *Daughters Win Sex-Abuse Case Against Father*, BOSTON GLOBE, May 18, 1990, at 17, which reports an all-female jury's award of $1.2 million to a Massachusetts woman who sued her father, a former F.B.I. agent and advisor, for sexually abusing her and her sister while they grew up).

255. *Id.*

CSA;[256] recalled events by siblings or other household members;[257] or a judgment of criminal conviction for the CSA.[258] However, as to the latter, caution is suggested. Current Texas law precludes reliance upon negligence findings in a civil suit where a prior conviction for an intentional crime is introduced into evidence at such trial.[259]

Finally, CSA plaintiffs and their counsel should be prepared to face the defendant's motion for summary judgment, based upon the statute of limitations. The Texas Supreme Court has distinguished between situations where the petition affirmatively shows that the limitations period has expired and the nonmovant seeks to avoid limitations in some manner, and those situations where the petition does not affirmatively show that the statute of limitations has run.[260] In the former situation, the nonmovant has the burden of producing evidence sufficient to raise a fact question as to the grounds for avoiding limitations; in the latter situation, the movant must establish that the suit is barred by limitations as a matter of law.[261] Hence, the CSA plaintiff should allege facts sufficient to show entitlement to the discovery rule.

---

256. *Accord* Flannagan v. State, 586 So.2d 1085, 1099 (Fla. Dist. Ct. App. 1991) (stating the doctor's testimony "established beyond peradventure that the condition of the child's private parts was consistent with repeated penetration").

257. FINKELHOR, *supra* note 15, at 4; Salten, *supra* note 9, at 196 n.44 *citing* S. BUTLER, CONSPIRACY OF SILENCE: THE TRAUMA OF INCEST 32 (1978). In one study of mothers whose daughters had been sexually abused by the father, the mothers recalled behavioral changes in the daughter which began at the time of such abuse. The behaviors included lying, vomiting, refusing to stay alone with the father, failing in school and sexually acting out. Despite the unusual nature of these behaviors, most of the mothers did not overtly question the circumstances. One mother was quoted as saying, "[a] couple of times I caught her with a pencil up her fanny in her bedroom during her nap. I thought it was kind of strange." Hubbard, *supra* note 73, at 37.

258. Petersen v. Bruen, 792 P.2d 18, 21 (Nev. 1990).

259. National Union Fire Ins. Co. v. Bourn, 441 S.W.2d 592, 596 (Tex. Civ. App.—Fort Worth 1969, writ ref'd n.r.e.).

260. Zale Corp. v. Rosenbaum, 520 S.W.2d 889, 891 (Tex. 1975) (recognizing that where a party seeks a summary judgment, the movant bears the burden to conclusively establish the bar of limitations; including the plaintiff's lack of an affirmative defense, which would have tolled the running of limitations); Oram v. General American Oil Co., 513 S.W.2d 533, 534 (Tex. 1974) (recognizing that if movant conclusively establishes the limitations defense, the non-movant would be required to raise a fact issue with respect to estoppel).

261. Whatley v. National Bank of Commerce, 555 S.W.2d 500, 503 (Tex. Civ. App.—Dallas, 1977, no writ) (stating that in cases involving fraud or duress, the statute of limitations does not begin to run until the fraud is discovered or duress removed); *see also* Black v. Wills, 758 S.W.2d 809, 816 (Tex. App.—Dallas 1988, no writ) ("when discovery facts are pleaded and proved, accrual of the plaintiff's cause of action occurs at the time plaintiff discovers . . . the nature of the injury . . . when the plaintiff fails to plead and prove discovery facts . . . the legal injury rule is still a viable concept for determining when the cause of action accrues").

4. *Punitive Damages*

There is no reason why CSA survivors may not seek punitive damages. The primary purposes of punitive damages are to punish the defendant and to deter him and others from engaging in similar conduct in the future.[262] To state a cause of action for punitive damages, the survivor must prove that the defendant's conduct was either willful and outrageous or grossly negligent.[263] The jury has the discretion to determine whether punitive damages should be awarded.[264] Because CSA is abhorrent conduct, it is a sufficient basis upon which to seek an exemplary damage award. To date, at least four courts have allowed jury awards of punitive damages to stand.[265]

VI. CONCLUSION

The policies favoring unenforceability of stale claims, as reflected in statutes of limitations, compared with those allowing a remedy to survivors of CSA, as reflected in the principles of delayed discovery and other equitable tolling provisions, stand in inescapable tension. Yet, societal policies are always reflected in judicial construction of the law. Our society has recognized the pain of CSA victims and acknowledged CSA's long and devastating effects. Now, our courts are beginning to see such effects in the growing number of lawsuits filed by CSA survivors. Texas will soon join those jurisdictions that have encountered these claims.

When CSA claims occur in Texas, our courts, too, will confront the procedural and substantive obstacles connected with such claims. However, Texas courts are no stranger to equity and have, in the past, interpreted the accrual rule to commence upon discovery of unknowable injuries. Since the current status of CSA law reflects a growing majority which recognizes CSA as an unknowable injury, Texas courts are likely

---

262. Hofer v. Lavender, 679 S.W.2d 470, 474 (Tex. 1984). In *Hofer*, the court enumerated four purposes of punitive damages: (1) to punish the wrongdoer; (2) to serve as an example to others; (3) to reimburse the plaintiff for losses too remote to be considered elements of strict compensation and (4) to compensate for inconvenience and attorney's fees.

263. Burk Royalty Co. v. Walls, 616 S.W.2d 911, 922 (Tex. 1981).

264. *Id.* at 921.

265. C.T.W. v. B.C.G. and D.T.G., 809 S.W.2d 788, 790 (Tex. App.—Beaumont 1991, no writ) (awarding 1.3 million dollars in actual damages and 1 million dollars in exemplary damages to each minor injured by stepgrandfather's pedophilic activity); Sessions v. Sessions, No. 85-542-3 in the 74th District Court, Waco, Texas, August 29, 1985 (Judge Derwood Johnson presiding); Father A and Mother A v. Moran, 469 N.W.2d 503, 507 (Minn. App. 1991) (awarding punitive damages to minor child sexually abused by a friend of the family, but holding that parents may not recover punitive damages); Elkington v. Foust, 618 P.2d 37 (Utah 1980) (upholding a punitive damage award of $30,000 where compensatory damages were $12,000); *cf.* State Auto Mutual Ins. Co. v. McIntyre, 652 F. Supp. 1177, 1221 (N.D. Ala. 1987) (affirming $75,000 punitive damage award for minor who was sexually abused).

to follow this trend. However, for now, it appears that the benefit of such rule will be given to survivors in Type 2 cases, as such cases are currently easier to resolve under traditional common law principles.* Perhaps, in the not so distant future, judicial nascence in these cases will provide a remedy for all CSA survivors.**

---

* Authors' note: After this article was released for press two additional jurisdictions addressed their first adult CSA claims. In *O'Neal v. Division of Family Services, State of Utah*, 821 P.2d 1139 (Utah 1991), the Utah Supreme Court held that a survivor in a Type 1 case could not toll the Statute of limitations on the basis of mental incompetency nor could he benefit from the discovery rule. However, the court reversed the issue as to its ruling on a Type 2 case, if such were presented in the future. *Id.* at 1145.

Similarly, the Oklahoma Supreme Court held that an adult survivor, who alleged continuous multiple personality disorders from CSA, could not toll limitations on the basis of a legal disability, nor could she benefit from the discovery rule. *Lovelace v. Keohane*, no. 74,848 (1992 WL 21444) (Okla. Feb. 11, 1992). However, the facts of *Lovelace*, are distinguishable from the usual CSA cases. In *Lovelace*, the plaintiff, who was abused by her father as a child, sought conunseling from Father Keohane as an adult. The counseling from Father Keohane resulted in further sexual injuries, for which the plaintiff sued. The Oklahoma Supreme Court noted the fact of plaintiff adulthood when considering her claim and held that the discovery rule would not be extended on her set of facts. 1992 WL 21444, *8.

** Carol: "Lex non deficit in justice exhibenda." T.S.

The Admissibility of Expert Testimony on Child Sexual Abuse Accommodation Syndrome as Indicia of Abuse: Aiding the Prosecution in Meeting Its Burden of Proof

I. INTRODUCTION

The number of child sexual abuse cases appearing in the criminal justice system has increased dramatically since the early 1980's.[1] These cases often present a prosecutor with unique problems of proof.[2] Therefore, some prosecutors have attempted to "bolster" their cases through the use of expert testimony.[3] This comment proposes that some form of this expert testimony should be admissible. In support of this proposition, this comment will begin by examining what is known as "child sexual abuse accommodation syndrome."[4] Next, it will discuss the evidentiary requirements which must be met in order for such expert testimony to be admissible. It will then examine how courts have ruled on the admissibility of expert testimony on child sexual abuse accommodation syndrome to prove that the abuse actually occurred.[5] Finally, it will conclude by defining and attempting to resolve any potential difficulties which can prevent the admission of this expert testimony before the trier of fact.

II. CHILD SEXUAL ABUSE ACCOMMODATION SYNDROME

Child sexual abuse accommodation syndrome was first described by Dr. Roland Summit, a Clinical Assistant Professor of Psychiatry at Harbor - UCLA Medical Center.[6] In his research, Dr. Summit identi-

---

1. *See generally* Roe, *Expert Testimony in Child Sexual Abuse Cases*, 40 U. MIAMI L. REV. 97, 97 (1985); Gardner, *Prosecutors Should Think Twice Before Using Experts in Child Sex Abuse Cases*, A.B.A. J. CRIM. JUST., Fall 1988, at 13 (caseload increase of 500 percent from 1981 to 1986 in the Madison County Prosecutor's Office, Alabama) [hereinafter Gardner].

2. Gardner, *supra* note 1, at 13. One problem is that the typical child sexual abuse case involves the child's word against the offender's word. *Id.* Often these cases involve accusations made by a child against individuals who seem to be respectable, such as the child's natural parent, a step-parent, a grandparent, some other type of relative, or a live-in companion. *Id.* Also, the prosecutor may find himself without any physical evidence of the abuse because of a delay in reporting. *Id.* In such situations, jurors find it difficult to convict an individual solely on the word of a child. *Id.*

3. *Id.*

4. Summit, *The Child Sexual Abuse Accommodation Syndrome*, 7 CHILD ABUSE & NEGLECT 177, 177 (1983) [hereinafter Summit].

5. McCord, *Expert Psychological Testimony About Child Complaints in Sexual Abuse Prosecutions: A Foray into the Admissibility of Novel Psychological Evidence*, 77 J. CRIM. L. & CRIMINOLOGY 1, 9 (1986) [hereinafter McCord].

6. Summit, *supra* note 4, at 177.

fied five phases of the syndrome.[7] The first two phases are preconditions to the abuse and are not actually caused by the abuse.[8] The first of these phases is secrecy.[9] Here the offender intimidates the victim into not disclosing the fact of the abuse.[10] This can be anything from a request of silence, to a threat of serious harm.[11] The second phase is helplessness.[12] In this phase, the victim feels powerless to prevent the abuse because of the authority the offender may have over the child.[13]

The final three phases are a direct result of the abuse.[14] The third phase is accommodation.[15] This is where the victim starts to accept the abuse in order to survive.[16] The fourth phase is when the victim discloses the abuse, which is often delayed and conflicted.[17] This behavior can be damaging to the victim's credibility as a witness, therefore, expert testimony should be utilized here to explain that this behavior is normal for sexually abused children.[18]

The final phase is the recantation by the victim of the original report.[19] The period following the disclosure can be traumatic for the child.[20] The disclosure will often be disbelieved by family members and the child may be extensively interviewed by lawyers, investigators, and social workers.[21] In some situations, the child may even be removed from his home. These events often result in the victim recanting their accusation. A sexually abused child may experience one or more of these phases as a result of the abuse.

III. EVIDENTIARY REQUIREMENTS OF EXPERT TESTIMONY

Expert testimony must meet several requirements before it is presented to the trier of fact.[22] The court must determine if the expert has sufficient skill, knowledge, experience, training, or expertise in

---

7. *Id.*
8. Hensley, *The Admissibility of "Child Sexual Abuse Accommodation Syndrome" in California Courts*, 17 PAC. L.J. 1361, 1365 (1986) [hereinafter Hensley].
9. Summit, *supra* note 4, at 181.
10. Gardner, *supra* note 1, at 14.
11. *See* State v. Haseltine, 120 Wis. 2d 92, 352 N.W.2d 673 (1984) (father told daughter he would kill her if she reported his abuse).
12. Summit, *supra* note 4, at 183.
13. Gardner, *supra* note 1, at 14.
14. Hensley, *supra* note 8, at 1366.
15. Summit, *supra* note 4, at 184.
16. *Id.* Dr. Summit states that during this stage, the child realizes that "the only healthy option left for . . . [him/her] is to learn to accept the situation and to survive." *Id.*
17. *Id.* at 186.
18. McCord, *supra* note 5, at 58-64. For a more detailed discussion on the use of expert testimony in this capacity, see *infra*, text accompanying notes 81-96.
19. Summit, *supra* note 4, at 188.
20. *Id.*
21. Gardner, *supra* note 1, at 14.
22. *See, e.g.,* FED. R. EVID. 702; FED. R. EVID. 703.

that particular area.[23] With this requirement met, individuals with practical experience in handling abuse victims, such as police officers, rape crisis counselors, victims advocates, and child protective service workers can be qualified as experts, as well as child psychologists and mental health professionals.[24] Therefore, this requirement is not difficult for the prosecution to establish as long as the proposed expert has some experience with child sexual abuse victims.

The second requirement is that the scientific, technical, or specific knowledge of the expert must be of such a nature as to assist the trier of fact to understand the evidence or to determine a fact in issue.[25] If the subject-matter of the expert testimony is within the scope of knowledge of the average juror, expert testimony is inadmissible.[26] Therefore, some explanation of the dynamics of child sexual abuse by an expert will be admissible since this knowledge is normally beyond the scope of the average juror.

The next hurdle is that the scientific evidence presented by the expert must meet the requirements of the *Frye* test.[27] *Frye* requires that before an expert can make a deduction based on scientific evidence, there must be general acceptance of that principle in the particular field from which it belongs.[28] The *Frye* test has been incorporated into the FEDERAL RULES OF EVIDENCE.[29] Therefore, before an expert can testify whether a particular child's behavior is in compliance with the symptoms of child sexual abuse accommodation syndrome, it must be established that the syndrome is generally accepted as valid in the field of child behavioral psychology.

The final requirement of expert testimony is that it must be relevant to the issue before the court. Evidence is relevant if it has "any tendency to make the existence of any fact that is of consequence to the determination of the action more or less probable than it would be without the evidence."[30] Once the expert testimony is deemed rele-

---

23. FED. R. EVID. 702. Rule 702 reads in pertinent part: "a witness qualified as an expert by knowledge, skill, experience, training, or education. . . ." *Id.*

24. Gardner, *supra* note 1, at 15.

25. FED. R. EVID. 702.

26. *Id.* The advisory committee's note states: "[w]hen opinions are excluded, it is because they are unhelpful and therefore superfluous and a waste of time." *Id.* advisory committee's note (quoting 7 WIGMORE § 1918).

27. Frye v. United States, 293 F. 1013 (D.C. Cir. 1923).

28. *Id.* at 1014. The court stated: "while courts will go a long way in admitting expert testimony deduced from a well-recognized scientific principle or discovery, the thing from which the deduction is made must be sufficiently established to have gained general acceptance in the particular field in which it belongs." *Id.*

29. FED. R. EVID. 703. Rule 703 reads in pertinent part: "[t]he facts or data in the particular case upon which an expert bases an opinion or inference may be . . . of a type *reasonably relied upon by experts in the particular field* in forming opinions or inferences upon the subject." *Id.* (emphasis added).

30. FED. R. EVID. 401. Expert testimony as well as all other types of evidence, must meet the relevancy requirements of Rule 401 to be admissible. *Id.*

vant, to be admissible, its probative value cannot be substantially outweighed by the danger of unfair prejudice.[31] Generally, the relevancy of expert testimony on child sexual abuse accommodation syndrome will depend on its effectiveness as a diagnostic analysis.[32]

Once these evidentiary requirements have been met, the prosecution will be allowed to present their expert testimony on child sexual abuse accommodation syndrome. However, as the next section of this comment will demonstrate, often these requirements have not been met and the expert testimony has occasionally been ruled inadmissible.

IV. USING EXPERT TESTIMONY ON CHILD SEXUAL ABUSE ACCOMMODATION SYNDROME TO PROVE THAT THE ABUSE ACTUALLY OCCURRED.

There is a split of authority with regard to the admissibility of expert testimony on child sexual abuse accommodation syndrome to prove that the victim actually was abused. Strong support for its admission can be seen in *People v. Payan*.[33] In *Payan*, the prosecution presented the testimony of a physician who was qualified as an expert on child sexual abuse accommodation syndrome.[34] The physician testified that sexually abused children often go through the first five phases of the syndrome.[35] The physician then testified that based upon his review of the preliminary hearing transcript and the police and mental reports, the children had in fact been sexually abused.[36] On appeal, the reviewing court held that the expert testimony was properly admitted since it aided the jury's understanding of an area in which they may have lacked adequate knowledge to form a proper basis for rendering a decision.[37] The defense argued that the expert's testimony failed to meet the *Frye* test.[38] However, the court rejected this claim by holding that the test was inapplicable to expert medical testimony.[39]

An earlier case decided by the Hawaii Supreme Court also found that expert testimony on child sexual abuse accommodation syndrome was admissible. In *State v. Kim*,[40] an expert testified that the victims

---

31. FED. R. EVID. 403.
32. The greater the acceptance of child sexual abuse accommodation syndrome in the medical and mental health field as a valid indicator of abuse, the greater the tendency it will have to make the existence of the abuse more probable.
33. 173 Cal. App. 3d 27, 220 Cal. Rptr. 126 (1985).
34. *Id.* at _____, 220 Cal. Rptr. at 128.
35. *Id.* As stated earlier, these five phases are secrecy, helplessness, accommodation, delayed disclosure and recantation. Summit, *supra* note 4, at 181-88. For discussion of these phases, see *supra*, text accompanying notes 7-20.
36. *Payan*, 173 Cal. App. 3d at _____, 220 Cal. Rptr. at 128.
37. *Id.* at _____, 220 Cal. Rptr. at 131-33.
38. *Id.* at _____, 220 Cal. Rptr. at 133.
39. *Id.*
40. 64 Haw. 598, 645 P.2d 1330 (1982).

displayed the same types of emotions which other victims of sexual abuse displayed.[41] The supreme court affirmed the trial judge's determination that the expert testimony assisted the jury and that its probative value was not substantially outweighed by the danger of unfair prejudice.[42] The court found the expert's testimony to be reliable based upon the expert's education, training, and experience with child sexual abuse victims.[43]

In *State v. Myers*,[44] an expert testified that the victim had the same symptoms as other sexually abused children.[45] The expert concluded that based on these similarities, the child was in fact sexually abused.[46] The Minnesota Supreme Court held that the testimony was properly admitted because it did assist the jury in determining a fact in issue and that its probative value was not substantially outweighed by the danger of unfair prejudice.[47] The court reasoned that the average juror did not possess any knowledge of a child's reaction to sexual abuse.[48]

As the preceding cases show, expert testimony of child sexual abuse accommodation syndrome to prove that the victim was in fact abused has been found to be relevant[49] and not unfairly prejudicial.[50] However, not all courts have ruled such testimony admissible. An example of this can be seen in *Bussey v. Commonwealth*.[51] In *Bussey*, the trial court permitted a psychiatrist to testify that the victim was displaying symptoms of the syndrome.[52] The Kentucky Supreme Court ruled this testimony was inadmissible because the state had failed to meet the *Frye* test, since it did not adequately establish that child sexual abuse accommodation syndrome was generally accepted in the medical community.[53]

---

41. *Id.* at 601, 645 P.2d at 1333.
42. *Id.* at 607, 645 P.2d at 1338-39.
43. *Id.* at 608, 645 P.2d at 1338.
44. 359 N.W.2d 604 (Minn. 1984).
45. *Id.* at 609. These symptoms were fear of men, nightmares of an assaultive nature, fear of blame or punishment and more sexual knowledge than normal for a child of that age. *Id.*
46. *Id.*
47. *Id.* at 610.
48. *Id.*
49. FED. R. EVID. 401. *See, e.g.*, People v. Payan, 173 Cal. App. 3d 27, ____, 220 Cal. Rptr. 126, 131-33 (1985); State v. Myers, 359 N.W.2d 604, 610 (Minn. 1984); State v. Kim, 64 Haw. 598, 607, 645 P.2d 1330, 1338-39 (1982).
50. FED. R. EVID. 402; *see, e.g., Myers*, 359 N.W.2d at 610; *Kim*, 64 Haw. at 607, 645 P.2d at 1338-39.
51. 697 S.W.2d 139 (Ky. 1985).
52. *Id.* at 140.
53. *Id.* at 141. The court stated that the testimony was inadmissible because the symptoms of the syndrome displayed by the victim could not be distinguished from symptoms which may have stemmed from abuse caused by someone other than the defendant. *Id.*

A second example of a court holding expert testimony inadmissible was *State v. Maule*.[54] In *Maule*, the expert offered by the state testified that the victim displayed the same characteristics as other sexually abused children.[55] The court stated that expert testimony must be based on facts which are reasonably relied upon by experts in the field.[56] The court went on to say that the expert's belief that sexually abused children shared the same characteristics was not shown to be reasonably relied upon by other experts in the field.[57] It further stated that there was no evidence presented by the expert that the characteristics displayed by these children were adequate indicia of abuse.[58]

It appears that the major obstacle to the admission of expert testimony of child sexual abuse accommodation syndrome has been a failure to show that the syndrome is reasonably relied upon by experts in the field. This brings the reliability of the syndrome into question. For prosecutors to use expert testimony for proving actual abuse when there is a lack of physical evidence, this hurdle must be eliminated. Possible solutions to this problem will be discussed in the next section of this comment.

V. Dealing with the Problems of Admissibility

It seems that the requirements of the *Frye* test pose the greatest obstacle to the admission of expert testimony for proving that the abuse actually occurred.[59] The purpose of the *Frye* test is to guarantee that the evidence relied upon by the jury has merit.[60] However, the *Frye* general acceptance requirement may deprive the jury of helpful evidence because of the time span between the adoption of a psychological analysis and its general acceptance in the field of mental health.[61] Prosecutors must find an alternative to the general acceptance requirement or work towards having child sexual abuse accommodation syndrome generally accepted in its field.

---

54. 35 Wash. App. 287, 667 P.2d 96 (1983).

55. *Id.* at ____, 667 P.2d at 97 n.1.

56. *Id.* at ____, 667 P.2d at 99. The court was referring to the requirement stated in Wash. Rule of Evid. 702 which is identical to Fed. Rule of Evid. 702.

57. *Id.* at ____, 667 P.2d at 96.

58. *Id.*

59. *See, e.g.*, Bussey v. Commonwealth, 697 S.W.2d 139, 141 (Ky. 1985) (expert testimony ruled inadmissible because state failed to establish that child sexual abuse accommodation syndrome was generally accepted in the medical community); State v. Maule, 35 Wash. App. 287, ____, 667 P.2d 96, 99 (1983) (expert's belief that children who had been sexually abused shared the same characteristics was not shown to be reasonably relied upon by experts in the field).

60. McCord, *supra* note 5, at 29.

61. *Id.* at 30. Furthermore, psychological evidence by virtue of its subjective nature may have more difficulty gaining general acceptance than a more mechanical objective technique. *Id.*

A. *Using an Alternative to the Frye Test to Determine if Expert Testimony on Child Sexual Abuse Accommodation Syndrome is Reliable as an Indicia of Abuse.*

An alternative to the general acceptance requirement of the *Frye* test is to propose a list of factors for a court to apply in order to determine the reliability and probative value of newly developed scientific and psychological evidence.[62] An advocate of this approach is Iowa Supreme Court Justice Mark McCormick.[63] Under this approach, in determining the reliability of scientific evidence, a trial court would apply pre-determined factors to the proposed evidence. In such a situation, Justice McCormick has suggested the following factors:

(1) The potential error rate in using the technique;
(2) The existence and maintenance of standards governing its use;
(3) Presence of safeguards in the characteristics of the technique;
(4) Analogy to other scientific techniques whose results are admissible;
(5) The extent to which the technique has .been accepted by scientists in the field involved;
(6) The nature and breadth of the influence adduced;
(7) The clarity and simplicity with which the technique can be described and its results explained;
(8) The extent to which the basic data are verifiable by the court or the jury;
(9) The availability of other experts to test and evaluate the technique;
(10) The probative significance of the evidence in the circumstances of the case; and
(11) The care with which the technique was applied in the case.[64]

This approach allows reliable scientific evidence which has not been in existence long enough to receive general acceptance in its field to be admitted.

Courts have used a factor analysis in determining the admissibility of other types of scientific evidence, such as forensic linguistic testimony,[65] blood stain expert testimony,[66] and expert testimony on the fallibility of eyewitnesses.[67] In following the factors established by Justice McCormick, the Iowa Supreme Court upheld the trial judge's decision to admit expert testimony on blood stain analysis.[68] The factors considered by the court in ruling that the testimony was admissible were:

---

62. *Id.* at 28.
63. *See* McCormick, *Scientific Evidence: Defining a New Approach to Admissibility*, 67 IOWA L. REV. 879 (1982) [hereinafter McCormick].
64. *Id.* at 911-12.
65. United States v. Clifford, 543 F. Supp. 424, 430 (W.D. Pa. 1982), *rev'd.*, 704 F.2d 86 (3d Cir. 1983).
66. State v. Hall, 297 N.W.2d 80, 84-85 (Iowa 1980), *cert. denied*, 450 U.S. 927 (1982).
67. People v. McDonald, 37 Cal. 3d 351, 690 P.2d 709, 208 Cal. Rptr. 236 (1984).
68. *Hall*, 297 N.W.2d at 86.

(1) [the expert's] considerable experience and his status as the leading expert in the field; (2) the existence of national training programs; (3) the existence of national and state organizations for experts in the field; (4) the offering of courses on the subject in several major schools; (5) use by police departments throughout the country in their day-to-day operations; (6) the holding of annual seminars; and (7) the existence of specialized publications.[69]

In response to the defendant's argument that there was inadequate foundation for the expert to testify on blood stain analysis, the court said the blood stain analysis "need not wait an assessment by the scientific community; the foundation evidence of reliability and the inherent understandability of the evidence itself provided sufficient bases [sic] for its admission."[70] Therefore, even though the blood stain analysis had not yet gained general acceptance in the scientific community, because it was inherently understandable and a proper foundation was laid for its reliability, the court held that the testimony was admissible.[71]

If a court applies a factor analysis such as the one suggested by Justice McCormick,[72] prosecutors will be in a better position for getting expert testimony on child sexual abuse accommodation syndrome admitted. The prosecution would not be required to prove that the syndrome was generally accepted in its field. In the alternative, the prosecutor can present evidence with regard to the syndrome which addresses the factors relied upon by the particular court. Whether a court finds expert testimony on child sexual abuse accommodation syndrome admissible as indicia of abuse will be subject to such variables as the specific expert providing the testimony and how the diagnosis of child sexual abuse accommodation syndrome was reached in the case at bar. However, if the factors can be met to the satisfaction of the judge, reliable scientific analysis such as child sexual abuse accommodation syndrome will be admissible as indicia of abuse before it is generally accepted by the scientific community.

---

69. *Id.* at 85.

70. *Id.* at 86. With regard to the court's discussion on reliability and understandability, McCord suggests that these are two of the four factors that a judge should consider in determining the admissibility of scientific evidence. McCord, *supra* note 5, at 31. These factors are: (1) necessity - how necessary the offered testimony is to the context of the case; (2) reliability - how reliable is the expert testimony likely to be; (3) understandability - the ability of the trier of fact to understand the offered testimony and give it its proper weight; and (4) importance - how critical the point is, in the circumstances of the case, on which the expert testimony is being offered. *Id.* at 31-33.

71. State v. Hall, 297 N.W.2d 80, 86 (Iowa 1980), *cert. denied*, 450 U.S. 927 (1982).

72. McCormick, *supra* note 63, at 911-12.

B. *Meeting the Requirements of the Frye Test by Having Child Sexual Abuse Accommodation Syndrome Generally Accepted in the Medical Community.*

In the event that a court continues to adhere strictly to the *Frye* test, there is still hope that child sexual abuse accommodation syndrome will gain general acceptance in the medical community. Other types of syndromes have been generally accepted by the medical community and subsequently passed the *Frye* test.[73] These are rape trauma syndrome,[74] battered wife syndrome,[75] battering parent syndrome[76] and battered child syndrome.[77] In fact, a California court found child sexual abuse accommodation syndrome to be a valid indicator of abuse by analogizing it with battered child syndrome.[78] The court stated that the victim's post-injury "behavior appears to be unique to children subjected to child abuse and [is] as valid an indicia of such abuse as the physical characteristics used to diagnose 'battered child syndrome.'"[79] This case shows how prosecutors can get expert testimony of the syndrome admitted by comparing it with other types of admissible syndromes. A comparison such as this should be considered by prosecutors when the issue centers on whether child sexual abuse accommodation syndrome has been generally accepted in its field.

In the event that a court will continue to strictly adhere to the *Frye* test, there is a possibility that expert testimony on child sexual abuse accommodation syndrome to show that the abuse actually occurred will eventually be admissible. This may be done either by receiving general acceptance in its field, as other types of syndromes have, or through comparisons with other types of syndromes which have been generally accepted in their areas.

C. *Using Expert Testimony on Child Sexual Abuse Accommodation Syndrome to Explain the Unusual Behavior of the Child Victim.*

Expert testimony on child sexual abuse accommodation syndrome does not have to be limited to proving that the abuse actually

---

73. McCord, *supra* note 5, at 28. McCord refers to these other syndromes as "novel" psychological evidence. *Id.*

74. *See* State v. Taylor, 663 S.W.2d 235, 240 (Mo. 1984) (reversed on other grounds); *contra* State v. Saldana, 324 N.W.2d 227, 230 (Minn. 1982).

75. *See* Ibn-Tamas v. United States, 407 A.2d 626, 638 (D.C. 1978); *contra* State v. Thomas, 66 Ohio St. 2d 518, 521-22, 423 N.E.2d 137, 140 (1981).

76. *See* State v. Loebach, 310 N.W.2d 58, 64 (Minn. 1981).

77. *See* People v. Jackson, 18 Cal. App. 3d 504, 507, 95 Cal. Rptr. 919, 921 (1971).

78. Matter of Cheryl H., 153 Cal. App. 3d 1098, 1117, 200 Cal. Rptr. 789, 800 (1984). This case was a non-criminal child custody matter where the father was accused of sexually abusing his three-year-old daughter. *Id.* at 1108-09, 200 Cal. Rptr. at 800.

79. *Id.* at 1117, 200 Cal. Rptr. at 800.

occurred. It can be used in many ways to aid the prosecution's case.[80] In the event that testimony on child sexual abuse accommodation syndrome is ruled inadmissible, the prosecution should consider these other methods to aid its case. One of these methods is to have the expert explain the unusual behavior of the child victim.[81]

As stated previously, two of the phases in child sexual abuse accommodation syndrome are delayed disclosure and recantation.[82] These facts can be used effectively by the defense on cross-examination to attack the credibility of the victim by implying that a child who had been sexually abused would have immediately reported it, and since the alleged victim did not do so, it is likely that the claim is untrue.[83] In rebuttal, the prosecution may rehabilitate the victim's credibility by presenting expert testimony which shows that even though the victim's behavior may appear to be inconsistent, it may in fact be consistent with sexual abuse.[84]

There is support for admitting expert testimony to explain why the victim may have delayed disclosure. One such case is *People v. Dunnahoo*.[85] In *Dunnahoo*, the defense brought out the fact that the two victims did not immediately report the sexual abuse to the police.[86] The prosecution rebutted this testimony with the testimony of two police officers qualified as experts in the field of child sexual abuse.[87] These experts testified that very often sexually abused children find it difficult to discuss their sexual abuse.[88] The appellate court ruled that this expert testimony was properly admitted as opinion testimony by an expert "because the subject of child molestation and more particularly, the sensitivities of the victims, is knowledge sufficiently beyond common experience such that the opinion of an expert would be of assistance to the trier of facts."[89]

Recantation is the other unusual behavior which defendants use to attack the credibility of the victim.[90] Many times, after a child

---

80. *See generally* McCord, *supra* note 5, at 41-67. Besides using the testimony to prove that the abuse actually occurred, McCord discusses three other possible uses. *Id.* They are: (1) using the expert to vouch for the complainant's credibility regarding the sexual abuse allegation; (2) using the expert to enhance the complainant's credibility by explaining the complainant's unusual behavior; (3) using the expert to enhance the complainant's credibility by explaining the capabilities of child witnesses. *Id.* The focus of this section of the comment will be on using the expert to explain the complainant's unusual behavior.
81. McCord, *supra* note 5, at 58-64.
82. Summit, *supra* note 4, at 186, 188.
83. McCord, *supra* note 5, at 59.
84. Gardner, *supra* note 1, at 15.
85. 152 Cal. App. 3d 561, 199 Cal. Rptr. 796 (1984).
86. *Id.* at 577, 199 Cal. Rptr. at 804.
87. *Id.*
88. *Id.*
89. *Id.*
90. McCord, *supra* note 5, at 59.

makes a claim of sexual abuse they will retract it. Later, during the trial, they will attempt to retract the recantation and reaffirm the original claim.[91] The defendant can impeach the child's credibility with the prior inconsistent statement.[92] The prosecutor can rebut this impeachment by using an expert to testify that it is not unusual for a child to retract an allegation of abuse out of fear and confusion.[93]

The Oregon Supreme Court in *State v. Middleton*,[94] held expert testimony which stated that child sexual abuse victims often retract their original accusations was properly admitted by the trial judge.[95] The court's reasoning in admitting the testimony was that such conduct was beyond the knowledge of the jury and it would aid the jury in determining the credibility of the victim's testimony.[96]

It appears that expert testimony to explain the victim's inconsistent behavior is admissible. In the event that expert testimony on child sexual abuse accommodation syndrome to prove that the abuse actually occurred is ruled inadmissible for failing to meet the *Frye* test, prosecutors should still consider using this evidence to cure other inherent weaknesses which arise in child sexual abuse prosecutions.

VI. CONCLUSION

Expert testimony on child sexual abuse accommodation syndrome can aid the prosecution in meeting its burden of proof, especially in cases where there is a lack of physical evidence. However, the syndrome's failure to receive general acceptance in its field often leads to it being held inadmissible as an indicia of abuse. Courts should determine the admissibility of such testimony by weighing certain factors which go directly to the reliability of the syndrome. Prosecutors can also show the reliability of child sexual abuse accommodation syndrome by analogizing it to other types of syndromes which have been generally accepted in their field. However, in the event that testimony on the syndrome is held to be inadmissible as a valid indicator of abuse, prosecutors should still consider its use to cure other inherent weaknesses in their case.

PATRICK LARSON

---

91. *Id.*
92. *Id.*
93. *Id.*
94. 294 Or. 427, 657 P.2d 1215 (1983).
95. *Id.* at ____, 657 P.2d at 1220.
96. *Id.*

COMMENTARY

BATTERED CHILD SYNDROME: EVIDENCE OF PRIOR ACTS IN DISGUISE

Michael S. Orfinger*

I. INTRODUCTION

In 1987, 1100 children across the United States died of child abuse;[1] the 1988 death toll may be even higher. While the naked statistics alone are shocking, they cannot begin to reflect the unreported quantum of physical, sexual, and emotional abuse that children endure each year.[2] Child abuse is a social epidemic that requires the joint efforts of the medical and legal communities; the former must recognize and

---

*Associate, Carlton, Fields, Ward, Emmanuel, Smith & Cutler, Orlando, Florida. B.A., 1986, Wake Forest University; J.D., 1989, University of Florida. The author thanks Professor Teree E. Foster, Professor Toni M. Massaro, and Dr. Michael C. Bell for their contributions to this commentary. The author is eternally grateful to his parents, Judge and Mrs. Melvin Orfinger, for their enduring support.

    1. NATIONAL CENTER FOR THE PROSECUTION OF CHILD ABUSE UPDATE, May 1988, at 1 (on file).

    2. There were 606,600 cases of child neglect and abuse reported nationwide in 1978. By 1985, that figure jumped to 1,299,400. Bureau of the Census, U.S. Dep't of Commerce, STATISTICAL ABSTRACT OF THE UNITED STATES 164 (1988) [hereinafter 1988 STATISTICAL ABSTRACT]. *But see* Fontana, *To Prevent the Abuse of the Future*, TRIAL, May-June 1974, at 14 (statistics grossly understate the problem of child abuse because only a fraction of abused children ever receive recognition or medical attention); Note, *The Testimony of Child Victims in Sex Abuse Prosecutions: Two Legislative Innovations*, 98 HARV. L. REV. 806, 806 n.7 (1985) (two out of every three victims of child sexual abuse never report the abusive act (citing D. FINKELHOR, SEXUALLY VICTIMIZED CHILDREN 106 (1979))).

treat it, while the latter must deter it. The medical community has responded with trained physicians and nurses able to recognize the indicia of child abuse. The legal community, on the other hand, has responded with mandatory reporting statutes for child abuse,[3] as well as stiff penalties for convicted abusers.[4]

Despite these laudable objectives and accomplishments, child abuse remains difficult to prosecute.[5] The young victim, if alive, often does not testify,[6] and rarely can the prosecution find a nonparty witness to the crime.[7] That a parent or guardian would intentionally harm a child is a difficult notion for many to accept.[8] Moreover, parents or those standing *in loco parentis* to the child are often able to fabricate plausible explanations for the child's injuries.[9] Thus, a child abuse prosecution may pit evidence of the child's injuries against the fabricated testimony of the alleged abuser, the plausibility of which may make the prosecutor's burden of proving guilt beyond a reasonable doubt insurmountable.

In this arena, as in many others, prosecutors have turned to expert testimony in an attempt to bolster child abuse prosecutions. The expert witness testifies as to whether the victim displays "battered child

---

3. *See, e.g.*, ALA. CODE § 26-14-3 (1986); CAL. PENAL CODE § 11166 (West 1982 & Supp. 1989); FLA. STAT. § 415.504 (1987); MINN. STAT. ANN. § 626.556(3) (West 1983 & Supp. 1989); TEX. FAM. CODE ANN. § 34.01 (Vernon 1986 & Supp. 1989). Under all these statutory schemes, anyone who is required to report child abuse and fails to do so commits a misdemeanor. For a discussion of the Florida statute, see Comment, *The Battered Child: Florida's Mandatory Reporting Statute*, 18 U. FLA. L. REV. 503 (1965) (analyzing FLA. STAT. § 828.041 (1965), an earlier but similar version of Florida's current statute).

4. For example, under Florida's statutory scheme, child abuse resulting in great bodily harm, permanent disability, or permanent disfigurement is a third-degree felony. FLA. STAT. § 827.04(1) (1987). Sexual abuse of a child is a second-degree felony. *Id.* § 827.071(2)-(5). One who kills a child while committing aggravated child abuse commits a capital felony. *Id.* § 782.04.

5. Morgan v. Foretich, 846 F.2d 941, 943 (4th Cir. 1988).

6. *Id.* at 951 (Powell, J. (retired), concurring in part and dissenting in part); *cf.* Cooper, *Child Abuse and Neglect — Medical Aspects*, in THE MALTREATMENT OF CHILDREN 9, 46-47 (S. Smith ed. 1978) (a child might fail to report child abuse because of "[f]ear of further abuse; loyalty to the family; feeling he deserved it; being overwhelmed by the assault and then by the medical attention; or not having an adequate vocabulary"); Comment, *Expert Medical Testimony Concerning "Battered Child Syndrome" Held Admissible*, 42 FORDHAM L. REV. 935, 939 n.35 (1974) ("Parents generally lie to protect each other, and children usually refuse to testify against their parents, primarily from fear of being removed from a parental figure.").

7. *Morgan*, 846 F.2d at 951 (Powell, J. (retired), concurring in part and dissenting in part).

8. Wasserman, *The Abused Parent of the Abused Child*, in VIOLENCE IN THE FAMILY 222, 223 (S. Steinmetz & M. Strauss eds. 1974).

9. *See* Comment, *supra* note 3, at 507.

syndrome," a term Dr. C. Henry Kempe coined in 1962.[10] Battered child syndrome is a medical diagnosis describing a pattern of serious and otherwise unexplained manifestations of physical abuse.[11] Expert testimony as to battered child syndrome has hardly been a point of judicial contention; every jurisdiction considering such evidence has held it admissible.[12] Nonetheless, this commentary suggests that the admissibility *vel non* of evidence of battered child syndrome deserves greater consideration, as most courts have failed to recognize or properly analyze the evidentiary issues. Careful analysis reveals that evidence of battered child syndrome is actually evidence of a defendant's prior acts. Courts therefore should treat it as such when prosecutors offer it into evidence.

Part II of this commentary traces the development of battered child syndrome and discusses the syndrome itself in detail. Part II also discusses battering parent syndrome, the psychological complement of battered child syndrome. Part III examines three leading cases in which courts have considered evidence of battered child syndrome, and attempts to distinguish cases of fatal and nonfatal child abuse. Part IV sets forth the proper evidentiary analysis under the Federal Rules of Evidence[13] and applies it to the cases examined in part III. The

---

10.   Kempe, Silverman, Steele, Droegemueller & Silver, *The Battered-Child Syndrome*, 181 J. A.M.A. 17 (1962) [hereinafter Kempe]. This article is thoroughly discussed in McCoid, *The Battered Child and Other Assaults Upon the Family: Part One*, 50 MINN. L. REV. 1, 9-12 (1965).

11.   H. Raffalli, *The Battered Child — An Overview of a Medical, Legal, and Social Problem*, 16 CRIME & DELINQ. 139, 140 (1970).

12.   *See, e.g.*, United States v. Bowers, 660 F.2d 527 (5th Cir. 1981); Eslava v. State, 473 So. 2d 1143 (Ala. Crim. App. 1985); State v. Moyer, 151 Ariz. 253, 727 P.2d 31 (Ct. App. 1986); People v. Jackson, 18 Cal. App. 3d 504, 95 Cal. Rptr. 919 (Ct. App. 1971); People v. Ellis, 41 Colo. App. 271, 589 P.2d 494 (Ct. App. 1978); State v. Dumlao, 3 Conn. App. 607, 491 A.2d 404 (App. Ct. 1985); People v. DeJesus, 71 Ill. App. 3d 235, 389 N.E.2d 260 (App. Ct. 1979); Bell v. Commonwealth, 684 S.W.2d 282 (Ky. Ct. App. 1984); State v. Conlogue, 474 A.2d 167 (Me. 1984); Commonwealth v. Labbe, 6 Mass. App. Ct. 73, 373 N.E.2d 227 (App. Ct. 1978); People v. Barnard, 93 Mich. App. 590, 286 N.W.2d 870 (Ct. App. 1979); State v. Loss, 295 Minn. 271, 204 N.W.2d 404 (1973); State v. Taylor, 163 Mont. 106, 515 P.2d 695 (1973); Bludsworth v. State, 98 Nev. 289, 646 P.2d 558 (1982); People v. Henson, 33 N.Y.2d 63, 304 N.E.2d 358, 349 N.Y.S.2d 657 (1973); State v. Wilkerson, 295 N.C. 559, 247 S.E.2d 905 (1978); *In re* R.W.B., 241 N.W.2d 546 (N.D. 1976); Commonwealth v. Rodgers, 364 Pa. Super. 477, 528 A.2d 610 (Super. Ct. 1987), *appeal denied*, 518 Pa. 638, 542 A.2d 1368 (1988); State v. Best, 89 S.D. 227, 232 N.W.2d 447 (1975); State v. Tanner, 675 P.2d 539 (Utah 1983) (superseded on other grounds by rule in State v. Walker, 743 P.2d 191 (Utah 1987)); State v. Mulder, 29 Wash. App. 513, 629 P.2d 462 (Ct. App. 1981).

13.   Because many state evidence codes pattern the Federal Rules of Evidence, this commentary assumes throughout, unless specifically indicated otherwise, that the Federal Rules of Evidence apply.

evidentiary ramifications of battering parent syndrome are discussed briefly in part V. This commentary concludes by suggesting that under the proposed analytical framework, battered child syndrome evidence is usually admissible prior act evidence. In contrast, evidence of battering parent syndrome is merely an attempt to introduce otherwise inadmissible evidence of the defendant's bad character.

II. THE MEDICAL AND PSYCHOLOGICAL PERSPECTIVE

Kempe did not suddenly discover the battered child syndrome. Earlier, several researchers studied unexplained injuries in children, many focusing on physical aspects of the injuries.[14] A survey of these early studies best begins with a 1946 article by Dr. John Caffey.[15] Caffey presented six cases in which children with subdural hematoma, a liquified blood clot on the brain, also exhibited multiple fractures of the long bones in the arms and legs.[16] No case evidenced a history of injury to which the fractures could be attributed, and none of the children had skeletal disease that would predispose them to pathological fractures.[17] Caffey concluded that fractures of the long bones were a common complication of subdural hematoma.[18] While puzzled by the lack of history of previous injury in these children, Caffey refused to attribute these injuries to intentionally inflicted harm.[19] Instead, he concluded that lay observers, who would provide the treating physician with medical history, often misunderstood the significance of childhood accidents such as falls on the head.[20]

Caffey's article posited a causal connection between subdural hematoma and long-bone fractures, but offered no conclusion as to what that connection might be. A 1955 article by Drs. John Woolley and William Evans[21] rejected any clinical or radiological connection between these injuries.[22] Instead, Woolley and Evans focused on the "injury-prone environment" in which the children they studied were

---

14. McCoid, *supra* note 10, at 4.

15. Caffey, *Multiple Fractures in the Long Bones of Infants Suffering from Chronic Subdural Hematoma*, 56 AM. J. ROENTGENOLOGY 163 (1946).

16. *Id.* at 163-70.

17. *Id.* at 171-72.

18. *Id.* at 173.

19. *Id.* at 172.

20. *Id.*

21. Woolley & Evans, *Significance of Skeletal Lesions in Infants Resembling Those of Traumatic Origin*, 158 J. A.M.A. 539 (1955).

22. *Id.* at 542.

living.[23] They deemed the family of each child they studied unstable, noting that emotionally erratic parents were the rule rather than the exception.[24] Perhaps most importantly, when the subject children were hospitalized and thus removed from their home environments, they suffered no new injuries and their previous injuries healed normally.[25] From this data, Woolley and Evans concluded that the injuries might be attributable to the presence of aggressive, immature, or emotionally ill adults in the household.[26]

Woolley and Evans, unlike Caffey, implicated parents as a cause of their children's injuries.[27] Caffey re-entered the debate in 1957, however, with an article that focused more thoroughly on the cause, rather than the physical manifestations, of unexplained skeletal injuries in children.[28] Caffey's new emphasis traced these injuries to "trauma."[29] In this respect, he followed the lead of Woolley and Evans, who had previously rejected the notion that infants' bones were predisposed to fracture.[30] However, while Woolley and Evans implied misconduct on the part of those standing *in loco parentis* to the child,[31] Caffey appeared more reluctant to do so. He recognized that a history of trauma rarely accompanied skeletal injuries in a child, and that the parent or guardian might be the only one able to furnish such a history.[32] Strangely, however, Caffey reasoned that the parent or guardian "may either omit the story of trauma because it is unknown to him, or conceal it intentionally because a true statement would imply *negligence* on his or her part."[33] Thus, while Caffey cautioned pedia-

---

23. *Id.* at 540-41.

24. *Id.* Woolley and Evans further noted that, with regard to the parents, "divorce, either earlier or following our contact with the cases, was commonplace." *Id.* at 541.

25. *Id.*

26. *Id.* at 542. Without directly accusing anyone, Woolley and Evans summarized their study by stating, "It is difficult to avoid the over-all conclusion that skeletal lesions having the appearance of fractures — regardless of history for injury or the presence or absence of intracranial bleeding — are due to undesirable vectors of force." *Id.* at 543; *see also* Adelson, *Slaughter of the Innocents — A Study of Forty-Six Homicides in Which the Victims Were Children,* 264 NEW ENG. J. MED. 1345, 1346 (1961) ("Frank psychosis in the assailant was the single most common factor in precipitating the fatal incident.").

27. Woolley & Evans, *supra* note 21, at 542-43.

28. Caffey, *Some Traumatic Lesions in Growing Bones Other Than Fractures and Dislocations: Clinical and Radiological Features,* 30 BRIT. J. RADIOLOGY 225 (1957).

29. *Id.*

30. *See* Woolley & Evans, *supra* note 21, at 542.

31. *See id.* at 540-42; *supra* notes 24-26 and accompanying text.

32. Caffey, *supra* note 28, at 226.

33. *Id.* (emphasis added).

tricians to consider the possibility of trauma when faced with an un-explained skeletal injury,[34] he seemed determined to ignore the possibility of intentional child abuse.

The above articles illustrate only two symptoms of child abuse: subdural hematoma and broken bones. But child abuse can manifest itself in countless repulsive ways. To fully appreciate the significance of battered child syndrome, one must recognize the depths to which some abusers can sink. Consider, for example, this summary from one study:

> The forms or types of abuse inflicted on these children is a negative testimony to the ingenuity and inventiveness of man. By far the greater number of injuries resulted from beatings with various kinds of implements [such as] [t]he hairbrush . . . bare fists . . . T.V. aerials . . . fan belts . . . bottles . . . chair legs, and . . . a sculling oar. Less imaginative, but equally effective, was plain kicking with street shoes or with heavy work shoes.
>
> Children had their extremities . . . burned in open flames. Others bore burn wounds inflicted on their bodies with lighted cigarettes, electric irons or hot pokers . . . . Still others were scalded by hot liquids . . . .
>
> Some children were strangled or suffocated by pillows held over their mouths or plastic bags thrown over their heads. A number were drowned in bathtubs and one child was buried alive.
>
> To complete the list — children were stabbed, bitten, shot, electric[ally] shock[ed], . . . stamped on and one child had pepper forced down his throat.[35]

These atrocities, coupled with the studies discussed above, set the stage for Kempe's classic 1962 article, *The Battered-Child Syndrome*.[36] Kempe studied 302 cases from 71 hospitals nationwide,[37] and found several common manifestations that he termed "battered child syndrome." The children, usually under three years of age, were in poor general health, and showed signs of neglect such as poor skin hygiene,

---

34. *Id.* at 227.

35. McCoid, *supra* note 10, at 15 (quoting DEFRANCIS, CHILD ABUSE — PREVIEW OF A NATIONWIDE SURVEY 5-7 (1963)); *see also* Adelson, *supra* note 26, at 1347 (causes of death in the 46 cases studied included gunshot wounds, asphyxiation, manual, pedal, and instrumental assault, stabbing, burning, and starvation).

36. Kempe, *supra* note 10.

37. *Id.* at 17.

malnutrition, and multiple soft tissue injuries.[38] Subdural hematoma was prevalent even in the absence of long bone fractures.[39] X-rays revealed a series of skeletal injuries to the arms and legs, all in various stages of healing.[40] Kempe attributed the frequency of these latter injuries to the fact that a child's arms and legs provided convenient "handles" for rough treatment.[41] As in the Woolley and Evans study, the children developed no new skeletal or soft tissue injuries while in the hospital.[42] Finally, Kempe emphasized that a major diagnostic feature of battered child syndrome was a marked discrepancy between clinical findings and the history provided by the parents.[43]

In short, Kempe advised physicians to consider battered child syndrome whenever a child presented subdural hematoma, unexplained fractures in different stages of healing, soft tissue swelling, skin bruising, signs of general neglect, or whenever the child's injuries clashed with the proffered history.[44] Kempe acknowledged that many physicians would resist believing that parents could be guilty of child abuse.[45] However, he strongly admonished these recalcitrant physicians that their duty to the children required a guarantee against re-injury.[46]

Kempe's analysis, unlike that of many of his predecessors, did not focus exclusively on the child's injuries. Rather, he also attempted to

---

38. *Id.* at 17-18.

39. *Id.* at 18. This finding plainly contradicts Caffey's 1946 finding. *See* Caffey, *supra* note 15, at 173.

40. Kempe, *supra* note 10, at 22.

41. *Id.* "The extremities are the 'handles' for rough handling, whether the arm is pulled to bring a reluctant child to his feet or to speed his ascent upstairs or whether the legs are held while swinging the tiny body in a punitive way or in an attempt to enforce corrective measures." *Id.*

42. *Id.* at 18; *see also* Woolley & Evans, *supra* note 21, at 541 (Woolley and Evans's corresponding findings).

43. Kempe, *supra* note 10, at 18; *cf.* Woolley & Evans, *supra* note 21, at 542 ("A history of injury in any clinical category of skeletal damage may be readily obtained, elicited only with difficulty, or not confirmed at all.").

44. Kempe, *supra* note 10, at 24; *see also* McCoid, *supra* note 10, at 18 (describing battered child syndrome as "multiple injuries in various stages of healing, primarily to the long bones and soft tissue and frequently coupled with poor hygiene and malnutrition, but peculiarly identified by the marked discrepancy between the clinical or physical findings and the historical data provided by the parents"); Cameron, Johnson & Camps, *The Battered Child Syndrome*, 6 MED. SCI. & LAW 2, 10 (1966) (other indicia of battered child syndrome are bruises indicative of fingerprints, and laceration of the skin which connects the upper lip to the gum).

45. Kempe, *supra* note 10, at 24.

46. *Id.*

flesh out the psychiatric aspects of child abusers themselves.[47] Kempe contended that at one extreme were patently psychotic child murderers, usually parents or close relatives of the child.[48] At the other extreme were anxious and guilt-ridden parents, usually mothers, who sought psychiatric help after fantasizing about hurting their children.[49] In the middle were parents whose children had suffered varying degrees of injury, and whose lives and health were at varying degrees of risk. As to these abusers, Kempe stated that

> [t]he parents, or at least the parent who inflicted the abuse, have been found to be of low intelligence. Often, they are described as psychopathic or sociopathic characters. Alcoholism, sexual promiscuity, unstable marriages, and minor criminal activities are reportedly common among them. They are immature, impulsive, self-centered, hypersensitive, and quick to react with poorly controlled aggression.[50]

Kempe emphasized that not all child abusers were poor or psychotic. In his opinion, however, even the well-educated and financially stable abuser possessed a character defect allowing unbridled expression of aggressive impulses.[51] Regardless of educational or socioeconomic status, abusers tended to adhere to a perverse "golden rule": they abused their children as their parents had abused them.[52] Thus, in Kempe's view, one could identify an abused child not only through the physical indicia of battered child syndrome, but also through a psychological assessment of the abusing parent.

The series of psychological traits thought to predispose an individual to abuse children is known as "battering parent syndrome."[53] Although Kempe worked with concededly meager psychological data,

---

47. *Id.* at 18.

48. *Id.*; *see also* Adelson, *supra* note 26 (assailant's psychosis as the most common factor in precipitating fatal assaults on children).

49. Kempe, *supra* note 10, at 18; *see also* Wecht & Larkin, *The Battered Child Syndrome — A Forensic Pathologist's Viewpoint,* in LEGAL MEDICINE 31, 32-34 (1980) (categories of child abusers).

50. Kempe, *supra* note 10, at 18. A national statistical survey of reported child abuse cases between 1976 and 1985 offers some demographic insight into child abusers. The majority of abusers were female, and white abusers far outnumbered blacks. The average abuser was in his or her early thirties; the average victim was slightly over seven years of age. 1988 STATISTICAL ABSTRACT, *supra* note 2, at 164.

51. Kempe, *supra* note 10, at 18.

52. *Id.*

53. *See, e.g.,* People v. Walkey, 177 Cal. App. 3d 268, 276-77, 223 Cal. Rptr. 132, 137 (Ct. App. 1986).

subsequent researchers have reached conclusions similar to his. In general, researchers agree that battering parents are usually former battered children.[54] Statistically, neuroses and psychoses are no more prevalent among battering parents than the population at large,[55] but certain psychological features are conspicuous. Battering parents tend to lack empathy for their children; they can neither recognize nor respond to their children's needs.[56] They also often have unrealistically high expectations of their children. These expectations can lead to the phenomenon of "role reversal," in which the parent treats the child like an adult, expecting the child to service the parent's emotional needs.[57] More generally, parents manifesting battering parent syndrome tend to be emotionally immature and disciplinarian. In addition to low self-esteem, they possess the lowest possible tolerance for inevitable childhood behaviors like crying and soiling diapers.[58]

In the years since Kempe's landmark article, the medical profession has become well-acquainted with battered child syndrome. Although classified as a medical diagnosis, obviously nothing within the victim causes the syndrome. Instead, it is directly attributable to the actions of those standing *in loco parentis* to the child. Its complement, battering parent syndrome, attempts to identify characteristics predisposing a parent to child abuse. An expert witness testifying to the presence of battered child syndrome plays the critical role of removing the rose-colored glasses through which the jury may view an accused parent. The evidentiary ramifications of such expert evidence are best analyzed by discussing the two contexts in which it is commonly used: child abuse prosecutions and homicide prosecutions.

---

54. *See, e.g.*, V. FONTANA, SOMEWHERE A CHILD IS CRYING 68 (1973); B. JUSTICE & R. JUSTICE, THE ABUSING FAMILY 92-93 (1976); Steele, *Psychodynamic Factors in Child Abuse*, in THE BATTERED CHILD 81, 83 (R. Helfer & R. Kempe eds. 1987). One author, writing about battering parents, has said, "The axiom about not being able to love when you have not known love yourself is painfully borne out in their case histories." R. INGLIS, SINS OF THE FATHERS 68 (1978).

55. Steele, *supra* note 54, at 82.

56. *Id.* at 84; *see also* Haynes-Seman, *Developmental Origins of Moral Masochism: A Failure-to-Thrive Toddler's Interactions with Mother*, 11 CHILD ABUSE & NEGLECT 319 (1987) (presenting a case study of one such parent).

57. V. FONTANA, *supra* note 54, at 64; B. JUSTICE & R. JUSTICE, *supra* note 54, at 94; Steele, *supra* note 54, at 85.

58. V. FONTANA, *supra* note 54, at 63-69; R. INGLIS, *supra* note 54, at 69; *see also* Comment, *Deliberate Premeditation, Extreme Atrocity and Cruelty, and the Battered Child Syndrome — A New Look at Criminal Culpability in Massachusetts*, 14 NEW ENG. L. REV. 812, 823 (1979) (outlining these characteristics in a discussion of the use of battering parent syndrome to mitigate guilt in a homicide prosecution).

III. BATTERED CHILD SYNDROME IN THE COURTROOM

A. *Nonfatal Child Abuse*

A California appellate court was the first to approve expert testimony on the issue of battered child syndrome.[59] In *People v. Jackson,*[60] the defendant was the live-in boyfriend of the thirteen-month-old victim's mother.[61] The mother left the child in defendant's custody, and returned home to find the child covered with burns.[62] At the hospital, a pediatrician found burns on twenty-three percent of the child's body, along with a distended abdomen, liver injury, subdural hematoma, bruises indicative of handprints, recent fractures in both forearms, and ten broken ribs.[63] The pediatrician testified at trial that these symptoms, coupled with defendant's inconsistent explanation of the initial burns, led to the diagnosis of battered child syndrome.[64] The defendant appealed his conviction, challenging the admissibility of the pediatrician's expert testimony.[65]

The California District Court of Appeal affirmed the conviction,[66] finding expert evidence of battered child syndrome admissible.[67] Defendant contended that the pediatrician's testimony constituted a personal opinion of defendant's guilt.[68] The court rejected this contention, stating that evidence of battered child syndrome "simply indicates that a child found with the type of injuries outlined above has not suffered those injuries by accidental means."[69] In other words, the expert testified only that *someone* had injured the child. From this evidence,

---

59. *See* People v. Jackson, 18 Cal. App. 3d 504, 95 Cal. Rptr. 919 (Ct. App. 1971). At least one earlier appellate court seems to have recognized evidence of battered child syndrome, although not identifying it as such, in Albritton v. State, 221 So. 2d 192 (Fla. 2d D.C.A. 1969). However, its admissibility *vel non* was not an issue before the appellate court. *Id.* at 196-98.

60. 18 Cal. App. 3d 504, 95 Cal. Rptr. 919 (Ct. App. 1971).

61. *Id.* at 506, 95 Cal. Rptr. at 920.

62. *Id.*

63. *Id.*

64. *Id.*, 95 Cal. Rptr. at 921.

65. *Id.* at 505-06, 95 Cal. Rptr. at 920. Defendant's counsel did not object to evidence of battered child syndrome at trial, and the court could have disposed of the appeal on that ground. However, the court chose to address the issue and thereby preempt a collateral attack of the conviction based upon the incompetence of counsel. *Id.* at 506, 95 Cal. Rptr. at 920.

66. *Id.* at 509, 95 Cal. Rptr. at 923.

67. *Id.* at 507, 95 Cal. Rptr. at 921.

68. *Id.*

69. *Id.* The expert testified that "'it would take thousands of children to have the severity and number and degree of injuries that this child had over the span of time that we had' by accidental means." *Id.*

the jury logically could conclude that only someone ostensibly caring for the child could inflict these injuries, because "an isolated contact with a vicious stranger would not result in this pattern of successive injuries stretching through several months."[70]

The latter statement from *Jackson* is perhaps the key to the admissibility of battered child syndrome evidence. Under the Federal Rules of Evidence, expert testimony is admissible only if it will help the fact finder understand the evidence or determine a fact in issue.[71] One might initially reject battered child syndrome evidence under this test, arguing that the injuries, once identified, speak for themselves and that the jury can draw upon its common experience and knowledge to determine the source of the injuries. Superficially, this might be an appealing argument. Yet *Jackson* shows that the injuries do not speak for themselves. The jury needs the expert to show that the injuries vary in age and occurred over time. The expert submits that the injuries could not be isolated accidents and that small children could not so injure themselves.[72] The expert testimony thus is valuable because it ties together cause and effect; it suggests a relationship between the injuries that might not otherwise occur to the jury.[73]

B.   *Homicidal Child Abuse*

In cases of nonfatal child abuse, the prosecutor uses battered child syndrome evidence primarily to prove that (1) the child could not have suffered the injuries accidentally, and (2) someone intentionally injured the child.[74] In homicide cases, however, its purpose is less clear. For example, in *State v. Tanner*,[75] the defendant was convicted of manslaughter for the death of her three-month-old daughter. The child

---

70.   *Id.*

71.   FED. R. EVID. 702.

72.   By drawing an inference of nonaccidental injury, the expert does not invade the province of the jury. The jury must still decide how much weight the expert's opinion deserves, and most importantly, whether the defendant caused the injuries. *See* State v. Toennis, 52 Wash. App. 176, 185, 758 P.2d 539, 545 (Ct. App. 1988) (citing State v. Mulder, 29 Wash. App. 513, 629 P.2d 462 (Ct. App. 1981)).

73.   *Cf.* People v. Clay, 227 Cal. App. 2d 87, 38 Cal. Rptr. 431 (Ct. App. 1964) (expert witness tying together the superficially unrelated acts of two individuals to establish the crime of till-tapping).

74.   *See, e.g.*, State v. Dumlao, 3 Conn. App. 607, 491 A.2d 404 (App. Ct. 1985); People v. DeJesus, 71 Ill. App. 3d 235, 389 N.E.2d 260 (App. Ct. 1979); State v. Durfee, 322 N.W.2d 778 (Minn. 1982).

75.   675 P.2d 539 (Utah 1983) (superseded on other grounds by rule in State v. Walker, 743 P.2d 191 (Utah 1987)).

died of "subdural hematoma associated with multiple contusions of the body."[76] Although defendant claimed the child had fallen,[77] the state's expert witness testified that the child's body displayed the characteristics of battered child syndrome, emphasizing the inadequacy of defendant's explanation for the injuries.[78] The trial court also allowed testimony regarding defendant's prior conduct toward the child.[79] On appeal, defendant challenged the trial court's admission of the state's expert testimony.[80]

The Utah Supreme Court affirmed the conviction[81] and held that a properly qualified expert witness could testify to the presence of battered child syndrome.[82] Defendant apparently argued that such evidence suggested her guilt as to prior offenses, and even if relevant, the evidence was far more prejudicial than probative.[83] The court rejected her arguments, reasoning, as did *Jackson*, that battered child syndrome evidence did not suggest the culpability of any particular individual.[84] As to the relevance of battered child syndrome evidence, the court found evidence of past injuries relevant to contradict any claim that the latest injury was accidental.[85] The court stated, however, that the evidence would be admissible whether or not a defendant raised the issue of accident or mistake.[86] Further, the court concluded that once the state established the existence of battered child syndrome, evidence of defendant's prior acts was admissible to show a pattern of conduct toward the child.[87]

Consider further in this regard *People v. Henson*,[88] in which the defendant-parents were convicted of criminally negligent homicide of

---

76. *Id.* at 541 (quoting autopsy report).

77. *Id.* at 544.

78. *Id.*

79. *Id.* at 545.

80. *Id.* at 541.

81. *Id.* at 551.

82. *Id.* at 543-44.

83. *Id.* at 543.

84. *Id.*; *see also* People v. DeJesus, 71 Ill. App. 3d 235, 389 N.E.2d 260 (App. Ct. 1979) (evidence of battered child syndrome describes only the nature of the injuries); State v. Wilkerson, 295 N.C. 559, 247 S.E.2d 905 (1978) (expert did not and would not have been allowed to testify that the child's injuries were caused by any one person).

85. *Tanner*, 675 P.2d at 543; *see also* Ashford v. State, 603 P.2d 1162, 1164 (Okla. Crim. App. 1979) ("The pattern of abuse is relevant to show the intent of the act.").

86. *Tanner*, 675 P.2d at 545. This statement appears to be only dicta, as defendant claimed that the latest injury was due to the child's fall. *Id.* at 544; *accord* People v. Kinder, 75 A.D.2d 34, 428 N.Y.S.2d 375 (App. Div. 1980).

87. *Tanner*, 675 P.2d at 549.

88. 33 N.Y.2d 63, 304 N.E.2d 358, 349 N.Y.S.2d 657 (1973).

their four-year-old son.[89] In *Henson*, the child died of bronchial pneumonia.[90] Defendants had tied the boy on his back in bed, which made it difficult for him to cough up the mucus accumulating in his throat.[91] An examining physician and the autopsy report revealed that the boy looked sallow and that his body was covered with bruises on the arms, legs, abdomen, chest, and genitals.[92] The mother attempted to explain these injuries, claiming that the boy had been falling out of bed for several days before his death, and that he had been stumbling around the house falling into furniture.[93] At trial, the prosecution attempted to introduce expert evidence of battered child syndrome; the court sustained defendants' objections to the questions.[94] The court nonetheless convicted defendants, who argued on appeal that the prosecutor's use of the phrase "battered child syndrome" in unanswered questions prejudiced the jury.[95]

The New York Court of Appeals affirmed the convictions,[96] finding the mere use of the phrase "battered child syndrome" nonprejudicial.[97] The court added that the questions would not have been prejudicial even had the trial court allowed the expert to answer, as the answers would have been relevant to prove that the boy's injuries were not accidental.[98] The court relied on the *Jackson* rationale, reasoning that the evidence would at most indicate that *someone* had injured the child.[99] This evidence of battered child syndrome, coupled with proof that the child was injured while in the sole custody of the parents, would support an inference that the parents inflicted the injuries.[100]

IV. THE EVIDENTIARY ANALYSIS

Despite its ready acceptance by the courts, battered child syndrome presents an evidentiary conundrum. That such evidence is helpful to

---

89. *Id.* at 65, 304 N.E.2d at 358-59, 349 N.Y.S.2d at 658.

90. *Id.* at 66, 304 N.E.2d at 359, 349 N.Y.S.2d at 659.

91. *Id.* at 70, 304 N.E.2d at 361, 349 N.Y.S.2d at 662. Defendants claimed the restraint "was necessary to prevent Kip [the victim] from 'wander[ing]' around and from 'pick[ing]' at scabs on his head." *Id.* at 67 n.2, 304 N.E.2d at 359 n.2, 349 N.Y.S.2d at 659 n.2.

92. *Id.* at 66, 304 N.E.2d at 359, 349 N.Y.S.2d at 658-59.

93. *Id.* at 67 n.3, 304 N.E.2d at 360 n.3, 349 N.Y.S.2d at 659 n.3.

94. *Id.* at 73, 304 N.E.2d at 363, 349 N.Y.S.2d at 664.

95. *Id.* Defendants also argued that the admission of evidence of previous injuries constituted reversible error because it was introduced to show propensity to commit the acts alleged. *Id.* at 72, 304 N.E.2d at 362, 349 N.Y.S.2d at 663.

96. *Id.* at 74, 304 N.E.2d at 364, 349 N.Y.S.2d at 666.

97. *Id.* at 73, 304 N.E.2d at 363, 349 N.Y.S.2d at 664-65.

98. *Id.*

99. *Id.* at 73-74, 304 N.E.2d at 363, 349 N.Y.S.2d at 665.

100. *Id.* at 74, 304 N.E.2d at 364, 349 N.Y.S.2d at 665-66.

jurors[101] is beyond peradventure. Thus, expert evidence of battered child syndrome should be admissible if relevant and not excluded by another rule of evidence.[102] Herein lies the evidentiary problem. Courts considering the admissibility of battered child syndrome evidence invariably reason that the evidence is relevant to prove that someone intentionally injured the child.[103] No doubt a product of the fervent desire to convict child abusers, the courts' reasoning reflects a result-oriented approach that often ignores rules of evidence. Unfortunately, these well-meaning courts have overlooked the evidentiary import of battered child syndrome.

The evidentiary analysis must first recognize that an expert testifying on the presence of battered child syndrome describes injuries the expert has observed.[104] In the expert's opinion, these injuries are themselves evidence of someone's intentional acts. That opinion without more is useless to the prosecution unless the prosecution can convince the jury that the defendant is the expert's "someone." Accordingly, the purpose of offering battered child syndrome evidence must be to prove that the defendant committed a series of prior acts, manifested by a series of prior injuries.[105]

The ultimate evidentiary issue is the admissibility of evidence of a defendant's prior acts under a given set of facts. Federal Rule of Evidence 404(b) sets forth the general rule:

> Evidence of other crimes, wrongs, or acts is not admissible to prove the character of a person in order to show that he acted in conformity therewith. It may, however, be admissible for other purposes, such as proof of motive, opportunity,

---

101. FED. R. EVID. 702.

102. FED. R. EVID. 402.

103. *See, e.g.*, State v. Moyer, 151 Ariz. 253, 727 P.2d 31 (Ct. App. 1986); People v. DeJesus, 71 Ill. App. 3d 235, 389 N.E.2d 260 (App. Ct. 1979); Bell v. Commonwealth, 684 S.W.2d 282 (Ky. Ct. App. 1984); People v. Barnard, 93 Mich. App. 590, 286 N.W.2d 870 (Ct. App. 1979); State v. Goblirsch, 309 Minn. 401, 246 N.W.2d 12 (1976); State v. Wilkerson, 295 N.C. 559, 247 S.E.2d 905 (1978); Commonwealth v. Rodgers, 364 Pa. Super. 477, 528 A.2d 610 (Super. Ct. 1987); State v. Best, 89 S.D. 227, 232 N.W.2d 447 (1975); State v. Mulder, 29 Wash. App. 513, 629 P.2d 462 (Ct. App. 1981).

104. People v. DeJesus, 71 Ill. App. 3d 235, 236, 389 N.E.2d 260, 261 (App. Ct. 1979).

105. *Cf. Tanner*, 675 P.2d at 553 (Stewart, J., dissenting) ("The majority asserts that the battered child syndrome evidence is not accusatory and only describes the cause of death . . . and on the other hand admits that such evidence incriminates the parents."); McCoid, *supra* note 10, at 18 (battered child syndrome "is really descriptive of a pattern of conduct on the part of the parents or others who are to guard the welfare of the child").

intent, preparation, plan, knowledge, identity, or absence of mistake or accident.[106]

Clearly, the prosecution cannot use evidence of prior acts to establish that the defendant has a criminal character and therefore more likely committed the act in question.[107] The prosecution may, however, introduce evidence of prior acts to establish motive, intent, or any of the other elements listed in Rule 404(b), provided that one of those elements actually is at issue.[108] Finally, the evidence must have sufficient probative value to outweigh its potential prejudice to the defendant.[109]

Viewing battered child syndrome as evidence of prior acts demonstrates the correctness of *Jackson*. The statute under which Jackson was convicted of child beating provided, in pertinent part:

> Any person who, under circumstances or conditions likely to produce great bodily harm or death, willfully *causes or permits any child to suffer*, or inflicts thereon unjustifiable physical pain or mental suffering, or having the care or custody of any child, willfully *causes or permits the person or health of such child to be injured*, or willfully causes or permits such child to be placed in such situation that its person or health is endangered, is punishable by imprisonment . . . .[110]

Under this statute, defendant may have been guilty of willfully causing the child to suffer, or causing injury to the child's health. These offenses do not necessarily arise from a single act; rather, the statutory language suggests offenses of a continuing nature. Thus, the injuries upon which the expert in *Jackson* based the diagnosis of battered

---

106. FED. R. EVID. 404(b).

107. *Id.*; Michelson v. United States, 335 U.S. 469 (1948); C. McCORMICK, EVIDENCE § 190 (3d ed. 1984); *see also* United States v. Myers, 550 F.2d 1036, 1044 (5th Cir. 1977) ("a defendant must be tried for what he did, not for who he is"), *cert. denied*, 439 U.S. 847 (1978).

108. C. McCORMICK, *supra* note 107, at § 190.

109. *Id.*; FED. R. EVID. 403.

110. CAL. PENAL CODE § 273a(1) (West 1973) (amended 1976, 1980, 1984) (emphasis added) (cited in *Jackson*, 18 Cal. App. 3d at 505, 95 Cal. Rptr. at 920). The opinion is unclear as to whether defendant was convicted under this subsection or subsection (2), which proscribes the same acts under circumstances or conditions other than those likely to produce great bodily harm or death. *See id.* § 273(a)(2); *Jackson*, 18 Cal. App. 3d at 505-06, 95 Cal. Rptr. at 920. Defendant also faced conviction under § 273d, which punished "[a]ny person who willfully inflicts upon any child any cruel or inhuman corporal punishment or injury resulting in a traumatic condition." CAL. PENAL CODE § 273d (West 1973) (cited in *Jackson*, 18 Cal. App. 3d at 505, 95 Cal. Rptr. at 920).

child syndrome were not prior acts in relation to the offense charged. Instead, the injuries manifested the very acts constituting the offense. The *Jackson* court therefore correctly reasoned that the expert evidence was relevant to prove that someone intentionally injured the child.[111] By proving that defendant ostensibly was caring for the child at the time the injuries were inflicted,[112] the prosecution could establish defendant's guilt under the relevant statute.[113]

Although the reasoning of *Henson* is blurrier than *Jackson*, one can square the *Henson* court's admission of battered child syndrome evidence on the same grounds. In *Henson*, the state's medical expert testified that while pneumonia was the "terminal event" causing the boy's death, the several injuries he suffered in his last days contributed to his death.[114] This testimony indicates that a series of acts, manifested by the injuries, caused the boy's death. Therefore, just as in *Jackson*, evidence of battered child syndrome would have established the very acts constituting the *actus reus* of homicide. Although the defendants in *Henson* were convicted anyway, evidence of battered child syndrome, coupled with proof that defendants had sole custody of the boy,[115] might have tied defendants even more strongly to the abusive acts.[116]

Although not addressed in the opinion, the excluded evidence arguably was admissible on at least two other grounds. First, defendants were convicted of criminally negligent homicide,[117] which the court defined as "'a culpable failure to perceive a substantial and unjustifiable risk' of death, constituting 'a gross deviation from the standard of care that a reasonable [parent] would observe.'"[118] Thus, the "intent" the prosecution had to prove was defendants' failure to perceive the

---

111. *Jackson*, 18 Cal. App. 3d at 507, 95 Cal. Rptr. at 921.

112. *Id.*

113. *Id.*; *see also* State v. Dumlao, 3 Conn. App. 607, 491 A.2d 404 (App. Ct. 1985), in which the prosecution used expert evidence of battered child syndrome to support a conviction under CONN. GEN. STAT. § 53-21 (1983). That statute proscribed causing or permitting a child under the age of 16 "'to be placed in such a situation that its life or limb is endangered, or its health is likely to be injured,'" as well as doing "'any act likely to impair the health . . . of any such child.'" *Id.* at 608 n.2, 491 A.2d at 408 n.2 (quoting CONN. GEN. STAT. § 53-21 (1983)).

114. *Henson*, 33 N.Y.2d at 71, 304 N.E.2d at 362, 349 N.Y.S.2d at 662.

115. *Id.* at 74, 304 N.E.2d at 364, 349 N.Y.S.2d at 665-66.

116. Whether this actually would have been necessary is another matter altogether, as the court found the evidence of guilt "overwhelming." *Id.* at 68, 304 N.E.2d at 360, 349 N.Y.S.2d at 660.

117. *Id.* at 65, 304 N.E.2d at 358-59, 349 N.Y.S.2d at 658.

118. *Id.* at 69, 304 N.E.2d at 361, 349 N.Y.S.2d at 661.

risk while under a legal duty to do so.[119] By showing defendants' conduct toward the child in the days immediately prior to his death, the prosecution might have established the indifference with which defendants viewed their son's plight. Of course, the court would then have had to conclude that the probative value of the evidence outweighed its prejudice.[120] The *Henson* court obviously was willing to reach this conclusion,[121] thus the evidence should have been admissible to prove defendants' intent.

Second, evidence of battered child syndrome should have been admissible to prove that the boy's injuries were not caused accidentally.[122] This issue arose in *Henson* when the defendant-mother insisted the boy was accident-prone.[123] The trial court admitted the testimony of several witnesses regarding the boy's injuries of previous years and the mother's constant claims of accidental injury.[124] If evidence of previous injuries was admissible to refute a claim of accidental injury, then evidence of battered child syndrome should have been admissible to prove the same thing.

In short, the New York Court of Appeals' analysis in *Henson*, while somewhat simplistic and incomplete, was correct. In contrast, the Utah Supreme Court's decision in *Tanner* reflects a hopelessly flawed analysis of battered child syndrome evidence. The autopsy report in *Tanner* stated that the child died of "'subdural hematoma associated with multiple contusions of the body.'"[125] This statement reflects that the child died from the subdural hematoma, and that the subdural hematoma and contusions somehow were related. The statement does not say the child died of multiple contusions. Therefore, the act constituting manslaughter in *Tanner* was the act causing the subdural hematoma, not the acts causing the contusions. The evidence of battered child syndrome, which in effect indicated that defendant intentionally inflicted these other injuries, thus was evidence of defendant's prior acts. The court therefore should have assessed its admissibility under Utah's equivalent of Rule 404(b).[126]

---

119. *Id.*, 304 N.E.2d at 360, 349 N.Y.S.2d at 660-61 (quoting People v. Haney, 30 N.Y.2d 328, 333, 284 N.E.2d 564, 567, 333 N.Y.S.2d 403, 407 (1972)).

120. *See* FED. R. EVID. 403.

121. *See Henson*, 33 N.Y.2d at 73, 304 N.E.2d at 363, 349 N.Y.S.2d at 664.

122. FED. R. EVID. 404(b); *see also supra* text accompanying note 106 (text of rule).

123. *Henson*, 33 N.Y.2d at 71, 304 N.E.2d at 362, 349 N.Y.S.2d at 663; *see also supra* text accompanying note 93 (describing mother's claims regarding cause of injuries).

124. *Henson*, 33 N.Y.2d at 71-72, 304 N.E.2d at 362, 349 N.Y.S.2d at 663.

125. *Tanner*, 675 P.2d at 541.

126. *See id.* at 552-53 (Stewart, J., dissenting) (quoting UTAH R. EVID. 55 (amended 1983, current version at UTAH R. EVID. 404(b), which permitted evidence of a defendant's prior acts

Instead, the *Tanner* court's analysis circumvented whether evidence of prior acts was admissible under the facts of the case. The court cited *Jackson* for the proposition that the evidence was relevant to show that the injuries did not occur accidentally.[127] The court reasoned that once a court admitted battered child syndrome evidence, it could also admit specific prior acts to prove a pattern of conduct toward the child.[128] In child abuse cases, the court contended, evidence of specific prior acts established a defendant's abusive pattern of conduct, rather than a general propensity for violence.[129]

Two flaws exist in the *Tanner* court's analysis. First, contrary to the court's assertion, *Tanner* was a homicide case, not a "child abuse" case. Unlike *Jackson* and *Henson*, the abusive acts to which the *Tanner* court referred did not constitute the offense for which defendant was convicted. In *Tanner*, evidence of battered child syndrome truly was "prior act" evidence; the majority's failure to recognize this was its second analytical flaw. A court engaged in more thoughtful evidentiary analysis would have asked whether evidence of battered child syndrome was relevant to prove something other than defendant's propensity for violence. Instead, the court's bootstrapping rationale allowed evidence of prior acts, masquerading as evidence of battered child syndrome, to create an issue justifying the admission of more prior acts.

Had the *Tanner* court correctly analyzed the evidentiary issue, not only would it have reached the same result, it would have provided future courts with an analytically sound point of departure. Battered child syndrome evidence should have been admissible in *Tanner*, as in *Henson*, to prove either absence of accident or intent.[130] The *Tanner* court upheld the trial court's admission of defendant's specific prior acts toward the child, reasoning that defendant's claim to physicians and police that the child had fallen raised the issue of accident.[131] Had the court recognized that battered child syndrome evidence really described defendant's prior acts, it would have upheld its admissibility on that basis.

---

to be admitted to prove "some other material fact including absence of mistake or accident, motive, opportunity, intent, preparation, plan, knowledge or identity" and arguing that the admission of battered child syndrome evidence violated this rule)).

127. *Tanner*, 675 P.2d at 542.

128. *Id.* at 549.

129. *Id.* at 546.

130. *See supra* note 126 (quoting pertinent provisions of UTAH R. EVID. 55, allowing admission to prove, among other things, intent or absence of accident or mistake).

131. *Tanner*, 675 P.2d at 547-48.

As to intent, defendant's manslaughter conviction under Utah law meant she recklessly caused the death of another.[132] Thus, the prosecution had to prove that defendant consciously disregarded a substantial and unjustifiable risk that the child would die.[133] Evidence of the way in which defendant acted in the face of an ever-increasing risk to the child's life should have been relevant to prove defendant's conscious disregard of that risk. Indeed, battered child syndrome evidence could have been the only way to prove the requisite intent, absent evidence of defendant's specific prior abusive acts. This evidentiary subtlety unfortunately was lost on the *Tanner* court; it admitted the battered child syndrome evidence to prove only that someone intentionally injured the child.[134]

A blanket application of the *Jackson* court's rationale will not apply in every case involving an abused child. In cases that involve continuing offenses, the *Jackson* analysis, although perhaps less lucid than it could be, is essentially correct. In cases that involve noncontinuing offenses, however, courts must apply Rule 404(b) or the state equivalent to reach the right result for the right reasons. While this analysis occasionally may result in the exclusion of battered child syndrome evidence,[135] courts must uniformly apply the rules of evidence. Having analyzed the evidentiary wrinkles of battered child syndrome, one must next consider those of its complement, battering parent syndrome.

V. BATTERING PARENT SYNDROME

Battering parent syndrome differs from battered child syndrome by describing character traits considered common in child abusers rather than manifestations of the abuse itself.[136] The two types of

---

132. *See* UTAH CODE ANN. § 76-5-205(1)(a) (1978) (amended 1985).

133. *Id.* § 76-2-103(3).

134. *Tanner*, 675 P.2d at 543.

135. For example, if the defendant concedes from the outset that the child has been battered, but claims not to have been the abuser, battered child syndrome evidence arguably would be admissible only to prove the identity of the assailant. To prove identity by prior acts, courts generally require that the acts be so identical as to be like the accused's signature. *See, e.g.,* United States v. Beasley, 809 F.2d 1273, 1277 (7th Cir. 1987); United States v. Myers, 550 F.2d 1036, 1045-46 (5th Cir. 1977), *cert. denied,* 439 U.S. 847 (1978); C. McCORMICK, *supra* note 107, at § 190. A battering parent might not resort to any one particular technique of abuse. As a result, the injuries the child manifests may be so dissimilar that the court would refuse to admit them into evidence.

136. *See supra* notes 53-58 and accompanying text.

evidence are similar, however, in that they trigger rules proscribing the use of character evidence.[137] Because battering parent syndrome evidence describes character traits rather than prior acts, Federal Rule of Evidence 404(a) governs its admissibility. The rule states that "evidence of a person's character or a trait of his character is not admissible for the purpose of proving that he acted in conformity therewith on a particular occasion . . . ."[138] An important exception to this rule is that a criminal defendant may introduce evidence of his or her good character. If the defendant so chooses, the prosecution may then introduce evidence of the defendant's bad character.[139] Battering parent syndrome and Rule 404(a) thus appear to be at loggerheads; a plain reading of the rule seems to bar the prosecution from introducing such evidence in its case-in-chief.

Guided by the precepts of this rule, every appellate court considering the issue has held that the prosecution cannot introduce evidence of battering parent syndrome unless the defendant first raises the issue of his or her own good character.[140] These courts uniformly reason that the prejudicial nature of battering parent syndrome evidence renders it inadmissible.[141] Despite this recognition of prejudice, how-

---

137. For a discussion of the general problems that psychological profile evidence presents, see Note, *The Syndrome Syndrome: Problems Concerning the Admissibility of Expert Testimony on Psychological Profiles*, 37 U. FLA. L. REV. 1035 (1985) (suggesting that the admissibility of novel psychological profile evidence turn on factors concerning relevance, that the "helpfulness" requirement of expert evidence be interpreted liberally, and that the fear of invading the jury's province affect weight rather than admissibility).

138. FED. R. EVID. 404(a).

139. FED. R. EVID. 404(a)(1); FED. R. EVID. 404 advisory committee's note.

140. *See* People v. Walkey, 177 Cal. App. 3d 268, 223 Cal. Rptr. 132 (Ct. App. 1986); Sanders v. State, 251 Ga. 70, 303 S.E.2d 13 (1983); Duley v. State, 56 Md. App. 275, 467 A.2d 776 (Ct. Spec. App. 1983); State v. Loebach, 310 N.W.2d 58 (Minn. 1981); *cf. In re Cheryl H.*, 153 Cal. App. 3d 1098, 200 Cal. Rptr. 789 (Ct. App. 1984) (expert testimony that defendant possessed character traits predisposing him toward sexual abuse was inadmissible character evidence); State v. Maule, 35 Wash. App. 287, 667 P.2d 96 (Ct. App. 1983) (admission of expert testimony that defendant was a member of a class predisposed toward child sexual abuse constituted reversible error).

141. *See, e.g.*, People v. Walkey, 177 Cal. App. 3d 268, 223 Cal. Rptr. 132 (Ct. App. 1986); Sanders v. State, 251 Ga. 70, 303 S.E.2d 13 (1983); Duley v. State, 56 Md. App. 275, 467 A.2d 776 (Ct. Spec. App. 1983); State v. Loebach, 310 N.W.2d 58 (Minn. 1981). Minnesota seems initially to have required evidence of battering parent syndrome to render evidence of battered child syndrome admissible. State v. Loss, 295 Minn. 271, 204 N.W.2d 404 (1973). The Minnesota Supreme Court disclaimed any such requirement three years later in State v. Goblirsch, 309 Minn. 401, 246 N.W.2d 12 (1976). Finally, in 1981, the same court found battering parent syndrome evidence inadmissible unless the defendant placed his character at issue. *Loebach*, 310 N.W.2d at 58.

ever, the courts consistently have upheld convictions of defendants against whom such evidence is introduced on the grounds of harmless error.[142]

In no reported case has the defendant placed his or her character in issue, thereby allowing the prosecution to introduce evidence of battering parent syndrome. Should it arise, such a case would present a far more interesting issue: whether evidence of battering parent syndrome should be admissible at all. The Federal Rules of Evidence attempt to resolve this issue by asking whether such evidence would be helpful to the fact finder.[143] To be helpful, of course, the evidence must be relevant to a fact in issue,[144] and the relevancy of scientific testimony is a function of its reliability.[145] Thus, if the defendant opens the door to the admission of bad character evidence, the specific issue becomes whether the underlying theory of battering parent syndrome is reliable enough to be relevant to prove a particular defendant committed a particular act of child abuse.

Even in the absence of guiding precedent, courts must answer this question in the negative. To admit the evidence would be to concede that human beings are so much a product of their background that they cannot help but behave according to statistical prediction. Such evidence would render the defendant a mere automaton in the jury's eyes. Certainly, the prosecution should be able to introduce evidence of the defendant's temper, emotional maturity, and manner of responding to the child.[146] After all, the defendant has opened the door to this evidence. However, lay testimony on these points should be sufficient to allow the jury to resolve any issue concerning the defendant's character. An expert's opinion would add little probative value to the equation.[147]

On the other hand, such testimony obviously has prejudicial effect. By identifying the defendant as one who manifests characteristics of battering parents, the expert places the defendant in a most loathsome

---

142. People v. Walkey, 177 Cal. App. 3d 268, 223 Cal. Rptr. 132 (Ct. App. 1986); Sanders v. State, 251 Ga. 70, 303 S.E.2d 13 (1983); Duley v. State, 56 Md. App. 275, 467 A.2d 776 (Ct. Spec. App. 1983); Loebach, 310 N.W.2d at 58.

143. FED. R. EVID. 702.

144. See FED. R. EVID. 402.

145. P. Gianelli, The Admissibility of Novel Scientific Evidence: Frye v. United States, A Half-Century Later, 80 COLUM. L. REV. 1197, 1235 (1980).

146. See supra notes 50-58 and accompanying text.

147. See Duley v. State, 56 Md. App. 275, 281, 467 A.2d 776, 780 (Ct. Spec. App. 1983) ("Such evidence is totally irrelevant because it does not tend to prove that [defendant] committed the acts of abuse attributed to him.").

class.[148] Theoretically, the evidence is irrelevant because it does no more than associate the defendant with a class of persons who, in the expert's opinion, often abuse children.[149] Realistically, however, the evidence simply stamps the defendant with the scientific community's imprimatur of guilt. The expert's opinion forces into a statistical framework the collected character traits upon which laypersons commonly base their character judgments.[150] Unfortunately, a jury confronted with such evidence may be dazzled by the expert and forget the impossibility of predicting human behavior beyond a reasonable doubt.[151]

VI. CONCLUSION

Battered child syndrome is a well-accepted medical diagnosis in both the physician's office and the courtroom. Every court considering the issue has admitted expert evidence of battered child syndrome,[152] yet almost all have done so on faulty reasoning. Courts have failed to recognize that such evidence is really disguised evidence of prior acts, the admissibility of which depends on evidentiary rules relating to proof of character. This sounder analytical framework usually would yield the same result and would provide courts initially considering the issue with the proper analytical point of departure.

Battering parent syndrome stands on another evidentiary footing. Expert evidence on this syndrome is inadmissible at least until the defendant raises the issue of his or her good character. No court has

---

148. *See id.*

149. *Id.*

150. *Cf. id.* (battering parent syndrome evidence "is no different than allowing an expert to testify that most homicides are committed by men. From that point of reference, only a dolt would not include [defendant] within the scope of the comment.").

151. *But see* State v. Conlogue, 474 A.2d 167 (Me. 1984), which on different facts flies in the face of the foregoing analysis. In *Conlogue*, defendant attempted to introduce evidence of battering parent syndrome in the victim's mother to prove that her earlier confession of guilt had been true and her subsequent recantation false. *Id.* at 172. The trial court excluded this evidence under Maine's identical counterpart to FED. R. EVID. 404(a). *Id.* The Supreme Judicial Court of Maine reversed the conviction, holding that the defendant's proffer was not of character evidence. *Id.* The holding seems grounded in the court's desire to give defendant every opportunity to exculpate himself. From an evidentiary standpoint, however, the dissent made the better argument. *See id.* at 173 (Scolnik, J., dissenting). The dissent recognized that the excluded evidence was offered to prove that the mother was an abusive parent who acted in conformity with her character on a given occasion. *Id.* at 174. *Conlogue* is perhaps best described as an aberration, and is offered here as such.

152. *See supra* note 12 and cases cited therein.

had the opportunity to consider whether such evidence should be admissible at all. As such evidence places the defendant within a class of typical child abusers, however, it provides the quintessential example of trying defendants for who they are, rather than for what they have done.[153] The expert can add nothing positive to the jury's understanding of defendants' character traits, but can tremendously prejudice these defendants by statistically declaring them child abusers.

In their laudable fervor to punish child abuse, courts still must adhere to fundamental rules of evidence. The rules exist to guarantee fair results based on objective standards. The odium with which the public views certain offenses cannot justify deviating from evidentiary norms. Accordingly, while courts should almost always admit evidence of battered child syndrome, they should not admit evidence of battering parent syndrome. Although the suggested analytical framework may change few results, the integrity of the adversary process requires that proper reasons support proper results.

---

153. *See* United States v. Myers, 550 F.2d 1036, 1044 (5th Cir. 1977) ("a defendant must be tried for what he did, not for who he is"), *cert. denied*, 439 U.S. 847 (1978).

Behavioral Sciences and the Law, Vol. 9, 201–215 (1991)

Expert Witnesses in Child Abuse Cases

Inger J. Sagatun, Ph.D.

This article discusses the need for expert testimony and the criteria for admissibility of such testimony in child abuse cases. It addresses the scope of expert testimony in both physical and sexual abuse cases with respect to (a) descriptive and diagnostic issues, (b) witness credibility issues, and (c) legal issues. In particular, the article focuses on the admissibility of expert testimony on the battered child syndrome, the child sexual abuse accommodation syndrome, and observations of behavior with anatomically correct dolls. The article concludes that medical expert testimony is more admissible in court than mental health expert testimony.

From a legal standpoint, child abuse is often difficult to prove. Maltreatment occurs in secret, and the child may be the only witness. Often the child may be too young to testify, or the testimony may be suspect precisely because the victim is a child. The problems created by a lack of testimony from the child victim are often compounded by a lack of clear physical evidence.

One way in which information relating to whether a child has been abused can be presented to the court is through an expert witness. More and more frequently, attorneys are turning to expert witnesses in child abuse cases. In theory, an expert witness can take the witness stand and give an opinion that based on the observations of the child he/she concludes that the child was physically or sexually abused. If the testimony is admissible and is sufficiently persuasive, the allegation can be found to be true even though the child may never have testified.

This article will discuss when expert testimony is admissible in court, and what types of questions experts are allowed to address. Expert testimony here refers primarily to either medical or mental health psychological/psychiatric testimony.

The use of experts in child abuse cases is not without controversy. As legal disputes become more complicated, lawyers and courts need experts with specialized knowledge and education to evaluate a case, help prepare litigation, or express an opinion. In complex cases, each side frequently has at least one expert. The result is often a battle of conflicting opinions. As the number of child abuse cases reaching the courtroom has increased, legal scholars have begun to examine the legal and scientific status of expert testimony in these cases (Borgida, Gresham, Swim, Bull, & Gray, 1989). The professional controversy generated by the admission of expert testimony in child abuse cases has become heated both within the psychological and legal

Inger J. Sagatun, Ph.D., is Professor of Administration of Justice at San Jose State University. Address reprint requests and correspondence to the author at Administration of Justice Department, San Jose State University, One Washington Square, San Jose, CA, 95192, USA.

0735-3936/91/020201-15$07.50

communities. For example, Faust and Ziskin (1988) argue that many clinicians seem to experience role conflict when they enter the legal arena as expert witnesses, and that they often become biased adversaries when they enter the unfamiliar court-room. Similarly, Levy (1989) argues that child abuse experts tend to be fiercely committed to the role of the child's advocate, and that often their objectivity and professional credibility must be called into question.

Allegations of child sexual abuse may be litigated in several different types of legal proceedings: criminal prosecution, dependency proceedings in juvenile court, child custody and visitation litigation in family court, proceedings to terminate paren-tal rights, civil proceedings brought by victims against perpetrators for monetary damages, or in civil litigation against social welfare agencies. The form of expert testimony will vary with the type of litigation involved (Myers, Bays, Becker, Berliner, Corwyn & Saywitz, 1989). Rules of evidence governing expert testimony vary some-what from state to state, but the law relating to expert testimony is similar across the U.S.

THE ADMISSIBILITY OF EXPERT TESTIMONY

In order for expert testimony to be admissible in courts of law the person testifying must first be qualified as an expert. In determining who is qualified to testify as an expert on child abuse, the courts should insist on a thorough showing of expertise before ruling that an individual is qualified. According to section 702 of the Federal Rules of Evidence (1990) and section 720(a) of the California Evidence Code (Stan-dard California Codes, 1990):

> A person is qualified to testify as an expert if he/she has special knowledge, skill, experience, training or education sufficient to qualify him or her as an expert on the subject to which his/her testimony relates. Against the objection of a party, such special knowledge, skill, experience, training, or education must be shown before the witness may testify as an expert

(Federal Rules of Evidences §702, 1990; Standard California Codes, Evidence Code Section 720(a), 1990, p. 20).

Secondly, in order for expert testimony to be admissible in courts of law, there must first be a judicial finding that:

(1) the testimony is relevant to the issue at hand,
(2) that the basis for the testimony is generally accepted by the scientific com-munity as reliable and valid, and
(3) that the testimony adds to the jurors' and the courts' understanding of the facts in the case.

The Issue of Relevance

Admissibility of expert testimony at trial depends first of all on a judicial finding that the testimony is relevant to the issues at hand. This means that the court must find a logical connection between the evidence presented by the expert and the issues that must be proved. The court must first evaluate the reliability of the evidence, and second balance the probative value and reliability of the evidence against factors mitigating against admission. (Myers *et al.*, 1989). For example, the more directly related the testimony is to a contested issue, the greater the need for the evidence, but the greater the potential harm if the testimony is unreliable or misused. The issue of relevance is particularly important with respect to expert testimony in child abuse cases where other types of evidence are often sorely lacking.

Acceptance in the Scientific Community

Another traditional requirement for acceptance of expert testimony is that the state of scientific knowledge in the relevant area must permit a reasonable opinion to be asserted by an expert (*Dyas v. U.S.*, 1977). To find that expert testimony is generally accepted by the relevant scientific community, the testimony must be subjected to the important *Frye* rule (*Frye v. United States*, 1923; *People v. Kelly*, 1976). According to this rule the evidence must be based on principles sufficiently established to have gained general acceptance in the particular field to which it belongs. While testimony subjected to the *Frye* rule has traditionally involved novel devices manipulating physical evidence (*People v. McDonald*, 1984), in recent years the test has also been applied to other types of evidence. In an important California Appellate Court decision (*In re Amber B*, 1987) the court found that the use of anatomically correct dolls to determine if a child had been sexually abused constituted a "new scientific tool" and hence would have to "pass" the *Frye* rule before expert testimony based on these observations could be admitted into evidence.

One of the criticisms of the *Frye* rule has been the difficulty in determining what should be classified as a new "scientific principle or discovery," (Giannelli, 1980). The critics charge that the test is too vague and that it is unclear when evidence can be considered acceptable by the scientific community (Myers, 1989). Faust and Ziskin (1988) argue that the clinical judgment of therapists is not reliable or valid enough to be used in court as expert testimony. According to their review of psychological studies, serious doubts must be raised about the diagnostic reliability of psychological tests, including, presumably, the use of anatomically correct dolls.

Testimony Adds to the Jurors' Understanding

The final court criterion for admitting testimony from expert witnesses is whether the expert has knowledge or information the jury would not otherwise have and which it would find useful in making findings of facts or law (Section 702 of the Federal Rules of Evidence). The expert's testimony must elucidate the basic understanding of the court or jury. The central issue here is whether the expert opinion will help the trier of fact to come to a rational determination. According to Levy (1989), this criterion has now become more important than satisfying the *Frye* rule of scientific acceptability.

The degree to which expert testimony in the area of child abuse can add to the jurors' understanding is also a subject for debate. According to Faust and Ziskin (1988) professional clinicians (psychologists) do not in fact make more accurate clinical judgment than laypersons. In response, Fowler and Matarazzo (1988) note that professional clinical assessments are more complex, but that it is difficult to translate such complex analyses into the simple "yes" or "no" responses required by the court. Recently, the Hawaii Supreme Court examined the admissibility of expert testimony in a child abuse case and concluded that even objective opinions of experts regarding a victim's credibility are no more reliable than the determination by the triers of fact (*State v. Batangan*, 1990).

THE SCOPE OF EXPERT TESTIMONY

In most legal proceedings involving child abuse, several important questions need to be answered. In order to get an answer to these questions the court may turn to expert testimony for help. Generally, courts face many descriptive or diagnostic issues, issues of witness credibility, and issues regarding the alleged legal facts in the case (e.g., whether the child was abused and who committed the abuse).

Descriptive and Diagnostic Issues

Important issues that may be presented in litigation include:

(1) What are the characteristics of abuse?
(2) What are the behaviors commonly observed in sexually abused children?
(3) Does the alleged victim have these characteristics and does he/she fit the "profile" of an abused child?
(4) Does the alleged offender fit an "offender profile"?

Meyer *et al.* (1989) note that appellate courts have held that the expert may give testimony as to descriptions of commonly observed behaviors in victims so long as they do not give an opinion whether the alleged victim was abused. Experts often also testify that *victims as a class* have certain characteristics which are consistent with what the *specific victim* states to have happened. This permits the expert to state something which does not directly address the third question above, but which nevertheless helps the jury to draw its own conclusions. The expert is not testifying that the alleged victim has the relevant characteristics of abuse, but that what the victim is describing is consistent with the characteristics of other persons in general who may have experienced similar events. In practice this is often what expert testimony does. This type of testimony, however, is complicated by the fact that reactions of victims to abusive behavior vary widely, and there are no fully established or agreed upon observable indicators of an "abused child victim profile."

In most cases experts are able to address what the characteristics of abuse are and whether the alleged victim has these characteristics. If the expert is testifying about victims as a class, it is up to the jury or the court as trier of fact to decide that because the alleged victim demonstrates behavior commonly seen in abused children, the victim probably was abused.

The expert may also be asked to address the issue of whether the alleged offender fits the "profile" of a child abuser (e.g., *People v. Lucero*, 1986). In a California state supreme court case (*People v. Stoll*, 1989), the court determined that expert testimony on whether the defendant fit the profile of an abuser need not be subjected to the *Frye* rule. Specifically the court held that the *Frye* rule did not apply to a psychologist's opinion based upon interviews and professional interpretations of standardized written personality tests. Note that this is one of the few cases that has allowed such testimony. More than 20 other states and federal courts have considered similar testimony and rejected it. In general, courts have found any kind of "profile testimony" to be unreliable.

Witness Credibility

Secondly, the court or jury must evaluate several issues related to witness credibility such as:

(1) is the child witness telling the truth?

(2) is the alleged perpetrator telling the truth?

Experts often testify generally about the capabilities of child witnesses (McCord, 1986). Expert testimony has also been used to enhance the child victim witness credibility by explaining any "unusual" behavior questioned by the defense (*People v. Dunnahoo*, 1984). Another category involves cases wherein an expert directly vouches for the complainant's credibility as a witness to the alleged sexual abuse, such as in *State v. Kim* (1982). (Parts of this ruling were later over-ruled in *State v. Batangan*, 1990.) According to *State v. Myers* (1984), the common experience of a jury may represent a less than adequate foundation for assessing the credibility of a young child who complains of sexual abuse. However, while experts may testify about the credibility of the various witnesses in court, it is still up to the jury or trier of fact to determine if the witness told the truth.

Serrato (1988) divides expert psychological testimony into several categories. The lesser impact categories include psychological testimony constituting a denial of defense claims, general testimony on common characteristics of sexually abused children, testimony about the general validity of child sexual abuse complaints, and expert opinion on the validity of a particular child witness. More important testimony involves linking general characteristics of sexually abused children with the particular child witness.

Legal Questions about the Alleged Facts

Thirdly, the court or jury needs to address the ultimate *legal* questions of:

(1)   whether the alleged victim was actually abused or traumatized in some way?, and/or

(2)   whether the alleged offender committed the abuse?

Expert testimony involving the diagnosis of sexual abuse has been used to "prove" that the abuse occurred (*State v. Myers*, 1984). However, as a rule courts have not allowed experts to address these important issues. As stated in the recent opinion, *State v. Batangan* (1990 p. 49):

> while testimony explaining "seemingly bizarre" behavior of child sex abuse victims is helpful to the jury and should be admitted, conclusionary opinions that abuse did occur and that the child victim's report of abuse is truthful and believable is of no assistance to the jury, and therefore, should not be admitted.

Courts agree that the expert *cannot* testify in the form of legal conclusions as to whether abuse occurred and, if so, who committed the abuse. Expert testimony may take the form of an opinion, an exposition of scientific principles relevant to the case, or an answer to a hypothetical question propounded by counsel. (Myers *et al.*, 1989). This sometimes creates problems in deciding whether an expert has crossed over from a professional opinion about child abuse to a legal opinion that the abuse occurred *(Johnson v. State*, 1987). Experts may not give opinions which in effect usurp the basic functions of the jury *(State v. Batangan*, 1990).

What is permissible expert testimony varies considerably depending on the type of court involved, the issue involved, the stage of the proceedings, and which side is presenting the expert witness. In order to examine in more detail when experts have been allowed to address and answer the questions listed above, we will now focus specifically on the different use of expert testimony in physical and sexual abuse cases. First, we will look at the field of physical child abuse and testimony on the battered child syndrome. Secondly, we will look at the field of sexual child abuse with testimony on the child sexual abuse accommodation theory and the use of anatomically correct dolls.

PHYSICAL ABUSE

Physical child abuse is legally defined as non-accidental physical injury to a child. The law often turns to experts in order to determine whether a child has been physically abused. Expert medical testimony may be indispensable to counter claims that the child's injuries were accidental (Berliner, 1988). When allegations of physical abuse are tried in court, the prosecution must first prove that the child's injuries were non-accidental, and second establish the identity of the perpetrator (Myers; 1989). In the past, expert testimony on physical abuse was restricted to a description of the nature of the injuries, and conclusions regarding whether a particular pattern of injuries was the result of abuse was left to the jury to make. In the last two decades, however, expert testimony on "the battered child syndrome" has been used to establish that a child's injuries were not accidental.

The Battered Child Syndrome

The term "battered child syndrome" was first coined by Kempe and his colleagues (Kempe, Silverman, Steele, Droegemueller & Silver, 1962). The battered child syndrome refers to a child who has received repeated and/or serious injuries by non-accidental means. Children with battered child syndrome usually show signs of repeated abuse, with injuries in different stages of healing. Characteristically, these injuries are inflicted by someone who is ostensibly caring for the child. Several elements are included in the "battered child syndrome". They are: (a) the child is usually under three years of age, (b) there is evidence of bone injury at different times, (c) there are subdural hematomas with or without skull fractures, (d) there is a seriously injured child who does not have a history that fits the injuries, (e) there is evidence of soft tissue injury, and (f) there is evidence of neglect. The battered child syndrome simply indicates that a child found with the type of injuries outlined above has not suffered those injuries by accidental means (Kempe *et al.*, 1962).

Not all physically abused children suffer from the battered child syndrome (Zumwalt & Hirsch, 1987). According to Zumwalt and Hirsch, many child fatalities result from a single beating or abuse.

The use of the battered child syndrome in court was affirmed in *People v. Jackson* (1971) based on the finding that the diagnosis of the "battered child syndrome" had become an accepted medical diagnosis (see Barta & Smith, 1963; Harper, 1963; Helfer & Kempe, 1968; McCoid, 1965; Paulson & Blake, 1967). Since *Jackson*, expert testimony on the syndrome has been routinely approved (e.g., *State v. Dumlao*, 1985; *State v. Tanner*, 1983). Nyers (1989) notes that every appellate court to consider expert testimony on the syndrome has approved such testimony. The "battered child syndrome" is now used as a well known medical diagnosis of physical child abuse (Helfer & Kempe, 1987; Schmitt, Bross, Caroll, Gray & Crosz, 1978).

Since the *Jackson* case, courts have allowed medical expert testimony on the *battered child* syndrome to do all of the following: (a) describe what the characteristics of abuse look like, (b) express an opinion as to whether the child in question exhibits the characteristics, and (c) express a professional opinion as to whether the child in question had been abused. In addition, many courts permit expert physicians to give opinions on the means used to inflict injuries (*People v. Jackson*, 1971; *State v. Jurgens*, 1988; *State v. McClary*, 1988; *State v. Tanner*, 1983).

However, an expert testifying on the battered child syndrome may not express an opinion as to whether the defendant in the case had committed the abuse, that is, offer an opinion about the identity of the perpetrator. Thus, even in the case of the battered child syndrome which represents the most "objective" medical criteria to ascertain the existence of abuse, expert testimony may not be used to establish the guilt of a particular defendant. If a physician has testified that a child's injuries comport with the accepted diagnosis of the battered child syndrome, the burden of proof shifts to the defendant who must show that the cause of the injury was accidental (Berliner *et al.*, 1988). If the defendant cannot provide an alternative explanation, the prosecution will have established a *prima facie* case of neglect and abuse (Fraser, 1974), but not of a criminal violation.

To answer the final *legal* question in criminal proceedings, that is, whether the defendant was guilty of the abuse, expert testimony cannot be used. Instead evidence of consciousness of guilt and implausible explanations may be admissible (*Payne v. State*, 1987). The testimony of eyewitnesses, including child victims, evidence that the caretaker has exclusive custody, and statements from caretakers may also be used (Myers, 1989).

CHILD SEXUAL ABUSE

Where there is medical evidence of sexual abuse, physicians also serve as expert witnesses in sexual abuse cases. In recent years, pediatricians and other medical experts on child sexual abuse have learned more about the medical manifestations of sexual abuse. Typically the major evidence sought is sperm or seminal fluid on the victim's skin, body openings, or clothing, or damage to vaginal and rectal areas (DeJong, 1989). When such medical evidence exists, it is generally admissible (DeJong & Rose, 1988). Frequently however, there is little or no medical evidence, and the courts must rely on other types of evidence.

Many mental health experts are prepared to testify that a child has been sexually molested based upon other types of behavior. Many sexually abused children demonstrate behavioral, cognitive, and emotional reactions to their abuse (Myers *et al.*, 1989). Courts often approve expert testimony describing behaviors observed in sexually abused children. Often the expert testimony is permitted to rehabilitate the child's credibility if his or her testimony has been questioned. Testimony offered to prove that the sexual abuse occurred has met with mostly negative results in court *(State v. Hudnall,* 1987; *State v. Moran,* 1986).

Child Sexual Abuse Accommodation Syndrome Theory

The most frequently utilized theory to explain children's reactions to sexual abuse is that supporting the *child sexual abuse accommodation syndrome* (Summitt, 1983). This theory describes the purportedly typical behavior of children who have been victims of repeated sexual abuse by a family member or an adult with whom the child has a trusting relationship. The proposed syndrome is comprised of one or more of five elements: secrecy, helplessness, entrapment and accommodation, delayed disclosure, and retraction (Summitt, 1983). According to the child sexual abuse accommodation syndrome it is typical for children to delay talking about the sexual abuse, if they do so at all.

A child who is molested by a trusted adult is often faced with intimidation to keep the molestation a secret. This atmosphere of secrecy conveys to the child that the molestation is bad and must not be exposed. Similarly, a child often fears punishment or loss of the adult's approval if sexual demands are not met, and may react with submission and helplessness. According to Summitt, the child may also learn to adjust to the traumatic situation, and may display outward manifestations of sexual abuse (Summitt, 1983, p. 185). For all of these reasons, sexually abused children may delay disclosure of the molestation and may often retract an accusation due to the traumatic reactions to disclosure (p. 188).

Some of the behaviors described in the child sexual abuse accommodation syndrome may be inconsistent with a judge's or jury's understanding of how a victim would respond to repeated sexual abuse. The judge or jury might conclude that it is likely that the child fabricated the story since he/she did not report it immediately or retracted an accusation. The child sexual abuse accommodation syndrome is therefore typically used to explain the child's behavior to the court and to establish a victim's credibility in light of such peculiar behavior.

The child sexual abuse accommodation syndrome has been permitted as evidence in several criminal court cases (e.g., *Keri v. State,* 1986; *People v. Gray,* 1986; *People v. Luna,* 1988; *People v. Payan,* 1985), while in other proceedings it has not been admitted (e.g., *Johnson v. State,* 1987; *Lantrip v. Commonwealth,* 1986; *People v. Bowker,* 1988; *People v. Roscoe,* 1985; *State v. Haseltine,* 1984). Whether such testimony was allowed depended on the type of proceeding, when in the proceedings the testimony was offered, and for what purpose.

In *People v. Gray* (1986), the trial court held that the testimony was admissible as rebuttal because the psychologist confined his testimony to child molestation victims *as a class* and did not render an opinion whether the victim in that case had been molested (pp. 219–220). The Court of Appeals affirmed, holding that the admission of expert testimony regarding the tendency of child victims to delay reporting of molestation and to give inconsistent accounts (the child sexual abuse accommodation syndrome) was permissible, so long as it did not express an opinion as to whether the specific child witness in the case at hand was telling the truth (p. 213).

The *Gray* court also disagreed with the appellant's contention that the trial court should have subjected the testimony to the *Frye* test. The court held that the test was not necessary when the expert testimony was simply based on the general experience of molestation victims—not to prove that molestation had occurred (*People v. Gray*, 1986), p. 219). In *People v. Payan* (1986) the lower court allowed expert testimony on the child sexual abuse accommodation syndrome for both credibility and diagnostic purposes. The appellate court, however, limited the admissibility of the syndrome to bolster the credibility of the children only. The appellate court opinion stated that expert opinion should be restricted to a discussion of victims as a class and prohibited any opinion on whether the prosecuting witness was in fact molested.

In *People v. Roscoe* (1985), the appellate court held that the lower court had been in *error* to admit a psychiatrist's testimony on the child sexual abuse accommodation syndrome, but held that the error was harmless. The court held that although expert testimony is admissible for certain purposes other than to establish defendant's guilt, the rule authorizing expert testimony to rehabilitate a complaining witness's credibility is limited to discussion of *victims as a class* supported by references to literature and experience. It does not extend to a diagnosis and discussion of the witness in the case at hand (p. 1093). In reaching this decision the court relied heavily on *People v. Bledsoe* (1984) which had noted that psychological syndromes relating to victims were developed not to determine whether a victim had been abused, but to assist mental health professionals in treating victims. Similarly, *State v. Haseltine* (1984) and *Johnson v. State* (1987) also rejected testimony that sexual abuse occurred based on the accommodation syndrome.

In summary, the child sexual abuse accommodation syndrome has been admitted in criminal court proceedings primarily as rebuttal to dispute the notion that the child's behavior was inconsistent with sexual abuse. Courts have rejected expert opinion on Summitt's (1983) accommodation syndrome when such testimony is offered to prove that abuse had occurred. In addition such testimony has been rejected because there was no showing that the syndrome was generally accepted in the relevant scientific community (*Lantrip v. Commonwealth*, 1986; *People v. Bowker*, 1988).

In general, criminal court proceedings have stricter rules for admitting evidence than juvenile dependency and family court proceedings. In dependency proceedings at the trial or jurisdictional stage, experts may address both diagnostic and credibility issues. However, even in such proceedings the expert may not address the legal issue of whether the defendant is the perpetrator. For example, In *Re Cheryl H.* (1984), although an opinion that the child had suffered abuse was permitted, the testimony of a psychiatrist that a child was sexually *abused by the father* was ruled inadmissible. The appellate court held that it was error to admit the expert opinion that Cheryl's father was the person who had committed the abuse because this testimony impermissibly drew inferences about conduct by a third party based primarily on hearsay. The court said that the psychiatrist should only have been permitted to express an opinion that Cheryl believed her father was the one who abused her (p. 1119).

Whether testimony on the child sexual abuse accommodation syndrome should be allowed to prove that sexual abuse has occurred is a hotly debated issue. Hensley (1986) believes that the child sexual abuse accommodation syndrome meets all the criteria for the *Frye* rule. He suggests that testimony on the syndrome is appropriate both to enhance the credibility of the child witness and to prove that the alleged familial sexual abuse occurred in cases in which the victim has been sexually abused by a relative or other trusted adult in a nonviolent manner.

Levy (1989) on the other hand concludes that evidence based on the child sexual abuse syndrome should never be admitted in court proceedings. According to Levy the symptoms of the syndrome are too broad and overlapping, unmeasurable, and based on impressionistic findings rather than scientific data. There is not enough information to determine whether the symptoms are indicative of sexual abuse.

Other experts contend that while the syndrome has a place in the courtroom, it should not be used for diagnostic purposes in court. Myers *et al.* (1989) note that many professionals simply assumed that, just like the battered child syndrome, the child sexual abuse accommodation syndrome could be used to detect abuse. However, while the battered child syndrome is medical in nature, based on "objective" evidence, the problem with the accommodation syndrome is that some of the components are not necessarily indicative of abuse. The purpose of the syndrome therefore is not to diagnose, but to help explain why so many children delay reporting the abuse and why so many recant and deny allegations of abuse (pp. 67–68).

Bulkley (1988) also notes that expert testimony on psychological reactions of child abuse victims should not be used to prove that a child was abused, due to the fact that there is such great variation in how children react to being abused. Many of the so-called common effects of abuse may be attributed to other trauma or exist in normal children.

The Use of Anatomically Correct Dolls

In criminal abuse cases the court is primarily interested in determining whether a particular person has been abused and who has committed the crime. Expert testimony on the child sexual abuse accommodation syndrome has not been permitted to address these questions.

In recent years, however, another possible behavioral manifestation of abuse, namely observations of abused children's play with anatomically correct dolls, has gained increasing popularity as a tool to determine whether in fact a child has been abused. Anatomically correct dolls usually come in "families" and may be quite diverse in their appearance (White & Santilli, 1988). The theory behind the use of anatomically correct dolls is that children who are unwilling or unable to talk about an abuse will somehow use the dolls to indicate whether they have been abused.

Two appellate court cases in California (*In re Amber, B.*, 1987; *In re Christine C.*, 1987) have addressed the use of anatomically correct dolls in court. In *Amber B.*, the trial court first found that a child had been sexually abused, based on a psychologist's testimony regarding the alleged victim's play with anatomically correct dolls. The appellate court however, concluded that analyzing a child's reports of abuse based on observations of behavior with anatomically correct dolls constitutes a new scientific process operating on purely scientific evidence which must be subjected to the scrutiny of the *Frye* test before it can be allowed in court. The appellate court excluded the testimony on the alleged victim's behavior with the anatomically correct dolls until it could be shown to be generally acceptable within the relevant scientific community (*In re Amber B.*, p. 682).

The *Amber B.* court further added that the entire field of child sexuality and abuse is beyond the scope of critical analysis by the average lay person. Thus, according to the opinion in *Amber B.* (1987, p. 686), a psychologist's examination using the technique of analyzing a child's play with anatomically correct dolls may be surrounded by an "aura of infallibility," and a trier of fact would tend to ascribe "an inordinately high degree of certainty" to the technique (*People v. McDonald*, 1984). While all parties would greatly benefit from reliable expert testimony addressing the question whether the child was abused, such expert testimony cannot be approved until its reliability is shown pursuant to the *Frye* rule, (*In re Amber B.*, p. 692). The court reversed the trial court judgment and remanded the case to establish the admissibility of the challenged testimony.

In the companion case, *In re Christine C.* (1987), the parent successfully challenged the expert opinion testimony of the alleged victim's behavior with anatomically correct dolls on the grounds that the testimony should have been subjected to the *Frye* test for admission of evidence. Unlike the *Amber B.* case, however, the appellate court concluded that the testimony was harmless since the children themselves had also testified and the trial judge had provided a detailed oral explanation of her ruling.

The scientific literature on the degree to which children's behavior with anatomically correct dolls can correctly assess whether abuse has occurred is rather scant. Three studies are commonly cited. In the first conducted by White, Strom, Santilli and Halpin (1986) two groups of children ($n = 25$ in each group) were interviewed to elicit their reactions to sexually anatomically correct dolls. Significant differences were found between the reactions of children who had not been referred for suspected sexual abuse and those who had. Children who had not been referred for abuse revealed very few behaviors indicative of abuse, whereas suspected abused children demonstrated significantly more sexually related behaviors when presented with the dolls. Younger children were more responsive to the dolls than older children. However, the study never specified whether the group referred for suspected child abuse had prior interviews with dolls, whether the experimenters who scored the behavior knew to which of the groups the children belonged, and the scoring categories were general and vague (Levy, 1989).

The second study also involved an assessment of the behavior of sexually abused children and the behavior of children who had not been sexually abused children, using anatomically correct dolls (Jampole & Weber, 1987). In this study a comparison was made between one group of children ($n = 10$) who all had been judged sexually abused by the child protection workers or the police, with another group ($n = 10$) of children who were not abused. Of the children who had been sexually abused, 9 demonstrated sexual behavior with the dolls; 1 did not. Of the children who had not been sexually abused, 8 did not demonstrate sexual behavior, 2 did. The authors concluded that anatomically correct dolls are a significant investigative tool. Although the differences between the two groups was clear, it should be noted that the number of children studied was very small. Secondly, all the children in the abused group had already been removed from their homes and had previously been interviewed and interrogated regarding their victimization. Such previous experiences may have affected the way they played with the dolls. Thirdly, no information was given about the nature of the researcher's behavior with the children (Levy, 1989).

The third study (Aman & Goodman, 1987) was somewhat different. Again the goal of the study was to assess the inferential value of children's reactions to anatomically correct dolls. The researchers focused on whether anatomically correct dolls facilitate children's abilities to report events accurately or whether they lead to false reports of abuse. A group of 3-year-olds ($n = 30$) and a group of 5-year-olds ($n = 30$) who were screened to eliminate any suspicions of sexual abuse participated in a real life play situation with a male confederate for 10 minutes. One week later, the children were interviewed by a female researcher under three different conditions. In the anatomically correct doll condition, children were questioned with the use of four anatomically correct dolls. In the second condition, the children were questioned with dolls that looked just like the anatomically correct dolls, but without the secondary sexual characteristics. In the third group, no dolls were used. All groups were asked several misleading questions implying a sexually inappropriate or abusive behavior on the part of the male confederate.

The researchers found that children's suggestibility did not significantly differ with use of the dolls. There were no significant interactions in the children's interactions with or without the dolls. The 5-year-olds answered the abuse questions more accurately than the 3-year-olds. On the basis of these findings the authors of the study concluded that playing with anatomically correct dolls does not lead to false reports of sexual abuse in children. However, this still doesn't answer the question of whether sexually abused children would make false statements or not. So far, a clear profile that clearly distinguishes abused children's play with dolls from non-abused children's play has not been developed.

The use of anatomically correct dolls in child abuse cases was developed primarily as a therapeutic tool, not as a means of investigation. It is still uncertain whether children who have been abused play with the dolls differently than children who have not been abused. The dolls in use are by no means standard, and investigators may use many different protocols in handling the play interviews with little or no training. Despite their value as a therapeutic tool in evaluating suspected sexual abuse of young children, evidentiary use of anatomically correct dolls in dependency or criminal proceedings has become increasingly controversial.

Given the lack of clarity in the interpretation of children's play with dolls, the importance of such play observations in a legal expert's testimony becomes problematic. Often the use of dolls is used more as "a sexual abuse detection device" that has the validity of a machine rather than the fallibility of an expert's observation (Levy, 1989). A noted legal expert in this area has concluded that the dolls should be used only as an investigative tool or as demonstrative evidence to aid children in testifying, not as a diagnosis of sexual abuse (Bulkley, 1988). Levy (1989) asserts that dolls testimony should be inadmissible altogether, even as an aid in a child's testimony. The fact that there is very little scientific evidence to support inferences about abuse from a child's play with anatomically correct dolls, combined with the possibility that such testimony by experts may nevertheless carry an "aura of infallibility" with jurors warrants the exclusion of expert testimony both as a descriptive and diagnostic tool.

CONCLUSION

In many cases in which the issues of abuse and victimization are raised, an expert's opinion may be offered concerning abuse generally or the facts of the case. Since the evidence at the hearing may not include testimony of the alleged victim, the expert's views may be determinative. For this reason the critical questions in these cases often are whether the expert can testify and on what issues he or she may render an opinion.

It is apparent from the cases cited above that there are some situations and issues on which an expert may testify, but there are other situations and issues in which he or she may not testify. A properly qualified expert may discuss the characteristics of an abused child, the characteristics of victims as a class, and the observed behavior of the child in question. However, that testimony may not be offered until someone has challenged the assertion that the child has been abused. Only medical experts have been allowed to link testimony on general characteristics about abuse and victims as a class to conclusions that the alleged victim has been abused. Although an expert may address the issue of a witness's credibility, it is not permissible for an expert to conclude that someone is telling the truth.

Expert testimony presented by the prosecution on typical characteristics of sex offenders or by the defense that the defendant does not fit the profile of an abuser has generally been excluded. The defendant, however, has more freedom in establishing that he/she does not fit the profile of an abuser by raising the issue of his/her character and his/her alleged propensity to engage in sexually deviant behavior. In no cases may an expert conclude that a certain individual is the perpetrator. Those issues are left to the trier of fact, the judge or jury.

Generally, the courts have permitted medical experts to address the more important issue of whether the child has been abused. Mental health experts have not been permitted to give that opinion. The child sexual abuse accommodation syndrome may be used to describe characteristics of abuse and behaviors that are typical of abused children. While play with anatomically correct dolls has been introduced as evidence that a particular child has been abused, only the battered child syndrome has conclusively been accepted as a basis for the diagnosis that a given child has in fact been abused.

The purpose of expert testimony is to assist the trier of fact by providing a resource for ascertaining truth in areas outside the knowledge of ordinary persons. Although such testimony may often be helpful, the possibility always exists that the trier of fact may be unduly influenced by the expert's testimony, especially if the knowledge has not yet been accepted by the relevant scientific community. Courts must proceed with caution in admitting expert testimony in child abuse cases. The trial court must be satisfied that the witness is indeed an expert and that the expert knowledge offered is recognized as valid and reliable by the relevant professional community.

Allegations of child abuse are difficult to prove, but they are equally difficult to defend against. Testimony that could be clearly prejudicial to the defendant must therefore be carefully considered and only accepted when it rests on sound scientific evidence.

These issues are far from resolved. More studies may call into question the child sexual abuse accommodation syndrome and observations of behavior with the anatomically correct dolls, or determine that these do in fact meet the *Frye* standards.

New techniques may be developed to provide better diagnostic tools to ascertain abuse.

It is important for the social sciences and the law to work hand in hand on these critical issues. The law has made some use of the battered child syndrome. It remains to be seen whether syndromes developed by mental health professions and the use of tools such as the anatomically correct dolls will be as useful. We need to develop better knowledge that will ensure a greater number of successful prosecutions of child abusers without violating the rights of defendants.

REFERENCES

Aman, C., & Goodman, G. (1987). *Children's use of anatomically detailed dolls: An experimental study.* Paper presented at the National Center on Child Abuse and Neglect, Symposium on Interviewing Children, Washington, DC.

Barta, R., & Smith, N. (1963). Wilful trauma to young children: A challenge to the physician. *Clinical Pediatrics, 2,* 545–554.

Berliner, L. (1988). Deciding whether a child has been sexually abused. In E. B. Nickolson (Ed.), *Sexual abuse allegations in custody and visitation cases* (pp. 48–62). Washington, DC: American Bar Association.

Borgida, E., Gresham, A., Swim, J., Bull, M., & Gray, E. (1989). Expert testimony in child sexual abuse cases: An empirical investigation of partisan orientation. *Family Law Quarterly, 23,* 433–451.

Bulkley, J. (1988), Legal proceedings, reforms, and emerging issues in child sexual abuse cases. *Behavioral Sciences & the Law, 6,* 153–180.

DeJong, A. R. (1989). Principles and pitfalls in forensic evidence data collection. *The Advisor, 2* (4), 8–9.

DeJong, A. R., & Rose, S. (1988). The frequency and significance of physical evidence in legally proven cases of child sexual abuse. *American Journal of Diseases in Children, 142,* 406.

Dyas v. United States, 376 A.2d 827 (D.C. App. 1977), *cert. denied,* 434 U.S. 973 (1977).

Faust, D., & Ziskin, J. (1988). The expert witness in psychology and psychiatry. *Science, 241,* 1143–1144.

Federal Rules of Evidence. (1990). St. Paul, MN: West.

Fowler, R. D., & Matarazzo, J. D. (1988). Psychologists and psychiatrists as expert witnesses. *Science, 241,* 1143.

Fraser, A. (1974). A pragmatic alternative to current legislative approaches to child abuse. *American Criminal Law Review, 12,* 103–117.

Frye v. United States, 293 F. 1013, 54 App. D.C. 46 (1923).

Giannelli, I. (1980). The admissibility of novel scientific evidence: *Frye v. United States* a half century later. *Columbia Law Review, 80,* 1197–1250.

Harper, F. (1963). The physician, the battered child and the law. *Pediatrics, 31,* 899–902.

Helfer, R., & Kempe, C. (Eds.). (1968). *The battered child* (1st ed.) Chicago, IL: University of Chicago Press.

Helfer, R., & Kempe, C. (Eds.). (1987). *The battered child* (4th ed.). Chicago, IL: University of Chicago Press.

Hensley, K. L. (1986). The admissibility of "child sexual abuse accommodation syndrome" in California criminal courts. *Pacific Law Journal, 17,* 1361–1391.

In re Amber B., 191 Cal. App.3d 682, 236 Cal. Rptr. 623 (1987).

In re Cheryl H., 153 Cal. App.3d 1098, 200 Cal. Rptr. 789 (1984).

In re Christine C., 191 Cal. App.3d 676, 236 Cal. Rptr. 630 (1987).

Jampole, L., & Weber, M. K. (1987). An assessment of the behavior of sexually abused and nonsexually abused children with anatomically correct dolls. *Child Abuse and Neglect, 11,* 187–192.

Johnson v. State, 292 Ark. 632, 732 S.W.2d 817 (1987).

Keri v. State, 179 Ga. App. 664, 347 S.E.2d 236 (1986).

Kempe, C. H., Silverman, F. N., Steele, B. F., Droegemueller, W., & Silver, H. K. (1962). The battered child syndrome. *Journal of American Medical Association, 181,* 17–24.

Lantrip v. Commonwealth, 713 S.W.2d 816 (Ky. 1986).

Levy, R. (1989). Using "scientific" testimony to prove child sexual abuse. *Family Law Quarterly, 23,* 383–411.

McCoid, A. (1965). The battered child and other assaults upon the family: Part one. *Minnesota Law Review, 50,* 1–58.

McCord, D. (1986). Expert psychological testimony about child complainants in sexual abuse prosecutions: A foray into the admissibility of novel psychological evidence. *Journal of Criminal Law and Criminology, 77*, 1–67.

Myers, J. (1989). Legal evidence of physical child abuse., *The Advisor, 2* (4), 3–4.

Myers, J., Bays, J., Becker, J., Berliner, L., Corwin D., & Saywitz, K. (1989). Expert testimony in child sexual abuse litigation. *Nebraska Law Review, 68*, 1–145.

Paulson, M. J., & Blake, R. (1967). The abused, battered and maltreated child: A review. *Trauma, 9* (4), 3–136.

Payne v. State, 21 Ark. App. 243, 731 S.W.2d 235 (1987).

People v. Bowker, 203 Cal. App.3d 385, 249 Cal. Rptr. 886 (1988).

People v. Bledsoe, 36 Cal.3d 236, 203 Cal. Rptr. 450, 681 P.2d 291 (1984).

People v. Dunnahoo, 152 Cal. App.3d 561, 199 Cal. Rptr. 796 (1984).

People v. Gray, 187 Cal. App.3d, 231 Cal. Rptr. 658 (1986).

People v. Jackson, 18 Cal. App.3d 504, 95 Cal. Rptr. 919 (1971).

People v. Kelley, 17 Cal.3d 24, 130 Cal. Rptr. 144, 549 P.2d 1240 (1976).

People v. Lucero, 724 P.2d 1374 (Colo. App. 1986).

People v. Luna, 204 Cal. App.3d 776, 250 Cal. Rptr. 878 (1988).

People v. McDonald, 37 Cal.3d, 351, 208 Cal. Rptr. 236, 690 P.2d 709 (1984).

People v. Payan, 173 Cal.App.3d 27, 220 Cal. Rptr. 126 (1985).

People v. Roehler, 167 Cal. App.3d 353, 213 Cal. Rptr. 353 (1985).

People v. Rosco, 168 Cal. App.3d 1093, 215 Cal. Rptr. 45 (1985).

People v. Stoll, 49 Cal.3d 1136, 265 Cal. Rptr. 111, 783 P.2d 698 (1989).

Schmitt, B., Bross, D., Caroll, C., Gray, J., Grosz, C., Kempe, C., & Lenherr, M. (1978). *Guidelines for the hospital and the clinic: Management of child abuse and neglect.* Washington DC: National Center on Child Abuse and Neglect, Children's Bureau.

Serrato, G. (1988). Expert testimony in child sexual abuse prosecutions: A spectrum of uses. *Boston University Law Review, 68*, 155–192.

Standard California Codes: *Civil procedure, evidence, probate, rules of court.* (1990). New York: Matthew Bender.

State v. Batangan, 71 Haw. 552, 799 P.2d 48 (1990).

State v. Dumlao, 3 Conn. App. 607, 491 A.2d 404 (1985).

State v. Haseltine, 120 Wis.2d 92, 352 N.W.2d 673 (1984).

State v. Hudnall, 293 S.C. 97, 359 S.E.2d 59 (1987).

State v. Jurgens, 424 N.W.2d 546 (Minn. App. 1988).

State v. Kim, 64 Haw. 598, 645 P.2d 1330 (1982).

State v. McClary, 207 Conn. 233, 541 A.2d 96 (1988).

State v. Moran, 151 Ariz. 378, 728 P.2d 248 (1986).

State v. Myers, 359 N.W.2d 604 (Minn. 1984).

State v. Tanner, 675 P.2d 539 (Utah 1983).

Summit, R. (1983). The child sexual abuse accommodation syndrome. *Child Abuse and Neglect, 7*, 177–193.

White, S., & Santilli, G. (1988). A review of clinical practices and research data on anatomically correct dolls. *Journal of Interpersonal Violence, 3*, 430–432.

White, S., Strom, G. A., Santilli, G., & Halpin, B. M. (1987). Interviewing sexual abuse victims with anatomically correct dolls. *Child Abuse and Neglect, 10*, 519–529.

Zumwalt, R. E., & Hirsch, C. S. (1987). Pathology of fatal child abuse and neglect. In R. E. Helfer & R. S. Kempe (Eds.), *The battered child* (4th ed., pp. 247–286). Chicago: University of Chicago Press.

PROFILING CHILD SEXUAL ABUSERS
Legal Considerations

JAMES M. PETERS

U. S. Attorney's Office, St. Croix, U.S. Virgin Islands

WILLIAM D. MURPHY

University of Tennessee, Memphis

Behavioral scientists have been presented as expert witnesses in child sexual abuse cases to testify that known child molesters perform differently on psychological tests than persons who do not molest children. Such testimony has been offered in a wide range of cases ranging from family court to the criminal arena, both for and against the accused. For a variety of reasons, appellate courts across the country have almost universally rejected this type of evidence, the notable exception being California. This article summarizes the case law on both sides of the issue and concludes that evidence regarding the supposed psychological profile of a child molester has no place in the courtroom. This article provides a brief summary of legal thought regarding the general admissibility of scientific evidence and then reviews published cases organized by the major legal underpinnings of each case. The analysis in this article is limited to laws within the United States and may not apply to other countries.

L awyers confronted with the complex task of proving or defending an allegation that an adult has sexually abused a child often turn to mental health professionals for advice and assistance. Clinicians who claim they can determine whether or not the alleged abused fits the so-called profile of a child molester using psychological tests have found a receptive audience among advocates for both alleged victims and suspected abusers. Typical is the following excerpt from the trial testimony of a Minnesota psychologist who testifies frequently on behalf of accused child molesters:

AUTHORS' NOTE: *Correspondence may be addressed to James M. Peters, c/o U.S. Attorney's Office, Box 3239, Christiansted, St. Croix, VI 00822.*

CRIMINAL JUSTICE AND BEHAVIOR, Vol. 19 No. 1, March 1992 38-53

A: . . . [T]here are ways in which confirmed sex abusers differ from non-sex abusers in their responses to these objective tests. . . . Both in terms of my own observations and also in terms of the more recent research evidence that's coming out, persons who are again determined by a finder of fact to have been perpetrators, for example, on the MMPI, will produce elevated scores on Scales 4, 7, and 8 and this is true in the research done by Kirkland and Bauer, the University of Colorado. In nine out of ten instances, there are elevated scores on two or three of those scales.

Q: Now, you had testified that you had Bill C. take the MMPI, is that correct?

A: Yes.

Q: Did you see any of the elevation that you have described in Scales 4, 7, and 8?

A: No. The MMPI Mr. C. produced is what we would call a dull, boring, normal profile. (*State v. Bill C.*, 1985)

Testimony of this nature enables the lawyer to argue that the accused is less (or more) likely to have committed the offense, based on his psychological profile. It has particular significance in criminal trials when offered by the defendant because, if it creates a reasonable doubt and results in an acquittal, the government is not permitted to appeal. That is true whether or not the trial judge's decision to admit the testimony was well-reasoned.

This article reviews the legal literature with special attention to appellate court opinions because of their value as precedents. With the notable exception of courts in California, we found that virtually every appellate court that has ruled on the admissibility of expert testimony regarding the psychological profile of child molesters has rejected it. Although the reasons they give for turning away the testimony vary, most seem to recognize that the fatal flaw of this type of evidence is that goodness of fit with a profile can never determine whether a given defendant committed a specific act at a specific time. Thus, for example, even if a psychological profile for child molesters who murder their victims existed and had perfect specificity and sensitivity, and even if notorious child molester/murderer John Wayne Gacy fit that profile, that fact would neither prove nor disprove whether Gacy molested and killed a specific child. This is consistent with the limitations of profiling outlined in the scientific literature (Murphy & Peters, 1992 [this issue]).

The reasons courts have given for spurning such testimony overlap and depend largely on the facts of each case. We discuss the published cases below. For purposes of clarity and organization, we have grouped the cases to reflect the major legal underpinnings of the courts' holdings. Before discussing the caselaw, however, we believe a brief discussion of the general admissibility of scientific testimony is in order.

METHODS EMPLOYED BY COURTS
TO EVALUATE SCIENTIFIC TESTIMONY

It is the trial judge's responsibility to decide whether the proposed expert testimony will assist the jury to understand the evidence or determine a fact in issue. Courts that have considered the admissibility of novel uses of psychiatric and psychological testimony, such as those discussed in this article, are far from uniform in their analyses of the issues. Some jurisdictions apply a strict standard adopted from the famous 1923 case in which a defendant's attempt to introduce evidence of a polygraph examination was rejected because he failed to prove that the scientific principle from which the deductions were drawn was sufficiently accepted in the scientific community (*Frye v. United States*, 1923). "The Frye rule furthers two valid objectives. It serves to assure that only scientific evidence that is reliable will be placed before the jury. Additionally, the generally accepted standard tends to assure that there will be a pool of available experts to which the opponent of the evidence can resort for advice and testimony" (McCord, 1986).

Many states have variations of the Frye rule. For instance, California's variant is generally referred to as the Kelly-Frye rule, based on *People v. Kelly* (1976), where the rule was redefined as a two-step process: (a) the reliability of the method must be established, usually by expert testimony, and (b) the witness furnishing such testimony must be properly qualified as an expert to give an opinion on the subject. Additionally, the proponent of the evidence must demonstrate that correct procedures were used in the particular case.

Other courts and commentators have suggested lists of factors to be used in analyzing proposed scientific evidence (McCormick, 1982). These include:

1. Potential error rate in using the technique.
2. Existence and maintenance of standards governing its use.
3. Presence of safeguards in the characteristics of the technique.
4. Analogy to other scientific techniques whose results are admissible.
5. Extent to which the technique has been accepted by scientists in the field involved.
6. Nature and breadth of the inference.
7. Clarity and simplicity with which the technique can be described and its results expanded.
8. Extent to which the basic data are verifiable by the court and jury.
9. Availability of other experts to test and evaluate the technique.
10. Probative significance of the evidence in the circumstances of the case.
11. Care with which the technique was applied in the case.

Another list of factors was proposed in Weinstein and Berger (1982). See also *State v. Maule* (1983) and *State v. Brown* (1984).

1. The technique's general acceptance in the field.
2. The expert's qualifications and stature.
3. Use made of the technique.
4. Potential rate of error.
5. Existence of specialized literature.
6. Novelty of the invention.
7. Extent to which the technique relies on the subjective interpretation of the expert.

SUMMARY OF THE MINORITY
VIEW ADMITTING PROFILE TESTIMONY

The leading case expressing the minority view that expert testimony regarding psychological profiles should be admitted for the purpose of raising an inference that a defendant is not the type of person likely to molest children is *People v. Stoll* (1989). In *Stoll*, the California

153

Supreme Court reversed a lower court and admitted a psychologist's opinion, based on interview and professional inter- pretation of standardized written personality tests (the MMPI and MCMI), that the defendant had a "normal personality function," had not in the past engaged in sexual deviancy of any kind and "showed no possibility for sexual deviancy in her personality profile." He expressed the opinion that it was "unlikely she would be involved in the events she's been charged with."

A year later in *People v. Ruiz* (1990), the California Court of Appeals stated that "it is now settled that psychological opinions based on personal examination and an analysis of accepted psychological tests, such as the MMPI and MCMI, may be admitted as character evidence tending to show that an individual was or was not likely to have committed a particular act, and that the admissibility of such evidence need not be tested under the *Kelly-Frye* standard."

Thus, in California, a psychologist's opinion that a defendant shows no obvious psychological or sexual problem is admissible circumstantial evidence that the accused did not commit the charged sexual offenses. In that state, an expert's opinion which meets traditional standards for competent expert opinion need not undergo additional screening procedures applicable to novel, or experimental "scientific" evidence. The *Stoll* court justified this departure from the majority rule by citing numerous other (non-child molestation) cases where standard psychological tests such as the MMPI were used to reach an opinion on the mental state of the accused. As of this writing (May 1991), *Stoll* has not been cited outside the state of California and thus has no authority outside that state.

MAJORITY VIEW: PSYCHOLOGICAL PROFILING IS NOT RELIABLE

Murphy and Peters (1992) demonstrate that scientific literature does not support the type of opinion rendered by the experts in the California cases cited above. The court in *United States v. St. Pierre* (1987) recognized the paucity of scientific support for this type of testimony. In that case the appellant sought to have an expert examine him to determine whether he fit the profile of a sexual offender. The motion was denied and he appealed. The court pointed out that the appellant had

> cited no decision or scientific treatise that recognizes the acceptability of such testimony. One of the standards for admissibility is that it must have gained the acceptance of the particular field or scientific community to which it belongs.

The court held that

> a review of the cases in other jurisdictions does not persuade us that it is generally accepted in the medical or legal communities that psychiatrists possess such knowledge or capabilities.

In a related case, a proceeding initiated by the New York Department of Social Services alleging that the respondent sexually abused his two preschool-aged boys, a psychologist was called by the department to help corroborate the older boy's out-of-court statements. After administering a battery of psychological tests to the respondent, the psychologist concluded that the accused suffered from difficulties in impulse control and feeling empathy for others, sexual problems, depression, inferiority, lack of confidence, and use of denial. She testified that she had developed a profile based on testing 18 incest offenders and was prepared to say that the father fit her profile of someone capable of sexual abuse. The trial court, however, held that 18 cases would not be an adequate statistical basis on which to base a profile of an incest offender. Her testimony was rejected on the grounds that the reliability of the profile was not adequately established to allow the court to use it as corroboration (*In the Matter of Arrigo*, 1986). In New York State Family Court, varied kinds of expert testimony are used to fulfill the requirement that there be some corroboration before certain hearsay statements of children will be admitted. In the *Arrigo* case, the evidence was offered by the alleged abuser and did not satisfy the court's minimum standard for admissibility.

The unreliability of this type of testimony was highlighted in a recent Oregon case where the defendant's psychologist testified that the defendant did not match the pedophile profile or have any serious sexual disorders. The admissibility of the opinion was not an issue on appeal. The Court of Appeals ruled that the lower court properly permitted the state to impeach the psychologist with evidence that he had given a similar opinion in another sexual abuse case and that defendant had later admitted the sexual abuse (*State v. Shearer*, 1990).

PENILE PLETHYSMOGRAPHY: AN UNPROVEN TECHNIQUE FOR DETERMINING PAST BEHAVIOR

Some mental health professionals have added the penile plethysmograph to their repertoire of assessment tools and attempted to use it in psychological profile testimony. Because of the apparent objectivity of this method, specific cases relevant to the admissibility of the procedure will be reviewed. For example, in an unreported case (*State v. Scott T.*, 1987), a clinical psychologist from Portland, Oregon, gave the following testimony regarding penile plethysmograph testing as part of the basis for his opinion that the defendant did not meet the so-called profile of a sexual offender:

> A: The first arousal assessment was completed on 5-27-87. Mr. T. viewed 14 slides, regarding some form of erotic materials, and five tapes describing sexual behavior. While responding to those materials — and these are mixed materials, Your Honor: some normal, some abnormal — his responses were quite low. There was not a lot of response while viewing the slides. There was very low arousal to four or five tapes, and by very low I mean nonexistent, and on the fifth tape he became moderately aroused to a normal tape describing sexual behavior with a female adult.
>
> Q: Was there any indication in those test results of predisposition . . . towards children?
>
> A: There was not any evidence or any inclination or information or data, I should say, that would suggest he had a predisposition toward engaging in sexual behavior with minors.

Testimony of this sort is frequently proffered and usually rejected by the trial judge. This testimony was ruled inadmissible by the trial court in *State of Washington v. Scott T., Clark County* (1987).

156

There are two reported cases involving the attempt to base an opinion that the accused did not fit the profile, in part, on the results of penile plethysmograph testing. (The methodology of this test is discussed in Murphy & Peters, 1992.) Both cases hold that the reliability of the technique is not yet sufficient for use in court. In *People v. John W.* (1986) the defendant was convicted of molesting his 11-year-old stepdaughter. He appealed on the grounds that the trial court refused to allow his psychologist to testify that he was not a sexual deviant. The psychologist drew that conclusion after giving the defendant the MMPI, two examinations on the penile plethysmograph and a standard psychological interview. The psychologist testified that the penile plethysmograph was in use at many diagnostic and treatment centers, but admitted that in his experience only 80% of convicted sex offenders showed a positive response to the deviant stimuli for which they were convicted. He also admitted that some men do not respond at all to external stimuli. Most important, he admitted there was no body of scientific knowledge based on either the MMPI or the penile plethysmograph that supported an opinion as to whether the defendant did or did not do anything to the victim.

The court observed that

> it is clear from Dr. Walker's candid responses . . . that he had to have based his opinion that appellant was not a sexual deviant primarily on the results of the physical test. . . . He conceded that it (the MMPI) had never been standardized in a sexual deviant population. Specifically, he stated that the publishers of the MMPI had not produced any profiles that one would expect from a person who is suffering from any sexual deviancy, so that the test is not particularly useful as applied to the topic of deviant sexuality. . . . He admitted that "the main usefulness of the MMPI is whether they were honest or not on the test." (*People v. John W.*, 1986)

The court applied the *Kelly-Frye* rule and held: "Based on these standards there was clearly no acceptable showing in this case that the physical test was a reliable means of diagnosing sexual deviancy."

The other reported case is from a trial-level Court in Duchess County, New York. A psychologist examined the respondent using a penile plethysmograph and concluded that because he did not become sexually aroused by children, the child in question would not be at risk living with him. Another expert testified that the penile plethysmograph has not gained acceptance by the scientific community as a reliable predictor of future behavior. The judge ruled that the results could not be considered as predictive of the father's behavior toward children and could not be considered to determine whether to terminate his parental rights. The court held that the plethysmograph has received questionable professional recognition and had a margin of error that was too great to forecast the child's safety (*Duchess County DSHS v. Mr. and Mrs. G.*, 1988).

Of interest is the Code of Ethics of the Association for the Treatment of Sexual Abusers (ATSA), an international organization established in 1984 to advance the development of professional standards and practices in the assessment and treatment of sexual abusers. ATSA is specific about the use of assessment data to determine criminal responsibility: "Assessments regarding a person's degree of sexual dangerousness, suitability for treatment, or other forensic referral questions shall not be determined solely on the basis of a penile plethysmographic assessment. Rather, such data must be properly integrated within a comprehensive assessment" (National Center for Prosecution of Child Abuse, 1988). The code further contains a provision stating, "Assessments should not be used to confirm or deny whether an event or crime has taken place" (National Center for Prosecution of Child Abuse, 1988). It should be recognized that even if a test was 100% accurate in profiling a sexual offender, it can never determine whether a defendant committed a specific act at a specific time.

PSYCHOLOGICAL PROFILE TESTIMONY IS IRRELEVANT TO THE DETERMINATION OF GUILT OR INNOCENCE

Psychological profile testimony has been offered in child sexual abuse cases for three purposes: (a) to prove the defendant did the crime, (b) to prove the defendant did not do the crime, and (c) to bolster the credibility of the defendant. The first step any court takes in analyzing admissibility of such testimony is to question whether it is relevant. Evidence is relevant if it has any tendency to make the existence of any fact of consequence to the determination of the case more or less probable than it would be without that evidence. Several courts have rejected proposed psychological profile testimony because it does not meet this test.

In *Williams v. State* (1983), the defense proposed to call a psychologist to testify that the defendant did not possess character disorders "virtually always found in child molesters," and therefore the statistical improbability of his committing the crimes was very high. The basis of testimony was an MMPI test and a mental status exam. The trial court refused to permit the testimony. The Texas Court of Appeals affirmed, stating that the opinion of one witness as to the state of mind of another is inadmissible because one person cannot possibly know another's state of mind, and such testimony is necessarily based on conjecture.

In *State v. Fitzgerald* (1986), a psychologist proffered testimony about "typical traits of pedophiles" in an effort to show that the defendant did not fit the profile. The trial court recognized that the basic requirement for admissibility of expert opinion is whether it would be helpful to the jury in understanding the evidence or resolving a factual dispute. The profile testimony was rejected as irrelevant, not generally accepted in the scientific community and confusing to the jury. The appellate court affirmed.

In *In the Matter of Cheryl H.* (1984), a psychiatrist had administered two standardized psychological tests to the accused, the MMPI and the Tennessee Self-Concept Scale. The tests indicated that the defendant exhibited personality traits (passive-dependent with highly guarded and defensive tendencies) that the psychiatrist testified were displayed by 85% of 200 fathers found to have sexually abused their daughters in a study by the UCLA Family Support Program. The trial court admitted the testimony and allowed the inference that because he possessed this propensity, he behaved in conformance with it in committing the crime. The California Court of Appeals ruled that admitting the psychiatrist's testimony was an error because, by statute, character evidence is inadmissible in civil cases. In dicta, the court also expressed reservations about the logic of such statistical evidence, suggesting it was too speculative and that its relevance may be "so marginal that it would be easily overcome by the tendency to mislead the trier of fact into fallacious reasoning" (*In the Matter of Cheryl H.*, 1984).

Similar reasoning is found in *State v. Claflin* (1984), *State v. Maule* (1983), and *State v. Petrich* (1983), in which reversals of child molestation convictions occurred because experts testifying on behalf of the state indicated that a large portion of persons who molest children are "father figures." The Washington courts, in each of these cases, viewed this testimony as tantamount to an opinion that the defendants were statistically more likely to have committed the crimes because of their membership in the group of father figures.

THE TESTIMONY INVADES THE PROVINCE OF THE JURY

In *State v. Tucker* (1990), the state presented a psychologist to testify about the general characteristics and behavior of sex offenders and their victims. After doing so, the expert testified that the defendant's conduct was consistent with the crime having occurred. The Arizona Court of Appeals reversed the conviction, pointing out that issues of ultimate fact may be the subject of expert testimony, however, witnesses are not permitted as experts on how juries should decide cases.

In *State v. Friedrich* (1987), the defendant was convicted of sexual assault in connection with crimes against his wife's 14-year-old niece. Defense counsel presented an offer of proof (a preview of proposed testimony, given outside the hearing of the jury) from a psychologist who had interviewed the defendant and given him psychological tests. The expert testified that he compared the defendant's psychological profile to the profile of known incest offenders and found them diametrically opposed. The defense argued that this finding tended to corroborate the defendant's testimony that he did not commit the alleged acts and also tended to negate the complaining witness' testimony that he did commit those acts. The trial court refused to allow the jury to hear the psychologist testify, concluding that admitting this evidence would result in a usurpation of the jury function of assessing witness credibility in that it "had the potential to cause the jury to substitute the expert's opinion for its own" (*State v. Friedrich,*

1987). The Supreme Court of Wisconsin affirmed, holding that the jury could draw its own conclusions on the question of the defendant's credibility without the help of the expert.

In *Dunnington v. State* (1987), the court was called on to decide whether the trial court properly allowed evidence in the form of rebuttal testimony proffered by the state from a purported expert in the field of child abuse. The expert testified about general profile characteristics of three recognized categories of pedophiles: fixated, regressed, and sadistic. The appeals court held that such evidence was not properly admitted because it infringed on the role of the jury as trier of fact, despite the defense allegation that the children were falsely accusing the defendant of sexually molesting them. The court also held that the probative value of the expert's testimony was outweighed by its potential for prejudice.

In *Pendleton v. Commonwealth* (1985), the defendant was accused of molesting his two daughters over a period of several years. He was convicted of rape and sodomy. The key issue involved excluded testimony from a psychologist who had administered tests and offered expert opinion that Pendleton's profile was not consistent with that of a sex offender. The defense sought to present the psychologist's opinion as to the probability that the defendant had committed the act. The court affirmed the conviction, ruling that the

> opinion as to whether the accused had the ability or propensity to commit such an act is improper because it is an opinion on the ultimate fact, that is, innocence or guilt. Consequently it invades the proper province of the jury. Such an opinion is not evidence of mental condition but is a factual conclusion on the ultimate issue before the jury which can be reached only by consideration of all the facts. (*Pendleton v. Commonwealth*, 1985)

PROBATIVE VALUE OUTWEIGHED
BY DANGER OF UNFAIR PREJUDICE

Another step courts use in analyzing the admissibility of evidence involves weighing whether the probative value of the testimony is substantially outweighed by the danger of unfair prejudice. This step recognizes that certain circumstances call for the exclusion of evidence that is of unquestioned relevance and which may meet the test of scientific reliability. There are six safeguards by which the trial judge may, in the exercise of discretion, exclude evidence that is otherwise relevant. These include the danger of unfair prejudice, confusion of the issues, misleading the jury, or considerations of undue delay, waste of time, or needless presentation of cumulative evidence (Federal Rules of Evidence 403).

In *Haakanson v. State* (1988), the trial court allowed testimony on behalf of the state from a police officer describing a "sex offender profile" and admitted physical evidence to fit the defendant within the profile description. The appeals court found this to be error and held that the prosecution may not introduce a profile to show that the defendant is more likely to have committed an offense because he fits within that profile. The Court stated that any probative value the evidence has is outweighed by the danger of unfair prejudice, confusion of the issues, or misleading the jury.

In *State v. Hanson* (1987), the state presented evidence through a police detective that children may delay in reporting sexual abuse because the perpetrator has established a relationship with them through "grooming techniques." The techniques include gift giving, much affection, praise, rewards, developing warm relationships with other persons who are close to the victim, and doing anything to establish emotional dependency. The state then offered evidence that the defendant had "groomed" the victim in an effort to prove he had molested them. The Oregon Supreme Court reversed, holding that profile evidence of a nonviolent child abuser was not probative of the issues at trial and there was a substantial danger of undue prejudice.

In *State v. Miller* (1985), testimony about a "typical psychological profile" of individuals who sexually molest children was offered by the accused. A psychologist was prepared to testify that persons who molest children generally have one or more of the following characteristics: (a) organic brain damage or other mental disorders, (b) a history of sexual assaults manifested before age 30, (c) under the influence of alcohol or drugs at the time the assault is committed, or

(d) suffer from depression. The trial court excluded the testimony on the grounds that it was irrelevant and speculative and would be confusing to the jury. The judge expressed concern that the jury would shift its attention in deciding the case from whether the appellant had committed the crime to whether the prosecution had proven that he fit within the typical psychological profile of a child abuser. The Utah Supreme Court held that even though the testimony was relevant to a pertinent trait of the appellant's character, namely, the incongruity of his personality with that of individuals likely to commit sexual offenses against children, the evidence was properly excluded because its probative value was substantially outweighed by the danger of confusion of the issues or misleading the jury.

In *Hall v. State* (1985), the Arkansas court held that expert testimony which included a description of the "typical" psychological profile of a child molester was distractive and prejudicial, and reversed the lower court ruling which allowed the testimony.

IMPROPER CHARACTER EVIDENCE

The Idaho Supreme Court reversed the conviction in *State v. Hester* (1988), in part because of testimony by a psychologist testifying for the prosecution regarding character traits of child abusers in general and Hester's traits in particular. The expert testified that the defendant exhibited character traits consistent with the characteristics of known child abusers. The opinion turned on Idaho Rule of Evidence 404 (which parallels the federal rule) prohibiting the admission of evidence of a person's character, even in the form of an expert opinion, if offered during the prosecution's case-in-chief to prove the accused's conduct on a specified occasion. The court held that the psychologist's opinion was relevant only if employed as a basis for an inference that the accused behaved in conformity with a particular propensity of disposition on a particular occasion. "This is merely an exotic variety of character evidence and is inadmissible under these circumstances" (*State v. Hester*, 1988).

CONCLUSION

Michael Martin, a professor of law at Fordham University, has written that "psychological profiles can be useful explanatory tools. However, courts are wise to give all profile evidence careful scrutiny for its propriety, relevance and potential prejudice" (Martin, 1988, p. 3). Most courts that have been asked to rule on the admissibility of the psychological profile of child molesters have heeded this reasoning and reached the result supported by the great bulk of scientific and legal literature cited in this article as well as in Murphy and Peters (1992). The notable exception is California. Perhaps a review of the literature cited in Murphy and Peters (1992), demonstrating the inapplicability of the major scientific tests cited in the California cases to the task of profiling child molesters, will encourage a renewed look at the admissibility of psychological profile testimony in that state.

REFERENCES

Cissell, J. (1987). *Federal criminal trials*. Charlottesville, VA: Michie.

Duchess County DSHS v. Mr. and Mrs. G., 534 N.Y. Supp.2d 64 (N.Y. Fam. Ct., 1988).

Dunnington v. State, 740 S.W.2d 899, 912 (Tex. Ct. App., 1987).

Federal Rules of Evidence, Sections 403, 404, 404(a)(1).

Frye v. United States, 293 F. 1013, 1014 (D.C. Cir., 1923).

Haakanson v. State, 760 P.2d 1030 (Alaska Ct. App. 1988).

Hall v. State, 692 S.W.2d 769 (Ark. Ct. App., 1985).

In the Matter of Arrigo, 503 N.Y. Supp. 2d 485 (N.Y. Fam. Ct., 1986).

In the Matter of Cheryl H., 153 Cal. App. 3d 1098, 200 Cal. Rptr. 789 (1984).

Martin, M. (1988, November 15). Profile evidence. *New York Law Journal*, p. 3.

McCord, D. (1986). Expert psychological testimony about child complaints in sexual abuse prosecutions. *Journal of Criminal Law and Criminology, 1*, 30.

McCormick, A. (1982). Scientific evidence: Defining a new approach to admissibility. *Iowa Law Revised, 879*, 911-912.

Murphy, W. D., & Peters, J. M. (1992). Profiling child sexual abusers: Psychological considerations. *Criminal Justice and Behavior, 19*, 24-37.

National Center for Prosecution of Child Abuse. (1988). Profiling child molesters. *Update, 1*(6).

Pendleton v. Commonwealth, 685 S.W.2d 549 (Ky., 1985).

People v. John W., 1985 Cal. App. 3d 801 229 Cal. Rptr. 783 (1986).

People v. Kelly, 17 Cal. 3d 24, 549 P.2d 1240 (1976).

People v. Ruiz, 272 Cal. Rptr. 368 (1990).

People v. Stoll, 265 Cal. Rptr. 111, 783 P.2d 698 (1989).

State v. Bill C., Anoka County, Minnesota (1985).

State v. Brown, 687 P.2d 751 (1984).

State v. Claflin, 690 P.2d 1186 (WA. Ct. App., 1984).

State v. Fitzgerald, 382 N.W.2d 892 (Minn. App., 1986).

State v. Friedrich, 398 N.W.2d 763 (Wis., 1987).

State v. Hanson, 743 P.2d 157 (1987).

State v. Hester, 760 P.2d, 27 (Idaho, 1988).

State v. Maule, 667 P.2d 96 (Wa. Ct. App., 1983).

State v. Miller, 709 P.2d 350 (Utah, 1985).

State v. Petrich, 683 P.2d 96 (Wa., 1983).

State v. Scott T., Clark County, Washington (1987).

State v. Shearer, 792 P.2d 1215 (Or. App. 1990).

State v. Tucker, 798 P.2d 1349 (Ariz. App. 1990).

United States v. St. Pierre, 812 F.2d 417 (8th Cir., 1987).

Weinstein, J., & Burger, M. (1982). *Weinstein's evidence.* New York: Bender.

Williams v. State, 649 S.W.2d 693 (Tx. Ct. App., 1983).

165

PROFILING CHILD SEXUAL ABUSERS
Psychological Considerations

WILLIAM D. MURPHY

University of Tennessee, Memphis

JAMES M. PETERS

U.S. Attorney's Office, St. Croix, U.S. Virgin Islands

Mental health professionals are increasingly being asked to provide expert testimony in the area of child sexual abuse. One controversial area is the provision of legal testimony regarding profiles of child sexual offenders. The current article addresses the scientific evidence of such testimony with a specific focus on current research with the Minnesota Multiphasic Personality Inventory and penile plethysmography. A companion article, by Peters and Murphy (in this special issue), addresses the legal issues surrounding such testimony. Conclusions from reviewing the existing literature suggest that there is limited empirical data to support contentions that mental health professionals can provide such testimony.

With increasing numbers of complex child sexual abuse cases reaching the courts, attorneys representing victims, those accused, and the government have sought advice and expert testimony from members of the mental health profession. Among the most controversial topics mental health professionals have been asked to address is the so-called psychological profile of a child sexual abuser. In the typical scenario, a mental health professional (psychiatrist, psychologist, social worker) will be asked to testify that there are identifiable characteristics or profiles of child sexual abusers according to published scientific research. The clinician may be asked first to assess the accused person, then to testify based on various tests and

AUTHORS' NOTE: *Correspondence may be addressed to William D. Murphy, Department of Psychiatry, University of Tennessee, 66 North Pauline, Suite 633, Memphis, TN 38105.*

CRIMINAL JUSTICE AND BEHAVIOR, Vol. 19 No. 1, March 1992 24-37
© 1992 American Association for Correctional Psychology

24

responses that the defendant either has or does not have those characteristics. Sometimes, too, the expert will be asked to offer an opinion
about the likelihood that the individual committed the crimes charged.

The purpose of this article is to address the scientific issues related
to the use of such testimony. This article reviews the scientific literature on the use of psychological procedures to develop profiles of the
sexual offender. A companion article (Peters & Murphy, 1992 [this
issue]) focuses on the legal issues involved in such profiling.

GENERAL CONSIDERATIONS

There have been numerous attempts by mental health professionals
to develop psychological profiles for the sexual offender. Many early
studies were flawed for a number of reasons including the use of
psychological instruments that were subjective in nature such as the
Rorschach, mixing different types of offenders in the same study (i.e.,
rapists, child molesters, and exhibitionists), and failure to employ
adequate control groups for comparison purposes (Levin & Stava,
1987; Murphy & Stalgaitis, 1987).

Recent studies, however, are based on what appear to be more
objective methods of assessment. The two most widely used instruments, both clinically and in research studies that will be the primary
topic at this point, are the Minnesota Multiphasic Personality Inventory (MMPI), a self-report measure of psychopathology, and penile
plethysmography. There have also been attempts to identify aspects
of the offender's history that match histories of known child sexual
offenders. One recurrent factor studied is the individual's own experience of sexual victimization. Although there are occasional references to other psychological instruments (Levin & Stava, 1987), they
are too few to warrant a conclusion.

MMPI

The MMPI is the most widely used psychological test in this
country and probably the world and has been used extensively with

sexual offenders. The MMPI consists of a 550 true-false questionnaire with 10 clinical scales assessing various areas of psychopathology and 3 validity scales. Two of the validity scales allow assessment of the patient's attempts, if any, to appear in a favorable light (Scales L and K), and the third (Scale F) allows some judgment concerning whether the person is "faking bad" or unable to comprehend the items. The MMPI is generally interpreted in terms of profiles, rather than a single scale, the most common interpretation being 2-point codes. That is, the test is interpreted for the 2 highest scale elevations usually requiring scores to be 2 standard deviations above the mean for interpretation. The MMPI has recently been revised (the MMPI II), although to date no literature has appeared relating MMPI II profiles to sex offenders.

A number of studies have looked at the mean MMPI profile of various groups of sex offenders (Levin & Stava, 1987) including a number addressing sex offenders against children. The majority of these studies have focused on correctional or hospital populations in which questions of guilt were not a major issue. As we will see, there are some doubts whether these data will generalize to a population of outpatient offenders and whether they will apply to individuals who are denying the charges.

Swenson and Grimes (1969), in an earlier study using a sample of predominantly child molesters, found a maximum mean elevation on Scale 4 (the Psychopathic Deviance Scale) with a somewhat elevated, although not 2 standard deviations above the mean, Scale 9 (the Hypomania Scale). The profile suggests that as a group, these sex offenders were rebellious, impulsive, defiant of authority, self-centered, and tended to act without considering the consequences of their behavior. Similarly, Langevin, Paitich, Freeman, Mann, and Handy (1978) found in a homosexual pedophile group (those who molest males) a peak elevation on Scale 4, but this was not observed in heterosexual pedophiles or incest cases. On the other hand, Panton (1979) found no difference between incestuous and nonincestuous child molesters, with both producing elevations on the Psychopathic Deviance Scale (Scale 4). Scott and Stone (1986) found that a group of outpatient incest offenders had basically normal profiles. Groff and Hubble (1984) found a 2-4 profile (the Depression Scale) for biological father incest offenders with young victims but a nearly normal profile for stepfathers and those who abused older children. McIvor and Duthie (1986) also found differences for incest cases with younger victims as compared to those with older victims but no profiles were presented.

Panton (1978), in a second study, compared rapists of adults, rapists of children, and nonviolent sexual molesters of children. He found that the two more aggressive groups showed elevations on Scales 4 and 8 (Schizophrenia Scale) that were interpreted as individuals who are very distrustful of others, fear emotional involvement, but have strong needs for attention. They tend to be seen as resentful, irritable, impulsive, and hostile. The finding of 4-8 profile as a second "average profile" in child molesters has been replicated by Armentrout and Hauer (1978), Anderson and Kunce (1979), and Quinsey, Arnold, and Pruesse (1980). In the above studies, Scale 2 (the Depression Scale) is also elevated; Kirkland and Bauer (1982) found a 8-7-4 profile in a group of 10 incest offenders and Kalichman (1991) found a 4-8-6 profile in offenders against children. The results of studies looking at the average profile would therefore suggest some commonalities among sex offenders. Common mean profiles involve elevations on Scale 4 of the MMPI, Scale 8 of the MMPI, with Scale 9 and Scale 2 also being elevated at times. One study with outpatient incestuous offenders found basically normal profiles (Scott & Stone, 1986).

Although on the surface such data seem to show consistency in sex offender profiles, questions arise. The first is how specific are these profiles to sex offenders? Quinsey et al. (1980) compared child molesters to a number of other groups seen in a forensic psychiatric facility. These other groups included rapists, murderers of family members, murderers of nonfamily members, arsonists, and property offenders. There were no differences among any of these groups, all showing peak elevations on Scales 4 and 8. In addition, elevations on Scale 4 alone or with Scale 9 are commonly seen in prison populations and 4-8/8-4 profiles are observed in a number of psychiatric populations and prison populations (Dahlstrom, Welsh, & Dahlstrom, 1972).

A second major problem with these studies is that they examine the mean profile which suggests that the groups are much more homogeneous than is actually observed. Three studies with large groups (Erickson, Luxenburg, Walbek, & Seely, 1987 [$n = 498$]; Hall, Maiuro,

Vitaliano, & Proctor, 1986 [n = 406]; Hall, 1989 [n = 81]) present the actual frequency of various profiles. In these studies, the 4-8 profile was the most frequent. However, in the Erickson et al. study, it occurred in only 13% of the child molesters, in the Hall et al. study, it occurred in only 7% of the population, and in the Hall (1989) study, 17% of the population. In these studies, almost every imaginable MMPI profile was observed and of the 45 theoretically possible 2-point codes, 43 were observed by Erickson et al. In the Erickson et al. study, 19% of the profiles fell within normal limits and in the Hall et al. study, 7% of the profiles were within normal limits. Presented this way, the data show no specific profile characterizing sex offenders; normal profiles are observed even among individuals who were incarcerated and convicted of sex offenses. This is further supported by a recent cluster analysis of MMPI profiles of child molesters showing 8 separate clusters (Duthie & McIvor, 1990).

There are also other factors that impact on MMPI profiles observed relevant to the legal situation, including prior criminal history and degree of denial. McCreary (1975) compared two groups of child molesters, one with no prior arrests and a second with one or more prior arrests. All of the individuals were convicted and the results indicated that the offenders with no previous convictions showed basically normal profiles while those with previous convictions showed the typical 4-8 profile.

Lanyon and Lutz (1984) investigated this issue of denial in a group of subjects indicted for sex offenses, including subjects both pre- and postconviction, although the percentages of each were not specified. It was found that subjects who admitted their offense produced the standard 4-8 profile, while subjects who either partially or fully denied produced basically normal profiles.

The literature related to the MMPI seems to clearly indicate that there is no one MMPI profile that describes child molesters and profiles produced by sex offenders against children are similar to other criminal and/or psychiatric populations. In addition, in the preconviction legal setting when an individual is probably unlikely to have had previous convictions, and is denying their charge, a normal profile would be expected.

PENILE PLETHYSMOGRAPHY

The direct measurement of erection responses to various types of stimuli has become a standard part of many treatment programs (Laws & Osborn, 1983) and is probably the most valid method of assessing sexual arousal (Zuckerman, 1972). In this section, we will attempt to review the state of the literature and outline why results from the procedure are being generalized into areas not supported by the literature.

Prior to reviewing the data, however, we should note how this assessment is conducted. Laws and Osborn (1983) have described general guidelines for conducting penile plethysmography assessments. However, it should be recognized that currently there is no accepted standard by experts nor is there any one set of standard stimulus material that is used. Most reputable programs do, however, follow some consistent patterns. In the general assessment procedure, the patient is seated in a comfortable chair in a room isolated from the equipment. In most situations, persons conducting the assessment are in verbal but not visual contact with the offender and the patient places a small transducer on his penis in the privacy of the laboratory. Most programs use a small device which only measures changes in the circumference of the penis, but some programs use a volumetric device which is a glass tube placed over the penis that measures changes in air displaced as a result of changes in erection. At the present time, the data are mixed as to whether the volumetric device is more sensitive (Murphy, Haynes, & Worley, 1991). Changes in the erection are recorded by various types of physiological monitors and are either visually displayed, written on chart paper or recorded by a computer.

In the majority of studies and in most clinical situations, two types of sexual material are most frequently used with offenders against children. These include slides generally depicting nude males and females of various ages. The second most frequently used stimulus are audiotapes describing in graphic details sexual interactions between adults and children that vary in amount of aggression used and/or type of sexual behavior performed. Video stimuli are less frequently employed. It is common for stimuli to be presented for 2 minutes, although this varies from study to study. In addition, it is common for the changes observed on the chart paper to be converted to some other unit such as percentage of full erection or actual millimeters of circumference change. In the clinical situation, one usually sets some minimum requirement for responding before the data are considered valid such as 10% to 20% of a full erection. In certain research studies, no minimum requirement is set and very small changes in erection response will be accepted. In interpreting erection data, there are also variations in clinicians' use of the results. Generally, one interprets the amount of arousal to the deviant stimuli (in this case the child stimuli) as compared to arousal to the adult control stimuli.

A number of studies have looked at actual responses of child molesters, and non-child molesters, to stimuli depicting females and males of various ages. Earlier studies by Freund (1965, 1967a, 1967b) resulted in significant statistical differences between the responses of pedophilic subjects versus normals. These results have been replicated by Quinsey, Chaplin, and Carrigan (1979), Quinsey, Steinman, Bergersen, and Holmes (1975), Marshall, Barbaree, and Christophe (1986), Marshall, Barbaree, and Butte (1988), Lang, Black, Frenzel, and Checkley (1988), Frenzel and Lang (1989), Freund and Blanchard (1989), and Freund and Watson (1991). Murphy, Haynes, Stalgaitis, and Flanagan (1986) showed similar results with child molesters, although no control group was employed. Further results from Quinsey's research indicated that, although nonfamilial child molesters showed more arousal to child stimuli than nonoffenders, this was not true of incestuous offenders who showed similar patterns to normals. The fact that incestuous offenders show patterns more similar to nonoffenders to slide material has also been found by Murphy et al. (1986) and Marshall, Barbaree, and Christophe (1986). However, Abel, Becker, Murphy, and Flanagan (1981) and Murphy et al. (1986) found that incestuous males displayed similar arousal as nonfamilial child molesters when audiotaped material was used, while Marshall et al. (1986) again found that incestuous offenders showed little arousal to audiotapes describing sexual interactions with children. Lang et al. (1988) and Frenzel and Lang (1989) found that in general the extrafamilial child molester showed more responding to prepubertal children than incest cases, although incest cases tend to respond more to adolescent cues than normal controls. Current data appears consistent in showing that nonfamilial child molesters show more arousal to children than control groups. In addition, the weight of the current evidence suggests that incest cases tend to be more similar to normals than they do to nonfamilial child molesters, although this issue is not totally resolved.

It has also been shown (Abel et al., 1981; Avery-Clark & Laws, 1984; Quinsey & Chaplin, 1988) that more aggressive pedophiles can be separated from less aggressive pedophiles on the basis of their sexual response to audiotapes describing aggressive sexual interactions. Lang et al. (1988) did not find statistical differences between aggressive and nonaggressive offenders, although their data indicated a trend similar to the other studies. Only two studies could be found that did not find statistical differences between child molesters and other offenders or normals on erection measures (Hall, Proctor, & Nelson, 1988; Haywood, Grossman, & Cavanaugh, 1990). However, both studies might have been invalid because subjects appeared to show very low levels of responding.

Except for the Hall et al. (1988) and Haywood et al. (1990) data, the above studies seem to suggest consistent patterns in this literature. However, it must be remembered that what is reported above are statistical differences of sufficient magnitude to allow clear separations between the groups. Other studies have presented data in a manner that allows one to determine the accuracy of classification using erection measures. Three studies use what is termed a pedophile index, which is the ratio of deviant arousal (arousal to material depicting children) to nondeviant arousal (arousal to material depicting adults). Two of these studies (Murphy et al., 1986; Abel et al., 1981) are of little use because they do not have control groups or use very small sample sizes. Using a pedophile index of 1.0, Abel et al. correctly classified 5/7 pedophiles and 7/7 incest cases while Murphy et al. with slide stimuli correctly classified 75% of heterosexual pedophiles, 78% of homosexual pedophiles, and 62% of mixed cases. Only 40% of incest cases had indexes above 1.0. Marshall et al. (1986) found that a pedophile index of 1.0 correctly classified only 40% of the nonfamilial child molesters as child molesters, although it classified the vast majority of nonoffenders as normals and the vast majority of incest cases appeared normal. A lower "cutoff" (that is a pedophile index of .6) correctly classified 60% of the child molesters and classified 82% of the normals correctly. What this means is that even with this very "loose" criteria, 40% of the known sex offenders were not correctly classified and 18% of the known normals were misclassified. Frenzel and Lang (1989) using largest responses to a stimulus category found that 68% of controls showed their largest responding to adult females, 66% of the incest cases showed their largest responses to adult females, and only 9.7% of incest cases showed a pedophilic pattern. Only 42% to 52% of the extrafamilial molesters evidenced clear pedophilic patterns. Freund and Blanchard (1989) found that only 55% of nonadmitters could be diagnosed as pedophiles, although 95% of controls were accurately classified. Freund and Watson (1991) found a sensitivity of from 44% to 88% for nonadmitting child molesters depending on number of victims, age of victims, and sex of victims. However, individuals with low responding or documented faking were excluded. Between 14% to 27% of patients were excluded for these reasons. In this study, 19% of controls were diagnosed as preferring minors.

There is also clear and long-standing evidence that individuals can fake and suppress erection responses when instructed (Abel, Barlow, Blanchard, & Mavissakalian, 1975; Freund, 1963; Laws & Holmen, 1978; Laws & Rubin, 1969; Quinsey & Bergersen, 1976; Wydra, Marshall, Earls, & Barbaree, 1983). In many of these studies, it would be impossible to detect such faking. This literature on individual's ability to control erection responses makes it clear that a subject's failure to respond in the laboratory cannot be interpreted because it could mean a number of things from intentional suppression to no true interest in the stimuli.

The results of the studies using erection data suggest that, although group differences are reliably found, the ability to classify an individual would produce error rates that would not be appropriate for the trial situation. In addition, in cases of incest or when patients deny charges, one would even expect to find either no responding in the laboratory or a normal response pattern. Further, it is clear that individuals can fake their responses and the absence of significant responding is basically meaningless in terms of a clinical interpretation. Like the MMPI literature, we find the conditions under which the test has been validated do not meet legal requirements.

BACKGROUND HISTORY

There is a good deal of clinical lore that a history of being sexually victimized is predominant in the backgrounds of sex offenders. However, there are a number of problems when extrapolating the clinical lore to the legal arena. First, one must realize that estimates currently suggest that somewhere between 1 in 8 children to 1 in 10 young males will be sexually abused before the age of 18 (Finkelhor, 1984). The vast majority of these children do not grow up to be sex offenders and therefore one could not classify someone as a sex offender based on the fact that they have been abused. In addition, even the estimate of the rate of sexual abuse in the history of known offenders varies widely (22% to 82%), at least in studies cited by Knopp (1984). Hanson and Slater (1988) reviewed data on 1,717 offenders included in 18 different studies. They found that the average rate of abuse across studies was 28%.

Also, of interest in this area, is a study reported by Hindman (1988). She reports data from a group of offenders seen before and after the introduction of a lie detection procedure in their clinic. Prior to the introduction of the lie detector, 67% of the offenders reported being victims as children and 29% reported beginning offending as adolescents. After the introduction of the polygraph, only 21% reported being abused as children, while 71% reported beginning their abuse in childhood or adolescence. Although this is only one study that was not completely controlled, it also raises serious questions of whether the actual reporting of victimization by offenders is accurate. Clearly there is insufficient evidence to correlate historical items with sex offending in any fashion that would be reliable enough for use in a courtroom.

CONCLUSION

The preceding review of the literature raises questions about the adequacy of our current data to allow any clear profiling of sex offenders. When judged against the legal requirements for expert testimony (see Peters & Murphy, 1991), there is doubt that psychological profiles have a place in a criminal trial where guilt and innocence is being determined. One could argue that clinical decision making and diagnosis is not based on interpretation of tests on a test-by-test basis, but is based on an overall integration of material based on clinical experience (Walker, 1990). This is generally true in the clinical situation. However, there is no research evidence to suggest that clinicians using all the tools available can profile sexual offenders with sufficient validity and reliability for use in criminal trials. This does not mean that psychological data are not valid for all uses. Psychological and physiological data are still valuable for treatment planning of known offenders and for empirical studies to increase our understanding of this population. Mental health professionals still have a role with the courts in presentencing situations once guilt or innocence has been determined.

REFERENCES

Abel, G. G., Becker, J. V., Murphy, W. D., & Flanagan, B. (1981). Identifying dangerous child molesters. In R. B. Stuart (Ed.), *Violent behavior: Social learning approaches to prediction, management, and treatment* (pp. 116-137). New York: Brunner/Mazel.

Anderson, W. P., & Kunce, J. T. (1979). Sex offenders: Three personality types. *Journal of Clinical Psychology, 35,* 671-676.

Armentrout, J. A., & Hauer, A. L. (1978). MMPIs of rapists of adults, rapists of children, and non-rapist sex offenders. *Journal of Clinical Psychology, 34,* 330-332.

Avery-Clark, C. A., & Laws, D. R. (1984). Differential erection response patterns of child sexual abusers to stimuli describing activities with children. *Behavior Therapy, 15,* 71-83.

Dahlstrom, W. G., Welsh, G. S., & Dahlstrom, L. E. (1972). *An MMPI handbook. Vol 1: Clinical interpretation.* Minneapolis: University of Minnesota.

Duthie, B., & McIvor, D. L. (1990). A new system for cluster-coding child molester MMPI profile types. *Criminal Justice and Behavior, 17,* 199-214.

Erickson, W. D., Luxenburg, M. G., Walbek, N. H., & Seely, R. K. (1987). Frequency of MMPI two-point code types among sex offenders. *Journal of Consulting and Clinical Psychology, 55,* 566-570.

Finkelhor, D. (1984). *Child sexual-abuse.* New York: Free Press.

Frenzel, R. R., & Lang, R. A. (1989). Identifying sexual preferences in intrafamilial and extrafamilial child sexual abusers. *Annals of Sex Research, 2,* 255-275.

Freund, K. (1963). A laboratory method for diagnosing predominance of homo and hetero erotic interest in the male. *Behavioral Research and Therapy, 1,* 85-93.

Freund, K. (1965). Diagnosing heterosexual pedophilia by means of a test for sexual interest. *Behavior Research and Therapy, 3*, 229-234.

Freund, K. (1967a). Diagnosing homo- or heterosexuality and erotic age-preference by means of a psychophysiological test. *Behavior Research and Therapy, 5*, 209-228.

Freund, K. (1967b). Erotic preference in pedophilia. *Behavior Research and Therapy, 5*, 339-348.

Freund, K., & Blanchard, R. (1989). Phallometric diagnosis of pedophilia. *Journal of Consulting and Clinical Psychology, 57*, 100-105.

Freund, K., & Watson, R. J. (1991). Assessment of the sensitivity and specificity of a phallometric test: An update of phallometric diagnosis of pedophilia. *Psychological Assessment: A Journal of Consulting and Clinical Psychology, 3*, 254-260.

Groff, M. G., & Hubble, L. M. (1984). A comparison of father-daughter and stepfather-stepdaughter incest. *Criminal Justice and Behavior, 11*, 461-475.

Hall, G.C.N. (1989). WAIS-R and MMPI profiles of men who have assaulted children: Evidence of limited utility. *Journal of Personality Assessment, 53*, 404-412.

Hall, G.C.N., Proctor, W. C., & Nelson, G. M. (1988). Validity of physiological measures of pedophilic sexual arousal in a sexual offender population. *Journal of Consulting and Clinical Psychology, 56*, 118-122.

Hall, G.C.N., Maiuro, R. D., Vitaliano, P. P., & Proctor, W. D. (1986). The utility of the MMPI with men who have sexually assaulted children. *Journal of Consulting and Clinical Psychology, 54*, 493-496.

Hanson, R. K., & Slater, S. (1988). Sexual victimization in the history of sexual abusers: A review. *Annals of Sex Research, 1*, 485-499.

Haywood, T. W., Grossman, L. S., & Cavanaugh, J. L. (1990). Subjective versus objective measurements of deviant sexual arousal in clinical evaluations of alleged child molesters. *Psychological Assessment: A Journal of Consulting and Clinical Psychology, 2*, 269-275.

Hindman, J. (1988). New insight into adult and juvenile sexual offenders. *Community Safety Quarterly, 1*, 3.

Kalichman, S. C. (1991). Psychopathology and personality characteristics of criminal sexual offenders as a function of victim age. *Archives of Sexual Behavior, 20*, 187-197.

Kirkland, K. D., & Bauer, C. A. (1982). MMPI traits of incestuous fathers. *Journal of Clinical Psychology, 38*, 645-649.

Knopp, F. H. (1984). *Retraining adult sex offenders: Methods and models.* Syracuse, NY: Safer Press.

Lang, R. A., Black, E. L., Frenzel, R. R., & Checkley, K. L. (1988). Aggression and erotic attraction toward children in incestuous and pedophilic men. *Annals of Sex Research, 1*, 417-441.

Langevin, R., Paitich, D., Freeman, R., Mann, K., & Handy, L. (1978). Personality characteristics and sexual anomalies in males. *Canadian Journal of Behavioral Science, 10*, 222-238.

Lanyon, R. I., & Lutz, R. W. (1984). MMPI discrimination of defensive and nondefensive felony sex offenders. *Journal of Consulting and Clinical Psychology, 52*, 841-943.

Laws, D. R., & Holmen, M. L. (1978). Sexual response faking by pedophiles. *Criminal Justice and Behavior, 5*, 343-356.

Laws, D. R., & Osborn, C. A. (1983). How to build and operate a behavioral laboratory to evaluate and treat sexual deviance. In J. G. Greer & I. R. Stuart (Eds.), *The sexual aggressor: Current perspectives on treatment* (pp. 293-335). New York: Van Nostrand Reinhold.

Laws, D. R., & Rubin, H. B. (1969). Instructional control of an autonomic response. *Journal of Applied Behavior Analysis, 2*, 93-99.

Levin, S. M., & Stava, L. (1987). Personality characteristics of sex offenders: A review. *Archives of Sexual Behavior, 16,* 57-79.

Marshall, W. L., Barbaree, H. E., & Butt, J. (1988). Sexual offenders against children: Sexual preference for gender, age of victim and type of behavior. *Behaviour Research and Therapy, 26,* 383-391.

Marshall, W. L., Barbaree, H. E., & Christophe, D. (1986). Sexual offenders against children: Sexual preferences for age of victims and type of behavior. *Canadian Journal of Behavioural Science, 18,* 424-439.

McCreary, C. P. (1975). Personality differences among child molesters. *Journal of Personality Assessment, 39,* 591-593.

McIvor, D. L., & Duthie, B. (1986). MMPI differences among child molesters. *Journal of Personality Assessment, 39,* 591-593.

Murphy, W. D., Haynes, M. R., Stalgaitis, S. J., & Flanagan, B. (1986). Differential sexual responding among four groups of sexual offenders against children. *Journal of Psychopathology and Behavioral Assessment, 8,* 339-353.

Murphy, W. D., Haynes, M. R., & Worley, P. J. (1991). Assessment of adult sexual interest. In C. R. Hollin & K. Howells (Eds.), *Clinical approaches to sex offenders and their victims* (pp. 77-92). West Sussex, England: Wiley.

Murphy, W. D., & Stalgaitis, S. J. (1987). Assessment and treatment considerations for sexual offenders against children: Behavioral and social learning approaches. In J. R. McNamara & M. A. Appel (Eds.), *Critical issues, developments, and trends in professional psychology* (Vol. 3, pp. 177-210). New York: Praeger.

Panton, J. H. (1978). Personality differences appearing between rapists of adults, rapists of children, and non-violent sexual molesters of female children. *Research Communications in Psychology, Psychiatry and Behavior, 3,* 385-393.

Panton, J. H. (1979). MMPI profile configurations associated with incestuous and non-incestuous child molesting. *Psychological Reports, 45,* 335-338.

Peters, J. M., & Murphy, W. D. (1992). Profiling child sexual abusers: Legal considerations. *Criminal Justice and Behavior, 19,* 38-53.

Quinsey, V. L., Arnold, L. S., & Pruesse, M. G. (1980). MMPI profiles of men referred for a pretrial psychiatric assessment as a function of offense type. *Journal of Clinical Psychology, 36,* 410-417.

Quinsey, V. L., & Bergersen, S. G. (1976). Instructional control of penile circumference in assessments of sexual preference. *Behavior Therapy, 7,* 489-493.

Quinsey, V. L., & Chaplin, T. C. (1988). Penile responses of child molesters and normals to descriptions of encounters with children involving sex and violence. *Journal of Interpersonal Violence, 3,* 259-274.

Quinsey, V. L., Chaplin, T. C., & Carrigan, W. F. (1979). Sexual preferences among incestuous and nonincestuous child molesters. *Behavior Therapy, 10,* 562-565.

Quinsey, V. L., Steinman, C. M., Bergersen, S. G., & Holmes, T. F. (1975). Penile circumference, skin conductance, and ranking responses of child molesters and "normals" to sexual and nonsexual visual stimuli. *Behavior Therapy, 6,* 213-219.

Scott, R. L., & Stone, D. A. (1986). MMPI profile constellations in incest families. *Journal of Consulting and Clinical Psychology, 54,* 364-368.

Swenson, W. M., & Grimes, B. P. (1969). Characteristics of sex offenders admitted to a Minnesota state hospital for pre-sentence psychiatric investigation. *Psychiatric Quarterly Supplement, 34,* 110-123.

Walker, L.E.A. (1990). Psychological assessment of sexually abused children for legal evaluation and expert witness testimony. *Professional Psychology, 21,* 344-353.

Wydra, A., Marshall, W. L., Earls, C. M., & Barbaree, H. E. (1983). Identification of cues and control of sexual arousal by rapists. *Behavior Research and Therapy, 21*, 469-476.

Zuckerman, M. (1972). Physiological measures of sexual arousal in the human. In N. S. Greenfield & R. A. Sternbach (Eds.), *Handbook of psychopathology* (pp. 709-740). New York: Holt, Rinehart & Winston.

DEBATE FORUM

Anatomically Correct Dolls:
Should They be Used as the Basis for Expert Testimony?

Background. Two decisions by the California Supreme Court of Appeal in the spring of 1987 have made it difficult to admit evidence based on anatomically correct doll interviews with children. An earlier court ruling (*People v. Shirley*) had implied that the Kelly-Frye rule on the admissibility of evidence (*Frye v. United States,* 1923; *People v. Kelly,* 1976) would extend from physical to include psychological evidence. In its reversal of lower court decisions (*In re Amber B. and Teela B.* and *In re Christine C. and Michael C.*) to accept testimony based on children's play with anatomically correct dolls, the California Supreme Court concluded that use of the dolls constitutes a new scientific method of proof and is admissible in court only if it has been accepted as generally reliable in the scientific community. In following the debate, two expert child and adolescent psychiatrists argue this issue of scientific reliability.

AFFIRMATIVE: ALAYNE YATES, M.D.

Ten years ago, anatomically correct dolls did not exist; now they are commonplace in mental health centers, law enforcement agencies, child protective service agencies, pediatric offices, and in child psychiatry playrooms. At present, the dolls are available in different colors and in sets of four, eight, or twelve. One company (Harnest, 1981) equips the male doll with a mustache, body hair, and detachable, exchangeable circumcized and uncircumcized penises. The female doll is supplied with a sanitary napkin and belt, a tampon, and a baby with an umbilical cord. Grandparent, baby, and toddler dolls are also available. A family of four dolls may cost several hundreds of dollars.

In spite of this manikin population explosion, there have been but two studies published in peer-reviewed journals that address the issue of whether abused children interact differently with the dolls than do nonabused children. Both of these articles were published in the journal *Child Abuse and Neglect* within the past 18 months. The first of these, by White et al. (1986), compared twenty-five 2- to 5.6-year-old children who were suspected sexual abuse victims with 25 control subjects who were not suspected victims. There were more girls among the suspected victims than among the controls and it is possible that some of the children who were suspected of having been abused had not been abused. Examiners were blind and the interview room was furnished with only a few other toys. The session began with at least 10 minutes of free play before the structured interview, which identified the dolls, assessed the child's knowledge of body parts, and inquired as to the existence/nonexistence of sexual abuse. The children suspected of having been abused demonstrated significantly more sexualized doll play ($p < 0.0001$) and described significantly more sexual abuse situations ($p < 0.0001$) than did the control children.

The second, smaller study by Jampole and Weber (1987)

Accepted October 20, 1987.

Dr. Yates is Chief of Child Psychiatry, Professor of Psychiatry and Associate Professor of Pediatrics, College of Medicine, University of Arizona, Tucson, Arizona. Dr. Terr is Clinical Professor of Psychiatry, University of California, San Francisco. Reprint requests to Dr. Yates or Dr. Terr, 450 Sutter St., San Francisco, CA 94108.

Commentary invited by the Journal of the American Academy of Child and Adolescent Psychiatry.

0890-8567/88/2702-0254 $02.00/0 © 1988 by the American Academy of Child and Adolescent Psychiatry.

compared 10 children whose sexual abuse had been confirmed with 10 nonabused controls. All 10 abused children were in custody as were six of the nonabused children. This study employed a nondirective approach in which most of the observations of sexual play were while the child was being observed through a one-way mirror. There were significant differences between the two groups in the occurrence of sexualized doll play.

In spite of differences in method and sample, the studies yielded comparable results, indicating that sexually abused children probably are more likely than nonabused children to engage in sexual play when exposed to the anatomically correct dolls. The results were not absolute: in both studies there were children who had been abused, or were suspected of being abused, who did not engage in sexual play, and in the Jampole study there were two children (20%) who had not been sexually abused but who engaged in sex play with the dolls. Thus, sexual play with the dolls indicates that abuse may have occurred, but it is not proof positive that abuse did occur. These studies are an important step in the right direction; they indicate that observations on anatomical doll play are in the process of being accepted by the profession.

Psychiatric research attempts to nail down assessment variables and to establish as far as possible indices of risk or probability. In sexual abuse assessment, there are many variables that have not been explored which may affect a given child's reaction to the anatomical dolls. These include the duration of the examination, which may be 10 minutes or an hour in length; the format of the interview; the location of the interview and availability of other toys; the number of prior interviews, with or without a similar set of dolls; and the training of the examiners. The dolls may not elicit the same kind of information from boys as from girls, as boys may have been taught not to play with dolls. Older boys or girls may avoid the dolls because they are "babyish" toys. Some children are more eroticized than others because of the family's style or living condition (Yates, 1987). They may exhibit more sexual interest and readiness to be involved in sexual play. Children who were reared in a liberal commune, a kibbutz, or in a one-bedroom apartment with six other children might respond in the same way as sexually abused children. We do not know how children who regularly watch the Playboy channel while their parents work would react either. If we are to fully appreciate the significance of sexual play, we would need to study the diversity of erotic expression in nonabused as well as abused children.

Events that were not defined as sexually abusive a decade or so ago, are now considered abusive. Examples include a child who chances on an exhibitionist in the alley or a 63-year-old, recently impotent grandfather who holds his 3-year-old grandaughter on his lap with his pants unzipped in the hope of obtaining an erection. Experiences such as this may or may not be perceived by the child as sexual and, if not, the child may not present the symptom of sexualized play with the anatomical dolls.

With all of these areas yet to be explored, why should we continue to use the anatomical dolls? For the same reasons that we continue to use puppets, dollhouses, anatomically absent dolls, and play dough in the playroom, even though there are not scientific studies that tell us what to expect from a given child with a given history in a given playroom with a certain examiner. The anatomical dolls are useful in enabling the examiner to understand the child and form an opinion. The fact that the examiner has the dolls and that the dolls have genitals gives the child tacit permission to explore sexual topics. Most articles in the playroom are asexual or ambisexual; Fisher-Price dollhouses come without bathrooms. The presence of succinctly sexual objects such as the anatomical dolls may help the child to focus on sexual topics. Dolls can be used to identify the child's names for the genitalia so that the child can talk about what happened. Through playing with the anatomical dolls the child can provide information that he or she is unable or unwilling to verbalize; the dolls are especially useful with children who are younger than age 3, retarded, very shy, or who speak a different language. It may be impossible to explore sexual issues with these children without using the dolls.

The California Supreme Court's interpretation of the Kelly-Frye rule restates a basic evidentiary position: that the opinion of an expert should be based on material or methods that are generally accepted within his or her profession. Ordinarily, a period of time will elapse between the introduction of diagnostic materials and their general acceptance. It would seem that the dolls are in the process of becoming accepted by the profession. If we were to abandon their use because of the courts' criticism they could never be fully accepted by the profession or introduced as evidence in court. Above all, we need to continue to use the dolls so that we may understand and further develop the technique. Before full acceptance of the procedure, expert witnesses must be careful not to overstate the importance of doll observations in forming their opinions.

Anatomically correct dolls are "new" only because of the addition of sexual characteristics. Child psychiatrists have used anatomically absent dolls since the birth of the profession. If we had not discriminated against the genitals initially, we would not be in the rather ludicrous position of being able to base an opinion on children's reactions to dolls but not on dolls with genitals. A case can be made for anatomical accuracy in the playroom regardless of the conditions of the court. Anxiety, guilt, and confusion about sexual issues are commonplace for children in a culture that strives to keep them from knowing about sex. When children demonstrate sexual interests or activities, their parents respond by condemning, mislabeling, or avoiding the subject (Gagnon and Simon,

1973), leaving children with unresolved emotional baggage. Child psychiatrists inadvertently subscribe to this bias by avoiding sexual issues through the selective elimination of genitals from the dolls used in therapy. If anatomically correct dolls with substantive genitals were standard equipment in the playroom, the therapist could explore and define children's concepts and concerns about genitalia. In time, this practice would lead to an appreciation of the range of children's responses to the genitals and a finer discrimination between abused and nonabused children, and, if the dolls were standard equipment, the court would not question their acceptance by the profession.

The majority of individuals who use the anatomically correct dolls are employed by public agencies and have little or no training in child development, child assessment, mental health, or human sexuality. Their credentials often consist of a weekend workshop in sexual trauma assessment. Yet the dolls are only as good as the people who use them. We need thoroughly qualified, skilled examiners who are comfortable in the playroom. Examiners need enough time to develop a relationship with the child. The child should spontaneously explore the dolls and their genitalia if the results are to be relatively uncontaminated. Examiners must have the ability to elicit a sexual history from the child so that the data obtained from the child's play with the dolls can be placed in perspective.

The Academy, the American Psychological Association, and the American Bar Association might collaborate in establishing reasonable standards of qualifications for those who examine children who are suspected of having been abused. They also might formulate guidelines for the use of the dolls in a manner that will not prejudice the child's responses. These guidelines would need to be reviewed periodically as more research data become available. In the interim, testimony concerning the child's behavior with the dolls needs to be regarded by the courts as an additional piece of evidentiary material that does not stand alone but that may or may not add to the suspicion that the child has been abused. The information obtained from doll play needs to be integrated with a compendium of other bits and pieces of information and observation that will enable the expert witness to render a considered opinion.

Although the validity and reliability of the use of the anatomically correct dolls may never be fully established, the procedure is in the process of being accepted by the profession because it facilitates the evaluation of young children who are suspected of having been abused. The dolls can be used to identify the terms the child uses for the genitals, to focus the interview, to provide the setting and the permission for the child to explore sexual topics, and to elicit information from very young, shy, retarded, or foreign language speaking children. If the dolls or comparable play materials were not available, some abused children would not be able to communicate their sexual concerns and experiences and, therefore, could not be protected by the courts.

NEGATIVE: LENORE TERR, M.D.

The preschooler enters the stranger's office. "Would you like to play?" the adult smiles. The child looks over the nice person's toys—a doll house, some clay, airplanes, cars, trucks, crayons, a Candyland game, and a family of rubbery puppets. There are some big soft dolls, too. These dolls have smallish eyes that do not open or shut, but their mouths open to reveal large, protruding tongues. Their hands are built like mittens with one thumb and four stuck-together fingers. Strange. They seem to have no clothes, so you can't play school with them, set them up for tea, or even undress them to take a bath. There is one, main thing you can see on these dolls—their sex. They have pubic hair, penises, scrotal sacs, rounded breasts, vaginas that indent, and buttocks with full folds. There is just about one game to play with these dolls—"sex."

For the ordinary youngster, the dolls I describe feel weird emotionally, although adults may consider them to be correct anatomically. Seeing the dolls on a professional toy shelf may tell the preschooler to play something that he or she thinks is bad inside an office he assumes to be good. The situation suggests, "Play sex," and the ordinary child feels odd complying to such a request coming from an adult.

As professionals, we have long seen demonstrated in our offices and in our literature that children will tell their best "truths" in response to friendly, open-ended questions and free play with ordinary toys. This is a proven technique. We understand that occasionally the psychiatrist must ask direct, closed-ended questions and that the researchers among us may wish to administer preset, structured interviews. For diagnostic purposes in ordinary child psychiatric practice, however, there is nothing superior to unstructured play and open-ended questions. These elicit the most, the "cleanest," information from youngsters.

These open-ended techniques take time, and they require high levels of training and expertise to administer. Sexually anatomically correct dolls, on the other hand, seem to allow for shortcuts both in time and in training—something that, of course, would appeal to our financially and morally pressed agencies. The anatomically correct dolls make but one request, "play sex." Many children seem to respond to them at once, even when untrained criminal investigators administer the doll sessions. The additional and tempting codicil: "Tell me. Did someone do something like this to you?" gathers up even more fast answers from certain children. And so a large, enthusiastic cohort of law enforcement and social personnel have come to rely upon this method for the main, and in some instances the only, method of investigation when preschoolers are alleged to have been sexually abused.

I watched a television tape recently that shows a policeman administering a sexually anatomically correct doll interview to a 3-year-old in a small room furnished with only two chairs and one set of dolls. When the youngster hesitated a moment after fiddling with the genitalia of the adult male doll, the officer asked, "Did your daddy do anything like that to you?" Such a question, asked in the midst of such stimulating, unusual play, might, I think, elicit any kind of answer from a confused young child, an answer, perhaps, having little to do with this particular youngster's life experiences. On the tape I watched, the boy answered, "Yes, Daddy did," and the prosecutor who presented the tape told us that he had obtained a criminal conviction of the boy's father on the basis of this. But *was* the boy really sexually abused? I felt at a loss to know.

Goodman and Aman (1987) presented a study recently in

which they had a male member of their team talk and play for 10 minutes with each of 31 normal 3-year-olds and 30 normal 5-year-olds. The children were then seen individually in a play session that was conducted a week later by a second investigator. The groups of children were divided as to what they were allowed to play in the sessions—with no dolls, with ordinary dolls, and with sexually anatomically correct dolls. Leading questions about "the man" were asked of each child as he or she played. "Show me where he kissed you." "Did he tell you secrets?" etc. Among the 3-year-olds playing with the sexually anatomically correct dolls, especially among the younger 3-year-olds, there were a number of "false positive" responses. As a matter of fact, 3-year-olds playing with any sort of doll tended to answer questions with less veracity than did the 5-year-olds. The 5-year-old child tended to give correct answers in any one of the three experimental situations. However, there were some false responses even in these "older" children.

It is primarily the 2-, 3-, and 4-year-old child for whom sexually anatomically correct doll interviews are geared, although the dolls, of course, may also be used in other contexts. It was thought that this sort of doll play would encourage young preschoolers to remember and to tell their bad experiences because it was recognized that very young children have trouble spontaneously bringing up memories of abusive episodes. As a matter of fact, most traumatized infants and toddlers, those under the approximate age of 28 to 36 months at the time they experience traumatic events, appear unable to bring out more than a few spot verbal recollections of documented episodes when asked months to years later, "Did anything very scary ever happen to you?" (Terr, 1988). The anatomically correct doll had seemed a promising way to get the preschooler to associate to the stimulus and to "tell" old events behaviorally, as opposed to the more difficult-to-obtain, purely verbal tellings of events. What has happened when the dolls actually are used, however, has not borne out the original enthusiasm for the concept. As a matter of fact, the dolls, when used without safeguards, may raise new problems.

White (1986) has suggested several safeguards. Sexually anatomically correct dolls should not be the only method of evaluation employed. They should be administered by well-trained professionals. A standardized, structured doll protocol should be used, and there must be a prohibition against asking certain direct, leading questions in conjunction with the doll play. I have suggested that child psychiatrists randomly, but regularly watch play sessions that are intended for courtroom use. This could be done through one-way mirrors or with tapes to determine whether the play, indeed, was part of an objective evaluation (Terr, 1986).

However, a problem would remain even if stringent safeguards were used along with the anatomically correct dolls—the problem of the occasional false negative or the false positive. Consider a hypothetically abused youngster, for instance. The sex abuse victim often habitually employs the defense of denial of external reality (Terr, 1987). This repeatedly stressed child may massively avoid, go mute, or otherwise hide from the world its impotent rage and sexual overstimulation (Burgess et al., 1981). Why should the mental health professional expect such a victim to play with sexually explicit dolls? The chronically abused preschooler, in fact, would probably be the very person to drop the doll, discard it, or ignore it altogether. A therapist would have to pursue this exceptional child with specific, leading questions in order to find what the therapist seeks. If anatomically correct doll play were to be the only option for evaluating such a child, I am afraid that this special youngster could easily be lost to treatment.

On the other hand, consider the exceptionally curious and uninhibited normal preschooler. This hypothetical child might be eager to please. She might be fascinated with sex and interested in the love relationships within her family. If the "right" mental health investigator invited such a child at just the "right" developmental time to play with sexually anatomically correct dolls, the youngster might give the investigator an eyeful or an earful. A tape of one such normal child did indeed confound the "blinded" experts in the Realmuto et al. (1986) preliminary study of blind raters' responses to taped doll interviews.

American law shudders at the possibility of imprisoning innocents. Our constitution also protects against needless interference with family functioning. In other words, our law does not tolerate the false positive. Yet, the law also wants to be of assistance to an ever-increasing multitude of children who have suffered abuses. Anatomically correct dolls embody this conflict between protection of rights and activism. This conflict within the law will not resolve itself until we in the behavioral sciences develop a series of meaningful studies of anatomically correct dolls that show just how serious and how prevalent false positives and false negatives actually are.

In the two lower court cases that were reversed or held "in error" by the California Court of Appeal, *In re Amber B.* (1987) and *In re Christine C.* (1987), each doctor, testifying about the evidence he had gleaned from anatomically correct doll play, was asked, on direct or cross-examination, the scientific basis for his reliance on the dolls. Neither doctor could give an acceptable answer. There probably *is* no acceptable answer. The only studies we currently have consider the anatomically correct doll play of *allegedly* abused children (White et al., 1986, for instance). Comparing allegedly abused children's play with anyone else's play probably will not give us a convincing answer. We would have to study the play of *definitely* abused children versus normal children's play before we could assess with some certainty the likelihood of false positive or negative responses.

It is up to the proponents of anatomically correct doll play to prove or to disprove their methods. These proofs have yet to be offered. The California Court of Appeal has communicated that the trial courts will require proofs. We in child psychiatry need the proofs, too. These proofs would not, I think, be hard to get. One study might go something like this: Large centers accumulate definite cases of childhood sexual abuse—definite because parents admit to it, pornographic pictures come in, or corroborating injuries establish the fact. An investigator interested in anatomically correct doll play could put together a group of 20 or so definitely abused children and a group of 20 or so normal matched control subjects, screened to eliminate known sex abuse and drawn

from pediatric or nursery school populations in the same city. A blind rater or a group of blind raters could then watch randomly arranged videotapes of the children's play sessions with anatomically correct dolls. They could decide from the play whether or not the child was abused. The known answers could then be compared with the guesses.

We need many kinds of convincing studies before we all fill up our toy shelves with 2-foot long dolls complete with detachable penises and menstrual pads. I have suggested one possible project. All studies must be done with thoughtful design and meticulous implementation. We may eventually have to consider re-engineering the dolls themselves in order to let the toys present more open-ended questions to children. All this is necessary because the consequences of legal action inside a family are grave. We must work to avoid both false positives and false negatives. One false negative response to an anatomically correct doll represents an abused child who might have been discovered, given open-ended questioning and an open-ended chance to play—in other words, a miscarriage of mental health professionalism. One false positive response to the sexually anatomically correct doll, on the other hand, may result in a miscarriage of the law.

References

Burgess, A. W., Groth, A. N. & McCausland, M. P. (1981), Child sex initiation rings. *Am. J. Orthopsychiatry*, 51:110–119.

Frye v. United States (1923), D. C. Cir. 293 F. 1013.

Gagnon, J. H. & Simon, W. (1973), *Sexual Conduct*. Chicago: Aldine.

Goodman, G. & Aman, C. (1987), *Children's use of anatomically correct dolls to report on an event*. Paper presented at the Annual Meeting, Society for Research in Child Development, Baltimore, Md.

Harnest, J. (1981), *Teach-a-Bodies*. Available from Teach-a-Bodies, 2544 Boyd St., Ft. Worth, Texas 76109.

In re Amber B. and Teela B. (1987), 191 Cal. App. 3rd 682.

In re Christine C. and Michael C. (1987), 191 Cal. App. 3rd 676.

Jampole, L. & Weber, M. K. (1987), An assessment of the behavior of sexually abused and nonsexually abused children with anatomically correct dolls. *Child Abuse Negl.*, 11:187–192.

People v. Kelly (1976), 17 Cal. 3d 24.

People v. Shirley (1982), 31 Cal. 3d 18, 53.

Realmuto, G., Jensen, J. & Garfinkel, B. (1986), *Interviewer and professional ratings of children interviewed with sexually anatomically correct dolls*. Poster Session presented at the Annual Meeting, American Academy of Child and Adolescent Psychiatry, Los Angeles, Cal.

Terr, L. (1986), The child psychiatrist and the child witness: travelling companions by necessity, if not by design. *J. Am. Acad. Child Psychiatry*, 25:462–472.

—— (1987), The trauma and extreme stress disorders: an outline and overview. Presented as the Samuel G. Hibbs Memorial Lecture, American Psychiatric Association Annual Meetings, Chicago.

—— (1988), Case study: What happens to early memories of trauma? A study of twenty children under age five at the time of documented traumatic events. *J. Am. Acad. Child Adolesc. Psychiatry*, 27:96–104.

White, S. (1986), Uses and abuses of the sexually anatomically correct dolls (Division of Child, Youth, and Family Services Newsletter, vol. 9, no. 1). Washington, D. C.: 9:1 American Psychological Association, Division 37, pp. 3–6.

—— Strom, G., Santilli, G. & Halpin, B. (1986), Interviewing young sexual abuse victims with anatomically correct dolls. *Child Abuse Negl.*, 10:519–529.

Yates, A. (1987), Psychological damage associated with extreme eroticism in young children. *Psychiatric Annals*, 17:257–261.

The Use of Anatomically Correct Dolls in the Evaluation of Sexually Abused Children

Cynthia C. Goldberg, Alayne Yates, MD

• There is confusion and controversy regarding the use of anatomically correct dolls in the evaluation of allegedly sexually abused children. Studies indicate that there is a significant difference between the play behavior of sexually abused children and that of nonabused children when using anatomically correct dolls. Other research suggests that nonabused children are not threatened, sexually stimulated, or excited to aggression by exposure to anatomically correct dolls. These dolls can be used by trained professionals to help make conclusions about a child's background. However, the dolls cannot be used to prove or disprove abuse.

(*AJDC.* 1990;144:1334-1336)

W hile dolls have been used in play therapy for years, anatomically correct dolls have only been introduced within the last decade. These dolls have been designed for use by child protection workers, mental health practitioners, physicians, and law enforcement workers as tools to diagnose and provide therapy for suspected victims of child abuse. The Eymann anatomically correct dolls (Eymann Dolls, Sacramento, Calif) are available in white, black, hispanic and Asian family sets. Each doll has a tongue, fingers, breasts, jointed legs, naval, anus, and appropriate male or female sex organs. There are both adult and child dolls; grandparent, baby, and toddler dolls are available from Teach-a-Bodies (Teach-a-Bodies, Ft Worth, Tex). This company provides the male doll with mustache, body hair, and exchangeable circumcised and un-

Accepted for publication June 4, 1990.
From the University of Arizona College of Medicine, Tucson.
Reprints not available.

circumcised penises. The female kit includes a sanitary napkin and belt, a tampon, and a baby with the umbilical cord. The genitalia and breasts of 17 sets of anatomic dolls were measured and found to be proportioned similarly to their human counterparts.[1]

RELEVANT STUDIES

Studies have assessed the play behavior of nonabused children and have compared the behavior of sexually abused children with the behavior of nonabused children during play with anatomically correct dolls. In one study,[2] 144 nonabused 3- to 8-year-children were observed in a playroom. Anatomically correct dolls were among the toys in the room. Each child was exposed to conditions in which an adult was present in the room, no adult was present, and the dolls were undressed. Results showed that for both genders and all age groups, a maximum of 26% of playtime was spent with the dolls. The children spent most of their time with the other toys. The children's interactions with the dolls were described in four behavioral categories. These were exploration (inspecting, touching, holding, moving, and looking), role play (feeding and caretaking), dressing, and aggression. The children most commonly fed the dolls, a role-play behavior. Aggressive behavior toward the dolls was rare; it accounted for less than 1% of the observed interactions. No aggression was observed when the dolls were left undressed. No sexually explicit behavior was observed.

Glasser and Collins[3] observed 91 nonabused children, aged 2 to 6 years, playing by themselves, with a friend, and in a group. Each child played individually with the examiner present, and then

played in a group with other children. The play sessions took place in a classroom with a central table on which the dressed anatomically correct dolls and other toys were placed. The examiner sat at a distance to observe play. Any child who did not engage in specific behaviors was encouraged to do so in a sequence predetermined by the examiners. For example, if the child did not undress the doll, the child was invited to do so. The child was then encouraged to play a "functions" game. In this game, the child names various body parts of the doll, beginning with eye, nose and mouth, and ending with genitalia. Time was also allotted for free play. Five of the 91 children observed refused to play with the dolls. Of the remaining 86 children, 64 (74%) undressed the dolls spontaneously, and 15 (17%) required significant encouragement. Only one child refused to undress the dolls. There were a variety of affective responses to the doll's genitals, ranging from shyness and avoidance to giggling and excitement. The age of the child and the peer setting had a statistically significant effect on the child's response. Older children and children in a group showed giggly and excited behavior. Seventy-eight (86%) of the observed children noticed, named, or touched the genitalia. Fifty-one (65%) touched the penis, three (4%) touched the vaginal opening, and 11 (14%) touched the anus. However, no child inserted a finger into either orifice. Only five of the children showed sexually explicit play. It was later revealed that two of them had been exposed to pornographic literature or videos, and the third child had observed sexual activity. The foundation of sexual knowledge of the remaining two children was unknown.

184

White et al[1] compared 25 children suspected to have been victims of sexual abuse with 25 nonreferred children. The ages of the children ranged from 2 to 5.6 years. Tests relating to suspected abuse, and scored on a scale of zero to four, were given to each child. Two different scores were given, one based on a report by the parent and medical evaluator, and another based on the child's behavioral response to the anatomically correct dolls. A statistically significant difference in awarded scores was found between the nonreferred children and the children suspected to have been abused. The two scores were more consistent for 3- and 4-year-old children than they were for 2- and 5-year-old children.

Jampole and Weber[5] studied 20 children aged 3 to 8 years. Ten of these children were victims of sexual abuse, and 10 were not. The two groups of children matched with respect to age, sex, and race. Each child was observed by an examiner in the room and by an examiner behind a two-way mirror. The playroom contained an assortment of toys, including anatomically correct dolls. If the child did not spontaneously play with the dolls within the first 10 minutes, the examiner presented the dolls to the child. If the child did not undress the dolls, the child was asked to undress them and name the body parts. The child was then left alone and the child's play was observed for an additional 15 minutes. A significant difference between the play behavior of the sexually abused children and that of the nonabused children was demonstrated. Nine (90%) of the abused children showed "sexual" behavior with the dolls (eg, demonstrated intercourse between dolls or between doll and child), while only 20% of the nonabused children showed such behavior. However, when the observer left the room, 19 of the abused and nonabused children (95%) demonstrated sexual behavior.

COMMENT

Current studies demonstrate a correlation between a background of sexual abuse and the behavior of abused children when playing with anatomically correct dolls. Both Jampole and Weber[5] and White et al[1] suggest that there is a significant difference in play behavior

between sexually abused and nonabused children. Sivan et al[2] and Glasser and Collins[3] suggest that presumably normal children are not threatened, sexually stimulated, or excited to aggression by exposure to anatomically correct dolls.

There are problems with these two comparison studies. First, both have small sample sizes. In addition, White et al used subjects who were suspected to have been sexually abused and subjects who may have been abused.[1] Jampole and Weber used abused subjects who had been interviewed previously regarding the abuse.[5] Also, too few boys were in their study. However, in all, similar conclusions have been made in each of these studies.

Hibbard et al[6] compared the drawings of 57 children who were allegedly sexually abused with those of 55 nonabused children. They found that the allegedly abused children were 5.4 times more likely to draw genitalia on human figures than the nonabused children. Although a child's drawing of genitalia on a human figure does not prove that the child has been sexually abused, research does indicate a relationship between a child's behavior and the child's background. Such behavior (ie, drawing genitalia) should alert care providers to the possibility that the child has been sexually abused.

The use of anatomically correct dolls in the evaluation of alleged victims of sexual abuse is a controversial issue, both in court and in the field of child and adolescent psychiatry. This stems from the lack of scientific data on children's play behaviors with anatomically correct dolls. The California Supreme Court of Appeal, in the spring of 1987, concluded that "the use of the dolls constitutes a new scientific method of proof and is admissible in court only if it has been accepted as generally reliable to the scientific community."[7] In other words, if a child plays with the dolls in a certain manner, this, in and of itself, is not proof that the child has been sexually abused, because there is no scientific evidence establishing a definite relationship between child play behavior and child abuse. Yates and Terr[8] debate whether these dolls should be used to assess sexually abused youngsters, because the child's play with the dolls does

not prove or disprove abuse. Yates points out that the only way that the necessary data can be gained is through the controlled use of anatomically correct dolls. However, she also points out that the evaluators of suspected abuse victims should not base their conclusions on the doll play alone. Terr believes that the presentation of the anatomically correct dolls biases the evaluation by prompting talk about sex. She also is concerned that doll play may ruin the child as a witness by "planting" new information and changing the memory in current storage.[8] She concludes that the use of anatomical dolls should be barred so that no false-positive or false-negative charges based on doll play are presented in court.[7]

There are still many variables to be explored that may affect a child's interaction with anatomically correct dolls: (1) the training of the interviewer; (2) the format of the interview; (3) the child's experiences with physical abuse and neglect; (4) the child's previous sexual exposure and sexual knowledge; and (5) the familiarity of the child with the interviewer and interview setting. Boat and Everson[9] surveyed 295 professionals, including physicians, child protection workers, law enforcement officers, and mental health practitioners regarding their use of anatomic dolls and their interpretations of child behavior with such dolls.[9] Most of the professionals were untrained and inexperienced in the use of anatomically correct dolls as a possible means of detecting evidence of child abuse. Fewer than half of the child protection workers and law enforcement officers had even minimum training. Approximately three quarters of the mental health practitioners and one quarter of the physicians had no training. Each group tended to use dolls with different body features. Few physicians had dolls with mouths and anal openings. Few law enforcement officers had dolls with vaginal openings and hands with five fingers. No group of professionals agreed on a description of "normal" play behavior of 2- to 5-year-old children. Boat and Everson conclude that evaluators should be trained before they begin to work with allegedly sexually abused children. They need to know how to conduct an objective evaluation using the anatomically correct dolls, and they need a basic understanding of early childhood development.

To make valid conclusions, the format of the interview and its setting should be standardized. It is also important for the interviewer to become familiar with the child, through introductions and play, before an official evaluation is made, as did Glasser and Collins.[1] The interview setting should contain the anatomically correct dolls as well as other types of toys. The evaluation sessions should proceed through a predetermined sequence of events, including an invitation to play with and undress the dolls if the child has not already done so. The "functions" game should also be played with the child so observations can be made. In addition, the interviewer should be sensitive to the child's reaction to a uniform, such as a white coat or a police officer's uniform, and adjust accordingly to make the child comfortable. To evaluate these sessions, they must either take place behind a two-way mirror with trained professionals observing from the other side or be videotaped and evaluated later.

It is also important to consider the child's background and how it contributes to the child's interactions with the dolls. The study by Glasser and Collins revealed that three of the five children who showed sexually explicit play with the dolls had previous sexual exposure and/or sexual knowledge.[1] Physical abuse and neglect could also affect the child's response to the dolls by making the child uncomfortable with the adult evaluator, thereby causing the child to alter or lessen play with the dolls. Physical abuse or neglect may also teach the child to treat the dolls as the child has been treated by an abuser. This background information is difficult to determine, but attempts can be made through structured parental interviews to disclose the child's background. These interviews can disclose not only demographic information, but also the child's familiarity with human anatomy, the parents' attitudes toward and practices of punishment, and the the parents' attitudes regarding the sexual education of their children.

Further research in this area should include a study comparing sexually abused children with a nonabused control group that matches the abused group for age, sex, race, socioeconomic status, and family background. This study should employ professionals who have completed standardized training and should take place in a standardized setting using a standard format; parental interviews should also be carried out.

Professionals specializing in child and adolescent psychiatry are likely to have prior training in the use of anatomically correct dolls and play therapy as means of making conclusions about the background of a child. Such training should enable them to conduct the standardized evaluation sessions described above. Research concludes that the behavior demonstrated by a child when playing with anatomically correct dolls correlates with the presence or absence of sexual abuse in the child's background. However, it is impossible, on the basis of current research, to prove or disprove abuse. It is possible, through such play-session evaluations, to identify the anxieties and concerns of children so that these issues can be targeted in future therapy sessions. Professionals should not attempt to run such evaluation sessions unless they have specific training in the use of ana-

tomically correct dolls. However, if a pediatrician sees a child exhibiting sexually explicit play, and the child has no history of being abused (ie, physical or laboratory evidence of abuse), it is important for the pediatrician to have the child's background investigated. The child may or may not have been abused, but it is important for the pediatrician to document these observations and request follow-up information.

At this time, we believe that anatomically correct dolls can be very valuable tools when used correctly by trained professionals. However, continued research is necessary if the child care community is to come to an agreement on the interpretive value of child play with anatomically correct dolls.

References

1. Bays J. Are the genitalia of anatomical dolls distorted? *Child Abuse and Negl.* 1990;14:171-175.
2. Sivan AB, Schor DP, Koeppl GK, Noble, LD. Interaction of normal children with anatomical dolls. *Child Abuse and Negl.* 1988;12:295-304.
3. Glasser D, Collins C. The response of young, non-sexually abused children to anatomically correct dolls. *J Child Psychol Psychiatry.* 1989;30:547-560.
4. White S, Strom GA, Santilli G, Halpin BM. Interviewing young sexual abuse victims with anatomically correct dolls. *Child Abuse and Negl.* 1986;10:519-529.
5. Jampole L, Weber MD. An assessment of the behavior of sexually abused and non-sexually abused children with anatomically correct dolls. *Child Abuse and Negl.* 1987;11:187-192.
6. Hibbard RA, Roghmann K, Hoekelman RA. Genitalia in children's drawings: an association with sexual abuse. *Pediatrics.* 1987;79:129-137.
7. Yates A, Terr L. Anatomically correct dolls: should they be used as the basis for expert testimony? *J Am Acad Child Adolesc Psychiatry.* 1988; 27:254-257.
8. Yates A, Terr L. Issue continued: anatomically correct dolls: should they be used as the basis for expert testimony? *J Am Acad Child Adolesc Psychiatry* 1988;27:387-388.
9. Boat BW, Everson MD. Use of anatomical dolls among professionals in sexual abuse evaluations. *Child Abuse and Negl.* 1988;12:171-179.

186

Child Abuse & Neglect, Vol. 15, pp. 567–573, 1991
Printed in the U.S.A. All rights reserved.

USE OF NONANATOMICAL DOLLS IN THE SEXUAL ABUSE INTERVIEW

HELEN L. BRITTON

Louisiana State University Medical Center, Children's Hospital of New Orleans

MARY ALLYCE O'KEEFE

Children's Hospital of New Orleans

Abstract—Controversy exists regarding use of anatomically detailed dolls in child sexual abuse evaluations because of concerns that such dolls may provoke false positive demonstrations of sexually explicit behavior. This study shows that children referred for medical evaluation of sexual abuse will use sexually explicit behavior to demonstrate what has happened to them with *nonanatomical* dolls as frequently as when they are interviewed with anatomically detailed ones. Over a two-year period, 136 children (aged 24 months to 10 years) were interviewed by the same pediatric interviewer. During the first year sexually anatomically detailed dolls (SAD) were used, and in the subsequent year nonanatomic dolls (NAD) were used. Data was analyzed according to age, sex, and demonstration of sexually explicit behavior. There were 67 children in the NAD group and 69 in the SAD group. Of the NAD group, 72% showed sexually explicit behavior compared to 68% in the SAD group. Comparisons using chi-square analysis revealed no significant differences between NAD and SAD. Results indicated that in the sexual abuse interview setting, use of sexually detailed dolls did not increase children's use of sexually explicit behavior to describe what had happened to them when compared to use of nonanatomical dolls, and that use of either type of doll provides similar information in the interview setting.

Key Words—Sexual abuse, Nonanatomical dolls, Child interview.

INTRODUCTION

METHODS USED to interview children who are being evaluated for possible sexual abuse have recently been severely criticized (Timnick & McGraw, 1990). Much criticism relates to the difficulty interviewers face in addressing the child at the developmentally appropriate level, taking into account age-related limitations in vocabulary, expressive language, and social frame of reference. Specifically, the use of anatomically detailed dolls has been questioned because of their potential "sexual suggestibility" (Yates & Terr, 1988). Dolls, however, are useful tools in the interview process allowing young children to point out body parts which they are unable or embarrassed to verbally identify, and providing a mechanism for them to act out scenes for which they may have no expressive language.

Several studies have investigated the use of anatomical dolls (Boat & Everson, 1988; Jampole & Weber, 1987; Leventhal, Hamilton, Rekedal, Tebano-Micci, & Eyester, 1989; White, Strom, Santill, & Halpin, 1986). Some studies compare using anatomical dolls in "abused" and "nonabused" populations (Jampole & Weber, 1987; White, et al., 1986), and others

Received for publication February 28, 1990; final revision received June 4, 1990; accepted June 5, 1990.

Requests for reprints should be sent to Helen L. Britton, M.D., Child Protection Team, Primary Children's Medical Center, 100 N. Medical Drive, Salt Lake City, UT 84113.

187

evaluate only nonabused children being interviewed with dolls (Sivan, Schor, Koeppl, & Noble, 1988). No studies have been published comparing the use of regular nonanatomical dolls with anatomically specific ones with children suspected of being sexually abused. This is an important concept. If children in this population demonstrate the same behaviors with both types of dolls, it not only indicates that the sexually detailed dolls are not suggestive, but also provides information about an interviewing method which may be considered less provocative.

The hypothesis of this study is that children who are referred for medical evaluation because of suspected sexual abuse will demonstrate sexually explicit behavior with nonanatomical dolls as frequently as when they are presented with anatomically detailed ones. Since parents and foster parents often indicate that sexually abused children engage in sexually explicit play with their dolls in the home setting, it seems likely that this same behavior should be observable in the interview arena.

METHODS

Study Design

The study was conceived as a direct result of the authors' past experience in interviewing suspected child sexual abuse victims over a five-year period using both anatomic and nonanatomic dolls. Although this is a prospective study, the design was simply to organize an already existing format into a more structured pattern for uniformity of data collection. Due to a relatively large geographic referral base, external control in experimental design such as randomization of subjects was not attempted. As use of both anatomically specific and nonanatomical dolls was generally accepted by the community, selection by the interviewer of one type of doll to use over a designated period of time was not a problem.

Subjects

The same female researcher interviewed 136 children aged 24 months to 10 years over a two-year period, the first year using anatomically detailed dolls ($n = 69$), and the second year using nonanatomical ones ($n = 67$). All children were referred by either the police or the community child protective service agency for medical evaluation as the result of a report of possible sexual abuse. These children therefore were highly suspected to have been abused and also had been interviewed by an intake worker prior to their visit. Unfortunately, information regarding possible use of anatomical dolls by the workers was not available. At the time of the medical evaluation, the cases were early in the investigative process, none of the suspected perpetrators had confessed, and none of the cases were considered "proven." We were unable to obtain long-term follow-up data. All children who met the above criteria during the time of the study were included in the data analysis. Consent was obtained from legal guardians of the children for conducting an interview and performing a physical examination to evaluate the possibility of sexual abuse. No additional consent was considered necessary as the evaluation process was not altered for purposes of this study.

Interview Methodology

All of the children were interviewed without an accompanying adult in the room. Occasionally one other observer (medical student, nurse) was present in the room but did not participate in the interview process. The child was told that the reason for the medical evaluation was that someone was worried something might have happened to their body and that this needed to be "checked out." The child was asked to tell who was worried and what they were worried about so that the appropriate evaluations could be done. If a physical complaint such as vaginal pain or dysuria was present, this complaint was the initial focal point. The dolls were presented early in the interview and were fully clothed. The children were instructed to use the dolls to show what happened to them and what parts of their body someone was worried about. Body parts were also pointed out on the dolls, and the children were asked what name they had for the body parts identified. The clothes were pulled aside on both the anatomical and the generic dolls to point out body parts covered by clothing. Interviews were scheduled to last for 30 minutes, and no free play was analyzed because of the medical nature of the visit.

On very young children (2- and 3-year-olds) who were less verbally skilled, some interviewing terms were slightly modified to meet the developmental needs of that population. Most children seemed to understand the word "worried," although sometimes the wording included phrases such as "worried about boo-boos or owies," using the child's own terminology to help modify or interpret adult vocabulary. Younger children used less verbal descriptions than older children and seemed to demonstrate events instead of verbalizing them, although this was not analyzed statistically.

When nonanatomical dolls were used, the children were allowed to choose from the Hart family dolls, Ken and Barbie, and related dolls, Cabbage Patch male and female dolls, and a variety of modified adult model dolls (i.e., Pee Wee Herman). Sometimes the child would demonstrate some activity with one set of dolls and then take another doll to point out more easily a different aspect of their history. Often the smaller Hart family dolls were used to act out a sequence of events, but a larger rag type doll would be used to demonstrate more exactly the area of the vagina or rectum where the child had been touched. Although the children were asked to "pick" the dolls they were going to use, they were allowed to change dolls when it seemed necessary for them to help complete a description.

Data Collection and Analysis

Data was collected from chart review of the 136 cases. The data was broken down by age, sex, and demonstration of sexually explicit behavior with the dolls. With the goal of keeping the data as objective as possible, sexually explicit positioning of the dolls was recorded only if the child indicated that what was being demonstrated had happened to her/him. Therefore, if a child placed the dolls on top of each other in a sexually suggestive position or stuck a finger into a body orifice but denied that that had happened to him, this was not included in the data.

Sexually explicit behavior was defined as follows: (1) fondling—child uses his own hand or that of a doll to touch the genital area of a doll; (2) oral–genital—child puts his own mouth or the face of a doll adjacent to the genital area of a doll, or the child puts the doll face adjacent to his own genital area; (3) sodomy—child places pubis of male doll to rectal area of another doll, or uses his own genital area and that of a doll to demonstrate the same activity; (4) attempted vaginal intercourse—child places pubic area of male doll adjacent to vaginal area of female doll, or adjacent to her own vaginal area. When children used nonanatomical dolls to demonstrate sexually specific behavior, they would often point to the male genital area while verbally referring to the Ken doll's "dick" or "pee-pee," or point to the area between the little girl doll's legs while referring to the "pussy" or the "private."

Data analysis was done using the chi-square analysis to evaluate frequency of sexually explicit behavior demonstrated when comparing children interviewed with the sexually anatomically detailed dolls (SAD group) to those interviewed with nonanatomical ones (NAD group). Data was further analyzed with respect to the child's age and sex.

189

Table 1. Demonstration of Sexually Explicit Behavior Using Sexually Anatomically Detailed (SAD) Versus Nonanatomical (NAD) Dolls; Ages 2–9 Years

	Male		Female		Both Sexes	
Behavior	SAD $n = 17$	NAD $n = 12$	SAD $n = 52$	NAD $n = 55$	SAD $n = 69$	NAD $n = 67$
Fondling	5[a]	4[a]	29*	34*	34*	38*
Oral–genital	2[a]	4[a]	10*	8*	12*	12*
Sodomy	2[a]	8[a]	8*	3*	10*	11*
Vaginal Intercourse	1[a]	0[a]	18*	14*	19*	14*
No explicit behavior	10*	4*	12*	15*	22*	19*
Percent showing explicit behavior	41%	66%	76%	72%	68%	72%

[a] Comparison of NAD and SAD groups by Chi-square not valid due to inadequate expected cell counts.
* No significant difference ($p > .05$) when comparing SAD and NAD groups by Chi-square analysis.

RESULTS

Results are shown for all ages combined in Table 1, and broken down into separate age groups in Tables 2, 3, and 4. As shown in Table 1, no significant differences in demonstrations of sexually explicit behavior were found between the SAD (anatomically specific dolls) and NAD (nonanatomical dolls) groups in the combined age range. This lack of significance was maintained when the data was further broken down by specific sexual act and by sex of the child.

The SAD and NAD groups were also analyzed after being divided in groups based on age. The age groups consisted of (1) 2- and 3-year-olds (Table 2); (2) 4-, 5-, and 6-year-olds (Table 3); and (3) 7-, 8-, and 9-year-olds (Table 4). Due to the limitations of sample size when the study population was thus divided, chi-square analysis was valid only for certain comparisons where the expected cell counts were adequate. These details are outlined in the accompanying tables. All of the analyses which were valid, however, continued to show no significant p values ($< .05$) when the SAD and NAD groups were compared. In some of the smaller groups (i.e., sodomy demonstrated by males, Tables 1 and 3) there appeared to be a trend to use NAD for sexual demonstration. Although other statistical techniques could be used to evaluate possible significance (i.e., Yates correction factor), the authors hesitated to make conclusions using such small numbers.

Table 2. Demonstration of Sexually Explicit Behavior in 2 and 3 Year Olds

	Male		Female		Both Sexes	
Behavior	SAD $n = 6$	NAD $n = 2$	SAD $n = 14$	NAD $n = 17$	SAD $n = 20$	NAD $n = 19$
Fondling	3	0	4*	9*	7*	9*
Oral–genital	0	1	2	2	2	3
Sodomy	0	1	1	0	1	1
Vaginal Intercourse	0	0	4	0	4	0
No explicit behavior	3	1	7*	8*	10*	9*
Percent showing explicit behavior	50%	50%	50%	53%	50%	52%

* No significant difference ($p > .05$) in SAD and NAD groups using Chi-square analysis. Comparison of unstarred groups not valid due to inadequate expected cell count.

190

Table 3. Demonstration of Sexually Explicit Behavior in 4, 5, and 6 Year Olds

	Male		Female		Both Sexes	
Behavior	SAD $n = 6$	NAD $n = 6$	SAD $n = 19$	NAD $n = 18$	SAD $n = 27$	NAD $n = 24$
Fondling	2	2	14*	11*	16*	13*
Oral–genital	2	2	2	2	4	4
Sodomy	2	6	4	0	6*	6*
Vaginal Intercourse	1	0	8*	5*	9*	6*
No explicit behavior	4	0	2	5	6*	5*
Percent showing explicit behavior	50%	100%	89%	72%	77%	79%

* No significant difference ($p > .05$) in SAD and NAD groups using Chi-square analysis. Comparison of unstarred groups not valid due to inadequate expected cell count.

DISCUSSION

The data clearly supports the study hypothesis that children being evaluated for suspected sexual abuse will demonstrate a similar frequency of sexually explicit behavior to describe what happened to them when being interviewed with either anatomical dolls (those with specific genital organs) or nonanatomically specific ones (i.e., Cabbage Patch, Ken, and Barbie). This lends further support to the theory that anatomical dolls *do not* provoke sexualized behavior since children in the study used nonanatomic dolls as frequently as they used those with sex organs to describe sexual events that happened to them. It also demonstrates that children who have been sexually victimized will act out situations that have occurred to them with dolls that are familiar, often naming and pointing to body parts that may not be physically apparent on whatever doll they use.

Although this data is helpful, further prospective studies should be done to ensure that these findings are reproducible in other interview settings and perhaps with other interview techniques. Limitations in personnel and unavailability of videotaping for the majority of interviews made independent ratings and rater reliability impossible to assess. The interviewer in this study used both anatomical and nonanatomical dolls in a manner that did not emphasize presence of genitals, and did not include as "positive" data nonspecific interest in sexual parts. Undoubtedly, a higher percentage of "positives" would have resulted had this type of behavior been included. Data, however, was not collected comparing frequency of nonspecific sexual play using the different types of dolls. Interpreting nonspecific behavior for research

Table 4. Demonstration of Sexually Explicit Behavior in 7–9 Year Olds

	Male		Female		Both Sexes	
Behavior	SAD $n = 3$	NAD $n = 4$	SAD $n = 19$	NAD $n = 20$	SAD $n = 22$	NAD $n = 24$
Fondling	0	2	11*	14*	11*	16*
Oral–genital	0	1	6*	4*	6*	5*
Sodomy	0	1	3	3	3	4
Vaginal Intercourse	0	0	6	9	6*	9*
No explicit behavior	3	1	3	2	6	3
Percent showing explicit behavior	0%	75%	84%	90%	72%	88%

* No significant difference ($p > .05$) in SAD and NAD groups using Chi-square analysis. Comparison of unstarred groups not valid due to inadequate expected cell count.

purposes may create a further dilemma, as children who have seen a lot of sexual behavior may perhaps demonstrate explicit acts which have not actually happened to them. This possibility also needs further investigation.

Finally, a larger prospective study needs to be done in order to ensure adequate sample size to statistically compare males and females in different age groups demonstrating specific sexual activities. It would also be helpful in a future study to use a standardized set of nonanatomical dolls resembling the anatomical dolls in all ways except for presence of genital organs in order to further clarify comparisons.

Perhaps the most important information to be extrapolated from this study is that dolls are useful in the child sexual abuse interview study, not because they may have anatomically detailed genital organs, but because they are props that allow children to express themselves more accurately and completely. Dolls help clarify vocabulary regarding body parts and events; they allow a child to demonstrate what he cannot yet developmentally verbalize; they allow the interviewer to observe behavioral response of the child to persons and events being depicted by the dolls; and they provide the child with a familiar and unthreatening method of relating events. All of these beneficial uses of the dolls are unrelated to whether or not the dolls have genital organs. Unfortunately, in some court settings, valuable information gained from use of the dolls gets lost in an argument about whether the anatomical dolls are "suggestive" props. This study helps to verify the necessity of gathering appropriate scientific information prior to rendering expert opinions in a court of law, and also helps to refocus the value of using dolls in the child sexual abuse interview.

REFERENCES

Boat, B. W., & Everson, M. D. (1988). Use of anatomical dolls among professionals in sexual abuse evaluations. *Child Abuse & Neglect*, **12**, 171–179.

Jampole, L., & Weber, M. K. (1987). An assessment of the behavior of sexually abused and nonsexually abused children with anatomically correct dolls. *Child Abuse & Neglect*, **11**, 187–192.

Leventhal, J. M., Hamilton, J., Rekedal S., Tebano-Micci, A., & Eyster, C. (1989). Anatomically correct dolls used in interview of young children suspected of having been sexually abused. *Pediatrics*, **84**, 900–906.

Sivan, A. B., Schor, D. P., Koeppl, G. K., & Noble, L. D. (1988). Interactions of normal children with anatomic dolls. *Child Abuse & Neglect*, **11**, 295–304.

Timnick, L., & McGraw, C. (1990, January 19). McMartin verdict: Not guilty. *Los Angeles Times*, p. 1.

White, S., Strom, G. A., Santill, G., & Halpin B. M. (1986). Interviewing young sexual abuse victims with anatomically correct dolls. *Child Abuse & Neglect*, **10**, 510–529.

Yates, A., & Terr, L. (1988). Anatomically correct dolls: Should they be used as the basis for expert testimony? *Journal of the American Academy of Child and Adolescent Psychiatry*, **27**, 254–257.

Résumé—Une controverse existe concernant l'utilisation des poupées détaillées sur le plan anatomique dans l'évaluation des sévices sexuels à l'égard des enfants, parce que ces poupées pourraient provoquer de fausses démonstrations de ce que les enfants ont vécu sur le plan sexuel. Cette étude démontre que les enfants référrés pour évaluation médicale après abus sexuel utilisent un comportement sexuel explicite pour mettre en scène ce qui leur est arrivé aussi bien avec des poupées normales qu'avec des poupées détaillées sexuellement. Cent trente-six enfants (agés entre deux et dix ans) ont été interrogés par le même enquêteur pédiatrique sur une période de deux ans. Les poupées détaillées sexuellement sur le plan anatomique (PSA) ont été utilisées au cours de la première année tandis que les poupées non détaillées sur le plan anatomique (PNA) ont été utilisées au cours de l'année suivante. Les données ont été analysées en tenant compte de l'âge, du sexe et du comportement sexuel explicite de l'enfant. Soixante-sept enfants faisaient partie du groupe PNA et soixante-neuf du groupe PSA. Soixante-douze pour-cent du groupe PNA a présenté un comportement sexuel explicite par rapport à 68 pour-cent du groupe PSA. Des comparaisons utilisant l'analyse chi-carré n'ont pas révélé de différence significative entre les deux groupes. Les résultats indiquent que l'utilisation de poupées détaillées sexuellement au cours de l'interrogatoire et de l'examen d'enfants abusés sexuellement n'augmente pas chez l'enfant le comportement sexuel explicite pour montrer ce qui lui est arrivé et que les deux sortes de poupées (corrigées ou non sur le plan sexuel) donnent le même type d'information.

Resumen—Existe cierta controversia en relación al uso de muñecas con detalles sexuales anatómicos en las evaluaciones de abuso sexual a los niños, por el temor de que éstas muñecas puedan provocar falsas demostraciones positivas de conductas sexualmente explícitas. Esta investigación demuestra que los niños que fueran evaluados por abuso sexual con muñecas no-anatómicas para que contaran lo que les había sucedido usarán conductas sexualmente explícitas con la misma frecuencia que cuando se evaluan con muñecas con detalles sexuales anatómicos. 136 niños (de 24 meses a 10 años de edad) fueron entrevistados por el mismo entrevistador pediátrico por un período de 2 años. Durante el primer año se usaron las muñecas con detalles sexuales anatómicos (SAD) y en el año siguiente se usaron muñecas no-anatómicos (NAD). Se analizaron los resultados según edad, sexo y demostraciones de conductas sexualmente explícitas. 67 niños estaban en el grupo NAD y 69 en el grupo SAD. 70% del grupo NAD mostró concuctas sexualmente explícitas comparado con un 68% en el grupo SAD. Las comparaciones usando el análisis del chi-cuadrado no revelaron diferencias significativas entre NAD y SAD. Los resultados indican que en el contexto de la entrevista por abuso sexual, el uso de muñecas con detalles sexuales no aumenta las conductas sexualmente explícitas para describir lo que les ha sucedido cuando se compara con el uso de muñecas no-anatómicas, y que ambos tipos de muñecas ofrecen similar información en el contexta de la entrevista.

Behavioral Sciences and the Law, Vol. 9, 43–51 (1991)

Assessment of Sexually Abused Children with Anatomically Detailed Dolls: A Critical Review

Cathy Maan, Ph.D.

The use of anatomically detailed (AD) dolls is widespread, especially with young children who have been, or may have been, sexually abused. A number of empirical studies have compared the responses of sexually abused and non-abused children to AD dolls. Additional research has assessed AD doll play among non-abused children only. Methodological limitations notwithstanding, virtually all empirical data support the use of AD dolls for data gathering in cases of sexual abuse.

Sexual abuse of children is widespread (Kempe & Kempe, 1984; MacFarlane, 1978; Russell, 1983) and constitutes a serious mental health problem with both short- and long-term consequences (Browne & Finkelhor, 1986). Anatomically detailed (AD) dolls are increasingly relied upon to assess the sexual knowledge and experience of children. These dolls are unique in that they "look like real people when their clothes are off" (White, Strom & Santilli, 1986, p. 7). Many investigators (Boat & Everson, 1986, 1988a; Jones & McQuiston, 1985; Walker, 1988) have suggested that AD dolls can be used by young children to demonstrate their experiences. Because so many victims of sexual abuse are very young—33% of incest victims are first abused prior to the age of six (Boat & Everson, 1986)—AD dolls can be a valuable assessment tool. In particular, the use of AD dolls may help those who are anxious about discussing sexual matters or those who have limited language capacity to describe their situations more freely and perhaps more accurately (Boat & Everson, 1986; Landers, 1988). The purpose of this article is to critically review and integrate the literature on the use of AD dolls in assessing children who may have been sexually abused.

Address correspondence and requests for reprints to: Cathy Maan, Ph.D. Psychology Department, University of Saskatchewan, Saskatoon, Saskatchewan, Canada, S7N 0W0.

The author thanks Susan Bryson and Albert Cota for their comments on an earlier draft of this paper. A preliminary version of this paper was presented at the Annual Convention of the Canadian Psychological Association (held in June 1989), Halifax, Nova Scotia.

0735–3936/91/010043–09$05.00

USE OF ANATOMICALLY DETAILED DOLLS BY PROFESSIONALS

Boat and Everson (1988c) conducted a survey of 295 child protection workers, law enforcement officers, physicians, and mental health practitioners concerning the use of AD dolls. Thirty-seven per cent of the respondents indicated that they used AD dolls, and an additional 25% indicated that they would be using them within a year. Few doll users had access to a manual, and many reported they had not received formal training in the use of AD dolls in sexual abuse cases.

Substantial differences were found in the features of the AD dolls being used. Features such as oral, vaginal, and anal openings were present in only some dolls. Physical aspects of AD dolls are important because certain features are necessary to allow children to demonstrate specific sexual acts. For example, dolls with hands that have individual fingers are needed for demonstrations of digital penetration (Boat & Everson, 1988c).

Anatomically detailed dolls interviews conducted by respondents in Boat Everson's (1988c) survey varied markedly. Users differed in the number of sessions they conducted with each child, in whether or not a parent was present, and in whether or not the alleged perpetrator was in the room. In clinical settings, variations in interviewing strategies across professionals may be associated with variations in the incidence and types of coercive behaviors reported by children.

Boat and Everson (1988c) also presented their respondents with scenarios of children engaging in sexualized play with AD dolls (e.g., vaginal penetration between the dolls) and asked them to judge how convincing such behavior was as evidence of sexual abuse. Responses varied as a function of respondents' group membership. For example, law enforcement officers were less likely than members of other professional groups to accept sexualized play as indicative of abuse. On a different point, all respondents were more likely to judge sexualized play as evidence of abuse when it was accompanied by a verbal description. Approximately 30% of law enforcement officers judged the demonstration of vaginal or anal penetration as "very convincing" evidence when it was not accompanied by a verbal description. With a verbal description, however, 62% of the law enforcement officers found the same acts "very convincing" evidence.

The final component of Boat and Everson's (1988c) survey concerned judgements made by respondents regarding whether certain play behaviors with AD dolls by young children could be considered "normal" (i.e., expected among children with no history of sexual abuse). Although no single behavior was unanimously rated "normal", most respondents concurred that undressing the dolls, staring at the dolls' genitals, and touching the dolls' genitals constituted normal behaviors. On the other hand, most respondents agreed that they would not expect to find acts of penetration between the dolls in the play of non-sexually abused children.

Boat and Everson's (1988c) survey indicated that many professionals use AD dolls and that many others intend to use them. It exposed the potential for misuse by demonstrating that few professionals were trained to work with the dolls. Results of the survey also indicated clearly that different professionals varied in their assessments of the same child behaviors during AD doll interviews. Researchers interested in replicating Boat and Everson's findings should consider including questions regarding respondents' experiences with, and training in, conducting interviews with sexually abused children. Such training would seem a necessary prerequisite to using AD dolls to assess sexually abused children.

METHODS OF STRUCTURED ASSESSMENT

In Boat and Everson's (1988c) study, many doll users "endorsed the need for a standard protocol to follow when presenting the dolls" (p. 173). Among the earliest attempts to standardize methods for using AD dolls were those of White, Strom and Santilli (1986) and Boat and Everson (1986, 1988a). These groups of researchers designed protocols for interviewing preschoolers with AD dolls. A primary goal of standardizing procedures was to provide the legal system with acceptable and reliable data from interviews with children involved in sexual abuse investigations.

Researchers (e.g., Walker, 1988; White & Santilli, 1986; White, Strom & Santilli, 1986) have suggested that the interviewer plays an important role in AD doll interviews. White and her colleagues emphasized this point in their interview protocol: the interviewer must feel comfortable with the dolls and have knowledge of normal developmental processes (e.g., motor skills and language development). Clearly, what the interviewer expects from young children influences her or his appraisal of the situation. Moreover, without knowledge of legal precedents and current laws, the clinician's input in the abuse investigation may be meaningless.

White, Strom and Santilli (1986) suggested that the interviewer be blind to the alleged abuse of the child being interviewed. If this is impossible, then referral information available to the clinician should be restricted. Unlike White, Strom and Santilli, Boat and Everson (1986) recommended that the interviewer draw upon information obtained from the referral source to guide the interview.

White, Strom and Santilli (1986) and Boat and Everson (1986, 1988a) recommended that the assessment procedure begin with an introduction of the AD dolls and a freeplay period. Two male adult dolls, two female adult dolls, two male child dolls, and two female child dolls are introduced with a statement such as the following: "These are special dolls which look like people when their clothes are off". The freeplay period allows the interviewer to make an informal assessment of the child's language usage, speech skills, mental abilities, and interactional skills.

In addition, during the freeplay period Boat and Everson (1986, 1988a) suggested that the interviewer obtain information about the child's understanding of key concepts, such as "where" and "when" with questions such as "Where do you live?" and "When do you eat breakfast?" The child should also be asked about a recent and memorable event with which the interviewer is familiar; this will enable the clinician to assess both the child's memory for recent events and her or his reliability as a reporter. Moreover, knowledge the interviewer gains in this stage of the interview can be useful in guiding the wording of questions later in the interview.

The protocols developed by White, Strom and Santilli (1986) and Boat and Everson (1986, 1988a) for sessions following the freeplay period share general features. The child is asked to choose a clothed doll, identify it as a boy or a girl, and name it. Here, the interviewer should test for body part identification and function by asking for names of neutral parts (e.g., arms and eyes) and their functions. Subsequently, the child is questioned about the sexual parts of at least three dolls, an adult doll of each gender and a child doll of the same gender as the child being

197

interviewed. The names the child gives for body parts should be recorded and these terms should be used throughout the interview. Issues about general body experiences are then addressed with questions such as "Has anyone put anything on or in any part of your body?" and "Have you seen anyone without clothes?" Positive responses to these questions should be explored.

For questions related to abuse history, Boat and Everson (1986, 1988a) and White, Strom and Santilli (1986) offer different recommendations. White, Strom and Santilli underscore the importance of asking only non-leading questions, particularly because of implications for courtroom testimony: a professional who asks leading questions may compromise his or her ability to present this data in a courtroom. Boat and Everson share White, Strom and Santilli's concerns regarding leading questions and offer clinicians some recommendations for how to avoid asking such questions (Boat & Everson, 1988a, p. 340). However, Boat and Everson argue that circumstances may compel a professional to ask leading questions regardless of the consequences for courtroom testimony. According to Boat and Everson, in cases where other sources of information suggest that the child has been abused, potentially leading questions may be necessary to obtain information to protect the child from further abuse. Clinicians, of course, should keep in mind that the use of leading questions is frowned upon by the legal system and may run the risk of eliciting false responses from some children.

EMPIRICAL STUDIES

Three main strategies have been used to examine how children interact with AD dolls. The *comparative* strategy involves comparing groups of abused and non-abused children. The *correlational* strategy involves observing how large samples of presumably non-abused children interact with AD dolls. The *analogue* strategy involves manipulating the experiences of non-abused children through the use of an adult confederate, and then probing the child's memory with AD dolls.

Comparative Studies

White, Strom, Santilli and Halpin (1986) compared the AD doll responses of children referred for sexual abuse and those of non-referred children. Each group contained 25 children ranging in age from two to six years (the referred and non-referred groups consisted of 64% and 52% girls, respectively).

Interviews were conducted by social workers and child psychologists trained to administer White, Strom and Santilli's (1986) standardized procedure. Interviewers were blind to group membership. Two indices of suspected sexual abuse were obtained. A *report indicator* consisted of parental reports of suspected child abuse and/or medical reports which were obtained on the referred children after their doll interviews. An *interview indicator* was computed based on children's responses during the doll interview. Both ratings were scored on a five point scale ranging from "no suspicion" to "high suspicion" of abuse. On both dependent measures, referred children obtained significantly higher scores than non-referred children.

The main limitation of White, Strom, Santilli and Halpin's (1986) study was that the two groups were not closely matched on demographic factors. Children in the non-referred group were recruited through a hospital employee newsletter and generally came from white, intact families. The referred children were recruited through social agencies and had mixed racial backgrounds; fewer than a third lived in intact homes. Socio-demographic differences between the two groups of children may have contributed to group differences in doll play.

Jampole and Weber (1987) also compared responses of referred and non-referred children. Children were matched on age, sex, and race. An interview protocol similar to White, Strom and Santilli's (1986) was developed by the authors. Jampole and Weber used dichotomous criteria for nonsexual versus sexual behavior within the interview. For example, they classified touching the dolls' genitals or breasts and exploration of the doll's genitals with fingers as nonsexual behaviors. In comparison, White, Strom, Santilli and Halpin (1986) classified these behaviors as negligible indicators of sexual abuse.

Jampole and Weber (1987) found that nine of ten referred children engaged in sexual play with the dolls. Examples of sexual behaviors were simulated intercourse between the dolls and intercourse between the child and the dolls. Eight of ten non-referred children did not show sexualized play.

Jampole and Weber (1987) noted several limitations of their study, including the use of small samples and the heterogeneous social backgrounds of the non-referred children. More specifically, all of the referred children were in state custody, yet only six of ten non-referred children were in such custody. In addition, and significantly, children in the two groups had different experiences with issues of abuse. Referred children had already been questioned extensively about sexual abuse.

The comparative method employed by White, Strom, Santilli, and Halpin (1986) and Jampole and Weber (1987) is one method to assess the construct validity (Anastasi, 1976) of AD doll interviews. This method, however, has limitations. Even with screening procedures, it is impossible to classify children within the non-referred group with certainty as having no history of sexual abuse (Goodman & Helgeson, 1988). Moreoever, in studies where group differences are found, researchers must consider the possibility that variables other than history of sexual abuse (e.g., socio-demographic characteristics) are contributing to group differences in doll play.

Studies With Non-Abused Children

Studies examining doll play by non-abused children are necessary before the doll play of abused children can be interpreted accurately (Helfer & Krugman, 1986). One consideration is that if large numbers of non-abused children show sexualized play with AD dolls, then the dolls themselves may be eliciting such behaviors. Two types of studies have examined non-abused children's play with AD dolls: correlational and analogue.

Correlational Research

The first published report concerning the play of presumably non-abused children with AD dolls was conducted by Gabriel (1985). Sixteen children, ranging in age from two to five years, were assessed individually for approximately 30 mintes. After 15 minutes of freeplay, the interviewer questioned each child about the dolls. Eight types of behaviors with the dolls were noted (e.g., identifying anatomy correctly, actively handling the dolls). Since many of these behaviors were found in the play of many children, Gabriel suggested that AD dolls may be of limited utility in cases where sexual abuse is suspected. However, because of serious methodological short-comings, Gabriel's findings and conclusions must be viewed cautiously. It is uncertain what protocol was used to interview children and it is unclear how the data were condensed to show specific behavior patterns. Finally, no attempts were made to screen children's backgrounds for sexual abuse.

Boat and Everson (1988b) investigated presumably non-abused children's reactions to AD dolls. Two hundred and nine children, ranging in age from two to five years, were administered a protocol similar to the one developed by the authors in 1986. It was found that exploratory behaviors such as touching, rubbing, and poking the dolls were common. In contrast, sexual intercourse between the dolls was demonstrated by only nine children. Boat and Everson suggested that such demonstrations are rare, and therefore noteworthy.

Sivan, Schor, Koeppl and Noble (1988) examined how 144 presumably non-abused three to eight year olds played with AD dolls. Each child was individually observed with several toys, including four AD dolls during three conditions. The first condition consisted of a seven minute freeplay session with a non-attentive adult. In the second condition, the adult left the room for seven minutes and upon his or her return asked the child to identify and give the function of neutral and sexual body parts. In the third condition, the adult left the room leaving the undressed dolls with the child for seven minutes.

Perhaps the most striking finding was that the dolls occupied little of the children's interest (Sivan, Schor, Koeppl & Noble, 1988). Before the dolls were undressed the most frequently occurring activity across the sample was the exploration of *other* toys in the playroom. Although the sexual parts of the dolls were inspected by many children, role playing of explicit sexual behaviors was never observed. The authors concluded that the children's reactions to AD dolls were similar to their reactions to other toys. Thus, they suggested that sexualized play observed in interactions with these dolls be explored.

Glaser and Collins (1989) conducted a study with 86 presumably non-abused children, ranging in age from two to six years. They examined children's interactions with dolls in a relatively unstructured play setting. The children were asked to undress the dolls, name the dolls' parts and their functions, and then dress the dolls. The majority of the children touched and explored the dolls' genitals, but the overwhelming majority did not show explicit sexual play with the dolls. Glaser and Collins investigated further the five children who showed explicit sexual play with the dolls. For two children the source of this play was unclear; for two others, sexual doll play seemed to be associated with a history of exposure to pornography; the fifth child had observed sexual activity between her friend and an older boy.

In keeping with Boat and Everson (1988b) and Sivan, Schor, Koeppl and Noble (1988), Glaser and Collins (1989) documented that AD dolls do not seem to elicit sexualized play in many non-abused children. A noteworthy feature of Glaser and Collins's study is that in the few cases in which sexualized play was observed, several potential reasons for this behavior emerged. Their findings imply that instances of sexual play with AD dolls should be explored by professionals with the awareness that several potential sources for this behavior may exist.

Analogue Research

Aman and Goodman (1989) also studied presumably non-abused children's use of AD dolls. They manipulated children's experiences with an adult confederate and then tested their memory for this event. Thirty children, aged three years and 30 children aged five years, were divided into three conditions: AD dolls, regular dolls, and no dolls.

All children were seen for two sessions. In the first session the child was introduced to an adult male confederate and was asked to play "Simon Says" or a similar game with him. In the second session, which took place in the same room a week later, a female interviewer questioned the child. Children were first asked to name body parts of the dolls (AD dolls for the AD doll condition and regular dolls for the remaining conditions). The dolls were then set aside and children were asked to tell what happened the week before in the same room. Children in the doll conditions were given dolls and encouraged to show and tell what happened. Each child was both asked objective and suggestive questions.

Results indicated that, especially for five year olds, AD dolls seemed useful in helping children to remember their interactions with the confederate. Five year olds recalled more correct information in the AD and regular doll conditions than in the non-doll condition. Aman and Goodman (1989) also found that the use of AD dolls did not lead to false reports of sexual abuse by these presumably non-abused children.

The major strength of the analogue approach is that the experimenter has control over all aspects of the interaction between the child and confederate. A limitation of the analogue approach, however, is that the results from such studies may not generalize to children who have been abused. Child sexual abuse is traumatic for victims (Browne & Finkelhor, 1986). Within analogue studies, it is impossible and unethical for the experimenter to subject children to traumatic interactions with an adult confederate.

OVERVIEW OF EMPIRICAL LITERATURE

A central issue addressed by all research, directly or indirectly, concerns the clinical usefulness of AD dolls. Clearly, AD dolls appear to be useful for data collection in child abuse investigations. For example, AD dolls seem useful as props to aid children in reconstructing events (Aman & Goodman, 1989; Walker, 1988). On the other hand, AD dolls are not a behavioral test for sexual abuse. Indeed, *"there is no behavioral test for child abuse"* (Melton & Limber, 1989, p. 1231, italics in original).

AD dolls are not useful, and should not be used, for determining whether or not sexual abuse has occurred (White & Santilli, 1986). There are two reasons for this. First, in comparative group studies, not all referred children show sexual play with AD dolls. Thus, it is likely that some sexually abused children will not show sexualized play during an AD doll interview. Second, in samples of children presumed to be non-abused (e.g., Boat and Everson, 1988b), some children showed sexualized play with AD dolls. The presence of sexualized play is, by itself, not a clear indicator of abuse.

The issue of suggestibility is salient among professionals who use AD dolls. The clinical usefulness of the dolls would be compromised if the dolls *per se* elicited sexualized play. From comparative, correlational, and analogue studies, evidence is accumulating to demonstrate that materials used in AD doll interviews are not suggestible. It is, however, worth emphasizing that the issue of suggestibility is multi-dimensional. One parameter concerns the dolls themselves, another concerns the testimony given by children, particularly young children (Penrod, 1988), and a third relates to the interview procedure (i.e., whether or not leading questions are asked). Further research is needed to delineate under what conditions, if any, AD dolls become suggestive (i.e., begin to elicit sexual play in samples of children presumed to be non-abused).

CONCLUSIONS

Researchers and clinicians hold a variety of opinions concerning the usefulness of AD dolls in sexual abuse investigations. For example, Shamroy (1987) stated that all clinicians who interact with sexually abused children will find AD dolls helpful (p. 166). On the other hand, King and Yuille (1987) argued that "dolls serve the function of a suggestive question with young children" (p. 31). Moreoover, Yuille (1988) recommended that dolls should not be used for investigative purposes. Others are more optimistic about the use of AD dolls in sexual abuse investigations (White & Quinn, in press; White & Santilli, 1986; Yates & Terr, 1988). In general, the latter groups of researchers have argued that AD dolls are beneficial when they are used by trained investigators for data gathering within a multidimensional assessment strategy.

Given the empirical evidence to date, the third perspective, that of cautious optimism, seems fitting. Professionals who choose to use AD dolls, or the results of AD doll interviews, should be aware of the strengths and limitations of these techniques to insure that their input into sexual abuse investigations is appropriate and beneficial.

REFERENCES

Aman, C. & Goodman, G. S. (1989). *Children's use of anatomically detailed dolls: An experimental study.* Unpublished manuscript, University of Denver, Denver, Colorado.

Anastasi, A. (1976). *Psychological Testing* (4th edn.). New York: Macmillan.

Boat, B. W. & Everson, M. D. (1986). *Using anatomical dolls: Guidelines for interviewing young children in sexual abuse investigations.* Unpublished manuscript, Department of Psychiatry, University of North Carolina, Chapel Hill, North Carolina.

Boat, B. W. & Everson, M. D. (1988a). Interviewing young children with anatomical dolls. *Child Welfare,* 67, 337–352.

Boat, B. W. & Everson, M. D. (1988b). Research and issues in using anatomical dolls. *Annals of Sex Research, 1,* 191–204.

Boat, B. W. & Everson, M. D. (1988c). Use of anatomical dolls among professionals in sexual abuse evaluations. *Child Abuse and Neglect, 12,* 171–179.

Browne, A. & Finkelhor, D. (1986). Impact of child sexual abuse: A review of the research. *Psychological Bulletin,* 99, 66–77.

Gabriel, R. M. (1985). Anatomically correct dolls in the diagnosis of sexual abuse of children. *Journal of the Melanie Klein Society, 3*(2), 40–51.

Glaser, D. & Collins, C. (1989). The response of young, non-sexually abused children to anatomically correct dolls. *Journal of Child Psychology and Psychiatry, 30,* 547–560.

Goodman, G. S. & Helgeson, V. S. (1988). Children as witnesses: What do they remember? In L. E. A. Walker (Ed.),*Handbook on sexual abuse of children* (pp. 109–136). New York: Springer Verlag.

Helfer, R. E. & Krugman, R. D. (1986). Editorial note. *Child Abuse and Neglect, 10,* 519.

Jampole, L. & Weber, M. K. (1987). As assessment of the behavior of sexually abused and nonsexually abused children with anatomically correct dolls. *Child Abuse and Neglect, 11,* 187–192.

Jones, D. P. H. & McQuiston, M. (1985). *Interviewing the sexually abused child.* University of Colorado School of Medicine: C. Henry Kempe National Center for the Prevention and Treatment of Child Abuse and Neglect.

Kempe, R. S. & Kempe, C. H. (1984). *The common secret: Sexual abuse of children and adolescents.* New York: W. H. Freeman.

King, M. A. & Yuille, J. C. (1987). Suggestibility and the child witness. In S. J. Ceci, M. P. Toglia and D. F. Ross (Eds.), *Children's eyewitness memory* (pp. 24–35). New York: Springer Verlag.

Landers, S. (1988, June). Use of "detailed dolls" questioned. *APA Monitor,* p. 24.

MacFarlane, K. (1978). The sexual abuse of children. In J. R. Chapman and M. Gates (Eds.), *The victimization of women.* (pp. 81–109). Beverly Hills: Sage.

Melton, G. B. & Limber, S. (1989). Psychologist's involvement in cases of maltreatment. *American Psychologist, 44,* 1225–1233.

Penrod, S. D. (1988). Psychology in courts: The child witness [Review of *Children's Eyewitness Memory*]. *Contemporary Psychology, 33,* 655–657.

Russell, D. E. H. (1983). The incidence and prevalence of intrafamilial and extrafamilial sexual abuse of female children. *Child Abuse and Neglect, 7,* 133–146.

Shamroy, J. A. (1987). Interviewing the sexually abused child with anatomically correct dolls. *Social Work, 32,* 165–166.

Sivan, A. B, Schor, D. P., Koeppl, G. K. & Noble, L. D. (1988). Interaction of normal children with anatomical dolls. *Child Abuse and Neglect, 12,* 295–304.

Walker, L. E. A. (1988). New techniques for assessment and evaluation of child sexual abuse victims: Using anatomically 'correct' dolls and videotape procedures. In L. E. A. Walker (Ed.), *Handbook on sexual abuse of children* (pp. 175–197). New York: Springer Verlag.

White, S. & Quinn, K. M. (in press). *Bulletin of the American Academy of Psychiatry and the Law.*

White, S. & Santilli, G. S. (1986). *Uses and abuses of sexually anatomically detailed dolls.* Unpublished manuscript, School of Medicine, Case Western Reserve University.

White, S., Strom, G. A. & Santilli, G. (1986). *Clinical protocol for interviewing preschoolers with sexually anatomically detailed dolls.* Unpublished manuscript, School of Medicine, Case Western University.

White, S., Strom, G. A., Santilli, G. & Halpin, B. M. (1986). Interviewing young sexual abuse victims with anatomically correct dolls. *Child Abuse and Neglect, 10,* 519–529.

Yates, A. & Terr, L. (1988). Anatomically correct dolls: Should they be used as the basis for expert testimony? *Journal of the American Academy of Child and Adolescent Psychiatry, 27,* 254–257.

Yuille, J. C. (1988). The systematic assessment of children's testimony. *Canadian Psychology, 29,* 247–262.

Trapped Within the System: Abused Children and Child Protective Service Agencies

I. Introduction

In the past two decades, child abuse and neglect have emerged and been recognized as widespread social problems warranting government intervention.[1] As the magnitude of the child abuse problem has increased, the public has demanded that state and federal legislators improve child protective services. Pursuant to this demand legislators in every jurisdiction[2] have enacted reporting statutes.[3] In 1974, Congress passed the Child Abuse Prevention and Treatment Act,[4] providing federal financial assistance to states implementing programs aimed at preventing and treating child abuse and neglect.[5] Consequently, many states passed statutes to ensure that their child protective services conformed to the Act.[6]

Since states enacted the first child abuse and neglect statutes, legislative focus has changed from requiring mere reporting of suspected abuse to initiating investigation and intervention proceed-

---

1. *See generally* Antler & Antler, *From Child Rescue to Family Protection: the Evolution of the Child Protective Movement in the United States,* CHILDREN AND YOUTH SERVICES REV. 1 (1979).

2. *See* Paulsen, *Child Abuse Reporting Laws: The Shape of the Legislation,* 67 COLUM. L. REV. 1 (1967); Paulsen, Parker & Adelman, *Child Abuse Reporting Laws — Some Legislative History,* 34 GEO. WASH. L. REV. 482 (1966); Paulsen, *The Legal Framework for Child Protection,* 66 COLUM. L. REV. 679 (1966).

3. Reporting statutes, although varying from state to state, generally require physicians, hospitals, teachers and school administrators to report cases of suspected child abuse. *See* Besharov, *The Legal Aspects of Reporting Known and Suspected Child Abuse and Neglect,* 23 VILL. L. REV. 458 (1978).

4. PUB. L. No. 93-247, 88 Stat. 4 (1974) (codified as amended at 42 U.S.C. §§ 5101-5106 (1976 & Supp. IV 1980)).

5. 42 U.S.C. § 5104(a)-(b)(1) (Supp. IV 1980). The Act allocates available funds once a state qualifies for them. In order to qualify, a state must: (1) have in effect a child abuse and neglect reporting law; (2) promptly investigate the accuracy of the report and take steps to protect the child; (3) demonstrate that the state has administrative procedures, training programs and multidisciplinary services in effect to deal with child abuse; (4) have the cooperation of courts, law enforcement officials and state agencies; (5) appoint a guardian ad litem to represent the child in legal proceedings; and (6) provide for public dissemination of information. 42 U.S.C. § 5103(b)(2) (1976 & Supp. IV 1980). Although the language of the Act is mandatory, strict compliance is not required in practice. Fraser, *A Glance at the Past, A Gaze at the Present, A Glimpse of the Future: A Critical Analysis of the Development of Child Abuse Reporting Statutes,* 54 CHI.[-]KENT L. REV. 641, 643 (1978).

6. Fraser, *supra* note 5, at 649.

773

ings.[7] The coalescence of state reporting laws and federal enactments has charged state, county, and municipal child protective service (CPS) agencies[8] with legal responsibilities of investigating reports of abuse and neglect, often substantiating such reports, and finally assisting the child and the family. Yet despite legislative duties imposed on child welfare agencies to ensure protection, many children suffer further abuse *after* their plight has been reported to a child welfare agency. No one knows precisely how many child abuse fatalities result from administrative breakdowns and judgment mistakes. Studies indicate that twenty-five percent of all child fatalities arising from abuse or neglect involve children already reported to a child protective agency.[9] Tens of thousands of other children sustained serious injury while under the supervision of CPS agencies.[10]

Until recently, recurrent malfeasance by child welfare agencies was attributed to inadequate funding and poor regulation.[11] This conclusion in turn sparked legislative reform. But increased regulation did not ensure that these problems would be solved. As a result, civil and even criminal liability of child protective agencies has emerged[12] as a powerful deterrent to negligent performance of their duties. The cost and publicity of holding CPS agencies liable for their inadequate response to reported child abuse both compensates the child for suffering and forces agency employees to become more aware of their responsibilities.

This comment examines the recent expansion in liability of CPS agencies and their employees when administrative breakdowns lead to continued abuse or death of a child. This comment also analyzes various aspects of child protection for which agencies have been held liable. Finally, it dissects the theories courts recognize to sustain a cause of action[13] and projects how far each goes in opening the door

---

7. *Id.* at 650.

8. At present, public agencies provide most child protective services. However, some agencies contractually delegate their duties to private welfare programs. The discussion of agency liability throughout this comment also applies to private organizations responsible for child protective services. Some federal courts have held private child care agencies "public in nature" and, thus, subject to suit under the Federal Civil Rights Act. *See, e.g.,* Perez v. Sugarman, 499 F.2d 761 (2d Cir. 1974).

9. D. BESHAROV, CRIMINAL AND CIVIL LIABILITY IN CHILD WELFARE WORK: THE GROWING TREND 5 (A.B.A. 1983) (citing Region VI Resource Center on Child Abuse and Neglect, *Child Deaths in Texas,* p.26 (1981)); Mayberry, *Child Protective Services in New York City: An Analysis of Case Management,* p.109 (1979).

10. Mayberry, *supra* note 9, at 105.

11. Besharov, *Child Protection: Past Progress, Present Problems, and Future Directions,* 17 FAM. L.Q. 151, 164 (1983).

12. *See, e.g.,* Boss, *Professional and Agency Liability for Negligence in Child Protection,* 11 LAW. MED. & HEALTH CARE 71 (1983); Schuck, *Suing Our Servants: The Court, Congress and the Liability of Public Officials for Damages,* 1980 SUP. CT. REV. 281.

13. Nearly all cases discussed in this comment involve a defendant's motion to dismiss a complaint. Therefore, the allegations by the plaintiff are untested since the court is deciding only whether the plaintiff has legal grounds for a claim, provided plaintiff's allegations are

774

to agency liability.

II. The Emergence of Agency Liability for Inadequate Child Protection

In order to compel CPS agencies to implement federal and state programs responsibly, those injured through agency negligence have sought relief in court. Criminal and civil liability of child welfare agencies has emerged because of centralization of child protection, recognition of agency employees as professionals, and increased facilitation of lawsuits against the state.

A. Centralized Agencies

Prior to enactment of mandatory reporting laws in the 1960s,[14] reports of suspected child abuse were handled by a variety of groups.[15] Reports could be forwarded to either a police agency, a public assistance agency, or one of the few CPS agencies in existence. Any agency receiving a report of suspected abuse could in turn refer it to one of the other agencies. Furthermore, schools, hospitals, social service agencies and community service organizations could report to any one of these agencies or go directly to court and file a child protective petition.[16]

With reports shuffled from agency to agency, important information concerning the child's safety often did not reach the appropriate agency. This patchwork of efforts left no one agency responsible for protecting the child,[17] and all too often resulted in the child's death.[18] Even cases initially accepted for investigation and checked into were often subsequently ignored.

Because of staff shortages and limited accountability, pending cases accumulated and were left untouched on caseworkers desks.[19] Workers tried to screen cases, giving priority to the most urgent situations. The protective staff in one western state, for example, accumulated a total of 140 uninvestigated pending cases. Three typical case files from this total included two general reports of neglect and one physician's report of severe malnutrition. This last case had still

---

true.

14. *See supra* note 2.

15. Besharov, *supra* note 9, at 2.

16. Horowitz & Davidson, *Improving the Legal Response of Child Protective Service Agencies*, 6 VT. L. REV. 381, 382 (1981).

17. C. HELFER & R. KEMPE, THE BATTERED CHILD, editor's note to Chapter 2 (2d ed. 1974).

18. For example, a New York legislative study revealed that in 1971 75% of child abuse fatalities involved child abuse victims previously reported to authorities. *New York State Assembly Select Committee on Child Abuse Report* ii-v (April 1972), *reprinted in* C. KEMPE & R. HELFER, THE BATTERED CHILD (2d ed. 1974).

19. Besharov, *supra* note 11 at 156.

not been investigated six months after the report had been filed.[20]

States were slow to address these problems inherent in their child protective programs. It was not until 1974 that federal efforts culminated in enactment of the Child Abuse Prevention and Treatment Act.[21] This Act directed the Secretary of Health, Education and Welfare[22] to establish a National Center on Child Abuse to serve as a clearinghouse for research and information about child protective programs. Perhaps the most important aspect of the Act was its development of a state grant program[23] which required states to establish comprehensive reporting and investigatory programs.[24] Although in 1973 only three states met the eligibility requirements,[25] state legislators rapidly passed laws setting up new child protective systems which would qualify for federal aid. By 1978, forty-three states had comprehensive child protective systems.[26]

Accordingly, child protection changed from fragmented efforts of numerous state agencies to the more focused duties of a specialized child protective agency. At the same time, this change created a legal entity that could be held responsible for inadequate protection. The duties of a public welfare agency included investigating reports of suspected child abuse and intervening to protect the child. Lawsuits brought against child protective agencies provided not only a means of compensation for those injured or killed as a result of agency malfeasance, but also provided a way to force CPS agencies to implement their duties responsibly. The undesired publicity and cost accompanying a judicial finding of agency negligence are powerful deterrents to inadequate performance of agency duties. Individually, no agency employee wants to face the repercussions of prosecution for negligent performance of his job. Thus, centralization of child protection services increased agency liability.

B. Agency Employees as Professionals

Agency liability also increased because caseworkers began to be regarded more as professionals than as mere bureaucrats. Caseworker liability can be analogized to liability of other profes-

---

20. *Id.* at 156.
21. *See supra* note 5.
22. The Department of Health, Education and Welfare is now known as the Department of Health and Human Services.
23. Title XX of the Social Security Act also provided the states with supplementary funds. States were allowed a 75% federal reimbursement for increases in their child protective staff. *See* BENTON, FIELD & MILLER, SOCIAL SERVICES: FEDERAL LEGISLATION V. STATE IMPLEMENTATION 72 (1978) (finding that the majority of state administrators and federal staff believed that Title XX had the most positive impact on children's protective services).
24. *See supra* note 5.
25. Besharov, *supra* note 11, at 158.
26. *Id.*

776

sionals such as physicians and teachers for failure to report suspected abuse.[27] During the 1960s, when public interest centered on the problems of child abuse, state legislatures responded by enacting laws requiring physicians, teachers and other professionals to report suspected abuse.[28] Legislators were convinced that such professionals were uniquely able to spot abused children and to evaluate their injuries. The threat of civil liability imposed through common law or statutory negligence theories[29] would promote more responsible behavior on the part of professionals.[30]

Recently, agency employees have been included in this category of responsible professionals in the child welfare system.[31] Like teachers and physicians, caseworkers aptly can investigate and monitor child abuse. Furthermore, caseworkers—like other professionals—must adhere to both statutory and common law duties.[32] Finally, imposing civil liability for a caseworker's failure to adequately investigate and monitor reported child abuse accordingly increases responsibility in child protection.

Extending civil liability to caseworkers as professionals is part of a general trend toward holding professionals responsible for their decisions.[33] The decision in *Tarasoff v. Regents of the University of California*[34] is the most controversial indication of this trend. In *Tarasoff*, a psychotherapist was held liable for his failure to warn a victim that one of his patients intended to cause her serious harm.[35] The court held that when a therapist knows or, according to the profession's standards, has reason to know that a patient presents a seri-

---

27. *See generally* Aaron, *Civil Liability For Teacher's Negligent Failure To Report Suspected Child Abuse*, 28 WAYNE L. REV. 183 (1981); Brown & Truitt, *Civil Liability for Failure to Diagnose and Report Child Abuse*, 54 CHI.[-]KENT L. REV. 753 (1978); Mazura, *Negligence-Malpractice-Physician's Liability for Failure to Diagnose and Report Child Abuse*, 23 WAYNE L. REV. 1187 (1977).

28. Between 1963 and 1965, all 50 states and the District of Columbia enacted laws requiring physicians and other professionals to report suspected abuse. *See* Kohlman, *Malpractice Liability for Failing to Report Child Abuse*, 49 CAL. ST. B.J. 119, 120 (1974).

29. *See, e.g.,* Landeros v. Flood, 17 Cal.3d 399, 551 P.2d 389, 131 Cal. Rptr. 69 (1976) (court found a physician's failure to comply with a state criminal statute making failure to report suspected abuse a misdemeanor constituted negligence *per se*).

30. *Reporting: Failure to Report Suspected Cases of Child Abuse*, 6 AM. JUR. PROOF OF FACTS 2d 345, 354 (1975). One author has suggested that private damage actions against physicians may be the sole means of securing widespread compliance with reporting statutes. *See* Kohlman, *supra* note 28, at 121.

31. Besharov, *supra* note 9, at 2.

32. Although the statutory duties of agencies vary from state to state, the Child Abuse Prevention and Treatment Act provides some national uniformity for states in constructing their statutes. *See supra* note 5. Courts have also found common law duties for which agencies have been held liable. *See infra* text accompanying notes 75-86.

33. Besharov, *supra* note 9, at 2.

34. 17 Cal.3d 425, 551 P.2d 334, 131 Cal. Rptr. 14.

35. After the patient informed the therapist of his intention to kill the young woman, the therapist contacted the police. The police questioned the patient and subsequently released him. Even though the therapist made these efforts to counter the patient's threats, the court found an unfulfilled duty to inform the intended victim. *Id.*

777

ous danger to a third party, the therapist has a duty to use reasonable care to protect the intended victims. The importance of *Tarasoff* for CPS agency employees is its expanded notion of professional duty, because the court was willing to recognize a duty where none existed before. Although this principle has been limited by subsequent decisions,[36] it exemplifies the general trend toward holding professionals liable for their decisions.

C. Increase in Government Liability

The increased liability of child protective agencies is also part of a general legislative and judicial trend facilitating lawsuits against the state. The abrogation of sovereign immunity[37] and the expansion of federal civil rights litigation[38] have caused a corresponding increase in litigation against the state.[39] States are no longer completely immune from liability for tortious acts by their individual agents. The expansion of state agency liability under state tort law mirrors expanded liability under section 1983 of the Federal Civil Rights Act.[40] These trends have created new opportunities for successful litigation against the state.

III. Areas of Liability

A. Failure to Investigate

Agencies have been prosecuted for negligent conduct in all aspects of child protection work. State law requires all agencies to initiate investigations pursuant to reports of suspected abuse on the same day the reports are received or shortly thereafter.[41] A caseworker can choose to reject a report, but such discretionary decisions are rare. Because a report need only convey a reasonable basis for suspecting abuse,[42] a caseworker must have sufficient grounds for rejecting the report.[43]

---

36. *See, e.g.,* Bellah v. Greenson, 73 Cal. App.3d 890, 893, 141 Cal. Rptr. 92, 95 (1977) (court limited duty to warn to situations where there is risk of violent assault as opposed to risk of self-inflicted harm or harm to property); Shaw v. Glickman, 45 Md. 718, 415 A.2d 625, 630-31 (1980) (court found no duty to warn where the therapist was dealing with a group psychotherapy program).

37. *See infra* note 87.

38. The Federal Civil Rights Act, 42 U.S.C. § 1983 (1970), establishes a cause of action against any person who, acting under color of state law, causes an individual to suffer a constitutional deprivation. *See infra* notes 111 and 112.

39. Besharov, *supra* note 9, at 2.

40. Since the United States Supreme Court's landmark decision in Monell v. Dept. of Social Services, 436 U.S. 658 (1978), individuals may sue local governments under section 1983.

41. Besharov, *The Legal Aspects of Reporting Known and Suspected Child Abuse and Neglect,* 23 VILL. L. REV. 458, 495 (1978).

42. *Id.* at 471.

43. Reports may be rejected if, for example, the allegations clearly fall outside the

778

Although failures to investigate reports are not common, the decision in *Mammo v. Arizona*[44] demonstrates that potential for liability exists. In *Mammo*, a father reported that he found bruises on two of his children during visitation, and that their mother would not allow him to visit his infant. The agency failed to investigate the report, and the infant died ten days later. The father successfully pursued a wrongful death action and received $300,000 in damages.[45]

B. Failure to Investigate Adequately

Even when an agency responds to a report of abuse, it may negligently conduct its investigation[46] or fail to place a child in protective custody.[47] Courts have held state social workers criminally liable for inadequate performance of these official duties. In *Steinberger v. District Court in and for the Tenth District*,[48] a caseworker and her supervisor were charged with failure to respond adequately to reported abuse. The child had been in foster care and was returned home. While the caseworker was on part-time leave, the agency received calls from the school to report large burns, cuts, and bruises on the child. Neither the caseworker nor her supervisor attempted to visit the child and verify the reports. After the child died, the caseworker and her supervisor were convicted under a criminal statute.[49]

Although no caseworker has yet been criminally convicted for failure to investigate adequately reports of abuse, the possibility of criminal charges is a deterrent for all agency employees. Courts are unlikely to expand criminal liability for CPS agency employees, since criminal liability is a harsh reprimand for an employee who was negligent on the job. On the other hand, awareness of criminal prosecutions may frighten CPS employees into increased compliance with agency policies and guidelines.

agency's definitions of child abuse or neglect, if the caller cannot provide sufficient information to identify or locate the child, or if specific evidence of malice exists. Besharov, *supra* note 9, at 7.

44. No. C-391550 (Maricopa County Super. Ct., Ariz., Sept. 19, 1980).

45. *Id.*

46. *See, e.g.,* Buege v. Iowa, No. 20521 (Allamakee, Iowa, July 30, 1980) (settlement amounted to $82,500 where agency investigated and substantiated reported abuse but failed to make follow-up visits, and child subsequently died).

47. For example, a complaint filed in the Federal District Court of Missouri alleged that a caseworker failed to remove a two-year-old child from a home when she witnessed, over a five-month period, the child's weight drop from 23 pounds to 13 pounds. Basharov, *supra* note 9, at 10.

48. 198 Colo. 59, 596 P.2d 755 (1979).

49. Both convictions were subsequently overturned upon finding the official misconduct statute void for vagueness. People v. Beruman, 638 P.2d 789, 794 (Colo. 1982).

C. Failure to Place in Protective Custody

Caseworkers must decide, based on their investigations, whether a child is in such imminent danger that protective custody is required.[50] The decision is difficult, and the consequences of making an error in judgment are harsh — unnecessarily placing a child in foster care and severing parental rights,[51] or wrongly deciding against foster care when a child is in serious danger. However, courts have held CPS agency employees liable for overlooking or ignoring signs of serious danger to a child and for failing to remove the child from the abusive environment.

In 1980, caseworkers and their supervisors in two states were prosecuted for criminal negligence in failing to place abused children in protective custody. In Kentucky, agency employees decided to close a case despite numerous reports of suspected abuse.[52] The child died of burns shortly thereafter. The charges were dismissed, however, because of negligence on the part of other agencies.[53] In Texas, three protective service agency employees were charged with criminal negligence when, despite hospital reports of severe burns, they did not remove the abused child from her home.[54] The child died subsequently. A month before the trial was to commence, the court quashed the indictments on all counts, finding that no indictable offense had been charged.[55]

D. Inadequate Foster Care

Most agency liability litigation arises from alleged inadequate foster care.[56] CPS agency employees are faced with a difficult choice in deciding whether to remove a child from his natural home. But once an agency decides to remove a child and place him in a foster home, the agency's responsibilities increase, as does its potential lia-

---

50. Child protection workers have great discretion to decide when it is appropriate to petition a court to award custody of the child to the state. Once the worker files the petition, the court may order the child's removal from his natural home. A worker may also remove a child without prior judicial approval if the worker determines that an emergency exists. Wald, *State Intervention on Behalf of Neglected Children: Standards for Removal of Children from their Homes, Monitoring the Status of Children in Foster Care and Termination of Parental Rights*, 28 STAN. L. REV. 623, 628-36 (1976).

51. *Id.*

52. Casper & Hutchinson, *CPS Indictments in Ky. and their Aftermath*, 4 NAT'L CHILD PROTECTION SERVICES NEWSLETTER 6 (1981).

53. Apparently, hospital physicians failed more than once to report treatment of the child. The judge found that since several agencies and numerous employees had caused the inadequate protection, it was unfair to charge the two caseworkers with criminal violations. *Id.*

54. Horowitz & Davidson, *Improving the Legal Response of Child Protective Service Agencies*, 6 VT. L. REV. 381, 384 (1981).

55. *Id.*

56. Foster care includes all state supervised placement of children, whether in institutional settings or in family homes.

780

bility.[57] One scenario typical of such cases illustrates why public outcry has been strongest in this area:

> Anna was placed in the legal custody of the New York Department of Social Services when she was two years old. At age three, she was put in a foster home by the Catholic Home Bureau, which had been delegated the responsibility of supervising her foster placement. As part of its decision to certify the foster home in which Anna was placed, the Bureau prepared a report, approving the foster parents as "reliable, helpful and endowed with Christian charity." By age ten, Anna was regularly beaten and sexually abused by her foster father. He threw her down stairs, whipped her repeatedly with a belt, lacerated her with a hunting knife, confined her to her room for days at a time and forced her to have sexual relations with him. In order to prevent discovery of her injuries, Anna's foster father withdrew her from school and threatened to institutionalize her if she disclosed his actions to anyone.
>
> Although the Catholic Home Bureau was charged by state law with periodically inspecting and annually recertifying the foster home, several years went by without a visit from Bureau personnel. When caseworkers did check up on the foster placement, they interviewed Anna only in the presence of her foster father and gave the home a favorable rating in spite of suspicions of child abuse. The Bureau was notified of Anna's removal from school and had been given psychiatric reports indicating that she was being sexually molested, yet the Bureau failed to protect Anna from continued abuse. At age sixteen, three years after strong evidence of child abuse had been revealed to the Bureau, Anna was removed from the foster home. Anna had been abused for over seven years while under the protective custody of the state of New York.[58]

In the past decade, national attention has focused increasingly on the failures of the foster care system.[59] The advent of reporting laws brought a corresponding increase in the number of children placed in foster care.[60] Presently, there are nearly one-half million

---

57. *See, e.g.,* Vonner v. State, 273 So. 2d 252 (La. 1973); Elton v. County of Orange, 3 Cal. App. 3d 1053, 84 Cal. Rptr. 27 (1970); Bartels v. County of Westchester, 76 A.D.2d 517, 429 N.Y.S.2d 906 (1980).

58. Doe v. County of Suffolk, 494 F. Supp. 1979 (E.D.N.Y. 1980).

59. In the past ten years, numerous articles have been written analyzing the foster care system. *See* Children's Defense Fund, *Children Without Homes: An Examination of Public Responsibility to Children in Out-of-Home Care* (1978); National Commission on Children in Need of Parents, *Who Knows? Who Cares?* (1979); Musewicz, *The Failure of Foster Care: Federal Statutory Reform and the Child's Right to Performance,* 54 S. CAL. L. REV. 633 (1981); Comment, *Foster Placement Review: Problems and Opportunities,* 83 DICK. L. REV. 487 (1979).

60. U.S. Nat'l Center on Child Abuse and Neglect, *Nat'l Study of the Incidence and Severity of Child Abuse and Neglect,* (DHHS 1981).

children under foster care in the United States.[61] Most frequently, children are placed in foster care because a court or social service agency has determined that the child was abused or neglected.[62] Unfortunately, sometimes deprivation and abuse faced by children under foster care is even more egregious than the original mistreatment from which the agency is claiming to protect them. Anna and those who have suffered similar cruelties from inadequate foster care services have sought remedy for these harms by suing the CPS agencies.

The many suits brought against agencies in this area of child protection result in part from the fact that abuse of foster children remains largely unchecked.[63] Although the federal government recently enacted the Adoption Assistance and Child Welfare Act of 1980[64] — aimed at improving foster care services — it failed to designate any specific programs.[65] The Act contains a foster care review provision which requires states to conduct a review of foster care placement through a court or administrative body. Theoretically, states will not receive matching funds if they fail to implement programs. However, there is no assurance that agencies and their employees will comply. Furthermore, the requisite standards described in the Act provide minimal protection for foster children. Even when agency regulations call for extensive monitoring of foster children, supervision of foster care is often sporadic and sometimes nonexistent.[66] Agency employees frequently do not abide by their own regulations because they have little incentive to do so.[67]

Furthermore, few avenues of redress are open for children left unprotected by the foster care system. Regulations and administrative procedures provide little recourse, and, usually, a child has no access to any grievance mechanism.[68] Legal advocates for foster children are rarely accessible. The children, even if old enough to ex-

---

61. Besharov, *supra* note 11, at 167.

62. "Abuse" and "neglect," usually defined by state statute, reflect the point at which the care provided by the natural parents is considered sufficiently inadequate for the state to take action. Abuse generally covers physical and emotional injury and denotes the commission of an act. Neglect occurs if parents fail to provide for a child's physical or emotional needs and is generally an omission. Bourne, *Child Abuse and Neglect: An Overview*, CRITICAL PERSPECTIVES ON CHILD ABUSE 1, 2 (R. Bourne & E. Newberger eds. 1979).

63. Besharov, *supra* note 11, at 168.

64. PUB. L. No. 96-272, codified in scattered sections of 42 U.S.C. The Act amended the AFDC foster care program which is operated under Title IV-A of the federal Social Security Act. 42 U.S.C. § 601 (1982).

65. The legislation merely promulgates minimum guidelines states must follow in operation of their foster care programs in order to qualify for certain federal funds. 42 U.S.C.A. § 627, 671(a) (West Supp. 1980).

66. *See* C. ROSE, SOME EMERGING ISSUES IN LEGAL LIABILITY OF CHILDREN'S AGENCIES (1978).

67. *Id.*

68. *Id.*

782

press their own views, are largely denied a voice in dependency proceedings and placement into foster homes or institutions.[69] Those children fortunate enough to have been represented by attorneys in the proceedings which lead to their foster placement have no subsequent contact with an attorney.[70] Even when a foster child has contacted a lawyer, further obstacles such as inaccessibility to the child's files or even to the child may hinder redress.[71] When children or their survivors finally bring lawsuits against a CPS agency, they provide a necessary incentive for better foster care services.

IV. Theories of Liability

Liability for inadequate child protective service is largely founded upon negligence theories. Both common law and statutory negligence theories have provided a basis for a cause of action. Courts have recently begun to consider a new avenue of redress based on section 1983 of the Civil Rights Act.[72] Section 1983 grants those seeking redress an alternative theory on which to base a claim of liability. An examination of the strengths and weaknesses of these two theories reveals the difficulty victims face in attempting to hold agencies responsible for malfeasance or nonfeasance.

A. Negligence

Most actions brought against agencies for inadequate child protective services have been founded upon the theory of negligence. In order to sustain a cause of action based on negligence, the plaintiff must show that a common law or statutory duty existed which the agency failed to perform and which proximately caused the plaintiff's injury.[73] The breach of duty and the injury to the plaintiff generally are not difficult to prove. The element of proximate cause as well as the defense of sovereign immunity[74] are the toughest hurdles a plaintiff must leap in establishing a cause of action under the theory of negligence.

1. Establishing the Cause of Action. — In general, courts have charged agencies with a duty of ordinary care in the implemen-

---

69. A few states allow the children to participate, through independent counsel, as parties in dependency proceedings. But, as a practical matter, children's preferences are often ignored. *Id.* at 21. Furthermore, the United States Supreme Court has refused to recognize a constitutional right for children to participate in dependency proceedings. Smith v. Offer, 431 U.S. 852 (1977).

70. Besharov, *supra* note 11, at 168.

71. *Id.*

72. *See infra* notes 111 and 112.

73. W. PROSSER, HANDBOOK OF THE LAW OF TORTS § 30 (4th ed. 1971).

74. *See infra* note 87.

tation of child protective services.[75] Courts have found the origin for an agency's duty of due care in both common law and statutory law. Most frequently, the agency has blatantly exposed its negligent actions or omissions by failing to comply with state statutes or agency regulations.[76] Courts have found this failure probative of negligence, but have not recognized such failure as negligence *per se*.

The court in *Bartel v. County of Westchester*[77] articulated both the common law and statutory bases for this duty. In *Bartel*, the representative of a three-year-old child brought action against the county for negligent placement and supervision of the child under foster care. The foster parents had carelessly scalded the child while bathing her. The court reasoned that the state had a duty to the child defined by both state law and common law. New York statutory law considered the state to be the *parens patriae*[78] of the child and, thus, charged it with the responsibility of supervising the foster home and removing the child if necessary. The court held that apart from the statutory duty creating liability, the agency could be sued for breach of its common law duty. The court cited a well established common law principle that one assuming to act, although not under a duty, must act with care, especially when caring for children.[79] Since the agency undertook the duty of protecting the infant, that duty, once assumed, had to be carried out with due care.[80]

Some courts look beyond duties enumerated in statutes and regulations and define the scope of an agency's responsibilities in broader terms of common law. In *Vonner v. State*,[81] a suit was brought by a child's mother against the state Department of Welfare for its negligence in failing to monitor foster parents who later eventually killed the child. Four foster children had been placed in the Vonner home. Despite the fact that the two oldest children had run away, complaining of continuous beatings by their foster parents, welfare workers failed to investigate the complaints thoroughly, as required by departmental rules. Specifically, the department failed to submit the two younger children to a yearly medical examination and failed to make regular visits to the foster home every two months.[82] The youngest child eventually died from physical abuse.

---

75. *See, e.g.*, Bradford v. Davis, 290 Or. 855, 626 P.2d 1376 (1981) (court recognized cause of action for an agency's failure to exercise ordinary care in discharge of statutory duty).

76. *See, e.g.*, Elton v. County of Orange, 3 Cal. App. 3d 1053, 84 Cal. Rptr. 27 (1970) (court sustained cause of action against a county for its failure to comply with regulations governing dependent children and foster homes).

77. 76 A.D.2d 517, 429 N.Y.S.2d 906 (1980).

78. *Parens patriae* refers traditionally to the role of the state as sovereign and guardian of persons under legal disability. BLACK'S LAW DICTIONARY 1003 (5th ed. 1979).

79. 2 HARPER & JAMES, THE LAW OF TORTS, § 18.6 at 1044-46 (1956).

80. Bartels v. County of Westchester, 76 A.D.2d 517, 429 N.Y.S.2d 906 (1980).

81. 273 So. 2d 252 (La. 1973).

82. *Id.*

784

In *Vonner,* the court recognized the department's negligent compliance with its own regulations but found that the department's duty rested on a broader base. Once the department took custody of the child, the court held that it was under a duty of due care to provide for that child's well-being. Indeed, the scope of the department's liability was not limited to compliance with its own regulations but rather was defined by general principles of tort liability.

As exemplified by *Bartel* and *Vonner,* courts generally derive an agency's duty to provide reasonable care from common law or statutory law. Courts next consider when the duty arises. Although courts have recognized an existent duty at various stages of child protection, they have been most willing to uphold the duty once the agency has taken custody and placed a child in foster care. Courts have refused to allow agencies to delegate this duty of due care to foster parents or others who temporarily care for the children on behalf of the state.

The court in *Andrews v. Courts of Ostego*[83] held that when an agency obtains custody of a child, it becomes directly responsible for the child's care and well-being. Thus, the court held that the agency could not insulate itself from responsibility by delegating that responsibility to others. This rationale is espoused frequently by courts dealing with an agency's inadequate supervision of foster care.[84]

Once a plaintiff has established an agency's breach of a duty, the plaintiff must then show a proximately caused injury. The injury and damage elements of liability are undeniable because of the child's injuries or death.[85] Finally, courts impose liability only for abuse sustained after the agency's negligent acts or omissions.[86]

2. Barriers to Establishing Negligence.—A plaintiff can frequently establish the breach of a common law or statutory duty which resulted in injury. Yet, the plaintiff may find the court reluctant to hold that the agency's negligence proximately caused the damage. Another significant problem a plaintiff may encounter is the defendant's claim of sovereign immunity[87] traditionally granted governmental agencies. These two barriers keep all but the most obvious

---

83. 446 N.Y.S. 2d 169 (Sup. Ct. Ostego Co. 1982).

84. *See, e.g.,* Vonner v. State, 273 So. 2d 252 (La. 1973).

85. The law of negligence requires proof of actual loss or damage to the interest of another. PROSSER, *supra* note 73, at 143.

86. *Id.* at 144-46.

87. The doctrine of governmental immunity is based on common law and holds that the government cannot be sued without its consent. In 1946, the United States waived its immunity from liability in tort by authorizing litigation of tort claims against it in the federal courts, under the Federal Tort Claims Act. 28 U.S.C. §§ 1346, 1402, 1504, 2110, 2401, 2402, 2411, 2412, 2671-2680 (1948). Likewise, all states have consented to suit via state tort claims statutes. PROSSER, *supra* note 73, at § 131.

cases of agency negligence out of court.

a. *Governmental Immunity.*—Even if a plaintiff establishes the elements constituting a cause of action for negligence, the claim may still be frustrated by the defense of governmental immunity.[88] In many states the child protective agency, as a political subdivision[89] of the state, is immune from suit for negligence if it was acting within its discretion when the injury occurred.[90] Discretionary functions have been defined as those made at planning or policy levels, not at administrative or ministerial levels.[91] Whether a court holds an agency liable for negligence may depend upon whether it finds the agency's acts or omissions of a discretionary or ministerial nature.

Courts have enumerated various reasons for finding the agency's decisions a discretionary matter of public policy. In *Elton v. County of Orange*,[92] the court held that a CPS agency could not claim the defense of governmental immunity because the investigation, placement and supervision of abused children were not basic policy decisions. In *Elton*, a dependent child sought damages for emotional and physical injuries inflicted by foster parents through the agency's negligence in supervising the foster home. The court held that discretionary actions would include, for example, recommending a child be declared independent. However, the court noted that subsequent ministerial acts that implement discretionary decisions—such as checking up on the child's status in a foster home—do not rise to the same level. In order to qualify for immunity, the court held that the agency must demonstrate that a policy decision took place in which risks and advantages were balanced.[93]

Other courts have presented a sound rationale for holding those

---

88. *See supra* note 87.

89. A political subdivision is a division of the state made by proper authorities for the purpose of carrying out a portion of those functions of the state which have always been regarded as public. State ex. rel. Marsano v. Mitchell, 155 Conn. 256, ____, 231 A.2d 539, 542 (1968).

90. The Federal Tort Claims Act as well as some state tort claims acts provide exceptions to the general rule of tort liability of the federal or state government. An exception is frequently provided for acts or omissions which are within the "discretionary function or duty" of an agency. *See, e.g.*, Smith v. Cooper, 256 Or. 485, 475 P.2d 78 (1969) (court held that persons acting as agents of government bodies are immune under common law from tort liability for conduct involving discretionary acts or functions).

91. In United Air Lines, Inc. v. Wiener, 335 F.2d 379, 393 (9th Cir. 1964), *cert. dismissed*, 379 U.S. 951 (1964), the court summarized the distinctions made between ministerial and discretionary acts as follows: "[It is] discretionary to undertake fire-fighting, lighthouse, rescue or wrecked-ship marking services, but not discretionary to conduct such operations negligently; discretionary to admit a patient to an army hospital, but not discretionary to treat the patient in a negligent manner; discretionary to establish a post office at a particular location but not to negligently fail to establish handrails; discretionary to establish control towers at airports and to undertake air traffic separation, but not to conduct the same negligently."

92. 3 Cal. App. 3d 1053, 84 Cal. Rptr. 27 (1970).

93. *Id.*

same duties to be discretionary in nature. In *Pickett v. Washington County*,[94] the court found an agency caseworker immune from liability for acts and omissions relating to the supervision, care, and custody of a child. In deciding whether the agency's acts were discretionary, the court considered the importance of the government function involved and the extent to which governmental liability might impair the exercise of that function. The court found that the government, acting through child welfare agencies, had undertaken an important function when it placed children in foster care. The court held that the agent employed by the government to implement this function is the caseworker, who continually must make complex judgments. These judgments require weighing risks that could hinder the child's development. The court held that decisions of this nature are highly discretionary and should not be subject to scrutiny by courts.

The designation of an agency's actions as discretionary or ministerial is a public policy decision, apparently largely based on notions of proximate cause. Agency employees can only be expected to forestall dangerous situations that are reasonably foreseeable. Courts seem to measure the degree of foreseeability that could be expected of the agency in relation to the type of injury involved. Based on this degree of foreseeability, courts decide whether or not agency decisions were discretionary and thus deserving of immunity. Court usually hold an agency's activities to be ministerial in cases in which the child has been severely injured or killed and the agency's negligence is alarmingly obvious.[95] Conversely, courts hold an agency's decision to be discretionary in cases involving minor injuries and weaker state controls.[96]

b. Proximate Cause.—Naturally, an agency should not be held liable for every injury suffered by a child at the hands of its foster parents. Common law notions of proximate cause require that legal responsibility be limited to cases where the causes are sufficiently connected with the result, such that the law may justifiably impose liability.[97] Most courts have held the connection between the agency's acts or omissions and the child's injury sufficiently connected if the agency knew[98] or should have known[99] of the foster

---

94. 31 Or. App. 1263, 572 P.2d 1070 (1977).
95. *See, e.g.,* Bartels v. County of Westchester, 76 A.D.2d 517, 429 N.Y.S.2d 906 (1980).
96. *See, e.g.,* Pickett v. Washington County, 31 Or. App. 1263, 572 P.2d 1070 (1977).
97. Prosser, *supra* note 73, at 237.
98. Hanson v. Rowe, 18 Ariz. App. 131, 500 P.2d 916 (1972); Commonwealth v. Coyle, 160 Pa. 36, 28 A. 634 (1894); Bartel v. County of Westchester, 76 A.D.2d 517, 429 N.Y.S.2d 906 (1980).
99. Vonner v. State, 273 So. 2d 252 (La. 1973); Commonwealth v. Coyle, 160 Pa. 36,

parent's abuse.

Proving that an agency employee knew or should have known that his actions would lead to the injury suffered by the child is a frequent roadblock to a negligence claim. Many courts required proof that the agency actually knew of the foster parents' violent proclivities and failed to safeguard against them.[100] This standard was espoused in the earliest reported case of agency liability, *Commonwealth v. Coyle*.[101] In *Coyle*, the county director of the poor was held liable for the negligent discharge of his duty in the care and placement of a seven-year-old child. The director had been warned of the foster father's cruelty, as evidenced by his treatment of other foster children. The court found the agency liable for knowingly permitting a child in its care to be grossly maltreated.

Courts hold that prior knowledge of a foster parent's propensity for violence does not necessarily mean actual knowledge. Some courts have supported a cause of action when the agency is put on sufficient notice that a child's health and safety is endangered.[102] In *Vonner v. State*,[103] the Department of Welfare was given notice of possible maltreatment when two of the four foster children placed in the Vonner home ran away, claiming they had been beaten regularly. The natural mother had also complained that her children were being abused by the foster parents. Yet in the face of such notice, welfare workers refused to investigate these complaints and circumstances of abuse. The *Vonner* court held that the element of proximate cause was established by the continuous course of beatings over an extended period that could and should have been discovered in the conscientious performance of the department's visitation duties.[104]

Because requisite foreseeability for proving proximate cause is difficult to establish, the court may find liability in only those cases of grossly inadequate performance by the agency. Courts have begun to recognize problems facing a plaintiff in trying to bring a legitimate negligence claim against an agency. Accordingly, some courts have made efforts to mitigate the plaintiff's burden of showing prior knowledge. In *Hanson v. Rome*,[105] for example, a surviving parent brought suit against a child protective agency for the death of one child and personal injuries to a second child at the hands of foster parents. The plaintiff's cause of action hinged on proving that the

---

28 A. 634 (1894).
100. *See supra* note 98.
101. 160 Pa. 36, 28 A. 634 (1894).
102. *See supra* note 99.
103. 273 So.2d 252 (La. 1973).
104. *Vonner*, 273 So. 2d at 255.
105. 18 Ariz. App. 131, 500 P.2d 916 (1972).

788

state had placed the two children in the home with knowledge of the foster parents' violent proclivities. In order to prove this, the plaintiff sought discovery of the name and address of other parents whose children had been placed in the same foster home. The state argued that such disclosure would violate federal regulations requiring confidentiality of records.[106] The court authorized discovery of the names and addresses despite federal regulations, because without such discovery the knowledge requirement would be insurmountable. The court reasoned that upholding difficulties faced by plaintiffs attempting to prove an agency's prior knowledge would only encourage lackadaisical supervision by the agency over its foster care program.[107]

Generally, courts have failed to find sufficient proximate cause when a child's injury resulted from foster parents' negligence, rather than from their intentional abuse.[108] The decision in *Parker v. St. Christopher's Home*[109] illustrates this point. In *Parker*, the court refused to hold a child welfare agency vicariously liable for a child's injuries, caused by a foster parent's negligent failure to prevent the child from spilling coffee on herself. The court held that the foster parents' control over the child was sufficiently independent from the agency to protect the agency from liability for unforeseeable acts of negligence.[110] In other words, the foster parents' act of setting a cup of hot coffee too close to the child was not sufficiently intentional to hold the agency liable for its failure to prevent the injury.

B. Section 1983

Victims also utilize a new theory of liability to attack CPS agencies — the civil rights violation suit.[111] Section 1983 of the Civil Rights Act provides a remedy against any person who "[u]nder color of any statute, ordinance, regulation, custom or usage of any state or

---

106. 42 U.S.C. § 602 allows the state to receive federal funds for foster home care if it enacts a plan to "provide safeguards which restrict use or disclosure of information concerning applicants and recipients to purposes directly connected with administration of aid to families with dependent children." *Id.*

107. *Hanson*, 18 Ariz. App. at 135, 500 P.2d at 920.

108. *See, e.g.*, Pickett v. Washington County, 31 Or. App. 1263, 572 P.2d 1070 (1977) (court found no liability when child was injured while horseback riding after being left unattended by foster parents); Fox v. Mission of Immaculate Virgin For Protection of Homeless and Destitute Children, 202 Misc. 478, 119 N.Y.S.2d 14 (Sup. Ct. Kings Co. 1952) (court rejected claim for personal injury when child fell through unguarded window in dormitory of foster institution); Parker v. St. Christopher's Home, 77 A.D.2d 921, 431 N.Y.S.2d 110 (2nd Dept. (1980)) (court found no cause of action against welfare agency when foster parent failed to prevent a 13-month-old child from spilling hot coffee on herself).

109. 77 A.D.2d 921, 431 N.Y.S.2d 110 (2nd Dept. 1980).

110. *Id.* at 112.

111. The United States Supreme Court has articulated three reasons why a person may choose to bring an action under 42 U.S.C. § 1983: (1) to override certain kinds of state laws; (2) to provide a remedy where state law is inadequate; and (3) to provide a federal remedy where the state remedy, though adequate in theory, is not available in practice. Monroe v. Pape, 365 U.S. 167, 173-74 (1961).

territory subject . . . any citizen to the deprivation of any rights . . . secured by the constitution and laws . . . [of the United States] . . . ."[112] Section 1983 was originally enacted in response to Ku Klux Klan activities, left uncontrolled by state and local governments in the South.[113] The statute created civil liability for representatives of the state who were unwilling to enforce state laws against the Klan.

During the first decades after its enactment, cases brought under section 1983 largely involved deprivation of voting rights.[114] However, the Act's coverage has since been expanded to include cases involving other constitutional violations,[115] as well as economic deprivations.[116] Most recently, section 1983 actions have appeared the area of child protection.

Four cases of CPS agency liability under section 1983 have already been litigated.[117] Accordingly, courts have begun to outline the requirements of a section 1983 action in the context of child welfare. On its face, a section 1983 action requires only three elements: (1) a state action that was (2) causally related to (3) a constitutional or federal statutory deprivation.[118] But courts have added another requirement — a standard of culpability[119] — in bringing a section 1983 action. It is this requisite state of mind that provides the greatest challenge to plaintiffs attempting to prosecute CPS agencies. Examining these four cases illustrates how courts have begun to analyze section 1983 actions in the area of child protection.

---

112. 42 U.S.C. § 1983 (1970) states: "Every person who, under color of any statute, ordinance, regulation, custom or usage, of any state or territory, subjects, or causes to be subjected, any citizen of the United States or other person within the jurisdiction thereof to the deprivation of any rights, privileges, or immunities secured by the Constitution and laws, shall be liable to the party injured in an action at law, suit in equity, or other proper proceeding for redress."

113. For a detailed discussion of the background of § 1983, see Comment, *Developments in the Law: Section 1983 and Federalism*, 90 Harv. L. Rev. 1133 (1977).

114. *See, e.g.*, Nixon v. Herndon, 273 U.S. 536 (1927); Myers v. Anderson, 238 U.S. 368 (1915).

115. Presently, the overwhelming majority of section 1983 cases arise in the context of alleged police misconduct. *See, e.g.*, Monroe v. Pape, 365 U.S. 167 (1961) (landmark case against police officers for making illegal search and interrogation of an innocent family).

116. *See, e.g.*, Burt v. City of New York, 156 F.2d 791 (2d Cir. 1946) (court found a section 1983 cause of action in allegations of a purposeful and discriminatory denial of an architect's permit).

117. Doe v. New York City Dep't of Social Servs., 649 F.2d 134 (2d Cir. 1981); Jensen v. Conrad (Jensen I), 570 F. Supp. 91 (4th Cir. 1983); Jensen v. Conrad (Jensen II), 570 F. Supp. 114 (4th Cir. 1983); Estate of Bailey v. County of York, 580 F. Supp. 796 (3d Cir. 1984).

118. *See supra* note 112.

119. The requisite standard of culpability in section 1983 actions is highly contested. Before the landmark case of Monroe v. Pape, 365 U.S. 167 (1961), courts generally read into the section a purposeful intent requirement. *Monroe* overruled this requirement but left unclear the role of defendant's state of mind in section 1983 actions. For a general discussion of the state of mind requirement of section 1983, see Comment, *The Evolution of the State of Mind Requirement of Section 1983*, 47 Tul. L. Rev. 870 (1973).

1. Doe v. New York City Dep't of Social Services.—Doe v. New York City Dep't of Social Services[120] is the only case in which the court upheld a cause of action under section 1983, in the context of child protection. The plaintiff, Anna Doe, had been abused by her foster father for more than six years.[121] The child welfare agency never became aware of the extent of Anna's abuse until six years after the abuse ceased because, Anna alleged, the agency failed to make thorough period investigations, in compliance with its statutory duties.[122]

In *Doe*, the court did not question Anna's allegation that her constitutional rights under the First, Fourth, Fifth, Ninth and Fourteenth Amendments had been violated. Rather, the court concentrated on the elements of causation and culpability. The court pointed out two fundamental requisites for imposing section 1983 liability: (1) omissions must have been a substantial factor leading to the denial of a constitutionally protected liberty interest; and (2) officials in charge of the agency being sued must have displayed a mental state of "deliberate indifference."[123] The *Doe* court discussed the deliberate indifference requirement, suggesting that gross negligence[124] creates a strong presumption of deliberate indifference. The court defined gross negligence as a state of mind between ordinary negligence and purposive intent.

The court further elaborated that deliberate indifference could be inferred not only when gross negligence is found, but also when the plaintiff establishes a pattern of defendant's failure to perform statutory duties.[125] The court found that the more a statute or regulation clearly mandates a specific course of conduct, the more it furnishes a plausible basis for inferring an agency's deliberate indifference from its failure to act, even without specific knowledge of the risk.[126] In *Doe*, the Catholic Home Bureau's failure to perform its statutory duties was held indicative of a pervasive pattern on indifference to the plaintiff's welfare.[127] In order to prove her allegation

---

120. *Doe*, 649 F.2d at 140.

121. *Id.* at 145.

122. N.Y. Soc. Serv. Law § 413 (McKinney 1970) (duty to report child abuse); N.Y. Soc. Serv. Law §§ 376, 378 (McKinney 1970) (duty to inspect periodically and annually recertify foster homes).

123. *Doe*, 649 F.2d at 140.

124. Gross negligence has been defined as "indifference to present legal duty and utter forgetfulness of legal obligations, so far as other persons may be affected, [and] a . . . manifestly smaller amount of watchfulness and circumspection than the circumstances require of a person of ordinary prudence." Burke v. Cook, 246 Mass. 518, ___, 141 N.E. 585, 586 (1923).

125. It is not violation of a statute *per se* that creates section 1983 liability, but rather injury to a constitutionally protected interest or violation of a constitutional right combined with requisite state of mind. *Id.*

126. *Doe*, 649 F.2d at 138.

127. *Id.*

791

of deliberate indifference, plaintiff sought discovery of the agency's policies, practices and procedures for ensuring child protection.[128] Plaintiff also sought information pertaining to other foster children handled by the agency. The *Doe* court held that discovery of official agency policy should be denied because the prospect of the agency having a policy encouraging child abuse was too remote.[129] However, the court held that discovery of the agency's actions in other cases of foster care should be permitted in order to allow plaintiffs to expose patterns of conduct amounting to deliberate indifference.[130]

The decision in *Doe* is important because it opens a new avenue of redress for victims who suffer from inadequate protection by a CPS agency.[131] Damage actions like the one in *Doe* have significant potential for increasing accountability of agencies and their employees. Further, *Doe* provides authority for discovery reaching beyond the scope of the individual plaintiff's circumstances. Such discovery is vital because the plaintiff will have a greater chance of maintaining a cause of action if he can prove that the agency's failure to prevent abuse was not an isolated incident.[132] Moreover the *Doe* court's extensive definition of deliberate indifference[133] as the appropriate standard of culpability should lend considerable guidance to litigants in pleading and proving similar claims.

2. Retreat from Doe.—Since *Doe*, three courts have examined section 1983 liability of CPS agencies.[134] These courts have accepted the *Doe* analysis, in form, by analyzing the defendant's culpability in terms of deliberate indifference. These decisions also reflect a substantive rejection of *Doe*, however, because in substance they make deliberate indifference an insurmountable obstacle for plaintiffs attempting to establish a cause of action under section 1983. Furthermore, these subsequent decisions have narrowed *Doe*'s scope, thus reconstructing the barriers *Doe* promised to eradicate.

---

128. The district court had barred such discovery and had excluded portions of an agency memorandum asserting that supervisory agencies were not meeting their responsibilities to report abuse of foster children. *Id.* at 147.

129. Official policy which demonstrates the requisite degree of culpability has been recognized as a possible basis for liability in section 1983 actions. *See* Monell v. Dept. of Social Services, 436 U.S. 658 (1978).

130. The court noted that a compelling reason for allowing limited discovery of agency action in other cases is provided by the rationale of Bishop v. Stoneham, 508 F.2d 1224 (2d Cir. 1974). In *Bishop* the court stated that "a series of incidents closely related in time, within several months [for example], may disclose a pattern of conduct amounting to deliberate indifference . . . ." *Id.* at 1226.

131. *See infra* notes 138-146.

132. For a discussion of "deliberate indifference" *see supra* text accompanying notes 123-133.

133. *Id.*

134. *See Jensen (Jensen I)*, 570 F. Supp. at 91; *Jensen (Jensen II)*, 570 F. Supp. at 114, *Bailey*, 580 F. Supp. at 794.

a. Jensen v. Conrad (Jensen I).—The first section 1983 child abuse case brought subsequent to *Doe* was *Jensen v. Conrad (Jensen I).*[135] Jensen, administratrix of the estate of Sylvia Brown, brought action against the South Carolina Department of Social Services for its deprivation of the Fourteenth Amendment right to life through failure to protect Brown from physical abuse inflicted by her parents. The complaint was dismissed in its entirety because of qualified immunity granted the agency. The court applied the United States Supreme Court standard for qualified immunity,[136] which shields government officials from civil liability insofar as their conduct does not violate "clearly established"[137] statutory or constitutional rights. The *Jensen I* court dismissed the case because although state statutes outlined general responsibilities of the agency at the time of its alleged misconduct, the statutes did not clearly state[138] that breach of the agency's duties would give rise to liability under section 1983. However, the court noted that *Doe* postdated the agency's conduct, thereby implying that *Doe* may abolish the immunity defense in subsequent section 1983 actions.

In a supplemental opinion issued four months later, however, the *Jensen I* court explained that even with abrogation of qualified immunity, no cause of action would be recognized. Most important to future litigants was the court's finding that the nexus[139] between the state and the abuser was too tenuous to hold the agency liable. The court distinguished *Doe* by pointing out that in *Doe* a sufficient nexus was established because the child abuser — the foster parent — was subject to direct state regulation. In *Jensen I*, however, the court held that no such nexus existed because natural parents are not obligated to accept agency supervision. The *Jensen I* court further

---

135. 570 F. Supp. 91 (4th Cir. 1983).

136. The doctrine of qualified immunity from suit available to public officials was recently articulated in the decision of Harlow v. Fitzgerald, 457 U.S. 800 (1982). There, the Court stated: " . . . government officials performing discretionary functions generally are shielded from liability for civil damages insofar as their conduct does not violate clearly established statutes or constitutional rights of which a reasonable person would have known." *Id.* at 810.

137. If the law at the time was not clearly established, an official could not reasonably be expected to anticipate subsequent legal developments, nor could he fairly be said to "know" that the law forbade conduct not previously identified as unlawful . . . . If the law was clearly established, the immunity defense ordinarily should fail, since a reasonably competent public official should know the law governing his conduct. *Id.* at 811.

138. The Court noted that whether or not a federal constitutional right is "clearly established" at the time of the alleged wrongful acts depends on a review of appropriate appellate courts' decisions. Although the plaintiff drew attention to the 1981 case of Doe v. New York City Dep't of Social Services, 649 F.2d 134 (2d Cir. 1981), *Doe* was decided subsequent to the acts complained of herein.

139. In 1982, the United States Supreme Court reaffirmed an essential dichotomy between state action and private conduct in Blum v. Yaretsky, 457 U.S. 991 (1982). The Court held that "the complaining party must show that there is a sufficiently close nexus between the state and the challenged action of the regulated entity so that the action of the latter may be fairly treated as that of the state itself." *Id.* at 351.

distinguished *Doe* because it involved a child in the state's legal custody.[140] Thus, *Jensen I* effectively narrowed the scope of *Doe* by confining *Doe*'s applicability to cases in which the state has taken custody of the child.

  b. Jensen v. Conrad (Jensen II).—In *Jensen v. Conrad (Jensen II)*[141] a different Fourth Circuit District Court echoed the finding of the *Jensen I* court that no cause of action under section 1983 would be recognized. In *Jensen II* the county department of social services failed to investigate thoroughly a report of child abuse. A department caseworker had decided, after interviewing the child, that its family should be contacted. However, the caseworker failed to locate the home and, after two months, classified the case as officially closed. The child died shortly thereafter, and the agency was charged with failure to properly train its workers. The *Jensen II* court accepted the *Doe* standard of culpability, but applied the "deliberate indifference"[142] test to effectively close the door to the plaintiff. The court held that in order to prove deliberate indifference the plaintiff must show that the agency was aware of serious inadequacies in the agency training program which posed known risks to the plaintiff. Further, the court held that the plaintiff must show that the agency declined to remedy the inadequacy.

  The court noted that plaintiff could raise a rebuttable presumption of deliberate indifference by showing a pattern of agency violations, or by showing the agency's gross negligence. But, according to the court, plaintiff's evidence that the agency failed to locate the child's home was not sufficient to prove the requisite intent for a section 1983 action.[143] The court found that even though the agency had received two separate reports of abuse and then had failed to thoroughly investigate them, plaintiff had not established deliberate indifference. Thus, *Jensen II* demonstrates that unless a plaintiff can clearly show a pattern of malfeasance or culpability close to actual intent, misconduct by the agency will go unrectified under section 1983.

  c. Estate of Bailey v. County of York.—The most recent case examining CPS agency liability under section 1983 is *Estate of Bai-*

---

  140. The court stated that "while the state and county officials may have been under a legal duty to offer protective services to the custodians of abused children, absent legal custody of a child by the state, the officials had no general duty to unequivocally ensure the safety of that child twenty-four hours a day." *Jensen I*, 570 F. Supp. at 110.

  141. 570 F. Supp. 114 (4th Cir. 1983). Although cited under the same name as the case previously discussed, this case — *Jensen II* — was brought by the administratrix of a different child whose situation was entirely different than that in *Jensen I*.

  142. *See supra* note 132.

  143. *Jensen II*, 570 F. Supp. at 120.

794

ley v. County of York.[144] In *Bailey*, an agency had taken custody of a child who had been abused by her mother's boyfriend. The agency had decided subsequently to return the child to her mother and to demand that the boyfriend move out of the mother's home. After the child was killed by the boyfriend, an action was brought against the agency for failing to discover that the boyfriend had continued to reside with the mother. In *Bailey*, the court followed the lead of *Jensen I*[145] by distinguishing *Doe* because it involved a child over which the state had actual legal custody. The *Bailey* court said that because the child's death was caused by a private individual and not the state, the requisite nexus[146] between the state actor and the child's death did not exist. The court did not discuss the fact that the state agency had custody and subsequently decided to return the child to a potentially unsafe environment. Rather, *Bailey* seems to fortify the holding in *Jensen I* that *Doe*'s application is limited to those cases in which the CPS agency has legal custody of the child.

V.   Conclusion

The debate concerning CPS agency liability transcends particular theories under which litigants seek to hold such agencies accountable. Analysis of causes of action and their attendant barriers to recovery reflects the tension between the rights of the abused child and those of CPS agencies facing resource shortages and financial cutbacks. Should the law hold agency employees liable for malfeasance and nonfeasance which may ultimately be caused by state and federal budgetary constraints? And if such liability is desirable, how egregious must misconduct be to sustain a cause of action against CPS agencies? These are precisely the questions which courts will address in the near future.

Presently, courts have begun to formulate CPS agency liability grounded on two bases: standard negligence claims and civil rights actions. Although courts seem prepared to adopt these causes of action for either gross agency misconduct or extreme cases of child abuse, it remains unclear whether they will extend these theories to incorporate more moderate forms of misfeasance or abuse. The embryonic stage of this area of litigation, however, should not relegate notions of CPS agency liability to idle speculation. As growing public awareness spawns further scrutiny of CPS agency practices, con-

---

144. 580 F. Supp. 794 (3d Cir. 1984).

145. *See supra* text accompanying notes 134-140.

146. *See supra* note 139.

tinuing judicial forays into such liability will become increasingly important to the attorney litigating in this field.

Shelly Urban

"Poor Joshua!":
The State's Responsibility
to Protect Children from Abuse

by Curry First

I. Introduction

On February 22, 1989, the Supreme Court, ruling in a child abuse case that it described as "undeniably tragic," declared that children have no substantive due process right to state protection from abuse at the hands of private actors.[1] Chief Justice William Rehnquist, writing for a six-to-three Court, ruled that the failure of a county social service agency in Wisconsin to protect a young boy from his father's brutality over two years did not violate the child's constitutional rights.

The decision upheld two lower federal courts' dismissals of a lawsuit filed on behalf of Joshua DeShaney, who, by the age of four, had suffered severe brain damage that left him retarded and institutionalized. His father, Randy DeShaney, was convicted of child abuse and sentenced to two to four years in prison.

Plaintiff Joshua, by his guardian ad litem and his mother, Melody DeShaney, brought the lawsuit under 42 U.S.C. § 1983 against three defendants: the Winnebago County Department of Social Services (DSS), the social worker who monitored Joshua, and the social worker's supervisor. The plaintiffs asserted that, due to the defendants' failure to act, Joshua suffered permanent brain injury from the physical abuse of his father. Causes of action were predicated on factual allegations asserting that the defendants were specifically aware of serious danger of physical abuse to an identifiable child; that the defendants had actively undertaken to protect the child over a time period in excess of 22 months; and that the defendants were the one state agency, by virtue of Wisconsin law, with child protection responsibility.

In his opinion, however, Chief Justice Rehnquist focused on the absence of a due process constitutional duty owed to Joshua by the state. "Because . . . the State had no constitutional duty to protect Joshua against his father's violence, its failure to do so—though calamitous in hindsight—simply does not constitute a violation of the Due Process Clause."[2] Because the case lost on the threshold constitutional duty issue, the Court did not consider the additional issue of whether the

government's misconduct was so aggravated as to surpass the negligence bar of *Daniels v. Williams* and *Davidson v. Cannon*.[3]

The purpose of this article is to give practitioners an understanding of the *DeShaney* case and the ramifications that it could have. The holding in *DeShaney* can affect various types of actions involving failure to protect generally and the mistreatment of children specifically, as well as attempts to impose liability upon the state. After a review of the factual and procedural background of the case, this article will explain the majority's opinion that the state does not have a constitutional duty to affirmatively protect children. The article will then survey the various types of cases affected by this opinion and suggest possible litigation strategies in light of *DeShaney*.

II. Factual Background

The facts in *DeShaney* must be detailed in order to demonstrate how pervasive was the state's actual knowledge of the precarious circumstances facing Joshua. Although *DeShaney* never went to trial, since the court granted defendants' motion for summary judgment, the pretrial record is voluminous and includes the defendant DSS's entire two-year child protection file on plaintiff Joshua. The parties, in support of and in opposition to the defendants' motion for summary judgment, also submitted affidavits and excerpts from the thousands of

1. DeShaney v. Winnebago County Dep't of Social Servs., 109 S. Ct. 998, 1012 (1989).
2. *Id.* at 1007 (footnote omitted).

3. Daniels v. Williams, 474 U.S. 327 (1986); Davidson v. Cannon, 474 U.S. 344 (1986). The Seventh Circuit in *DeShaney* held that the misconduct was sufficiently aggravated as to surpass that bar. DeShaney v. Winnebago County Dep't of Social Servs., 812 F.2d 299, 302 (7th Cir. 1987). However, the Seventh Circuit found against *DeShaney* when it undertook a constitutional causation analysis under Martinez v. California, 444 U.S. 277 (1980), discussed *infra*. It is submitted that the Supreme Court followed the proper analytical task in its constitutional approach in *DeShaney*. "Resolving the threshold question of duty in terms of causation can only confuse both issues. Greater clarity and precision would be achieved if courts would recognize the distinction between duty and causation and analyze each in its own terms." Eaton, *Causation in Constitutional Torts*, 6 Iowa L. Rev., 443, 479 (1982).

pages of deposition.[4] Because the case never went to trial, the fact characterizations and fact conclusions drawn by the Seventh Circuit and Supreme Court, discussed below, might be viewed with skepticism.

Joshua was born in Wyoming in 1979 to Melody, his mother (a petitioner in the United States Supreme Court), and Randy DeShaney, his father. One year later, a court in Wyoming granted the couple a divorce and awarded custody of Joshua to his father. Shortly thereafter, the father, Randy, moved to Wisconsin, bringing Joshua with him. There, he married (and shortly afterward divorced) a woman, Maria, whose lawyer told the Oshkosh, Wisconsin, police in 1982 that Randy had "hit the boy, causing marks and is a prime case for child abuse."[5]

A year later, Joshua paid the first of his many visits to the emergency room. At this time, in January 1983, the defendants believed Joshua to be a possible victim of child abuse and arranged for temporary legal custody of him to be taken, nominally, by the hospital, while the defendants investigated. The investigation resulted in a multidisciplinary team meeting held in accordance with Wisconsin law. This meeting involved a physician, a child psychologist, a nurse, a police officer, the defendant county's civil attorney, and the two individual defendants—the DSS caseworker and her supervisor. All present acknowledged that Joshua had probably been abused, but the defendant county's civil attorney indicated his belief that there was insufficient evidence of abuse to seek a judicial hearing as authorized by state law.[6] Joshua was then returned to his father.

The defendant DSS caseworker met with the family about a dozen times over the next year. Sometimes she saw Joshua, sometimes not. For example, just three weeks after the court closed the child protection case that DSS had brought, the defendant social worker received word from the hospital that Joshua had again been treated for suspicious injuries. "But after talking to the hospital's social worker, she concluded that there was no evidence of child abuse."[7] The defendant social worker's file thereafter contains entries documenting (1) police notification and/or hospital emergency room treatment twice

> The holding in *DeShaney* can affect various types of actions involving failure to protect generally and the mistreatment of children specifically, as well as attempts to impose liability upon the state.

during September 1983; (2) observations by the social worker during home visits of injuries to Joshua in October and November 1983; and (3) reports during this period of physical abuse by the father, Randy, against his girlfriend, Maria. On November 30, 1983, Joshua was taken to the emergency room again with serious lacerations on his forehead and shoulders.

During the next year, 1984, the social worker made several home visits, but did not insist on seeing Joshua when told that he was in bed sick or asleep. On March 7, 1984, the social worker made an unannounced home visit; her notes indicate, "I don't know why, but I did not ask to see Joshua." The next day, Joshua's father beat him so severely that he suffered critical and permanent brain damage. The neurosurgeon who treated Joshua found evidence of previous traumatic head injury. The boy's body was covered with bruises and lesions of varying age.[8] As a result of the injuries Joshua suffered, he will remain confined to an institution for the profoundly retarded for the rest of his life.

III. Proceedings in District and Appellate Courts

Suit was filed in the District Court for the Eastern District of Wisconsin under 42 U.S.C. § 1983.[9] The section 1983 constitutional predicate for the action was the due process clause, which prohibits state deprivations "of life, liberty, or property, without due process of law."[10] The trial court, in an unpublished opinion dated June 20, 1986, rejected the substantive due process and special relation contentions of the plaintiff when it granted defendants' motion for summary judgment.[11] The trial court reasoned that "[t]he Fourteenth Amendment's concept of liberty does not include the right to basic public services" in the absence of a "special relationship" between

---

4. For example, the court record contains the defendant social worker's client file on Joshua, including throughout personally articulated comments and opinions. E.g.

> I continue to have a great deal of concern over the welfare of Joshua . . . my primary concern with this family continues to remain the innumerable accidents that Joshua has suffered, which I seriously question as simply a child being accident-prone. In addition, I am concerned about the physical fighting that occurs within the home . . . . I cannot help but hypothesize that the probability of Randy [Joshua's birth father] becoming upset with Maria [the father's girlfriend]—using physical violence, and Maria not knowing what to do with her frustration and anger, possibly taking them out on Joshua.

Attachment G to plaintiffs' memorandum and affidavits opposing defendants' motion for summary judgment, DeShaney v. Winnebago County Dep't of Social Servs., No. 85-C-310 (E.D. Wis. June 20, 1986) (Clearinghouse No. 44,786).

5. *DeShaney*, 812 F.2d at 299.
6. WIS. STAT. § 48.205(1)(a).
7. *DeShaney*, 812 F.2d at 300.

---

8. *Id.* Joshua's mother, Melody, was then summoned from Wyoming. When she arrived, the caseworker told her, "I just knew the phone would ring someday and Joshua would be dead." *Id.*
9. "Every person who, under color of any statute, ordinance, regulation, custom or usage of any State . . . subjects or causes to be subjected, any . . . person within the jurisdiction thereof to the deprivation of any rights, privileges, or immunities secured by Constitution and laws, shall be liable to the party injured in an action at law." 42 U.S.C. § 1983.
10. U.S. CONST. amend. XIV, § 1.
11. *DeShaney*, No. 85-C-310.

the individual and the state.[12] The court also held that, although there was "no bright line by which the existence of a special relationship for Section 1983 purposes may be determined," there was no such relationship on the facts of the case.[13]

The Seventh Circuit unanimously affirmed in a decision written by Judge Posner. The court set forth two different "rights" of which Joshua might claim to have been deprived: (1) "a right—a form of liberty or property—to be protected by the Department of Social Services from the brutalities perpetrated by his father"; and (2) "his right to bodily integrity (again viewed as a form of liberty or property within the meaning of the due process clause)."[14]

The Seventh Circuit disposed of the first argument summarily by invoking "the rule, well-established in this Circuit, that the State's failure to protect people from private violence . . . not attributable to the conduct of its employees, is not a deprivation of constitutionally protected property or liberty."[15] Focusing on the second "right" at greater length, the Seventh Circuit restated the question as whether "the State was complicit in the beatings"[16] and then proceeded to discuss the issue in terms of causation.[17] In finding a lack of causation, the court distinguished *DeShaney* from the case "where the State places the victim in a situation of high risk, thus markedly increasing the probability of harm and by so doing becoming a cause of the harm."[18] The court also explicitly "reject[ed] the proposition embraced by a divided panel of the Third Circuit in *Estate of Bailey ex rel. Oare v. County of York*, 768 F.2d 503, 510-11 (3d Cir. 1985), that once the State is aware of the danger that a particular child may be abused, a special relationship arises between it and the child and places on the State a constitutional duty to protect the child from the abuse."[19] In rejecting the Third Circuit's analysis, the Seventh Circuit acknowledged that prison custodial situations may be appropriate for conceptualizing the constitutional special relationship analysis, but the court

was unwilling to extend this concept to this setting, which it viewed as noncustodial.[20]

IV. The Supreme Court's Opinion in *DeShaney*

When the Court granted certiorari on March 21, 1988, the case immediately caught the nation's attention.[21] This attention was not a surprise, given that child abuse—sexual and physical—had become a major national issue. Interest in the subject of child abuse first surfaced in the 1960s; in 1974, Congress passed the Child Abuse Prevention and Treatment Act,[22] which authorized funds to states to assist in efforts to respond to child abuse.[23]

By the 1980s, child abuse was recognized as a serious national problem. There were an estimated 2.25 million reports of suspected child abuse or neglect in 1987.[24] In addition, an estimated 1,132 deaths were attributable to child abuse that year.[25] By 1988, child abuse was a significant socio-legal problem of menacing proportions.

The resultant lineup in the United States Supreme Court reflected the tension between the competing societal and constitutional values. The amici supporting the *DeShaney* petitioners included the American Civil Liberties Union Children's Rights Project, Legal Services for Children, the Juvenile Law Center, Bay Area Coalition Against Child Abuse, the National Women Abuse Prevention Project, and the Massachusetts Committee for Children and Youth. Among the states and governmental organizations supporting the defendants were Wisconsin, New York, Connecticut, Maryland, Oregon, and Pennsylvania, as well as the National Association of Counties, the Council of State Governments, the U.S. Conference of Mayors, the National Conference of State Legislators, the National League of Cities, the International City Management Association, and the Nation-

---

12. *Id.*, slip op. at 7.
13. *Id.*, slip op. at 9.
14. *DeShaney*, 812 F.2d at 301. "This appeal requires us to decide whether a reckless failure by Wisconsin welfare authorities to protect a child from a parent's physical abuse deprives the child of liberty or property within the meaning of the Fourteenth Amendment." *Id.* at 299.
15. *Id.* at 301 (citations omitted).
16. *Id.*
17. *Id.* at 302-03.
18. *Id.* at 303. The Seventh Circuit, by this analysis, and later the Supreme Court, engaged in critical factfinding and fact characterization in a case that will never go before a jury. The important factor of whether government defendants, in a case of this type involving a failure to protect, in fact markedly increase the probability of harm, and, if so, the significance, if any, of such analysis and finding is discussed *infra*. Indeed, in his dissent, Justice Brennan focused directly on what he perceived to be the constitutional and decisionmaking harm when the majority prematurely mischaracterized the misconduct alleged. "This [characterization about positive and negative liberties and the facts] is more than a quibble over dicta; it is a point about perspective, having substantive ramifications." *DeShaney*, 109 S. Ct. at 1008.
19. *DeShaney*, 812 F.2d at 303.

20. Finally, the Seventh Circuit did hold that the misconduct alleged was so extreme as to escape the negligence bar of *Daniels*, 474 U.S. 327. *DeShaney*, 812 F.2d at 302. "The recklessness in this case came later, when Ann Kemmeter [defendant-social worker] inexplicably failed to act on mounting, and eventually overwhelming, evidence that Joshua was in great peril from his father." *Id.* at 303.
21. The next day, the *New York Times* wrote a lengthy, 18-paragraph story, "High Court to Decide on Liability of Local Officials in Child Abuse." The attention continued throughout that year, including a cover story in the *ABA Journal*, Reidinger, *Why Did No One Protect This Child?*, Dec. 1988.
22. 42 U.S.C. § 5101.
23. The Wisconsin child protection system, like the child protection systems of the 46 states that receive federal child welfare funds, comprehensively covers this subject. The federal act requires an adequate system for reporting possible abuse or neglect, and a prompt investigation of the report, so that "upon a finding of abuse or neglect, immediate steps shall be taken to protect the health and welfare of the abused or neglected child." 42 U.S.C. § 5103(B)(C). *See generally* Wald, *State Intervention on Behalf of Neglected Children: Standards for Removal of Children from their Homes, Monitoring the Status of Children in Foster Care, and Termination of Parental Rights*, 28 STAN. L. REV. 623 (1976).
24. NATIONAL CENTER ON CHILD ABUSE PREVENTION RESEARCH, CHILD ABUSE FATALITIES REMAIN HIGH: RESULTS OF THE 1987 ANNUAL FIFTY-STATE SURVEY 3 (Mar. 1988).
25. *Id.* at 7.

231

al School Boards Association. In addition, the United States filed an amicus brief supporting the defendants/respondents and, further, an assistant attorney general within the Office of the Solicitor General presented oral argument in support of the defendants.

In the Court, Joshua DeShaney and his mother, as petitioners, maintained two primary claims. First, they asserted that the respondents violated their constitutional rights by allowing Randy DeShaney to take from Joshua his liberty interests and personal security, which are protected against state deprivation by the due process clause—an "interest in freedom from bodily harm." Second, petitioners argued that the Wisconsin Children's Code[26] gave children such as Joshua an entitlement—a form of "liberty"—to receive social welfare services in accordance with the terms of that statute, and that a failure thereof constituted a "deprivation of that interest that is proscribed by the Constitution." Petitioners placed primary reliance upon *Taylor v. Ledbetter*.[27]

The Court decided that DSS did not have a constitutional duty to affirmatively protect the vulnerable child from his brutalizing father.[28] As the Court addressed this issue and before it concluded that "the State had no constitutional duty to protect Joshua,"[29] Chief Justice Rehnquist traced the majority's view of due process in this duty context. In his analysis, Justice Rehnquist was careful to juxtapose due process as a "limitation on the State's power to act" versus an attempt to read due process as affirmatively requiring the state to protect an individual against private violence. "If the Due Process Clause does not require the State to provide its citizens with particular protective services, it follows that the State cannot be held liable under the Clause for injuries that could have been averted had it chosen to provide them."[30]

Justice Rehnquist also examined the "special relationship" doctrine as asserted by petitioners and as analyzed by several of the courts of appeal. Those appellate courts that had based liability on such a special relationship had done so on a reliance theory—*i.e.*, the state promised its protection and the victim relied upon this promise. The majority indicated that the Supreme Court had limited this relationship for liability purposes under the due process clause to circumstances in which the state had physical custody of the victim.

> But these [special relationship] cases afford petitioners no help. Taken together, they stand only for the proposition that when the State takes a person into its custody and holds him there against his will, the Constitution imposes upon it a corresponding duty to assume some responsibility for his safety and general well-being.
>
> . . . .
>
> The affirmative duty to protect arises not from the State's knowledge of the individual's predicament or from its expressions of intent to help him, but from the limitation which it has imposed on his freedom to act on his own behalf.[31]

Because *DeShaney* lost on the threshold constitutional duty issue, the Supreme Court explicitly stated that it would not address certain other liability issues. The petitioners would have had to overcome these additional elements to complete their section 1983 presentation.

First, Chief Justice Rehnquist indicated that the Court need not, and would not, address DSS's alternative argument that the individual state actors lacked the requisite "state of mind" to make out a due process violation.[32] The Seventh Circuit had found the misconduct to be so aggravated as to escape the *Daniels* bar.[33]

---

26. Wis. Stat. Ann. §§ 48.01 *et seq.* (West 1987).
27. Taylor v. Ledbetter, 791 F.2d 881 (11th Cir. 1986), *aff'd in part, rev'd in part on reh'g,* 818 F.2d 791 (11th Cir. 1987) (en banc), *cert. denied,* 109 S. Ct. 1337 (1989). In *Taylor,* the Eleventh Circuit en banc found a substantive due process deprivation by virtue of the state's "action in assuming the responsibility of finding and keeping a child in a safe environment [which] placed an obligation on the State to insure the continuing safety of that environment." *Id.,* 818 F.2d at 795. *Taylor,* unlike *DeShaney,* involved placement by the state with foster parents. That fact was noted by Chief Justice Rehnquist in *DeShaney* as a possible distinguishing factor and issue for another day, 109 S. Ct. at 1006 n.9. The majority in *Taylor* noted "contemporary society's outrage at the exposure of defenseless children to gross mistreatment and abuse It is time that the law give to these defenseless children at least the same protection afforded adults who are imprisoned as a result of their own misdeeds." *Taylor,* 818 F.2d at 797 (citation omitted)
28. To understand further the Supreme Court's decision in *DeShaney,* one must also recognize liability issues that the court did not address. The Court did not decide the case, as did the Seventh Circuit, based on a *Martinez* causation analysis. Martinez v. California, 444 U.S. 277 (1980). Further, the Court did not decide by analyzing the defendants' contention that the individual defendants lacked the requisite "state of mind" to make out a due process violation vis-a-vis *Daniels,* 474 U.S. at 334 n.3. The court did not decide *DeShaney* by addressing the defendants' further contention that liability was lacking because the defendants were entitled to a qualified immunity. Finally, although the majority cited the substantive due process "conscience-shocking" decision in Rochin v. California, 342 U.S. 165, 172 (1952), the case was not decided on such grounds. *DeShaney,* 109 S. Ct. at 1004.
29. *Id.* at 1009.

---

30. *Id.* at 1005 (footnote omitted).
31. *Id.* at 1005-06 (citation omitted). The Court seemed to want to send its message in broad terms applicable to "protection" situations in addition to child protection. "As a general matter, then, we conclude that a State's failure to protect an individual against private violence simply does not constitute a violation of the Due Process Clause." *Id.* at 1004.
32. *DeShaney,* 109 S. Ct. at 1007 n.10. Citing *Daniels,* 474 U.S. at 334 n.3, the Court concluded that due process is designed to control abuses of governmental power (and therefore not mere negligence) but does proscribe intentional deprivations. After *Daniels* and *Davidson,* the courts have resolved the question of whether 42 U.S.C. § 1983 liability attaches for gross negligence in a number of different ways. Two circuits have held that gross negligence is sufficient for liability. Colburn v. Upper Darby Township, 838 F.2d 663, 668 n.3 (3d Cir. 1988); Metzger v. Osbek, 841 F.2d 518, 520 n.1 (3d Cir. 1988). One circuit has held that even recklessness is not sufficient for liability. Washington v. District of Columbia, 802 F.2d 1478, 1481 (D.C. Cir. 1986). Another circuit has held that recklessness or deliberate indifference is necessary for liability. Bass v. Jackson, 790 F.2d 260, 262-63 (2d Cir. 1986).
33. *DeShaney,* 812 F.2d at 302.

In addition, the Supreme Court majority rejected the individual respondents'/defendants' contention that the Court should affirm based on defendants' entitlement to qualified immunity.[34]

Finally, the court also declined to address defendants'/respondents' argument that the defendant county should be dismissed as it was not alleged or proven to be a "person" for purposes of section 1983.[35]

In his dissent, Justice Brennan, joined by Justices Marshall and Blackmun, took exception to the majority's framing of the issues and its narrow interpretation of the special relationship doctrine. With respect to the majority's holding that the Constitution creates no general right to basic governmental services, Justice Brennan decried the efforts of the majority to decide an issue that was not before the Court and that the petitions had specifically avoided. He also rebuked the majority for proclaiming that the Constitution safeguards negative, but not positive, liberties.[36] Indeed, Justice Brennan saw this characterization of the issues and of the fourteenth amendment as wrong, not simply for the likelihood to confuse, but also for the potential dispositive effect.

> This is more than a quibble over dicta; it is a point about perspective, having substantive ramifications. In a constitutional setting that distinguishes sharply between action and inaction, *one's characterization of the misconduct alleged-ly under 1983 may effectively decide the case.* Thus, by leading off with a discussion (and rejection) of the idea that the Constitution imposes on the States an affirmative duty to take basic care of their citizens, the Court foreshadows—perhaps even preordains—its conclusion that no duty existed even on the specific facts before us.[37]

In his dissent, Justice Brennan focused on (1) actions taken by the authorities in Wisconsin with respect to Joshua, (2) the in-place child protection statute and protection system in Wisconsin, including the duty of investigation, and (3) the conclusion that Joshua in effect was worse off because of the institutions and individuals that were relying on DSS to care for Joshua. Justice Brennan did not see a bright line between action and inaction or between incarceration and freedom. He argued

> **The Supreme Court decided that the Department of Social Services did not have a constitutional duty to affirmatively protect Joshua from his brutalizing father.**

that the authorities in Wisconsin "effectively confined Joshua DeShaney within the walls of Randy DeShaney's violent home until such time as DSS took action to remove him."[38] The result, then, is that Joshua may have been *"made worse off* by the existence of this program when the persons and entities charged with carrying it out failed to do their jobs."[39]

To foreclose this inevitability, Justice Brennan states that the analysis must begin from the opposite direction.

He asserts that the question of constitutional deprivation should turn on the "action" that Wisconsin took with respect to Joshua, rather than on the actions that the state failed to take.[40] He indicates that *Youngberg* and *Estelle* should be read as standing for the more generous proposition "that, if a State cuts off private sources of aid and then refuses aid itself, it cannot wash its hands of the harm that results from its inaction."[41] One predicate of liability is the state's removal of private sources of aid, effectively making the individual worse off. This analysis flows from the pervasive elements of the Wisconsin Child Protection Act, which provides for various governmental institutions relying on the social worker to protect such children. On the other hand, the majority's factual analysis asserts that Joshua was not made "more vulnerable" by virtue of a failure

---

34. *DeShaney,* 109 S. Ct. at 1007 n.10 (*citing* Anderson v. Creighton, 483 U.S. 635 (1987)). *See* Jensen v. Conrad, 747 F.2d 185 (4th Cir. 1984), *cert. denied,* 470 U.S. 1052 (1985) (the Court found liability on a special relationship theory but then ultimately denied liability by granting defendants' dispositive motion based on their constitutional qualified immunity). In *DeShaney,* several amici even asserted that the individual defendants/respondents had absolute immunity. *See generally* Imbler v. Pachtman, 424 U.S. 409 (1976) (prosecutor).

35. *See* Monell v. New York City Dep't of Social Servs., 109 S. Ct. at 1007 n.10. As to municipal liability and the liability of the individual defendant supervisor, see generally City of Canton v. Harris, 109 S. Ct. 1197 (1989); St. Louis v. Praprotnik, 108 S. Ct. 915 (1988); Oklahoma City v. Tuttle, 471 U.S. 808 (1985).

36. *Monell,* 109 S. Ct. at 1008.

37. *Id.* (emphasis added).

38. *Id.* at 1011.

39. *Id.* (emphasis added). Indeed, Archie v. City of Racine, 826 F.2d 480 (1987), *rev'g in part and aff'g in part* 627 F. Supp. 766 (E.D. Wis. 1986), with facts as compelling as those in *DeShaney,* involved a black woman who died of respiratory failure while in her apartment. On the day prior to her death, her friend had called the fire department for emergency rescue service and had spoken to a government dispatcher. The dispatcher refused to send the service, and told the woman to breathe into a "little paper bag" and to stay in her apartment. Eight hours later, a second call was received by the same dispatcher from the woman's same friend. The friend stated that he was scared, that the woman's condition was the same, and inquired whether her condition would "beat the heart out." The dispatcher responded "no" twice to the inquiry, again instructed the woman to breathe into a paper bag, and again refused rescue service. The stricken woman had relatives nearby with an automobile but, relying on the dispatcher's advice, she did not call them. She died hours later.

According to a unanimous three-judge Seventh Circuit panel, *Archie* stated a cause of action sufficient to permit the claims to go back to the district court for a trial. However, the full Seventh Circuit en banc reversed the panel opinion by an eight-to-three vote, 847 F.2d 1211 (7th Cir. 1988). The Supreme Court subsequently denied certiorari, 109 S. Ct. 1338 (1989), three weeks after *DeShaney* was decided.

40. *DeShaney,* 109 S. Ct. at 1011. Justice Brennan then cited and relied upon the decisions in Estelle v. Gamble, 429 U.S. 97 (1976), and Youngberg v. Romeo, 457 U.S. 307 (1987).

41. *DeShaney,* 109 S. Ct. at 1009.

233

to protect.[42] The majority also propounded that "[t]he most that can be said of the State functionaries in this case is that they stood by and did nothing when suspicious circumstances dictated a more active role for them."[43] As to this last statement by the majority, Justice Brennan indicated, "This description of respondents' conduct tells only part of the story."[44] Justice Blackmun, in his separate dissenting opinion, noted that the facts involve more than mere passivity as set forth by the majority.[45] DeShaney poignantly demonstrates that judicial characterization of the principle can take on a life of its own.

In his brief, the Solicitor General asserted to the Supreme Court that the men who wrote the Bill of Rights were not concerned that the government might do too little but that it might do too much.[46] But one can characterize cases such as Archie and DeShaney as examples of the government doing "too much" to the victim petitioner. When the defendant social worker in DeShaney visited and monitored Joshua's case directly and did so individually and personally on 18 occasions over a 22-month period, she was doing "too much" in the sense that she was telling all others—police, day care teachers, neighbors, other relatives, emergency room personnel, etc.—that she was the one government official in charge, monitoring and fulfilling the responsibilities for all state agencies. Had she done less, the others may have been alerted to step in. By her inaction/actions, she was in that sense markedly increasing the probability of harm or further harm to Joshua.

Looking at the facts in this light, and applying the majority's interpretation that due process secures the individual from the arbitrary exercise of the powers of government,[47] one

---

Advocates pursuing protection or rescue litigation after *DeShaney* must understand that an aggravated "abuse of power" by state defendants is not actionable if a constitutional duty is absent.

---

may interpret the result as power exercised by government in an arbitrary, pervasive, and oppressive manner. The characterization of the facts or actions may be determinative.[48]

V. Child Protective Litigation After *DeShaney*

Eleven days after issuing its opinion in *DeShaney*, the Supreme Court denied certiorari in *Taylor v. Ledbetter*, in which the child victim prevailed in the appeals court.[49] Other failure-to-protect cases reaching the Court after *DeShaney* have been denied certiorari or remanded for review in light of *DeShaney*.[50] The following section reviews litigation strategies and arguments that may be made on behalf of plaintiff victims in child protective litigation brought after *DeShaney*.

A. Substantive Due Process and Constitutional Duty

DeShaney was not actionable under the substantive components of the due process clause in spite of the fact that defendants' actions and inactions were unquestionably "conscience-shocking" under *Rochin v. California*.[51] Advocates pursuing protection or rescue litigation after *DeShaney* must understand that an aggravated "abuse of power" by state defendants is not actionable if a constitutional duty is absent. Although the due process clause provides protection to the individual not only by requiring appropriate procedural safeguards, but also by placing "substantive limitations upon State actions,"[52] and although these substantive limitations protect the individual against a government defendant's conduct that "shocks the conscience,"[53] the substantive protections to the

---

42. *Id.* at 1006.
43. *Id.* at 1007.
44. *Id.*
45. In the Seventh Circuit en banc decision in *Archie*, the majority commented upon a failure to rescue case decided ten years ago, White v. Rochford, 592 F.2d 381 (7th Cir. 1979) (police arrested the driver of a car and took him away, leaving small children to fend for themselves on an interstate). The majority in *Archie*, commenting upon *White*, indicated that the court need not decide "whose characterization of the facts in *White* was best; we are concerned here only with the principle." *Archie*, 847 F.2d at 1223 n.11.
    But the characterization, development, and analysis of the facts can be controlling. These propositions are important in cases decided on dispositive motions in the trial court and cases that never will go to a jury. Indeed, in *Archie* the majority concluded that the dispatcher did not hinder the deceased from seeking other sources of aid, 847 F.2d at 1223. However, that conclusion was very much in dispute and a large part of the case. The dissent noted the availability of other sources of private aid, their utilization in the past, and the fact that, but for the dispatcher's "unconstitutional abuse of a power," the decedent would have been rescued with an appreciable chance of surviving. *Id.* at 1227 (*citing* 826 F.2d 480, 497-498).
46. Brief of the Solicitor General at 12, *DeShaney*, 109 S. Ct. 998 (*citing* Jackson v. City of Joliet, 715 F.2d 1200, 1203 (7th Cir. 1983), *cert. denied*, 465 U.S. 1049 (1984)).
47. *DeShaney*, 109 S. Ct. at 1003 (*quoting from* Daniels v. Williams, 474 U.S. at 331).

48. *See* Hohfeld, *Some Fundamental Legal Concepts as Applied in Judicial Reasoning*, 23 YALE L.J. 16 (1913) (right and duty are the flip side of each other, such that finding that a defendant has no duty to a plaintiff is a holding that the plaintiff has no right against that defendant).
49. Taylor v. Ledbetter, 791 F.2d 881 (11th Cir. 1986), *aff'd in part, rev'd in part on reh'g*, 818 F.2d 791 (11th Cir. 1987) (en banc), *cert. denied* 109 S. Ct. 1337 (1989).
50. *See* Archie v. City of Racine, 847 F.2d 1211 (7th Cir. 1988), *cert. denied*, 103 L. Ed. 2d 809 (U.S. 1989) (No. 88-576); City of New Kensington v. Horton, 857 F.2d 1463 (3d Cir.), *vacated and remanded for further consideration in light of DeShaney*, 109 S. Ct. 1334 (1989); Smith v. Stoneking, 856 F.2d 594 (3d Cir.), *vacated and remanded for further consideration in light of DeShaney*, 109 S. Ct. 1333 (1989).
51. *Rochin*, 342 U.S. 165.
52. Paul v. Davis, 424 U.S. 693, 711 n.5 (1976).
53. *Rochin*, 342 U.S. 165, 172.

234

individual only exist if there is initially the breach of a governmental constitutional duty. Thus, governmental power that "shocks the conscience" does not violate the Constitution in the absence of an infringement of a constitutional duty.[54]

If constitutional—not state—law[55] duty is the threshold issue, then what is the constitutional duty? The Constitution assigns rights and duties: rights on individuals and duties on the government. Many of the duties are prohibitory. Other provisions impose affirmative duties, such as the requirement that the government obtain a search warrant before taking certain actions. Whether the duties are couched in negative or positive terms, a court considering a constitutional claim will invariably have to make a determination as to the existence and scope of the constitutional duty involved.

This simply points out the obvious—duties do not come into play except in situations where they are applicable. The fact remains that, at some point in the government's dealings with a citizen, affirmative duties compelled by the Constitution will arise. Further, there is reason to believe that constitutional tort cases will involve affirmative constitutional duties more frequently than other types of cases. Because the range of constitutional duties is much less comprehensive than the range of ordinary tort duties, it will often be the case that official conduct causing injury violates a common-law duty but not a constitutional one.[56] Six years before *DeShaney*, in *Baker v. McCollan*,[57] Justice Rehnquist stated, "Section 1983 imposes liability for violations of rights protected by the Constitution, not for violations of *duties* of care arising out of tort law."[58]

B. Litigation Strategies

In constitutional damage litigation, attorneys for plaintiff victims have one primary goal during pretrial maneuvering: get the case to the jury. Obviously, the defendants' goal is to prevent this, and defendants typically begin their process by filing anywhere from a few to a dozen affirmative defenses in their answer and by filing dispositive motions under Fed. R. Civ. P. 12(b)(6), 12(c), and 15 to dismiss the case or to withdraw various causes of action from the jury. In *DeShaney*, summary judgment was granted on all causes of action for all defendants, and the Supreme Court affirmed that judgment.[59]

One litigation tactic to end-run *DeShaney* is to bring the child protection damage action in state court under the appropriate state torts.[60] However, in considering such litigation in state court under state statutes, advocates should recognize that many states will give social workers absolute, not qualified, immunity from damages.[61]

Given the pervasive nature of the holding in *DeShaney*, how—if at all—is one to frame a pleading and proof to survive pretrial dispositive motions when one represents a victim of

---

54. Judicial statements such as "the tort alleged was accomplished by an abuse of governmental power sufficient to raise an ordinary tort by a governmental agent to the stature of a violation of the Constitution" do not state the law unless, as an initial precept, a constitutional duty has been breached by those governmental defendants. Suthoff v. Yazoo County Indus. Dev. Corp., 637 F.2d 337, 340 (5th Cir. 1981), *reh'g denied*, 642 F.2d 822, *cert. denied*, 454 U.S. 1157 (1982). "The 'shocks-the-conscience' approach of *Rochin v. California*, 342 U.S. 65 (1952), is not an ambulatory source of authority to impose damages on public officials for sins of omission or everyday torts . . . unless he violated a duty imposed by [constitutional] law." *Archie*, 847 F.2d 1215.

55. As to state statutory and common-law duties under tort concepts respecting duties to protect and duties to rescue, see generally RESTATEMENT (SECOND) OF TORTS §§ 314(A)(4), 324; PROSSER & KEETON, THE LAW OF TORTS, 378-82 (5th ed. 1984). The right-protecting provisions of the Constitution, similar to ordinary tort duties, deal with "the problem of the relation between" individuals and the government "which imposes on one a legal obligation for the benefit of the other . . . to conform to a particular standard of conduct." *Id.* at 356.

56. *See generally* Note, *A Theory of Negligence for Constitutional Torts*, 92 YALE L.J. 683 (1983); Wells & Eaton, *Affirmative Duties and Constitutional Torts*, 16 U. MICH. J.L. REF. 1 (1982).

57. Baker v. McCollan, 443 U.S. 137 (1983).

58. *Id.* at 146 (emphasis added). Much of the analysis in this section is based on the forthcoming law review article by Associate Professor of Law William Burnham, Wayne State University. Burnham, *Separating Constitutional and Common-Law Torts: A Critique and a Proposed Constitutional Theory of Duty*, 73 MINN. L. REV. (forthcoming 1989).

59. Justice Brennan, dissenting, indicated that he would allow Joshua and his mother "the opportunity to show that respondent's failure to help him arose, not out of the sound exercise of professional judgment that we recognized in *Youngberg* as sufficient to preclude liability, see 457 U.S. at 322-323, but from the kind of arbitrariness that we have in the past condemned." *DeShaney*, 109 S. Ct. at 1011 (citations omitted).

60. For recent cases in which state courts have found child protection system personnel liable for failing to protect a child from abuse at a parent's hands, see, *e.g.*, Turner v. District of Columbia, 532 A.2d 662 (D.C. 1987) (child protection statute creates a special relationship between the agency and abused children); Florida Dep't of Health & Rehabilitative Servs. v. Yamuni, 529 So. 2d 258 (Fla. 1988) (child protection statute created a duty on agency to provide protective services to abused children); Coleman v. Cooper, 366 S.E.2d 2 (N.C. Ct. App. 1988).

In *DeShaney*, it was explicitly recognized by the judiciary that the petitioners avoided the Wisconsin courts because of the damage ceiling in the amount of $50,000 under WIS. STAT. § 893.80(3). Judge Posner, who authored the opinion in the Seventh Circuit and who specifically concurred in *Archie* had this concurring comment in the latter case: "And although [the defendant dispatcher's] gross negligence, which may well have cost [plaintiff] her life, cries out for a remedy in damages, the plaintiffs' tort remedy under Wisconsin law is inadequate because of the $50,000 ceiling on damages that Wisconsin imposes in suits against public agencies and employees. This ceiling is too low, under modern concepts of the value of life, to provide adequate compensation and deterrence in a wrongful death case on behalf of a 43-year-old woman." *Archie*, 847 F.2d at 1224-25. Judge Posner continued, "I think that the State of Wisconsin may well be open to criticism for having placed what appears to be an arbitrary limitation on the damages that may be awarded for torts committed by its State and local agencies and employees." *Id.* at 1226-27. But then Judge Posner continues his discourse by assuming or hypothesizing that this low ceiling in effect increases the extent of rescue services because it discourages lawsuits and thus reduces the cost of such public services. *Id.* at 1227. *See* Posner, *Wealth Maximization Revisited*, 2 NOTRE DAME J.L. ETHICS & PUB. POL'Y 85 (1985) ("Wealth maximization as ethically attractive norm for social and political choices").

61. Mushlin, *Unsafe Havens: The Case for Constitutional Protection of Foster Children from Abuse and Neglect*, 23 HARV. C.R. - C.L. L. REV. 199, 245-49 (1988).

government misconduct in the context of an egregious "abuse of power"[62] in failing to protect or rescue? Every attempt should be made to slot the case, facts, and liability arguments into two Seventh Circuit cases that have a long progeny: *Byrd v. Brishke*[63] and *White v. Rochford.*[64] In *Byrd*, the Court held that police officers who stood by and watched other police officers beat a person in a public place could be held liable under section 1983 for their failure to act. That case has been adopted and followed by every circuit in the country.[65] In *White*, the Court held that police officers could be sued under section 1983 for recklessly exposing children to danger by leaving them in a car on the freeway after lawfully arresting their guardian for drag racing. The Court stated that "the unjustified and arbitrary refusal of police officers to lend aid to children endangered by the performance of official duty" did amount to a violation of the due process clause.[66] Note that in *White* liability attached under a finding that there had been a deprivation of liberty, even though the plaintiff children were not in the state's actual custody.[67]

Advocates prosecuting child protection cases should argue that the government, by its conduct, acts, and actions,[68] deprived the plaintiff victim of a constitutional right. One should not only emphasizes the litany of actions taken by the government, but also must allege that those actions markedly increased the probability of harm coming to the plaintiff. This reasoning confronts Judge Easterbrook's negative constitutionalism[69] by asserting that the defendants did too much. Emphasize factually that, absent the vulnerability-increasing actions taken by the defendants, the plaintiff could have avoided injury. That is, there are so many facts suggesting this result that a jury, under proper instructions, must decide this issue.

Advocates should note that traditional "custody" constitutional damage litigation involving prisoners and mental patients injured by nonstate actors continues to be good law, because the state has custody of such individuals.[70] It is still well established that the mentally ill and retarded, residents of state juvenile training schools, suspects in police custody, and pretrial detainees have a constitutional right to protection.[71]

C. Foster Care and Governmental Liability

Although *DeShaney* seems to preclude any state liability for maltreatment of children at the hands of their natural parents, the case may provide some oblique support for actions against the state for the placement of children in abusive foster homes. The majority opinion acknowledged the imposition by other federal appellate courts of liability upon the state for failing to protect children in foster homes. The Court then stated that this fact situation was not before it, and thus it would not express a view on liability in the foster care setting.[72]

The strongest support for this characterization of foster homes as state custodial care is *Doe v. New York City Department of Social Services.*[73] In that case, a foster child had been beaten and sexually abused by her foster father. She alleged that

---

62. Aside from the threshold dispositive issue of constitutional due process duty, one must also allege and prove that the misconduct was analogous to the type of misconduct condemned as arbitrary in the past. *See, e.g.*, Daniels v. Williams, 474 U.S. 327, 331 (1986). *See also* two "soft" readings of *Daniels* holding that gross negligence is actionable: Colburn v. Upper Darby Township, 838 F.2d 663, 668 & n.3 (3d Cir. 1988); Metzger v. Osbek, 841 F.2d 518, 520 n.1 (3d Cir. 1988). *But see* Washington v. District of Columbia, 802 F.2d 1478, 1481 (D.C. Cir. 1986). In this context, counsel should urge the historical purpose of the remedial statute—42 U.S.C. § 1983—as cogently articulated in Monroe v. Pape, 365 U.S. 167 (1961). "While one main scourge of the evil—perhaps the leading one—was the Ku Klux Klan, the remedy created was not a remedy against it or its members but against those who, representing a State in some capacity, were *unable* or *unwilling* to enforce a state law." *Id.* at 175, 176 (emphasis in original) (footnote omitted).

   See generally Keynes, The Fourteenth Amendment, 42 U.S.C. § 1983 and State Inaction: Did the Authors of the Enforcement Act of 1871 Intend Civil Liability for the States' Failure to Protect Individual Rights? (unpublished 1988 research by Prof. Edward Keynes, Penn State Univ., and appended to *DeShaney* petitioners' Supreme Court reply brief).

63. Byrd v. Brishke, 466 F.2d 6 (7th Cir. 1972).

64. White v. Rochford, 592 F.2d 381 (7th Cir. 1979).

65. *See, e.g.*, Fundiller v. City of Cooper City, 777 F.2d 1436, 1441-42 (11th Cir. 1985). This is a variation of the "snake pit" metaphor. "If the State puts a man in a position of danger from private persons and then fails to protect him, it will not be heard to say that its role was merely passive; it is as much an active tortfeasor as if it had thrown him into a snake pit." Bowers v. DeVito, 686 F.2d 616, 618 (7th Cir. 1982).

66. *White*, 592 F.2d at 383.

67. In *Archie*, the panel commented on *White*, noting that the police "markedly increased a particular person's risk of danger from others," 826 F.2d at 497. In *DeShaney*, the majority indicated that, while the defendants/respondents may have been aware of Joshua's danger, they nevertheless "played no part in [its] creation, nor did [they] do anything to render him any more vulnerable." *DeShaney*, 109 S. Ct. at 1006. Thus, supportable allegations that government misconduct rendered the victim more vulnerable to danger are necessary. Or, stated differently, one must allege that the government has "monopolize[d] the avenues of relief." *Archie*, 847 F.2d at 1222. This analysis was important in Justice Brennan's dissent in *DeShaney*, see, *e.g.*, 109 S. Ct. at 1010-11.

68. Justice Brennan, dissenting in *DeShaney*, stated that he "would focus first on the action that Wisconsin has taken with respect to Joshua and children like him, rather than on the actions that the State failed to take." *Id.* at 1008.

69. "The men who wrote the Bill of Rights were not concerned that Government might do too little for the people but that it might *do too much to them.*" Jackson v. City of Joliet, 715 F.2d at 1203 (emphasis added).

70. *Id.* at 1004-05 (Chief Justice Rehnquist commenting on four Supreme Court precedents in this area).

71. *E.g.*, City of Revere v. Massachusetts Gen. Hosp., 463 U.S. 239, 245 (1983).

72. *DeShaney*, 109 S. Ct. at 1009 n.9. Foster care cases may subject the state to due process liability through analogy to the state custodial requirement invoked in *DeShaney*. "In the substantive due process analysis, it is the State's affirmative act of restraining the individual's freedom to act on his own behalf—through incarceration, institutionalization, or other similar restraint of personal liberty—which is the 'deprivation of liberty' triggering the protections of the Due Process Clause." *Id.* at 1007. Foster care would seem to provide such a custodial relationship, as the state, operating under state laws, transfers a child from a parent (or other custodian) to a state-licensed and state-approved foster home.

73. Doe v. New York City Dep't of Social Servs., 649 F.2d 134 (2d Cir. 1981), *cert. denied*, 464 U.S. 864 (1983).

236

the foster care agency was deliberately indifferent to her welfare. The Second Circuit viewed the case as involving a failure
to perform an affirmative responsibility. The court referred to
the custodial aspects of foster care, which it suggested might
render appropriate constitutional protection and duty concepts
analogous to prison cases.[74] The court then focused on the state
law requirement explicitly directing the agency to report incidents of abuse.

In the face of these statutory requirements, the court
indicated that, under section 1983, a deliberate lack of concern
for the plaintiff's welfare could be inferred from "a pattern of
omissions revealing deliberate inattention to specific duties
imposed for the purpose of safeguarding plaintiffs from abuse."[75]

Taylor v. Ledbetter[76] presents the most recent indication
that foster care will be decided in the context of custodial care
analysis. In *Taylor*, plaintiffs alleged that a two-year-old girl
had been beaten by her foster mother as well as given an
overdose of unnecessary medication, which caused her to become permanently comatose. The action, brought under section
1983, claimed that the defendants had violated the child's
constitutional right to safety by failing to investigate adequately
the foster home before placing the child, by failing to supervise
the foster home, and by failing to provide complete medical
information to the child's physician.[77]

On rehearing, the Eleventh Circuit found that the situation of a child in foster care is sufficiently analogous to that of
involuntarily confined prisoners and mental patients that similar
rules of law should apply.[78] Thus, the liberty interest involved
is the kind of substantive due process right protected in *Youngberg
v. Romeo*[79] and *Estelle v. Gamble*.[80] The *Taylor* court found that
"the state's action in assuming responsibility of finding and
keeping the child in a safe environment placed an obligation on
the state to insure the continuing safety of that environment."[81]
The court remanded to allow the state officials to demonstrate
the public policy reasons that might balance the liberty interests
of the individual.

The sympathetic equities of the vulnerable child present
in *DeShaney* continue their force in the foster care cases. The
foster care cases are stronger because they involve the dispositive
factor absent in *DeShaney*—namely, that it is the state that
affirmatively reaches out and changes the one custodial setting
of the child and, by state power, transfers the child to a
state-licensed and state-approved foster home. A state's power
vis-a-vis vulnerable children, whether characterized as police
power or *parens patriae*, is based primarily on the presumption
that younger children lack the mental capacity and maturity to

> **Although *DeShaney* seems to preclude any state liability for maltreatment of children at the hands of their natural parents, the case may provide some oblique support for actions against the state for the placement of children in abusive foster homes.**

protect themselves.[82] This puts foster care cases squarely in line
with custodial cases in which the Supreme Court and lower
courts have found a constitutional duty to protect those persons
who, because of their custody, have no alternative but to rely on
the state for their safety and well-being.

D. *Roth* Due Process Entitlement

In their brief to the Supreme Court, petitioners had
asserted that the Wisconsin child protection statute created an
entitlement under *Board of Regents v. Roth*[83] recognizing a clear
and specific statutory intent to protect children. In response, the
respondents asserted that child protection legislation did not use
the requisite language to create a fourteenth amendment entitlement
as, for example, state law provides for a state statutory immunity from liability. Respondents argued that an expectation or
entitlement is absent when the state statute does not use language "of an unmistakably mandatory character."[84] The majority opinion in *DeShaney* expressly acknowledged that the *Roth*
entitlement issue, raised for the first time before the Supreme
Court, would not be decided, as it was not raised or decided by
either court below.

Advocates in child protection litigation brought after
DeShaney should cogently touch all of the *Roth* liability bases:
(1) a protection or rescue state statute must be mandatory
(nondiscretionary), thus creating a fourteenth amendment
entitlement property right; (2) this property right must be
afforded procedural protection under the due process clause;
and (3) the procedural protection, if any, that the state gives
must be inadequate, thus creating liability under section 1983.

Advocates should argue that a due process interest can
arise entirely as a result of a legitimate expectation that the

---

74. However, the court also went on to distinguish foster care institutions from institutions such as prisons with respect to lines of
authority. *Id.*, 649 F.2d at 142.
75. *Id.* at 145.
76. Taylor v. Ledbetter, 791 F.2d 881 (11th Cir. 1986), *aff'd in part,
rev'd in part & remanded*, 818 F.2d 791 (11th Cir. 1987).
77. *Id.* 791 F.2d at 881, 882.
78. *Id.* 818 F.2d at 796.
79. Youngberg v. Romeo, 457 U.S. 307 (1982).
80. Estelle v. Gamble, 429 U.S. 97 (1976).
81. *Taylor*, 818 F.2d at 795.

82. *See* Wald, *Children's Rights: A Framework for Analysis*, 12 U.
CAL. D.L. REV. 255-56, 262-63, 266-70, 273-74 (1979). "The
State, of course, has a duty of the highest order to protect the
interests of minor children, particularly those of tender years."
Palmore v. Sidoti, 466 U.S. 429, 433 (1984).
83. Board of Regents v. Roth, 408 U.S. 564 (1972). *See* WIS. STAT. §
48.981(4).
84. *See generally* Hewitt v. Helms, 459 U.S. 460 (1983). Petitioners,
in turn, in their reply brief before the Court, relied again upon
Taylor v. Ledbetter, 818 F.2d 791 (11th Cir. 1987). *Taylor* has now
been remanded by the Supreme Court, and advocates should follow
its progress as it goes back to the federal court in Atlanta for a trial
on liability and damages.

government creates by assuring individuals that substantive protection will arise in a given situation. In determining whether a *Roth* interest exists, courts will look for indication that the protection is conferred by a clearly prescribed statute or rule. This analysis will enable a court to discern entitlement interests without any reference to the presence or absence of core interests, viz avoidance of the constitutional duty analysis.[85]

E. Fourteenth Amendment Equal Treatment Under Law

Attorneys scrutinizing a failure to rescue/failure to protect fact situation should always investigate the possibility of a fourteenth amendment equal protection claim.[86] Indeed, the Chief Justice in *DeShaney* noted that the government may not "selectively deny its protective services to certain disfavored minorities without violating the Equal Protection Clause."[87] In a challenge to police response to domestic violence calls, the Ninth Circuit recently reversed the trial court in *Balistreri v. Pacifica Police Department*[88] and acknowledged that evidence produced by the female plaintiff was sufficient to suggest "an animus against abused women." In that case, the plaintiff had, on more than one occasion, advised the police that her former spouse was threatening her, and the police failed to protect

---

85. *See also* Board of Pardons v. Allen, 107 S. Ct. 2415, 2417-22 (1987). By way of caution, note also that the Supreme Court has suggested two circumstances that may preclude the recognition of the *Roth* entitlement: (1) when the deprivation of the benefit will have minor consequences; and (2) when the decision is "traditionally entrusted to the expertise" of the government official. Hewitt v. Helms, 459 U.S. 460, 470 (1983). However, these factors may be somewhat fluid; *see generally* Thompson v. Kentucky Dep't of Corrections, 833 F.2d 614, 618 (6th Cir. 1987), *cert. granted* 108 S. Ct. 2869 (1988). *See also* Comment, *Entitlement Enjoyment and Due Process of Law*, 1974 DUKE L.J. 89.
86. Typically, as discussed *infra*, the claim will be race- or sex-based, although there may also be a situation involving extreme arbitrariness. It is inconsistent with notions of fundamental fairness and due process for a state official, consciously indifferent, to single out one individual for denial of state-provided services. In Logan v. Zimmerman Brush Co., 455 U.S. 422 (1982), six Justices agreed that the denial of a state-created benefit of an administrative remedy for physical disability discrimination to one claimant solely because the state agency failed to process the claim on time was arbitrary and failed a rational basis standard of review under the equal protection clause. Id. at 441-442 (Blackmun, J.), 444 (Powell, J., concurring in judgment).
87. *DeShaney*, 109 S. Ct. at 1004 n.3 (citation omitted).
88. Balistreri v. Pacifica Police Dep't, 855 F.2d 1421 (9th Cir. 1988).

> With the holding in *DeShaney*, the Supreme Court has severely limited the possibility of successful causes of action against negligent governmental social service providers and governments in the failure to protect/failure to rescue area.

her.[89] She alleged a deliberate failure by the police to protect women threatened by domestic violence.

Equal protection claims continue to be viable. They will always be the first line of attack where a factual basis exists.

VI. Conclusion

With the holding in *DeShaney*, the Supreme Court has severely limited the possibility of successful causes of action against negligent governmental social service providers and governments in the failure to protect/failure to rescue area. By focusing on the lack of any constitutional duty, the Court has foreclosed any examination of government officials' often egregious neglect of their responsibilities to protect the welfare of children who cannot protect themselves. Cases like *DeShaney* and the death of Lisa Steinberg in New York City bring to light the massive problem of child abuse and the bureaucratic unwillingness on the part of the state and local agencies to perform their duties.

The ruling in *DeShaney* means that it will be difficult to apply direct incentives to social service agencies to correct or improve their behavior. It will also be hard to punish these agencies for negligence that truly shocks the conscience. In this respect, the *DeShaney* holding flies in the face of common sense and common sensibility according to which the public would demand some accountability from governmental entities whose actions leave identifiable children in the path of harm. For now, the Supreme Court has immunized child protective services from responsibility for their blundered attempts at protecting children.

Curry First is the Litigation Director at Legal Aid Society of Milwaukee, Inc., 1204 W. Wisconsin Ave., Milwaukee, WI 53233, (414) 765-0600. He was guardian ad litem for Joshua in the *DeShaney* case.

---

89. *Cf.* Hynson v. City of Chester Legal Dep't, 864 F.2d 1026 (3d Cir. 1988).

238

Moral Ambition, Formalism, and the "Free World" of *DeShaney*

Aviam Soifer*

> [T]he arbitrary quality of thoughtlessness can be as disastrous and unfair to private rights and the public interest as the perversity of a willful scheme.[1]

Introduction: For Arthur S. Miller

Arthur S. Miller was a scholarly friend of mine. We never met, however, and I do not remember that we ever talked by phone. Arthur befriended me and taught me through his written words. He wrote an amazing array of books, articles, op-ed pieces, and the like, but he still found time to write letters—charming, vigorous, challenging letters. He corresponded with me faithfully over a decade or so. Regretfully, my side of the correspondence was much less regular. Nevertheless, Arthur sent a stream of reprints and drafts; I occasionally sent along something I'd finally finished. If there is

---

* Professor of Law, Boston University. B.A. 1969, M.U.S. 1972, J.D. 1972, Yale.

1. Hobson v. Hansen, 269 F. Supp. 401, 497 (D.D.C. 1967) (Skelly Wright, J.), *aff'd sub nom.* Smuck v. Hobson, 408 F.2d 175 (D.C. Cir. 1969), *further relief ordered*, 320 F. Supp. 409 (1970), *order denying motion to hold defendants in contempt*, No. 82-66 (D.D.C. Feb. 17, 1973).

For a critical account of Judge Skelly Wright's continued active involvement in this long litigation that attempted to desegregate and equalize the public schools in the District of Columbia, see D. HOROWITZ, THE COURTS AND SOCIAL POLICY 106-70 (1977). For a better account of the benefits as well as the costs of institutional litigation, or at least an account much closer to the views about the appropriate judicial role expressed in this Essay, see L. YACKLE, REFORM AND REGRET: THE STORY OF FEDERAL JUDICIAL INVOLVEMENT IN THE ALABAMA PRISON SYSTEM (1989) (recounting the study of federal Judge Frank M. Johnson and the Alabama prison litigation).

August 1989   Vol. 57   No. 6

such a thing as a scholar's scholar, Arthur Miller served as a worthy example of that threatened genus.

Arthur Miller used the written word provocatively. He provoked new thoughts and contributed fresh ideas across a number of areas, including some he staked out virtually by himself. His passionate concern for improving humanity's chances for the future, despite the threat of nuclear and population explosions and what he called the Positive State, led Arthur to probe prevailing categories of legal thought. He helped his readers see through legalism to what was going on behind the façade. Some of his best work used skeptical realism to challenge core concepts, often heavily laden with barnacles, such as separation of powers, the private/public distinction, and national security. Arthur Miller's work was driven in large measure by passionate concern for posterity and by a kind of populist faith that greater understanding might produce reform, not merely resignation and cynicism.

In this Essay, I discuss a recent United States Supreme Court decision, *DeShaney v. Winnebago County Department of Social Services*.[2] This case underscores an important point Arthur developed decades ago about the crucial role of major premises in judicial decisions.[3] *DeShaney* also illustrates why he was concerned about misleadingly static categories that float above reality and prompt lawyers to ignore the pervasive role of government and of flux in the modern welfare state.[4] Finally, it contrasts sharply with Arthur's concern that constitutional law should reflect "moral precepts of action as well as legal limitations," in keeping with his repeated message that "[f]reedom is a *social* right as well as something of value for an individual."[5]

Chief Justice Rehnquist's opinion for the majority in *DeShaney* is an abomination. It is illogical and extremely mechanistic; it also abuses history, fails to consider practical impact, and demonstrates moral insensitivity. Not only that, it is wrong The decision holds that the state has no constitutional duty to protect a child not in custody. In Part I, I explore some of *DeShaney*'s shortcomings as judicial craftsmanship. In Part II, I briefly assess its historical stance and its dangerous practical implications. In the Conclusion, I comment on the profoundly troubling lack of "moral ambition"[6] in

---

2. 109 S. Ct. 998 (1989).

3. Miller, *On the Choice of Major Premises in Supreme Court Opinions*, 14 J. Pub. L. 251 (1965) [hereinafter Miller, Major Premises].

4. *See, e.g.*, A.S. Miller, The Supreme Court and American Capitalism (1968) [hereinafter A.S. Miller, American Capitalism]; Miller, *An Affirmative Thrust to Due Process of Law?*, 30 Geo. Wash. L. Rev. 399 (1962) [hereinafter Miller, *Affirmative Thrust*].

5. Miller, *Affirmative Thrust, supra* note 4, at 422, 417. One of Arthur's favorite quotations, from a decision he considered a watershed in American constitutional law, says in part: "[T]he liberty safeguarded [by due process] is liberty in a social organization which requires the protection of law against the evils which menace the health, safety, morals and welfare of the people." West Coast Hotel Co. v. Parrish, 300 U.S. 379, 391 (1937) (Hughes, C.J.).

6. *DeShaney*, 109 S. Ct. at 1012 (Blackmun, J., dissenting) (quoting A. Stone, Law, Psychiatry, and Morality 262 (1984)).

DeShaney. It is primarily this failure that makes DeShaney's compartmentalized, neo-Social Darwinian approach so chilling. Tragically, DeShaney exemplifies the moral obtuseness in legal thinking that was Arthur Miller's primary target throughout his distinguished scholarly career.

The DeShaney majority delights in machismo conceptualism. The opinion of the Court is a terrible example of the familiar judicial quest for safe-houses designed by drawing rigid lines. Judges strive for some mythical locus of certainty where they, at least, can escape the more complicated relationships of common humanity. The powerful dissenting opinions in DeShaney highlight a competing perception of reality that is full of change and connection. The dissenters' worldview involves a complex continuum rather than a world that can be run with a simple on/off switch.[7] Unfortunately, the DeShaney majority's binary *weltanschauung* has an intuitive appeal, though its pedigree is hardly sympathetic. This approach echoes opinions by justices such as Peckham, Brewer, and McReynolds. Its "fixation on the general principle that the Constitution does not establish positive rights"[8] is also reminiscent of the tough and efficient principles proclaimed by many state court judges, a century or so ago, while they engaged in cold-blooded expansion of common law doctrines such as assumption of risk, the fellow-servant rule, and a property right to operate a business free of labor strife.[9]

---

7. This realistic approach adopted by the dissenters has been key to our most important constitutional law decisions since 1937. See, e.g., the decisions following West Coast Hotel Co. v. Parrish, 300 U.S. 379 (1937), that constituted the 1937 "revolution," discussed in A.S. MILLER, AMERICAN CAPITALISM, *supra* note 4, at 76-114; the line of cases begun in the famous footnote 4 in United States v. Carolene Products Co., 304 U.S. 144 (1938), and expanded in Brown v. Board of Education, 347 U.S. 483 (1954), and its progeny, discussed and built upon in J. ELY, DEMOCRACY AND DISTRUST: A THEORY OF JUDICIAL REVIEW (1980); and the factually sensitive First Amendment decisions such as New York Times Co. v. Sullivan, 376 U.S. 254 (1964), flowing out of the civil rights movement, discussed in H. KALVEN JR., THE NEGRO AND THE FIRST AMENDMENT (1965).

8. *DeShaney*, 109 S. Ct. at 1008 (Brennan, J., joined by Marshall and Blackmun, JJ., dissenting).

9. These judges also were particularly concerned to have judges patrolling to keep the boundaries of the free world crisply defined and thereby to make the free world free for individual autonomy. It was an age with a "dominant . . . gospel of greed," as Charles Sanders Peirce put it, when men " 'seemed to relish a ruthless theory.' " R. WILSON, IN QUEST OF COMMUNITY: SOCIAL PHILOSOPHY IN THE UNITED STATES, 1860-1920, at 56 (1968) (quoting Peirce). Yet even these American followers of Herbert Spencer made exceptions for children and others they perceived as in need of protection despite their vigorous celebration of struggle in the world of "Nature, red in tooth and claw." *See* DARWINISM AND THE AMERICAN INTELLECTUAL 98-99 (R. Wilson ed. 1967) ("If there was a genuine American Spencerian it was [John] Fiske . . . who had one important original idea in his long and prolific scholarly life: that the family introduced a moral buffer between man and the law of struggle."); *see also* E. CORWIN, THE TWILIGHT OF THE SUPREME COURT: A HISTORY OF OUR CONSTITUTIONAL THEORY (1934); B. TWISS, LAWYERS AND THE CONSTITUTION: HOW LAISSEZ-FAIRE CAME TO THE SUPREME COURT (1942); Avery, *Images of Violence in Labor Jurisprudence: The Regulation of Picketing and Boycotts, 1894-*

In some respects, however, *DeShaney* may go even further. It is an opinion that cries out for the curmudgeonly critique of blatant constitutional law fallacies exemplified by Thomas Reed Powell or Adolf A. Berle Jr.'s destruction of category mistakes. Arthur Miller's similar puncturing of pompous posturing would easily show us that the *DeShaney* majority has turned its back on realism in favor of the false symmetry of categorical constructs invoked to decide the case. (There is some comfort in knowing that Arthur would have warned against overestimating the import and impact of any constitutional law decision). It is a trifle ironic, therefore, but also sadly fitting, to write about *DeShaney*, a tragic throwback to last century's high formalism, in memory of Arthur S. Miller and the "capacity for outrage"[10] he celebrated in others and embodied himself.

I. "Poor Joshua!"[11] *Creating the Present Through Judicial Craftsmanship*

Chief Justice Rehnquist begins his opinion with a bare-bones description: "Petitioner is a boy who was beaten and permanently injured by his father, with whom he lived."[12] Standing alone, this opening sentence encapsulates the majority opinion. (This first sentence also hides how much more complicated and appalling the facts of this case turn out to be, as Justice Brennan's dissent makes painfully clear). Because this "boy" lived with his father, the majority holds, the state could not be implicated in the horrific series of beatings Joshua endured as a toddler, culminating in "brain damage so severe that he is expected to spend the rest of his life confined to an institution for the profoundly retarded."[13] Though state officials knew of and easily could have protected Joshua from his terrible situation, the state owed the boy no constitutional duty of protection. "While the State may have been aware of the dangers that Joshua faced *in the free world,*" Rehnquist writes, "it played no part in their creation, nor did it do anything to render him any more vulnerable to them."[14] Therefore, Joshua, who was two years old when the police were first told of his beatings and four years old at the time of the severe final beating, could not validly claim that he had

---

1921, 37 Buffalo L. Rev. 1 (1988/89); Hurvitz, *American Labor Law and the Doctrine of Entrepreneurial Property Rights: Boycotts, Courts, and the Juridical Reorientation of 1886-1895,* 8 Indus. Rel. L.J. 307 (1986).

10. *See, e.g.,* A.S. Miller, A "Capacity for Outrage": The Judicial Odyssey of J. Skelly Wright (1984) [hereinafter A.S. Miller, Judicial Odyssey]. The phrase itself is Abraham Sofaer's worthy description of J. Skelly Wright. *Id.* at 5.

11. *DeShaney,* 109 S. Ct. at 1012 (Blackmun, J., dissenting).

12. *Id.* at 1001.

13. *Id.* at 1002. Rehnquist does note that "[t]he facts of this case are undeniably tragic," *id.* at 1001, and that the state's failure to protect Joshua was "calamitous in hindsight," though it "simply does not constitute a violation of the Due Process Clause." *Id.* at 1007. The Court also notes that Joshua's father was later convicted of child abuse. *Id.* at 1002.

14. *Id.* at 1006 (emphasis added). An indication of how easy it would have been for the majority to reach the opposite result, and to do so on narrow grounds, is contained in a footnote, in which Rehnquist states that a claim of " 'entitlement' " to protection premised on Wisconsin statutes was not timely raised. *Id.* at 1003 n.2.

been deprived of liberty in violation of the Due Process Clause of the Fourteenth Amendment.

In order to get to this hard-nosed response to a tragic situation, Rehnquist must severely diminish the actual extent of involvement by the Winnebago County Department of Social Services (DSS). It is left to Brennan's dissent to detail the repeated visits by DSS staff—and their persistent, inexplicable failure to act. Even in holding against Joshua DeShaney's claim in the lower court, Judge Richard Posner framed the constitutional question to be whether "a reckless failure by Wisconsin welfare authorities" to protect Joshua might violate the Due Process Clause.[15] With the exception of Rehnquist's stark attempt to minimize the facts, his majority opinion closely tracks Posner's approach below in this case, and in a series of other decisions in which Posner has led the Seventh Circuit to deny that any government has any constitutional duty to protect its citizens in any way.[16]

Although Posner purports to use history to support this radical claim, the Supreme Court majority primarily relies upon a divide-and-conquer tactic that is true neither to text nor to logic. Rehnquist does allude to history with a blatantly ahistorical methodology that I will criticize in the next section, but the decision is mainly ipse dixit derived from ideology rather than from the occurrences or ideas of the past.

Rehnquist begins with arid generalities about the scope of due process. He asserts that "nothing in the language of the Due Process Clause itself requires the State to protect the life, liberty, and property of its citizens against invasion by private actors."[17] Moreover, he says, the language of the Due Process Clause cannot be

---

15. DeShaney v. Winnebago County Dep't of Social Servs., 812 F.2d 298, 299 (7th Cir. 1987).

16. In Bowers v. DeVito, 686 F.2d 616, 618 (7th Cir. 1982), for example, Posner wrote: "The Constitution is a charter of negative liberties; it tells the state to let people alone; it does not require the federal government or the state to provide services, even so elementary a service as maintaining law and order." *See also* Jackson v. City of Joliet, 715 F.2d 1200, 1203 (7th Cir. 1983) (stating that "the Constitution is a charter of negative rather than positive liberties. . . . The men who wrote the Bill of Rights were not concerned that government might do too little for the people but that it might do too much to them," so that even gross negligence by a police officer at the scene of a fatal automobile accident could not be a deprivation of due process). Apparently, under *DeShaney*'s reasoning, even a police officer who arrested an adult driver and then left young children unattended in a car would not be liable for their subsequent injuries. *See* White v. Rochford, 592 F.2d 381 (7th Cir. 1979) (holding for the Pre-Posner Seventh Circuit that such police conduct could violate the Due Process Clause).

17. *DeShaney*, 109 S. Ct. at 1003. This assertion sounds somewhat persuasive until you think about it. That is, nothing in the Due Process Clause specifies what its grand outlines mean in any context, even when it comes to protecting property rights. Yet Rehnquist and the other justices in the majority did not require specificity when they recognized the right of a beach owner to rebuild without being required to grant an easement to the public to reach the beach, thereby overruling the views of state officials

extended "to impose an affirmative obligation on the State."[18] Finally, with the cold and false logic Rehnquist seems to favor these days—reasoning that revolves around the theme that greater power necessarily includes lesser power—he writes: "If the Due Process Clause does not require the State to provide its citizens with particular protective services, it follows that the State cannot be held liable under the Clause for injuries that could have been averted had it chosen to provide them."[19]

Here abstraction even triumphs over its own premises. Rehnquist glides from a state's choice to provide services, in the sense of establishing and funding protective services for its citizens, to the choice, by the very state employees who are thereby "provided," to withhold such services from someone like Joshua. Moreover, he ignores the powerful preemptive quality of the state's initial protective decision, thereby ousting other institutions that might provide such services. Finally, he is blind to the fact that even in the majority's mere nightwatchman theory of government, it surely is significant when the nightwatchman falls asleep on the job.

It is difficult, to be sure, to argue in the abstract as to precisely what a governmental duty to protect encompasses and how it should be limited. That is why history and some awareness of flux in the meaning of constitutional words, structures, and interpretations, are crucial. It is also why the majority's failure to come to grips with the facts of this case, and with the repeated, tragic interventions by the state, is particularly appalling.

But Rehnquist seeks the high road. He purports to be bound by

---

and the California Court of Appeals. *See* Nollan v. California Coastal Comm'n, 483 U.S. 825 (1987) (Justice Stevens joined in *DeShaney* but dissented in *Nollan*, along with the three *DeShaney* dissenters, Justices Brennan, Blackmun, and Marshall; Justice Kennedy was not yet on the Court). This type of beachfront property regulation surely was not addressed with any more specificity in the Fourteenth Amendment than was Joshua DeShaney's liberty claim, nor does Justice Scalia's holding in *Nollan* show reverence for leaving plaintiffs exclusively to state remedies.

The requirement of a textual basis for a Due Process Clause interpretation would also undo the Court's settled "reverse incorporation" approach to the denial of equal protection by the federal government, *see* Bolling v. Sharpe, 347 U.S. 497 (1954), to say nothing of the selective incorporation of the Bill of Rights that has dominated constitutional discourse during much of this century. What virtually all the justices in the majority in *DeShaney* are willing to invent—with even less textual basis—in the service of inherent executive power and the "reason of state" doctrine provides a particularly glaring contrast with *DeShaney*'s niggardly approach to "liberty." See, e.g., the decisions discussed and criticized in A.S. Miller, THE SECRET CONSTITUTION AND THE NEED FOR CONSTITUTIONAL CHANGE (1987); Miller, *Reason of State and the Emergent Constitution of Control,* 64 MINN. L. REV. 585 (1980).

18. *DeShaney,* 109 S. Ct. at 1003.

19. *Id.* at 1004 (The confusing *them* reference in the quotation is not the only awkward syntax in this decision.). It is worth noting that this sentence, and the entire thrust of *DeShaney*, marks the decision's potential utility when judges are asked to decide, for example, if a school district may close its public schools, so long as it does so without obvious, provable invidious discriminatory motivation. For a fine description and critique of the greater-includes-the-lesser approach, see Sullivan, *Unconstitutional Conditions,* 102 HARV. L. REV. 1413 (1989). *Cf.* Epstein, *Foreword: Unconstitutional Conditions, State Power, and the Limits of Consent,* 102 HARV. L. REV. 4 (1988) (stating a view closer to that of the *DeShaney* majority). It should be sobering to note that one of the primary justifications for slavery was that the greater power to kill captives was said to include the lesser power to enslave them and their progeny.

text and logic as he works from his crucial initial premises.[20] Yet this high road is so rarefied that its abstractions climb toward cloud-cuckoo-land. The majority offers textualism without consideration of the textual context of the specific words at issue; indeed, the textual structure of the Fourteenth Amendment as a whole and the history of the amendment and the statutes based upon it are treated as entirely irrelevant.

The majority's next step in pursuit of its "neat and decisive divide between action and inaction"[21] is simply to divide the world into two universes, reminiscent of the heyday of the Cold War, when Rehnquist studied law. Joshua has no cause to complain against the state, the Chief Justice insists, because the problems confronting this two- to four-year-old child were "dangers Joshua faced in the free world."[22] In the free world, government has no constitutional duty to its citizens; in the other world, the world of incarceration and institutionalization, the state may owe some affirmative duty to an individual, derived entirely "from the limitation . . . imposed on his freedom to act on his own behalf."[23]

Because no government had locked up Joshua, he ought to have taken care of himself.[24] That is what individuals, rugged or not, are

---

20. Brennan's dissent drives home the extent to which the majority's decision is preordained by its initial "perspective" and its "baseline," to the point that Brennan accuses the majority of proclaiming a general principle that is really a product of the justices' own "fixation." *DeShaney*, 109 S. Ct. at 1008 (Brennan, J., dissenting). *See generally* Miller, *Major Premises, supra* note 3 (describing and decrying the judicial tendency to follow initial premises unrealistically and uncritically).
21. *DeShaney*, 109 S. Ct. at 1009 (Brennan, J., dissenting).
22. *Id.* at 1006.
23. *Id.* This dichotomy may be an adaptation of the binary choice drawn by the state officials to distinguish "state custody" from which Joshua was "at liberty." Brief for Respondents at 25, *DeShaney* (No. 87-154). Rehnquist's use of *free world* is innovative, however. A LEXIS search discloses that the relatively rare previous uses of the phrase in Supreme Court opinions, all since World War II, have been primarily in political or military contexts. *See, e.g.,* Silkwood v. Kerr-McGee Corp., 464 U.S. 238, 282 n.12 (1984) (Powell, J., dissenting); Reid v. Covert, 354 U.S. 1, 86 (1957) (Clark, J., dissenting); Dennis v. United States, 341 U.S. 494, 581 (1951) (Douglas, J., dissenting); Schneiderman v. United States, 320 U.S. 118, 120 (1943). The only exceptions to the usual usage—*e.g.,* "United States troops are stationed in many countries as part of our own national defense and to help strengthen the Free World struggle against Communist imperialism," Wilson v. Girard, 354 U.S. 524, 548 (1957)—were in Hutto v. Finney, 437 U.S. 678, 681 (1978) (quoting the district court's description of routine prison conditions in Arkansas as " 'a dark and evil world completely alien to the free world' "), and in Bute v. Illinois, 333 U.S. 640, 677 n.1 (1948) (Douglas, J., dissenting) (quoting Cohen & Griswold, *Denial of Counsel to Indigent Defendant Questioned,* N.Y. Times, Aug. 2, 1942, at 6E, col. 5) (attacking Betts v. Brady, 316 U.S. 455 (1942), and claiming a greater right to counsel for a criminal defendant). These earlier usages conflict with Rehnquist's distinction between the free world and the world of incarceration, because they were concerned with criminal processes *within* the free world.
24. After all, as District Judge Reynolds found, the social worker had noted that Joshua, "who was four years old at the time, was trained to make his bed and prepare his own breakfast every morning." DeShaney v. DeShaney, No. 85-C-310 (E.D. Wis. June 20, 1986), in Petition for Cert., app. at 58, *DeShaney* (filed July 17, 1987) (No. 87-154).

expected to do in the free world. The majority concedes that the state "may have been aware of the dangers that Joshua faced in the free world," but insists that state intervention "placed him in no worse position than that in which he would have been had it not acted at all."[25] To hold otherwise, even in the face of the state's "expressions of intent to help him," would transform the state into "the permanent guarantor of an individual's safety by having once offered him shelter."[26]

The idea that the state did not worsen Joshua's situation by appearing to protect him, that it is absolved because it did not affirmatively erect an obstacle, is belied by the record.[27] But the either/or approach seems even more forced when it is compared to Rehnquist's own, directly inconsistent words in another recent decision involving the rights and constitutional status of children.

In *Schall v. Martin,*[28] in order to uphold extensive pretrial detention of accused juvenile delinquents, then-Justice Rehnquist's majority opinion argued that a juvenile's interest in freedom "must be qualified by the recognition that juveniles, unlike adults, are always in some form of custody."[29] For pretrial detainees, then, there are more than two worlds. Any attempt to reconcile the approaches in the two decisions, perhaps using a distinction between "juveniles" and younger children, immediately fails. That is because, Rehnquist continued, "Children, by definition, are not assumed to have the capacity to take care of themselves. They are assumed to be subject to the control of their parents, and if parental control falters, *the State must play its part as* parens patriae."[30] Thus, the state *must* play its role as parens patriae when it comes to detaining children. Without any textual basis, Rehnquist simply took notice in *Schall* that children are, after all, not really free. They are "always in some form of custody."[31] In stark contrast, *DeShaney* says we must find a

---

25. *DeShaney*, 109 S. Ct. at 1006.
26. *Id.*
27. The Court relies on Harris v. McRae, 448 U.S. 297, 317-18 (1980) (finding that the government has no obligation to fund medically necessary abortions), and Martinez v. California, 444 U.S. 277 (1980) (holding that state officials who released a parolee were not liable for the death of a private citizen he killed), to make a causal claim: the state officials did nothing equivalent to erecting an obstacle or hurdle in the plaintiff's path. *DeShaney*, in turn, became an important precedent for Rehnquist's argument for the plurality in the abortion decision, Webster v. Reproductive Health Services, 109 S. Ct. 3040 (1989). Because the state need not operate hospitals at all, according to Rehnquist, it is free to prohibit any use of public facilities and personnel for performing abortions. In contrast to his own rigidity about the meaning of due process in *DeShaney*, it is ironic that Rehnquist criticizes Roe v. Wade, 410 U.S. 113 (1973), and several abortion decisions following it, for creating a "virtual . . . Procrustean bed," *Webster*, 109 S. Ct. at 3056, in their interpretation of due process.
28. 467 U.S. 253 (1984).
29. *Id.* at 265.
30. *Id.* (emphasis added).
31. That this inconsistency is not a mere slip of the judicial pen is clear when one considers other Rehnquist opinions about the status of children, *e.g.*, Michael M. v. Superior Court, 450 U.S. 464, 476 (1981) (concluding that teenage males are not "in need of the special solicitude of the courts"); Craig v. Boren, 429 U.S. 190, 218-19 (1976) (Rehnquist, J., dissenting) (rejecting the argument that heightened scrutiny is warranted for statutes discriminating on the basis of gender and age), as well as other opinions in

specific text in the Due Process Clause before any obligation as parens patriae is owed to Joshua. Without such language, the state's greater power—it need not do anything, according to Rehnquist— necessarily includes its lesser power to do something that worsens the situation, so long as the ineptitude is not intentionally invidious discrimination.[32] Joshua must be left to his father's hands, to the everyday struggle of a violent state of nature, to "the dangers of the free world."[33] Poor Joshua!

II. Transforming the Past, Controlling the Future

A. History: The Past

In his opinion for the Seventh Circuit in *DeShaney*, Posner proclaimed: "The state does not have a duty enforceable by the federal courts to maintain a police force or a fire department, or to protect children from their parents."[34] Posner knows this. He does not need any authority. Conflating 1787 with 1866, he claims to have history as well as some Libertarian totem on his side: "The men

---

which he joined. *E.g.*, New Jersey v. T.L.O., 469 U.S. 325 (1985) (holding that the constitutional rights of children are more restricted in the school setting); Lehman v. Lycoming County Children's Servs. Agency, 458 U.S. 502 (1982) (holding that federal habeas corpus sec. 2254 does not extend to a constitutional challenge to a state statute under which a mother lost parental rights involuntarily, given federalism and finality interests); Bellotti v. Baird, 443 U.S. 622, 634-35 (1979) (noting that the status of minors is unique in many respects, and requiring that "constitutional principles be applied with sensitivity and flexibility to the special needs of parents and children").

32. *DeShaney*, 109 S. Ct. at 1004 n.3. The Court here notes that the Equal Protection Clause prohibits selective denial of protective services to certain (unspecified) disfavored minorities. For an attempt to address the overwhelming practical problem of proof of such bad motive, and its lack of support in the Court's precedents prior to Washington v. Davis, 426 U.S. 229 (1976), see Soifer, *Complacency and Constitutional Law*, 42 OHIO ST. L.J. 383 (1981). If anything, Supreme Court decisions since 1981 have made it even less possible to meet such a burden in the practical world of litigation.

33. State officials apparently received information on 11 occasions strongly indicating severe child abuse of Joshua. The respondents dispute the number, just as they dispute whether the social worker involved knew of cigarette burns or only "wondered" whether the marks she saw were cigarette burns. Brief for Respondents at 4-5 n.7, *DeShaney* (No. 87-154). Any fair reading of the record, however, suggests that a dispute over the precise number of incidents fades into unimportance in light of the horrific life Joshua obviously led. State officials did nothing to aid him even after the state had taken temporary custody, set up the interdisciplinary "Child Protection Team," established a plan as a condition of returning Joshua to his father's custody to which Joshua's father consented but which he blatantly failed to follow, and had a social worker visit Joshua's home who repeatedly and dutifully made entries revealing evidence of abuse but did nothing. The record discloses more than ten separate police and emergency room contacts with Joshua during his two years in Wisconsin, and approximately the same number of social worker visits. DeShaney v. DeShaney, No. 85-C-310 (E.D. Wis. June 20, 1986), in Petition for Cert., app. at 52-61, *DeShaney* (filed July 17, 1987) (No. 87-154).

34. DeShaney v. Winnebago County Dep't of Social Servs., 812 F.2d 298, 301 (7th Cir. 1987). This statement actually may be a slight modification of Posner's even more radical position in Bowers v. DeVito, 686 F.2d 616, 618 (7th Cir. 1982). *See supra* note 16.

who framed the original Constitution and the Fourteenth Amendment were worried about government's oppressing the citizenry rather than about its failing to provide adequate social services."[35] Supplemented only by the claim that political remedies, and any remedies that the states in their discretion saw fit to provide, "were assumed to be adequate,"[36] this assertion is the entirety of Posner's historical argument.[37] It must be comforting to have a direct line to what worried an undefined cohort of Framers who achieved consensus as they floated together across a century. And it cannot be said that Posner is guilty of "law office history."[38] Instead, he practices *ex cathedra* history. He is so in tune with the ghostly voices that harmonized in the Constitution adopted in 1789 and amplified in 1868—or perhaps in 1787 and 1866, when the constitutional texts were formally proposed—that he need never venture down to the dirty world of historic evidence.

Had Posner actually considered the historic context of the Constitution makers, he would have noticed disagreement, confusion, ambivalence, and the general messiness of mixed motives and ambitions. People surely did not talk about social workers or "child protection teams." Congressmen did not even debate the problem of child abuse, though there was concern about apprenticeship as a form of forbidden involuntary servitude. Thus, Posner might have claimed support for the argument that the Due Process Clause was not intended to reach Joshua DeShaney's terrible situation. But he also would have found a long history of communal responsibility for children perceived to be in trouble, and little support for the proposition that the state had left such children, or their families, alone,

---

35. *DeShaney*, 812 F.2d at 301. This assertion is a fine example of the argument-from-false-dichotomy technique favored by Posner and by the majority in *DeShaney*. Posner's claim is belied not only by the considerable force Congress attempted to place behind the panoply of civil rights statutes it passed between 1866 and 1875 (including military occupation of the recalcitrant South), but also by section 1 of the Fourteenth Amendment itself, which specifically mentions "protection" as well as "privileges or immunities" as constitutional claims that states may not deny. Posner's argument also ignores the rest of that amendment and the context of its passage, and the Thirteenth and Fifteenth Amendments, which hardly suggest willingness to leave law and order and everything else to the discretion of the states, or to political remedies as administered by the states, in the wake of the Civil War.

36. *Id.*

37. The ratification of the Fifteenth Amendment in 1870 surely undercuts Posner's claim that political remedies were assumed to be adequate in the immediate post-Civil War political climate. He does concede, however, that a state "may not invidiously withdraw its protection from a disfavored minority without violating the equal protection clause in its most fundamental sense." *Id.* at 301. His only other "concession" is a tip of the word processor to an article by his colleague, David Currie, in which, according to Posner, the exceptions to Posner's principle of a constitution are "well discussed" but not applicable. *Id.* (citing Currie, *Positive and Negative Constitutional Rights*, 53 U. CHI. L. REV. 864 (1986)). It might be added that Currie neither ventures into historical details nor directly confronts Posner's radical claims in this article.

38. For criticisms of the "law office history" methodology, see Casper, Jones v. Mayer: *Clio, Bemused and Confused Muse*, 1968 SUP. CT. REV. 89; Kelly, *Clio and the Court: An Illicit Love Affair*, 1965 SUP. CT. REV. 119; Wiecek, *Clio As Hostage: The United States Supreme Court and the Uses of History*, 24 CAL. W.L. REV. 227 (1988). The standard critique charges lawyers and judges with ripping citations out of historical context, but Posner uses no citations at all.

entirely "free" to do their own thing.[39]

The notion of rights in 1787-89 was hardly exclusively negative, moreover, and those who gathered in Philadelphia hardly met there in order to leave all relationships between individuals and government to the discretion of the states. Perhaps Posner regards Chief Justice John Marshall as merely eccentric when he wrote in *Marbury v. Madison:*[40] "The very essence of civil liberty certainly consists in the right of every individual to claim the protection of the laws, whenever he receives an injury. One of the first duties of government is to afford that protection."[41]

This is hardly the place to delve into the complexity of the first constitutional period, nor to explore the active role of government on both state and federal levels to create new rights and vested expectations through "the release of energy" across what white Americans perceived to be an unsettled continent.[42] The very effort to adopt a national Constitution was inconsistent with the idea of a purely negative government. Additionally, any close reading of the entire constitutional text—including the Necessary and Proper Clause and the Ninth Amendment, for example—must confront open-ended governmental powers and unenumerated rights that cannot be reconciled with Posnerian history.[43]

---

39. *See, e.g.,* M. GROSSBERG, GOVERNING THE HEARTH: LAW AND THE FAMILY IN NINE-TEENTH-CENTURY AMERICA 236-37, 289-307 (1985) (noting that during the antebellum period, judges began to emphasize child welfare concerns over the exclusive family preferences of the common law, and this trend accelerated after the Civil War); R. MORRIS, GOVERNMENT AND LABOR IN EARLY AMERICA 14-21, 363-89 (1981) (explaining that town governments were responsible for supervising and providing for the poor, and supervised apprenticeship systems for needy children); D. ROTHMAN, THE DISCOVERY OF THE ASYLUM: SOCIAL ORDER AND DISORDER IN THE NEW REPUBLIC 14-15, 169-72, 210-16 (1971) (discussing governmental intervention to protect children in postcolonial and Jacksonian society); Bardaglio, *Challenging Parental Custody Rights: The Legal Reconstruction of Parenthood in the Nineteenth-Century American South,* 4 CONTINUITY & CHANGE 259, 269-80 (1989) (recognizing that even in the South, which lagged behind the North in elevating child welfare concerns over family interests, judges invoked the idea that the state had the duty as parens patriae to protect children, and noting that this idea became widespread after the Civil War); Zainaldin, *The Emergence of a Modern American Family Law: Child Custody, Adoption, and the Courts, 1796-1851,* 73 Nw. U.L. REV. 1038, 1050 (1979) (discussing the burst of pre-Civil War social reforms in the United States, unparalleled in other countries, premised on responding to the particular needs of children). *Cf.* M. LESY, WISCONSIN DEATH TRIP (2d ed. 1983) (revealing photographs suggesting the harsh 19th-century life in a small Wisconsin town).

40. 5 U.S. (1 Cranch) 137 (1803).

41. *Id.* at 163.

42. J. HURST, LAW AND THE CONDITIONS OF FREEDOM IN THE NINETEENTH-CENTURY UNITED STATES 3-70 (1956). *See generally* O. HANDLIN & M. HANDLIN, COMMONWEALTH (1947); L. HARTZ, ECONOMIC POLICY AND DEMOCRATIC THOUGHT: PENNSYLVANIA, 1776-1860 (1948); and the articles by Harry Scheiber and Paul Gates available in AMERICAN LAW AND THE CONSTITUTIONAL ORDER: HISTORICAL PERSPECTIVES (2d ed. 1988).

43. For recent explorations of the ideas and politics surrounding 1787, see, e.g., excellent collections of essays published to mark the Bicentennial, BEYOND CONFEDERATION: ORIGINS OF THE CONSTITUTION AND AMERICAN NATIONAL IDENTITY (1987), and THE FRAMING AND RATIFICATION OF THE CONSTITUTION (1987). For a cogent affirmative

If anything, Posner's ahistorical fallacy is even less convincing about the immediate post-Civil War period. Speeches surrounding the passage and ratification of the Thirteenth, Fourteenth, and Fifteenth Amendments brim over with declarations of a national obligation to assure federal protection of the rights of citizens, including but not limited to the rights of former slaves. The debates over the numerous civil rights acts from 1866 to 1875 are replete with vehement pronouncements about the reciprocal relationship of allegiance and protection. Sponsors and supporters of these acts repeatedly emphasized the federal duty to provide protection when state officials invaded or failed to protect the full and equal rights of all citizens.[44]

The title and the context of the Ku Klux Klan Act of 1871, the precursor of 42 U.S.C. § 1983 at issue in *DeShaney*, surely indicates concern to protect private citizens from private violence. Also, as the Supreme Court has noted many times in recent decades, this statute was part of a transformation of federalism. For example: "The Civil Rights Act of 1871, along with the Fourteenth Amendment it was enacted to enforce, were crucial ingredients in the basic alteration of our federal system accomplished during the Reconstruction Era."[45] Section 1983 was primarily intended to interpose federal protection against unconstitutional state action, whether done by the state legislatures or by state judges or by executive branch officials. Finally, although surely not models of clarity, the relevant speeches in Congress and the historical context of the 1860s and early 1870s make clear that "deliberate inactivity"[46] by state and local officials, in the face of brutal depredations, was a central concern of the post-Civil War period.

The Ku Klux Klan Act of 1871, for example, "was aimed at least as much at the abdication of law enforcement responsibilities by Southern officials as it was at the Klan's outrages."[47] To be sure,

---

reading of the text of the pre-Civil War Constitution, see, e.g., C. BLACK, THE PEOPLE AND THE COURT: JUDICIAL REVIEW IN A DEMOCRACY (1960); Black, *On Reading and Using the Ninth Amendment*, in POWER AND POLICY IN QUEST OF LAW: ESSAYS IN HONOR OF EUGENE VICTOR ROSTOW 187 (1985); Black, *Further Reflections on the Constitutional Justice of Livelihood*, 86 COLUM. L. REV. 1103 (1986).

44. The historical literature is voluminous, of course, but I still favor Soifer, *Protecting Civil Rights: A Critique of Raoul Berger's History*, 54 N.Y.U. L. REV. 651 (1979), for a discussion of historical sources and a detailed introduction to the widespread perception of the national government's duty to protect the "full and equal" rights of all citizens in the context of section 1 of the 1866 Civil Rights Act, unquestionably the precursor of section 1 of the Fourteenth Amendment.

45. Patsy v. Florida Bd. of Regents, 457 U.S. 496, 503 (1982); *see also, e.g.*, Mitchum v. Foster, 407 U.S. 225, 242 (1972); McNeese v. Board of Educ., 373 U.S. 668 (1963).

46. Note, *Developments in the Law—Section 1983 and Federalism*, 90 HARV. L. REV. 1133, 1154 (1977).

47. *Id.* at 1154; *see also* M. CURTIS, NO STATE SHALL ABRIDGE: THE FOURTEENTH AMENDMENT AND THE BILL OF RIGHTS 156-64 (1986); E. FONER, RECONSTRUCTION: AMERICA'S UNFINISHED REVOLUTION 1963-1877, at 412-59 (1988); H. HYMAN & W. WIECEK, EQUAL JUSTICE UNDER LAW: CONSTITUTIONAL DEVELOPMENT 1835-1875, at 335-515 (1982); J. JAMES, THE FRAMING OF THE FOURTEENTH AMENDMENT (1956); J. JAMES, THE RATIFICATION OF THE FOURTEENTH AMENDMENT (1984); R. KACZOROWSKI, THE POLITICS OF JUDICIAL INTERPRETATION: THE FEDERAL COURTS, DEPARTMENT OF JUSTICE AND CIVIL RIGHTS, 1866-1876, at 53-57 (1985); Note, *supra* note 46, at 1153-56. The very

Congress was not precise. It did not specify what rights were covered, what degree of state abdication would make a federal case, nor to what extent coverage was to be truly national, rather than merely aimed at the protection of blacks and their white allies from both governmental and private depredations in the South. But that murkiness only underscores what is amiss in Posner's attempt to blast away original intent, to the extent it can be discovered, leaving conceptual constructs that only purport to be based in history.

Rehnquist bothers with history even less than does Posner. The entire historical discussion in *DeShaney* is a précis of Posner's argument about the purpose of the Due Process Clause: "Its purpose was to protect the people from the State, not to ensure that the State protected them from each other. The Framers were content to leave the extent of governmental obligation in the latter area to the democratic political processes."[48] Rehnquist himself once noted that the "Civil War Amendments to the Constitution . . . serve as a sword, rather than merely as a shield, for those whom they were designed to protect."[49] But he now carves a gaping hole in the shield and buries the sword altogether. On Rehnquist's peculiar view, the Civil War was fought to protect state sovereignty. The amendments and statutes to guarantee the fruits of Union victory merely sought to return discretionary power to the states, so long as state officials did not restore slavery.

It is impossible, of course, to be certain about what Representative Jonathan Bingham or Senator Lyman Trumbull might have decided if faced with a legal question such as that presented in *DeShaney.* In a less anonymous world of a small Wisconsin town a century ago, it is hard to imagine, but conceivable, that Joshua's father would have been left alone to commit repeated acts of violence against his son. Yet it is also hard to construct the precise analogy for the "child protection team" that "stood by and did nothing

---

terms of the Ku Klux Klan Act, as they survive in 42 U.S.C. § 1983, suggest affirmative federal protection of "rights, privileges, or immunities" against both active and passive deprivations. Every person is liable who, under color of law, "custom, or usage," either "subjects, *or causes to be subjected*" any citizen or other person within the jurisdiction of the United States to deprivation of any rights or privileges, as well as immunities. 42 U.S.C. § 1983 (1982) (emphasis added).

48. *DeShaney*, 109 S. Ct. at 1003.

49. Edelman v. Jordan, 415 U.S. 651, 664 (1974). There have been indications that this statement was not mere rhetoric to cushion the restrictive holding in *Edelman*, which found an Eleventh Amendment barrier to federal judicial remedies against state officials. *See, e.g.,* Fitzpatrick v. Bitzer, 427 U.S. 445 (1976) (holding that Congress could use power under section 5 of the Fourteenth Amendment to overcome Eleventh Amendment barriers); Rehnquist, *The Notion of a Living Constitution,* 54 TEX. L. REV. 693 (1976) (arguing that the Civil War Amendments were intended to provide limitations on the authority of state governments, and to empower Congress to resolve the problems society might confront even a century later).

when suspicious circumstances dictated a more active role,"[50] which is Rehnquist's "protection" description of how the state officials performed as Joshua's tragedy unfolded.

Actually, history cannot answer Rehnquist's question directly. Moreover, history complicates the neatness of using ideology as the decisive reference point, but does not support the Court's misdirected nostalgia for a continuous golden age of laissez-faire, conveniently said to be reflected throughout the Constitution. If anything, the post-Civil War Amendments suggest an entirely different thrust: an attempt to interpose the federal government against state action and inaction that deprive "any citizen . . . or other person" of what the politicians of the era considered to be "rights, privileges, or immunities secured by the Constitution and laws."[51]

The *DeShaney* majority's binary approach and *ex cathedra* history misses another crucial factor—the development of due process doctrine since Reconstruction. Taken at its word, the majority would not accept incorporation of any of the Bill of Rights through the Due Process Clause of the Fourteenth Amendment. The Rehnquist-Posner account of due process does not seem to accept any constitutional requirements on the states to protect any citizens other than those in custody or victims of overt, intentional invidious discrimination by state officials. Moreover, the majority in *DeShaney* rejects a point made by Justice Frankfurter—certainly not generally considered a judicial activist—who once noted: "Representing as it does a living principle, due process is not confined within a permanent catalogue of what may at a given time be deemed the limits or the essentials of fundamental rights."[52] Yet the *DeShaney* majority requires just such a catalogue, allegedly to be found in history, text, and logic. As the next sections show, *DeShaney* is actually grounded in ill-conceived, anti-democratic policy and in a rigid, ideological commitment that produces considerable moral obtuseness.

B. Being Practical: On Not "Yielding to That Impulse" of "Natural Sympathy"[53]

A major thrust of the majority opinion in *DeShaney* concerns the slippery-slope danger of "transform[ing] every tort committed by a state actor into a constitutional violation."[54] To be sure, several recent decisions support the Court's claim that " 'not all common-law duties owed by government actors were . . . constitutionalized by the Fourteenth Amendment.' "[55] But it took *DeShaney* to transmogrify

---

50. *DeShaney*, 109 S. Ct. at 1007.

51. 42 U.S.C. § 1983 (1982).

52. Wolf v. Colorado, 338 U.S. 25, 27 (1949), *overruled on other grounds*, 367 U.S. 643 (1961) (overruling *Wolf* insofar as it held that evidence obtained by searches and seizures in violation of the federal Constitution was nevertheless admissible in state criminal proceedings).

53. *DeShaney*, 109 S. Ct. at 1007.

54. *Id.*

55. *Id.* (quoting Daniels v. Williams, 474 U.S. 327, 335 (1986)).

"not all" into "none." *DeShaney* turns the category of all constitutional torts that are not intentional into an empty set for all citizens who are not in custody. It is ironic that the Court might have used a crabbed version of state action to accomplish the same result,[56] but its restrictive view of what liberty constitutionally entails is more radical and more clearly designed for use in future cases.

Why is the Court so anxious to eliminate constitutional protection? Questionable assumptions about federalism, federal court docket control, and state and local treasuries obviously enter the majority's calculation. Yet it still would have been very easy to decide this case on the narrow basis of its appalling facts, because the particular governmental inaction, despite repeated contact by state officials, surely rises to the level of "deliberate indifference," "recklessness," or "gross" negligence made actionable even under this Court's recent, stingy precedents.[57] There are two additional and central, albeit unspoken, "practical" elements of the *DeShaney* Court's revision of the relevant statute, 42 U.S.C. § 1983. First, the Court wishes to keep sympathetic cases away from juries, and second, it desires to impose an extreme, statist view under the guise of leaving matters to the political process. Rehnquist relies on the common urge to separate law from politics. In fact, however, the *DeShaney* majority aggressively uses political ideology to enable judges to control the barrier between legal and political spheres, even as Rehnquist claims that to do otherwise would be judicial arrogation.

In recent years, the Court has used a variety of devices to restrict constitutional torts. The Court has abused longstanding doctrines of standing and ripeness and has made an inedible porridge, both overly sweet and overly bitter, in its attempts to define what constitutes a protected property right.[58] *DeShaney* is the culmination of the gambit either to reject the plaintiff's choice of a federal forum entirely or, failing that, to make sure that such a choice turns out to be a mistake, because sympathetic factual issues will never get to the

---

56. *See, e.g.,* Flagg Bros., Inc. v. Brooks, 436 U.S. 149 (1978) (holding that state action could not be found in the exercise by a private party of power delegated it by the state, which is traditionally associated with sovereignty); Jackson v. Metropolitan Edison Co., 419 U.S. 345 (1974) (finding that the state was not sufficiently connected with the termination of services to an individual by a privately owned and operated utility corporation to support a section 1983 action, even though the utility corporation operated under a state-issued certificate of public convenience).

57. *See, e.g.,* Daniels v. Williams, 474 U.S. 327 (1986); Davidson v. Cannon, 474 U.S. 344 (1986); City of Los Angeles v. Lyons, 461 U.S. 95 (1983); Paul v. Davis, 424 U.S. 693 (1976); Rizzo v. Goode, 423 U.S. 362 (1976).

58. For excellent recent discussions of the problematic cases in this realm, see Beermann, *Government Official Torts and the Takings Clause: Federalism and State Sovereign Immunity,* 68 B.U.L. REV. 277 (1988); Whitman, *Government Responsibility for Constitutional Torts,* 85 MICH. L. REV. 225 (1986).

jury.[59]

The idea of leaving matters to the political processes, a notion that Posner and Rehnquist purport to find reassuring as they send plaintiffs away, does not preclude these judges from significantly amending a basic civil rights statute in *DeShaney*. A statute intended to afford broad protection from the Ku Klux Klan and from inaction by state officials in the face of Klan outrages was clearly not limited to affirmative state action. Because Posner and Rehnquist dislike the implications of this statute, however, they take it upon themselves to transform it to be true to the logical implications of what they think it should have said. Nor does their proclaimed respect for the popular will extend to the democracy of the jury box. There is to be no opportunity for checks and balances across the borderlines of their federalism. No federal jury will be allowed to hold state officials accountable for their tortious acts or failures to act, absent proof of invidious and discriminatory motive.

Paradoxically, the *DeShaney* majority's failure to grasp the reality of the modern role of the Positive State produces an approach that is anything but individualism. Its practical import is to allow bureaucrats to do nothing. They may come face-to-face with easily remediable suffering and blink. They may decide to intervene in a manner that is directly and terribly harmful, yet they still will not be held to have caused the harm unless they actually, actively inflicted it themselves. They may give the appearance of acting to remedy a terrible situation, and thereby deter any attempts by third parties to rescue a battered child, yet they will still not be constitutionally liable for the void they create.

Because the state need not render any service, it will not be held constitutionally to have created the harm. This is the clear implication of the greater-includes-the-lesser reasoning of *DeShaney*. State officials may be secure in the knowledge that, at least as a matter of federal law, to fail to improve, and even to make a tragic situation far worse, is entirely acceptable. Rehnquist concedes that even if a person does not have an initial duty to rescue, once that person undertakes a rescue, as a matter of common law, liability may ensue if the rescue attempt is done negligently. But, he argues, to follow

---

59. An obvious basis for the plaintiffs' effort to get and keep the federal forum was the $50,000 cap on damages recovery under Wisconsin law. WIS. STAT. ANN. § 893.80(3) (West 1983). Justice Frankfurter, who surely was not an advocate of expansive interpretation of section 1983, nevertheless noted "how important providing a federal trial court was among the several purposes of the Ku Klux Act." Monroe v. Pape, 365 U.S. 167, 251 (1961) (Frankfurter, J., dissenting), *rev'd on other grounds*, 436 U.S. 658 (1978) (overruling *Monroe* "insofar as it holds that local governments are wholly immune from suit under § 1983"); *see also* Lane v. Wilson, 307 U.S. 268, 274-75. (1939). Likewise, Justice Holmes often emphasized the importance of respecting a plaintiff's choice of a federal forum when Congress had provided for that choice. For example, in a due process case he wrote that resort to state remedies could not be required because "[a]ll their constitutional rights . . . depend upon what the facts are found to be," which meant that plaintiffs could not be "forbidden to try those facts before a court of their own choosing." Prentis v. Atlantic Coast Line Co., 211 U.S. 210, 228 (1908); *see also* Oklahoma Natural Gas Co. v. Russell, 261 U.S. 290, 293 (1923).

that approach for state officials would be to "thrust upon"[60] the people of Wisconsin an unworthy expansion of the Due Process Clause.

III. The Moral Dimension: Where " 'Doing Nothing Can Be the Worst Mistake' "[61]

In its haste to confine the liberty protected by the Due Process Clause and to eviscerate section 1983 and thereby reduce access to federal courts, the *DeShaney* majority follows a cruel, purported logic that is aptly labeled "sterile formalism"[62] in Justice Blackmun's dissent. In doing so, the Court is so "indifferent to . . . indifference"[63] as to shock the conscience. A remarkably creaky fiction drives the majority opinion; it is a fiction that demands a leap of illogical faith and rejects attention to history, text, and context. Rehnquist strives for what Holmes long ago called "the logical method and form [that] flatter that longing for certainty and for repose which is in every human mind."[64] Yet Rehnquist fails to heed Holmes's next words: "But certainty generally is illusion, and repose is not the destiny of man."[65]

Obviously, the definition of a duty to intervene is difficult in itself and rife with the potential for paternalistic abuse or for inefficiencies of various kinds.[66] This moral issue cries out for context. Joshua DeShaney's horrible experience demands nuanced attention to relationships and to the specific facts of the case before the court,[67] not some purportedly neutral general principle.

As Mary Ann Glendon points out, the Court's response in *DeShaney* is all too reminiscent of that moment in the first year of law school when a student learns that there is no legal duty to rescue a

---

60. *DeShaney*, 109 S. Ct. at 1007.
61. *Id.* at 1012 (Blackmun, J., dissenting) (quoting A. STONE, LAW, PSYCHIATRY, AND MORALITY 262 (1984)).
62. *Id.*
63. *Id.* (Brennan, J., dissenting).
64. Holmes, *The Path of the Law*, 10 HARV. L. REV. 457, 466 (1897).
65. *Id.*
66. For a fine discussion of the moral quandry surrounding the question of the Good Samaritan, see Thomson, *The Trolley Problem*, 94 YALE L.J. 1395 (1985). For a compelling argument in favor of the duty to intervene against injustice, premised in classical political theory, see Shklar, *Giving Injustice Its Due*, 98 YALE L.J. 1135 (1989).
67. District Court Judge Reynolds decided *DeShaney* on a motion to dismiss, which he treated as a motion for summary judgment. DeShaney v. DeShaney, No. 85-C-310 (E.D. Wis. June 20, 1986), in Petition for Cert., app. at 48-49, *DeShaney* (filed July 17, 1987) (No. 87-154).

baby drowning in a pond.[68] Most students absorb that lesson without accepting a complete segregation of moral and legal worlds.[69] And some come to believe that constitutional law is more aspirational than common law, that "a judge's highest calling is to ensure in his every decision that the implementation and enforcement of the laws of this country must be to upgrade and civilize the manner in which these laws are enforced,"[70] and that, in pursuit of "goodness,"[71] it is even sometimes appropriate for a judge to "take the short run into account."[72]

The *DeShaney* majority, by contrast, proclaims an abstract, purportedly certain, and general constitutional principle: the state has a limited degree of responsibility. State officials are constitutionally bound to avoid grossly harmful acts or omissions that grievously harm people who live within the confined sphere of state custody. In the much larger world, however, everyone else is fully free and able to take part in the great national free-for-all. Every child, woman, and man, no matter how actually encumbered, is properly relegated exclusively to the political processes and the states for any refuge or redress. No one in this free world—no matter what that person's condition or age—may look to the federal Constitution for relief, with the possible exception of those rare individuals who are able to prove that invidious discriminatory motivation was the cause of their suffering at the hands of government officials.

Blackmun's brief dissent in *DeShaney* offers a devastating attack on the majority's lack of "moral ambition."[73] At first it may seem odd for Blackmun to invoke Robert Cover's *Justice Accused* (1975), a study of antebellum Northern judges who retreated into formalistic legal reasoning rather than grant relief to fugitive slaves with whom they

---

68. M. Glendon, Rights and Responsibilities in Modern Legal Language (1989) (unpublished manuscript).

69. Law schools fail to give adequate attention to the issue of when and if to maintain the moral/legal gap. Arthur Miller's last book, A.S. MILLER & J. BOWMAN, DEATH BY INSTALLMENTS: THE ORDEAL OF WILLIE FRANCIS (1988), provides a fine text for study of such matters. It vividly details events leading up to the Court's decision in Louisiana ex rel. Francis v. Resweber, 329 U.S. 459 (1947), to allow a second execution attempt of a poor, incompetently defended black teenager, after drunken deputies botched the first execution attempt on Louisiana's portable electric chair. Justice Frankfurter's role particularly merits attention. Frankfurter fought hard to keep a majority together behind the proposition that Francis was the victim of "one of those contingencies which is not the fault of man." *Id.* at 93 (quoting a note from Frankfurter to Justice Reed, Dec. 14, 1946). Once he achieved that result by a 4-1-4 vote, however, Frankfurter tried unsuccessfully to use his Harvard Law School connections to arrange, behind the scenes, to have the Louisiana governor commute the death sentence. Unfortunately, Willie Francis's experience provides a grisly precedent for recent events. *See* Applebome, *2 Electric Jolts in Alabama Execution*, N.Y. Times, July 15, 1989, at A6, col. 1 (discussing the execution of a mildly retarded murderer—the first retarded person to be executed since the Supreme Court voted to allow such executions in June 1989—that took 19 minutes and two jolts of electricity).

70. Johnson, *Foreword* to A.S. MILLER, *supra* note 10, at x.

71. A.S. MILLER, JUDICIAL ODYSSEY, *supra* note 10, at 7.

72. *Id.* at 35 (quoting Judge J. Skelly Wright).

73. *DeShaney*, 109 S. Ct. at 1012 (quoting A. STONE, LAW, PSYCHIATRY, AND MORALITY 262 (1984)).

personally sympathized. The analogy, however, is actually (and terribly) appropriate. It lends powerful support to Blackmun's plea for a " 'sympathetic' " reading of the Fourteenth Amendment, which "comports with dictates of fundamental justice and recognizes that compassion need not be exiled from the province of judging."[74]

Blackmun may have a particularly strong reason for the sense of outrage that permeates his dissent. He may be echoing, but also in part atoning for, his own majority opinion in *Wyman v. James.*[75] In that opinion, his first for the Court, Blackmun held that compulsory home visits by social workers were constitutional even if they forced a welfare mother to choose between continuing to receive her welfare benefits or waiving her Fourth Amendment rights.[76] Blackmun characterized the social worker as "a friend to one in need."[77] Thus Blackmun's own early, idealized portrait of a "helping professional" may exacerbate his outrage in *DeShaney*, where the record clearly shows that social workers, and other members of Joshua's "Child Protection Team," grossly and repeatedly failed to help the child. Blackmun began by wanting to trust experts, but he has learned that he often cannot. These experts—and through them the state—purported to come to the aid of "one in need," yet they remained eerily aloof from the suffering of a helpless child.[78]

A crucial lesson of our bleak century, and of the Holocaust in particular, is that it can be morally reprehensible to do nothing in the face of evil. There are, in fact, Supreme Court precedents that suggest that "a State may be found complicit in an injury even if it did not create the situation that caused the harm."[79] Even if there were no such precedents, however, judges as well as other officials of the state ought to be held accountable when they are complicit with evil, even when they operate in the guise of "merely following the rules."

Judges are people, too. They ought not to be entirely immune

---

74. *Id.*

75. 400 U.S. 309 (1971).

76. Blackmun directly rejected the unconstitutional conditions argument in the welfare context: "Mrs. James has the 'right' to refuse the home visit, but a consequence in the form of cessation of aid . . . flows from that refusal. The choice is entirely hers, and nothing of constitutional magnitude is involved." *Id.* at 324. More in keeping with his *DeShaney* dissent, he also stressed the child's separate interest and the particulars of the individual child's case, because "[a]ll was not always well with the infant Maurice (skull fracture, a dent in the head, a possible rat bite)." *Id.* at 322 n.9.

77. *Id.* at 323.

78. Justice Brennan notes that the social worker dutifully recorded her perceptions of what Joshua was undergoing, in detail that is "almost eerie in light of her failure to act upon it." *DeShaney*, 109 S. Ct. at 1010. For a cogent analysis of the attitudes about family violence embedded in law, see M. Minow, Law and Violence (Mar. 24, 1989) (unpublished manuscript).

79. *DeShaney*, 109 S. Ct. at 1009 (Brennan, J., dissenting) (citing Shelley v. Kraemer, 334 U.S. 1 (1948); Burton v. Wilmington Parking Auth., 365 U.S. 715 (1961)).

from the blame we share if we collaborate passively upon encountering reprehensible acts. It is horrific to be so complacent as to lack ambition to do better. It may be even worse to purport to help someone but to do nothing. We are to blame, surely, if we attend only to ourselves and our business as usual, while we claim to seek justice. We fail legally as well as morally if we do nothing when we have the direct chance—but lack adequate aspiration—to promote "the betterment of the human condition."[80]

---

80. A.S. MILLER & M. FEINRIDER, NUCLEAR WEAPONS AND LAW at x (1984).

JOURNAL OF FAMILY LAW

University of Louisville School of Law

Volume Twenty-Eight	1989-90	Number One

ALLEGATIONS OF CHILD SEXUAL ABUSE IN CUSTODY AND VISITATION LITIGATION: RECOMMENDATIONS FOR IMPROVED FACT FINDING AND CHILD PROTECTION

By John E.B. Myers*

Elizabeth Morgan, M.D. languished in the Washington, D.C. jail for more than two years. Dr. Morgan committed no crime. She was incarcerated for civil contempt because she refused to disclose the whereabouts of her six-year-old daughter to the judge presiding over custody litigation between Morgan and her former husband, Dr. Eric Foretich. Morgan claims that during periods of visitation, Foretich molested their daughter; a claim Foretich denies.[1]

---

* Professor of Law, University of the Pacific, McGeorge School of Law, Sacramento, CA.

I wish to express thanks to David Corwin, M.D. for his valuable comments on drafts of this article.

[1] For information on Dr. Morgan's case see Lewis, *The Limits of the Law*, N.Y. Times, Dec. 22, 1988, at A23, col. 1; Lewis, *Judgment of Solomon*, N.Y. Times, Dec. 15, 1988, at A39, col. 1; McGrory, *Morgan's Choice*, Wash. Post, Dec. 15, 1988, at A2; *A Mother's Tale: Why I'm Taking No Chances With the Courts*, U.S. NEWS & WORLD REP., June 13, 1988, at 30; Chin & Podesta, *Stalemate for High Stakes*, PEOPLE, Jan. 23, 1989, at 84; Szegedy-Maszak, *Who's to Judge?*, N.Y. Times, May 21, 1989 (Magazine), at 28; Elson, *A Hard Case of Contempt: Elizabeth Morgan: Mother Courage or a Paranoid Liar*, N.Y. Times, Sept. 18, 1989, at 66.

On September 23, 1989, President Bush signed a bill designed to free Dr. Morgan. The bill establishes a one year limit on the time individuals can be incarcerated for civil contempt in the District of Columbia. Dr. Morgan has been released. *See* Dowd, *Bush Signs a Bill to Release a*

Elizabeth Morgan is not alone in defying the law. Convinced that courts are failing to protect children from sexual abuse by former spouses, a growing number of parents are hiding their children.[2] Some, like Morgan, go to jail when they refuse to comply with decisions regarding custody or visitation. Other parents disappear with their children, vanishing into what some call the "new underground railway." Like its 19th century counterpart that aided runaway slaves, the new railway is a loose affiliation of normally law abiding citizens who are willing to risk prosecution to help people flee what they perceive as an unjust system.

The fact that hundreds—perhaps thousands—of parents are giving up on the legal system to protect their children indicates that public confidence in the law is eroding. The time is ripe to grapple with the tremendously complex issues that arise when allegations of child sexual abuse occur in custody and visitation litigation. To that end, Section I of this Article discusses the prevalence of child sexual abuse. Section II notes the harmful psychological effects of sexual abuse. Section III discusses evidentiary and constitutional issues cutting across all forums in which allegations of child sexual abuse are litigated.[3] Section IV fo-

---

Mother, N.Y. Times, Sept. 24, 1989, at 14, col. 4.

Dr. Morgan commenced a civil action in federal court on behalf of her daughter against Dr. Foretich. *See* Morgan v. Foretich, 846 F.2d 941 (4th Cir. 1988).

[2] *See Mothers on the Run*, U.S. NEWS & WORLD REP., June 13, 1988, at 22; Podesta & Chin, *Run for Their Lives, Saving the Children: Parents on the Run*, PEOPLE, Jan. 23, 1989, at 71. *See also* Apel, *Custodial Parents, Child Sexual Abuse, and the Legal System: Beyond Contempt*, 38 AM. L. REV. 491 (1989).

[3] Allegations of child sexual abuse arise in at least eight types of legal proceedings.
   (1) The past decade has witnessed a marked increase in criminal prosecution of child sexual abuse.
   (2) Because a significant number of perpetrators are minors, prosecution in juvenile court is also common.
   (3) Under its abuse and neglect jurisdiction, the juvenile court plays the key judicial role in protecting sexually abused children.
   (4) Allegations of sexual abuse arise in litigation to terminate parental rights.
   (5) An increasing number of victims are employing civil litigation to seek monetary damages from perpetrators. *See, e.g.*, Snyder v. Boy Scouts of Am., Inc., 305 Cal. App. 3d 1318, 253 Cal. Rptr. 156 (1988)(action barred by statute of limitations); E.W. v. D.C.H., 754 P.2d 817 (Mont. 1988)(action barred by statute of limitations); Saint Michelle v. Robinson, 52 Wash. App. 309, 759 P.2d 467 (1988)(action not barred by statute of limitations).
   (6) Civil actions are commenced against child protective service agencies and professionals for failing to protect children from sexual abuse. *See* DeShaney v. Winnebago Co. Dep't Social Servs., 109 S. Ct. 998 (1989)(state not liable under 28 U.S.C. § 1983 for failure to protect child from physical abuse inflicted by parent; child was not in state custody at time of abuse).

cuses on issues of special concern in child custody and visitation litigation incident to divorce. Finally, Section V offers recommendations for improving the response of the legal system to allegations of child sexual abuse arising in custody and visitation litigation.

I. INCIDENCE OF CHILD SEXUAL ABUSE

It is difficult to estimate how many children are sexually abused each year.[4] Estimates of sexual abuse come primarily from two sources. The first is the child abuse reporting laws which exist in every state. These laws require professionals who interact with children to report suspected abuse and neglect to law enforcement or child protection authorities.[5] The American Humane Association compiled reporting statistics from a sample of states and estimated that in 1986 there were 132,000 substantiated cases of child sexual abuse.[6] Most child sexual

---

(7) State regulatory agencies bring administrative proceedings against day care operators and professionals to suspend or revoke licenses. *See, e.g.,* Seering v. Dep't of Social Servs., 194 Cal. App. 3d 298, 239 Cal. Rptr. 422 (1987).

(8) In a small but increasing number of cases, allegations of child sexual abuse arise in custody and visitation litigation in family court.

[4] *See* Peters, Wyatt & Finkelhor, *Prevalence*, A SOURCEBOOK ON CHILD SEXUAL ABUSE 15, 16 (D. Finkelhor ed. 1986)[hereinafter *Prevalence*]("The reality is that there is not yet any consensus among social scientists about the national scope of sexual abuse. No statistics yet exist that fully satisfy the request that journalists and others so frequently make for an accurate national estimate").

[5] *See generally* J. MYERS & W. PETERS, CHILD ABUSE REPORTING LEGISLATION IN THE 1980s (1987).

The approach of most reporting statutes is to require professionals who come in contact with children to report suspected physical abuse, sexual abuse, and neglect to designated law enforcement and/or child protection authorities. In addition to mandated reports from professionals, the statutes permit lay people to report suspected abuse.

[6] American Humane Association, HIGHLIGHTS OF OFFICIAL CHILD NEGLECT AND ABUSE REPORTING 1986, 23 (1988)[hereinafter American Humane]. The Highlights indicate that the estimated rate of child sexual abuse is 20.89 cases per 10,000 children. *Id.*

One of the persistent problems in determining the incidence of child abuse is determining when a report of abuse is substantiated. American Humane acknowledges this dilemma, writing:

A precise definition of case substantiation cannot be offered because the definition and policy varies from state to state. Nevertheless, all definitions imply a degree of certainty that the involved child is in fact at risk, and in many states that some level of intervention is warranted in the child's behalf.

Id. at 11.

The report notes a continuing trend toward increased reports of child sexual abuse. "The percent of sexual abuse cases increased between 1983 and 1986, from approximately nine percent to 16 percent of all maltreated children." *Id.* at 22. The report goes on to state that:

[E]stimates of the number of children sexually maltreated and the rate of sexual maltreatment have increased significantly between 1976 and 1986. In particular, the increase in 1985 in the proportion of sexual maltreatment translates into an increase of

abuse is never reported,[7] however, and the true incidence rate is probably substantially higher.[8]

The second source of data on the incidence of child sexual abuse comes from a small but growing number of sociological studies.[9] While these studies employ differing methodologies and definitions of sexual abuse, they consistently point to one finding: Child sexual abuse is widespread. In 1986, Peters, Wyatt, and Finkelhor reviewed nineteen studies estimating the percentage of females subjected to sexual abuse.[10] The average rate of sexual abuse across the studies was 22.7%. In other words, more than twenty percent of girls apparently experience some form of sexual abuse. Thirteen of the studies reviewed by Peters and her colleagues estimate the percentage of males subjected to abuse. The average rate for boys was 10.2%. Whatever the methodological shortcomings of individual studies, their cumulative weight cannot be ignored.

Addressing child sexual abuse in day care is also important. In 1988, David Finkelhor and his colleagues published the results of a national study of sexual abuse in day care.[11] The "study attempted to identify all cases of sexual abuse in day care reported nationwide during the period of January 1983 through December 1985."[12] The research disclosed 270 substantiated cases of sexual abuse, involving a total of 1,639 child victims.[13] Extrapolating from available data, the researchers estimate that the actual incidence is "500 to 550 reported and substantiated cases and 2500 victims for the three-year period. . . . [We] estimate that the risk to children is 5.5 children sexually abused

---

about 27 percent from 1984 in the estimated number of children who are reported as sexually maltreated throughout the country.
Id. at 23-24.

[7] *See* Russell, *The Incidence and Prevalence of Intrafamilial and Extrafamilial Sexual Abuse of Female Children,* 7 CHILD ABUSE & NEGLECT 133 (1983).

[8] *See Prevalence, supra* note 4, at 18. The authors refer to American Humane Association estimates of sexual abuse for years through 1983 and write that "most people consider the scope of the problem reflected in such figures to be a substantial underestimate."
See also D. Whitcomb, EXEMPLARY PROJECTS ASSISTING CHILD VICTIMS OF SEXUAL ABUSE 1, 12 (1982)("As many as 100,000 to 500,000 children may be sexually abused each year").

[9] The studies are discussed and critically analyzed in D. FINKELHOR, A HANDBOOK ON CHILD SEXUAL ABUSE (1986).

[10] *See Prevalence, supra* note 4.

[11] *See* D. Finkelhor, *Sexual Abuse in Day Care: A National Study, Executive Summary* (Family Research Laboratory, University of New Hampshire, 1988).

[12] *Id.* at 3.

[13] *Id.*

for 10,000 enrolled" in day care.[14] Thus, while the percentage of children abused in day care is small,[15] the number of incidents and victims is cause for considerable concern.

Age offers no protection from sexual abuse.[16] Victims range from infants[17] to adolescents.[18] One pedophile organization has a slogan, "Sex by year eight or else it's too late."[19]

II. HARMFUL EFFECTS OF CHILD SEXUAL ABUSE

Clinical and scientific research establishes that for many children, sexual abuse has serious short and long-term consequences.[20] In partic-

---

[14] *Id.* at 4 (original emphasis removed).

[15] Finkelhor cautions that while the estimate of 500 to 550 cases is a "large number, it must be put in the context of 229,000 day care facilities nationwide serving seven million children." *Id.* at 3.

[16] *See* American Humane, *supra* note 6, at 21, table 5, which reads:

Comparison of Age Descriptions

Child Abuse and Neglect

Age	All U.S. Children	Involved Children
0 - 5	34%	43%
6 - 11	31%	33%
12 - 17	35%	24%

[17] *See In re* D.T., 229 N.J. Super. 509, 552 A.2d 189 (1988)(four-month-old victim).

Not only are there many young victims, a surprising number of perpetrators are children too. *See* Cantwell, *Child Sexual Abuse: Very Young Perpetrators,* 12 CHILD ABUSE & NEGLECT 579 (1988); Johnson, *Child Perpetrators—Children Who Molest Other Children: Preliminary Findings,* 12 CHILD ABUSE & NEGLECT 219 (1988)(describing perpetrators ranging in age from four to thirteen).

[18] *See* Powers & Eckenrode, *The Maltreatment of Adolescents,* 12 CHILD ABUSE & NEGLECT 189 (1988)("Research clearly refutes the myth that young children are the main victims of abuse and neglect and that the risk of maltreatment declines as children grow older").

[19] de Young, *The Indignant Page: Techniques of Neutralization in the Publications of Pedophile Organizations,* 12 CHILD ABUSE & NEGLECT 583 (1988). Dr. de Young discusses American pedophile organizations, all of which "advocate similar goals: the abolition or lowering of age of consent laws; an end to the social harassment and legal prosecution of pedophiles; and the demythologizing of adult sexual behavior with children." *Id.* at 584.

[20] *See* LASTING EFFECTS OF CHILD SEXUAL ABUSE (G. Wyatt & G. Powell eds. 1988); Browne & Finkelhor, *Initial and Long-Term Effects: A Review of the Research,* A SOURCEBOOK ON CHILD SEXUAL ABUSE 143 (D. Finkelhor ed. 1986); Finkelhor & Browne, *Initial and Long-Term Effects: A Conceptual Framework,* A SOURCEBOOK ON CHILD SEXUAL ABUSE 143 (D. Finkelhor ed. 1986); Myers, Bays, Becker, Berliner, Corwin & Saywitz, *Expert Testimony in Child Sexual Abuse Litigation,* 68 NEB. L. REV. 1, 52-61 (1989)[hereinafter *Expert Testimony*]("child sexual abuse often has devastating long-term consequences"); Sgroi, Porter & Blick, *Validation of Child Sexual Abuse,* HANDBOOK OF CLINICAL INTERVENTION IN CHILD SEXUAL

ular, sexual abuse is related to a variety of medical and mental health problems. Lucy Berliner and her colleagues describe research on the effects of child sexual abuse:

> The earliest systematic reports focused on incest victims who were receiving psychotherapy, and found that incest victims have more severe symptoms than patients who have not been sexually abused. Since then, a number of studies of women in the general population have confirmed that abuse survivors experience higher levels of symptomatic distress. Adult survivors are more depressed, more anxious, have more dissociative and somatic symptoms, and have lower self-esteem. Survivors are also at significantly higher risk of developing depression, various anxiety disorders, including post traumatic stress disorder (PTSD), substance abuse disorders, and sexual dysfunction. High rates of sexual abuse are found in the histories of patients with conversion reactions, suicidality, self mutilation, multiple personality disorder, chronic pelvic pain, and in women with eating disorders. Childhood sexual abuse is found in a large percentage of adolescent prostitutes and runaways.
>
> Since the late 1970s, numerous publications have described the negative effects of sexual abuse on children. These publications described certain general patterns of reaction found in clinical samples of sexually abused children. For the most part, children described in these studies were victims of incest. Numerous negative effects are described, including fears and anxieties, feelings of guilt, shame and anger, self-destructiveness, and inappropriate sexual or aggressive behavior.[21]

The relevant literature refutes any notion that child sexual abuse is benign. While most sexually abused children go on to lead productive adult lives, there is no doubt that sexual abuse leaves lasting psychological scars in many victims.

III. EVIDENTIARY AND CONSTITUTIONAL ISSUES IN CHILD SEXUAL ABUSE LITIGATION

Child sexual abuse is often exceedingly difficult to prove. Medical evidence is lacking in most cases.[22] The victim is usually the only eyewitness; therefore, the ability to prove abuse and to identify the perpetrator frequently hinge on the child's ability to testify. While the great majority of children age four and older possess the psychological capacity to testify, some are intimidated into silence, some recant, and others are poor witnesses. The paucity of evidence that plagues child sexual

---

ABUSE 39 (S. Sgroi ed. 1982); *The Lasting Effects of Child Sexual Abuse*, 2 J. INTERPERSONAL VIOLENCE 347 (1987).

[21] *Expert Testimony, supra* note 20, at 53 (footnotes omitted).

[22] *See id.* at 34.

abuse litigation combines with the unique capabilities, limitations, and needs of child witnesses to create complex evidentiary and constitutional issues.[23] Four of these issues are discussed below.

A. Testimonial Competence of Children

Many adults have doubts about child witnesses.[24] Psychological research conducted during the early years of this century fueled this skepticism.[25] One researcher asked, "When are we going to give up, in all civilized nations, listening to children in courts of law?"[26] The picture is different today. Children testify with increasing frequency, and contemporary psychological research indicates that children are better witnesses than many adults expect.[27]

Courts have not required that children attain a minimum age before allowing them to testify.[28] In a minority of jurisdictions, children under certain ages (typically ten, twelve, or fourteen) are presumed to be incompetent unless the trial judge determines after questioning that they possess the capacity to testify.[29] Under the influence of the Federal Rules of Evidence, a growing number of states hold that "[e]very person is competent to be a witness,"[30] including children.[31] Legislatures in a few states have gone a step further by enacting statutes designed to ensure that child victims of sexual abuse are always permitted to testify.[32] To be competent to testify, a child must possess the

---

[23] *See generally* J. MYERS, CHILD WITNESS LAW AND PRACTICE (1987)[hereinafter CHILD WITNESS].

[24] For discussion of psychological research on the reaction of mock jurors to child witnesses, see PERSPECTIVES ON CHILDREN'S TESTIMONY (S. Ceci, D. Ross & M. Toglia eds. 1989); *Expert Testimony, supra* note 20, at 92-106.

[25] *See* Goodman, *Children's Testimony in Historical Perspective*, 40 J. SOC. ISSUES 9 (1984).

[26] Varendonck, *Les temoignages d'enfants dans un process retentissant*, 11 ARCHIVES DE PSYCHOLOGIE 129 (1911).

[27] *See Expert Testimony, supra* note 20, at 92-106 for discussion of relevant psychological literature.

[28] *See* Wheeler v. United States, 159 U.S. 523, 524 (1895); CHILD WITNESS, *supra* note 23, at § 3.2 (citing cases).

[29] *See* Head v. State, 519 N.E.2d 152 (Ind. 1988); CHILD WITNESS, *supra* note 23, at § 3.10.

[30] FED. R. EVID. 601.

[31] *See, e.g.*, State v. Dwyer, 143 Wis. 2d 448, __, 422 N.W.2d 121, 126 (Wis. Ct. App. 1988)(following adoption of state counterpart of FED. R. EVID. 601, the court of appeals wrote: "Our supreme court has specifically found that the former questions of competency are now credibility issues to be dealt with by the trier of fact"); CHILD WITNESS, *supra* note 23, at § 3.8.

[32] *See, e.g.*, COLO. REV. STAT. § 13-90-106(1)(b)(II) (1987); MO. ANN. STAT. § 491.060(2)(Vernon 1989); UTAH CODE ANN. § 76-5-410 (1988).

See also State v. Williams, 729 S.W.2d 197 (Mo.), *cert. denied*, 108 S. Ct. 296 (1987)(up-

capacity to observe,[33] sufficient memory to recollect events,[34] the capacity to communicate,[35] an appreciation of the moral duty to tell the truth,[36] and an understanding of the difference between truth and falsehood.[37]

Adults sometimes assume that young children are less observant than older children and adults. Psychological research discloses, however, that young children are not necessarily less discerning observers. Even preschool children possess the sensory capacity to observe the world around them and to register accurate perceptions.[38]

Do young children have the ability to remember what they observe? The answer is yes for the great majority of children.[39] While older children and adults are better at some memory tasks than young children, psychological research discloses that "given simple, supportive questions, even young children generally have sufficient memory skills to respond to the recall demands of testimony."[40] Children are particularly good at remembering the central details of relatively simple events that have personal meaning for them.

Children generally possess the capacity to communicate with sufficient clarity to make themselves understood.[41] The fact that a youngster uses childlike language does not render the child incompetent.[42] Furthermore, a child is not incompetent because he or she hesitates to

---

holding constitutionality of Missouri statute permitting all child victims to testify); CHILD WITNESS, *supra* note 23, at § 3.11.

[33] CHILD WITNESS, *supra* note 23, at § 3.12.

[34] *In re* A.H.B., 491 A.2d 490, 492 (D.C. 1985); CHILD WITNESS, *supra* note 23, at § 3.14.

[35] Rhea v. State, 705 S.W.2d 165 (Tex. Ct. App. 1985)(three-year-old child not competent; child could not communicate adequately); CHILD WITNESS, *supra* note 23, at § 3.15.

[36] *See In re* R.R., 79 N.J. 97, 398 A.2d 76 (1979); CHILD WITNESS, *supra* note 23, at § 3.19.

[37] *See* Heckathorne v. State, 697 S.W.2d 8 (Tex. Ct. App. 1985); CHILD WITNESS, *supra* note 23, at § 3.18.

[38] *See* CHILD WITNESS, *supra* note 23, at § 3.12 (discussing relevant psychological literature).

[39] *See id.* at §§ 3.14, 10.17-10.27; Melton, *Children's Competency to Testify,* 5 L. & HUMAN BEHAVIOR 73 (1981); Myers, *The Testimonial Competence of Children,* 25 J. FAM. L. 287 (1986-87); *Expert Testimony, supra* note 20, at 95-7; Saywitz, *The Credibility of Child Witnesses,* 10 FAM. ADVOC. 38, 40 (1988).

[40] G. MELTON, J. PETRILA, N. POYTHRESS & C. SLOBOGIN, PSYCHOLOGICAL EVALUATIONS FOR THE COURTS § 5.06 at 102 (1987).

[41] *See* Jones & Krugman, *Can a Three-Year-Old Child Bear Witness to Her Sexual Assault and Attempted Murder?,* 10 CHILD ABUSE & NEGLECT 253 (1986)(answering yes).

[42] State v. Lairby, 699 P.2d 1187, 1206 n.23 (Utah 1984), *overruled on other grounds,* State v. Ossana, 739 P.2d 628 (Utah 1987)(fact that six-year-old victim of sexual abuse used word *winky* to describe penis did not render her incompetent).

answer questions.[43] Even a total refusal to answer some questions does not lead automatically to a finding of incompetence. In one case, for example, a six-year-old took the stand; "[t]owards the end of her cross-examination, she refused to listen to questions and placed her fingers in her ears."[44] Despite this rather emphatic unwillingness to communicate, the court ruled that the child was competent.[45]

When communication breakdowns occur with child witnesses, the problem usually rests with the attorney, not the child. Try as they might, attorneys have difficulty avoiding legal terminology that children do not understand. Psychologist Karen Saywitz reminds us that "[t]o young children, a *case* is something you carry papers in, a *hearing* is something you do with your ears, *charges* are something you do with a credit card, *motion* is like waving your arms, *parties* are for getting presents, a *minor* is someone who digs coal."[46]

The great majority of children understand the obligation to tell the truth in court.[47] Furthermore, most children are sufficiently aware of the difference between truth and falsehood to testify competently.[48] Adults sometimes wonder, however, whether the rich fantasy life of childhood causes children to confuse the real and the imagined. While children pretend in their play, they seem to know when they are pretending. During play tea parties, for example, preschoolers take imaginary sips from empty cups, but they do not attempt to eat plastic cookies. Modern research indicates that children may be less likely than adults to differentiate fact from fantasy in some situations, but not in others.[49] At this point in time, there is insufficient scientific evidence to support an argument that children's testimony should be excluded because children cannot differentiate fact from fantasy. In the majority of cases, children can distinguish the real from the imaginary.

With proper support and preparation, children as young as three

---

[43] *See* State v. Armstrong, 453 So. 2d 1256, 1259 (La. Ct. App. 1984); State v. Weisenstein, 367 N.W.2d 201, 204 (S.D. 1985).

[44] Pendleton v. Commonwealth, 685 S.W.2d 549 (Ky. 1985).

[45] *Id.* at 551.

[46] Saywitz, *Bullying Children Won't Work*, 10 FAM. ADVOC. 16, 18 (1988)(emphasis in orginal); Saywitz, *Children's Conceptions of the Legal System: "Court Is a Place to Play Basketball*," PERSPECTIVES ON CHILDREN'S TESTIMONY 131 (S. Ceci, D. Ross & M. Toglia eds. 1989).

[47] *See* CHILD WITNESS, *supra* note 23, at § 3.19.

[48] *See id.* at § 3.18.

[49] *See Expert Testimony, supra* note 20, at 103-04 for discussion of psychological research on children's ability to distinguish fact from fantasy.

can testify effectively.[50] The fact that the individual on the stand is a child whose head is barely visible above the rail of the witness box, and whose feet dangle far above the floor should not automatically discredit the testimony. Young children provide accurate, often compelling, testimony.

B. *Admissibility of Children's Hearsay Statements*

Children's hearsay statements assume extraordinary importance in sexual abuse litigation.[51] The child's out-of-court description of abuse is sometimes the most important evidence in the case.[52] While there are many exceptions to the hearsay rule, only a handful play a role in child sexual abuse litigation.[53] The excited utterance exception is used most frequently.[54] The exception for statements to physicians providing diagnostic or treatment services is also important.[55] In states that have a residual or catchall exception, reliable hearsay that does not fit within a traditional exception is admissible.[56] Beginning in 1982, a growing number of jurisdictions adopted special hearsay exceptions for children.[57] The child hearsay exceptions authorize the admission, in child abuse cases, of reliable out-of-court statements by children under speci-

---

[50] *See* State v. Hussey, 521 A.2d 278 (Me. 1987)(three-year-old competent).

[51] *See* Note, *A Comprehensive Approach to Child Hearsay in Sex Abuse Cases*, 83 COLUM. L. REV. 1745 (1983). *See generally* CHILD WITNESS, *supra* note 23, at §§ 5.1-5.41.

[52] It is important to note that many of a child's out-of-court verbal utterances and acts related to sexual abuse are not hearsay because they are not assertions. *See* CHILD WITNESS, *supra* note 23, at §§ 5.2-5.11 for a discussion of the importance of nonassertive verbal and nonverbal conduct in child abuse litigation. *See, e.g., In re* Penelope B., 104 Wash. 2d 643, 709 P.2d 1185 (1985) for a case discussing nonassertive utterances in child abuse litigation.

[53] The following hearsay exceptions play an important role in child abuse litigation: excited utterances, statements for purposes of diagnosis or treatment, state of mind, present sense impression, business records exception, the residual exception, and special exceptions designed to admit statements by child victim/witnesses.

Also of great importance in child sexual abuse litigation are children's statements that are admissible under the theory of fresh complaint of rape. Theoretically, a fresh complaint is not hearsay, thus fresh complaint evidence is not barred by the hearsay rule. *See* CHILD WITNESS, *supra* note 23, at § 5.34 for a discussion of fresh complaint evidence.

[54] FED. R. EVID. 803(2). *See* Morgan v. Foretich, 846 F.2d 941 (4th Cir. 1988)(excellent discussion of excited utterance and other exceptions); CHILD WITNESS, *supra* note 23, § 5.33, at 329.

[55] FED. R. EVID. 803(4). *See* Mosteller, *Child Sexual Abuse and Statements for the Purpose of Medical Diagnosis or Treatment*, 67 N.C.L. REV. 257 (1989); CHILD WITNESS, *supra* note 23, at § 5.36.

[56] FED. R. EVID. 803(24), 804(b)(5). *See* CHILD WITNESS, *supra* note 23, § 5.37, at 362.

[57] *See, e.g.,* WASH. REV. CODE ANN. § 9A.44.120 (1987 Supp.). *See* CHILD WITNESS, *supra* note 23, § 5.38, at 372.

fied ages. The child hearsay exceptions have withstood constitutional challenge.[58] In child custody and visitation litigation incident to divorce, the state of mind exception plays an important role. This exception is discussed in the subsection below addressing evidentiary recommendations.

C. *Video Testimony and the Confrontation Clause*

Testifying is difficult for most witnesses, but when the witness is a child, the experience can be overwhelming.[59] In criminal trials especially, many professionals believe selected children should be spared the ordeal of testifying in open court before the defendant and a room full of strangers. Many states responded to this belief with legislation authorizing video testimony from young children. The video testimony statutes fall into four categories: (1) videotaped interviews, (2) videotaped depositions, (3) videotaped preliminary hearing testimony, and (4) live trial testimony via closed-circuit television. Most video testimony statutes contemplate circumstances in which children testify outside the physical presence of the defendant.

While video testimony raises several constitutional issues,[60] the question receiving the greatest judicial attention is the impact of video testimony on the criminal defendant's sixth amendment right to confront accusatory witnesses.[61] Does the state interest in protecting children from the rigors of testifying ever outweigh the defendant's constitutional right to a face-to-face encounter with the child? With its 1988 decision in *Coy v. Iowa*,[62] the U.S. Supreme Court made clear that face-to-face confrontation is the rule, and any exceptions must be based on an individualized showing of necessity.

---

[58] *See, e.g.*, Cogburn v. State, 292 Ark. 564, 732 S.W.2d 807 (1987); Perez v. State, 536 So. 2d 206 (Fla. 1988); State v. Myatt, 237 Kan. 17, 697 P.2d 836 (1985); State v. Loughton, 747 P.2d 426 (Utah 1987); State v. Ryan, 103 Wash. 2d 165, 691 P.2d 197 (1984)(en banc); Buckley v. State, 758 S.W.2d 339 (Tex. Ct. App. 1988); CHILD WITNESS, *supra* note 23, at § 5.38.

[59] *See* Schwartz-Kenny, Wilson & Goodman, *An Examination of Child Witness Accuracy and the Emotional Effects on Children of Testifying in Court*, UNDERSTANDING AND MANAGING CHILD SEXUAL ABUSE (K. Oates ed. Sydney, Australia: Harcourt, Brace, Janovich, in press)[hereinafter *Emotional Effects*].

[60] For a discussion of constitutional issues raised by video testimony see CHILD WITNESS, *supra* note 23, at §§ 6.1-6.9.

[61] The U.S. CONST. amend. VI provides in part that "[i]n all criminal prosecutions, the accused shall . . . be confronted with the witnesses against him."

For a summary of recent cases see the supplement to CHILD WITNESS, *supra* note 23, §§ 6.1—6.9.

[62] 108 S. Ct. 2798, 2803 (1988).

Post-*Coy* decisions hold that the right to face-to-face confrontation is not absolute, and in selected cases, the Constitution permits children to testify outside the physical presence of the defendant.[63] Courts agree, however, that before the right to face-to-face confrontation may be abridged, the state must make a convincing showing that the child requires the special accommodation of video testimony.[64] Courts take several views on what the state must show before it can permissibly dispense with face-to-face confrontation. Some courts hold that confrontation may be curtailed only when a face-to-face encounter would render the child unavailable as a witness.[65] A second approach links the use of video testimony to a finding that a face-to-face encounter would impair the child's ability to testify accurately.[66] Courts adopting the second approach hold that the most important consideration must be the accuracy of the child's testimony, not the psychological trauma of testifying.[67] A third approach focuses primary attention on the trauma to the child.[68] If the court is convinced that testifying would be sufficiently traumatic to the child, it may dispense with face-to-face confrontation.[69]

---

[63] *See, e.g.*, State v. Vincent, 159 Ariz. 418, 768 P.2d 150 (Ariz. 1989)(en banc). The Arizona Supreme Court upheld the constitutionality of an Arizona statute permitting videotaped depositions to be taken out of the presence of the defendant. The court emphasized, however, that dispensing with face-to-face confrontation must be based on an individualized showing of necessity. It is not permissible to rely on generalized assumptions about the trauma of testifying. There must be specific evidence about the impact of testifying on the particular child.

See also Glendening v. State, 536 So. 2d 212 (Fla. 1988); *In re* B.F., 230 N.J. Super. 153, 553 A.2d 40 (1989).

But see Long v. State, 742 S.W.2d 302 (Tex. Ct. App. 1987), *cert. denied*, 108 S. Ct. 1301 (1988)(striking down on confrontation grounds a statute permitting admission of videotaped interviews). *See also* Powell v. State, 765 S.W.2d 435 (Tex. Ct. App. 1988).

[64] *See, e.g., Vincent*, 768 P.2d at 150; *In re* B.F., 230 N.J. Super. at 153, 553 A.2d 40 (state must carry burden of proving necessity by clear and convincing evidence).

[65] *See, e.g., Vincent*, 768 P.2d 150; State v. Black, 537 A.2d 1154 (Me. 1988); State v. Twist, 528 A.2d 1250 (Me. 1987); Wildermuth v. State, 310 Md. 496, 530 A.2d 275 (1987); State v. Lindner, 142 Wis. 2d 783, 419 N.W.2d 352 (Ct. App. 1987); CAL. PENAL CODE § 1347(b)(2)(West Supp. 1988).

[66] *See, e.g.*, State v. Bonello, 210 Conn. 51, 554 A.2d 277 (1989); State v. Jarzbek, 204 Conn. 683, 529 A.2d 1245 (1987), *cert. denied*, 108 S. Ct. 1017 (1988).

[67] *Bonello*, 554 A.2d at 277; *Jarzbek*, 529 A.2d at 1244.

[68] *See, e.g.*, Glendening v. State, 536 So. 2d 212 (Fla. 1988).

[69] Recent psychological research on the trauma of testifying indicates several factors that appear to be related to the likelihood children will experience emotional problems following involvement in the legal system. Schwartz-Kenney, Wilson & Goodman compared the psychological well-being of sexually abused children who testified in court with sexually abused children who did not testify. The researchers write:

[O]n average children who testified fared worse than children who did not have to take the stand. This generalization was only true for a subset of children, however. That is,

The confrontation clause does not apply in child custody and visitation litigation.[70] Moreover, the complex sixth amendment issues discussed above do not arise in family court. Most courts hold that in custody and visitation litigation the trial judge may interview children in chambers, outside the physical presence of the child's parents.[71] The preferred policy is to permit counsel to attend the interview and to question the child. The child's testimony should be recorded. Finally, it is advisable for the court to make a finding that testimony outside the parents' presence will serve the child's best interest and will assist the child to be more forthcoming while testifying.

D. *Expert Psychological Testimony*

Few aspects of child sexual abuse litigation generate more confusion and disagreement than expert psychological testimony.[72] Uncertainty abounds for several reasons. First, psychological knowledge about child sexual abuse is still developing, and many questions remain

---

some children who testified did indeed improve over time whereas others did not. What factors distinguished the two groups? Children who were fortunate to have maternal support, whose cases were strengthened by corroborative evidence, or who only had to testify once were more likely to improve than children who did not have these benefits. Surprisingly, a number of factors thought to affect children's reactions to legal involvement did not predict their well-being, including psychological counseling, abuse severity (e.g., length of abuse, type of sexual act), and number of times the children were questioned by authorities such as police or social workers, during the investigation. These findings suggest that courtroom testimony has adverse effects on the well being of a subgroup of children.
Emotional Effects, supra note 59, at 65.

[70] For a discussion of the right to confrontation in juvenile court proceedings to determine abuse and neglect, see *In re* Mary S., 186 Cal. App. 3d 414, 230 Cal. Rptr. 726 (1986)(persons accused of child abuse in juvenile court have a right to confront witnesses against them. This right is not without exception, however. Trial judge may permit children to testify out of the physical presence of parents when children testify they are afraid of parents); *In re* Long, 313 N.W.2d 473, 478-79 (Iowa 1981)(court stated that sixth amendment does not apply in neglect proceedings. Court assumed without deciding that persons accused of neglect have a right to confront accusatory witnesses); *In re* James A., 505 A.2d 1386 (R.I. 1986); *In re* M.W., 374 N.W.2d 889, 893 (S.D. 1985)("The constitutional implications of the confrontation clause . . . are not present in a civil action. . . . We have recently held that dependency and neglect proceedings are civil in nature.").

[71] *See, e.g.,* Diggs v. Tyler, 525 So. 2d 1263, 1266 (La. Ct. App. 1988)(in child custody litigation incident to divorce, the court may interview the child in chambers without the parents present). *See also* H. Clark, Domestic Relations § 14.4, at 54-42 (2d ed. 1988).

[72] For in-depth treatment of expert testimony in child sexual abuse litigation see McCord, *Expert Psychological Testimony About Child Complainants in Sexual Abuse Prosecutions: A Foray into the Admissibility of Novel Psychological Evidence*, 77 J. Crim. L. & Criminology 1 (1986)[hereinafter McCord]; *Expert Testimony, supra* note 20.

unanswered. Second, some professionals who are permitted to testify as experts on sexual abuse lack genuine expertise. Third, some attorneys, mental health professionals, and courts misunderstand what is often called "syndrome" evidence.[73] Finally, attorneys sometimes fail to articulate the specific reason why expert psychological testimony is offered. For example, is the testimony offered as substantive evidence of abuse, or is the purpose of the testimony to rehabilitate a child witness' impeached credibility? Certain types of expert testimony are admissible for one purpose but not the other.

In an effort to dispel some of the confusion surrounding psychological testimony, a brief description of five categories of such testimony follows. A clear distinction is drawn between testimony offered as substantive evidence of sexual abuse, and testimony offered to rehabilitate a child's impeached credibility.

1. Expert Psychological Testimony as Substantive Evidence of Sexual Abuse

Psychological testimony designed to prove sexual abuse takes two forms.

(a) Expert Psychological Testimony Describing Behaviors Commonly Observed in Sexually Abused Children

Many sexually abused children demonstrate behavioral, cognitive, and emotional reactions to their abuse.[74] There is no single reaction observed in all sexually abused children. Approximately twenty percent of sexually abused children demonstrate no observable reaction.[75] Researchers have observed a substantial variety of reactions in sexually abused children, including anxiety, regression, sleep disturbance, acting out, depression, and nightmares.[76] An examination of these behaviors

---

[73] For discussion of "syndrome evidence" see *Expert Testimony, supra* note 20, at 58. Evidence of syndromes plays an important role in child abuse litigation. In physical abuse litigation, expert testimony describing the battered child syndrome is admissible to prove that a child's injuries were nonaccidental. *See* Myers & Carter, *Proof of Physical Child Abuse*, 53 Mo. L. Rev. 189 (1988). In child sexual abuse litigation, the child sexual abuse accommodation syndrome is useful to rehabilitate child victims' impeached credibility.

[74] *See Expert Testimony, supra* note 20, at 52-62.

[75] *See id.* at 58.

[76] *See generally* Sgroi, Porter & Blick, *Validation of Child Sexual Abuse*, Handbook of Clinical Intervention in Child Sexual Abuse 39, 40-41 (S. Sgroi ed. 1982); *Expert Testimony, supra* note 20, at 53-61.

quickly reveals, however, that they are also associated with a wide range of psychological problems that are not associated with sexual abuse.

While some of the behaviors observed in sexually abused children are consistent with a number of problems, others are linked more strongly with personal or vicarious sexual experience. Examples of such behaviors include age-appropriate knowledge of sexual acts or anatomy, sexualized play, and genitalia in young children's drawings.[77]

The presence of behaviors commonly observed in sexually abused children can be probative of abuse, and expert psychological testimony describing such behaviors should be admissible in selected cases. The probative value of such testimony is highest when there is a coalescence of three types of behaviors: (1) a central core of sexual behaviors which are strongly associated with sexual abuse; (2) nonsexual behaviors which are commonly observed in sexually abused children; and (3) medical evidence of sexual abuse. Probative value declines as sexual behaviors and medical evidence decrease in proportion to nonsexual behaviors. When the only evidence consists of a number of ambiguous, nonsexual behaviors, the evidence may lack any probative value, or its probative worth may be outweighed by the potential for unfair prejudice to the person accused of abuse.

A number of appellate courts which have considered the theory of substantive proof outlined above, reject it.[78] This across-the-board rejection is unwarranted, however. Evidence offered under this theory passes the test of relevance because the presence of behaviors commonly observed in sexually abused children increases the likelihood that the child was abused.[79] Furthermore, clinical and scientific literature supports cautious reliance on such evidence.[80] Rejecting this type of evidence is particularly inappropriate in bench trials where the possibility of jury confusion is eliminated. The argument for admission of

---

[77] *See Expert Testimony, supra* note 20, at 62-63.

[78] *See* State v. Moran, 151 Ariz. 378, 728 P.2d 248 (1986); State v. Hundnall, 293 S.C. 97, 359 S.E.2d 59 (1987). *See also Expert Testimony, supra* note 20, at 80-84.

In Anderson v. State, 749 P.2d 369, 374 (Alaska Ct. App. 1988), the court indicated that when expert testimony describing reactions commonly observed in sexually abused children is offered to prove abuse, the proponent must establish that the relevant scientific community accepts the ability of professionals to detect abuse in this fashion.

[79] *See* FED. R. EVID. 401 (defining relevant evidence).

[80] *See Expert Testimony, supra* note 20, *passim.* For a contrary view see McCord, *supra* note 72.

this evidence is persuasive when the probative value of evidence offered under this theory is considered in light of the difficulty of proving sexual abuse of young children.

The theory of proof discussed above is based on an assessment of behaviors commonly observed in sexually abused children. It is important to realize that this theory is not based on a psychological syndrome. Currently, a professional consensus does not exist on whether there is a psychological syndrome that detects or diagnoses child sexual abuse. Unfortunately, the theory of proof described above is too often mislabeled as syndrome evidence. In particular, the theory is confused with the child sexual abuse accommodation syndrome described by Dr. Roland Summit.[81] The accommodation syndrome was not intended as a diagnostic device. The fact that a child demonstrates characteristics seen in the accommodation syndrome does not prove abuse. By contrast, the fact that a child demonstrates behavior commonly observed in sexually abused children can be probative of sexual abuse. To reiterate, the theory of proof discussed above should not be confused with child sexual abuse accommodation syndrome. The theory is not based on a psychological syndrome and should not be labeled syndrome evidence.

(b)   Expert Psychological Testimony on Whether a Particular Child Was Sexually Abused

Expert psychological testimony on whether a particular child was sexually abused differs from the testimony discussed in the preceding subsection in one important respect. In the preceding subsection, the expert did not venture an opinion on whether a particular child was abused. Rather, the expert's testimony was limited to behaviors observed in the class of sexually abused children.[82] The testimony described in the present subsection goes the next step to an opinion that a particular child was abused.[83]

---

[81] Summit, *The Child Sexual Abuse Accommodation Syndrome*, 7 Child Abuse & Neglect 177 (1983).

[82] When expert testimony is limited to reactions observed in sexually abused children, the testimony takes one of two forms:

(1) The expert confines his or her testimony to a description of behaviors commonly observed in the class of sexually abused children, and lay testimony is adduced to establish that the particular child demonstrates such behaviors; or

(2) The expert describes behaviors commonly observed in the class of sexually abused children, and then goes on to testify that the child in the case at bench demonstrates such behaviors.

[83] Such testimony can take several forms. *See Expert Testimony, supra* note 20, at 70-71.

The admissibility of expert psychological testimony on whether a child was abused is a divisive issue. Some courts hold that such testimony is improper in all or nearly all circumstances.[84] Other courts reach the opposite conclusion.[85] The commentators are also divided.[86] In view of the current controversy surrounding expert psychological testimony on whether a child was sexually abused, it may be appropriate at the present time to eschew such testimony in criminal jury trials. Proceedings in family and juvenile court are another matter, however, and psychological testimony on whether abuse occurred is sometimes appropriate in these forums. Clinical and scientific literature supports cautious reliance on the ability of qualified professionals to formulate accurate clinical judgments about sexual abuse.[87] Recall that child sexual abuse is often very difficult to prove. The court needs all the relevant evidence that is available. Because cases are tried to the court, concern about jury confusion is eliminated. In juvenile and family court, the need to consider all relevant evidence works in tandem with the compelling state interest in protecting children from abuse to justify admission of expert psychological testimony on whether sexual abuse occurred.[88] The New York courts admit such testimony in dependency cases and there is much to commend the New York approach.[89]

---

[84] *See, e.g.*, Johnson v. State, 292 Ark. 632, 732 S.W.2d 817 (1987); Russell v. State, 289 Ark. 533, 712 S.W.2d 916 (1986); In re Amber B., 191 Cal. App. 3d 682, 236 Cal. Rptr. 623 (1987)(court determines that reaching a clinical judgment about whether a child was sexually abused on the basis of interviewing the child and the child's play with anatomically detailed dolls constitutes a novel form of proof; before such evidence can be admitted, the proponent must establish that the technique is generally accepted in the relevant professional community); State v. Haseltine, 120 Wis. 2d 92, 352 N.W.2d 673 (Ct. App. 1984).

[85] *See, e.g.*, Seering v. Dep't of Social Servs., 194 Cal. App. 3d 298, ___, 239 Cal. Rptr. 422, 432 (1987); Glendening v. State, 536 So. 2d 212 (Fla. 1988); Townsend v. State, 103 Nev. 113, 734 P.2d 705 (1987).

[86] *Compare* McCord, *supra* note 72 *with Expert Testimony*, *supra* note 20.

[87] *See Expert Testimony*, *supra* note 20, at 69-85.

[88] The state has a compelling parens patriae interest in protecting children from harm. *See* New York v. Ferber, 458 U.S. 747, 756 (1982); Globe Newspaper Co. v. Superior Court, 457 U.S. 596 (1982); Ginsberg v. New York, 390 U.S. 629 (1968); Prince v. Mass., 321 U.S. 158 (1944); State v. Jarzbek, 204 Conn. 683, ___, 529 A.2d 1245, 1253-54 (1987), *cert. denied*, 108 S. Ct. 1017 (1988); People v. Kahan, 15 N.Y.2d 311, 312, 206 N.E.2d 333, 334, 258 N.Y.S.2d 391, 392 (1965)(Fuld, J., concurring)(characterizing society's interest in the welfare of children as "transcendent").

[89] *See In re* Dona D., 141 Misc. 2d 46, 532 N.Y.S.2d 696 (Fam. Ct. 1988); In re E.M., 137 Misc. 2d 197, 520 N.Y.S.2d 327 (Fam. Ct. 1987); In re Donna K., 132 A.D.2d 1004, ___, 518 N.Y.S.2d 289, 290 (1987). The New York approach is discussed in *Expert Testimony*, *supra* note 20, at 79-80.

2. *Expert Psychological Testimony to Rehabilitate a Child's Impeached Credibility*

Courts are more accepting of expert psychological testimony designed to rehabilitate a child's credibility than they are of psychological testimony offered as substantive evidence of abuse. This subsection briefly discusses three types of rehabilitation testimony.

(a) Expert Psychological Testimony to Explain Behaviors
Such as Delay in Reporting and Recantation

In many child sexual abuse cases, the person accused of abuse hopes to impeach the child's credibility by pointing out that the child changed the story over time or recanted. Another common mode of impeachment is to establish that the child delayed reporting the abuse. Such impeachment is legitimate. However, when the defense concentrates its attack on delay, inconsistency, and recantation, the party attempting to prove abuse has a legitimate need to rehabilitate the child's credibility. Such rehabilitation often takes the form of expert testimony. The great majority of courts allow such testimony[90] to explain why sexually abused children delay reporting their abuse,[91] why children recant,[92] why childrens' descriptions of abuse are sometimes in-

---

[90] *See, e.g.,* State v. Davis, 422 N.W.2d 296, 299 (Minn. Ct. App. 1988)(court approves expert testimony to inform jury that running away from home is common among sexually abused adolescents); State v. Bailey, 89 N.C. App. 212, ___, 365 S.E.2d 651, 655 (1988)(expert could state why child would continue to cooperate with abuser); State v. Robinson, 431 N.W.2d 165 (Wis. 1988).

[91] *See, e.g.,* People v. Bowker, 203 Cal. App. 3d 385, 393-94, 249 Cal. Rptr. 886, 891 (1988); People v. Gray, 187 Cal. App. 3d 213, 216, 231 Cal. Rptr. 658, 660 (1986); People v. Dunnahoo, 152 Cal. App. 3d 561, 577, 199 Cal. Rptr. 796, 804 (1984); People v. Hampton, 746 P.2d 947 (Colo. 1987)(adult rape victim; rape trauma syndrome admitted to explain delay); Wheat v. State, 527 A.2d 269 (Del. 1987); People v. Matlock, 153 Mich. App. 171, ___, 395 N.W.2d 274, 277 (1986); State v. Sandberg, 406 N.W.2d 506, 511 (Minn. 1987); State v. Myers, 359 N.W.2d 604, 610 (Minn. 1984); *Davis,* 422 N.W.2d at 299; Smith v. State, 100 Nev. 570, 688 P.2d 326, 326-27 (1984); People v. Benjamin R., 103 A.D.2d 663, ___, 481 N.Y.S.2d 827, 831-32 (1984); State v. Garfield, 34 Ohio App. 3d 300, 302, 518 N.E.2d 568 (1986); State v. Hicks, 148 Vt. 459, ___, 535 A.2d 776, 777 (1987); State v. Petrich, 101 Wash. 2d 566, 683 P.2d 173, 179-80 (Ct. App. 1984); Scadden v. State, 732 P.2d 1036, 1046 (Wyo. 1987).

But see Dunnington v. State, 740 S.W.2d 896, 898-99 (Tex. Ct. App. 1987)(delay in reporting not beyond ken of jurors, therefore expert testimony not needed).

[92] *See, e.g.,* State v. Lindsey, 149 Ariz. 472, ___, 720 P.2d 73, 75 (1986); People v. Luna, 204 Cal. App. 3d 394, 250 Cal. Rptr. 878 (1988); People v. Bowker, 249 Cal. Rptr. 891 (1988); *Wheat,* 527 A.2d at 269; State v. Middleton, 294 Or. 427, ___, 657 P.2d 1215, 1220 (1983); *Davis,* 422 N.W.2d at 299-300.

consistent,[93] why abused children are angry,[94] and why some children want to continue living with the person who sexually abused them.[95]

(b)   Expert Psychological Testimony to Explain Developmental Differences Between Adult and Child Witnesses

The expert testimony described in this subsection is designed to rehabilitate a child's credibility following impeachment which asserts that children are less credible witnesses than adults. The thrust of such impeachment is that the child's developmental immaturity renders his or her testimony suspect. The impeaching attorney may try to raise doubts about the child's ability to resist suggestive questioning or to distinguish fact from fantasy. In light of psychological research indicating that some adults view children as less credible witnesses than adults,[96] such impeachment may be effective. To counter such impeachment, the court may permit expert testimony which informs the factfinder of psychological research indicating that children are not necessarily less reliable witnesses than adults.[97] For example, recent research indicates that children are less suggestible than many adults believe them to be.[98] When the defense seeks to capitalize on commonly held misconceptions about the testimonial capacity of children, expert rebuttal testimony is sometimes appropriate.[99]

(c)   Expert Psychological Testimony Regarding Credibility of Children

In child sexual abuse litigation, the child is often the most important witness. Thus, the child's credibility is critical. Is it proper for the proponent of a child's testimony to offer expert testimony regarding the truthfulness of sexually abused children as a class, or the truthfulness

---

[93] *See, e.g.,* State v. Moran, 151 Ariz. 378, ___, 728 P.2d 248, 255 (1986); *Lindsey,* 149 Ariz. at ___, 720 P.2d at 75 (1986); State v. Black, 537 A.2d 1154, 1156 (Me. 1988); State v. Pettit, 66 Or. App. 575, ___, 675 P.2d 183, 185 (1984); State v. Rogers, 293 S.C. 505, ___, 362 S.E.2d 7, 8 (1987).

[94] *See, e.g., Moran,* 151 Ariz. at ___, 728 P.2d at 253-54 (defendant argued the child was angry due to his parental discipline; the expert supplied an alternative explanation for the child's anger at defendant).

[95] *Id.*

[96] For a summary of this research see *Expert Testimony, supra* note 20, at 92-107.

[97] *Id.*

[98] For a discussion of psychological literature on childhood suggestability see *id.* at 100-03.

[99] *See* United States v. Azure, 801 F.2d 336 (8th Cir. 1986); State v. Brotherton, 384 N.W.2d 375 (Iowa 1986); Head v. State, 519 N.E.2d 151 (Ind. 1988).

of a particular child? Unlike some aspects of expert testimony on sexual abuse, courts are nearly unanimous regarding expert testimony on credibility. Most courts reject testimony which comments directly on the credibility of individual children or sexually abused children as a class.[100] The Oregon Supreme Court did not mince words in its condemnation of such testimony:

> We have said before, and we will say it again, but this time with emphasis—we really mean it—*no psychotherapist may render an opinion on whether a witness is credible in any trial conducted in this state.* The assessment of credibility is for the trier of fact and not for psychotherapists.[101]

In the final analysis, the rationale underlying the rejection of expert testimony on credibility is the well-settled belief that assessing credibility is the exclusive province of the fact finder.[102]

IV. ISSUES OF SPECIAL CONCERN IN CHILD CUSTODY AND VISITATION LITIGATION

This section discusses three issues that make child custody and visitation litigation involving allegations of sexual abuse particularly difficult.

A. Concern Regarding Fabricated Allegations

There is increasing concern that a wave of fabricated charges of child sexual abuse is sweeping the country. A newspaper story warns of a "wave of false allegations."[103] The byline of a magazine article warns

---

[100] *See, e.g.,* State v. Moran, 151 Ariz. 378, ___, 728 P.2d 248, 254 (1986); People v. Oliver, 745 P.2d 222, 225 (Colo. 1987); *Head,* 519 N.E.2d at 152-53. *See also Expert Testimony, supra* note 20, at 121-27 (collecting and discussing cases).

[101] State v. Milbradt, 305 Or. 621, ___, 756 P.2d 620, 624 (1988)(emphasis in original). The Arizona Supreme Court was nearly as emphatic in State v. Lindsey, 149 Ariz. 472, ___, 720 P.2d 73, 76 (1986), where it wrote that "we explicitly state at this time that trial courts should not admit direct expert testimony that quantifies the probabilities of the credibility of another witness."

[102] *See* United States v. Barnard, 490 F.2d 907, 912 (9th Cir. 1973), *cert. denied,* 416 U.S. 959 (1974)("the jury is the lie detector in the courtroom"); *Lindsey,* 149 Ariz. at ___, 720 P.2d at 76; Townsend v. State, 103 Nev. 113, ___, 734 P.2d 705, 709 (1987); State v. Holloway, 82 N.C. App. 586, ___, 347 S.E.2d 72, 73 (1986); Commonwealth v. Davis, 514 Pa. 77, ___, 541 A.2d 315, 317 (1988); Commonwealth v. Seese, 512 Pa. 439, ___, 517 A.2d 920, 922 (1986); State v. Friedrich, 135 Wis. 2d 1, ___, 398 N.W.2d 763, 770 (1987).

For an argument in favor of a limited role for expert testimony on credibility in child sexual abuse litigation, see *Expert Testimony, supra* note 20, at 127.

[103] Coleman, *Therapists are the Real Culprits in Many Child Sexual Abuse Cases,* Oakland

that "trumpted-up charges of child abuse are divorce's ugly new weapon."[104] Is there a tidal wave of fabricated allegations? There is little doubt that an increasing number of parents embroiled in custody litigation are willing to broach the subject of sexual abuse. There is no systematic evidence, however, that the number of allegations has reached flood stage. Nor is there convincing evidence that a substantial portion of the allegations are fabricated. In fact, the research that exists points the other way.[105] Allegations of child sexual abuse occur in a small but increasing number of custody cases.[106] Allegations occur in approximately two to four percent of cases.[107]

Several researchers have investigated the rate of fabricated reports of child sexual abuse. A few of the studies focus on fabricated allegations in custody disputes, while most concentrate on fabricated reports in the general population. One of the best studies in the latter group is by Jones and McGraw, who evaluated all cases of suspected child sexual abuse reported to the Denver Social Services Department during 1983.[108] The research disclosed that eight percent of the reports were probably fictitious.[109] Other researchers found similar rates of fabricated allegations.[110]

When the focus of research narrows to custody cases, several authors report much higher rates of fabricated reporting than those discussed above. Green evaluated eleven suspected victims of child sexual

---

Tribune, Apr. 24, 1987, at B-6.

[104] Hopkins, *Fathers on Trial*, N.Y., Jan. 11, 1988, at 42. *See also* R. GARDNER, THE PARENTAL ALIENATION SYNDROME AND THE DIFFERENTIATION BETWEEN FABRICATED AND GENUINE CHILD SEXUAL ABUSE 274 (1987)(in the author's experience with child custody, "the vast majority of children who profess sexual abuse are fabricators"); Gordon, *False Allegations of Abuse in Child Custody Disputes*, 2 MINN. FAM. L.J. 225 (1985)("For many parents engaged in seriously contested child custody disputes, false allegations of child abuse have become an effective weapon for achieving an advantage in court").

[105] *See* ASSOCIATION OF FAMILY AND CONCILIATION COURTS, THE SEXUAL ABUSE ALLEGATIONS PROJECT, FINAL REPORT (1988)[hereinafter FINAL REPORT]; ASSOCIATION OF FAMILY AND CONCILIATION COURTS, ALLEGATIONS OF SEXUAL ABUSE IN CUSTODY AND VISITATION CASES: AN EMPIRICAL STUDY OF 169 CASES FROM 12 STATES (1988)[hereinafter EMPIRICAL STUDY]. Information on the the FINAL REPORT and the EMPIRICAL STUDY may be obtained by writing to Nancy Thoennes, Ph.D., Association of Family and Conciliation Courts, Research Unit, 1720 Emerson Street, Denver, Colorado 80218 (303) 837-1555.

[106] *See* FINAL REPORT, *supra* note 105, at 6.

[107] *See* EMPIRICAL STUDY, *supra* note 105, at 3.

[108] Jones & McGraw, *Reliable and Fictitious Accounts of Sexual Abuse of Children*, 2 J. INTERPERSONAL VIOLENCE 27 (1987)[hereinafter Jones & McGraw].

[109] *Id*. at 38. Among the small percentage of false reports, most were made by adults. Children rarely made fabricated allegations. *Id*. at 36-38.

[110] The research is discussed in *Expert Testimony*, *supra* note 20, at 112-13.

abuse and concluded that four of the allegations were fabricated (36%).[111] Benedek and Schetky were unable to document abuse in ten of eighteen cases (55%).[112] Commenting on these studies, Quinn writes that "these are very small clinical samples with a selective pattern of referrals."[113] Berliner adds that these and similar studies "describe a limited number of cases referred for evaluation . . . . In most of the cases described, there were multiple evaluations and conflicting opinions among professionals. Ultimately, there is no way of knowing that the authors' assessments are accurate."[114]

Jones and Seig studied twenty cases in which sexual abuse allegations arose in custody disputes.[115] They found that twenty percent of the allegations probably were fictitious.[116] The researchers conclude that "the setting of the divorce and custody dispute does seem to raise the likelihood that clinicians will find an increased number of fictitious allegations. However, in this study nearly ¾ (70%) were reliable, arguing strongly against the practice of dismissing allegations in custody disputes contexts as most likely false."[117]

Fabricated allegations of sexual abuse occur in custody and visitation litigation, and there is reason to proceed cautiously in such cases. As Jones and Seig point out, however, the higher percentage of fabricated allegations should not lead to exaggerated skepticism about such allegations. Many are true.

Part of the confusion over false allegations of sexual abuse comes from a misunderstanding of data generated through state child abuse and neglect reporting statutes. In 1986, more than 2,000,000 reports of

---

[111] Green, *True and False Allegations of Sexual Abuse in Custody Disputes*, 25 J. AM. ACAD. CHILD PSYCHIATRY 449 (1986). For cricitism of Dr. Green's article see Corwin, Berliner, Goodman, Goodwin & White, *Child Sexual Abuse and Custody Disputes*, 2 J. INTERPERSONAL VIOLENCE 91 (1987).

[112] Benedek & Schetky, *Allegations of Sexual Abuse in Child Custody and Visitation Disputes*, EMERGING ISSUES IN CHILD PSYCHIATRY AND LAW 145 (D. Schetky & E. Benedek eds. 1985).

[113] Quinn, *The Credibility of Children's Allegations of Sexual Abuse*, 6 BEHAVIORAL SCIENCES & L. 181 (1988).

[114] Berliner, *Deciding Whether a Child Has Been Sexually Abused*, SEXUAL ABUSE ALLEGATIONS IN CUSTODY AND VISITATION CASES 48, 52 (B. Nicholson & J. Bulkley eds. 1988).

[115] Jones & Seig, *Child Sexual Abuse Allegations in Custody and Visitation Disputes*, SEXUAL ABUSE ALLEGATIONS IN CUSTODY AND VISITATION CASES 22 (B. Nicholson & J. Bulkley eds. 1988).

[116] *Id.* at 29.

[117] *Id.*

suspected abuse and neglect were registered in the United States.[118] The American Humane Association indicates, however, that only forty to forty-two percent of the reports were substantiated.[119] One might conclude from this low substantiation rate that more than half of all the reports were fabricated. However, this is not true. There is an important distinction between unsubstantiated reports and fabricated reports. A fabricated report is a deliberate falsehood. In contrast, an unsubstantiated report is one without enough evidence to determine whether or not abuse occurred. There are innumerable reasons why an accurate report nevertheless may find its way into the "unsubstantiated" column. In some cases, no investigation is conducted. In others, an investigation is conducted but there is insufficient evidence to substantiate abuse. Perhaps the child is too young to describe what happened, or witnesses have moved away or refuse to cooperate. The fact that a majority of child abuse reports are unsubstantiated says little about the incidence of child sexual abuse, and less about the rate of fabricated allegations.

Deliberately fabricated allegations of child sexual abuse should be distinguished from what may be called misperception allegations. In some cases, parents acting in good faith misperceive information about their child, leading to suspicion of sexual abuse where none exists. For example, Jones and McGraw describe a divorced woman with custody of her five-year-old daughter. The woman suspected that her former husband was molesting the child because the girl experienced vaginal redness and irritation following weekend visits with her father. On the advice of her pediatrician, the mother reported her suspicion. Subsequent investigation uncovered no evidence of abuse.[120]

The likelihood of misperception allegations is particularly high among divorced and divorcing couples who experience continuing animosity. Already suspicious of one another, these spouses may misperceive innocent or ambiguous activity as evidence of sexual abuse. Coincidentally, the incidence of deliberately fabricated allegations is higher among divorcing parents. Thus, in custody and visitation cases it is very difficult to distinguish between true, misperceived, and fabricated allegations. Yet, every effort must be made to discover the

---

[118] American Humane, *supra* note 6, at 6.

[119] *Id.* at ii. At a 42% rate of substantiation, it is estimated that 737,000 American children were abused or neglected during 1986. *Id.*

[120] Jones & McGraw, *supra* note 108, at 43 n.1.

truth. If the allegation is true, the child requires protection. Even when there is no abuse, it is important to determine whether an allegation was deliberately fabricated or based on misperception. A court may doubt the custodial fitness of a parent who lodges a deliberately fabricated allegation, whereas, it may be appropriate to award custody to a parent who makes a good faith but misperceived allegation.

Another factor contributing to misunderstanding and a resulting climate of fear regarding fabricated allegations is a by-product of the McMartin preschool case in Los Angeles, and other multiple victim cases. Such cases are exceedingly complex, and problematic. Some articles in the popular press give the impression that the cases are a cruel hoax, and that the police, prosecutors, and mental health professionals involved are at least incompetent, if not corrupt.[121] This perception is inaccurate. Nevertheless, media fallout from McMartin and similar cases fuels concern about fabricated charges.

An additional ingredient in the fabricated charges conundrum is the appearance of opportunism that attaches when allegations of sexual abuse arise for the first time in child custody litigation. Seemingly, if sexual abuse had really occurred, the innocent parent would have discovered it and acted sooner. Charges of sexual abuse coinciding with a bitter custody dispute are intuitively suspicious. Couple this suspicion with the perception that angry parents will "stoop to anything" to gain custody, and the stage is set for disbelief.

While the stakes involved in custody litigation do push some parents over the edge of honesty, the fact that allegations of abuse arise for the first time when a family breaks up does not mean the allegations are false. Mental health professionals confirm that many children first disclose or experience sexual abuse when their parents divorce. Corwin and his colleagues write:

> There are several reasons abused children may be more likely to disclose abuse by a parent and to be believed by the other parent following separation or divorce. With the breakup of the parents comes diminished opportunity for an abusing parent to enforce secrecy as there is increased opportunity for the child to disclose abuse separately to the other parent. Decreased dependency and increased distrust between parents increases willingness to suspect child abuse by the other parent.
>
> Additionally, the losses, stresses, and overall negative impact of separa-

---

[121] Downing, *Pioneer Case at McMartin Called Hoax*, The Commercial Appeal, Memphis, TN, Jan. 17, 1988.

tion and divorce may precipitate regressive "acting out" by parents, including child sexual abuse.[122]

A final aspect of the fabrication problem deserves mention. Skepticism regarding allegations arising in custody litigation may be reinforced through unwarranted comparisons between custody litigation and criminal litigation. In the aggregate, the evidence available in criminal cases seems stronger than the evidence offered in custody cases. One might conclude that the paucity of evidence in family court results from a high rate of fabricated allegations. A moment's reflection exposes the error of this reasoning. In criminal litigation, charges are seldom filed when the evidence is weak. By contrast, a parent who suspects sexual abuse takes whatever evidence there is, no matter how slight, and attempts to protect the child. Unlike the prosecutor, parents cannot decline to press charges. Thus, the disparity between evidence presented in criminal and family court bears little relation to the truth of the allegations.

In the final analysis, the allegation most likely to be false is the one asserting there is a "wave of fabricated allegations." The problem of fabricated allegations is serious, but distorting the issue has the undesirable effect of casting a pale of unwarranted skepticism over all allegations of child sexual abuse.

B.   *The Long Shadow of John Henry Wigmore*

No scholar has had greater impact on the law of evidence than John Henry Wigmore. Wigmore's monumental treatise on evidence, first published in 1904, remains an important and viable work.[123] Like many others of his time, Wigmore was influenced by the emerging discipline of psychiatry and, in particular, by Sigmund Freud. Through the Oedipus Complex, Freud theorized that adult neurosis was linked to childhood sexual fantasy.[124] Freud's tremendous influence bolstered

---

[122] *See* Corwin, Berliner, Goodman, Goodwin & White, *Child Sexual Abuse and Custody Disputes*, 2 J. INTERPERSONAL VIOLENCE 91 (1987).

[123] J. WIGMORE, EVIDENCE IN TRIALS AT COMMON LAW (Chadbourne rev. 1970)[hereinafter WIGMORE].

[124] Originally, Freud believed that neurosis was linked to actual childhood sexual experience. Freud presented this thesis, called the seduction theory, to the Vienna psychoanalytic circle in 1896, and was roundly criticized. He withdrew the seduction theory and replaced it with the Oedipus Complex. For discussions of Freud's turnabout see J. MASSON, THE ASSAULT ON TRUTH: FREUD'S SUPPRESSION OF THE SEDUCTION THEORY (1984); SUMMIT, HIDDEN VICTIMS, HIDDEN PAIN: SOCIETAL AVOIDANCE OF CHILD SEXUAL ABUSE 39 (G. Wyatt & G. Powell eds.

the belief that child sexual abuse was rare, and that allegations of abuse were often the product of fantasy. Since most allegations of sexual abuse are made by women, an aura of disbelief surrounding such claims affixed itself to women and girls. Caught up in this gender based suspicion, Wigmore wrote:

> Modern psychiatrists have amply studied the behavior of errant young girls and women coming before the courts in all sorts of cases. Their psychic complexes are multifarious, distorted partly by inherent defects, partly by diseased derangements or abnormal instincts, partly by bad social environments, partly by temporary physiological or emotional conditions. One form taken by these complexes is that of contriving false charges of sexual offenses by men. The unchaste (let us call it) mentality finds incidental but direct expression in the narration of imaginary sex incidents of which the narrator is the heroine or the victim. On the surface the narration is straightforward and convincing. The real victim, however, too often in such cases is the innocent man . . . .
>
> *No judge should ever let a sex offense charge go to the jury unless the female complainant's social history and mental makeup have been examined and testified to by a qualified physician.*[125]

Wigmore's influence added scholarly support to judicial skepticism about women and girls as witnesses in sex offense cases. Courts frequently subjected females to psychiatric examination on the issue of credibility.[126] Furthermore, many courts ruled that testimony from sex offense victims was so suspicious that a conviction could not be based on the victim's uncorroborated testimony.[127] Psychiatric examination and corroboration were not required of victims of other crimes.

The influence of men like Freud and Wigmore led to what one psychologist describes as an official "endorsement of incredulity" regarding victims of sexual abuse.[128] The message went out: Child sexual abuse does not occur with any frequency; such claims are a product of fantasy or depravity; whatever the case, they are not to be believed.

1988)[hereinafter SUMMIT]; Myers, *Protecting Children from Sexual Abuse: What Does the Future Hold?*, 15 J. CONTEMP. L. 31 (1989).

[125] WIGMORE, *supra* note 123, § 924a, at 736-37 (emphasis in original).

[126] *See, e.g.*, Ballard v. Superior Court, 64 Cal. 2d 159, 49 Cal. Rptr. 302 (1966); Annotation, *Requiring Complaining Witness in Prosecution for Sex Crime to Submit to Psychiatric Examination*, 18 A.L.R.3d 1433 (1968). *See also* CHILD WITNESS, *supra* note 20, § 3.27. For criticism of court ordered psychiatric examinations in sex offense cases see Note, *Psychiatric Examination of Sexual Assault Victims: A Reevaluation*, 15 U.C. DAVIS L. REV. 973 (1982).

[127] For discussion of the corroboration requirement see CHILD WITNESS, *supra* note 23, § 4.21.

[128] Goodwin, *Credibility Problems in Multiple Personality Disorder Patients and Abused Children*, CHILDHOOD ANTECEDENTS OF MULTIPLE PERSONALITY 2, 5 (R. Kluft ed. 1985).

During the past thirty years, mental health professionals have changed their views about the propensity of females to fabricate accusations of rape and molestation. Today, Wigmore's suspicions are flatly rejected as legally[129] and psychologically[130] unsound. Nevertheless, suspicion about the credibility of sex offense victims is deeply ingrained in the American psyche. Consciously or unconsciously, this suspicion may contaminate decision making about sexual abuse. The shadow of doubt cast by John Wigmore's writings continues to obscure objective analysis of allegations of child sexual abuse, especially when such allegations are made by women.

In addition to the distrust arising from Freudian theory, other factors influence gender bias. For example, widening suspicion that allegations are fabricated sparks the belief that no male is immune from suspicion, and that it is not safe to hug or touch a child for fear of being reported to the authorities.[131] For some men, this personal sense of jeopardy may engender undue skepticism of allegations of sexual abuse. Other men may unconsciously identify with the plight of their accused brethren.

Finally, consider the "Catch-22" faced by women who raise the possibility of sexual abuse. A mother is idealized as her child's natural protector—possessing "woman's intuition" about the welfare of her offspring. When allegations of sexual abuse arise for the first time at divorce, some may wonder how a mother could possibly fail to notice that her child was being sexually abused. Thus, even if the allegation is established, there may be reservations about the woman's maternal competence. And if the allegation is not established, the woman is stigmatized as a false accuser. There seems to be no safe way to raise the possibility of sexual abuse.

C. Society's Blind Spot

Psychiatrist Roland Summit observes that society has a blind spot for child sexual abuse—a powerful desire to deny the problem. Summit

---

[129] *See, e.g.*, People v. King, 41 Colo. App. 177, ___, 581 P.2d 739, 741 (1978); State v. Romero, 94 N.M. 22, 606 P.2d 1116 (Ct. App. 1980). *See also* WIGMORE, *supra* note 123, § 924a, Supp., collecting numerous cases rejecting Wigmore's original position.

[130] *See Expert Testimony, supra* note 20, at 110; *Romero*, 94 N.M. at 22, 606 P.2d at 1116.

[131] For an interesting account of two explosive custody cases see Wilkinson, *Witchhunting in Hattiesburg*, THE AM. LAW., May 1988, at 107 (One of the attorneys involved observed that "[f]rom a male standpoint, it's frightening").

writes:

> Anyone proclaiming [the reality of child sexual abuse] imposes a dismal flaw in our hope for a just and fair society. All our systems of justice, reason and power have been adjusted to ignore the possibility of such a fatal flaw. Our very sense of enlightenment insists that anything *that* important could not escape our attention. Where could it hide? Parents would find it out. Doctors would see it. The courts would stop it. Victims would tell their psychiatrists. It would be obvious in psychological tests. Our best minds would know it. It is more reasonable to argue that young upstarts are making trouble. You can't trust kids. Untrained experts are creating a wave of hysteria. They ask leading questions. No family is safe from the invasion of the child savers. It's time to get back to common sense.[132]

In other words, it is time to suppress the ugly reality of child sexual abuse. One avenue to suppression lies in disbelief.

The issues discussed above add a psychological veneer to the complexity of custody and visitation litigation involving allegations of sexual abuse—a psychic film which distorts objective analysis. Professionals should increase their sensitivity to the historical, cultural, and psychological forces that may influence their views of child sexual abuse.

V.   Recommendations for Improving the Response of Family Courts to Allegations of Child Sexual Abuse

This section offers suggestions for improving the judicial response to allegations of child sexual abuse in custody and visitation litigation. Subsection A summarizes the recommendations of a national research project on allegations of child sexual abuse in custody and visitation cases. Subsection B suggests substantive and evidentiary approaches to resolving certain cases.

A.   *Recommendations of the Sexual Abuse Allegations Project*

Concerned about allegations of child sexual abuse in custody and visitation litigation, the federal government's National Center for Child Abuse and Neglect[133] supported a national research project known as the "Sexual Abuse Allegations Project." The Association of Family and Conciliation Courts and the ABA Center on Children and the Law

---

[132] Summit, *supra* note 124, at 51 (emphasis in original).

[133] The National Center on Child Abuse and Neglect is part of the U.S. Department of Health and Human Services.

conducted this research.[134] These groups released the Final Report on the research in March, 1988.[135] The Final Report contains important recommendations for improving the judicial response to custody and visitation cases involving allegations of sexual abuse. A summary of these recommendations follow.

1. Improving the Relationship Between the Family Court and the Child Protective Services Agency

Several agencies respond to allegations of child sexual abuse, including law enforcement, the prosecutor's office, and child protective services (hereinafter CPS). It is not uncommon for judicial proceedings to be underway simultaneously in juvenile court, family court, and criminal court. Not surprisingly, when several complex bureaucracies become involved with the same family, opportunities for miscommunication abound.

The Final Report points out that the potential for misunderstanding is particularly high between CPS agencies and family court workers. The Report offers five recommendations to "improve the currently tenuous relationship between the domestic relations court and the child protective service agency."[136]

(1) Family court and CPS workers should receive cross-training to increase understanding of their respective "mandates, options and vocabulary."[137]
(2) Formal liaisons should be established between family courts and CPS agencies to facilitate communication.[138]
(3) Formal policies should be established to facilitate communication between family courts and CPS.[139]
(4) Professionals from the family court staff should be invited to participate in interagency, interdisciplinary committees which

---

[134] The ABA Center on Children and the Law is sponsored by the Young Lawyer's Division of the American Bar Association. The Center produces many valuable publications relating to children and the law. For information on the Center write to Howard A. Davidson, Director, or Robert M. Horowitz, Associate Director, ABA Center on Children and the Law, 1800 M St., N.W., Washington, D.C. 20036.

[135] For information regarding FINAL REPORT and a related study, write to Nancy Thoennes, Ph.D., Association of Family and Conciliation Courts/Research Unit, 1720 Emerson St., Denver, CO 80218.

[136] FINAL REPORT, *supra* note 105, at 86.

[137] *Id.* at 86-87.

[138] *Id.* at 87.

[139] *Id.* at 88.

meet to discuss child abuse cases.[140]
(5) Training on child sexual abuse should be provided to family
court personnel and the family law bench and bar.[141]

2. Improving the Relationship Between Family Court and Juvenile Court

Clearly, family court and juvenile court must communicate. The
Final Report suggests that formal policies be implemented to ensure
such communication.[142] The Final Report also recommends that child
advocates be used in family court as well as in juvenile court "to help
promote expeditious and efficient case processing."[143]

3. Use of Mental Health Professionals in Family Court

Mental health professionals play an important role in evaluating
allegations of child sexual abuse. The Final Report offers several recommendations regarding consulting professionals. The Final Report
points to the possible benefits of court-appointed clinicians, noting:

> [C]ourt-appointed professionals have a better likelihood of obtaining access to
> all the parties in a case—an important prerequisite for a useful evaluation.
> The use of court-appointed experts may also discourage the parties from
> "shopping" for experts until someone is located who supports the client's posi-
> tion. These "shopping trips" are costly to the parent, stressful for the child
> who is repeatedly interviewed, and increase the risk that the court will be
> subjected to "battles of the experts."[144]

The Final Report suggests that judges and other professionals receive training on the elements of a proper psychological evaluation of
suspected child sexual abuse.[145] Since the degree of relevant expertise
varies considerably among professionals, the judge must know enough
about the psychological literature to differentiate the real expert from
the imagined.

The Report suggests that prosecutors provide training for mental
health professionals to acquaint them with the forensic implications of
their interaction with children. For example, mental health workers

---

[140] *Id.* at 87.
[141] *Id.* at 88.
[142] *Id.* at 89.
[143] *Id.*
[144] *Id.* at 90-91.
[145] *Id.* at 91.

benefit from training on interviewing techniques that avoid overly leading and suggestive questions.[146] Furthermore, clinicians need to know the types of information that have forensic relevance so they can frame appropriate interview questions.[147]

Finally, the Report reminds the reader that in many cases, no amount of expertise will determine whether abuse occurred.[148] Too often it is impossible to be sure. There is no litmus test for child sexual abuse. In fact, the opinion of an "expert" who claims absolute certainty should be examined critically.

4. *Factors to Consider in Judicial Determinations*

The Final Report addresses two recommendations directed to family court judges. First, the Final Report recommends that courts consider alternatives to monitored or supervised visitation, suggesting that such visitation interferes with meaningful parent-child interaction and leads to resentment.[149] One alternative is "therapeutic supervised visitation in which psychologists or graduate students provide family therapy and family observations, as well as supervision."[150] Second, the Report stresses the importance of avoiding generalizations about the validity of allegations of child sexual abuse that arise in custody and visitation litigation.

The Final Report of the Sexual Abuse Allegations Project provides concrete suggestions that can be implemented quickly and without significantly disrupting existing systems. The Report deserves serious study.[151]

B. *Substantive and Evidentiary Recommendations for Selected Cases*

This subsection makes eight recommendations regarding evidentiary and substantive issues in custody and visitation cases involving allegations of child sexual abuse. The recommendations are not intended to apply in all cases. In some particularly difficult situations, however, one or more of the recommendations may assist the court.

---

[146] *Id.*
[147] *Id.* at 92.
[148] *Id.*
[149] *Id.* at 92-93.
[150] *Id.* at 93.
[151] *See supra* note 135 for information on obtaining FINAL REPORT.

1. Shifting the Burden of Proof When Evidence of Identity Fails[152]

In civil litigation, the burden of proof generally rests on the plaintiff. In child custody litigation, however, the burden of proof rests equally on both parents.[153] Each parent has the burden of proving that the child's best interests will be fostered by an award of custody to that parent.[154] This means that, when one parent accuses the other of sexually abusing their child, the accusing parent bears the burden of proof on that issue. If the accusing parent succeeds in proving that sexual abuse has occurred, but fails to establish that the accused parent committed the abuse, traditional burden of proof analysis dictates dismissal of the allegation, with the conclusion that nothing can be done that interferes with the accused parent's right to custody or visitation.[155] This result may leave the child in jeopardy, however, because the accused parent indeed may be the perpetrator. It is also true, of course, that the accuser, or someone associated with the accuser, may be the perpetrator.[156] In a narrow range of cases, an alternative approach to the traditional allocation of burden of proof seems warranted. When abuse is established, but proof of identity is lacking, the court may require each parent—accuser and accused alike—to prove that they are not the perpetrator.

This approach was employed by the Appellate Division of the New Jersey Superior Court in a juvenile court protective proceeding. In *In*

---

[152] For a discussion of methods to prove identity in child abuse litigation see Myers & Carter, *Proof of Physical Child Abuse*, 53 Mo. L. Rev. 189, 218-24 (1988).

[153] *See* 3 J. McCahey, M. Kaufman, C. Kraut, D. Gaffner, R. Schwartz & M. Silverman, Child Custody & Visitation Law and Practice § 20.02[1], at 20-6 (1983), where the authors write:

The ordinary burden of proof on the plaintiff in a legal action does not apply to the plaintiff in a divorce action seeking custody of a minor child. In contested custody-visitation disputes, the true objective is the best interests of the child. The parents stand on equal footing at the outset of the proceeding.

[154] *See* 2 C. Markey, California Family Law § 22.111, at 22-76 (1978, 1988)("If the contest is between the parents at a hearing during their dissolution, the issue is the best interests of the child, and each party will have the burden of establishing that the best interests of the child require that custody be given to him or her.").

[155] Failure to prove that an accused parent sexually abused a child, however, does not result in simple dismissal of the accusation. On the contrary, the accusing parent may be branded a false accuser, and denied custody or visitation for that reason.

[156] In practice, the person alleging sexual abuse is usually the mother. In response, the father may allege that the actual pepetrator is a male associate of the mother.

re D.T.[157] there was medical evidence that a four-month-old child had been sexually abused. However, there was insufficient evidence to establish the identity of the perpetrator. Turning to principles of tort law, the court wrote:

> Were this a tort suit brought against a limited number of persons, each having access or custody of a baby during the time frame when a sexual abuse concededly occurred, no one else having such contact and the baby being then and now helpless to identify her abuser, would we not recognize an occasion for invocation of [the doctrine requiring defendants to exculpate themselves from liability]? The burden would then be shifted, and such defendants would be required to come forward and give their evidence to establish non-culpability . . . .
>
> Shifting the burden is no less appropriate here, particularly as neither punitive relief nor damages are sought, but only continued limited monitorship of an admittedly abused child.[158]

The New Jersey court's allocation of the burden of proof finds support in the overriding public policy of protecting children from abuse. A similar approach is appropriate in child custody and visitation litigation incident to divorce when: (1) there is convincing evidence of sexual abuse; (2) both parents had the opportunity to abuse the child; and (3) the likelihood of further abuse is significant. If either or both parents fail to carry their burden of proof, the court may enter appropriate orders to ensure the child's safety.

The approach adopted in *In re D.T.* is not immune from criticism. In a partial dissent, Judge Shebell argued against shifting the burden of proof, writing that the court's solution "might unjustly serve to place guilt upon a parent for the heinous offense of sexual abuse merely because of the parent's inability to prove innocence."[159] Another concern is that parents may refrain from raising legitimate claims of sexual abuse because they fear the burden of proving innocence will be cast on them if they fail to convince the court of the accused parent's guilt.

2. Failure to Protect a Child as Justification for Temporary Supervision of Custody and/or Visitation

In cases where sexual abuse is established but proof of identity is lacking, there is an alternative to shifting the burden of proof. Parents

---

[157] 229 N.J. Super. 509, 552 A.2d 189 (1988).

[158] *Id.* at 192-93 (footnote omitted).

[159] *Id.* at 193 (Shebell, J., concurring in part and dissenting in part).

have a duty to protect their children from harm. When parents fail to protect their child from sexual abuse, the court can subject both parents to temporary supervision or monitoring to ensure the safety of the child.[160] Under this approach, neither parent is stigmatized as a child abuser. Although stigma accompanies a finding of failure to protect, such oprobrium is of lesser magnitude than the stigma attached to a finding of abuse.

3. *The State of Mind Exception to the Hearsay Rule*

The state of mind exception to the hearsay rule plays a minor role in criminal child abuse litigation.[161] In custody and visitation litigation, however, the exception occupies an important position.[162] The state of mind exception authorizes admission of out-of-court statements "of the declarant's then existing state of mind [or] emotion, . . . but not including a statement of memory or belief to prove the fact remembered or believed."[163]

In custody and visitation cases, evidence of a child's state of mind is relevant to determine the child's best interest, and hearsay statements describing the child's state of mind are admissible for that purpose.[164] For example, it is proper under the state of mind exception to admit hearsay statements describing a child's "intimidation by the father and desire to live with the mother."[165] Similarly, a child's hearsay statements describing parental misconduct are admissible insofar as the

---

[160] If monitoring is required, it may be appropriate to transfer the case to the juvenile court.

[161] *See* CHILD WITNESS, *supra* note 23, § 5.35.

[162] For custody and visitation cases discussing the state of mind exception see Griffin v. Griffin, 81 N.C. App. 665, 344 S.E.2d 828 (1986); Crabtree v. Crabtree, 716 S.W.2d 923, 927 (Tenn. Ct. App. 1986).

Hearsay issues often do not arise into appellate decisions on child custody and visitation. There is no doubt, however, that the hearsay rule applies in such proceedings. *See In re* Marriage of Williams, 303 N.W.2d 160 (Iowa 1981)(report of court appointed custody evaluator was heresay and should have been excluded); *In re* Marriage of Cavitt, 564 S.W.2d 53 (Mo. Ct. App. 1978)(social agency report was inadmissible hearsay, but its admission was harmless error in bench trial); Murdoch v. Murdoch, 200 Neb. 429, 264 N.W.2d 183 (1978)(statement of child to father expressing affection was not hearsay because it was not offered for the truth. The child's statement was relevant simply because it was made); Griffin v. Griffin, 81 N.C. App. 665, 344 S.E.2d 828 (1986); Fuhrman v. Fuhrman, 254 N.W.2d 97 (N.D. 1977)(error requiring reversal to admit and consider hearsay report of social worker regarding custody); Crabtree v. Crabtree, 716 S.W.2d 923 (Tenn. Ct. App. 1986).

[163] FED. R. EVID. 803(3).

[164] *See Griffin*, 81 N.C. App. at ___, 344 S.E.2d at 831.

[165] *Id.* at ___, 344 S.E.2d at 830.

statements reveal the child's fear of a parent.[166]

When offering a child's out-of-court statement under the state of mind exception, the party must take care to ensure that the evidentiary purpose of the statement is limited to proof of the child's state of mind at the moment the statement was made. The exception does not apply to evidence of a child's memory or belief to prove the truth of facts remembered or believed. Thus, a child's out-of-court statement describing sexual abuse would be admissible under the state of mind exception to prove the child's fear or dislike of the perpetrating parent. However, the statement would not be admissible under this exception to prove that the child actually was abused.[167]

The case of *In re Custody of Jennifer*[168] illustrates the limits of the state of mind exception. In this care and protection proceeding, the trial court determined that Jennifer had been sexually abused by her father.[169] Over the father's objection, the judge relied on the state of mind exception to admit testimony from teachers, social workers, psychologists, and others regarding Jennifer's statements describing the sexual abuse.[170] The Massachusetts Appeals Court ruled that the trial judge misapplied the state of mind exception. The appellate court wrote:

> Under the state of mind exception to the hearsay rule an out-of-court statement of a declarant's then existing (i.e., at the time the statement is made) state of mind is admissible if his mental condition is relevant to a material issue in the case . . . . However, "[a]n extrajudicial statement of a declarant is not ordinarily admissible if it is a statement of memory or belief to prove the fact remembered or believed." . . . We have no question that a child's state of mind may be a material issue in a care and protection proceeding. The problem here is that the judge's findings make clear that he substantially relied on evidence as proof of critical past events which he, on admission, limited to state of mind (and used apparently at least to some extent on that question). The evidence was inadmissible for the former purpose. This is no less so because of the nature of the proceedings.[171]

---

[166] *Crabtree*, 716 S.W.2d at 927 (visitation case involving allegations of sexual abuse by one parent).

[167] The statement would be admissible as substantive evidence of the abuse if the statement fit the requirements of another hearsay exception, such as the excited utterance exception. *See, e.g.,* Morgan v. Foretich, 846 F.2d 941 (4th Cir. 1988).

[168] 25 Mass. App. Ct. 241, 517 N.E.2d 187 (1988).

[169] The father was found to have abused two daughters. *Id.*

[170] 25 Mass. App. Ct. at ___, 517 N.E.2d at 189.

[171] *Id.* (citing Commonwealth v. Lowe, 391 Mass. 97, 461 N.E.2d 192 (1984)).

In child custody and visitation cases involving allegations of sexual abuse, the state of mind exception is particularly important.[172] For example, in some cases there is substantial evidence of sexual abuse, but it is impossible to determine who molested the child.[173] In other cases, the evidence creates a strong suspicion of sexual abuse by a parent but falls short of a preponderance of the evidence. In both scenarios the child is at risk of further sexual abuse, yet, under traditional notions of burden of proof, there is not enough evidence to justify a custody or visitation order that will protect the child from the likely perpetrator.[174] The court may fear that doing nothing consigns the child to further sexual abuse, yet feel powerless to take action. In a proper case, statements admissible under the state of mind exception can be used to protect the child despite the fact that sexual abuse or identity cannot be substantiated. For instance, the child's out-of-court statements expressing fear or dislike of the parent accused of sexual abuse can constitute sufficient evidence to support a custody or visitation order.[175] Similarly, if the child believes he or she has been molested by the accused parent, placing limits on interaction with the parent may be in the child's best interest.[176] This use of state of mind evidence does not avoid the requirement that allegations of sexual abuse be established. Rather, evidence of a child's feelings, beliefs, and fears constitutes an independent and sufficient source of proof regarding a child's best interests.

4.   Temporary Custody

Every state authorizes temporary child custody during the pendency of divorce proceedings. When a petition for temporary custody alleges sexual abuse, special considerations arise. Most importantly, the psychological literature convincingly establishes that a child who is sex-

---

[172] *See, e.g.,* Crabtree v. Crabtree, 716 S.W.2d 923 (Tenn. Ct. App. 1986).

[173] *See, e.g., In re* D.T., 229 N.J. Super. 509, 552 A.2d 189 (1988)(juvenile court protective proceeding. There was medical evidence that the four-month-old infant was sexually abused, but insufficient evidence to identify the perpetrator).

[174] *See Crabtree,* 716 S.W.2d at 926 (visitation case involving allegations of sexual abuse. "While the simple allegation of sexual abuse sets off a strong reaction in each of us and galvanizes our determination to protect the child, the allegation of abuse still must be proved.").

[175] *See Crabtree,* 716 S.W.2d at 923. In civil proceedings, the general rule is that hearsay is sufficient to support a finding of fact or judgment. *See* CHILD WITNESS, *supra* note 23, § 5.20. In criminal litigation, hearsay may not suffice to support a conviction. *See id.*

[176] *See Crabtree,* 716 S.W.2d at 927 ("Where the child's state of mind shows that he or she has a real fear of one parent based on the real or imagined mistreatment by that parent, that is sufficient to persuade this court to exclude the child from the company of that parent except under proper supervision.").

ually abused is at risk of serious harm. The harm is sufficiently grave that courts should award temporary custody to the nonabusing parent whenever there is reason to believe sexual abuse has occurred or is likely to occur.

While the evidence needed to establish reasonable belief comes from many sources, it is important to remember that child sexual abuse is often very difficult to prove. Because a petition for temporary custody comes early in the proceeding, before complete evaluation is possible, courts should not place a heavy burden of proof on the petitioner. The threat to the child's welfare is so high if abuse is occurring that temporary custody should be granted when the petitioner raises "questions going to the merits so serious, substantial, difficult and doubtful, as to make fair ground for litigation and thus for more deliberate investigation."[177]

In most cases the court makes the correct decision regarding a petition for temporary custody. However, courts cannot ignore the possibility of two types of errors. First, the judge may deny a petition when abuse is occurring, and a child is at risk. Second, the judge may grant a petition when abuse is not occurring, and a child is not at risk. Bearing in mind the effects of sexual abuse, and the interim nature of temporary custody, the court should err in the direction of protecting sexually abused children. That is, improvidently granting temporary custody is less likely to harm a child than improvidently denying such custody.

When a parent alleging child sexual abuse is denied temporary custody, that parent should be permitted to repetition the court on a showing that new evidence of sexual abuse is available. New evidence includes information coming to light following the hearing on the petition for temporary custody, as well as evidence that existed prior to the hearing, provided the alleging parent was unaware of the evidence at the time of the original petition.[178]

---

[177] Hamilton Watch Co. v. Benrus Watch Co., 206 F.2d 738, 740 (2d Cir. 1953).

[178] In ordinary civil litigation, when a party seeks relief on the basis of newly discovered evidence, the party must establish that the evidence could not have been discovered with reasonable diligence. *See* Fed. R. Civ. P. 60(b)(2). In child custody litigation, the court's primary interest is the child's best interests. To protect the child, courts should not ordinarily deny the right to repetition for temporary custody simply because the petitioning parent failed to exercise reasonable diligence. The parent's failure to discover evidence of sexual abuse must not be visited on the child. The court can remedy lack of due diligence through appropriate sanctions directed against the petitioning parent and/or counsel.

5. Character Evidence and Uncharged Misconduct Evidence in Custody Litigation

A basic principle of American law holds that evidence of a person's character generally is not admissible to prove that the person acted in conformity with his or her character on a particular occasion.[179] In certain types of litigation, however, character is said to be "in issue," and in such cases character evidence is admissible. Parental character is "in issue" in child custody litigation because the custody decision turns on parental fitness.[180]

When character evidence is offered in custody litigation involving allegations of child sexual abuse, the logical relevance of the evidence is predicated on the following inferences: (1) the accused parent has a history of sexual abuse of children; (2) based on this history, one infers that the accused parent has a propensity for child sexual abuse; (3) based on the intermediate inference of propensity, one further infers that the accused parent probably acted in conformity with that propensity and sexually abused the child.

The character evidence described above is not the only evidentiary use of parental misconduct. Evidence of a parent's uncharged crimes, wrongs, or acts is admissible for non-character purposes as well. In particular, evidence of uncharged misconduct may be admitted to prove motive, opportunity, intent, preparation, plan, knowledge, identity, or absence of mistake or accident.[181] Each of these purposes plays an important role in criminal child abuse litigation.[182] At the present time, uncharged misconduct evidence is used rarely in custody and visitation litigation involving allegations of sexual abuse. Counsel seeking to prove sexual abuse may want to consider expanded use of uncharged misconduct evidence.

6. Misinterpretation of Parental Behavior

It is important to guard against misinterpreting the behavior of parents who make accusations of child sexual abuse. Such parents are under extraordinary, sometimes disabling, stress. At the outset, many

---

[179] *See* Michelson v. United States, 335 U.S. 469 (1948); FED. R. EVID. 404(a).

[180] *See* WIGMORE, *supra* note 123, § 69.1, at 1457.

[181] FED. R. EVID. 404(b).

[182] *See* Myers, *Uncharged Misconduct Evidence in Child Abuse Litigation*, 1988 UTAH L. REV. 479 (1988). *See generally* E. IMWINKELRIED, UNCHARGED MISCONDUCT EVIDENCE (1984).

parents believe the court will come quickly to their child's rescue. When the accused parent denies the allegation, however, accusing parents soon realize they carry a difficult burden of proof, and that if they fail to convince the judge, they may be branded false accusers who are unfit for custody. Desperate to protect their children, such parents may act in ways that appear irrational. For example, a parent searching for evidence of sexual abuse may take a child to one professional after another in the hope that someone, somewhere, will supply the missing proof. In the context of a heated custody battle, such parental behavior is understandable. Unfortunately, some individuals misinterpret such behavior, concluding that a parent who "shops around" for evidence probably has none. Even worse, an extreme skeptic may conclude that a parent who takes a child to several professionals is guilty of child abuse for subjecting the child to "unnecessary" examinations.[183]

The supercharged atmosphere surrounding allegations of child sexual abuse sometimes breeds unusual and even bizarre behavior in parents. The professionals involved in such cases must step back and evaluate parental action with an understanding of the pressure experienced by both parents.

7. Modification of Custody Awards

All jurisdictions permit modification of custody and visitation awards on a showing of substantially changed circumstances. When an allegation of child sexual abuse is made at the initial custody trial, the court's determination becomes res judicata regarding facts litigated at that time. If the parent alleging sexual abuse fails to establish the allegation, the accusing parent cannot relitigate the issue on the basis of the same evidence. However, if further evidence regarding sexual abuse comes to light, the matter should be reopened. In other words, a showing of additional evidence should constitute the substantially changed circumstances required to relitigate custody or visitation. Once the matter is reopened, the court should consider the additional evidence as well as the evidence presented at the earlier trial. This does not mean earlier evidence is relitigated. Rather, viewing new evidence in light of the old allows the court to see the entire picture. Often new evidence is

---

[183] *See Wilkinson, supra* note 131 (describing a case in which a mother accused her former husband of sexually abusing their daughter. The trial court found that the father did not abuse the child. But the court did not stop there. It went on to rule that the mother had abused the child by subjecting the youngster to numerous unwarranted visits to the doctor).

meaningless unless it is evaluated along with everything else that is known about the child, including facts developed in earlier proceedings.[184]

8. *Transfer Selected Cases from Family Court to Juvenile Court*

In some cases involving allegations of child sexual abuse, the family court should transfer the matter to the juvenile court. The relationship between the family court and juvenile court is thoroughly analyzed in an excellent law review article by Leonard Edwards, a respected California jurist who has served both courts.[185] Judge Edwards concludes that in some cases transfer from one court to the other is appropriate. Edwards writes:

> Family court was designed to provide litigants with a forum in which to resolve the issues relating to the custody, care and control of children. Juvenile court was created to protect children from parental abuse or neglect.[186]
>
> . . .
>
> [In California], the juvenile court is better equipped to investigate and try child abuse allegations, and subsequently protect and supervise an abused child.[187]
>
> . . .
>
> When child protection is the issue, the courts should be prepared to work together to insure that adequate resources are available to protect the child. In most cases this means the juvenile court should have an opportunity to decide if it will intervene. If it chooses not to intervene, the family court must use all of its resources to meet the child's needs. The family court should also be prepared to turn to the juvenile court for help in extraordinary cases in which the parties are in such conflict that the child is seriously suffering.[188]

CONCLUSION

Decision making in custody and visitation litigation is always difficult, but when allegations of child sexual abuse arise, the task assumes Herculean proportions. Clear evidence of abuse is seldom available. Some children cannot or will not testify. Others are inconsistent, am-

---

[184] *See* J.P. v. P.W., 772 S.W.2d 786 (Mo. Ct. App. 1989).

[185] Edwards, *The Relationship of Family and Juvenile Courts in Child Abuse Cases*, 27 SANTA CLARA L. REV. 201 (1987).

[186] *Id.* at 204.

[187] *Id.* at 235.

[188] *Id.* at 269.

bivalent, and confused. The possibility of coaching and fabricated allegations cannot be ignored. The perception of parental credibility is influenced by the very nature of the proceeding. But paucity of evidence and questionable credibility are not the only problems. Added to these is the psychological dimension, including a legacy of skepticism of women who allege sexual offenses, distrust of children, unwillingness to believe that parents could sexually abuse their children, and disgust that some do.

The legal and psychological complexity of litigation involving allegations of child sexual abuse places extraordinary demands on bench and bar. Each professional must come to terms with the feelings generated by such cases, including the possibility of gender bias. As rumors circulate of a "wave" of false allegations, it is tempting to dismiss allegations of child sexual abuse as the work of false accusers. Disbelief is one way to shut out the unpalatable reality of child abuse. Yet, scientific and clinical literature refutes the rumors. The task is not to shut our eyes, but to respond with measured objectivity and neutrality, tempered with compassion.

Why Parents Run

DEBORAH FISHER

One morning last May, Juanita Lammer was in her home in Bothell, Washington, with her four children, Jesse, Nicholas, Jaimie, and Andre, when half a dozen FBI agents burst through the front door. As the agents handcuffed Juanita, they sequestered Jesse and Nicholas, ages eight and six, in the kitchen, preparing to turn them over to Washington Child Protective Services. Fourteen months earlier, Juanita and Michael, her current husband, had left the state of Minnesota to protect the two boys from sexual and physical abuse the boys say was perpetrated by their biological father. The family had already fought through a bitter two-and-one-half year custody dispute in family court. Despite multiple allegations, physical evidence, and the testimony of experts and witnesses, the judge handling the case eventually transferred custody of Jesse and Nicholas to their biological father. When Juanita and Michael were faced with the choice of sending the children back to what they believed would be certain abuse or themselves going to jail for custodial interference, they decided to commit what they describe as an act of civil disobedience — they ran.

The Lammers are not alone in their decision to defy a court order. When the Lammers appeared on a Seattle talk show to discuss their case, a woman called in to say she had spent 41 days in jail for custodial interference after being arrested on the run. The caller said three of her four cellmates had been in jail for the same thing. Dr. Elizabeth Morgan spent two years in a Washington, DC jail for refusing to tell a judge where her daughter Hilary was hidden from the child's father, whom Hilary says sexually abused her. After the courts failed to protect her daughter years ago, Faye Yager of Atlanta now openly operates an "underground" system, hiding parents trying to protect their kids.

Although the Lammers' story differs in detail from other cases reported in the press, the outline is the same. Juanita and her ex-husband divorced in 1983. They shared legal custody. Jesse and Nicholas lived with Juanita and visited their father frequently. In the summer of 1985, the children complained their biological father was hitting, slapping, pinching, and shaking them. Though the father admitted in a counseling session to hitting Jesse, he balked at any more counseling and then filed suit for full custody.

As visitations continued, the boys began displaying behavior disturbing to Juanita, who is a counselor in private practice specializing in family issues, chemical dependency, and sexual abuse. In March of 1986, Jesse disclosed to a psychologist what he had not yet told his mother—that his biological father, while nude from the waist down, had rubbed his penis in front of him. The psychologist reported the incident to Child Protective Services, who investigated and ruled the report "unable to substantiate." A CPS worker later told the mother that if the report had involved a next door neighbor something could be done, but because the person was the biological father, it tended to be labeled "poor judgment."

Before the family went into hiding, both boys reported over a period of two years several incidents of being sexually and physically abused. Juanita and her new husband, Michael, consistently pressed the Family Court system to act to protect the children. As time went on, the allegations included anal penetration, masturbation of the boys' penises, and the father telling the children to touch his penis. Even so, Juanita and Michael were willing to allow the boys' father continued contact with them if he was monitored and sought treatment. At the very least, the family wanted adequate supervision.

After CPS marked the initial allegation "unable to substantiate," Juanita and Michael went to Family Court Services, who'd become involved because of the custody action. While Court Services evaluated the custody matter CPS refused to investigate any further reports. Court Services wouldn't handle the allegations, either, saying they were not qualified to determine sexual abuse. The Lammers tried filing criminal charges. A police officer videotaped an interview of the children and took the tape and her report to the county attorney's office. An assistant county attorney wouldn't press charges because of the boys' ages and because the case lacked adult corroboration and physical evidence. Then a court-appointed psychologist evaluated the children for the custody matter, but never interviewed them about their allegations of anal penetration and masturbation of their penises by their father. Three conclusive reports by a pediatrician and sexual abuse expert, who said the children had been sexually abused, were ignored. Physical evidence was not allowed into the evidentiary hearing.

The final straw for the Lammers came when Nicholas returned home from a visitation with a welt and bruises on his face. Nicholas told his mother and stepfather that his father had hit him when he asked him when the sexual abuse would stop. CPS told the Lammers that because the matter was before a judge and the file by now was so full of allegations, they would no longer accept any reports.

After the family fled the state, the judge ruled that if any abuse *had* occurred, it would "constitute such a minimal degree" that it did not warrant interrupting the father's relationship with his children. The judge did decide, however, that Juanita's efforts to protect her children warranted taking them away from her and giving the biological father full custody. In the court's final order, Juanita was not even allowed any visitation rights.

At a time when the criminal courts are telling the public to tolerate the abuse of children no longer, some family courts are still telling parents and children to accept a level of abuse in order to maintain family ties. Parents are desperate enough to go into hiding with their children because they exhaust all conventional legal options and their children remain unprotected. Appeals are an unattractive option because, in many cases, a disputed custody change remains in effect during the process. There comes a time when a parent who truly believes his or her child has been abused cannot look that child in the eye and say "You go back or else I go to jail." When such parents — usually women — take strong measures to protect their kids, they are often accused of simply acting vindictively toward an ex-spouse. But what parent would give up home, career, family, friends, support, identity, and safety just to punish an ex-spouse?

One of the problems women and children still confront in the legal system in custody cases is one battered women encountered years ago — they are simply not believed. Despite recent changes in the law validating children as competent witnesses on their own behalf, they are still not viewed as credible. In the Lammer case, for example, the judge refused to speak with the children. When Jesse asked to talk to him, the judge told counsel in chambers that he "didn't want some six-year old" telling him what to do. Children are rarely recognized in court records as having initiated the allegations. Mothers are often described as having made the allegations, and because the reports arise in a custody case, the mothers automatically become suspect.

Statistics do not support the belief that false sexual abuse allegations commonly arise in custody cases. In a two-year study of custody cases conducted by the Association of Family and Conciliation Courts, data were collected from 200 court personnel in Denver, Los Angeles, Madison, Seattle, and Cambridge. The study revealed that sexual abuse allegations occur in only 2% to 10% of all family cases involving custody or visitation disputes. The study's authors found that "[d]eliberately false allegations made to influence the custody decision or to hurt the ex-spouse do happen, but they are viewed by knowledgeable professionals as rarities."

In fact, many custody cases are actually initiated and won by fathers, not mothers. In her book, *Mothers on Trial: The Battle for Children and Custody*, Phyllis Chesler noted that in 70% of the cases she surveyed, fathers won custody. After interviewing 55 men who sued for custody of their children, Chesler found that the primary reason they did so was because they didn't want to pay child support or alimony. Other reasons included having a patriarchal concept of children as property and a desire to punish ex-wives.

In the midst of the turbulent feelings often associated with divorce and custody cases, professionals suspect sexual abuse allegations that arise at the same time. However, David Corwin, M.D., psychiatric consultant to the Multidisciplinary Child Abuse Team at Oakland, California's Children's Hospital, theorizes that children are actually more likely to disclose abuse by a parent during a divorce action. "With the breakup of the parents," says Corwin, "comes diminished opportunity for an abusing parent to enforce secrecy." Corwin suggests that the child feels safe enough at last to disclose the abuse, or that under the stresses of a divorce, a parent might even begin to abuse a child.

Another problem facing professionals and parents is that when a report is made, many family courts lack the coordinated examination of a multidisciplinary team that often benefits criminal court cases. In the Lammer case, for example, neither CPS nor Court Services — though aware of each other's involvement — quite knew what to with the allegations. A lack of coordination can lead to an impossible double-bind being imposed upon the parents. When Juanita asked CPS and Court Services at various times for advice on whether she should withhold visitation when the children continued reporting the abuse, she was told that if she *didn't* protect the children, she could be charged with neglect or the children might be removed to a foster home. Later on, she was charged with contempt for withholding visitation. The judge eventually dismissed those charges.

Still another problem with these cases is that the system is designed to respond to "underdogs." When parents or their children don't "act" the part, they are viewed with suspicion. A concerned and assertive mother is viewed as hysterical or vindictive. An articulate, assertive child is discounted as coached. When professionals involved in the case see the difficulties children are having, they feel compelled to find a source for the problem. If it is not entirely clear to them that the problem is the accused, then blame falls on the other parent. In our culture today, it is still easier to believe that an ex-wife is viciously making up charges of sexual abuse than to believe that a father is abusing his kids.

Ultimately, the judge writes an opinion that indicts the mother's fitness rather than providing a plan of protection for the children. The problem is exacerbated by judges who may not be well educated about child sexual abuse. In the Lammer case, for instance, the judge hypothetically asked Dr. Carolyn Levitt — the pediatrician and sexual abuse specialist who confirmed in three separate examinations that the children had been sexually abused — if it wasn't actually *the doctor* who had abused the boys and if they weren't simply transferring the abuse to their father?

After years of telling their story to dozens of professionals — and being sent back over and over again — the children in this case begged for relief from the abuse, suggesting at one point that the family run away. For Jesse, Nicholas, and their family, the initial euphoria of flight was eventually dampened by the realities of life on the road. They left already strapped by the expense of the custody case. After trying to find safety and documentation on their own, they made contact with the underground for a short time. But the underground turned out to be even more precarious than going it alone. After leaving the underground, traveling again (and delivering the Lammers' fourth baby while in hiding), the family settled in Washington State. The Lammers wanted to maintain safety and stability long enough for the boys to get old enough to be considered credible witnesses on their own behalf. When the FBI took Jesse and Nicholas away from their mother in May, the boys were still telling their story, pleading not to be sent back — a fact the FBI even acknowledged to the press.

Like other children on the run, Jesse and Nicholas certainly had great difficulties. They were coping with the aftermath of sexual abuse, the loss of their faith in the legal system, and the fear of being discovered and sent back to face more abuse. Yet, it was also a time of respite for them. The boys had neighborhood chums, bicycles, and Cub Scouts. They knew that, at least for a time, they wouldn't have to face the man they say abused them.

The day after Juanita and Michael were arrested, Jesse and Nicholas returned to Minnesota to the custody of their biological father. While in the custody of Washington Child Protective Services, the children, once again, repeated their story. Washington CPS took the extraordinary step of writing Minnesota, suggesting the state reinvestigate the case. The Lammers spent five days in jail, and when they were later extradited to Minnesota, received bail of $10,000 a piece. The Lammers face two years in prison for felony charges of custodial interference. Minnesota law recognizes a parent's belief of abuse of a child as a legitimate defense. If the Lammers are acquitted, they will try to regain custody of Jesse and Nicholas in family court. If they are convicted, their lawyers say they probably won't see the boys again. No matter what happens, the boys will someday face the personal ordeal of healing from all that's happened. When that time comes, their parents believe the boys will have at least this from which to start: they were believed by someone they loved and trusted.

Deborah Fisher is a writer and consultant in child abuse prevention and education. As former legal affairs reporter for Minnesota Public Radio, she specialized in covering children's issues such as the Scott County sexual abuse cases. The author became interested in researching and writing about sexual abuse allegations in the custody cases as a result of testifying on behalf of the children in the Lammer case.

COMMENTS

THE VOICE OF A CHILD: INDEPENDENT LEGAL REPRESENTATION OF CHILDREN IN PRIVATE CUSTODY DISPUTES WHEN SEXUAL ABUSE IS ALLEGED

KERIN S. BISCHOFF†

Children are our most precious resource, and it is fundamental that they have a chance to be brought up in an environment where they are not abused or neglected. To that end, it is the duty of our courts to use every available legal means to see that such a goal be attained.[1]

Children represent the future of society and the promise of humankind. Yet children are vulnerable, impressionable, and in need of guidance. When court proceedings will immutably alter childrens' lives, their interests must be voiced.[2]

"The right to representation by counsel is not a formality . . . it is of the essence of justice."[3] Children are now guaranteed legal representation in juvenile delinquency proceedings. Children in state-initiated investigations of suspected abuse are also provided with counsel, based on the premise that a child is an independent individual with the right to articulate her own interests in matters so fundamentally affecting the quality of her life.[4] When allegations of sexual abuse occur during a private custody battle, however, independent representation for the child is not required and is rarely provided. While some children's rights advocates urge requiring counsel to

---

† B.S. 1988, Bowling Green State University; J.D. Candidate 1991, University of Pennsylvania. This Comment is dedicated to Susan Knecht Smith, with many thanks.

[1] C.J.(S.)R. v. G.D.S., 701 S.W.2d 165, 169-70 (Mo. Ct. App. 1985).

[2] *See generally* J. WALLERSTEIN & S. BLAKESLEE, SECOND CHANCES: MEN, WOMEN & CHILDREN A DECADE AFTER DIVORCE (1989) [hereinafter SECOND CHANCES] (exploring the psychological impact of divorce on children); Foster & Freed, *A Bill of Rights for Children*, 6 FAM. L.Q. 343 (1972) (offering a framework of rights incorporating minors' expectations).

[3] Kent v. U.S., 383 U.S. 541, 561 (1966).

[4] *See* Stapleton v. Dauphin County Child Care Serv., 228 Pa. Super. 371, 381-382, 324 A.2d 562, 568 (1974).

represent children in all disputed custody cases,[5] little attention has been given to the special concerns raised by allegations of incest during custody disputes.

This Comment argues that allegations of sexual abuse made during custody disputes raise a particular need for independent legal representation of children. The predominant current legal standard, judicial discretion, often allows this need to go unmet. Independent legal representation of all potential victims of sexual abuse is essential to protect effectively the "best interests" of these children.

I. CURRENT STATE OF THE LAW REGARDING CHILDREN'S ADVOCATES IN PRIVATE CUSTODY DISPUTES

In general, present law does not require independent legal representation of children in private custody disputes. When parents divorce or separate, the court is vested with the authority to make a determination[6] regarding the custody of children.[7] The virtually universal standard mandated by legislatures to determine child custody disputes is the "best interests" standard.[8] While the substantive law of custody gives children a right to a determination made in

---

[5] Many of the sources cited in this Comment argue for appointing a guardian *ad litem* or a child advocate in all custody or disputed custody cases. While accepting the validity of these arguments, the author views those situations involving allegations of sexual abuse to implicate far more serious concerns.

[6] The court has jurisdiction to consider all issues surrounding the custody of children whenever parents appear in court for a divorce, annulment, or separation. *See e.g.*, CAL. CIV. CODE § 4600 (West 1983 & Supp. 1989); CONN. GEN. STAT. ANN. § 466-56 (West 1986). Courts typically incorporate the parties' privately reached custodial agreement into the judgment. However, the court's best interests inquiry is not precluded by a private agreement. *See* Mnookin & Kornhauser, *Bargaining in the Shadow of the Law: The Case of Divorce*, 88 YALE L.J. 950, 955 (1979).

[7] A "child" is a person who has not reached the age of state-determined civil majority, generally eighteen years. *See* Soler, Costello & O'Hearn, *Legal Rights of Children in the United States of America*, in LAW AND THE STATUS OF THE CHILD 675, 683 (A. Pappas ed. 1983) [hereinafter *Legal Rights of Children*]. Under the common law, a child under the age of seven was deemed incapable of forming the requisite intent to commit a crime. *See id.* at 683. Notably, the seven-year cut-off is often used as the age at which children are deemed to be competent to direct their attorneys. *See, e.g.*, JUVENILE LAW CENTER OF PHILADELPHIA, MODEL OF REPRESENTATION IN DEPENDENT COURT 7 (1986) ("When representing clients under age seven, we will assert rights on our client's behalf.").

[8] *See e.g.*, CAL. CIV. CODE § 4600(b) (West 1983 & Supp 1989); CONN. GEN. STAT. ANN. § 466-54 (West 1986); D.C. CODE ANN. §§ 16-911(a)(5), -914(a) (1981); HAW. REV. STAT. § 571-46(1) (1985); KY. REV. STAT. ANN. § 403.270 (Michie/Bobbs-Merrill 1984); MASS. ANN. LAWS ch. 208, § 31 (Law. Co-op 1989); N.Y. DOM. REL. LAW § 240 (McKinney 1986 & Supp. 1990); *see also* UNIFORM MARRIAGE & DIVORCE ACT § 402 (1974); Bazemore v. Davis, 394 A.2d 1377, 1383 (D.C. 1978) (holding that child's best interests are sole criterion in custody dispute between [biological] parents).

their "best interest," children generally do not have the right to have their views regarding their interests presented to the court.[9]

Recent standards issued by the American Bar Association would require the appointment of independent counsel in custody cases.[10] Only two states, however, mandate the appointment of a representative in all divorce-related custody disputes.[11] In most states, the appointment of a representative for children in private custody disputes is a matter of judicial discretion, either by statute[12] or by the judge's inherent power.[13]

---

[9] See Note, Due Process for Children: A Right to Counsel in Custody Proceedings, 4 N.Y.U. REV. L. & SOC. CHANGE 177, 177 (1974) [hereinafter Due Process].

[10] See A.B.A.-I.J.A. STANDARDS RELATING TO COUNSEL FOR PRIVATE PARTIES (1980), reprinted in CHILDREN'S RIGHTS CHRONICLE, Dec. 1983, at 3; see also A Divorce Reform Act, 5 HARV. J. ON LEGIS. 563, 583 (1968) (model act for child advocacy drafted by the Legislative Research Bureau of Harvard Law School which would require the appointment of independent counsel for all children whose rights might be affected in a divorce proceeding).

[11] See N.H. REV. STAT. ANN. § 458:17-a (Supp. 1989); WIS. STAT. ANN. § 767.045 (West 1981); Lane, The Guardian ad Litem in Divorce Cases, in FOUNDATIONS OF CHILD ADVOCACY 161, 164 (D. Bross & L. Michaels eds. 1987) (noting that Wisconsin and New Hampshire are the only two states which require the appointment of a guardian ad litem). Neither of these statutes makes special provisions for allegations of sexual abuse; counsel is provided in all disputed custody cases.

[12] See, e.g., CAL. CIV. CODE § 4606 (West 1983 & Supp. 1989) (providing for appointment of counsel upon court finding that appointment would be in child's best interests); CONN. GEN. STAT. ANN. § 466-54 (West 1971) (same); D.C. CODE ANN. § 16-918(b) (1981) (same); HAW. REV. STAT. § 571-46(8) (1985) (providing for appointment of guardian ad litem); MASS. ANN. LAWS. ch. 215, § 56A (Law. Co-op. 1986) (providing for appointment of guardian ad litem for investigative purposes); N.Y. JUD. LAW § 249 (McKinney 1983) (providing for appointment of law guardian where child is party to certain proceedings if child is sought to be placed in protective custody); WASH. REV. CODE ANN. § 26.09.110 (1986) (allowing for appointment of attorney if in child's best interests); WIS. STAT. ANN. § 767.045 (West 1981) (allowing for appointment of attorney where court has reason for "special concern"). States are split as to whether or not the appointed person must be an attorney. The Uniform Marriage and Divorce Act permits the appointment of an attorney in private custody disputes to act as an advocate on behalf of the child. See UNIF. MARRIAGE & DIVORCE ACT § 310, 9A U.L.A. 443 (1987). States may attempt to follow a policy of representation although the statutory language is permissive. See Lane, supra note 11, at 164. But see Foster & Freed, supra note 2, at 355 n.40 (stating that while Dom. Rel. Law. § 215-c, enacted in California, Iowa, Oregon, and New York, authorizes the appointment of a guardian in divorce cases, such authority is rarely exercised).

[13] See, e.g. Villareal v. State Dep't of Transp., 160 Ariz. 474, 481, 774 P.2d 213, 220 (1989) (stating that to ensure protection of rights of children, a trial judge may, upon his or her own motion, appoint a guardian ad litem); Gardner v. Gardner, 545 So.2d 339, 340 n.1 (Fla. Dist. Ct. App. 1989) (stating that in a custody case, the trial court has the option of appointing guardian ad litem if circumstances demand it); In re Marriage of Strauss, 183 Ill. App. 3d 424, 539 N.E.2d 808, 811 (1989) (holding that the courts have inherent power to appoint guardian ad litem for minors' interest in litigation); Parrillo v. Parrillo, 495 A.2d 683, 686 (R.I. 1985) (stating that "[i]t is well

Statutes granting discretionary power typically permit a judge to appoint a guardian *ad litem*[14] or an attorney when the court determines that such appointment would be in a child's "best interests" during custody, support, and visitation proceedings.[15] This standard is inherently indeterminate. Statutes may specify factors for consideration,[16] but a judge's discretion in determining what constitutes a child's best interests is accorded great latitude. When evidence is contradictory, as it typically is in sexual abuse cases, the trial judge is

---

settled that the trial justice has the inherent power to appoint a guardian ad litem whenever there are interests of a minor to be protected"). The statutes merely supplement the court's inherent equity jurisdiction and do not displace it. *See Due Process, supra* note 9, at 179 n.13.

[14] A guardian *ad litem* is generally defined as "a person invested during a legal proceeding with the power and duty to protect the rights and interests of a child (or an incompetent) involved in litigation." Davidson, *The Guardian* Ad Litem, CHILDREN TODAY, Mar.-Apr. 1981, at 1. There is no consensus as to the duties of the guardian *ad litem. See id.* The child advocate traditionally is granted some discretion to determine what the child's best interests may be. *See* Genden, *Separate Legal Representation for Children: Protecting the Rights and Interests of Minors in Judicial Proceedings,* 11 HARV. C.R.-C.L. L. REV. 565, 588 (1976); *infra* text accompanying notes 51-67.

[15] *See, e.g.,* CAL. CIV. CODE § 4606 (West 1989) (providing that in a proceeding in which custody is an issue, the court may, "if it finds it would be in the best interests of the minor child," appoint a guardian *ad litem*). Other statutes have enunciated this "best interests" standard in different ways. *See, e.g.,* N.D. CENT. CODE § 14-09-06.4 (1981) (providing that a guardian *ad litem* may be appointed where there is "special concern as to the future of the minor children"); OHIO R. CIV. P. § 75(B)(2) (Anderson 1989) (providing for the guardian *ad litem* when "essential to protect the child's interests").

The "best interests" standard is vague because society lacks a consensus about the determining values which define what is "best." The standard is even more difficult because unlike traditional litigation based on past conduct, a best interests analysis requires a prediction of future behavior. *See* Lane, *supra* note 11, at 176 (noting that continued use of the best interest standard promotes the denial of a child's due process right); Mnookin, *Child-Custody Adjudication: Judicial Functions in the Face of Indeterminacy,* 39 LAW & CONTEMP. PROBS. 226, 258-59 (1975) (noting that the determination of what is "best" or "least detrimental" for a child is usually speculative).

[16] *See e.g.,* UNIF. MARRIAGE & DIVORCE ACT § 402, 9A U.L.A. 561 (1987) (specifying parent's wishes as to custody, child's wishes as to custodian, child's interaction with parents, siblings, and others who may significantly affect best interests, child's adjustment to home, school, and community, and mental and physical health of all individuals involved, all taken into consideration); COLO. REV. STAT. § 14-10-124 (Supp. 1984) (Court shall consider all relevant factors including [those of UMDA § 402] and the ability of the custodian to encourage child's relationship with noncustodial parent); 1984 MINN. LAWS 518.17 Subdiv.1 (including wishes of parents, reasonable preference of child if deemed old enough, continuity of environment, and cultural background); *cf.* ALA. CODE § 30-3-1 (1983) (articulating standard as custody that may seem right and proper having regard to parents' prudence and moral character).

the sole evaluator of the credibility of evidence and subsequent review presumes reasonableness.[17]

Some courts have recognized the need for independent counsel in particularly bitter and protracted custody proceedings.[18] Divorced or divorcing parents' hostility toward one another may overshadow concern for the child's interests; as a result, the children's rights likely will not be fairly represented by the parents' counsel.[19] Appointing a legal representative "assure[s] that one voice will be raised in sole representation of the best interests of th[e] minor child."[20]

Operating under a discretionary statute, the Minnesota Court of Appeals found a trial court to have erred by failing to appoint a representative for two teenage girls in a custody suit in which sexual abuse by the step-father was alleged.[21] The court recognized that when physical and emotional safety are in question, the interests of children are different from their parents and will not adequately be represented without "vigorous, independent representation of the children by counsel acting only in their interest."[22]

Similarly, a Missouri Court of Appeals held that it is an abuse of discretion not to appoint a representative when the choice of custodian is at issue and the "court has knowledge, from the pleadings or from any other source, that the children . . . have been, or are being, abused."[23]

When the sexual molestation of a child is even a remote possibility, allegations of sexual abuse should automatically evoke the "special concern" necessary under a discretionary standard to compel the appointment of an independent representative. Because of the com-

---

[17] *See* Atkinson, *Criteria for Deciding Child Custody in the Trial and Appellate Courts*, 18 FAM. L.Q. 1, 40 (1984) (describing a recent study which found that 30 states' appellate courts will affirm a trial court's custody decision unless it is a "clear abuse of discretion" or is "against the manifest weight of the evidence").

[18] *See, e.g.,* Yontef v. Yontef, 185 Conn. 275, 284, 440 A.2d 899, 904 (1981) (stating that the better course is to appoint independent counsel in seriously contested cases); Gennarini v. Gennarini, 2 Conn. App. 132, 477 A.2d 674, 675 n.3 (1984) (same).

[19] *See* Martinez v. Martinez, 101 N.M. 493, 496, 684 P.2d 1158, 1161 (1984) (stating that when a child's welfare is at stake, the court would carefully review the record to ensure the child's interests were protected); Higgins v. Higgins, 629 S.W.2d 20, 22 (Tenn. Ct. App. 1981) (stating that in cases of intense hostility, children should have the benefit of independent counsel).

[20] Clark v. Clark, 358 N.W.2d 438, 441 (Minn. Ct. App. 1984).

[21] *See* M.M. v. R.R.M., 358 N.W.2d 86, 89 (Minn. Ct. App. 1984).

[22] *Id.* at 89.

[23] C.J.(S.)R. v. G.D.S., 701 S.W.2d 165, 169 (Mo. Ct. App. 1985).

peting notions of *parens patriae* and family autonomy,[24] and the skepticism with which such allegations tend to be received by judges, however, this is not the case. Possible sexual abuse in a custody dispute does not uniformly trigger the appointment of counsel. Discretion allows some children who may have been sexually abused to go unrepresented.[25]

For example, in *Sucher v. Sucher,*[26] a Minnesota appeals court upheld a trial court's refusal to appoint a guardian *ad litem* to represent three children in a custody battle.[27] Despite allegations and some evidence of sexual abuse, the trial judge's failure to appoint a representative was held not to be an abuse of discretion.[28] The child's story vacillated during an in camera interview and was therefore considered insufficient evidence to trigger the discretionary standard.[29] While the child's role in this case was critical, counsel was denied based on the court's opinion that all the circumstances of the children had been fully litigated and that there were no alternatives which a guardian could have presented.[30]

II.   WHY REQUIRE INDEPENDENT REPRESENTATION?

Children must be provided with independent representation whenever allegations of sexual abuse are made because neither the judge nor the child's parents can adequately represent the child's interests. For the child, fundamental bodily and psychological integrity is at stake. "Independent representation by counsel [whenever the child's welfare is at stake] is the most significant and practical reform that can be made in the area of children and the law . . . reform should be directed at [permitting] all interested parties—including children—to have independent counsel."[31]

As stated earlier, the substantive law guarantees all children in divorce cases the right to custody determinations made in their best

---

[24] *See* discussion *infra* notes 68-94 and accompanying text.

[25] *See Who's Taking Care of the Children? They May Need Counsel,* CAL. LAW., Nov. 1987, at 12 [hereinafter *Who's Taking Care*] (stating that many judges, while authorized under California Civil Code § 4606, are reluctant to appoint attorneys for children, and adding that children often go unrepresented for want of available attorneys).

[26] 416 N.W.2d 182 (Minn. Ct. App. 1987).

[27] *See id.* at 185.

[28] *See id.*

[29] *See id.* at 183.

[30] *See id.* at 185 (stating that foster care was the only alternative which a guardian could have presented).

[31] Foster & Freed, *supra* note 2, at 356.

interests.[32] The resolution of sexual abuse allegations will significantly shape the judge's assessment of the child's best interests.[33] Yet the difficulties of proving sexual abuse[34] are exacerbated by the divorce context and, therefore, abuse is often not legally established despite significant physical and psychological evidence.[35] The ramifications of an erroneous decision—either ordering continued contact when a child is in actual jeopardy[36] or constraining the relationship with a falsely accused parent[37]—make improved procedural standards at both the fact-finding and disposition stages essential in order to meet the statutory best interests mandate.[38]

Mandatory legal representation will ensure that the child's voice is heard.[39] Representation is the sole procedure which assures that

---

[32] See supra notes 6-9 and accompanying text.

[33] See e.g., Md. Fam. Law Code Ann. § 9-101 (Supp. 1989) (stating that unsupervised visitation and custody shall be denied to a party whom the court finds has abused a child, unless it is specifically found that there is no likelihood of further abuse).

[34] Sexual abuse is difficult to prove because of the lack of corroborating witnesses, the victim's age, real and perceived problems in the credibility and competency of the child witness, clashes with the defendant's sixth amendment confrontation rights, and various cultural prejudices. See Apel, Custodial Parents, Child Sexual Abuse, and the Legal Systems: Beyond Contempt, 38 Am. U.L. Rev. 491, 495-501 (1989); Keating, Children in Incestuous Relationships: the Forgotten Victims, 34 Loy. L. Rev. 111, 112-113 (1988).

[35] See Keating supra note 34, at 113-15 (stating that societal disbelief of the frequency of incest leads to judicial prejudice against accusing parents); see also infra text accompanying notes 101-04.

[36] See Goldson, Child Development and the Response to Maltreatment, in Foundations of Child Advocacy 3, 13 (D. Bross & L. Michaels eds. 1987) (noting common symptoms of withdrawal, self-abusive behavior, and internalized guilt resulting from disruption of normal psychological development); Kerns, The Pediatric Perspective, in Foundations of Child Advocacy, supra, at 23, 33 (stating that the psychological impact of sexual abuse ranges from acute trauma to the catastrophic and continuing developmental damage associated with continued incest).

[37] See Second Chances, supra note 2, at 257 (recognizing the importance of maintaining two parents in the postdivorce family for the child's self-esteem and psychological well-being).

[38] See Besharov, The Need to Narrow the Grounds for State Intervention, in Protecting Children from Abuse & Neglect: Policy and Practice 47 (C. Thomas ed. 1988), reprinted in Child Abuse and Neglect 32, 36 (American Bar Ass'n. Nat'l Legal Resource Center for Child Advocacy and Protection eds. 1989); Genden, supra note 14, at 565 (noting that children's rights and interests are jeopardized when their best interests are determined without an independent advocate).

[39] See Hansen, Guardians Ad Litem in Divorce and Custody Cases: Protection of the Child's Interests, 4 J. Fam. L. 181, 184 (1964) (discussing the Milwaukee Family Court system of appointing a guardian ad litem whenever custody is disputed and stating that having an advocate ensures court concern for the rights of children); cf. Who's Taking Care, supra note 25, at 12 (noting the perception of a Juvenile Court

all matters of law will be available for the determination of the child's best interests.[40] Without independent representation, the child, whether an actual victim of incest or not, risks needless abuse by the legal system charged to protect her best interests. Even if sexual abuse is not ultimately proven,[41] the allegations themselves generate the need for representation because of the physical, psychological, and emotional probing of the fact-finding process. Any court adjudicating claims of sexual abuse without the participation of the child's advocate is relying on indirect, secondary evidence from parents, psychologists, and physicians. It is curious that when the potential harm to a child is so great, the judicial system would grant such importance to secondary evidence "when direct evidence is so easily obtainable. The best interests of a child can best be determined on the basis of objective, independent evidence . . . made available to the court [by] independent counsel."[42]

The family court forum in which a judge considers allegations of sexual abuse made during divorce proceedings poses unique problems for the sexually abused child which necessitate according the child the extra procedural protection of a voice.[43] Family courts are traditionally concerned with the equitable distribution of property and the reasonable access of both parents to their children. In fact, good faith allegations are insufficient summarily to halt continued contact with an alleged abuser. In "normal" divorce cases, preserving the continued contact of children with both parents is justifiable. When a child is subjected to sexual molestation, however, continued contact is exceedingly harmful.[44]

Sucher v. Sucher[45] demonstrates the potential dangers of a system in which appointment of independent representation is discretionary. The trial judge is not in a position to determine whether the

---

Commissioner that an advocate is needed when there are serious allegations of child abuse or when a controversial issue such as religious lifestyle threatens to overwhelm the child's interests).

[40] *See Due Process, supra* note 9, at 185.

[41] Commentators have observed that in many cases "presexual conditioning," a precursor to molestation, has taken place, even if actual sexual abuse has not yet occurred. *See* Walker & Edwall, *Domestic Violence and Determination of Visitation and Custody in Divorce, in* DOMESTIC VIOLENCE ON TRIAL 127, 136 (D. Sonkin ed. 1987).

[42] Inker & Perretta, *A Child's Right to Counsel in Custody Cases,* 5 FAM. L. Q. 108, 115 (1971).

[43] *See* Keating, *supra* note 34, at 112 (noting that "[s]uch courts are set up to compromise and settle difficulties between two spouses").

[44] *See id.*

[45] 416 N.W.2d 182 (Minn. Ct. App. 1987). *See supra* notes 26-30 and accompanying text for discussion.

child's circumstances, from the child's point of view, have been fully litigated. Rather, the advocate for the child, who is obligated to represent the child's interests, should make this determination. As the court stated in *M.M. v. R.R.M.*,[46] when "the missing element [is] vigorous, independent representation of the children by counsel," the record available for the trial judge will be "woefully incomplete."[47]

Finally, the discretionary standard is an inadequate safeguard when the consequences of a wrong decision are as devastating as those following incest.[48] The legal representation of children is one affirmative step that can help the legal system operate in favor of abused children. While independent legal representation does not promise a complete solution to the dilemmas posed by sexual abuse allegations in divorce cases, the appearance of an attorney for the child may help a judge make "reasoned determinations of fact and . . . disposition."[49] Suspected victims of sexual abuse need the "assistance of counsel to cope with problems of law, to make skilled inquiry into the facts, [and] to insist upon regularity of the proceedings."[50] In order to determine the best interests of children, the child's voice must be heard in all cases in which sexual abuse is alleged.

III. The Role of the Child's Representative

Ambiguity about the attorney's role in family litigation has emerged as an important issue in recent years.[51] The role of chil-

---

[46] 358 N.W.2d 86 (Minn. Ct. App. 1984).

[47] *Id.* at 89.

[48] The effects of incest follow its victims into adulthood: creating cynical, troubled, and possibly dangerous adults and perpetuating a vicious cycle as the adults who were child-victims become offenders. *See supra* note 36. It is only by breaking the cycle of grossly inadequate parent-child relationships that society stands to gain capable parents for the future. *See* J. Goldstein, A. Freud & A. Solnit, Beyond the Best Interests of the Child 7 (1983). Teaching children that the abuser will be sanctioned helps to break the cycle. Acting to ensure the proper adjudication of allegations of sexual abuse is not merely an act of humane concern for children, but also an act of enlightened societal self interest. *See* Delaney, *The Battered Child and the Law,* in Helping the Battered Child and His Family, 187, 193 (C. Kempe & R. Helfer eds. 1972) [hereinafter Helping the Battered Child]

[49] *In re* Gault, 387 U.S. 1, 40 (1967) (quoting N.Y. Family Court Act § 241 with approval and holding that a juvenile has a right to counsel in a serious delinquency proceeding) (discussed *infra* at notes 117-22 and accompanying text).

[50] *Id.* at 36.

[51] *See* Isaacs, *The Role of the Lawyer in Child Abuse Cases,* in Helping the Battered Child, *supra* note 48, at 225 (stating that acceptance of social work techniques and objectives in the judicial process has created much uncertainty as to the role of counsel in family litigation).

dren's counsel is often undefined and, consequently, hotly disputed.[52] Should she play the role of a guardian *ad litem,* who determines what is best for a child,[53] or that of an advocate, who is obligated to present the wishes of her client? Also, should the child's representative, regardless of role, be required to be an attorney?

In order to ensure that the child's voice is heard in court, a representative should be an advocate who will advance the child's position and not make independent judgments of the child's best interests.[54] An advocate, unlike a traditional guardian *ad litem,*[55] insures that the child's voice is heard with full force in legal proceedings. To be effective, such an advocate should also be a lawyer.[56] The following credo characterizes the role the attorney should play:

---

[52] *See, e.g.,* Redeker, *The Right of an Abused Child to Independent Counsel and the Role of the Child Advocate in Child Abuse Cases,* 23 VILL. L. REV. 521, 539 (1978) (arguing that the guardian *ad litem* representation of state-determined "best interests" does not fulfill the child's need for counsel); *Representing Dependent Children,* CHILDREN'S RIGHTS CHRONICLE, Dec. 1983, at 1 (discussing the lack of a clear model of representation in dependency cases).

[53] *See supra* note 14 (defining guardian *ad litem*).

[54] *See* Redeker, *supra* note 52, at 539-42 (advocating the need for legal counsel representing the child, and criticizing the concept of guardians *ad litem*); Genden, *supra* note 14, at 588-89; *see also* Bross, *An Introduction to Child Representation,* in FOUNDATIONS OF CHILD ADVOCACY 85, 86 (D. Bross & L. Michaels eds. 1987) (noting that confusion as to the role of the attorney, even when the child cannot express her wishes is not justified, since "[i]t is no longer a question that objective standards can be established for representation of incompetent adults or other individuals"). Even when a client is too young to direct an attorney, the closest approximation of a normal attorney-client relationship, uninfluenced by third parties, best achieves the desired representation. *See* Comment, *Speaking For a Child: The Role of Independent Counsel for Minors,* 75 CALIF. L. REV. 681, 701-05 (1987) (advocating a doctrine of substituted judgment whereby an attorney focuses on what the particular child, if mature, would desire).

[55] *See* Note, *Lawyering for the Child,* 87 YALE L. J. 1126, 1140-41 (1978) (noting that the traditional guardian *ad litem* is a nonadvocate representative, more properly termed an investigator).

[56] While not dismissing those child advocacy programs which have utilized non-lawyers, *see, e.g.,* Blady, *Special Child Advocates: A Volunteer Court Program,* CHILDREN TODAY, May-June 1981, at 2 (discussing the benefits of court appointed special advocate volunteer programs in representing children); Comment, *The Non-Lawyer Guardian* ad Litem *in Child Abuse and Neglect Proceedings,* 58 WASH. L. REV. 853, 864-67 (1983) (describing a program using non-lawyer volunteers backed up by lawyers), this Comment is based on the premise that the child's voice must be one "guided by relevant legal tradition and principles." Bross, *supra* note 54, at 85. The child's advocate must handle the maze of legal rules in order to "facilitate the legal process so that the child is not damaged or compromised by a system whose goals should be to protect the child, but which . . . may . . . lose sight of the child's needs and capacities." Goldson, *supra* note 36, at 17-18.

A tension between social work and law is unavoidable in this context. Each has its role for the child and, in the ideal situation, there will be an attorney advocate and

We are, first, lawyers charged with representing clients. . . . [E]ven though our client may be young, when he or she is capable of exercising minimal judgment we will represent the client's position to the court. . . . We will not represent a position to the court that is contrary to our client's wishes. . . . We do not believe that it is appropriate for [us] to assume the function of the court . . . .[57]

The court ultimately is responsible for the child's best interests: "the trial court does not function solely as an arbiter between . . . private parties [but must] determine what . . . would best guarantee an opportunity for the children involved to grow [in]to mature and responsible citizens."[58] A preliminary assessment by an advocate of these best interests usurps the judge's authority and prejudices the determination. While social and psychological expert testimony aids the judge in her determination of the child's "best interests," the child's voice must be heard and must inform any truly valid determination.

The child's advocate should represent only the interests of the child, and not consider the competing claims of the parents in the custody case. Once a parent's claim affects the representation, the child effectively has lost her advocate. For example, even when a child expresses terror and pleads with her "advocate" not to send her to an alleged abuser, the counsel who is affected by parents' concerns may fail to oppose visitation.[59] In this scenario, what force does the child's voice really have? Who protects the child from the lawyer, and why have a lawyer at all?[60]

When the attorney is guided by her conception of a child's best interests and not by the voice of the child, interest conflicts or diminished representation may be overlooked. For example, in one paren-

---

a guardian *ad litem*. If there is only one representative, it ought to be the attorney, and the social worker can testify as a witness for the child as the American Bar Association has suggested. *See infra* notes 64-66.

[57] Juvenile Law Center of Philadelphia, JLC Model of Representation in Dependent Court (draft Feb. 24, 1986).

[58] Hansen, *supra* note 39, at 184 (quoting Kritzik v. Kritzik, 21 Wis. 2d 442, 124 N.W.2d 581 (1963)).

[59] *See, e.g.*, Apel, *supra* note 34, at 492-93 (containing an excellent chronology of the Morgan case); *Hilary's Guardian: A Breach of Trust*, Legal Times, Feb. 20, 1989, at 19, col. 4 (letter to editor claiming that although empowered to cancel or interrupt visits, the guardian of Hilary Foretich, the child in the highly publicized Morgan-Foretich case, did not do so despite the child's express wishes). This scenario is especially problematic because of the preference for keeping families and parent-child relationships intact. *See infra* note 80 and accompanying text.

[60] *See* Juvenile Law Center of Philadelphia, *supra* note 57, at 2 (expressing concern that lawyers will "present a case that is contrary to a client's wishes").

tal rights termination proceeding where abuse was alleged, the "advocate of the child's best interests" standard permitted the dual representation of two children whose wishes were diametrically opposed. One child wanted to return to her mother while the other child did not.[61] Because the children's counsel's role was to advocate the children's best interests, however, the Iowa Supreme Court found no "actual" conflict.[62] Furthermore, because it was a juvenile proceeding, the court was unwilling to presume prejudice from the dual representation "even if under ordinary [criminal] standards a substantial possibility of conflict would be shown."[63]

Standards proposed jointly by the American Bar Association and the Institute for Judicial Administration expressly reject the traditional guardian *ad litem* model of representing children and urge advocacy of the child's interests.[64] In protective proceedings "where the juvenile is capable of considered judgment on his or her own behalf, determination of the client's interest in the proceeding should ultimately remain the client's responsibility."[65] The introduction to the Standards claims that this model of the lawyer-client relationship is necessary to achieve fundamental goals of the legal system, including enforcement of the child's substantive rights and facilitation of accurate determination of factual and legal issues through the adversary process.[66]

Whenever there is suspicion that children have been sexually abused, representation by an attorney acting as an advocate should be required.[67] Any legislation requiring representation must clearly

---

[61] *See In re* J.P.B. and C.R.B., 419 N.W.2d 387 (Iowa 1988) (claiming that the dual representation did not prevent the effective representation of the child who wished to remain with the petitioner).

[62] *See id.* at 390.

[63] *Id.* at 392.

[64] *See* IJA-ABA JOINT COMMISSION ON JUVENILE JUSTICE STANDARDS, STANDARDS RELATING TO COUNSEL FOR PRIVATE PARTIES Standard 3.1(a) (1976).

[65] *Id.* at Standard 3.1(b)(ii)(b). However, the Standard continues that in cases involving "very young persons" the child

> may be incapable of considered judgment, in which case responsibility passes to the guardian *ad litem*. If no guardian *ad litem* has been appointed, the attorney is to determine the child's interest after inquiring into all relevant circumstances or may elect to confine her role to fact finding only and take no position before the court.

Id. at Standard 3.1(b)(ii)(c) and comment.

[66] *See id.* at 3-5 (introduction to standards).

[67] *See* de Montigny v. de Montigny, 70 Wis. 2d 131, 138, 233 N.W.2d 463, 467 (1975) ("It is clear that a guardian *ad litem* appointed to represent children is more than a nominal representative appointed to counsel and consult with the trial judge. Rather, he has all the duties, powers, and responsibilities of counsel who represents a

delineate the responsibility of the child advocate in order to provide all incest victims the voice needed to protect their interests.

IV. ADDRESSING THE ARGUMENTS AGAINST INDEPENDENT LEGAL REPRESENTATION

A. *Parens Patriae*

Children in private custody battles where sexual abuse is alleged currently must rely on judicial discretion for independent legal representation.[68] *Parens patriae*, a derivative of English common law, is often used as a spearhead against the use of children's advocates; the notion is that "[t]he king should protect all who have no other protector, that he is the guardian above all guardians . . . . The king's justices see no great reason why every infant should have a permanent guardian, because they believe that they can do full justice to infants."[69] Many judges believe that the parents' representatives and the "independent investigative powers and duties of the court . . . adequately protect the children's interests and renders unnecessary the extra expense and delay of cases by court appointment of counsel to independently represent the children."[70] According to the *parens patriae* doctrine, children do not need independent legal representation because their interests are protected by the court itself. The legal system relies heavily on this premise.[71]

As noted in a *Bill of Rights for Children,* it is an anomaly that children in any divorce proceeding are unrepresented. "The major disputed issue may be their custody and visitation rights, and in a very real sense, they may be the principal parties in interest since the ultimate issue . . . is their welfare and best interests."[72] This argument has greater force when sexual abuse is alleged, because the court

---

party to litigation."); *c.f.* Vande Hoven v. Vande Hoven, 336 N.W.2d 366, 368 (N.D. 1983) (stating in dicta that where sexual abuse is alleged, "it appears to be in the best interests of the children to have their guardian *ad litem* bestowed with full advocacy authority"). Note that the court in *Vande Hoven* was operating under a statutory requirement that a guardian *ad litem* was to advocate the best interests. *See* N.D. CENT. CODE § 14-09-06.4 (1981).

[68] *See supra* notes 12-17 and accompanying text (describing the discretionary standard as the current state of the law).

[69] II F. POLLOCK & F. MAITLAND, THE HISTORY OF ENGLISH LAW 445 (2d ed. 1899).

[70] Chalupa v. Chalupa, 220 Neb. 704, 705-06, 371 N.W.2d 706, 707-08 (1985).

[71] *See Legal Rights of Children, supra* note 7, at 677 n.14 (noting current American law).

[72] Foster & Freed, *supra* note 2, at 355.

decides not only which parent will have custody but whether or not the child's body and mind will continue to be invaded. Regrettably, these children are legally no more entitled to a "voice" than children in any other custody dispute.

If the victim of incest is to realize her right to legal protection, her story must first be heard.[73] As a Milwaukee family court judge who has instituted the appointment of guardians *ad litem* in all disputed custody cases has noted:

> When two terriers fight over a bone, the bone does not join the fighting. But a child is not a thing or an object to go as a prize to the winner of a contest . . . . The whole future life of the child will be affected by the court's decision . . . . Will such basic interests of the child be adequately represented or even presented to the court by the attorneys for the warring litigants? . . . Is not a minor and dependent child whose parents are involved in a divorce case entitled to . . . representation [similar to that given to a child in a tort or probate action] at least in those cases in which custody becomes a matter of dispute between the parties or concern to the court?[74]

Judges who serve as protectors of children's social and legal interests sacrifice impartiality.[75] The composite voices of social psychologists, physicians, parents, and young children upon which judges may rely cannot equal the autonomous legal voices of children themselves.[76] Professor Laurence Tribe recognized the potential limits of wise and benevolent paternalism, stating:

> If the universality of the childhood experience . . . could guarantee empathy from adult lawmakers despite the absence of children from legislative assemblies, there would be no occasion to regard children as an isolated and unrepresented minority in need of special protection; but if adults instead look with contempt at a stage they have "outgrown" and will never re-enter, then every privilege withheld . . . from the young must become a source of suspicion.[77]

---

[73] *See id.* ("The right to be heard includes the right to have standing in legal proceedings to assert one's claims of interest.").

[74] Hansen, *supra* note 39, at 181-82.

[75] *See* Isaacs, *The Role of the Lawyer in Child Abuse Cases,* in HELPING THE BATTERED CHILD AND HIS FAMILY 225, 229 (C. Kempe & R. Helfer eds. 1972) ("Even the judge cannot adequately serve as protector of the legal . . . interests of the child without seriously sacrificing the appearance of impartiality").

[76] *See* Tribe, *Childhood, Suspect Classifications, and Conclusive Presumptions: Three Linked Riddles,* 39 LAW & CONTEMP. PROBS. 8, 12 n.14 (Summer 1975) (stating that the basic message of *In re Gault,* discussed *infra* at notes 117-22 and accompanying text, is that "the best paternalistic intentions toward children cannot substitute for procedurally fair juvenile hearings").

[77] *Id.* at 9 (footnote omitted).

In order to ensure the vitality of the legal system, judges must recognize that today's children may view situations such as custody and visitation in unique and unprecedented ways. The need for an individualized voice is critical in this context because determinations are based on the best interests analysis, and society lacks a consensus regarding what is "best" for children.[78] Thus, when the consequences of a disposition may be irreparably harmful, as in the case of sexual abuse,[79] individualized children's voices must be heard. Independent legal representation that articulates the voice of each child is the best way to accomplish this objective.

B. Familial Privacy

Another obstacle to the independent representation of allegedly abused children in private custody cases stems from a perception of the American family as an autonomous "private government" with protected interests.[80] Because children legally are incapable of determining what is in their best interests, and parents legally are presumed competent to represent their children's interests, appointing counsel for children is often seen as infringing on parental rights.[81]

Society protects the right of individuals to marry,[82] to procreate or not to procreate,[83] and, increasingly, to define themselves as

---

78 See id. at 27 (calling for individualization when the dissolving moral consensus affects agreed-upon fundamental rights, such as the circumstances warranting depriving a parent of the right to raise her child).

79 See supra note 36 (discussing the consequences of sexual abuse).

80 See Griswold v. Connecticut, 381 U.S. 479, 485-86 (1965) (reserving a constitutionally protected sphere of privacy within a family). The view of the family as a private "corporation" dictates that the state will do everything to support the unification of the family. Therefore, it is rare for a court to deny visitation rights even if there is known physical and sexual abuse of the child. See DOMESTIC VIOLENCE ON TRIAL: PSYCHOLOGICAL AND LEGAL DIMENSIONS OF FAMILY VIOLENCE 149 (D. Sonkin ed. 1987).

81 See J. GOLDSTEIN, A. FREUD & A. SOLNIT, supra note 48, at 9-14 (discussing the legal status of children); Guggenheim, The Right to be Represented But Not Heard: Reflections on Legal Representation for Children, 59 N.Y.U. L. REV. 76, 121-22 (1984) (arguing that because the best interests test makes virtually all aspects of a parent's life relevant, a child advocate may probe into "deeply held secrets" which parents have privately agreed to keep out of the court's consideration).

82 See Zablocki v. Redhail, 434 U.S. 374, 383 (1978) (holding that the right to marry is fundamental).

83 See Griswold, 381 U.S. at 483-85 (creating a marital privacy right derived from Bill of Rights guarantees). A drastically different approach would be to require state licensing of all prospective biological and adoptive parents. See LaFollette, Licensing Parents, 9 PHILOSOPHY AND PUBLIC AFFAIRS 182 (1980) (supporting such licensing).

"families" for many purposes.[84] Families may protect themselves against state intrusion by invoking constitutionally protected rights of privacy.[85] It is incongruous, however, to restrict the exercise of such rights to traditional family units while ignoring the individual rights of children from shattered families.[86] The theory of the family as an inviolable unit presumes that the family is intact and can be counted on to protect its members.[87] When divorce and abuse disintegrate the family social unit, viewing the family as paramount may fail to protect the child.[88]

Parents embroiled in custody disputes involving allegations of abuse are particularly inappropriate representatives of their child's welfare or wishes.[89] When one parent alleges sexual abuse by the other, the accused parent's judgment and parental fitness is ques-

---

[84] *See, e.g.*, Moore v. City of East Cleveland, 431 U.S. 494 (1977) (invalidating a housing ordinance which did not recognize a grandparent and grandchild as a "family," arbitrarily cutting off the protection of family rights at the boundary of the nuclear family); Smith v. Organization of Foster Families, 431 U.S. 816, 842-47 (1977) (suggesting that foster families have sufficient indicia of "family" to entitle them to some constitutional protection); Santa Barbara v. Adamson, 27 Cal. 3d 123, 610 P.2d 436, 164 Cal. Rptr. 539 (1980) (relying on a state constitutional privacy provision to strike down city zoning ordinance that defined family to exclude groups of more than five unmarried people); Braschi v. Stahl Assocs. Co., 74 N.Y.2d 201, 543 N.E.2d 49, 544 N.Y.S.2d 784 (1989) (holding that a homosexual relationship constitutes a "family" under New York City's rent-control regulations); Gutis, *What Is A Family? Traditional Limits Are Being Redrawn*, N.Y. Times, August 31, 1989, at C1, col. 5 (discussing *Braschi* and "domestic partnership laws," noting that as society changes, the definition of family also changes, and quoting Professor Robert F. Kelly: "the law is basically trying to catch up to these transformations in family structure").

[85] *See* Richards, *The Individual, the Family, and the Constitution: A Jurisprudential Perspective*, 55 N.Y.U. L. REV. 1, 4 & n.35 (1980).

[86] *See supra* text accompanying note 72.

[87] *See* SECOND CHANCES, *supra* note 2, at 17 (noting that the present understanding of child development and family life is almost entirely based on the intact family form).

[88] *See* J. GOLDSTEIN, A. FREUD & A. SOLNIT, *supra* note 48, at 66 (stating that "the presumption [of parental representation] should not prevail . . . once the child's placement becomes the subject of a dispute" taken to the courts and in other situations where there is no "conflict-free interest" in representing the child). In these cases, the child should be accorded party status and given independent representation. *See id.*; Inker & Perretta, *supra* note 42, at 111; Podell, *The "Why" Behind Appointing Guardians Ad Litem for Children in Divorce Proceedings*, 57 MARQ. L. REV. 103, 103 (1973) (stating that the child of divorce is a "disenfranchised victim used as a pawn in a game of chess being played between its warring parents who frequently want the court to physically cut up and divide the child between them in the same manner that they have [done] emotionally").

[89] *See* Lempp, *Child Welfare and the Law: A Medical and Psychiatric Viewpoint*, in THE CHILD AND THE LAW 213, 221 (F. Bates ed. 1976) (discussing the protection of children's interests in divorce actions).

tioned.[90] As an interested party, each parent should be presumed incapable of presenting a voice that contradicts his or her own.[91] Neither parent can be relied upon to speak for the child; consequently, an extremely deferential approach to the parents is no longer viable. For this reason, the child's voice must be heard in order to procedurally protect her best interests. This need outweighs competing concerns.[92] To assume that the parents' attorneys have covered the entire agenda ignores the reality that "in countless circumstances a juvenile's rights and interests . . . are at sharp variance with those of his parents."[93] The possibility of abuse and allegations of such certainly constitute one of those circumstances. Indeed, "[w]ithout a separate advocate, the court may not perceive the existence of the special needs of the child."[94]

V. LEGAL FOUNDATIONS FOR INDEPENDENT REPRESENTATION

This Comment has argued that when sexual abuse is alleged, a statutory commitment to a best interests determination requires the procedural protection of independent legal representation for a child. In addition to the best interests rationale, reform in the private custody dispute context may be based on analogous statutory authority or on constitutional grounds. Ultimately, finding constitutional authority is less important[95] than sensitizing courts and legislators to the need of every child for independent counsel when allegations of sexual abuse are asserted. In the end, however, judicial discretion is too slim a reed upon which to rest the right to be free from sexual molestation. Legislators have already recognized that when the state alleges abuse, a child must be provided represen-

---

90 See Bross, supra note 54, at 86.

91 See Redeker, supra note 52, at 527-28. Just as the rights of the parent or custodian and the rights of a child conflict in a child abuse action, so too does a conflict exist between the child and her parents in a custody suit where abuse is alleged. Just as the state is an "interested party" when it initiates abuse proceedings against a parent, parents suing for custody are also parties with interests distinct from the child's. See id.

92 cf. Podell, supra note 88, at 107 (dismissing parental objections to counsel as lacking merit in light of the child's interests). Arguments in favor of parental privacy rights rely heavily on the premise that both parents in a custody dispute are fit and, therefore, that a child without counsel faces only a small risk of damage. See Guggenheim, supra note 81, at 121-22. Continued sexual abuse by one of the parents obviously negates this underlying premise.

93 In re Clark, 21 Ohio Op. 2d 86, 87, 185 N.E.2d 128, 130 (1962).

94 Genden, supra note 14, at 573.

95 See id. at 581 (noting that avoiding constitutional issues may be advantageous as a matter of litigation strategy).

tation. This right of representation must be extended to include the children in private custody disputes who are possible victims of abuse.

A.   *Analogy to State-Initiated Investigations of Abuse*

When a state alleges abuse, the child who is the subject of the custody proceeding is generally statutorily guaranteed representation. Such a guarantee is strongly supported by the federal government, particularly in cases of child *sexual* abuse.[96] The Child Abuse Prevention and Treatment Act[97] conditions the granting of federal funds for the handling of child abuse cases on a state's provision of a guardian *ad litem* to represent the child in "every case involving an abused or neglected child which results in a judicial proceeding."[98] State statutes commonly require that when the state alleges abuse,

---

[96] While it was once assumed that the judge, the attorney for the child's parents, and the attorney for the agency bringing proceedings were capable of adequately representing the child's interests, an "analysis of the roles and responsibilities of these attorneys shows that they cannot fully represent the interests of the child and that there is a clear and demonstrable need to provide the child with independent representation in abuse and neglect proceedings." NAT'L CENTER ON CHILD ABUSE & NEGLECT, U.S. DEP'T OF HEALTH & HUMAN SERVS., REPRESENTATION FOR THE ABUSED AND NEGLECTED CHILD: THE GUARDIAN AD LITEM AND LEGAL COUNSEL 2 (1980).

Congress has recognized that child abuse is a steadily increasing problem of significant national magnitude that imposes both social and economic costs on its victims and on society. *See* H.R. REP. No. 135, 100th Cong., 2d Sess. 18, 20-21, *reprinted in* 1988 U.S. CODE CONG. & ADMIN. NEWS 72, 75, 77. In recognition of the problem, Congress has acted to impose responsibilities on the states and federal government to monitor the effectiveness and facilitate the improvement of the independent legal representation of children in abuse cases. *See, e.g.,* Child Abuse Prevention, Adoption, and Family Services Act of 1988, Pub. L. No. 100-294, 102 Stat. 102, 118 (codified as amended at 42 U.S.C.A. § 5105 note (West Supp. 1989)) (requiring the National Center on Child Abuse and Neglect to study the provisions of legal representation of children in each state as well as the effectiveness of such representation); *id.* at 113-16 (codified as amended at 42 U.S.C.A. § 5106c(c)-(e) (West Supp. 1989)) (requiring as a predicate for federal funding of the handling of child abuse cases, particularly cases of sexual abuse, that each state designate a task force whose recommendations must be adopted).

[97] 42 U.S.C.A. § 5101-07 (West 1983 & Supp. 1989). The 1988 amendments to the Act seek to (1) improve the quality of the administration of the National Center on Child Abuse and Neglect; (2) strengthen the coordination of its efforts with other federal agencies to implement a unified approach to guide national priorities; (3) expand the activities to be performed with regard to the collection and dissemination of research and data; and (4) emphasize the importance of identification and prevention efforts. *See* H.R. REP. No. 135, *supra* note 96, at 22-25, *reprinted in* 1988 U.S. CODE CONG. & ADMIN. NEWS 72, 78-82.

[98] 42 U.S.C.A. § 5106a(b)(6) (West Supp. 1989). The statute's effectiveness may be questioned given that it does not specify whether the guardian *ad litem* must be an attorney.

the child must be provided with independent representation.[99] The federal and state governments, however, have not extended this right to the many potentially sexually abused children in private custody disputes. Given Congress' express recognition of the importance of representation in sexual abuse cases brought by the state, the different treatment of children in private cases is unjustified. Their interests are coextensive with those of children in state-initiated proceedings.

One might attempt to draw distinctions between sexual abuse proceedings initiated by the state and those which are not, in an effort to argue that the child's need for representation is less critical in a private custody dispute. As demonstrated below, these distinctions are specious.

1.   The Veracity of Allegations Made in the Divorce "War"

There is a commonly held assumption that allegations of sexual abuse made by "warring" spouses are more likely to be false than allegations made by a state agency.[100] Based on this assumption, the need for procedural safeguards, such as independent representation, is perceived as less critical in private custody disputes. Recent studies have shown this assumption to be unfounded:

> The number of sexual abuse charges arising during divorces and/or custody/visitation disputes are small in number, only a very small percentage of even the contested cases.
>
> The number of cases involving such allegations has increased in recent years, as have sexual abuse reports in the general population. . . .
>
> At present, there is no evidence to suggest that allegations arising at the time of divorces or custody disputes are more likely to be false.

---

[99] *See, e.g.,* ALASKA STAT. § 47.17.030(e) (1984) (providing for representation by a guardian *ad litem*); CAL. WELF. & INST. CODE § 326 (West 1984) (making official who files petition alleging abuse the child's guardian *ad litem*); N.J. STAT. ANN. § 9:6-8.23 (West 1976) (providing for appointment of law guardian in abuse cases); WIS. STAT. ANN. § 48.23(3m) (1987) (requiring appointment of counsel under certain conditions when abuse is alleged); *see also* MODEL CHILD ABUSE & NEGLECT REP. LAW § 15A (1975) (providing that child subject to any judicial proceeding regarding child abuse or neglect shall be entitled to legal counsel).

[100] *See* Keating, *supra* note 34, at 113 (noting that the assumption may be attributed to society's belief that the allegations in such a situation are almost always false); Sege, *Some Say Ruling Will Silence Other Women,* Boston Globe, June 22, 1989, at 1 (stating that the percentage of true allegations of sexual abuse in private cases is similar to that in cases begun by child protective agencies).

Deliberately false allegations made to influence the custody decision or to hurt an ex-spouse do happen but they are viewed by knowledgeable professionals as rarities.[101]

Society doubts the truthfulness of the allegations because "[i]t is an easier psychological rationalization to believe that an ex-spouse would make up these charges to get even than it is to believe that a parent would molest his own child."[102] Articles suggesting that children are frequently "brainwashed" by vindictive spouses to believe that they were molested, have misled legal and clinical decisionmakers.[103] Because of feelings that allegations of abuse are likely to be false, courts may ignore such allegations in making custody determinations.[104] This harms both the protective parent and the abused child. As one observer noted, "[w]hat we really need to be stressing to the legal and mental health community is to look at each case as an allegation of child sexual abuse and ignore the fact that there's a custody battle going on . . . . That, in and of itself, will probably tell you very little."[105] Ensuring that the child's independent voice is heard is one method of counteracting misperception regarding abuse in custody disputes.

2.   Societal Stereotypes About Incest

Distinguishing sexually abused children in private custody disputes from those in state-initiated proceedings also may be attributed to general reluctance to believe that incest sweeps across the socioeconomic spectrum. The tragic death of Lisa Steinberg in New York City chillingly illustrated that child abuse is not solely an incident of poverty or lack of education.[106] The erroneous assumption

---

[101] Keating, *supra* note 34, at 117 (quoting N. Thoennes & J. Pearson, Summary of Findings from the Sexual Abuse Allegations Project 17-19 (1987) (unpublished paper prepared by the Research Unit of the Association of Family and Conciliation Courts, Denver, Colorado)).

[102] *Id.* at 115.

[103] *See* Letter from Graeme Hanson, M.D., to Melvin Lewis, M.D., editor, 27 J. AM. ACAD. CHILD & ADOLESCENT PSYCHIATRY 258 (1988) (criticizing Green, *True and False Allegations of Sexual Abuse in Child Custody Disputes,* 25 J. AM. ACAD. CHILD & ADOLESCENT PSYCHIATRY 449 (1986) (concerning fabrication and collusion)).

[104] *See* Keating, *supra* note 34, at 113.

[105] Sege, *supra* note 100 (quoting Nancy Thoennes, director of the Sexual Abuse Allegations Project in Denver).

[106] Lisa Steinberg died after suffering extensive physical abuse at the hands of her stepfather, Joel Steinberg. Steinberg, an attorney, was convicted of first-degree manslaughter. *See* Sullivan, *Steinberg Is Guilty of First-Degree Manslaughter,* N.Y. Times, Jan. 31, 1989, at A1, col. 1.

that one can assess sex abusers by "type"[107]—education, wealth, or other socioeconomic factors—means that legislators and judges are less likely to view accusations levelled in the divorce context as truthful.[108] When abuse proceedings are initiated by the state, they more typically involve parents and children of lower socioeconomic levels. Reporting patterns significantly obscure the economic and social distribution of child abuse. A poor family in a clinic or emergency room setting is far more likely to be suspected, evaluated, and reported than is an affluent family whose child is treated in a private practitioner's office.[109] In less affluent neighborhoods, child protection agencies are more likely to learn of potential danger to the child, to force the family into the child protective system, and to provide the child with representation. In short, abuse, including sexual abuse, is less likely to be detected by the state if the family is of moderate or substantial economic means. As a result, some allegations of sexual abuse may come to the state's attention only when the parties are engaged in a custody dispute. Unfortunately for these children, their right to representation is often denied simply because their abuse is revealed during a private custody dispute.[110]

---

[107] See Keating, supra note 34, at 120 ("Courts all too often base a decision solely on an evaluation of the accused parent. If he does not fit the profile of what the evaluating professional sees as the 'type' to molest children, the court does not deem it possible that he has molested the child.").

[108] This is not to say that only people in higher socioeconomic clases have private custody disputes. Legislators and judges may be less likely to view accusations levelled in the divorce context as truthful not because fewer of the stereotypical high-risk abusers—the poor and the uneducated—are in divorce court, but because of the view that private custody proceedings are only a secondary, and therefore relatively unimportant, source of protection for abused children. Such a view sees abuse as occurring primarily in lower class families. According to this view, because such abuse is likely to be detected by state agencies, triggering representation at a judicial determination stage, there is little need for independent representation in the divorce context; the child's interests will be protected in the state-initiated proceeding.

[109] See Kerns, supra note 36, at 24; see also Martin, The Child and His Development, in HELPING THE BATTERED CHILD, supra note 48, at 93, 93-94 (noting that a public child development center does not serve many middle- or upper-class families).

[110] This result may be seen as discriminating against both the interests of the children of middle to upper economic means, whose voices are not heard, and against the parents of lower economic means, who are prosecuted with greater frequency. Is there any reason to provide better representation to the child in state-initiated proceedings or to provide greater protection of privacy to wealthier parents?

B.   *Constitutional Authority*

Children clearly possess certain constitutional rights.[111] The scope of these rights, however, is unclear. Professor Tribe has noted that children's rights, like those of "discrete and insular minorities," are difficult to safeguard because they are not represented in the legislature.[112] Although there may be reasons to treat children differently from adults at times, children's rights prevail over competing considerations when

> the issue . . . involves the exercise of a right we have come to regard as constitutionally 'fundamental,' such as the right to bodily liberty or the right to be heard in one's own defense. . . . [W]hen such a right is at stake, the general fact of youth *alone* cannot automatically justify the right's abridgement.[113]

Sexual molestation is an invasion of bodily liberty and integrity. Just as a person has a right to refuse medical treatment[114] and a right to be free from forced sterilization,[115] each individual has the right to be free from incestuous sexual molestation.[116] A child's right to

---

[111] *See, e.g.,* Planned Parenthood v. Danforth, 428 U.S. 52, 74 (1976) (holding that minors, as well as adults, are protected by the Constitution); Tinker v. Des Moines Indep. Community School Dist., 393 U.S. 503, 511 (1969) (holding that public school students have constitutionally protected freedom of speech); *In re* Gault, 387 U.S. 1, 13 (1967) (concluding that "whatever may be their precise impact, neither the Fourteenth Amendment nor the Bill of Rights is for adults alone"); Coe v. Gerstein, 376 F. Supp. 695, 698 (S.D. Fla. 1973) (stating that with reference to " 'fundamental', *'personal,'* constitutional rights," a pregnant woman under 18 years of age could not be distinguished from one of majority age), *appeal dismissed,* 417 U.S. 279 (1974); Genden, *supra* note 14, at 581 (discussing the nature of a child's constitutional rights).

Although the rights of children now appear to be firmly established, constitutional protection for children is a fairly recent development. The first Supreme Court case involving the rights of children was not heard until 1966. *See* Kent v. United States, 383 U.S. 541, 561-62 (1966) (holding that due process entitles a juvenile to representation by counsel).

[112] *See* Tribe, *supra* note 76, at 9 (citing United States v. Carolene Prods. Co., 304 U.S. 144, 153 n.4 (1938)).

[113] *Id.* at 11.

[114] *See* Tune v. Walter Reed Army Medical Hosp., 602 F. Supp. 1542 (D.D.C. 1985); Superintendent v. Saikewicz, 373 Mass. 728, 370 N.E.2d 417 (1977); Schloendorff v. Society of New York Hosp., 211 N.Y. 125, 105 N.E. 92 (1914), *overruled on other grounds,* Bing v. Thunig, 163 N.Y.S.2d 3, 143 N.E.2d 3 (1957).

[115] *See* Skinner v. Oklahoma, 316 U.S. 535 (1942).

[116] It is acknowledged that the threat to bodily integrity is not state initiated and that the fourteenth amendment applies only to state actors or those acting under the color of state authority. *See* The Civil Rights Cases, 109 U.S. 3, 11 (1883) (stating that only state actions are the subject matter of the fourteenth amendment). Even when parents agree on custody, however, the court's approval of this determination is a prerequisite to its validity. In deciding whether to approve the agreement, the

be heard in "self-defense" is as critical a protective measure in a sexual abuse case as in a juvenile delinquency proceeding. All children who are suspected sexual abuse victims and who are the subjects of private custody disputes have important interests which are weighty enough to warrant explicit consideration in a constitutional analysis.

A due process argument that children in divorce custody cases are constitutionally entitled to representation may be based on *In re Gault*.[117] This landmark case established a minor's right to counsel in juvenile delinquency proceedings which may result in commitment to an institution.[118] While the Court limited its decision to a determination of a juvenile's entitlement to counsel in delinquency proceedings,[119] the case has been the impetus for extending the legal rights of minors.[120]

Ordinarily, the requirements of procedural due process apply only when there is a threat to life, liberty, or property, as protected by the fourteenth amendment.[121] *Gault* expressed such a strong belief in the critical role of counsel in the American judicial system, however, that many commentators have argued that the right of counsel in *Gault* is independent of the type of interest affected. They assert that this right will eventually extend beyond those cases involving a deprivation of liberty to all judicial proceedings involving children.[122]

In any case, a child has a liberty interest in remaining in her family's custody. The Supreme Court has recognized that family

---

state also may be adjudicating whether abuse will continue; that decision will be enforceable by the state against the parties. *See* Bergstrom v. Bergstrom, 478 F. Supp. 434, 439 (D.N.D. 1979) (holding that enforcement of a court custody order invoked the full powers of the District of Columbia, sufficient to meet the "federal action" requirement, the analog of state action, of the fifth amendment), *vacated on other grounds*, 623 F.2d 517 (8th Cir. 1980).

[117] 387 U.S. 1 (1967).

[118] *See id.* at 41. The extent to which the opinion depends on the juvenile's interest in freedom from confinement is unclear. *See infra* notes 121-22 and accompanying text.

[119] *See Gault*, 387 U.S. at 13-14.

[120] *See* Bersoff, *Representation for Children in Custody Decisions: All that Glitters is not Gault*, 15 J. FAM. L. 27, 27 (1976-77) (attributing to *Gault* a general "alteration of the balance of power in child-populated, adult-dominated institutions," such as juvenile courts, schools, and mental hospitals).

[121] *See* Board of Regents v. Roth, 408 U.S. 564, 569 (1972).

[122] *See, e.g.*, Genden, *supra* note 14, at 582 (discussing the extension of *Gault*); Inker & Perretta, *supra* note 42, at 113 (stating that a dynamic system would logically extend the protections of *Gault* to all proceedings involving children); *Due Process*, *supra* note 9, at 177 (stating that *Gault* was the Court's recognition that children are not best served by informal treatment in a paternalistic system).

relationships are interests which entitle parents to due process.[123] The Court has also stated that liberty encompasses the right to establish a home, bring up children, and to "enjoy those privileges long recognized at common law as essential to the orderly pursuit of happiness."[124]

Just as a parent's liberty is affected by state decisions concerning her relationship with her child, a child's liberty is similarly affected. Therefore, the liberty interests of both the parent and the child must be protected by due process of law. The Second Circuit noted this reciprocity of rights in stating:

> This right to the preservation of family integrity encompasses the reciprocal rights of both parent and children. It is the interest of the parent in the "companionship, care, custody and management of his . . . children . . . and of the children in not being dislocated from the emotional attachments that derive from the intimacy of daily association," with the parents.[125]

A child's right to representation is derived from this right to continued parental contact, and its exercise guards against unnecessary disruption of parent-child relationships. In the context of state-initiated custody proceedings, it has been recognized that: "[t]he physical liberty interest of a child in a neglect proceeding is sufficiently similar to the liberty interest of a child in a delinquency proceeding to require the same right to counsel."[126] Similarly, it has been noted that: "[a] change of parental bondage during the tender years is hardly less upsetting of one's pattern of life than is the denomination and possible commitment of a child as a 'juvenile delinquent.'"[127] While the representation of allegedly abused chil-

---

[123] *See* Stanley v. Illinois, 405 U.S. 645, 651 (1972) (stating that a parent's interest in the care, companionship, and custody of children are rights deserving of due process); Armstrong v. Manzo, 380 U.S. 545, 550 (1965) (requiring notice and a hearing before depriving a parent of the custody of a child).

[124] Meyer v. Nebraska, 262 U.S. 390, 399 (1923).

[125] Duchesne v. Sugarman, 566 F.2d 817, 825 (2d Cir. 1977) (citing *Stanley*, 405 U.S. at 651); *See also* Smith v. Organization of Foster Families for Equality and Reform, 431 U.S. 816, 844 (1977) ("No one would seriously dispute that a[n] . . . interdependent relationship [exists] between an adult and a child in his or her care"); Smith v. Fontana, 818 F.2d 1411, 1418 (9th Cir. 1987) ("companionship and nurturing interests of parent and child in maintaining tight familial bond are reciprocal"); *In re* S.A.D., 382 Pa. Super. 166, 175, 555 A.2d 123, 126 (1989) (recognizing the child's interest in a dependency hearing as concomitant to the parents' rights).

[126] Long, *When the Client is a Child: Dilemmas in the Lawyer's Role*, 21 J. Fam. L. 607, 628 (1982-83).

[127] Brown v. Chastain, 416 F.2d 1012, 1027 (5th Cir. 1969) (Rives, J.,

dren in state-initiated proceedings is governed by statutes, it is frequently argued that such a procedure is constitutionally compelled.[128] If resting on constitutional grounds, the right ought to extend to private proceedings as well. The child's interest in a continuing relationship with a non-abusive parent is no less important when another parent, rather than the state, seeks effectively to terminate the relationship.

In all private custody disputes, cognizance of the constitutionally protected interest in family integrity begs the question of whether all children have a constitutionally protected right to be free from state interference with an ongoing parent-child relationship. Arguably, the court has no authority to inhibit a child's relationship with a non-custodial parent unless that relationship would cause the child articulable harm.[129] One commentator has suggested that even when the institutionalization or foster care of a child is not contemplated, the child's liberty is always invoked by a change in custody, because of the potential deprivation to the child of the company and control of one parent.[130] While a child does not normally have the liberty to choose her custodian, when a situation arises which calls for a judicial choice, failure to consider the child's

---

dissenting) (asserting the importance of not denying access to the courts because of statutory financial burdens).

[128] *See* Inker & Perretta, *supra* note 42, at 116-19; Redeker, *supra* note 52, at 530; *Due Process*, supra note 9, at 184. The Constitutional basis of a child's right to counsel in this context is an open question in view of Lassiter v. Department of Soc. Serv., 452 U.S. 18 (1981) (holding that the due process clause did not require the appointment of counsel for the parent in every case in which parental rights may be terminated). When sexual abuse is alleged in the private dispute, the termination of visitation, as well as custody, is sought.

[129] *See* 4 L. WARDLE, C. BLAKESLEY & J. PARKER, CONTEMPORARY FAMILY LAW § 39:12, at 91 (1988). Refusing to protect a child's relationship with either single parent is inconsistent with expanding definitions of family. *Cf. supra* note 84 and accompanying text.

[130] *See Due Process*, *supra* note 9, at 180-181 & n.32 (recognizing that any change in custody, whether the child is removed to an institution or is shifted between parents, affects the same interests of the child and that there should be no distinction drawn for due process purposes). The child's interest has been viewed not merely as liberty, but as "[t]he basic human right to maintain and enjoy the relationship which normally exists between the parents and the children." State v. Wade, 19 Or. App. 314, 319, 527 P.2d 753, 755 (1974) (affording independent counsel to children involved in proceedings regarding the termination of parental rights), *overruled on other grounds, In re* D., 24 Or. App. 601, 547 P.2d 175, *cert. denied,* 429 U.S. 907 (1976); *see also* Genden, *supra* note 14, at 581 (discussing the characterization of the interests in *Wade*).

voice is arguably a denial of liberty under the fourteenth amendment.[131]

When sexual abuse is alleged, however, the liberty interests implicated are yet greater than those in general private custody disputes. Because a parent-child relationship is far more imperilled when sexual abuse is alleged, the child's liberty interest merits the same procedural safeguards in such cases as in state-initiated proceedings. While the potential for harm is generally less in private custody cases than in juvenile delinquency cases, this is not true of private custody cases in which sexual abuse is alleged. All allegations of child sexual abuse raise the need for the procedural protection of independent counsel to represent the suspected victims.

Conclusion

The nation has declared war on the critical social problem of child abuse, particularly sexual abuse. Because establishing sexual abuse in private custody disputes is so complex and difficult, and because the consequences of erroneous determinations are so pernicious, an attack on child abuse which does not include the private forum is incomplete.

In private custody disputes, the child's dual interests in avoiding continued molestation and in maintaining healthy relationships with non-abusing parents merit legal recognition. Because those interests differ from the parents' and are insufficiently protected by *parens patriae*, they warrant separate legal representation.

Whether or not it is recognized as constitutionally compelled, the present statutory and judicial commitment to making custody determinations that are in a child's best interests mandates the independent legal representation of all children when sexual abuse is alleged. This will not eradicate the damage done to victims of sexual

---

[131] *See Due Process, supra* note 9, at 180; *see also* Brown v. Chastain, 416 F.2d 1012, 1027 (5th Cir. 1969) (Rives, J., dissenting) (professing that because a well-founded parental relationship is a necessity in that the formation of life habits is at stake, "there could hardly be a better case for Fourteenth Amendment protection"), *cert. denied*, 397 U.S. 951 (1970); *cf.* Hannah v. Larche, 363 U.S. 420, 442 (1960) (stating that "whether the Constitution requires that a particular right [of due process] obtain in a specific proceeding depends upon a complexity of factors," including the nature of the alleged right, the nature of the proceeding, and the possible burden on the proceeding). Custody proceedings will have great effects on the later lives of the children involved. In light of these effects, the flexible approach articulated in *Hannah* indicates that the due process right of independent legal representation should be provided to children in custody proceedings. *See* Inker & Peretta, *supra* note 42, at 116-18.

abuse; it can, however, provide a means for reducing the damage by insuring that the victim's interests are not neglected.

"The legal profession is the one most identifiable group in control of our nation's destiny. It must lead the way in providing for the needs of helpless children whose lives are tangled in the law."[132] The independent legal representation of all children who are suspected victims of sexual abuse is a vital step towards tipping the scales of justice in the children's best interests.

---

[132] Lane, *supra* note 11, at 177.

Amer. J. Orthopsychiat. 61(1), January 1991

POSSIBLE EXPLANATIONS FOR CHILD SEXUAL ABUSE ALLEGATIONS IN DIVORCE

Kathleen Coulborn Faller, M.S.W., Ph.D.

Based on a clinical sample of 136 cases, four classes of child sexual abuse cases in divorce are proposed: divorce precipitated by discovery of sexual abuse; long-standing sexual victimization revealed after marital breakup; sexual abuse precipitated by marital dissolution; and false allegations made during or after divorce. Implications for clinical practice are discussed.

Professional beliefs about children's claims of sexual victimization have fluctuated rather strikingly during this century. Until the 1970s, the claims were commonly assumed to be fantasies and perhaps based upon children's unconscious wishes to have sexual relationships with the adults in question *(Freud, 1896/1962; Lerman, 1988; Masson, 1984)*. However, this interpretation lost much of its support in the 1970s as the number of cases reported to child protection agencies increased. Child protection investigators and other mental health professionals have since tended to take children's accounts at face value and assume they were true unless there was evidence to the contrary *(Faller, 1984; McCarty, 1981)*. Moreover, studies such as that of New England college students by Finkelhor *(1979)* and of San Francisco area women by Russell *(1983)*, demonstrated the pervasiveness of sexual abuse during childhood and diminished the skepticism of professionals toward such allegations.

Nevertheless, in the past five years, doubt about sexual victimization has again become an issue, especially when accusations are made in situations where parents are divorcing or divorced *(Benedek & Schetky, 1985; Blush & Ross, 1986; Gardner, 1989; Green, 1986; Kaplan & Kaplan, 1981; Renshaw, 1987; Schuman, 1986)*. This has happened despite research *(Jones & Seig, 1988; Paradise, Rostain, & Nathanson, 1988; Thoennes & Pearson, 1988)* indicating that some allegations made in the context of divorce are false, but by no means the majority.

In this article, a range of dynamics leading to allegations of sexual abuse in divorce is explored, and four categories of cases are proposed. The classification system is based on a review of the literature, discussions with other mental health professionals, and a careful examination of a clinical research sample of 136 cases. These cases had been referred to the University of Michigan Project on Child Abuse and Neglect for diagnosis and/or treatment, 58% of them by child protection agencies and 20% by another agency or a court; 22% were self-referred, about half of them with the agreement of both parents.

The cases in the sample involve allega-

A revised version of a paper submitted to the Journal in December 1989. The author is at the University of Michigan School of Social Work, Ann Arbor.

86

tions against fathers (N = 94), mothers (N = 8), stepparents (N = 18), other relatives (N = 7), boyfriends or girlfriends (N = 3), and unrelated persons (N = 6). As the numbers suggest, the vast majority (91%) of the offenders were male, and most were fathers. Therefore, the accused parent will be referred to herein as the father and the non-accused parent as the mother. The perpetrator-victim dyad was used as the level of analysis in order to accommodate those instances in which abuse of the child was allegedly by more than one person or in which the accused was alleged to have more than one victim.

Forty-nine (36%) of the alleged victims were male and 87 (64%) female. The mean age of the victims at assessment was 6.2 years for the boys and 5.4 for the girls.

PROPOSED CATEGORIES

The four identified dynamics resulting in allegations of sexual abuse during or after the dissolution of a marriage are as follows: *1)* the mother finds out about the sexual abuse and decides to divorce her husband; *2)* long-standing sexual abuse is only revealed during the marital breakup; *3)* sexual abuse has been precipitated by the marital dissolution; or *4)* the allegation is false.

Information on strategies and criteria for validation of sexual abuse allegations can be found elsewhere *(Faller, 1988a,b).* It should be noted that, in a series of chi-squares and analyses of variance, no differences were found based on the circumstances of the allegation and victim's age, victim's sex, the perpetrator-victim relationship, or the perpetrator's sex.

Abuse Leading to Divorce

In the author's clinical experience, approximately half of the women who discover that their husbands have sexually abused their children divorce them. How they reach this decision varies. In some cases, the woman learns of the sexual abuse from the victim, from others, or from observation. She then leaves the offender, tak-

ing the children, and sues for divorce *(Berliner, 1988; Corwin, Berliner, Goodman, Goodwin, & White, 1987).* The sexual abuse may come to official or professional attention only when issues of visitation with the offending parent are being decided in the divorce proceedings. Eleven cases in the clinical sample of 136 were of this type.

In other instances, upon discovering the sexual abuse the woman contacts the police, child protective services, a therapist, or other professionals. In still others, the mother learns of the sexual abuse from an outside agent (e.g., the school, protective services, or the police). Thus, in these two instances the sexual abuse is known to authorities before the woman initiates divorce action, and the professionals with whom she deals are often instrumental in her decision to divorce.

When, as in the first instance, the woman independently chooses to end a marriage in which her children are being sexually abused, her concerns about visitation by her husband are more likely to be questioned than they are when the authorities have addressed the sexual abuse before the divorce action. In the former cases, it may be alleged that the mother is accusing the father of sexual abuse in order to restrict his access to the children. In the latter cases, however, the woman may have ignored sexual abuse or required persuasion by authorities to act protectively, indicators she may be a less than capable parent.

Abuse Revealed During Divorce

Early clinical literature described "classical incest" as a pattern of father-daughter incest that persists for years. It is only reported by the victim when she reaches adolescence, or it is revealed when the parental couple divorces *(Berliner, 1988; Faller, 1988a).* It thus appears that clinicians have understood for some time that long-standing sexual abuse may not surface until marital breakup. In the clinical sample under discussion, 26 cases fall into this category.

The reasons for revelation at this time

can be several. The child may finally feel safe enough to report long-standing sexual abuse because the perpetrator is out of the home and no longer able to punish her for disclosure *(Berliner, 1988)*. Second, the mother may have consciously or unconsciously avoided looking into possibly indicative behavior during the marriage, but as the marriage dissolves she is able or willing to consider the implications of that behavior. Third, the mother may have known about the sexual abuse during the marriage, but been fearful of making it known or chosen to tolerate it because the marriage had beneficial aspects.

Abuse Precipitated by Divorce

Divorce is usually traumatic for all parties—husband, wife, and children. In this context, behavior not previously exhibited may develop, and may include sexual abuse. The offending party may be either the mother or the father, although, as with other sexual abuse, the abuser is more likely to be male. Fifty-two cases in the clinical sample were of this type.

In many of the cases, there had been prior indications of sexual attraction to children that had apparently been held in check by the structure of the marriage. The following types of behavior were reported: an unusual amount of touching and caressing of the child, tongue kissing, sleeping with the child, and erections when wrestling, during other body contact, or while bathing with the child.

One of the consequences of divorce is the loss of family structure. Often, there is no longer another adult present to monitor a parent's behavior during unsupervised visitation or custody. Rules which regulate where children and parents sleep, when they go to sleep, and with whom they bathe may no longer exist. Such a situation may lead to the expression of sexual feelings toward children.

Two other dynamics may contribute to sexual abuse as a marriage dissolves. The parent who becomes the abuser may feel a tremendous emotional loss with the separation from the spouse. In the author's clinical experience, the offending parent is usually not the instigator of the divorce, and is often bewildered and overwhelmed by the marital demise. In this vulnerable psychological state, the parent turns to the child for emotional support, and because this parent has some sexual attraction to children, the relationship becomes sexual. Second, the parent who becomes an abuser is often very angry at the spouse for destroying the marriage and for other perceived or actual transgressions. Direct expression of that anger may be impossible or insufficient for satisfactory retaliation. The child then becomes the vehicle for that expression or retaliation. The intensity of these feelings may result in physical injury from the sexual maltreatment.

It is important to be aware that the offender may be in such a state of emotional turmoil that he cannot control his sexually abusive behavior, even when he knows his former spouse, protective services, or the court is monitoring his contact with the child. Therefore, repeated incidents are not uncommon in this type of sexual abuse. In some cases, repetition is interpreted by mental health experts as a way of keeping the former spouse involved; in others it is seen as a cry for help.

False Allegations During Divorce

Proportionately more false accusations of sexual abuse may be made in the context of divorce than in other situations. Most false allegations are made by adults, not children *(Berliner, 1988; Faller, 1988a; Jones & McGraw, 1987)*. In this sample, 19 of the cases were categorized as false and 12 as inconclusive (therefore possibly false).

The higher proportion of false allegations can be understood by contrasting the divorce situation with others. In intrafamilial sexual abuse, it is usually a major issue to convince nonabusive family members that the abuse occurred. Mothers may find it very difficult to believe that the man to whom they are married could sexually victimize their children. Quite the opposite problem may arise when parents are divorcing. These adults may be convinced that their estranged spouses are capable of almost anything, including sexual abuse, and they may overreact rather than underreact to suspicious circumstances.

There are several variations to this pattern. Under the stress of divorce and its aftermath, parental perceptions may become distorted *(Benedek & Schetky, 1985)* and the behavior of former partners perceived as pathological. Occasional drinking episodes may be redefined as alcoholism. A desire for certain sexual activities or for frequent sex may be characterized as perversion. A single slap during an argument may lead to the label of batterer. Having developed a distorted view of the ex-partner, the parent may conclude that anyone who is an alcoholic, a pervert, or a batterer would also sexually abuse a child.

In addition, these parents may have distorted perceptions of the child's relationship to the ex-spouse. For example, when the child returns from a visit with the noncustodial parent without seeming particularly disturbed, the custodial parent may conclude that the child has been drugged or brainwashed. Since the ex-partner has such a disturbing effect on the custodial parent, it must be the same for the child and, if not, the ex-spouse must have manipulated the child in some devious way.

Second, the parent or others may observe behavior by the child that could indicate sexual abuse, but could just as well have other explanations. Typical examples are resistance to visits with the suspected abuser, having nightmares before or after the visits, wetting the bed, or masturbation. Such behavior could be precipitated by stress related to the divorce, by fear of losing the custodial parent if loyalty to the other parent is shown, or by an appreciation that the custodial parent would welcome negative reactions to or comments about the ex-

partner. Even masturbation is not necessarily related to sexual abuse; it is normal among children, as well as among adults. Excessive masturbation is regarded as possibly symptomatic of sexual abuse, but who is to say what is excessive? Furthermore, self-stimulation is pleasurable, and children may need to comfort themselves in a divorce situation, especially if their parents are too preoccupied to nurture properly.

Alternatively, the child may return from visits and say such things as "Daddy touched me," "Daddy hurt me," or "Daddy takes baths with me." Statements like these, which could relate to innocent parent-child interactions, are then assumed to be accounts of sexual abuse.

Third, parents may correctly perceive that their children have been sexually abused, but incorrectly attribute it to their ex-partners. In four cases in the sample, medical or behavioral evidence indicated sexual misuse, and the mothers were convinced that the fathers were the perpetrators. However, after a careful evaluation, it appeared that in two instances the stepfathers were the abusers, while in a third it was the mother's boyfriend. In the fourth case, precocious sexual knowledge came from sexual interaction with other children.

Finally, the parent may consciously lie in making the allegation, although this seems to be quite rare *(Faller, 1988a; Jones & McGraw, 1987; Nicholson & Bulkley, 1988; Thoennes, 1987; Thoennes & Pearson, 1988)*. Three cases in the sample appeared to be calculated untruths, evidently motivated by the desire to exclude the accused parent from the life of the child and of the accusing parent. Counterallegations may also be fabricated by an accused parent.

CLINICAL IMPLICATIONS

These findings indicate that mental health professionals who are assessing sexual abuse accusations in divorce contexts should maintain an open mind and an appreciation of the range of potential circumstances and dynamics that might result in such a report.

Four proposed categories among the cases examined in this study have been described, but there may also be others. The largest proportion of cases were those in which the marital dissolution precipitated the sexual abuse, followed by those in which divorce triggered disclosure. Excluding 16 cases (12%) whose dynamics were not related to divorce and are therefore not germane to this discussion, at least 15% and perhaps as much as a 25% were apparently false. The least common circumstance was that in which discovery of sexual abuse caused the divorce.

As with other sexual abuse cases, the child interview is the most important factor in determining the truth of the allegation (Conte, Sorenson, Fogarty, & Dalla Rosa, 1988; Faller, 1984, 1988a,b; Jones & McQuiston, 1986; Sgroi, 1982). However, when the accusation is made by an estranged or former spouse, evaluating that parent appears to be the second most important aspect of assessment. Understanding of the dynamics of the allegation will be facilitated by careful evaluation of the source of the accuser's suspicions, reactions to the stress of marital dissolution, and overall functioning. In exploring the source of her concern, a chronological account, as well as details of her specific observations of child behavior and other such indications, can facilitate correct classification of the case. The consistency of her description of her ex-partner with observations by others will be a helpful clue, as will an assessment of the level of her hostility toward him. A past history of emotional problems or a propensity to distort the truth or to lie may also be enlightening, as positive findings in these areas may indicate a false allegation. Interestingly, it appears that the interviews with accusing parents are more helpful than those with the accused in this type of case.

This study offers some useful guidelines to the practitioner, but its limitations must be recognized. The sample is circumscribed geographically and, insofar as all were cases referred to the Interdisciplinary Project, perhaps in terms of other client characteristics as well.

Additional work is need to further our understanding of abuse allegations in divorce cases. Of particular interest would be investigations comparable to this one, in which cases are identified by child protective services and the courts. Longitudinal studies of sexual abuse allegations in divorce proceedings could have both heuristic and clinical implications.

REFERENCES

Benedek, E., & Schetky, D. (1985). Allegations of sexual abuse in child custody and visitation disputes. In E. Benedek & D. Schetky (Eds.), *Emerging issues in child psychiatry and the law*. New York: Brunner/Mazel.

Berliner, L. (1988). Deciding whether a child has been sexually abused. In E.B. Nicholson & J. Bulkley, (Eds.), *Sexual abuse allegations in custody and visitation cases*. Washington, DC: American Bar Association.

Blush, G., & Ross, K. (1986). *Sexual allegations in Divorce: The SAID syndrome*. Unpublished manuscript.

Conte, J., Sorenson, E., Fogarty, L., & Dalla Rosa, J. (1988). *Evaluating children's reports of sexual abuse: Results from a survey of professionals*. Chicago: University of Chicago School of Social Service Administration.

Corwin, D., Berliner, L., Goodman, G., Goodwin, J., & White, S. (1987). Child sexual abuse and custody disputes: No easy answers. *Journal of Interpersonal Violence, 2*(1), 91–105.

Faller, K.C. (1984). Is the child victim of sexual abuse telling the truth? *Child Abuse and Neglect, 8*, 473–481.

Faller, K.C. (1988a). *Child sexual abuse: An interdisciplinary manual for diagnosis, case management and treatment*. New York: Columbia University Press.

Faller, K.C. (1988b). Criteria for judging the credibility of children's statement about their sexual abuse. *Child Welfare, 57*, 389–401.

Finkelhor, D. (1979). *Sexually victimized children*. New York: Free Press.

Freud, S. (1962). The aetiology of hysteria. In J. Strachey, (Ed. and Trans.), *The standard edition of the complete psychological works of Sigmund Freud* (Vol. 3, pp. 189–221). London: Hogarth Press. (Original work published 1896)

Gardner, R. (1989). Differentiating between bona fide and fabricated allegations of sexual abuse of children. *Journal of the American Academy of Matrimonial Lawyers, 5*, 1–27.

Green, A. (1986). True and false allegations of sexual abuse in child custody disputes. *Journal of the American Academy of Child Psychiatry. 25*, 449–456.

Jones, D. & McGraw, E.M. (1987). Reliable and fictitious accounts of sexual abuse to children. *Journal of Interpersonal Violence, 2*(1), 27–45.

Jones, D., & McQuiston, M. (1986). *Interviewing the sexually abused child.* Denver: Kempe National Center for the Prevention and Treatment of Child Abuse and Neglect.

Jones, D. & Seig, A. (1988). Child sexual abuse allegations in custody or visitation cases: A report of 20 Cases. In E.B. Nicholson & J. Bulkley, (Eds.), *Sexual abuse allegations in custody and visitation cases.* Washington, DC: American Bar Association.

Kaplan, S.L., & Kaplan, S.J. (1981). The child's accusation of sexual abuse during a divorce and custody struggle. *Hillside Journal of Clinical Psychiatry, 3,* 81–95.

Lerman, H. (1988). The psychoanalytic legacy: From whence we come. In L. Walker, (Ed.). *Handbook on sexual abuse of children.* New York: Springer.

McCarty, L. (1981). Investigation of incest: Opportunity to motivate families to seek help. *Child Welfare, 60,* 679–689.

Masson, J. (1984). *The assault on the truth: Freud's suppression of the seduction theory.* New York: Farrar, Straus, & Giroux.

Nicholson, E.B., & Bulkley, J. (Eds.). (1988). *Sexual abuse allegations in custody and visitation cases.* Washington, DC: American Bar Association.

Paradise, J., Rostain, A., & Nathanson, M. (1988). Substantiation of sexual abuse charges when parents dispute custody or visitation. *Pediatrics, 81,* 835–839.

Renshaw, D. (1987). Child sexual abuse: When wrongly charged. *Encyclopedia Britannica Medical and Health Annual,* 301–303.

Russell, D. (1983). The incidence and prevalence of intrafamilial and extrafamilial sexual abuse among female children. *Child Abuse and Neglect, 7,* 133–146.

Schuman, D. (1986). False allegations of physical and sexual abuse. *Bulletin of the American Academy of Psychiatry and Law, 14,* 5–21.

Sgroi, S. (1982). *Handbook of clinical intervention in child sexual abuse.* Lexington, MA: Lexington Books.

Thoennes, N. (1987, April). *Sexual abuse allegations in custody disputes.* Paper presented at the National Conference on the Victimization of Children, Anaheim, CA.

Thoennes, N., & Pearson, J. (1988). *Allegations of sexual abuse in custody and visitation cases.* Denver: Association of Family and Conciliation Courts Research Unit.

For reprints: Kathleen Coulborn Faller, University of Michigan, School of Social Work, 1065 Frieze Building, Ann Arbor, MI 48109

International Journal of Law and Psychiatry, Vol. 14, pp. 269–286, 1991
Printed in the U.S.A. All rights reserved

Sexual Abuse Allegations in Child Custody Disputes

Michael F. Elterman* and Marion F. Ehrenberg**

Since the 1970s the emerging roles of men and women, and the associated changes in family structure and parent-child relationships, have been mirrored in custody and visitation laws (Levine, Ewing, & Hager, 1987; Wallerstein, 1985). Sociocultural developments, such as concerns about sexual discrimination, the movement of mothers into the work force, and the emergence of no-fault divorce (Ricks, 1984) have influenced courts to shift gradually from the presumption of maternal custody — *the tender years presumption* — toward greater equality in the claims of mothers and fathers. At present custody decisions tend to be based more on the needs of the child, than the rights of the parents.

This situation has set the stage for a proliferation of custody disputes (Zarski, Knight, & Zarski, 1985) and a concomitant search for standards and guidelines to govern *the best interests of the child* criterion (Hauser, 1985). Mental health professionals have aimed to assist in the interpretation of this criterion by attempting to match the needs of the child with the parent whose resources and skills are best suited to meet these requirements (Jaffe, Austin, Leschied, & Sas, 1987; Weiner, Simons, & Cavanaugh, 1985). Joint custody is being widely prescribed as representing the best interests of the child. However, its practical consequences (Roman & Dichter, 1985) and psychological implications (Melton, Petrila, Poythress & Slobogin, 1987) are still being explored.

During a divorce and custody dispute embittered spouses may resort to extremes of behaviour (Kaplan & Kaplan, 1981). In the early 1970s adultery was the main contentious issue used to draw attention to a parent's moral fitness (Murray, 1987). Prior to 1974 an adulterous parent was presumed to have forfeited custody and, in some cases, even visitation rights (McCahey, 1987). Within the past 15 years, both social mores and custody laws regarding the sexual conduct of parents have changed dramatically (*Brinkley v. Brinkley*, 1985; *Dykes v. Dykes*, 1986). As a general rule, evidence of a parent's sexual conduct standing by itself will no longer support a denial of custody to that parent (McCahey, 1987).

The recent increase in reported cases of child sexual abuse and incest, as

---

*Director of Psychology, University Hospital — Shaughnessy Site, 4500 Oak Street, Vancouver, British Columbia, Canada V6H 3N1.
**Department of Psychology, University of Victoria, P.O. Box 3050, Victoria, British Columbia, Canada V6H 3P5.

well as the accumulation of evidence for its traumatic and far-reaching effects on child victims (Browne & Finkelhor, 1986; Haugaard & Reppucci, 1988; Pine, 1987), have resulted in an increased awareness of this phenomenon by mental health professionals, lawyers, judges, and law enforcement personnel. Mass media coverage of cases has contributed to public consciousness (Green, 1986).

Enough anecdotal and case study evidence has been collected to ascertain that parents may accuse one another of sexual molestation of their children during child custody battles (Benedek & Shetky, 1984, 1985; deJong, 1986; Green, 1986; Jaffe et al., 1987; Kaplan & Kaplan, 1981; Klajner-Diamond, Wehrspann, & Steinhauer, 1987; Murray, 1987). If such allegations are substantiated, the perpetrator is excluded from contact with the children, and the plaintiff is usually awarded full custody. Mental health professionals involved in making recommendations for a case of this kind tend to lean conservatively in the direction of least possible risk to the child (Murray, 1987) by overpredicting the dangerousness of the accused parent. The problem of false positive errors resulting from this practice has been discussed extensively in the general prediction of dangerousness literature (e.g., Schiffer, 1978) and should be considered in this more specific context.

Judges are faced with the difficulty of making decisions that strike an appropriate balance between parental rights and child protection based on continually evolving child and family law/policy (Levine et al., 1987). The problem faced directly by the court, and indirectly by mental health professionals requested to assist the courts, is that where there is uncertainty, the choice between two potential errors must be made: (a) To deprive an innocent parent of a relationship with their child; or (b) To put a child back into a situation where they may be sexually abused. If an error is made, a child's physical and psychological security may be jeopardized *or* a parent's family life and career may be destroyed (Green, 1986). Case studies of falsely accused fathers in the popular press (e.g., "Child abuse", 1987; "Guilty until", 1987) have aptly illustrated that attempting to prove one's innocence can be emotionally and financially devastating. At present, the potential shortterm and longterm psychological effects of false allegations of sexual abuse on the *children* involved in the case remain unexplored.

Trends in the Believability of Children

The credence given to children's allegations has fluctuated considerably with socio-cultural changes. Historically, the occurrence of child sexual abuse was denied (Alter-Reid, Gibbs, Lachenmeyer, Sigal, & Massoth, 1986). Although the prevalence of child sexual abuse was documented in the nineteenth century (Benedek & Shetky, 1985). Freud attributed patients' memories of seduction and sexual violence to Oedipal fantasies rather than fact (Freud, [1933], 1965). His emphasis on the repression of sexual wishes and unconscious fantasy became the foundations of the then dominant body of psychoanalytic literature. Freud's colleagues were influenced to similarly discredit the possibility of child sexual abuse (Benedek & Shetky, 1985). More recently, it has been proposed that many of Freud's patients were in fact victims of sexual abuse (Jortner, 1985; Masson, 1984).

When the reality of sexual abuse was first accepted, there was a tendency to blame the victim for its instigation and to deny the extent of its negative effects on the child. Currently, blame is more likely to be attributed to the psychopathology of the offender than to the characteristics of the child (Alter-Reid et al., 1986). The psychiatric/psychological literature has, in recent years, tended to emphasize the perpetrator's exploitation vis-à-vis the child's subordinate position. An attitude of outrage at incestuous activity (Baily, 1980) has created an atmosphere where a child's account of sexual abuse is often accepted without question (Faller, 1984).

This credo "that children must be believed" (Klajner-Diamond et al., 1987) appears to have led to uncritical evaluations of some sexual abuse allegations which not only damage those falsely accused, but also undermined the credibility of true victims (Klajner-Diamond et al., 1987). The media coverage of several notable cases—such as the preliminary hearing testimony of the alleged victims in the McMartin Preschool case; and the charges dropped against a large number of citizens accused of sexual abuse in Jordan, Minnesota (de-Jong, 1986)—has called into question the credibility of children's allegations. Although children generally do not tend to fabricate allegations of sexual abuse (e.g., Haugaard & Reppucci, 1988; Jones, 1987), mental health professionals are reaching a consensus that there are factors present in custody and access situations which will increase the likelihood of improbable allegations (Benedek & Shetky, 1985; deJong, 1986; Gardner, 1987; Green, 1986; Kaplan & Kaplan, 1981). Goodwin, Sahd, & Rada (1978) review of the literature suggests that this psycholegal problem is not limited to the North American context.

In our continuing discussion of sexual abuse allegations in custody and access disputes, the reader is alerted to two points. *First,* we will be referring to the alleging and the accused parent in gender-free terms to actively promote an unbiased and nonstereotyped perspective on this problem. The empirical literature on incest has consistently documented that between 75 and 90% of reported cases involve female victims and male perpetrators (e.g., Browne & Finkelhor, 1986; Faller, 1984), and the clinical/legal literature (Gardner, 1987; Green, 1986) has tended to focus its discussion of sexual abuse allegations in custody and access disputes on cases where mothers allege sexual abuse of their children against fathers. However, recent reports of natural fathers accusing mothers, mothers' boyfriends, or the children's stepfathers of sexually abusing their children have demonstrated that the phenomenon is not limited to this more frequently discussed scenario. *Second,* we will be referring to probable and improbable—rather than true and false—allegations of sexual abuse. "True" and "false" implies a dichotomy of "sexual abuse" and "not sexual abuse," rather than the much less clearly defined continuum of relative appropriateness in adults' interactions with children (Haugaard & Reppucci, 1986). Also, a true/false dichotomy misrepresents the level of confidence that can be associated with the evaluation of sexual abuse allegations. It is a serious methodological problem that is practically impossible to validate an evaluation of the truthfulness of the allegation using any absolute, scientifically acceptable criterion measure or "gold standard." Instead, we rely on an indirect measure as an intermediate criterion—the court's decision—which is assumed to be correlated with the ultimate criterion or "truth." *Probable* and *improb-*

able reflect this issue more accurately. Finally, true/false terminology in the context of children's statements may suggest malicious intentionality on the part of the alleging child. This is neither a finding supported by the existing evidence, nor a point to be taken from this paper.

Research on Probable and Improbable Allegations of Sexual Abuse

Despite the recent increase in research on child sexual abuse, the issue of improbable accusations has been largely neglected by behavioral scientists. The available evidence is limited to case reports, anecdotal references, and a few empirical studies.

Peters (1976) reported four improbable accusations of sexual molestation in a total of 64 children brought to a hospital's emergency room and evaluated by their staff. Unfortunately, the actual relationship between the alleged offender and the victim, and whether the offender was living in the child's home were not specified. Goodwin, Sahd, and Rada (1978) found that 3 of 46 sexual abuse cases reported to a child abuse agency were based on improbable allegations. One of these cases involved the allegation of an adolescent girl, and two the accusations of a psychotic mother. The authors provide virtually no information on how the probability or probability of an allegation was determined, although it is clear that the judgements were made by a team of mental health professionals. A recent and more extensive archival study (Jones, 1987) demonstrated that of 576 sexual abuse cases only 7.81% of the cases could not be substantiated; of these, 6.25% were allegations made by an adult, and 1.56% by a child. These studies suggest that between 6 and 8% — a small, but significant, number — of reported sexual abuse cases could not be substantiated.

The proportion of improbable allegations of sexual abuse made by parents during court litigation, involving custody and visitation issues, has been significantly greater (Green, 1986). Benedek and Shetky (1984) were unable to document 10 of 18 (55%) charges of sexual abuse in children evaluated during custody and visitation disputes. It is not clear from these studies whether the allegations were made by the parent or by the child in a spontaneous disclosure. This is a potentially critical difference. Green (1986) reported four improbable and seven probable allegations of sexual abuse made by the custodial, against the noncustodial, parent (36%). The shortcomings of this study include the small sample size, and a possibly biased sample (Corwin, Berliner, Goodman, Goodwin, & White, 1987).

The courts have held that the admissibility of a child's testimony is dependent upon the trial judge's determination of the "capacity and intelligence of the child, his appreciation of the difference between truth and falsehood, as well as his duty to tell the former" (Melton, 1985). The current literature on the reliability of child testimony in the courts has provided clear evidence that children can be as reliable as adults in telling the truth (Goodman, 1984; King & Yuille, 1985). Direct and leading questions can distort memory both in children and adults (Goodman, 1984; Loftus & Davis, 1984). In particular, children appear to be susceptible to suggestion in situations where they are trying to conform to the wishes of an adult (Green, 1986; Klajner-Diamond et al., 1987). However, if interviewing methods are modified to support their age-specific cognitive and social sensitivities, the accuracy of their reports increases dramatically (King & Yuille, 1987; Yuille, 1988). With this qualification, the available research generally supports the potential of children, as young as age four, to present testimony which is as reliable as that of adults (Melton, 1985).

In summary, the current literature suggests that children are accurate in their disclosures of sexual abuse in noncustody cases in 92 to 94% of the cases (Goodwin et al., 1978; Jones, 1985; Peters, 1976). However, in the context of custody disputes the corresponding figures are significantly lower (Benedek & Shetky, 1984; Green, 1986; Jones, 1987). These findings propose that there are factors present in custody situations which are related to higher proportions of improbable allegations. The need for further empirical investigations, employing larger sample sizes, and more rigorous research designs, are needed to clarify the phenomenon of improbable sexual abuse allegations.

Allegations of sexual abuse have been most common in child custody disputes that arise immediately after a divorce has been granted, and center around issues of visitation (Benedek & Shetky, 1984; Green, 1986). An allegation of sexual abuse by the custodial parent will capture the judge's attention and effect an immediate suspension of the noncustodial parent's visitation rights, and it may permanently terminate contact between the accused parent and the child. A noncustodial parent may allege sexual abuse in an attempt to get the court to change the permanent custody that was awarded at the time of divorce.

The accusations may be completely without foundation, but are usually based on a "core of reality" (Green, 1986; Klajner-Diamond et al., 1987). Emotionally stressed parents may pick up on "marginal symptoms" (Elterman, 1987), jump to unfounded or inappropriate conclusions, and generally assume the worst. There are several situations in which the noncustodial parent will be particularly vulnerable to accusations by the custodial parent. The child may display regressive symptoms (crying, nightmares, bedwetting, or clinging), depression, anger, noncompliance, or aggressiveness after a visit with the noncustodial parent. The custodial parent may misinterpret the child's general feelings about separating from the noncustodial parent — feelings which will be heightened at the end of a visit — as signs of sexual abuse. Similarly, custodial parents may misperceive increases in physical contact — hugging, kissing, holding — between the child and the other parent as sexual. In reality, these physical displays of affection may be triggered by long and unaccustomed absences. The child may exhibit physical symptoms upon return from a visit, such as constipation (change in diet during visits) or redness in the genital area (inexperienced bathing or toileting), and these signs may be misinterpreted. Post-visit interrogations may ensue, "did he touch you down there?" to confirm the custodial parent's suspicions. The literature on children's memory (Yuille, 1988) indicates that children are likely to assimilate the adult's suggestions as fact, especially when the adult is perceived as a credible figure. The child's fears of abandonment by the "other" parent, an emotional reaction commonly noted in children of divorce (e.g., Garbarino & Vondra, 1987), may strengthen this tendency.

Once the parent has alleged sexual abuse, a predictable chain of events is set into motion – including involvement of police, social service workers, lawyers, and mental health professionals – in preparation for a court hearing (Murray, 1987). Repeated interviewing may shape the child's report of events (King & Yuille, 1987; Yuille, 1988). Typically, the visitation or custody rights are immediately suspended. Even in cases where there is insufficient evidence to substantiate the sexual abuse accusation, or charge the accused parent, the court may restore only supervised access. The court and professionals involved will, most often under these conditions, systematically hedge to protect the child. Although a decision in this direction is ethically and practically unavoidable, the strong possibility remains that innocent parents are being removed from their children's lives.

If the accused parent is cleared, the months or years that have elapsed with the completion of proceedings may have irrepairably damaged the relationship with the child. The potential effects on the child may be devastating (Elwell & Ephross, 1987; Pine, 1987).

The Evaluation of Sexual Abuse Allegations in Custody Disputes

The preceding discussion has attempted to illustrate how improbable allegations may arise in custody and visitation disputes, to underline the extent and scope of this problem, and to emphasize its potentially devastating consequences for the accused parents and their children. It should be noted here, that in some cases the allegations may be based on the accurate perceptions of one parent that the other parent – unable to cope with the stresses of familial separation, and exposed to the child in an unsupervised context – has initiated a sexually abusing relationship. These circumstances point to a need for increased sensitivity, awareness and sophistication about the possibility of improbable allegations, and about their evaluation.

A number of indicators that may be associated with improbable allegations have emerged from the literature, and are summarized in the following section of this paper. These indicators are derived from three main sources. The *first* source of these indicators is the few empirical studies on improbable allegations cited above. *None* of these studies involved the systematic measurement and analysis of a priori-generated indicators. Instead, sex abuse allegation cases, that could not be substantiated, were subjectively analyzed on a post-hoc basis for factors that differentiated them from substantiated cases. *Second*, the recommendations of experienced mental health professionals working in the area of sex abuse allegations in custody and access disputes are included. *Third*, findings from the general child sexual literature, which are relevant to but have not been researched in the context of custody and access disputes, are reviewed. An attempt has been made to alert the reader to how these general findings might be applied more specifically to the custody situation. These indicators are *not* intended to be used as a checklist. Instead they summarize what little information is available, and are presented to point to specific directions for empirical investigation. This type of research will be necessary for the development of criteria for differentiating probable and improbable allegations of sexual abuse arising during custody and access disputes.

346

1. General Circumstances of the Sexual Abuse Allegation

Improbable allegations are substantially more often brought about (a) by the parent than by the child, and (b) after a separation or divorce rather than during the marriage (Benedek & Shetky, 1984, 1985; Gardner, 1987). However, the *specific* circumstances under which the allegation is made by a parent should be explored carefully. The presence of an abusing marital relationship may delay a disclosure of child sexual abuse until after a separation or divorce. On the other hand, the severity of the stress caused by a marital separation may increase the likelihood of impulsive behaviour. Thus, incestuous behaviour may in fact begin, and be reported, during this stressful life period (Mac-Farlane, 1986). Changes in the family structure (e.g., remarriages), and what they mean to the child or children and both parents should also be considered in research studies.

2. Child's Disclosure of Alleged Sexual Abuse

In probable cases children rarely report the sexual abuse quickly; rather, delayed and conflicted disclosures are expected (deJong, 1986; Faller, 1984; Sgroi, Porter, & Blick, 1982). Abused children are resistant to direct questioning about sexual details (Green, 1986), and may retract their disclosures (Gardner, 1987). Summit (1983) has described a common sequence of reactions of children to sexual molestation as the *Abuse Accommodation Syndrome (AAS)*. The components of secrecy, helplessness, entrapment, and accommodation — associated with sexual victimization — may be followed by an initial disclosure, and a subsequent retraction of these disclosing statements. This retraction is in part related to the child's intense fears of the offender, and/or guilt about the consequences of their statements for the offender and other family members (deJong, 1986; Green, 1986; Klajner-Diamond et al., 1987). The existence of AAS was recently acknowledged by legal authorities (*State* v. *Middleton*, 1985).

In improbable cases, details of sexual activity are generally more spontaneous and more easily obtained during the first interview. The child is outspoken and nondefensive in his or her description without significant changes in mood or affect. Their emotions are inconsistent with what is being said (i.e., absence of negative affect, crying, blushing, stuttering, etc.) (Green, 1986; Haugaard & Reppucci, 1988). In the custody/access context the evaluation of the child's disclosure may become extremely complex. A child's improbable allegation of sexual abuse may be accompanied by emotional responses similar to those documented in relation to probable disclosures, due to emotional blackmail on the part of the alleging parent. Careful documentation of disclosures in probable versus improbable cases of sex abuse allegations in this specific context may reveal differences in the nature and patterns of the child's disclosure. Legal professionals should be alerted to these psychological issues relevant to children's disclosures. Retractions must be considered very carefully to avoid the erroneous dismissal of allegations. Court dates and other legal deadlines should accommodate children's patterns of disclosures over the course of a *series* of interviews.

3. Details of the Alleged Sexual Abuse

In probable cases the child is more often able to provide specific details of the abuse, by recalling details of the event (e.g., "daddy's red car") associated with their internal visual image. In improbable cases reports of details are more likely to change between interviews, because there is no permanent image from which the child is describing his experience. However, a *lack* of specific details will not necessarily suggest that an allegation is *improbable*. For example, Goodman's (1984) research suggests that young children who experienced a frightening event were less able than those who perceived a nonfrightening event to recall details, but were equivocal in their ability to recall more central events. This example points to a recommendation for individuals planning to conduct research on the evaluation of sex abuse allegations brought forth during custody/access disputes. Researchers should focus on *active* signs of both probable and improbable allegations, rather than *negative* signs (i.e., "the lack of . . . "). There is an important difference between the presence of a sign suggesting the accusation is more probable or improbable, and the lack of the same sign being interpreted in the opposite direction.

In improbable cases the details are generally less credible. They may have the flavour of a scenario "borrowed" from a movie or television program about sexual abuse. The details may be altogether incorrect. For example, when asked what the color of the father's sperm was, the child may respond "yellow" (Gardner, 1987). However, such details must always be evaluated in the context of the child's idiosyncratic use of language, such as in this example, the use of color concepts.

4. Secrecy Details

In more probable cases the offender has often created a "secret" and told the child not to tell. The more details of pressure for secrecy the child is able to report, the more probable the allegation (Gardner, 1987). The nature of the secrecy details should be investigated carefully in custody cases to evaluate whether they stem from pressure for secrecy about genuine sex abuse or pressure for secrecy in supporting the improbable allegation of a parent. One hypothesis for empirical investigation would be that direct threats for secrecy in genuine sexual abuse would effect the child's report differently, than more subtly communicated threat in the case of an improbable allegation.

5. Appropriateness of the Child's Terminology and Perspective

In improbable cases the vocabulary or grammar used to recall the sexual abuse details may be inappropriate to the child's age (e.g., "made love to me" from a five-year-old). The child may use adult expressions, adult sexual terminology or colloquialisms, and may speak from an adult perspective (Gardner, 1987; Green, 1986; Haugaard & Reppucci, 1988; MacFarlane, 1986). Here it may be important to compare the language used by the alleging parent, and by the accused parent, with that of the child in question.

In probable cases the child uses age-appropriate, idiosyncratic terminology (e.g., pain is "ouwie"; vagina is "bum"). Children at the preoperational stage of development (between two and three years of age) may not see objects as the same if they change in appearance (e.g., erect penis and nonerect penis will not be viewed as the same penis), and will tend to categorize objects in terms of function (e.g., ejaculation is "peeing") (deJong, 1986). MacFarlane and Krebs (1986) have underlined the importance of establishing common terminology with the child at the onset of interview, in terms of names for people, things, body parts, and sexual acts. In improbable cases it may be hypothesized that children will be unable to translate a report of sexual abuse originally described from an adult perspective to more age-appropriate, idiosyncratic terminology. One suggestion for empirical work might be that a child, who has spontaneously employed an adult perspective and adult terminology in describing the sexual abuse, be interviewed further to determine the more child-like idiosyncratic terminology they use to name anatomical parts on a daily basis. Once this terminology has been determined, they may be asked to recall the abusive episode/s in "their own words." The response of children involved in probable and improbable cases could then be compared.

6. Presence of Sexually Specific Symptoms

The presence of sexually specific symptoms is consistent with probable allegations of sexual abuse. Some form of "traumatic sexualization" (Browne & Finkelhor, 1986) is usually associated with the child's experience of sexual abuse. The perpetrator tends to reward the child for sexual behaviour, and this shapes the child's sexual feelings and attitudes in developmentally and interpersonally inappropriate ways. As a result the child may learn sexual behaviour as a strategy for approaching, manipulating, and appeasing others (Haugaard & Reppucci, 1988).

Sexually abused children may become sexually aggressive (Browne & Finkelhor, 1986) by reenacting sexual behaviour in their play with other children — either as the aggressor or as the victim (Faller, 1984). Younger children who have been sexually abused tend to masturbate excessively (Friedrich, Urquiza, & Beilke, 1986), whereas older children are more frequently sexually seductive with adults (Faller, 1984).

7. Sexual Knowledge

In improbable cases the child may *lack* inappropriate sexual knowledge. Conversely, sexually abused children will be far more aware of sexual matters than their peers (Faller, 1984). They may have an obsessive interest in sex and knowledge of adult sexual functioning, and themes of sex are usually present in their drawings and play (Gardner, 1987; Green, 1986). The play of sexually abused children may involve reenactment of the abuse as a means of desensitizing the trauma (Gardner, 1987). Information about the type of "sexual/adult" knowledge learned through an improbable allegation has not been discussed in the literature and should be explored.

8. Child's Interactions with the Accused Parent

In probable cases the child will rarely confront the accused parent with the allegation, even if the alleging parent is present. The sexually abused child will often be fearful and withdrawn in the presence of the offender and may cling to the other parent (Haugaard & Reppucci, 1988). This intense fear may generalize to all individuals perceived to be similar to the offender — for example, men with dark beards (Faller, 1984; Gardner, 1986). The reaction of the child to a male examiner should be noted (Faller, 1984), and the interactions between the alleging parent and the child should be observed as a baseline upon which to compare the relationship between the child and the alleged offender (Green, 1986).

Gardner (1987) has noted that in improbable cases the child will often confront the accused parent with the allegation in the alleging parent's presence, especially when prompted by nonverbal messages by the alleging parent (Green, 1986). Manipulative parents often control the child by monitoring his or her responses through eye contact and subtle facial expressions (Green, 1986). The "brainwashed" child responds by checking with the alleging parent before proceeding. In these improbable cases there will be a discrepancy between the child's angry accusations and the apparent comfort in the accused parent's presence, when the alleging parent is absent (Benedek & Shetky, 1984; Green, 1986). Research comparing videotapes of these interactions in probable sex abuse allegation cases, improbable sex abuse allegation cases, and in custody cases where no allegations of sexual abuse have been made may reveal differences in these patterns of behaviour.

9. Presence of Child Sexual Abuse Symptoms

Numerous signs and symptoms, present in some children who have been sexually abused, have been identified in the literature (e.g., Alter-Reid et al., 1986; Browne & Finkelhor, 1986). The empirical literature suggests that a large proportion of child sexual abuse victims (Bresee, Stearns, Bess, & Packer, 1986; Browne & Finkelhor, 1986) exhibit some specific emotional reactions (e.g., fear, anxiety, feelings of betrayal, depression, anger), self-perceptions (low self-esteem, disempowerment, stigmatization), physical consequences and somatic complaints (sleep and eating disturbances, nausea). Similarly, their sexuality (sexually specific behaviour) and social functioning (underachievement at school, problems in peer relations) will be affected.

Recent reviews of the empirical literature (Haugaard & Reppucci, 1988; MacFarlane & Waterman, 1986) have summarized factors influencing the effects of child sexual abuse. These factors include: (a) Child characteristics (age, sex, prior emotional health); (b) Characteristics of the abuse experience (duration, relationship with perpetrator, amount of coercion); and (c) Events subsequent to the abuse. A sexual abuse allegation may be evaluated in terms of its consistency with this information. Research in the area of sex abuse allegations during custody/access disputes will need to address the problem of differentiating a child's emotional reactions to sexual abuse (sexual exploitation) versus responses to involvement in an improbable accusation (psychological exploitation) and a distressing family environment. It is conceivable that there may be considerable overlap in the emotional burden carried by the children in both circumstances.

10. Characteristics of the Accused Parent

Given the range of pathology thought to underlie instances of incest, no single profile of the incest offender can be identified. However, there are certain clinical observations that may raise concerns about the risk of molestation (Bresee et al., 1986). The literature on the characteristics of incestuous parents provides little specific information on sexually abusing mothers.

Incestuous fathers may exhibit impulse control problems and difficulties monitoring or directing emotional reactions; excessive self-centeredness (Bressee et al., 1986); strong dependency needs; poor self-esteem (Famularo, Stone, Barnum, & Wharton, 1986); and a tendency to regress when faced with stressful circumstances (Benedek & Shetky, 1984; Green, 1986; Gardner, 1987). These findings are based on the ad hoc analysis of admitted sex abuse offender characteristics. Therefore, the absence of these characteristics will not necessarily rule out sexually abusive behaviour in an accused parent. Furthermore, there is no evidence to suggest that these features are present solely in sexually abusing adults, but are also associated with a variety of other conditions.

In probable cases, there may be signs of symbolic or overt sexual play with the father, if the molestation progressed slowly over a longer period of time and was relatively unthreatening (Benedek & Shetky, 1984). In improbable cases the father and child will more likely engage in more age- and role-appropriate interactions. If a father is incorrectly accused, he may react with indignation, whereas incest offenders may respond more sheepishly or may resort to threats and bribes (Gardner, 1987).

Probable offenders may display other sexual deviations or have a history of sexual abuse (Browne & Finkelhor, 1986; Gardner, 1987; Green, 1986). It has been suggested that, in some cases, sexual abuse of a child may represent active mastery of the parent's own childhood trauma. Finally, abusing parents may tend to overestimate their children's capabilities and have developmentally unrealistic expectations of them (Azar & Rohrbeck, 1986). The Adult-Adolescent Parenting Inventory (AAPI; Barotek, 1984) is one psychometrically sound inventory that may be used to assess the appropriateness of parents' developmental expectations of the child, empathy toward the child's needs, and potential reversal of parent-child roles.

Although phallometric techniques have been recommended for therapeutic purposes, their use in the assessment of sexual abuse allegations remains highly controversial. The research to date suggests that positive phallometric findings may be useful for evaluation processes (i.e., when a sexual response is shown to deviant cues), whereas negative responses are virtually meaningless (O'Shaughnessy, 1987).

11. Characteristics of the Alleging Parent

In improbable cases the alleging parent has been reported to present underlying pathology in the form of paranoid, histrionic, or borderline tendencies, or may even exhibit psychotic features (Benedek & Shetky, 1984). However, it is important to recognize, that a disturbed mother with vengeful motives may, nevertheless, have discovered genuine evidence of sexual abuse (Bresee et al., 1986).

In improbable cases the alleging parent seems overzealous about the allegation, but reluctant to have the child interviewed alone. S/he may, in fact, insist on being present during the interview, and will prompt the child when s/he is asked about the abuse. S/he will appear unwilling to consider the possibility that the child was *not* abused (Bresee et al., 1986), and will reject any other explanations for the child's behaviour without giving them any consideration. These parents will appear unaware or indifferent about the impact of the investigative process on the child, and will not appreciate the psychological trauma connected with child sexual abuse (Gardner, 1987). They will not be sensitive to the psychological loss for the child, should their relationship with the accused parent be terminated. One possible variable to be examined in future empirical work might be the parent's perspective-taking ability.

When the alleging parent is asked to report the initial scenario upon which the allegations are based, s/he will build up and stretch the available information out of proportion. In probable cases alleging parents will tend to reduce or deny indicators of sexual abuse. In improbable cases the alleging parent will not be able to give specific information about the events leading up to the alleged abuse (Bresee et al., 1986; Gardner, 1987).

The alleging parent's interactions with the evaluator should also be noted. In improbable cases alleging parents will prefer a "hired gun" evaluator. S/he may check with the examiner to see if s/he has asked the child the appropriate questions and will tend to fill in missing details. S/he may demand that the investigation continue regardless of the impact the process is having on the child. In some cases these alleging parents will attempt to contact other evaluators if they feel the initial examiner is not confirming their suspicions (Bresee et al., 1986). Finally, in probable cases, alleging parents will likely feel ashamed or stigmatized, and may blame themselves for not having protected their child more adequately. In improbable cases the alleging parent will not have this attitude, and may be relatively free with the information.

The information presented in the above two sections (10 and 11) is based largely on the impressions of mental health professionals experienced in custody evaluations. For the purposes of this paper these impressions are provided for hypothesis-generating purposes. These hypotheses should be addressed by research documenting the characteristics of alleging and accused parents and their relationships with their children in probable versus improbable cases.

12. Vulnerability of the Child

The literature suggests that some children are more vulnerable to sexual abuse than others. These generally more susceptible children are younger, have little accurate sexual knowledge, lack self-protective coping skills, have been sexually abused earlier in their lives, have a stepfather living in their homes, are weakly or conflictually bonded with their mothers, and are overly compliant (deJong, 1986; Gardner, 1987). This knowledge may be useful for the evaluation of sex abuse allegations in custody proceedings. Information about disclosures, or lack thereof, by siblings and step-siblings may provide a context for the evaluation of an allegation about the child in question.

Evaluative Procedures and Considerations

Judges tend to seek the expertise of mental health professionals to assist them in gathering information relevant to custody and access determinations (Felner, Gillespie & Smith, 1985; Foster, 1984; Wyer, Gaylord & Grove, 1987). The information obtained by a psychiatrist or clinical psychologist through the completion of a requested psychological evaluation may or may not be used by the fact finders in their final determination. In a psychological/psychiatric assessment conducted for these purposes the evaluators must clearly articulate the facts and observations that form the data base for their conclusions. This data base should be comprised of the clinical interview and psychological testing with the child, a developmental history as a basis for the assessment of potential changes in the child's behaviour or emotions following the alleged abuse, medical reports of any physical signs of abuse, as well as psychiatric evaluations including sexual histories of *both* the accusing and the accused parent (Bresee et al., 1986). Both mental health (e.g., Gardner, 1987) and legal professionals (e.g., Bala & Anweiler, 1986) have agreed that failure to at least *attempt* to interview all parties involved could be fatal to the weight given to an expert's opinion. The evaluators must use their clinical judgement as to whether the child and the alleged offender should be seen together for the purposes of the assessment to protect the child from unmanageable distress.

The evaluator should also attempt to resist time restrictions. Evaluations of sexual abuse allegations will require more frequent contact with the child over a longer period of time. Consistent and consensual sensitization of legal professionals to this necessity may in time create an atmosphere of more realistic time expectations for child sex abuse interviewers. The interviewer should work toward creating an atmosphere of safety and trust, where the child is protected at all times from further trauma (Bresee et al., 1986).

Some authors (e.g., Colby & Colby, 1987; Faller, 1984) have recommended the use of audio- and video-taping, as a convincing and valid source of evidence both for evaluative purposes and for presentation in the courts. The recent amendment of the *Canada Evidence Act* (Bill C-15) permits videotapes of children's evidence to be admitted in court.

Gardner (1987) has noted that the sequence of the evaluation should progress from general to specific questions (Benedek & Shetky, 1985) to minimize the contamination of interview data by examiner statements. When evaluating the child, the media of play, pictures and stories are generally less threatening means for eliciting sexual themes, memories, and content than interviewing (Benedek & Shetky, 1984; Faller, 1984). However, in selecting these methods, evaluators must be aware of the potentially suggestive, contaminating and leading influences these materials may have on the child. The use of anatomically correct dolls for investigative purposes has become a questionable practice until further empirical studies have been completed (Faller, 1984; Goranson, 1986; Yuille, 1988). Although a number of authors have adopted the use of anatomically detailed dolls to aid younger children in recalling and expressing experiences of sexual abuse, there are no standardized protocols for their use, and there is no agreement on what behaviours constitute evidence of abuse (Yuille, 1988). The major problem associated with the dolls is their suggestibility. Furthermore, recent studies (Boat & Everson, 1987; Goranson, 1986; Grams & Herbert, 1987) indicate that nonabused children exhibit some of the behaviours that have been considered by clinicians as evidence of sexual abuse. The age of the child permitting, objective measures of self-esteem, depression, body image, level of depression and the relationship with parents should be employed (Bresee et al., 1986).

DeJong (1986) has suggested that the evaluator get a "base reading" from adult caretakers as to the child's physical, emotional, and behavioural functioning before the time of the alleged abuse, and to then document the nature and extent of any changes – taking into consideration other stressors. These would include those related to parental divorce or separation, and to adjustment to visits with the noncustodial parent. Therefore, the evaluator must be familiar with the current literature describing the psychological effects of divorce, as well as that documenting post child sexual abuse signs and symptoms.

The assessment of the child should include an evaluation of cognitive functioning. The evaluator needs to interview the child and interpret their responses with sensitivity to the cognitive idiosyncrasies related to specific developmental levels (Waterman, 1986). For example, young children may not be able to affix dates or exact times to incidents of abuse, but will be able to locate such acts in relation to significant events in their lives (e.g., "the day it snowed"; "at breakfast time") (Faller, 1984). A review of the literature (Yuille, 1988) suggests that a child's memory for an event is a function of attentional capacity for an event and the cognitive structure to which the event can be assimilated. The younger the child, the more likely these two factors will limit the details of the event stored in memory. Recall may be further reduced by limitations in the number and complexity of retrieval strategies. In free recall, younger children tend to remember less details than older children and adults, but what they remember is accurate (Loftus & Davis, 1984; Melton, 1985). Memory distortions may occur in two ways in a young child. First, a child of less than two years may confuse (misinterpret an event) and fuse (two events become one) memories believing these recollections are accurate. Second, they will have problems ordering events according to time (Klajner-Diamond et al., 1987; Melton, 1985). Yuille (1988) has presented *Statement Validity Analysis*, a method of interviewing children and assessing the validity of their statements, which may be useful for the evaluation of sex abuse allegations in custody/access disputes, because of its sensitivity to the child's level of cognitive development.

Orzek (1985) has emphasized the child's tendency to rely on trusted adults to aid them in interpreting novel events. The custodial parent may play the role of translating the noncustodial parent's behaviour to the child. This role may be crucial immediately after the parents' separation, when the fears of abandonment by the custodial parent are most salient, and when the context of the visiting relationship is still foreign to the child.

The evaluator of sexual abuse allegations must be aware not only of the effects of sexual abuse on child victims, but also of the variables contributing to these effects. There is literature to suggest that the duration and frequency of abuse, the type of sexual act, the amount of force and aggression, the child's age at onset, the sex and age of the offender will modify the child's reactions and symptoms (e.g., Browne & Finkelhor, 1986; Elwell & Ephross, 1987; Main, Wehrspann, Klajner-Diamond, LeBaron & Winder, 1986). The evaluator may use this information to assess whether the signs of possible sexual abuse in the child, and the reports of the alleging parent, are consistent with the details of the abuse. Recently, researchers (e.g., Pierce & Pierce, 1985; Sebold, 1987) have delineated sex differences in the responses of child victims of sexual abuse. For example, male adolescent victims tend to respond to sexual abuse with homophobic concerns. This type of information may be important in assessing the credibility of sexual abuse allegations — as active signs increasing confidence that sexual abuse has occurred, rather than as negative signs that abuse is not likely to have occurred.

Finally, the evaluator should be aware of the family dynamics associated with child sexual abuse (Haugaard & Reppucci, 1988; MacFarlane & Waterman, 1986; Pettis & Hughes, 1985). For example, the fact that stepfathers and father substitutes are overrepresented among abusers (e.g., Giles-Sims & Finkelhor, 1984) should not be dismissed. Thus, if an evaluator perceives clear signs of sexual abuse in the child, this does not necessarily lead to the conclusion that the accused father is the perpetrator. This underlines the necessity for interviewing the alleged offender. Some authors (e.g., Gray & Cosgrove, 1985) have suggested that cultural issues, such as childrearing practices, should be considered in evaluating potential abuse cases.

Conclusions

This paper has attempted to capture the extent and complexity of the problem of sexual abuse allegations in custody disputes. This problem is psycholegal in nature and will require the attention and collaboration of legal and mental health professionals. This sentiment has been expressed more generally in the area of custody evaluations and family policy (e.g., Felner et al., 1985) and is particularly appropriate in our context. Legal professionals will be most concerned with the potential abuse of existing custody and sexual abuse laws. Mental health professionals will need to increase their sophistication in evaluating sexual abuse allegations arising from the custody context, and behavioural scientists should support their efforts by conducting the needed research. Communication between mental health professionals/scientists and legal professionals, as well as mutual education, will be necessary in formulating a psycholegally integrated and socioculturally responsible approach to this problem.

The 12 indicators outlined in this paper may serve a hypothesis-generating function for future empirical studies designed to identify factors that will be useful in the differentiation of probable and improbable allegations. A control group of families involved in custody or access disputes, but not in sex abuse allegations, should be included to establish a reasonable comparative context. The outcome criterion will have to be defined carefully and with greater sophistication than positive versus negative court outcome. One possibility would be to specify the criterion measure in probabilistic terms on a continuum ranging from highly probable to highly improbable allegations. For example, the content of the court's decision (e.g., amount and type of access permitted) and the presence/absence of medical evidence of sexual abuse may represent factors contributing to the relative position on this continuum. The most highly probable and the most highly improbable cases would then weigh most heavily in the analyses. Potentially relevant factors (as outlined in the 12 areas of indicators) may then be investigated through a comparison of the control and experimental groups.

An additional concern for the psychologist will be the shortterm and long-term effects on the child involved in an improbable allegation case. Follow up studies may be useful for this purpose. A comparison of the characteristics of alleging parents in improbable cases and accused parents in probable cases may further our understanding of the dynamics of child abuse. The exploitation of a child as a pawn in a custody dispute is a form of child maltreatment that will need to be addressed by both mental health and legal professionals.

References

Alter-Reid, K., Gibbs, M. S., Lachenmeyer, J. R., Sigal, J., & Massoth, N. A. (1986). Sexual abuse of children: A review of the empirical findings. *Clinical Psychology Review, 6*(4), 249–266.

Azar, S. T., & Rohrbeck, C. A. (1986). Child abuse and unrealistic expectations: Further validation of the Parent Opinion Questionnaire (POQ). *Journal of Consulting and Clinical Psychology, 54*(6), 867–868.

Bala, N., & Anweiler, J. (1986, June). *Allegations of sexual abuse in a parental custody dispute: Smoke-screen or fire?* Paper presented at the Symposium on Custody Litigation, Law Society of Upper Canada Continuing Legal Education Program, Toronto, Canada.

Baily, T. F. (1980). Observations on dynamics and practice of sexual abuse. In W. M. Holder (Ed.), *Sexual abuse of children: Implications for treatment* (pp. 45–57). Englewood, CO: American Humane.

Barotek, S. J. (1984). *Handbook for adult-adolescent parenting inventory.* Eau Claire, WI: Family Development Associates.

Benedek, S., & Shetky, D. (1984, October). *Allegations of sexual abuse in child custody cases.* Paper presented at the Annual Meeting of the American Academy of Psychiatry and the Law, Nassau, Bahamas.

Benedek, S., & Shetky, D. (1985). Allegations of sexual abuse in child custody and visitation disputes. In D. Shetky & E. Benedek (Eds.), *Emerging issues in child psychiatry and law* (pp. 145–158). New York: Brunner/Mazel.

Boat, B., & Everson, M. (1987, April). *Correspondence between beliefs of doll users and the behaviour of non-abused and sexually abuse children with anatomical dolls.* Paper presented at the Society for Research in Child Development Biennial Meeting, New York.

Bresee, P., Stearns, G. B., Bess, B. H., & Packer, L. S. (1986). Allegations of child sexual abuse in child custody disputes: A therapeutic assessment model. *American Journal of Orthopsychiatry, 56*(4), 560–569.

Brinkley v. Brinkley, 336 SE 2d 90, Va App, (1985).

Browne, A., & Finkelhor, D. (1986). Impact of child sexual abuse: A review of the research. *Psychological Bulletin, 99*(1), 66–77.

Child abuse used to win custody feuds. (1987, January). *Toronto Globe and Mail*, P.Bl.

Colby, I., & Colby, I. (1987). Videotaping the child sexual abuse victim. *The Journal of Contemporary Social Work, 68*(2), 117–121.

Corwin, D. L., Berliner, L., Goodman, G., Goodwin, J., & White, S. (1987). Child sexual abuse and custody disputes. *Journal of Interpersonal Violence, 2*(1), 91–105.

deJong, M. (1986). A conceptual model for judging the truthfulness of a young child's allegations of sexual abuse. *American Journal of Orthopsychiatry, 56*(4), 550–559.

Dykes v. Dykes, 488 So 2d 368 LaApp (1986).

Elwell, M. E., & Ephross, P. H. (1987). Initial reactions of sexually abused children. *Social Casework, 68*(2), 109–116.

Elterman, M. F. (1987, March). *Differentiating true and false allegations of child sexual abuse in custody cases.* Paper presented to Annual Conference of Family Court Counsellors, Vancouver, Canada.

Faller, K. (1984). Is the child victim of sexual abuse telling the truth? *Child Abuse and Neglect, 8,* 473–481.

Famularo, R., Stone, K., Barnum, R., & Wharton, R. (1986). Alcoholism and severe child maltreatment. *American Journal of Orthopsychiatry, 56*(3), 481–485.

Felner, R. D., Gillespie, J. F., & Smith, R. (1985). Risk and vulnerability in childhood: A reappraisal. *Journal of Clinical Psychology, 14*(1), 2–3.

Foster, H. H. (1984). Child custody and divorce: A lawyer's view. *Annual Progress in Child Psychiatry and Child Development, 6,* 474–487.

Freud, S. (1965). *The complete introductory lectures on psychoanalysis* (Edited/translated by J. Strachey; originally published 1933). New York: Norton.

Friedrich, W., Urquiza, A. J., & Beilke, R. L. (1986). Behaviour problems in sexually abused young children. *Journal of Pediatric Psychology, 11*(1), 111–121.

Garbarino, J., & Vondra, J. (1987). Psychological maltreatment: Issues and perspectives. In M. R. Brassard, R. Germain, & S. N. Hart (Eds.), *Psychological maltreatment of children and youth.* New York: Pergamon Press.

Gardner, R. A. (1987). *The parental alienation syndrome and the differentiation between fabricated and genuine sex-abuse.* Cresskill, NJ: Creative Therapeutics.

Giles-Sims, J., & Finkelhor, D. (1984). Child abuse in stepfamilies. *Family Relations: Journal of Applied Family and Studies, 33*(3), 407–413.

Goodman, G. S. (1984). The child's testimony in historical perspective. *Journal of Social Issues, 6,* 401–476.

Goodwin, J., Sahd, D., & Rada, R. (1978). Incest hoax: False accusations, false denials. *Bulletin of the American Academy of Psychiatry and the Law, 6,* 269–276.

Goranson, S. E. (1986). *Young child interview responses to anatomically correct dolls.* Unpublished master's of social work thesis, University of British Columbia, Vancouver, Canada.

Grams, G. D., & Herbert, C. P. (1987, November). *Responses of "non-abused children" to the anatomically detailed dolls: An exploratory study.* Paper presented at Conference on Sexual Abuse Allegations, Continuing Legal Education Society, Vancouver, Canada.

Gray, E., & Cosgrove, J. (1985). Ethnocentric perception of childrearing practices in protective services. *Child Abuse and Neglect, 9*(3), 389–396.

Green, A. H. (1986). True and false allegations of sexual abuse in child custody disputes. *Journal of the American Academy of Child Psychiatry, 25*(4), 449–456.

Guilty until proven innocent. (1987, June). *New York Times,* p. 11.

Haugaard, J. F., & Reppucci, N. D. (1988). *The sexual abuse of children.* San Francisco: Jossey-Bass.

Hauser, B. B. (1985). Custody in dispute: Legal and psychological profiles of contesting families. *Journal of the American Academy of Child Psychiatry, 24*(5), 575–582.

Jones, D. P. H. (1987). Reliable and fictitious accounts of sexual abuse in children. *Journal of Interpersonal Violence, 2*(1), 27–45.

Jaffe, P., Austin, G., Lescheid, A., & Sas, L. (1987). Critical issues in the development of custody and access dispute resolution services. *Canadian Journal of Behavioural Science, 19*(4), 405–417.

Jortner, S. (1985). To what degree was Freud wrong—and how much difference does it make in psychotherapy? *Journal of Contemporary Psychotherapy, 15*(2), 114–122.

Kaplan, S. L., & Kaplan, S. J. (1981). The child's accusation of sexual abuse during a divorce and custody struggle. *Hillside Journal of Clinical Psychiatry, 3*(1), 81–95.

King, M. A., & Yuille, J. C. (1985). *An investigation of children's eyewitness abilities.* Unpublished manuscript, University of British Columbia, Vancouver, Canada.

King, M. A., & Yuille, J. C. (1987). Suggestibility and the child witness. In M. P. Toglia, S. Ceci, D. Ross (Eds.), *Child witnesses* (pp. 52–74). New York: Springer-Verlag.

Klajner-Diamond, H., Wehrspann, W., & Steinhauer, P. (1987). Assessing the credibility of young children's allegations of sexual abuse: Clinical issues. *Canadian Journal of Psychiatry, 32*(10), 610–614.

Levine, M., Ewing, C. P., & Hager, R. (1987). Juvenile and family mental health law in sociocultural context. *International Journal of Law and Psychiatry, 10,* 91–109.

Loftus, E., & Davis, G. (1984). Distortions in memory of children. *Journal of Social Issues, 40*(2), 51–67.

MacFarlane, K. (1986). Child sex abuse allegations in divorce proceedings. In K. MacFarlane and J. Waterman (Eds.), *Sexual abuse of young children,* pp. 121–150. New York: Guilford.

MacFarlane, K., & Krebs, S. (1986). Techniques for interviewing and evidence gathering. In K. MacFarlane and J. Waterman (Eds.), *Sexual abuse of young children,* (pp. 67–100). New York: Guilford.

MacFarlane, K., & Waterman, J. (1986). *Sexual abuse of young children*. New York: Guilford.

Main, M., Wehrspann, W., Klajner-Diamond, H., LeBaron, D., & Winder, C. (1986). Review of 125 children who were sexually abused. *Child Abuse and Neglect, 10*, 223-229.

Masson, J. M. (1984). *The assault on truth*. New York: Farran, Straus & Giroux.

McCahey, J. P. (Ed.) (1987). *Child custody and visitation: Law and Practice*. New York: Matthew Bender.

Melton, G. B. (1985). Sexually abused children and the legal system: Some policy recommendations. *American Journal of Family Therapy, 13*(1), 61-67.

Melton, G. B., Petrila, J., Poythress, N. G., & Slobogin, C. (1987). Child custody and divorce. In Melton et al. (Eds.), *Psychological evaluations for the courts: A handbook for mental health professionals and lawyers*. New York: Guilford Press.

Murray, M. L. (1987). Child sexual abuse: The new stick. *Family Practice Journal, 1*(1), 1-2.

Orzek, A. M. (1985). The child's cognitive processing of sexual abuse. *Journal of Child and Adolescent Psychotherapy, 2*(2), 110-114.

Peters, J. (1976). Children who are victims of sexual assault and the psychology of offenders. *American Journal of Psychotherapy, 30*, 398-421.

Pettis, K. W., & Hughes, R. D. (1985). Sexual victimization of children: A current perspective. *Behavioural Disorders, 10*(2), 136-144.

Pierce, R., & Pierce, L. H. (1985). The sexually abused child: A comparison of male and female victim (Special issue: C. Henry Kempe memorial research issue. *Child abuse and Neglect, 9*(2), 191-199.

O'Shaughnessy, R. (1987, November). *Sex abuse allegations in custody litigation: Role of the mental health professional*. Paper presented to the Continuing Legal Education Society of British Columbia, Vancouver, Canada.

Pine, B. A. (1987). Forum: When helping hurts—the double jeopardy for sexual abuse victims. *Social Casework: The Journal of Contemporary Social Work, 68*(2), 126-127.

Ricks, S. S. (1984). Determining child custody: Trends, factors, and alternatives. *Conciliation Courts Review, 22*, 65-70.

Roman, M., & Dichter, S. (1985). Fathers and feminism: Backlash within the women's movement. *Conciliation Courts Review, 23*(2), 37-45.

Schiffer, M. E. (1978). *Mental disorder and the criminal trial process*. Toronto, Canada: Butterworths.

Sahd, D. (1980). Psychological assessment of sexually abusing families and treatment implications. In W. M. Holder (Ed.), *Sexual abuse of children: Implications for treatment* (pp. 71-86). Englewood, Colorado: American Humane.

Sebold, J. (1987). Indicators of child sexual abuse in males. *The Journal of Contemporary Social Work, 68*(2), 75-80.

Sgroi, S. M., Porter, F. S., & Blick, L. C. (1982). Validation of child sex abuse allegations. In S. M. Sgroi (Ed.), *Handbook of clinical intervention in child sexual abuse* (pp. 201-235). Lexington, Mass.: Lexington Books.

State v. Middleton, 9.F.L.R.-263. "Expert testimony on 'Familial Child Sex Abuse Syndrome' was admissable. (1985).

Summit, R. (1983). The Child sexual abuse accommodating syndrome. *Child abuse and neglect, 7*, 177-193.

Wallerstein, J. S. (1985). Children of divorce: Emerging trends. *Psychiatric Clinics of North America, 8*(4), 837-856.

Waterman, J. (1986). Developmental considerations. In K. MacFarlane & J. Waterman (Eds.), *Sexual abuse of young children* (pp. 15-29). New York: Guilford.

Weiner, B. A., Simons, V. A., & Cavanaugh, J. L. (1985). Child Custody and Sexual Abuse. In D. H. Shetky & E. P. Benedek (Eds.), *Emerging issues in child psychiatry and the law* (pp. 59-75). New York: Brunner/Mazel. Wyer, M. M., Gaylord, S. L., & Grove, E. T. (1987). The legal context of child custody evaluations. In L. A. Weithorn (Ed.), *Psychology and child custody determinations: Knowledge, roles and expertise*. Lincoln, NE: University of Nebraska Press.

Yuille, J. C. (1988). The systematic assessment of children's testimony. *Canadian psychology, 29*(3), 247-262.

Zarski, L. P., Knight, R., & Zarski, J. J. (1985). Child custody disputes: A review of legal and clinical resolution methods. *International Journal of Family Therapy, 7*(2), 96-106.

Birth Control as a Condition of Probation for Those Convicted of Child Abuse: A Psycholegal Discussion of Whether the Condition Prevents Future Child Abuse or is a Violation of Liberty

Emily Campbell*

TABLE OF CONTENTS

---

*B.A., Mercer University, 1987; M.A., University of Nebraska, 1991; J.D., University of Nebraska, 1991; Doctoral Candidate (Social Psychology), University of Nebraska. The author is currently a first-year litigation associate at Sullivan & Cromwell (not yet admitted to the New York Bar).

Sullivan & Cromwell takes no responsibility for the views of the author expressed in this article.

The author wishes to thank Dr. Ross Thompson and Dr. Alan Tomkins for their helpful comments in revising this article for publication. The author would also like to thank Dr. Gary Melton for providing invaluable reference materials used in preparation of this article.

Correspondence regarding this article should be addressed to the author at Sullivan & Cromwell, 125 Broad Street, New York, New York 10004.

I. INTRODUCTION

Child abuse is a pervasive problem in the United States.[1] With the growing number of reports of abuse, there has been a public outcry for some resolution.[2] Judges, in particular, who are faced with the issues of punishment and rehabilitation of abusers, have periodically conditioned an abuser's probation on the use of birth control. Such a condition prevents conception of future children who might be abused.[3]

---

1. Almost 24,000 maltreated children experienced serious physical injury in 1983. *See* DEBORAH DARO, CONFRONTING CHILD ABUSE: RESEARCH FOR EFFECTIVE PROGRAM DESIGN (1988). Some children die as a result of physical abuse. *See* Rosalie Anderson et al., *Child Deaths Attributed to Abuse and Neglect: An Empirical Study*, 5 CHILDREN & YOUTH SERVICES REV. 75 (1983); P.T. D'Orban, *Women Who Kill Their Children*, 134 BRITISH J. PSYCHIATRY 560 (1979); Leah G. Fein, *Can Child Fatalities, End Product of Abuse, Be Prevented?*, 1 CHILD & YOUTH SERVICES REV. 31 (1979); Janine Jason et al., *Homicide as a Cause of Pediatric Mortality in the United States*, 72 PEDIATRICS 191 (1983); Philip J. Resnick, *Child Murder By Parents: A Psychiatric Review of Filicide*, 126 AM. J. PSYCHIATRY 325 (1969); Philip J. Resnick, *Murder of the Newborn: A Psychiatric Review of Neonaticide*, 126 AM. J. PSYCHIATRY 1414 (1970). *See also* MARIA W. PIERS, INFANTICIDE: PAST AND PRESENT (1978); Centers for Disease Control, *Child Homicide—United States*, 31 MORBIDITY & MORTALITY WKLY. REP. 292 (1982).

2. There has been an increasing awareness in the United States of the need to prevent child maltreatment. *See* U.S. Surgeon General, *Control of Stress and Violent Behavior*, in HEALTHY PEOPLE: THE U.S. SURGEON GENERAL'S REPORT ON HEALTH PROMOTION AND DISEASE PREVENTION (1979) ("By 1990, injuries and deaths to children inflicted by abusing parents should be reduced by at least 25%"). Children should be able to be safe, especially in their own homes. For information on an increased awareness of children's rights, see HOWARD COHEN, EQUAL RIGHTS FOR CHILDREN (1980); MICHAEL D.A. FREEMAN, THE RIGHTS AND WRONGS OF CHILDREN 104-146 (1983) (abuse and neglect); THE RIGHTS OF CHILDREN: LEGAL AND PSYCHOLOGICAL PERSPECTIVES (James S. Henning ed., 1982); United Nations Declaration of the Rights of the Child, *noted in* FREEMAN, *supra*, at 283-85; COLIN WRINGE, CHILDREN'S RIGHTS: A PHILOSOPHICAL STUDY (1981).

3. *See generally* John C. Williams, Annotation, *Propriety of Conditioning Probation on Defendant's Remaining Childless or Having No Additional Children During Probationary Period*, 94 A.L.R. 3d 1218 (1979).

In May 1988, an Arizona judge sentenced a teenage mother, who left her two sons alone in a sweltering apartment for three days, to practice birth control throughout her child bearing years. The apartment had no air conditioning, and when both children were found, they were dehydrated and near death. The judge had said that the "birth control stipulation was the only way to make sure [she] did not have other children to abuse."[4] However, the order was subsequently reversed.[5]

In September 1988, an Indianapolis judge encountered a woman who in 1986 had fatally poisoned her first child with psychotropic drugs. An autopsy revealed that the child died of poisoning from antidepressant and antipsychotic drugs which had been prescribed for his mother.[6] The mother had pleaded guilty to charges of neglect, carrying a prison term of six to twenty years. She was undergoing treatment in a psychiatric ward, and because she was pregnant again, she was being fed intravenously to ensure nourishment of the fetus. The judge offered to reduce her prison sentence if she would agree to be sterilized. He stated: "Here is a woman who should not be a mother, someone who has killed her child and pleaded guilty to neglect. I think she needs to recognize that the same thing can happen again and take steps to control that it doesn't."[7] The mother agreed to undergo a tubal ligation after giving birth because she was well aware of the risk of her engaging in similar behavior in the future.[8]

More recently, in January 1991, a California judge[9] sentenced a woman

---

4. *Court Tells Mother to Use Birth Control*, L.A. TIMES, May 26, 1988, at 11, col. 6; *Judge Put Woman on Birth Control*, CHI. TRIB., May 26, 1988, at 14; *Woman Is Pregnant Despite Court Order For Birth Control*, N.Y. TIMES, Aug. 31, 1988, at A24; *Woman's Sentence is Birth Control*, N.Y. TIMES, May 26, 1988, at A22.

5. *Birth Control Order Is Overturned*, N.Y. TIMES, Sept. 3, 1988, at 8. In another Arizona case, a woman was convicted of child abuse in the 1986 death of her ten-month-old son when the baby died after suffering a skull fracture and brain damage when the mother threw him onto a bathroom floor because he would not stop crying. The judge apparently conditioned probation upon her use of birth control, but refused to find her in violation when she was again found to be pregnant. UPI, Jan. 5, 1988, *available in* Lexis, Nexis Library, UPI file.

6. Joseph R. Tybor, *Does Sterilization Fit the Crime? Women Must decide*, CHI. TRIB., Sept. 25, 1988 at C4.

7. *Id.*

8. *Id.*

9. Judge Howard Broadman has been known for his creative sentencing. In 1990, he put an ex-convict who stole two six packs of beer on probation with a condition that the defendant wear a T-shirt proclaiming that he was a felon. *Judge: Birth Control Implant Ruling Stands*, CHI. TRIB., Jan. 11, 1991, at M4. This judge also required an alcoholic to swallow Anabuse, a drug that would make the defendant violently ill if he drank alcohol. He ordered a man who stole a boat to give his own car to the county to see how it feels "to lose a prized possession." Mark A. Stein, *Judge Stirs Debate with Ordering of Birth*

to three years probation on the condition that she use a Norplant[10] birth control implant. The mother had criminally abused her four- and six-year-old children by physically assaulting them with a belt, belt buckle, and extension cord, while being pregnant with her fifth child.[11] The judge also ordered the mother to quit smoking, and explained, "if you can't quit smoking for the betterment of your baby, how are you ever going to get your act together not

---

Control; Courts: A Mother of Four Agrees to have a Contraceptive Implant in Pleading Guilty to Child Abuse. Critics Call It Unconstitutional, L.A. TIMES, Jan. 10, 1991, at A3 (quoting Charles Rothbauam, lawyer representing the defendant). Furthermore, in a civil divorce case, he ordered ex-spouses to take turns staying in their former home so that the children would not have their lives disrupted by moving back and forth between parents. *Id.* The judge has decided not to be further involved in this case because he was recently shot at by a man upset about the implications of this decision as it relates to abortion. *See Abortion Opponent is Arraigned on Charge of Trying to Murder Judge*, L.A. TIMES, Mar. 7, 1991, at A26; Bill Ainsworth, *"I Take Away People's Rights All the Time*, LEGAL TIMES, at 10; *Controversial Judge Quits Abuse Case*, L.A. TIMES, Apr. 14, 1991, at A30; *Controversial Judge Steps Aside*, WASH. POST, Apr. 15, 1991, at A6; *Gunshot Fired at Judge is Tied to Norplant Case*, N.Y. TIMES, Mar. 6, 1991, at A20; John Hurst, *Controversial Judge Dodges Not Only Critics, But Bullet*, L.A. TIMES, Apr. 29, 1991, at A3; *Judge in Birth Control Ruling Quits Case*, CHI. TRIB., Apr. 14, 1991, at 26; *Judge Removes Himself in Birth Control Case*, N.Y. TIMES, Apr. 15, 1991, at A13; *Man is Arraigned in Court Shooting*, N.Y. TIMES, Mar. 7, 1991, at A22; *Possible Motive Told in Court Shooting*, L.A. TIMES, Mar. 6, 1991, at A20.

10. Norplant works by slowly releasing levonorgestrel, a synthetic form of progesterone, at a steady rate to maintain blood hormone levels sufficient to suppress ovulation. It also causes the mucus that lines the cervix to thicken, trapping sperm that try to enter the cervical canal. This method is 99.7% effective. It must be inserted in a doctor's office under a local anesthetic. Sylvia Rubin, *Birth Control Breakthrough: The Long-Awaited Norplant—The First Contraceptive to Hit the Market*, SAN FRANCISCO CHRON., Jan. 28, 1991, at B3.

11. The case has generated a great deal of criticism and comment. *See* B.D. Colen, *Sterilization: Unacceptable Penalty*, NEWSDAY, Jan. 29, 1991, at 73; Bruce Fein, *This Birth-Control Sentence is Correct*, USA TODAY, Feb. 4, 1991, at 8A; John P. MacKenzie, *Whose Choice Is It Anyway?*, N.Y. TIMES, Jan. 28, 1991, at A22; Helen R. Neuborne, *In the Norplant Case, Good Intentions Make Bad Law*, L.A. TIMES, Mar. 3, 1991, at M1; James Willwerth, *Should We Take Away Their Kids? Often the Best Way to Save the Child is to Save the Mother as Well*, TIME, May 13, 1991, at 62. The case was appealed but was declared moot. *See Appeal Filed; Birth Control Implant Order is Appealed*, L.A. TIMES, Feb. 2, 1991, at B18; William Booth, *Judge Orders Birth Control Implant in Defendant*, WASH. POST, Jan. 5, 1991, at A1; *Child Abuser's Birth Control Case Ends: No Legal Precedent*, CHI. TRIB., April 15, 1992, at M8; *Implant Order Appealed*, SAN FRANCISCO CHRON., Apr. 26, 1991, at A27; Desda Moss, *Court-Ordered Birth Control Draws Fire*, USA TODAY, Jan. 10, 1991, at 2A; *Woman in Abuse Case Agrees to Birth Control*, N.Y. TIMES, Jan. 5, 1991 at 6. This case is being appealed, *Appeal Filed in Norplant Case*, L.A. TIMES, July 26, 1991, at A25.

to beat your children?"[12] This latter case has drawn a great deal of national attention.[13]

These types of probationary conditions are apparently based on the premise that a woman who has abused one or more of her children will likely abuse future children; if the woman is "going to" abuse future children, these children should be protected by not being allowed to be born. There are many constitutional concerns raised by such orders. The American Civil Liberties Union (ACLU) believes that these types of orders involve involuntary sterilization, a form of cruel and unusual punishment prohibited by the Eighth Amendment.[14] Others see this as violative of the right of privacy.[15] Similarly, others see this as dangerously close to the eugenics movement prevalent in the early part of this century.[16] One commentator said: "I think it is an effort by government to say to certain people you shouldn't have children."[17] Another commentator described the conditions of probation by stating, "The government is saying we want a certain class of people not to breed. . . . It smacks of population control."[18]

This preventive measure is constitutionally suspect. Although the U.S. Supreme Court has never directly ruled on sterilization in this context,[19] it did

---

12. *Judge to Reconsider Probation Requiring Birth Control*, L.A. TIMES, Jan. 9, 1991, at 16.

13. This story appeared on CBS, "This Morning," January 1991. *See also* sources cited at note 11.

There has been an even more recent case involving conditioning probation on the use of birth control. For example, a nineteen-year-old in Houston agreed to have the Norplant implant to avoid a prison term for shaking her two-month-old son hard enough to cause brain damage. John Makeig, *Mom Convicted of Child Abuse Picks Birth-Control Implant Over Prison*, HOUSTON CHRON., March 6, 1992 at A1.

14. U.S. CONST. amend. VIII.

15. *See* Roe v. Wade, 410 U.S. 113 (1973).

16. *See* MARK B. ADAMS, THE WELLBORN SCIENCE: EUGENICS IN GERMANY, FRANCE, BRAZIL AND RUSSIA (Mark B. Adams ed., 1990); JACQUES DUPAQUIER & ANTOINETE FAUVE-CHAMOUX, *ET. AL.*, MALTHUS PAST AND PRESENT (1983); HARRY H. LAUGHLIN, THE LEGAL STATUS OF EUGENICAL STERILIZATION: HISTORY AND ANALYSIS OF LITIGATION UNDER THE VIRGINIA STERILIZATION STATUTE, WHICH LED TO A DECISION OF THE SUPREME COURT OF THE UNITED STATES UPHOLDING THE STATUTE (1929). *See generally* THOMAS LITTLEWOOD, THE POLITICS OF POPULATION CONTROL (1977); THOMAS M. SHAPIRO, POPULATION CONTROL POLITICS: WOMEN, STERILIZATION, AND REPRODUCTIVE CHOICE (1985); Phillip Reilly, *Involuntary Sterilization in the United States: A Surgical Solution*, 62 Q. REV. BIOLOGY 153 (1987); Clyde Spillenger, *Reproduction and Medical Interventionism: An Historical Comment*, 13 NOVA L. REV. 385 (1989).

17. Booth, *supra* note 11, at A1 (quoting Sheldon Segal, Rockefeller Foundation, originator of implantable contraceptives and driving force behind development of Norplant).

18. Stein, *supra* note 9, at A3.

19. Defendants have little incentive to appeal because they often are avoiding lengthy sentences by agreeing to these conditions.

strike down an Oklahoma statute that allowed sterilization for certain groups of felons, stating that "procreation is one of the basic civil rights of man."[20] The few appellate cases that have dealt with this issue have all decided that such conditions violate "procreative rights" protected by the constitution.[21] However, these courts do not carefully address *why* these types of conditions are violative of constitutional rights.

This article will consider the reasons that such conditions are not proper. First, psychological research indicates that it is very difficult to predict whether future children will be abused. Just because one child is abused does not mean that other children in a particular family are being or will be abused.

Second, even if potential abusers could be identified with a high degree of accuracy, individuals have a constitutional right to bear children that would have to be overridden by a compelling state interest with no less restrictive alternatives available.[22] In these cases, neither the state interest in protecting nonexistent life, nor the fact that the state would possibly have to support the child through state money in foster care, appear compelling. Even when a parent has abused an existing child, his or her parental rights cannot be terminated without due process protections, *e.g.*, a hearing.[23] Thus, a woman who is on probation might or might not be able to keep a child that she would have depending on what was found at a hearing to determine her fitness as a parent with respect to *that* child. After having spent some time in prison for the child abuse, plus having undergone counseling—a condition of probation routinely imposed on such an individual, her circumstances likely would have changed (assuming, of course, that these activities are rehabilitative), and at a hearing, it is possible that she would be found to be able to care for her child.[24] Furthermore, even if the child were to be put in foster care until the mother was fit, she might very well regain custody of the child after showing

---

20. Skinner v. Oklahoma, 316 U.S. 535 (1942).

21. *See infra* notes 26-65 and accompanying text.

22. G. GUNTHER, CONSTITUTIONAL LAW (1980).

23. *See infra* note 171 and accompanying text.

24. In this article, women are the focus because the major cases have all been directed at women. However, it should be noted that a court could require a man to use birth control. In fact, there is one case that discussed the legality of such a condition as applied to a man. In Howland v. State, 420 So. 2d 918 (Fla. Dist. Ct. App. 1982), the defendant was convicted of negligent child abuse. The judge had conditioned probation upon the defendant not having further contact with his child and not residing with a minor child under the age of 16. These two conditions were upheld as reasonably related to the crime and future criminality. However, the defendant was also prohibited from fathering a child. This condition was declared invalid because it was not reasonably related to the crime of child abuse and dealt with noncriminal conduct, i.e., "begetting" a child. Such a condition could only relate to criminal conduct if the father had custody or contact with the child, possibilities which the court believed had been foreclosed by the other valid conditions of probation.

that she was competent to care for him or her. If she were not allowed to have the child in the first instance, her constitutional right to rear a child, which is firmly established in the constitution,[25] would be abridged, rather than merely her ability to bear the child.

II. THE PROBATIONARY BIRTH CONTROL CASES

While there has been a recent resurgence of interest in prescribing birth control as a condition of probation in child abuse cases, there have been four major appellate cases that have found such conditions to be void.[26] These cases will be considered below.

A. *Ohio v. Livingston*

In 1976, Ohio was the first state whose appellate court dealt with this issue. In *Ohio v. Livingston*,[27] the lower court had decided that the defendant who had been convicted of child abuse was to bear no other children during a five-year probationary period. The defendant had placed her seven-month-old child on a space heater, causing second degree burns on about 7% of the child's body.[28] Although the court of appeals recognized that a judge has broad discretion, the court is "not free to impose arbitrary conditions that significantly burden the defendant in the exercise of her liberty and bear only a remote relationship to the crime for which she was convicted and to the objectives sought by probation of education and rehabilitation."[29]

---

25. *See infra* note 158 and accompanying text.

26. There have been several minor cases that have considered the same or similar conditions of probation, but not in the case of child abuse. *See* Ex rel. V.B., 533 N.E.2d 1150 (Ill. App. Ct. 1989) (adjudicated juvenile delinquent who had kidnapped child was required to participate in counseling and "not to get pregnant;" court did not discuss the conditions of probation); Thomas v. State, 519 So. 2d 1113 (Fla. Dist. Ct. App. 1988) (convicted of stealing; special condition of probation prohibiting defendant from becoming pregnant bore no relation to the offense); People v. Dominguez, 64 Cal. Rptr. 290 (Cal. Ct. App. 1967) (defendant was convicted of second-degree robbery; condition that defendant not become pregnant without being married was invalid); State v. Norman, 484 So. 2d 953 (La. Ct. App. 1986) (woman convicted of forgery was required not to give birth to any illegitimate children during two-year probationary period; condition was invalid because not reasonably related to preventing criminal conduct); Wiggins v. State, 386 So. 2d 46 (Fla. Dist. Ct. App. 1980) (probation condition prohibiting probationers who were convicted of burglary from engaging in sexual intercourse with individuals to whom they were not lawfully married was not reasonably related to the probationers' past and future criminality or to the rehabilitative process).

27. 372 N.E.2d 1335 (Ohio Ct. App. 1976).

28. *Id.* at 1336.

29. *Id.* at 1337.

The appellate court found that the condition of probation was void. Relying on *People v. Dominguez*,[30] the court implicitly found that the only justification for the condition was to prevent yet-to-be-conceived children from becoming wards of the state, and thus, reduce public expenditures. However, the court did not consider whether it would be likely that the mother would abuse her future children.

B. *Rodriguez v. State*

Three years later, a Florida court considered the same issue. In *Rodriguez v. State*,[31] the judge had placed the defendant on probation for ten years, subject to conditions prohibiting marriage, pregnancy and custody of children. Here, the defendant had entered a plea of nolo contendere to a charge of aggravated child abuse. The defendant had hit her nine-year old child about the face and pushed the child against a car resulting in bruises.[32] The defendant appealed arguing that she had a fundamental right to procreation, marriage, and custody of her children.[33] She claimed that a compelling state interest would have to be demonstrated in order to override her constitutional rights.[34]

The state argued that the conditions were reasonable and necessary to protect her children, that the defendant had no right to give birth to children that would be placed for adoption,[35] and that, while she was a prisoner, she would have no right to become pregnant.[36] The trial court relied on an American Bar Association (ABA) standard which suggests that "conditions imposed by the court should be designed to assist the probationer in leading a law-abiding life" and "be reasonably related to . . . rehabilitation and not unduly restrictive of . . . liberty."[37] The court applied the following test:

> In determining whether a condition of probation is reasonably related to rehabilitation, . . . a condition is invalid if it (1) has no relationship to the

---

30. 64 Cal. Rptr. 290 (Cal. App. 1967). For a discussion of this case, see *infra* notes 167-70 and accompanying text.

31. 378 So. 2d 7 (Fla. Dist. Ct. App. 1979).

32. *Id.* at 8.

33. *Id.* at 8 n.1 (basing her claims on Skinner v. Oklahoma, 316 U.S. 535 (1942), and Loving v. Virginia, 388 U.S. 1 (1967)).

34. *Id.* at 8 n.2.

35. It is unclear whether there is such a right. *Compare* the unwed fathers cases, *infra* note 163.

36. The state also claimed that she would not be able to marry without the court's consent if she were still a prisoner. 378 So. 2d at 9.

37. *Id.* (citing INSTITUTE OF JUDICIAL ADMINISTRATION, STANDARDS RELATING TO PROBATION § 3.2(b) (1970)).

crime of which the offender was convicted, (2) relates to conduct which is not in itself criminal, and (3) requires or forbids conduct which is not reasonably related to future criminality.[38]

Noting that trial courts have broad discretion to impose conditions of probation, the appellate court stated that conditions cannot be imposed if they are so punitive as to be unrelated to rehabilitation.

Therefore, while upholding the condition of probation that prohibited the defendant from having custody of her children, the court struck down the conditions relating to marriage and pregnancy. Although the court recognized that these conditions could relate to future criminality if the pregnancy resulted in custody of the minor child, the court held that could not be the case since the mother was not entitled to custody of any children.[39] "Thus, the conditions prohibiting . . . pregnancy [would] add nothing to decrease the possibility of further child abuse or other criminality."[40]

C. *People v. Ruby Pointer*

Another five years passed before a California court was presented with the very same issue in *People v. Pointer*.[41] Here, Ruby Pointer had been on a macrobiotic diet[42] despite the objections of her children's father and her physician. She was feeding her two children, ages two and four, the same diet. Breast feeding the two-year-old while she was on the diet was especially hazardous to his health because the mother's diet influences the nutrient content of breast milk; the child would not receive certain vital nutrients needed for growth and development.

Despite a lengthy involvement with Child Protective Services, the child continued to be in Pointer's custody and subjected to the diet, until he almost died and had to be hospitalized.[43] Nevertheless, the child had already "suffered severe growth retardation and permanent neurological damage."[44] After discharge, the child was placed in foster care. However, Pointer abducted her child from foster care[45] and was subsequently arrested. She was

---

38. *Id.*

39. *Id.* at 10.

40. *Id.*

41. 199 Cal. Rptr. 357 (Cal. Ct. App. 1984).

42. Such a diet consists mostly of grains, beans, and vegetables with emphasis on eliminating fruit, milk, and meat products. *Id.* at 359 n.2.

43. Pointer continued to bring him macrobiotic food even in the hospital. *Id.* at 360.

44. *Id.*

45. Pointer claimed to be concerned about the type of food he was being fed in foster care, *e.g.*, eggs. *Id.*

found guilty of child endangerment. She was then sentenced to five years probation on the conditions that she serve one year in county jail; participate in an appropriate counseling program; not be informed of the permanent whereabouts of her son who had been placed in foster care; have no unsupervised visits with her son; have no custody of any children (including her own children) without court approval; and that she not conceive during the probationary period.[46] Pointer challenged the last condition of probation[47] as violative of her fundamental right of privacy and procreation.[48]

The probation report used to support this condition had stated that it would at least prevent her from becoming pregnant and injuring "another small child in the future."[49] A psychologist also testified that "[a]ny new born child to Ms. Pointer would encounter similar risks as those of her previous children."[50]

The court in *Pointer* began to assess the validity of the condition of probation first along the criterion of "reasonableness." In California, the test for reasonableness of a condition of probation is as follows: "A condition of probation will not be held invalid unless it (1) has no relationship to the crime of which the offender was convicted, (2) relates to conduct which is not in itself criminal, and (3) requires or forbids conduct which is not reasonably related to future criminality. . . ."[51] Applying the test to the case, the court concluded that the condition was reasonable, explaining:

> [I]n this unusual case the condition is related to child endangerment, the crime for which the appellant was convicted. Although cases in other jurisdictions have concluded that a defendant not become pregnant has no relation to the crime of child abuse or to future criminality, those cases relied heavily upon the fact that the abuse could be entirely avoided by removal of any children from the custody of the defendant. This case is distinguishable, however, because of evidence that the harm sought to be prevented by the trial court may occur before birth. Since the record fully supports the trial court's belief that appellant would continue to adhere to a strict macrobiotic diet despite the dangers it presents to any children she might conceive, we

---

46. *Id.* at 360.

47. The trial judge had given careful consideration to this condition stating: "I have never considered imposing as a condition of probation the requirement that someone not conceive during the period of probation, and I have never considered requiring as a condition of probation that a defendant not have custody of her children without approval by the sentencing court following a hearing, but that's certainly what I intend to do in this case. This is an extremely serious case." *Id.* at 362.

48. *Id.*

49. *Id.*

50. *Id.*

51. *Id.* at 363.

cannot say that the condition of probation prohibiting conception is completely unrelated to the crime for which appellant was convicted or to the possibility of future criminality.[52]

The court in Pointer stated that courts have broad discretion to prescribe conditions of probation that "foster rehabilitation and protect the public to the end that justice may be done."[53] Nevertheless, discretion is not boundless but is limited by constitutional safeguards.[54] Although the government may impose conditions of probation which qualify or impinge upon constitutional rights when circumstances permit such interference, where a fundamental right such as privacy is implicated, there must be a compelling state interest that would justify the intrusion.[55] While some would argue that a sentencing court may impose such restrictions because they may withhold the benefit of probation entirely, the U.S. Supreme Court held a probationer can "no longer be denied due process" because "probation is an 'act of grace.'"[56]

Thus, the *Pointer* court could not stop at a reasonableness analysis. The condition imposed by the judge infringed upon "the exercise of a fundamental right to privacy protected by both the federal and state constitutions."[57] The condition must be narrowly tailored to meet the compelling state interest when a fundamental constitutional right is implicated, as the court stated: "If available alternative means exist which are less violative of a constitutional right and are narrowly drawn so as to correlate more closely with the purpose contemplated, those alternatives should be used."[58] Finding no rehabilitative purpose but rather an interest "to protect the public by preventing injury to an unborn child," the court determined that there were less restrictive alternatives available, including having the mother follow a strict neonatal program, and if she was unable to care for the child, place the child in foster care as was done with the existing children.[59]

---

52. *Id.* at 364.

53. *Id.*

54. • *See* JOANNA L. WEISSMAN, CONSTITUTIONAL PRIMER ON MODERN PROBATION CONDITIONS (1982).

55. *See generally* GUNTHER, *supra* note 22.

56. Gagnon v. Scarpeli, 411 U.S. 778 (1973).

57. 199 Cal. Rptr. at 364. *See* Roe v. Wade, 410 U.S. 113 (1973); Griswold v. Connecticut, 381 U.S. 479 (1968).

58. 199 Cal. Rptr. at 365.

59. *Id.* at 365.

D. *State v. Mosburg*

Again, another five years passed, and this time a Kansas judge decided to try the same condition of probation for a child abuser. In *State v. Mosburg*,[60] the defendant had been convicted of child endangerment. She had taken her baby to a restaurant parking lot, found an unlocked truck with a bag of items in it, and left the baby in the truck without any identification or intent to return.[61] The defendant was given two years probation with the condition that she would refrain from becoming pregnant during the term of her probation.[62] Relying on *People v. Pointer*[63] and *State v. Livingston*,[64] the court found Mosburg's right to privacy was unduly intruded upon by the probation condition. Like the *Pointer* and *Livingston* courts, the *Mosburg* court struck down the probation condition of refraining from getting pregnant. The court did not consider whether there was a constitutional right to bear a child per se. Furthermore, it did not consider expressly the alternatives to such a requirement. Rather, the court seemed to be concerned with the practical constraints, concluding that: "There would be significant enforcement problems should Mosburg become pregnant, forcing her to choose among concealing her pregnancy (thus denying her child adequate medical care), abortion, or incarceration."[65]

E. *With Unanimity Among the Appellate Cases That These Conditions Violate the Rights of Probationers, Why Do Judges Continue to Prescribe Birth Control?*

In general, courts recognize that a judge is not free to condition probation on "anything" that he or she wants. Rather, the condition of probation should be reasonably related to both the past crime and potential future crimes and not be violative of fundamental constitutional rights, such as privacy, unless there is a compelling reason for doing so. In these appellate cases, courts have been unwilling to allow birth control conditions to stand because the conditions are viewed as violative of fundamental privacy rights without a compelling justification and without being narrowly drawn. These courts have not allowed the state's apparent financial interest in preventing the conception of children who *may* have to be put into foster care at the state's expense to act as a justification. Furthermore, the least restrictive means of

---

60. 768 P.2d 313 (Kan. Ct. App. 1989).
61. *Id.* at 313-14.
62. *Id.* at 314.
63. 199 Cal. Rptr. at 357.
64. 372 N.E.2d 1335 (Ohio Ct. App. 1976).
65. 768 P.2d at 315 (1989).

dealing with the problem of child abuse has been to put the child, *if necessary*, into foster care rather than preventing his or her birth altogether.

While the results of these cases seem to comport with modern notions of individual liberties,[66] there are those who would argue that such conditions are not improper.[67] Daniel Polsby, a constitutional and criminal law professor at Northwestern University, indicated that the condition is proper under these circumstances:

> The question is obviously very, very sensitive and constitutionally unresolved, but in sentencing, judges consider the need of the public to be protected and that includes the treatment of children. . . .
>
> The state takes kids away from unfit parents all the time. What is proposed here is not the taking away of children that actually exist, but those who don't exist and, arguably, that's less invasive than removing a natural child from its parent.[68]

Such reasoning assumes (1) abusers will abuse future children, and (2) the woman has no protected interest in bearing a child even if that child may be removed (temporarily) upon his or her birth and placed in foster care. Both these assumptions are flawed, as will be demonstrated in Parts II and III *infra*.

III. THE LIKELIHOOD OF ABUSING FUTURE CHILDREN: THE SOCIAL SCIENCE RESEARCH

In order to support the validity of conditioning probation upon the use of birth control, a judge would have to believe that (1) this woman is likely to

---

66. Constitutional law during the past twenty years has seen an increase in individual rights. *See, e.g.*, Roe v. Wade, 410 U.S. 113 (1973). However, with the composition of the court more conservative, this trend is changing. *See* Webster v. Reproductive Health Servs., 492 U.S. 490 (1989).

67. One woman stated:

I applaud the [California judge's decision] to order the use of Norplant. . . . He has taken an important step toward preventing an abusive parent from abusing another child, who is yet unborn. Norplant is the ideal contraceptive for the brainless people (of all races and socioeconomic groups) who have unprotected sex and bring unwanted children into this world only to beat them.

For all the smug ACLU lawyers preparing to leap to [the child abuser's] defense, I ask, what is more just, allowing this woman to bear children and abuse them in the name of protecting her rights, or thinking of and defending the unspoken rights of the abused children?

The Norplant Sentence, WASH. POST, Jan. 24, 1991, at A20 (letter to the editor by Jessica L. Tracy).

68. Joseph R. Tybor, *Does Sterilization Fit the Crime? Woman Must Decide*, CHI. TRIB., Sept. 25, 1988, at 4C (quoting Daniel Polsby).

be abusive in the future based on her past history of abuse, and (2) the future child will be the target of the abuse. These are questions to which social science could conceivably contribute in order to reach decisions based upon "empirical reality."[69]

Social scientists have done much research to describe and ultimately identify potential child abusers. Yet, predicting future abuse is not as easy as it might sound. While there has been some evidence that abuse can be predicted, there are often high rates of false positives, that is, identifying people who would not abuse children as abusers. While the type of predictive instruments used in this research might be proper in providing services to clients,[70] for example, when constitutional rights are made contingent upon the accuracy of such instruments, problems arise. With predictive ability of any less than 100%, some people would be improperly denied the ability to procreate.[71]

Furthermore, there has been virtually no research on identifying the likelihood of abusing any one child. Thus, the research that would be most relevant to the problem at hand has not been conducted. While inferences can be made with respect to the likelihood of abusing future children from the research that has been conducted, the evidence does not suggest that an additional child would be "guaranteed" to be abused by an identified child abuser.[72] The research on abusive families simply does not support the idea that if one child is abused, all children will be.

Therefore, social science research may shed light on the problem not by supporting those who would seek to prohibit abusers from bearing future children, but rather suggesting that such predictions are not possible in light of constitutional constraints. Social science research that describes and attempts to explain characteristics of abusers, patterns of abusers' interactions with children, predictions of who will abuse, the rate of recidivism of abusers,

---

69. *See, e.g.*, Gary Melton, *The Clashing of Symbols: Prelude to Child and Family Policy*, 42 AM. PSYCHOLOGIST 345 (1987) (giving examples with respect to children's rights cases, Melton advocates that courts use empirical reality to make decisions).

70. Distinctions should be made between treatment and legal consequences. In treatment, it is probably better to err on the side of caution. The same is not true in the legal arena because of constitutional restraints.

71. *See infra* notes 138-141 and accompanying text. While it is true that predictive ability of less than 100% is not necessarily constitutionally suspect, as a practical matter, where there are any errors in judicial judgment, the cost to the parent is great because she will be denied the right to have additional children.

72. After doing a thorough literature review, I contacted several experts in the field, including Ross Thompson and Gary Melton of the University of Nebraska, and they were unable to point to any research that directly bears on this question. Melton suggested that I contact the American Association for Protecting Children and the Clearinghouse on Child Abuse and Neglect, but they were also unable to lead me to research directly bearing on this issue. Thus, I must conclude that no such research exists.

and the likelihood of abusing more than one child in a family is relevant to a discussion of this particular condition of probation. This research is discussed below.

A. *Characteristics of People Physically Abusing Children*

Much research has been done on describing who "child abusers" are.[73] Female perpetrators[74] tend to be young[75] and undereducated.[76] Women are concerned with social factors affecting the control they have over their environment.[77] History of abuse in their own lives has been important,[78] and they abuse male children significantly more often than female children.[79]

Personality characteristics of abusers include lack of confidence and low self-esteem.[80] Abusive parents also tend to have less social support than other people.[81] These parents are often under a great deal of stress and have difficulty coping with that stress.[82]

---

73. In this article, physical abuse will be the focus rather than sexual abuse or neglect. Furthermore, in this article, female abusers will be the focus because the major cases discussing birth control probationary conditions have been directed at women. It is important to note, however, that similar conditions could be, and in one case have been, directed at males. *See supra* note 24.

74. Phyllis A. Jameson & Cynthia Schellenbach, *Social and Psychological Factors in the Backgrounds of Male and Female Perpetrators of Child Abuse*, 1 CHILD ABUSE AND NEGLECT 77 (1977).

75. Most male perpetrators were between the ages of 31 and 40. *Id.* at 80.

76. The same was not true for males, however. Over sixty percent of the males had completed high school. *Id.*

77. Males were concerned primarily with achievement and employment. *Id.* at 81.

78. History of abuse was not important for males. *Id.*

79. Male perpetrators abused both female and male children with equal frequency. *Id.* at 81.

80. *See* Carl Pollock & Brandt Steele, *A Therapeutic Approach to Parents*, in HELPING THE BATTERED CHILD AND HIS FAMILY (Henry Kempe & Ray Helfer eds., 1972).

81. *See* Dorothy Howze & Jonathan Kotch, *Disentangling Life Events, Stress and Social Support: Implications for the Primary Prevention of Child Abuse and Neglect*, 8 CHILD ABUSE & NEGLECT 401, 404 (1984); Betty Johnson & Harold Morse, *Injured Children and Their Parents*, 15 CHILDREN 147 (1968); Selwyn M. Smith, *The Battered Child Syndrome: Some Research Findings*, 3 ROYAL SOC'Y OF HEALTH J. 148 (1975).

82. Howze & Kotch, *supra* note 81; Margaret Lynch, *Ill-Health and Child Abuse*, 2 LANCET 317 (1975). *See also* THE TRANSITION TO PARENTHOOD: CURRENT THEORY AND RESEARCH (Gerald Y. Michaels & Wendy Goldberg eds.,, 1988) (parenting itself can be stressful); Harry Adamakos et al., *Maternal Social Support As a Predictor of Mother-Child Stress and Stimulation*, 10 CHILD ABUSE & NEGLECT 463, 468-69 (1986); Dave Crnic et al., *Effects of Stress and Social Support on Mothers and Premature and Full-Term Infants*, 54 CHILD DEV. 209 (1983); James Garbarino & Ann Crouter, *Defining the Commitment Context for Parent-Child Relations*, 49 CHILD DEV. 604 (1978); James Garbarino & S. Holly

Abusers often view their children as the instigators of the violence.[83] Many researchers now emphasize the social interactive nature of violent incidents.[84] Parents often have unrealistic expectations of a child's abilities, for example, they often treat a child in an age-inappropriate manner.[85]

One study[86] examined the justifications abusers gave for their abuse.[87]

Stocking, *The Social Context of Child Maltreatment*, in PROTECTING CHILDREN FROM ABUSE AND NEGLECT 1-14 (James Garbarino & S. Holly Stocking eds., 1980); Blair Justice & David F. Duncan, *Life Crisis as a Precursor to Child Abuse*, 91 PUB. HEALTH REP. 110 (1976); John Pascoe et al., *The Association Between Mothers' Social Support and Provision of Stimulation to their Children*, 2 DEVELOPMENTAL AND BEHAVIORAL PEDIATRICS 15 (1981); John Pascoe & Jo Anne Earp, *The Effects of Mothers' Social Support and Life Changes on the Stimulation of Their Children in the Home*, 74 AM. J. PUB. HEALTH 358 (1984); Murray A. Strauss, *Stress and Physical Child Abuse*, 4 CHILD ABUSE & NEGLECT 75 (1980).

83. *See* Betty Johnson & Harold Morse, *Injured Children and Their Parents*, 15 CHILDREN 147 (1968); Deborah Larrance & Craig Twentyman, *Maternal Attributions and Child Abuse*, 92 J. ABNORMAL PSYCHOL. 449, 455-56 (1981); Mindy Rosenberg & N. Dickon Reppucci, *Abusive Mothers: Perceptions of Their Own and Their Children's Behavior*, 51 J. CONSULTING & CLINICAL PSYCHOL. 674 (1983); Sherry Wood-Shuman & John D. Cone, *Differences in Abusive, At-Risk For Abuse, and Control Mothers' Descriptions of Normal Child Behavior*, 10 CHILD ABUSE & NEGLECT 397, 398-99 (1986) (at-risk mothers rated more children's behaviors as negative than did control mothers and were more like the abusive mothers who were the most negative of all).

84. *See* ALFRED KADUSHIN & JUDITH A. MARTIN, CHILD ABUSE: AN INTERACTIONAL EVENT (1981); MURRAY A. STRAUSS *ET. AL.*, BEHIND CLOSED DOORS: VIOLENCE IN THE AMERICAN FAMILY (1980); Ross D. Parke & Candace Whitmer-Collmer, *Child Abuse: An Interdisciplinary Analysis*, in 5 REV. OF CHILD DEV. RES. 509 (E. Mavis Hetherington ed., 1975); David A. Wolfe, *Child-Abusive Parents: An Empirical Review and Analysis*, 97 PSYCHOL. BULL. 462 (1985).

85. *See* Sandra T. Azar et al., *Unrealistic Expectations and Problem-Solving Ability in Maltreating and Comparisons Mothers*, 52 J. OF CONSULTING AND CLINICAL PSYCHOL. 687 (1984); Arthur H. Green, *Psychiatric Elements of Abusing Parents*, AUDIO DIG. 19 (1973); Craig T. Twentyman & Ron C. Plotkin, *Unrealistic Expectations of Parents Who Maltreat Their Children: An Educational Deficit that Pertains to Child Development*, 38 J. CLINICAL PSYCHOL. 497 (1982).

86. Dorthee Dietrich et al., *Some Factors Influencing Abusers' Justifications of Their Child Abuse*, 14 CHILD ABUSE & NEGLECT 337 (1990).

87. One theory posits that powerful persons' aggressive actions are mostly an attempt at coercion carried out to stop the others' offending behavior and to make them accede to the powerful person's wishes. *See* David Finkelhor, *Common Features of Family Abuse*, in THE DARK SIDE OF FAMILIES: CURRENT FAMILY VIOLENCE RESEARCH 17 (David Finkelhor et al. eds., 1983). Another theory, however, posits that there is a deliberate attempt to hurt someone else. While not denying that violence can bring about intended goals, i.e., getting the child to act as the parent wants, aggression can be used to inflict injury because the parent himself or herself is feeling badly and wants to attack an available target which may or may not be the source of the negative emotions. Leonard Berkowitz, *Frustration-Aggression Hypothesis: Examination and Reformulation*, 106 PSYCHOL. BULL. 59 (1989); Leonard Berkowitz, *The Goals of Aggression*, in THE DARK SIDE OF FAMILIES:

The researchers interviewed abusers and examined (1) whether the abuser felt remorse about the abusive behavior, (2) whether the abuser indicated that he or she would react in a similar manner if the same situation arose again, the assumption being that the adult would react the same if he or she viewed his or her action as appropriate, and (3) whether the abuser "blamed" the child for the abuse. The results of the study indicated that about 40% of abusers had no regrets about the abuse, over 50% blamed the victim, and over 60% felt "justified" for the abusive behavior.[88] A large number of adult caretakers interpreted the child's behavior as having been intentional, and in virtually all of these cases, the adult perceived the incident as "having been aimed at them personally."[89] The abusers indicated that it was appropriate for them to hit their children when they openly defied their authority or when the children had been annoying at a time the parent was under a great deal of stress.[90]

B. Patterns of Abusers' Interactions with Children

Families that exhibit various kinds of deviant behavior tend to have fewer positive contacts among family members.[91] They are less talkative and less active than "normal" families.[92] One study examined three different family types in which the mother was responsible for the negative interactions: (1) families with one or more abused children, (2) families where one or more children had been neglected, and (3) families where no official records of abuse or neglect existed but who were matched for various factors such as the age of the parents and children, number of children, income, and parents'

CURRENT FAMILY VIOLENCE RESEARCH 166 (David Finkelhor et al. eds., 1983).

88. Dietrich, *supra* note 86, at 341.

89. *Id.*

90. However, the adults were concerned about their loss of control over their own behavior, *i.e.*, losing their temper, indicating that they not only wanted control over their children's behavior, but also over their own behavior. *Id.* at 344.

91. *See* ELLIOT MISCHLER & NANCY E. WAXLE, INTERACTION IN FAMILIES (1968). *See also* David M. Bousha & Craig T. Twentyman, *Mother-Child Interactional Styles in Abuse, Neglect, and Control Groups: Naturalistic Observations in the Home*, 93 J. ABNORMAL PSYCHOL. 106 (1984); Robert L. Burgess & Rand D. Conger, *Family Interaction in Abusive, Neglectful and Normal Families*, 49 CHILD DEV. 1163 (1978); Kim N. Dietrich et al., *Infant Maltreatment: Caretaker-Infant Interactions and Developmental Consequences at Different Levels of Parenting Failure*, 72 PEDIATRICS 532 (1983); Arthur H. Green et al., *Child Abuse: Pathological Syndrome of Family Interaction*, 131 AM. J. PSYCHIATRY 882 (1974); S.M. Smith & R. Hanson, *Interpersonal Relationships and Child-rearing Practices in 214 Parents of Battered Children*, 126 BRIT. J. OF PSYCHIATRY 404-07 (1975); .

92. *See* William D. Winter & Antonio J. Ferreira, *Talking Time as an Index of Interfamilial Similarity in Normal and Abnormal Families*, 74 J. OF ABNORMAL PSYCHOL. 574 (1969).

educational levels.[93] The researchers found that mothers in abusive families were particularly distinctive. They directed 20% fewer verbal contacts to other family members than did the mothers in the normal families. In addition, mothers in the abusive families allocated 14% fewer verbal contacts to their children.[94] The abusive parents as a unit tended not to interact on a "physical level." This was true for both positive and negative interactions, *e.g.*, affectionate behavior or hitting. The researchers concluded that "These adults, especially the mothers, are unskilled in the use of physical contacts and when they do employ physical behavior, they do so inappropriately or excessively."[95]

Another study examined the type of negative physical contacts that both abusive and nonabusive parents have with their children when the children misbehave. The researchers found that parents who abuse their children more often use "hitting with a belt or paddle" than do other parents even when a child does something dangerous, fails in school, steals, or destroys others' property. Fewer abusers utilize "spanking with the hand" for the same type of situations.[96]

Still another study compared parents who abused and who did not abuse their children by examining responses to the child's behaviors. When a child would not cooperate, would not stop crying, got angry with the parent, embarrassed the parent, screamed, or yelled, abusers reacted more negatively with either a negative physical or verbal encounter, while nonabusers would either do nothing, pick up, hug, or distract the child.[97]

C. *Predicting Who Will Abuse*

Despite descriptive studies that depict abusers' characteristics and

---

93. Robert L. Burgess & Rand D. Conger, *Family Interaction Patterns Related to Child Abuse and Neglect: Some Preliminary Findings*, 1 CHILD ABUSE & NEGLECT 269 (1977).

94. *Id.* at 272. Similar patterns were found for families with neglected children. *Id.* at 274.

95. *Id.* at 274.

96. M.A. Disbrow, Deviant Behavior and Putative Reference Persons (1968) (unpublished doctoral dissertation, University of Washington), *cited in* M.A. Disbrow et al., *Measuring the Components of Parents' Potential for Child Abuse and Neglect*, 1 CHILD ABUSE & NEGLECT 279 (1977).

97. *Id. See also* John A. Aragona & Sheila M. Eyberg, *Neglected Children: Mothers' Report of Child Behavior Problems and Observed Verbal Behavior*, 52 CHILD DEV. 596 (1981); Frodi & Lamb, *Child Abusers' Responses to Infant Smiles and Cries*, 51 CHILD DEV. 238 (1980); David A. Wolfe et al., *Child Abusive Parents' Physiological Responses to Stressful and Non-Stressful Behavior in Children*, 5 BEHAVIORAL ASSESSMENT 363-71 (1983).

interactions with children, research that tries to predict who will abuse their children has been riddled with difficulties. In retrospective studies, some of the strongest predictors of abuse have included frequent changes in residency;[98] a low self-image;[99] more opportunity to encounter their children at home because the parents are unemployed, and thus, in the home more often and under stress because of the lack of income;[100] large family size;[101] unwanted pregnancy;[102] and crowding.[103]

While these characteristics may appear to clearly differentiate abusive parents, many of these same characteristics may be found in nonabusive parents.[104] Abusive parents are a heterogenous group, and factors making some of them susceptible to violence-generating influences are not necessarily the same as factors producing this susceptibility in other caretakers.[105]

---

98. *See* Brian Lauer et al., *Battered Child Syndrome: Review of 130 Patients*, 54 PEDIATRICS 67, 69 (1974).

99. R. Parke & C. Collmer, Child Abuse: An Interdisciplinary Analysis, 5 REV. OF CHILD DEV. RES. 509 (E.M. Hetherington ed., 1975).

100. A lot of research has been conducted to examine the relationship between unemployment and child abuse. *See* Michael Segal, *Economic Deprivation and the Quality of Parent-Child Relations: A Trickle Down Framework*, 5 J. APPLIED DEVELOPMENTAL PSYCHOL. 127-44 (1984); Laurence D. Steinberg et al., *Economic Antecedents of Child Abuse and Neglect*, 52 CHILD DEV. 975 (1981). Most research in this area indicates that there is a positive relationship between unemployment and child abuse. However, most researchers have been unable to determine whether it is the increased psychological stress, an increased number of hours a potential abusive adult has with a child, or other factors that may be associated with unemployment such as alcohol or substance abuse. Richard D. Krugman et al., *The Relationship Between Unemployment and Physical Abuse of Children*, 10 CHILD ABUSE & NEGLECT 415 (1986).

101. Parke & Collmer, *supra* note 99, at 511.

102. Selwyn M. Smith et al., *Social Aspects of the Battered Baby Syndrome*, 125 BRIT. J. OF PSYCHIATRY 568 (1974); Theo Solomon, *History and Demography of Child Abuse*, 51 PEDIATRICS 773 (1973).

103. *See* Barry Melnick & John R. Hurley, *Distinctive Personality Attributes of Child Abusing Mothers*, 33 J. OF CONSULTING & CLINICAL PSYCHOL. 746 (1969); James L. Spearly & Michael Lauderdale, *Community Characteristics and Ethnicity in the Prediction of Child Maltreatment Rates*, 7 CHILD ABUSE & NEGLECT 91 (1983); John J. Spinetta & David Rigler, *The Child Abusing Parents: A Psychological Review*, 77 PSYCHOL. BULL. 296 (1972).

104. *See, e.g.*, Spinetta & Rigler, *supra* note 103.

105. Some researchers have begun to examine the factors involved in fatal maltreatment. In one study, women who had killed a child were interviewed in prison. Jill E. Korbin, *Incarcerated Mothers' Perceptions and Interpretations of Their Fatally Maltreated Children*, 11 CHILD ABUSE & NEGLECT 397 (1987). The charges ranged from willful cruelty and felony child endangering to second degree murder. *Id.* at 399. The study found that difficulties during the prenatal and perinatal periods may foreshadow parenting problems. One woman reported that she felt the child was "hurting her from inside and disfiguring her by creating moles on her face and neck." *Id.* at 400. Another

One study compared the ability of professionals and nonprofessionals to evaluate parent-child interactions in order to determine which parents were "abusive" based on behavior recorded on videotape.[106] The results indicated that both the professionals' and the undergraduates' prediction ability was only at chance levels. For example, the control family in one pair of tapes was more likely to be seen as abusive by both the professionals and undergraduates. Experience with abusive families was only slightly correlated with predictive accuracy. The relationship was curvilinear, with the professionals with no experience and those with the highest levels of experience being most accurate in their judgments.

Because experience appeared to be relatively unimportant in making correct judgments, the written justifications for the professionals' choices were examined. Their observations were not systematic. This study raises

---

woman who had been a prostitute was surprised to find herself pregnant with a "'trick baby.'" *Id.* However, not all problems were readily apparent during that period, *i.e.*, postpartum depression might have been responsible in at least one case. *Id.*

Another factor identified was separation from the mothers. Two of the mothers' children were premature and required hospitalization; three of the mothers were hospitalized. Four of the children had been in foster care and/or had been removed to a protective placement following abuse by the mother. *Id.*

Three of the mothers believed their children to be developmentally delayed. Only two of those who viewed their children as developmentally delayed had professional validation, but even for two of the mothers who believed that the children were developmentally advanced, they had unrealistic expectations of their childrens' capabilities. One mother was fearful that her sons were "so mature that she was incapable of raising them correctly. She believed that the four-year-old brother of the fatally abused child tried to seduce adult women." *Id.* at 402. Another mother believed that her precocious daughter was "conceived in a bargain with the devil." *Id.* She was certain that the advanced development was an indication of the infant's capacity for inflicting harm on others. Nevertheless, those who viewed their children's behavior as "normal" also displayed age-inappropriate expectations, such as expressing disappointment that her very young daughter could not "sit up and talk to her." *Id.* at 402-03.

Most interesting was a recurring theme of feeling rejected by their children. For example, one mother believed that her "child wouldn't cry if she really loved her." *Id.* Another woman's feeling of rejection began in the delivery room. She felt that the newborn looked at her husband and not at her. *Id.*

These mothers also blamed their children for instigating the abuse. Persistent crying, refusal to eat, toilet accidents, sassing, racial slurs, or wanting to return to a foster home were among the difficult behaviors. Although the researchers did not want to blame the victim, they noted that the parent-child interaction could not be ignored. Other factors that seemed important included deprivation and abuse in the abusers' own childhoods, and insufficient social support systems. *Id.* at 404.

The results of this research did not really segregate abused children versus fatally abused children, rather their cases just seem more extreme, and the mothers had more psychological pathologies.

106. Raymond H. Starr, *Clinical Judgment of Abuse-Proneness Based on Parent-Child Interactions*, 11 CHILD ABUSE & NEGLECT 87 (1987).

questions about the ability of professionals, who would presumably be evaluating abusers, to determine the likelihood of future abuse and to accurately do such evaluations.[107]

However, another study claimed an 85% ability to select parents who would abuse, having a 15% rate of *false negatives*.[108] This false negative rate is important because instead of getting false positives, that is, parents who did not abuse being identified as abusers, the researchers only failed to identify 15% of the abusers. The researchers selected parents' background, including whether the parents were abused; personality characteristics; events that would prevent early attachment, such as separation; social network resources; attitudes about child rearing; ways of handling irritating child behaviors; and parent-child interactions.   They reported that these behaviors and characteristics were able to discriminate with a high percentage of success who would and would not abuse.

The success of this study is extremely misleading because of the methods used. The bulk of this study was conducted by observing *behavior in the home*.[109] Rather than using more subjective interviewing techniques, the researchers used objective, identifiable behaviors. While these methods may be useful in research, in the "real world," it may not be feasible to go into the abusers' homes and make these observations for a variety of reasons, including cost, as well as possible legal constraints, such as the fourth amendment's prohibition on unreasonable searches and seizures.[110] With respect to the criminal justice system,[111] it seems unlikely that investigators would be able to enter the families' homes for purposes of observing these behaviors.[112]

---

107. *Id.*

108. M.A. Disbrow et al., *Measuring the Components of Parents' Potential for Child Abuse and Neglect*, 1 CHILD ABUSE & NEGLECT 279 (1977). The study claimed an 89% accuracy rate for identifying nonabusers, with 11% false negatives. *Id.* at 293.

109. The researchers also measured *physiological responses* in the laboratory. Beyond practical problems, there may be fourth amendment problems. *But see* Schmerber v. California, 384 U.S. 757 (1964) (holding that a compelled blood test for alcohol intoxication was not a violation of the fourth amendment).

110. U.S. CONST. amend. IV.

111. The department of social services, for example, can enter homes to investigate family interactions. However, agencies and the criminal justice system are likely subject to different legal restrictions on their behavior.

112. It seems unlikely that for purposes of issuing a warrant that there will be definable lists of behaviors with sufficient specificity so as to pass fourth amendment scrutiny. It would probably be insufficient to say that they are looking for "abusive behavior." That would be similar to saying that you are looking for "illegal activity," rather than specifying "dealing cocaine." Although the state could rely on a statute to specify such behaviors such as "excessive hitting," the verbal behaviors that were of interest in the study and the less stringent forms of physical abuse may not be identifiable by statute.

Another study claiming a high rate of success involved observations made during prenatal, labor/delivery, and postpartum periods.[113] Observations were made about events such as the mother's denial of pregnancy, including not willing to gain weight; not making plans for the baby; statements that the child would be "one too many;" hostile reactions to the child; no eye-contact with the baby; negative verbal interactions; and the mother being bothered by crying. A questionnaire did not add significantly to the accuracy of the prediction made in the delivery room. The researchers stated that the observations made in the delivery room "are noninvasive and should be part of obstetrical and postpartum routine."[114] However, such a procedure would entail making observations of all mothers and having a way to maintain that data base. The potential for identifying abusers might be great, but that would mean that this method could also be applied to a *first* child. If a woman is identified as a potential abuser, would the government be willing to prevent her from having even her first child?

Besides direct observation, other techniques have been used to try to predict who will be abusive. In studies that use "paper and pencil" measures and/or interviewing techniques, low predictive utility has been demonstrated. One study typifies this type of research. Examining predictors such as having a child removed from the home, feeling bad when the woman learned she was pregnant and did not want the child, reacting negatively to the child when she is tired and the child keeps irritating her, and having negative feelings when she hears the baby screaming, only 6% of the families identified as being at risk for abuse actually reported abuse within two years.[115] Thus, there was an excessive rate of false positives. While the researchers stated that the problem of such a high false positive rate is that there is the waste of resources in cases where intervention is expensive but not needed, the researchers did not mention the legal implications of basing decisions such as not to have children on such results. Clearly, as this typical study indicates, the high rate of false positives demonstrates that there is not an easy way to predict who will abuse using a more easily administered, more common social science technique of "paper and pencil" measures.[116]

---

113. June D. Gray et al., *Prediction and Prevention of Child Abuse and Neglect*, 1 CHILD ABUSE & NEGLECT 45 (1977).

114. *Id.* at 53.

115. William A. Altemeier et al., *Prediction of Child Abuse: A Prospective Study of Feasibility*, 8 CHILD ABUSE & NEGLECT 393 (1984).

116. Another study did not specifically target abusive parenting, but targeted simply "problem parenting," *i.e.*, parents who have difficulty raising their children. William R. Avison, et al., *Screening for Problem Parenting: Preliminary Evidence on a Promising Instrument*, 10 CHILD ABUSE & NEGLECT 157 (1986). While the researchers claimed to be able to identify 90% of the abusers, the researchers cautioned that this would only be true depending on the base rate for the maladaptive behavior. The lower the maladaptive

D. *Effectiveness of Interventions in Child Maltreatment: The Recidivism Rate for Abuse is High*

Once an abuser is identified for being at risk of abuse through predictive clinical measures, or has actually abused and is usually recommended for treatment by social services or a court,[117] treatment ensues. Because of the costs of abuse,[118] much attention has been focused on what society can do to prevent further child abuse.[119] Interventions for parents who abuse and neglect their children exist, including projects by the federal government; Parents Anonymous; family treatment programs; and individual, family, and group therapy. However, recidivism rates for abusers who participate in treatment programs vary tremendously.[120] For physical abuse, 16 to 60% of parents reabuse their children following the initial incident; in these physical

---

behavior in the population, the greater likelihood of false positives. *Id.* at 166. Child abuse has a low base rate compared to other behaviors. Thus, in assessing the predictive utility of any instruments, it will be important to remember that the lower the base rates in the population, the greater likelihood of identifying false positives. Thus, it will depend on many factors including what the likelihood of reabuse is and what the likelihood of abusing future children is.

117. One common feature of court-ordered treatment plans for abusive parents is parent education classes. Presumably, if the parent is able to improve his or her behavior, the child can be returned to the home when he or she had been removed due to the abuse. In one study, a parental education program called "Hugs 'n' Kids: Parenting Your Preschooler," was examined to see if it was effective. Judith S. Golub et al., *A Videotape Parent Education Program for Abusive Parents*, 11 CHILD ABUSE & NEGLECT 255 (1987). Participants demonstrated increased knowledge of the alternatives to physical punishment and understanding of normal child development, as well as changed attitudes toward their children's misbehavior. However, recidivism of actual abuse was not studied.

118. *See, e.g.,* Howard Dubowitz, *Cost and Effectiveness of Interventions in Child Maltreatment*, 14 CHILD ABUSE & NEGLECT 177 (1990).

119. *See* C. Henry Kempe, *A Practical Approach to the Protection of the Abused Child and Rehabilitation of the Abusing Parents*, 51 PEDIATRICS 804 (1973).

120. Studies show differing rates of recidivism based upon the type of abuse, *i.e.,* physical or sexual, and the type of treatment program. *See, e.g.,* Anne H. Cohn & Deborah Daro, *Is Treatment Too Late? What Ten Years of Evaluative Research Tells Us*, 11 CHILD ABUSE & NEGLECT 433 (1987) (more than one-third of the families maltreated their children while in treatment; over one-half of the families were judged likely to mistreat their children following termination); C.W. Morse et al., *A Three-Year Follow-Up Study of Abused and Neglected Children*, 120 AM. J. OF DISEASES OF CHILDREN 439 (1970) (33% recidivism rate); A.E. Skinner & R.L. Castle, *Battered Children: A Retrospective Study* (1969) (60% recidivism rate). *But see* James Garbarino, *Can We Measure Success in Preventing Child Abuse? Issues in Policy, Programming and Research*, 10 CHILD ABUSE & NEGLECT 143 (1986).

abuse cases, 20 to 87% of families are unchanged or worse at the end of treatment.[121]

One program evaluation found that in a group of eleven treatment programs involving 1,724 parents, 30% were reported to have "severely" abused or neglected their children during treatment.[122] Those who had most severely abused their children before treatment were more likely to reabuse. Recidivism was lowest in treatment programs that employed highly trained workers to manage cases.[123] Of the 1,190 parents assessed by clinicians, 42% were judged to have a reduced potential for maltreatment.[124] Parents who physically abused their children were more likely to improve than parents who simply neglected them.

In a second study evaluating nineteen clinical demonstration projects, researchers found similar results.[125] Despite the fact that parents had improved their knowledge of child development and their understanding of their child's needs, decreased their need to have their child obey commands, and improved their self-esteem, over 50% of the adult clients were judged as likely to maltreat their children in the future.

E. *Likelihood of Abusing More than One Child*

When a person is accused of child abuse, the public may assume that all of that person's children are being abused, or that a parent who would abuse one child is, therefore, unfit to care for the other children. One study found that in 45.3% of the families, more than one child was a target of abuse.[126] Nevertheless, research in the area indicates that not all children are always abused in a family. Many times only one child is singled out for abuse.[127]

---

121. David P.H. Jones, *The Untreatable Family*, 11 CHILD ABUSE & NEGLECT 409 (1987).

122. BERKELY PLANNING ASSOCIATES, CHILD ABUSE AND NEGLECT TREATMENT PROGRAMS: FINAL REPORT AND SUMMARY OF FINDINGS FROM THE EVALUATION OF THE JOINT OCD/SRS NATIONAL DEMONSTRATION PROGRAM IN CHILD ABUSE AND NEGLECT 1974-1977, *cited in* Dubowitz, *supra* note 118, at 180-81.

123. *Id.*

124. *Id.* Parental age, employment status, and race did not predict outcomes, but alcohol and drug abuse were important predictors.

125. BERKLEY PLANNING ASSOCIATES, THE EXPLORATION OF CLIENT CHARACTERISTICS, SERVICES, AND OUTCOME: EVALUATION OF THE CLINICAL DEMONSTRATION OF CHILD ABUSE AND NEGLECT (1982), *cited in* Dubowitz, *supra* note 118, at 180-81.

126. Roy C. Herrenkohl et al., *The Repetition of Child Abuse: How Frequently Does It Occur?*, 3 CHILD ABUSE & NEGLECT 67 (1979).

127. C. Henry Kempe et al., *The Battered Child Syndrome*, 181 JAMA 17 (1962).

What makes the abused children targets rather than their siblings?[128] This question is especially important if a person will be prevented from having future children. If the parent can be deemed to be abusive "no matter what" (and the high recidivism rates may lead many to believe this to be the case), an argument could be made that he or she not be allowed to have additional children. However, if that parent could have another child and not abuse him or her, that individual should be allowed the opportunity to rear that child.

Research has been conducted to compare children who are abused and their siblings who are not abused.[129] One study compared twenty-five abused children with their nonabused siblings. The study described several factors that were significantly more prevalent prior to, at, and following the birth of the abused children including: (1) abnormal pregnancy, (2) abnormal labor and delivery, (3) neonatal separation, (4) other separation during the first six months, and (5) illnesses in the first year.[130] Another study analyzed records of fifty-one abused children and found that more than one third of them had either been seriously ill or had a congenital defect.[131]

Others have suggested a high incidence of early separation of infant and mother.[132] However, no research has been done to predict the likelihood of other children being abused where one child of that parent has already been

---

128. See E. Elmer & G.S. Gregg, *Developmental Characteristics of Abused Children*, 40 PEDIATRICS 596 (1967); Margaret Lynch, *Risk factors in the Child: A Study of Abused Children and Their Siblings*, in THE ABUSED CHILD: A MULTIDISCIPLINARY APPROACH TO DEVELOPMENTAL ISSUES AND TREATMENT 43 (Harold P. Martin ed., 1976); Harold P. Martin, *Which Children Get Abused: High Risk Factors in the Child*, in THE ABUSED CHILD: A MULTIDISCIPLINARY APPROACH TO DEVELOPMENTAL ISSUES AND TREATMENT 27 (Harold P. Martin ed., 1976).

129. There may be something "different" about children who are abused. See Ann M. Frodi, *Contribution of Infant Characteristics to Child Abuse*, 85 AM. J. MENTAL DEFICIENCY 341 (1981); Irvin D. Milowe & Reginold S. Lourie, *The Child's Role in the Battered Child Syndrome*, 65 J. PEDIATRICS 1079-81 (1964).

Although not all children in a particular family may be abused, the siblings of abused children may suffer from their brothers' or sisters' abuse. One study compared the perceptions of the family of children who are abused with their siblings' perceptions of their family. The researchers found no differences in the way that children in abusive families perceive the family regardless of whether they themselves were abused. All children in abusive families viewed their parents more negatively than children in nonabusive homes. Sandra M. Halperin, *Family Perceptions of Abused Children and Their Siblings*, 7 CHILD ABUSE & NEGLECT 107 (1983).

130. Margaret A. Lynch, *Ill-Health and Child Abuse*, 2 LANCET 317 (1975).

131. Leo Stern, *Prematurity as a Factor in Child Abuse*, 8 HOSP. PRAC. 117 (1973).

132. See Avory A. Farnaroff et al., *Follow-Up of Low Birth Weight Infants: The Predictive Value of Maternal Visiting Patterns*, 49 PEDIATRICS 287 (1972); M.H. Klaus & H.J. Kennell, *Mothers Separated From Their Newborn Infants*, 17 PEDIATRIC CLINICS OF N. AM. 1005 (1970).

abused. Presumably this research would be the most relevant to the question presented in this article. It is possible that the probabilities could be compiled from existing data bases. Nevertheless, this important information has not been made available.

F. *Conclusions from the Research: The Problems of Prediction*

Social scientists have been very interested in child abuse.[133] Researchers have been interested in identifying characteristics of abusers in an effort to predict who will be in need of services. This research has been based on describing characteristics of abusing parents,[134] abusing families,[135] and abused children,[136] as well as devising measurement devices that allow for screening potential abusers.[137] These devices have the most use in service

---

133. LEONTINE YOUNG, WEDNESDAY'S CHILD: A STUDY OF CHILD NEGLECT AND ABUSE (1964); Jay Belsky, *Child Maltreatment: An Ecological Integration*, 35 AM. PSYCHOLOGIST 320 (1980); Angela Browne & David Finkelhor, *Initial and Long-Term Effects: A Review of the Research*, in A SOURCE-BOOK ON CHILD SEXUAL ABUSE 143 (David Finkelhor ed., 1986); James Garbarino, *The Human Ecology of Child Maltreatment: A Conceptual Model for Research*, 39 J. OF MARRIAGE & THE FAMILY 721 (1977); James Garbarino & Ann Crouter, *Defining the Community Context for Parent-Child Relations: The Correlates of Child Maltreatment*, 49 CHILD DEV. 604 (1978); Richard J. Gelles, *Child Abuse as Psychopathology: A Sociological Critique and Reformulation*, 43 AM. J. OF ORTHOPSYCHIATRY 611 (1973); Richard J. Gelles, *Demythologizing Child Abuse*, 25 FAM. COORDINATOR 135 (1976); Richard J. Gelles & Clair P. Cornell, *International Perspectives on Child Abuse*, 7 CHILD ABUSE & NEGLECT 375 (1983); Richard J. Light, *Abused and Neglected Children in America: A Study of Alternative Policies*, 43 HARV. EDUC. REV. 556 (1973); Antonio Martinez-Roig et al., *Psychological Implications of the Maltreated Child Syndrome*, 7 CHILD ABUSE & NEGLECT 261 (1983); Joan McCord, *A Forty-Year Perspective on Effects of Child Abuse and Neglect*, 7 CHILD ABUSE & NEGLECT 265 (1983); Raymond H. Starr, *Child Abuse*, 34 AM. PSYCHOLOGIST 872 (1979).

134. *See supra* notes 73-90, 98-103 and accompanying text.

135. *See supra* notes 91-97 and accompanying text.

136. *See supra* notes 129-132 and accompanying text.

137. *See* Raymond H. Starr, *A Research-Based Approach to the Prediction of Child Abuse*, in CHILD ABUSE PREDICTION: POLICY IMPLICATIONS 105-34 (Raymond H. Starr ed., 1982). *See also* M.A. Disbrow et al., *Measuring the Components of Parents' Potential for Child Abuse and Neglect*, 1 CHILD ABUSE & NEGLECT 279 (1977); Jane D. Gray et al., *Prediction and Prevention of Child Abuse*, 1 CHILD ABUSE & NEGLECT 45 (1977); Joel S. Milner & Ronald C. Wimberly, *An Inventory for the Identification of Child Abusers*, 35 J. CLINICAL PSYCHOL. 95 (1979); Joel S. Milner & Ronald C. Wimberly, *Predication and Explanation of Child Abuse*, 36 J. CLINICAL PSYCHOL. 875 (1980); Roy C. Muir et al., *Prenatal Screening for Risk of Major Parenting Problems: Further Results from the Queen Mary Maternity Hospital Child Care Unit*, 10 CHILD ABUSE & NEGLECT 369 (1986) (success in identifying at risk mothers during the prenatal period); Carol Schneider et al., *A Predictive Screening Questionnaire for Potential Problems in Mother-Child Interactions*, in CHILD ABUSE AND NEGLECT: THE FAMILY AND THE COMMUNITY 393 (Ray E. Helfer

provision but might also be used in the legal arena. When they are used in the legal system, however, concerns about the accuracy of such devices are paramount; people's rights should not be violated without sufficient foundation. The rates of prediction are not 100%. For this reason, there is the likelihood that people will be misclassified and will lose their rights to procreate based on a prediction device that is wrong with respect to them.[138]

While it is common for people to want to be able to predict who is going to be an abuser or who will reabuse their children, it is unclear whether this task is even possible. The problem of prediction is persistent in the law and psychology arena. The legal system, for example, frequently asks psychologists, "What is the likelihood that this criminal will commit a future dangerous act?" While research by forensic psychologists indicates that factors in the assessment of dangerousness such as number of prior violent episodes, the precipitants of prior violence, and the severity of the original offense, do predict future dangerousness, most experts agree that such mental health forecasting has very little to offer the legal system.[139]

Most social scientists agree that prediction is not readily within the purview of social science.[140] The legal system's reliance on such predictions merely increases the rate of false positives, that is, restraining people who, in fact, would not be dangerous in the future despite the fact that the predictors so indicate. In the context of child abuse, the rates of false positives[141] would indicate that the risk of misidentifying a potential abuser is too high for the legal system to rely on that data.

Besides looking at the identification of abusers, it would seem relevant to the question of child abuse to look also at the target of that abuse, namely the child. However, social science research has not investigated the

---

& C. Henry Kempe eds., 1976); Carol Schneider et al., *Screening for the Potential to Abuse: A Review*, in THE BATTERED CHILD (C. Henry Kempe & Ray E. Helfer eds., 3d ed., 1980); Carol Schneider et al., *The Predictive Questionnaire: Preliminary Report*, in HELPING THE BATTERED CHILD AND HIS FAMILY 271 (C. Henry Kempe & Ray E. Helfer eds., 1972).

138. Milton Kotelchuck, *Child Abuse and Neglect: Prediction and Misclassification*, in CHILD ABUSE PREDICTION: POLICY IMPLICATIONS 67 (Raymond H. Starr ed., 1982). *See also* Jessica H. Daniel et al., *Child Abuse Screening: Implications of the Limited Predictive Power of Abuse Discriminate From a Controlled Family Study of Pediatric Social Illness*, 2 CHILD ABUSE & NEGLECT 247 (1978).

139. *See, e.g.*, John Monahan, *Prediction Research and the Emergency Commitment of Dangerous Mentally Ill Persons: A Reconsideration*, 135 AM. J. PSYCHIATRY 198 (1978); Vernon L. Quinsey & Mireille Cyr, *Perceived Dangerousness and Treatability of Offenders*, 1 J. INTERPERSONAL VIOLENCE 458-71 (1986); P.D. Scott, *Assessing Dangerousness in Criminals*, 131 BRIT. J. PSYCHIATRY 127 (1977).

140. *See* JOHN MONAHAN & LAURENS WALKER, SOCIAL SCIENCE IN LAW: CASES AND MATERIALS 160-207 (1985).

141. *See supra* notes 115-16 and accompanying text.

likelihood of abusing *future* children. While this would seem a likely research area, virtually no useful research exists that would assist the legal system in predicting when any one child will be abused.[142]

Even with the research indicating high rates of recidivism,[143] this research does not address the question of which children are being abused. Is it the same child who is returned to a family from foster care, for example, or is it another child? These answers are simply not available in the literature.

Nevertheless, even if it were shown that there was a 100% likelihood of abusing a future child, there might still be other restraints on a court's ability to condition probation on the use of birth control.[144] These constitutional restraints will be discussed below.

IV. CONSTITUTIONAL LIMITATIONS ON CONDITIONING PROBATION ON THE USE OF BIRTH CONTROL

A. *The U.S. Supreme Court Cases on Sterilization*

There have been no Supreme Court cases directly on the issue of whether women who have been convicted of child abuse should be prevented from having children as a condition of probation. However, two Supreme Court cases regarding sterilization may be important in determining how best to evaluate these probation cases.[145] In *Buck v. Bell*,[146] the Court upheld a Virginia sterilization law that allowed individuals with mental retardation to be sterilized involuntarily. The law was upheld because it was considered beneficial to the patient and to society due to the fact that it allowed people to be discharged from state institutions, to return to the community, and to become self-supporting without creating a risk of thrusting onto society children whose parents would be unable to care for them and who might be retarded themselves.

Even if one disagrees whether mentally retarded persons would be good

---

142. *See supra* notes 126-32 and accompanying text.

143. *See supra* notes 117-25 and accompanying text.

144. Even if social science proved to be correct, penalties are generally not imposed upon people for conduct that has not yet occurred. For example, all children are *not* routinely removed from a home where only one child has been abused. Similarly, criminals are not kept locked up beyond the term of a sentence even if recidivism is likely.

145. There have been a variety of lower court decisions invalidating "sterilization," *i.e.*, using drugs to reduce sex drive. *See, e.g.*, People v. Dominguez, 64 Cal. Rptr. 290 (Cal. Ct. App. 1967); Hammer v. State, 377 N.E.2d 638 (Ind. 1978), *cert. denied sub nom.* Hammer v. Indiana, 439 U.S. 969 (1978); State v. Gauntlett, 352 N.W.2d 310 (Mich. App. 1984), *modified*, 353 N.W.2d 463 (Mich. 1984), *appeal denied*, 394 N.W.2d 437 (Mich. App. 1986); State *ex rel.* Coats v. Rakestraw, 610 P.2d 256 (Okla. Crim. 1980).

146. 274 U.S. 200 (1927).

parents,[147] today it seems untenable that persons, who would otherwise be contributing members of society, could be kept in an institution for fear that they would give birth to a "defective" child that would in turn be "thrust" upon society. If the concern was to prevent society from becoming responsible for the care of the mentally retarded individuals' children, should not female child abusers, who would otherwise be kept in prison, be required to utilize birth control to prevent society from paying for the care of their children, *i.e.*, foster care?

The *Buck* case, however, was not simply concerned with society's financial interest in the care of children born to persons with mental retardation. The real thrust of *Buck* was clarified in another sterilization case, *Skinner v. Oklahoma*.[148]

In *Skinner*, the Supreme Court declared unconstitutional an Oklahoma statute providing for compulsory sterilization of persons convicted three times of felonies involving "moral turpitude," but which did not apply to all crimes, *e.g.*, embezzlement. The Court saw little distinction between grand larceny and embezzlement.[149]

The Court distinguished *Buck* because, unlike criminal behavior, there was considerable evidence that mental retardation was inherited.[150] Because mental retardation was seen as inheritable, the state had a compelling state interest in preventing the birth of additionally retarded individuals.[151] The *Skinner* Court found that the state had no interest in preventing children being born to criminals because these children were not likely to follow in the footsteps of their criminal parents.[152]

---

147. *See* Elizabeth Scott, *Sterilization of Mentally Retarded Persons: Reproductive Rights and Family Privacy*, 1986 DUKE L.J. 806; Elizabeth W. Seagull & Susan L. Scheurer, *Neglected and Abused Children of Mentally Retarded Parents*, 10 CHILD ABUSE & NEGLECT 493 (1986); Alexander J. Tymchuk & Linda Andron, *Mothers with Mental Retardation Who Do or Do Not Abuse or Neglect Their Children*, 14 CHILD ABUSE & NEGLECT 313 (1990); Patrick Werner, Comment, *Terminating the Rights of Mentally Retarded Parents: Severing the Ties that Bind*, 22 J. MARSHALL L. REV. 133 (1988).

148. 316 U.S. 535 (1942).

149. *Id.* at 538-39.

150. *Id.* at 541-42. The real problem may be in child rearing, as mental retardation is often not genetic but environmental. Thus, perhaps persons with mental retardation should be allowed to bear children but then turn them over to the custody of the state so that they might be able to get the proper education/stimulation. *See* John A. Robertson, *Procreative Liberty and the Control of Conception, Pregnancy, and Childbirth*, 69 VIRGINIA L. REV. 405, 413 (1983) (arguing that mentally retarded people who can appreciate the consequences of sex should be allowed to bear, not necessarily raise, children).

151. Later court decisions seem to be in direct contravention, *e.g.*, the rights of the mentally retarded include a right to special education.

152. *Skinner*, 316 U.S. at 542.

If the interest had been the prevention of individuals that would have to be supported by society financially, the same would be true of children born to women who would be prevented from caring for them because of their abusive nature. Yet, financial interests do not seem to be the heart of *Buck* or *Skinner*. Rather, heritability of "defects" seems key.[153] Given this interest in preventing "defectives," there is no evidence that the women would be giving birth to children who would be mentally retarded or abusive.[154] Conversely, these children would probably become contributing members of society, assuming reasonable rearing conditions. Nevertheless, the state must be asserting some interest; otherwise, the condition would be void on its face. Where is the interest in preventing such individuals from being born?

It seems that the state interest in preventing the birth of children to probationers is in preventing future abuse of these children. However, unless the harm is in vitro,[155] the child can be removed to state custody after his or her birth. The state can intervene on behalf of the child once he or she is born to prevent his or her abuse or neglect, but the state may not necessarily be able to prevent the birth completely.

B. *A Constitutional Right to Bear Children*

Despite the fact that childbearing has always been intricately tied with marriage and family[156] in cases of contraception or abortion, the U.S. Supreme

---

153. *See also* Jeffrey F. Ghent, *Validity of Statutes Authorizing Asexualization or Sterilization of Criminals or Mental Defectives*, 53 A.L.R. 3D 960 (1973).

154. History of abuse is but one factor used to characterize abusers. *See supra* notes 73-82 and accompanying text.

155. *See* People v. Pointer, 199 Cal. Rptr. 357 (Cal. App. 1984) discussed at notes 41-59 and accompanying text. A state may prohibit actions by a pregnant woman that might reasonably be thought to harm a viable fetus. For example, some states prohibit pregnant women from using alcohol, tobacco, or drugs likely to damage the fetus. When a woman violates these laws, she may be sent to prison. However, women who are alcoholics, smokers, or drug addicts are *not prevented* from becoming pregnant; even though there is a high degree of likelihood that such individuals will continue to drink, smoke, or use drugs during their pregnancy, these individuals are not prohibited from becoming pregnant. They are essentially given the "benefit of the doubt" because it is possible that they would quit for the time that they are pregnant and resume after childbirth. If they do continue the proscribed behavior, they will be penalized, but they are at least allowed the freedom to make that choice. *See generally* James M. Wilson, *Compelled Hospitalization and Treatment During Pregnancy & Mental Health Statutes as Model for Legislation to Protect Children from Prenatal Damage and Alcohol Exposure*, 25 FAMILY LAW QUARTERLY 149 (1991). *But see* Rorie Sherman, *Pregnant Drug Abusers Sue for Treatment*, Nat'l J., Nov. 2, 1992, at 9 (some alcohol and drug treatment programs refuse to treat pregnant women.)

156. In fact, in Roe v. Wade, 410 U.S. 113 (1974), the court found the right to privacy in the context of family law decisions such as Meyer v. Nebraska, 262 U.S. 390 (1923) (discussing parent's rights to control education of their children); Loving v. Virginia, 388

Court has recognized the rights of all persons to avoid conception.[157] Thus, the right *not* to procreate has been recognized.

One commentator has argued that because there is a right *not* to procreate, there must be a corresponding freedom to procreate. Furthermore, such a right may be derived from the right to rear children.[158] While it could be argued that there is a distinction between the decision to prevent conception and the right to conceive because the Supreme Court cases only speak of the individual's right to decide to prevent conception,[159] this conclusion is untenable.[160] Broad statements by the Court suggest that there *is* a right to procreate.[161] The Court has stated that the right of privacy protects the decision whether to "bear or beget" a child.[162] Though the Court stated this in dicta originally, having been quoted over many decades, it has become part

---

U.S. 1 (1967) (declaring unconstitutional a state's prohibition of interracial marriages); and Pierce v. Society of Sisters, 268 U.S. 510 (1925) (striking state statute requiring parents to send children to public schools). Furthermore, when discussing the psychological harm that might result from having an unwanted child, the *Roe* Court stated: "There is also the distress, for all concerned, associated with the unwanted child, and there is the problem of bringing into a *family* already unable, psychologically and otherwise, to care for it." 410 U.S. at 153 (emphasis added).

157. *See, e.g.,* Griswold v. Connecticut, 381 U.S. 479 (1965). Birth control is generally made available to all persons regardless of age or marital status. The use of birth control in such situations is voluntary. Thus, the present cases are completely different because the use of birth control is being forced upon these women by court order.

158. Bruce C. Hafen, *The Constitutional Status of Marriage, Kinship, and Sexual Privacy - Balancing the Individual and Social Interest*, 81 MICH. L. REV. 463 (1983).

159. Carey v. Population Servs. Int'l, 431 U.S. 678, 688 (1977).

160. What rights these particular individuals have is crucial. Is it a right generally to bear children, or only to rear children? In a seminal 1983 article by Bruce Hafen, *supra* note 158, it was argued that the only individual interests that are to be recognized are those that also benefit society. Hafen pointed out that in more recent years, societal interests have been overpowered by individual interests:

> While the Court's early marriage cases 'turned on the importance of marriage to society,' its more recent cases "turn on the importance of the relationship to the individual." . . . [T]he individual and social interests are so intertwined in family cases that meaningful analysis of the competing interest is rendered impossible by current civil liberties approaches that always give the individual interest a procedurally exalted priority over the social interest. Great needs exist for a method of constitutional analysis that will allow for explicit consideration of the social interest in domestic relations.

Id. at 470-71. Although Hafen's article is concerned with the relationship between marriage, kinship, and sexual privacy, and although he does not deal with the issue concerned in this article, much of his analysis is applicable because of the potentially conflicting needs of society to prevent further abuse and/or to prevent itself from becoming financially responsible for abusers' children and individuals' rights to bear children.

161. *See infra* notes 180-182 and accompanying text.

162. Eisenstadt v. Baird, 405 U.S. 438, 453 (1972).

of constitutional tradition. While the actual holdings of the contraceptive and abortion cases have only addressed the ability of one to prevent conception or child birth, more recent unwed fathers' cases[163] suggest that a woman has the right to have a child which may be placed up for adoption and that the father, much less the state, has little legal right to interfere with her decision.

If a constitutional right existed only for child rearing or deciding not to have a child, the state could interfere with decisions to become pregnant with only rational justification.[164] If only a rational justification was required, certainly the potential cost of having these abusers' children being placed in foster care (even temporarily) would be sufficient to uphold probationary conditions requiring the probationer to use birth control.[165]

The "cost-justification," *i.e.*, preventing society from having to care for these children, has been rejected for imposing birth control on a probationer.[166] In one California case, a woman had been convicted of

---

163. *See* Lehr v. Robertson, 463 U.S. 248 (1983); Caban v. Muhammed, 441 U.S. 380 (1979); Quilloin v. Walcott, 434 U.S. 246 (1977); Stanley v. Illinois, 405 U.S. 645 (1972). Arguably, the relevance of these cases is questionable as the state interests are different, and the basis for the unwed fathers' rights are different. However, practically, the fathers have little voice in the ultimate decision by the mother to abort, place the child up for adoption, or rear the child alone. *See generally* Ruthann Macolini & Kara Boucher, *The Parental Rights of Unwed Fathers: A Developmental Perspective*, 20 N.C. CENT. L.J. 45 (1992).

164. GUNTHER, *supra* note 22.

165. When financial interests are permissible justifications, concerns arise about the potential regulation of poor persons' families. The government already offers a wide variety of family planning services for the poor. Many argue that if these probationary conditions were upheld, they would be but a first step to deciding who should have children. The chance of forcing contraceptives on welfare mothers, for example, seems likely with Norplant, which requires no pills to be taken; once implanted, it lasts up to five years. *See* Virginia Ellis, *Witnesses Criticize Norplant Proposals*, L.A. TIMES, Oct. 17, 1991, at A3, col. 1 (Kansas lawmaker proposes that welfare mothers who agree to have the implant be paid a $500 cash bonus); Joyce Price, *Forced Norplant Use Assailed*, WASH. TIMES, April 2, 1992, at A5 (American Medical Association objects to state proposals to pay women on welfare to use Norplant). The Norplant implant is often used in Third World countries. *Birth Control Advocates Like Choice Less and Less*, WASH. TIMES, Jan. 17, 1991, at G2.

166. Can the state also assert an interest in preventing the abuse of children who have not yet been conceived? In Roe v. Wade, 410 U.S. 113 (1973), the Court asserted that states have an interest in potential life. *Id.* at 150. There, potential life was defined from the point of viability. *Id.* at 163-64. Here, however, the state might wish to assert an interest in a non-entity. Since there has been no conception, no person's interests are being advocated. The interest is not that of preventing genetic deficiencies as in *Buck*, *supra* note 146, or prohibiting the transference of criminal tendencies as in *Skinner*, *supra* note 148, but rather to prevent harm to *future* children. Each woman being subject to the condition of probation was adjudicated with respect to *existing* children. Any restraints should be made with respect to those children in terms of custody. Such a condition seems much more reasonable than prohibiting her from conceiving. In fact, some evidence suggests that not all children are abused. One child may be singled out for abuse, and when that child is

robbery.[167] She had two small children, was pregnant with her third child, and had never been married. As a condition of her probation, the trial judge had ordered her not to become pregnant again. She was found to be in violation of her probation due to her pregnancy.

The rationale the state proposed was the fact that society would be responsible for the care of her children, as she had been receiving public financial assistance with respect to her first two children. The judge stated in connection with revocation of her probation due to the pregnancy, "It appears to me this woman is irresponsible; she is foisting obligations upon others, and one of the objectives of probation is to teach and encourage responsibility in all phases including the economics of life and being able to support the dependents who will naturally flow from this sort of conduct."[168]

On appeal, however, the court found that this condition of probation was void. Although the California Penal Code authorized courts to

impose any . . . reasonable conditions, as it may determine are fitting and proper to the end that justice may be done, that amends may be made to society for the breach of the law, for any injury done to any person resulting from such breach and generally and specifically for the reformation and rehabilitation of the probationer . . . ,[169]

the court found that the prohibition of future pregnancy was unrelated to the crime for which she had been convicted, *i.e.*, the robbery. A future pregnancy was not in and of itself criminal and did not relate to future criminality; there was no demonstration that unmarried pregnant woman were more likely to commit crimes. When responding to the monetary arguments made by the state, the court concluded:

The motive was to prevent the appellant from producing offspring who might become public charges. The burden upon the taxpayers to maintain illegitimate children at the public expense is a grave problem, but a court cannot use its awesome power in imposing conditions of probation to vindicate the public interest in reducing the welfare rolls by applying unreasonable conditions of probation. The interest of the public in saving money for the taxpayers is by no means the same thing as the public interest in the reformation and rehabilitation of offenders.[170]

---

removed, the family is "healthy" again.
167. People v. Dominguez, 64 Cal. Rptr. 290 (Cal. App. 1967).
168. *Id.* at 292.
169. *Id.*
170. *Id.* at 294.

The cost to taxpayers for a child in foster care is great. It is not likely that these children could be placed for adoption immediately, thereby obviating the need for foster care. Constitutional restraints require factual findings at a hearing before parental rights can be terminated,[171] with termination being a prerequisite to adoption. It is unclear whether the state would be able to show that parental rights should be terminated immediately[172] because often a parent is given some time to demonstrate that he or she has reformed, especially when the state is providing counseling services to help the parent achieve that goal.[173]

Nevertheless, if the woman has a constitutional right to *bear* children, the state's financial interests would be nil. Procreation is the basis of the continuation of the human race. If persons are not allowed to continue their genes, some have argued that they would be denied a basic human right.[174] One commentator has proposed that a minimum condition for the right to procreate would be the ability to take care of the child or to transfer the obligation to one who could fulfill it.[175] Social mechanisms, *e.g.*, the

---

171. There are high standards that must be met before parental rights can be terminated.

172. It is quite common for courts to use prior bad acts involving siblings or other relatives, such as the abuse of other children, in the termination case of a child or in prosecuting a parent for child abuse. *See, e.g.,* Matter of Juv. Dep't. Action #96290, 785 P.2d 121 (Ariz. App. 1990); Crabtree v. State, 547 N.E.2d 286 (Ind. App. 1989); Matter of Welfare of M.D.O., 462 N.W.2d 370 (Minn. 1990); State v. Fraction, 782 S.W. 2d 764 (Mo. App. 1989); State v. Christeson, 780 S.W.2d 119 (Mo. App. 1989); *In re* K.B., 577 A. 2d 277 (Vt. 1990). For cases involving nonrelatives, *see, e.g.,* People v. Moffat, 560 N.E.2d 352 (Ill. App. 1990), *cert. denied,* 567 N.E.2d 338 (Ill. 1991); *In re* A.D. & C.D., 556 N.E.2d 338 (Ill. App. 1990); *In re* P.A.D., 792 P.2d 159 (Wash. App. 1990). However, the findings must still be with respect to *that* child.

173. Query whether the state, which may be unable to show that parental rights should be terminated, will be able to prove that this mother is likely to abuse her future children. Such a finding would be necessary for sustaining a challenge to the condition of probation itself; it must be presupposed that she will neglect or abuse the child because that is the only "justifiable" basis for imposing this particular condition of probation.

174. The analysis may depend on what constitutional right is identified. Is it the right to be free from interference with bodily integrity? *See* Robertson, *supra* note 150, at 413 n.20 (arguing that with sterilization or contraception, the test would be a compelling state interest to justify the involuntary interference with bodily integrity; Robertson finds that this test would not be met by a desire to conserve taxpayer money). Is the right simply to bear children period, or is the right further qualified by having the right to bear children that would then be placed in state care or up for adoption? The framing of the constitutional right at stake is critical. *See generally* Bowers v. Hardwick, 470 U.S. 106 (1986) (framing the issue as a right to homosexual sodomy rather than as a right to privacy, and thus, the Court had no difficulty finding no such constitutional right).

175. Conora O'Neill, *Begetting, Bearing and Rearing,* in HAVING CHILDREN: PHILOSOPHICAL AND LEGAL REFLECTIONS ON PARENTHOOD 25 (Conora O'Neill & William Ruddick eds., 1979).

Department of Social Services, exist to assure that a child will be cared for in the event that the parent is unable to care for the child; thus, the problem is solved if one believes that a person is always able to transfer that custody to the state.

V. CONCLUSION

Judges continue to order abusive mothers to use birth control as a condition of their probation[176] in an effort to rectify the pervasive problem of child abuse.[177] However, such a condition is not proper. First, the empirical evidence does not support the assumptions underlying the condition, that is, that a woman who has abused a child will abuse again[178] and that she will abuse that *particular* child who is yet unborn. Second, and more important,[179] the constitutional right of privacy confers upon these women a right to bear children.

The Supreme Court has stated that the decision whether to have children is at the very heart of the choices protected by the constitutional right of privacy.[180] Bearing children is by definition one of the most intimate of

---

176. *Cf.* Young, Alverson & Young, *Court-Ordered Contraception*, 55 A.B.A.J. 223 (1969) (response to teenage pregnancy problem for adjudicated juvenile delinquents).

177. For more information on child abuse, *see* MARLA R. BRASSARD ET AL., PSYCHOLOGICAL MALTREATMENT OF CHILDREN AND YOUTH (1987); DEBORAH DARO, CONFRONTING CHILD ABUSE: RESEARCH FOR EFFECTIVE PROGRAM DESIGN (1988); DAVID FINKELHOR, CHILD SEXUAL ABUSE: NEW THEORY & RESEARCH (1984); JAMES GARBARINO ET AL., THE PSYCHOLOGICALLY BATTERED CHILD: STRATEGIES FOR ASSESSMENT AND INTERVENTION (1986); JAMES GARBARINO, S. HOLLY STOCKING ET AL., PROTECTING CHILDREN FROM ABUSE & NEGLECT: DEVELOPING AND MAINTAINING EFFECTIVE SUPPORT SYSTEMS FOR FAMILIES (1980); JEFFREY J. HAUGAARD & N. DICKON REPUCCI, THE SEXUAL ABUSE OF CHILDREN: A COMPREHENSIVE GUIDE TO CURRENT KNOWLEDGE AND INTERVENTION STRATEGIES (1988); NIGEL PARTON, THE POLITICS OF CHILD ABUSE (1985); DAVID A. WOLFE, CHILD ABUSE: IMPLICATIONS FOR CHILD DEVELOPMENT AND PSYCHOPATHOLOGY (1987); Annie H. Cohn, *Effective Treatment of Child Abuse and Neglect*, 24 SOC. WORK 513 (Nov. 1979); Herrenkohl, *supra* note 126 (meta-analysis). *See also* ROSS RIZLEY & DANTE CICCHETTI, DEVELOPMENTAL PERSPECTIVES ON THE ETIOLOGY, INTERGENERATIONAL TRANSMISSION, AND SEQUELAE OF CHILD MALTREATMENT (1981); James Garbarino, *The Elusive "Crime" of Emotional Abuse*, 2 CHILD ABUSE & NEGLECT 89 (1978); Philip G. Ney, *Child Abuse: A Study of the Child's Perspective*, 10 CHILD ABUSE & NEGLECT 511 (1986); Oates et al., *Risk Factors Associated with Child Abuse*, 3 CHILD ABUSE & NEGLECT 547 (1979).

178. *See also* Isaacs, *A Brief Review of the Characteristics of Abuse-Prone Parents*, 4 THE BEHAVIOR THERAPIST 5 (1981).

179. Even if the social science evidence were able to predict whether the woman will abuse with 100% accuracy, constitutional restraints exist that limit the judge's discretion to impose such conditions on a probationer's right to procreate.

180. Carey v. Population Servs. Int'l, 431 U.S. 678, 685 (1977).

human activities and should be encompassed within the right of privacy.[181] The Court has stated: "If the right of privacy means anything, it is the right of the individual, married or single, to be free of unwanted governmental intrusion into matters so fundamentally affecting a person as the decision whether to bear or beget a child."[182] Thus, the abusive mother should have a right to bear children that could only be overridden by a compelling governmental interest, which in these cases is absent.

---

181. *Id.*
182. Eisenstadt v. Baird, 405 U.S. 438, 453 (1972).

Sterilization Ordered for Child Abuser

From Tennessee to Texas, judges order procedure when defendants volunteer

Barbara Gross sat in a small eastern Tennessee courtroom in January listening to the lawyers talk about her future. The 26-year-old woman and her husband, Ronald, 33, had pleaded guilty to charges of sexually abusing their four children—all under the age of 13.

She heard the lawyers tell the judge about the incestuous relationship in which her family allegedly was involved. They said that her four children already had been taken away from her by social workers, that her first son apparently was fathered by her own father, and that she was pregnant again.

Despite the horrible allegations, the prosecutor agreed that the couple needed help, not prison, and recommended probation. Washington County, Tenn., Criminal Court Judge Lynn Brown agreed, but said the couple must agree to very severe conditions.

The solution settled on by two defense lawyers, the prosecutor and the judge was simple: stop Barbara Gross from having children again. But by making her sterilization a condition to probation, Brown thrust the case into the national spotlight. Among those criticizing the decision is the county district attorney, whose deputy prosecutor agreed to the idea.

"It's not a proper punishment and cannot be enforced," said District Attorney David Crockett. If the woman changes her mind, he said, "the judge's only remedy is to put her in prison. And I think that would be overturned on appeal. I do not approve of how this case was handled."

A Rare Order

Legal experts say they learn of court-ordered tubal ligations and castrations two or three times a year in the United States. Most judges withdraw the decisions, and the appellate courts overturn the rest.

A sentencing law requiring repeat sex offenders to be sterilized was held unconstitutional in the 1942 U.S. Supreme Court case, *Skinner v. Oklahoma*, 316 U.S. 535. Procreation, the justices said, is "one of the basic civil rights of man."

Since then, various courts have tried making sterilization a condition of a reduced sentence, but appellate courts have resisted. In the mid-1980s, the supreme courts of Arizona and South Carolina and a Michigan appeals court overturned such orders.

Only one, South Carolina's high court, based its decision on constitutional grounds, finding that castration violated the state prohibition on cruel and unusual punishment. *State v. Brown*, 326 S.E.2d 410 (1985).

More recently, a judge in Houston, Texas, last year ordered a man convicted of sexually assaulting a 13-year-old to be sterilized after the defendant volunteered to be castrated if the judge would spare him any jail time. However, the judge later rescinded the order after no doctor could be found who would perform the surgery.

Judge Lynn Brown, who ordered a sexual abuser to be sterilized: "There was no ultimatum."

The judge who ordered Gross to undergo tubal ligation in *Tennessee v. Gross*, No. 19507, claims that his order is different from ones that were struck down because the defendant voluntarily agreed to sterilization.

"There was no ultimatum," said Brown. "The fact that she agreed to it, completely voluntarily, makes this case different from all the rest. You can waive your constitutional rights and that's what she did that day."

Public defender Jeff Kelly, who represents Gross, doesn't agree that her decision was voluntary.

"She believed she was going to prison, she had just lost custody of her children and she was eight months pregnant, so she was under severe mental stress," said Kelly. "And she was asked to make the decision in 20 minutes."

The transcript shows that Kelly expressed reservations that Gross was "limited mentally" but nonetheless at Brown's request agreed to discuss sterilization with his client. At that point, Brown said he would sentence the woman to probation.

After speaking with Gross during a 20-minute recess, Kelly said she had agreed to be sterilized.

"That's a good choice," Brown said. "The court is more inclined actually to put you on probation in making that voluntary condition. When she goes in to have this child at the hospital, she is to tell them she has chosen to get her tubes tied. That is a condition with which she has agreed. That's appropriate. Five children is enough."

Gross has given birth to her fifth child, but her lawyer and Brown aren't sure if she has had the tubal ligation. And her probation officer isn't returning phone calls.

Since Gross agreed to sterilization and it is the order of the court, Brown said, she can't change her mind. "Until she or her lawyer comes to court and makes a motion to modify the conditions of probation, she should have it done or face some kind of penalty," Brown declared.

Civil libertarians take issue with that view. Gross "could no more waive her right to procreation than a pickpocket could waive his right to bodily integrity and allow his hand to be cut off rather than go to jail," said Lynn Paltrow of the Center for Reproductive Law and Policy.
—*Mark Curriden*

ACKNOWLEDGMENTS

Bharam, Durga M. "Statute of Limitations for Child Sexual Abuse Offenses: A Time for Reform Utilizing the Discovery Rule." *Journal of Criminal Law & Criminology* 80 (1989): 842–65. Reprinted with the special permission of the Northwestern University School of Law, *Journal of Criminal Law and Criminology*. Courtesy of Yale University Law Library.

Porto, Brian L. "New Hampshire's New Statute of Limitations for Child Sexual Assault: Is It Constitutional and Is It Good Public Policy?" *New England Law Review* 26 (1991): 141–72. Reprinted with the permission of the New England School of Law. Copyright New England School of Law 1991. All rights reserved. Courtesy of *New England Law Review*.

Snelling, Tina, and Wayne Fisher. "Adult Survivors of Childhood Sexual Abuse: Should Texas Courts Apply the Discovery Rule?" *South Texas Law Review* 33 (1992): 377–415. Reprinted with the permission of the *South Texas Law Review*. Courtesy of Yale University Law Library.

Larson, Patrick. "The Admissibility of Expert Testimony on Child Sexual Abuse Accommodation Syndrome as Indicia of Abuse: Aiding the Prosecution in Meeting Its Burden of Proof." *Ohio Northern University Law Review* 16 (1989): 81–91. Reprinted with the permission of the *Ohio Northern University Law Review*. Courtesy of *Ohio Northern University Law Review*.

Orfinger, Michael S. "Battered Child Syndrome: Evidence of Prior Acts in Disguise." *Florida Law Review* 41 (1989): 345–67. Reprinted with the permission of the *University of Florida Law Review*. Copyright 1989. Courtesy of Yale University Law Library.

Sagatun, Inger J. "Expert Witnesses in Child Abuse Cases." *Behavioral Sciences & the Law* 9 (1991): 201–15. Reprinted with the permission of John Wiley & Sons Ltd. Courtesy of Yale University Law Library.

Peters, James M., and William D. Murphy. "Profiling Child Sexual
   Abusers: Legal Considerations." *Criminal Justice and Behav-
   ior* 19 (1992): 38–53. Reprinted with the permission of Sage
   Publications, Inc.

Murphy, William D., and James M. Peters. "Profiling Child Sexual
   Abusers: Psychological Considerations." *Criminal Justice and
   Behavior* 19 (1992): 24–37. Reprinted with the permission of
   Sage Publications, Inc.

Yates, Alayne, and Lenore Terr. "Anatomically Correct Dolls:
   Should They Be Used as the Basis for Expert Testimony?"
   *Journal of the American Academy of Child and Adolescent
   Psychiatry* 27 (1988): 254–57. Reprinted with the permission of
   Williams & Wilkins.

Goldberg, Cynthia C., and Alayne Yates. "The Use of Anatomically
   Correct Dolls in the Evaluation of Sexually Abused Children."
   American Journal of Diseases of Children 144 (1990): 1334–36.
   Reprinted with the permission of the American Medical Asso-
   ciation. Copyright (1990).

Britton, Helen L. and Mary Allyce O'Keefe. "Use of Nonanatomical
   Dolls in the Sexual Abuse Interview." *Child Abuse & Neglect*
   15 (1991): 567–73. Reprinted with the permission of Elsevier
   Science Ltd. Courtesy of Yale University Law Library.

Maan, Cathy. "Assessment of Sexually Abused Children with
   Anatomically Detailed Dolls: A Critical Review." *Behavioral
   Sciences & the Law* 9 (1991): 43–51. Reprinted with the per-
   mission of John Wiley & Sons Ltd. Courtesy of Yale University
   Law Library.

Urban, Shelly. "Trapped Within the System: Abused Children and
   Child Protective Service Agencies." *Dickinson Law Review* 89
   (1985): 773–96. Reprinted with the permission of the Dickinson
   School of Law. Courtesy of *Dickinson Law Review*.

First, Curry. "'Poor Joshua!': The State's Responsibility to Protect
   Children from Abuse." *Clearinghouse Review* 23 (1989): 525–
   34. Reprinted with permission. Copyright 1989, National Clearinghouse for Legal Services, Inc. Courtesy of Yale University
   Law Library.

Soifer, Aviam. "Moral Ambition, Formalism, and the 'Free World'
   of *DeShaney*." *George Washington Law Review* 57 (1989): 1513–
   32. Reprinted with the permission of the *George Washington
   Law Review*. Copyright 1989. Courtesy of Yale University Law
   Library.

Myers, John E.B. "Allegations of Child Sexual Abuse in Custody and Visitation Litigation: Recommendations for Improved Fact Finding and Child Protection." *Journal of Family Law* 28 (1989–90): 1–41. Reprinted with the permission of the *Journal of Family Law*. Courtesy of Yale University Law Library.

Fisher, Deborah. "Why Parents Run." *Journal of Interpersonal Violence* 5 (1990): 123–27. Reprinted with the permission of Sage Publications, Inc.

Bischoff, Kerin S. "The Voice of a Child: Independent Legal Representation of Children in Private Custody Disputes When Sexual Abuse Is Alleged." *University of Pennsylvania Law Review* 138 (1990): 1383–1409. Reprinted with the permission of the *University of Pennsylvania Law Review* and Fred B. Rothman & Company. Copyright 1990 by the University of Pennsylvania. Courtesy of Yale University Law Library.

Faller, Kathleen Coulborn. "Possible Explanations for Child Sexual Abuse Allegations in Divorce." *American Journal of Orthopsychiatry* 61 (1991): 86–91. Copyright (1991) by the American Orthopsychiatric Association Inc. Reprinted by permission.

Elterman, Michael F. and Marion F. Ehrenberg. "Sexual Abuse Allegations in Child Custody Disputes." *International Journal of Law and Psychiatry* 14 (1991): 269–86. Reprinted with the permission of Elsevier Science Ltd.

Campbell, Emily. "Birth Control as a Condition of Probation for Those Convicted of Child Abuse: A Psycholegal Discussion of Whether the Condition Prevents Future Child Abuse or Is a Violation of Liberty." *Gonzaga Law Review* 28 (1992/3): 67–102. Reprinted with the permission of the *Gonzaga Law Review*. Courtesy of the *Gonzaga Law Review*.

Curriden, Mark. "Sterilization Ordered for Child Abuser." *American Bar Association Journal* 79 (1993): 32. Reprinted with the permission of the *ABA Journal, The Lawyer's Magazine,* published by the American Bar Association. Courtesy of Yale University Law Library.

SERIES INDEX BY AUTHOR

Please Note: Numbers at the end of each entry refer to the volume in which the article appears.